TCP/IP Administration

TCP/IP
Administration

Craig Zacker

IDG Books Worldwide, Inc.
An International Data Group Company

Foster City, CA ◆ Chicago, IL ◆ Indianapolis, IN ◆ Southlake, TX

TCP/IP Administration

Published by

IDG Books Worldwide, Inc.

An International Data Group Company

919 E. Hillsdale Blvd., Suite 400

Foster City, CA 94404

www.idgbooks.com (IDG Books Worldwide Web site)

Library of Congress Catalog Card No.: 97-077231

ISBN: 0-7645-3158-1

Printed in the United States of America

10 9 8 7 6 5 4 3 2 1

1E/RY/RS/ZX/FC

Distributed in the United States by IDG Books Worldwide, Inc.

Distributed by Macmillan Canada for Canada; by Transworld Publishers Limited in the United Kingdom; by IDG Norge Books for Norway; by IDG Sweden Books for Sweden; by Woodslane Pty. Ltd. for Australia; by Woodslane Enterprises Ltd. for New Zealand; by Longman Singapore Publishers Ltd. for Singapore, Malaysia, Thailand, and Indonesia; by Simron Pty. Ltd. for South Africa; by Toppan Company Ltd. for Japan; by Distribuidora Cuspide for Argentina; by Livraria Cultura for Brazil; by Ediciencia S.A. for Ecuador; by Addison-Wesley Publishing Company for Korea; by Ediciones ZETA S.C.R. Ltda. for Peru; by WS Computer Publishing Corporation, Inc., for the Philippines; by Unalis Corporation for Taiwan; by Contemporanea de Ediciones for Venezuela; by Computer Book & Magazine Store for Puerto Rico; by Express Computer Distributors for the Caribbean and West Indies. Authorized Sales Agent: Anthony Rudkin Associates for the Middle East and North Africa.

For general information on IDG Books Worldwide's books in the U.S., please call our Consumer Customer Service department at 800-762-2974. For reseller information, including discounts and premium sales, please call our Reseller Customer Service department at 800-434-3422.

For information on where to purchase IDG Books Worldwide's books outside the U.S., please contact our International Sales department at 415-655-3200 or fax 415-655-3295.

For information on foreign language translations, please contact our Foreign & Subsidiary Rights department at 415-655-3021 or fax 415-655-3281.

For sales inquiries and special prices for bulk quantities, please contact our Sales department at 415-655-3200 or write to the address above.

For information on using IDG Books Worldwide's books in the classroom or for ordering examination copies, please contact our Educational Sales department at 800-434-2086 or fax 817-251-8174.

For press review copies, author interviews, or other publicity information, please contact our Public Relations department at 415-655-3000 or fax 415-655-3299.

For authorization to photocopy items for corporate, personal, or educational use, please contact Copyright Clearance Center, 222 Rosewood Drive, Danvers, MA 01923, or fax 508-750-4470.

The IDG Books Worldwide logo is a trademark under exclusive license to IDG Books Worldwide, Inc., from International Data Group, Inc.

ABOUT IDG BOOKS WORLDWIDE

Welcome to the world of IDG Books Worldwide.

IDG Books Worldwide, Inc., is a subsidiary of International Data Group, the world's largest publisher of computer-related information and the leading global provider of information services on information technology. IDG was founded more than 25 years ago and now employs more than 8,500 people worldwide. IDG publishes more than 275 computer publications in over 75 countries (see listing below). More than 60 million people read one or more IDG publications each month.

Launched in 1990, IDG Books Worldwide is today the #1 publisher of best-selling computer books in the United States. We are proud to have received eight awards from the Computer Press Association in recognition of editorial excellence and three from *Computer Currents'* First Annual Readers' Choice Awards. Our best-selling *...For Dummies*® series has more than 30 million copies in print with translations in 30 languages. IDG Books Worldwide, through a joint venture with IDG's Hi-Tech Beijing, became the first U.S. publisher to publish a computer book in the People's Republic of China. In record time, IDG Books Worldwide has become the first choice for millions of readers around the world who want to learn how to better manage their businesses.

Our mission is simple: Every one of our books is designed to bring extra value and skill-building instructions to the reader. Our books are written by experts who understand and care about our readers. The knowledge base of our editorial staff comes from years of experience in publishing, education, and journalism — experience we use to produce books for the '90s. In short, we care about books, so we attract the best people. We devote special attention to details such as audience, interior design, use of icons, and illustrations. And because we use an efficient process of authoring, editing, and desktop publishing our books electronically, we can spend more time ensuring superior content and spend less time on the technicalities of making books.

You can count on our commitment to deliver high-quality books at competitive prices on topics you want to read about. At IDG Books Worldwide, we continue in the IDG tradition of delivering quality for more than 25 years. You'll find no better book on a subject than one from IDG Books Worldwide.

John Kilcullen
CEO
IDG Books Worldwide, Inc.

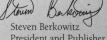

Steven Berkowitz
President and Publisher
IDG Books Worldwide, Inc.

Eighth Annual
Computer Press
Awards ≥1992

Ninth Annual
Computer Press
Awards ≥1993

Tenth Annual
Computer Press
Awards ≥1994

Eleventh Annual
Computer Press
Awards ≥1995

Credits

ACQUISITIONS EDITOR
Anne Hamilton

DEVELOPMENT EDITOR
Katharine Dvorak

TECHNICAL EDITORS
Kelli Adam
Dan Garcia

COPY EDITOR
Nicole Fountain

PRODUCTION COORDINATOR
Tom Debolski

BOOK DESIGNER
Jim Donohue
Kurt Krames

GRAPHICS AND
PRODUCTION SPECIALISTS
Dina F Quan
Trevor Wilson

QUALITY CONTROL SPECIALIST
Mark Schumann

ILLUSTRATOR
Jesse Coleman

PROOFREADER
Jennifer K. Overmeyer

INDEXER
Lynnzee Elze Spence

About the Author

Craig Zacker is a writer and editor whose computing experience began in the halcyon days of teletypes and paper tape. After making the move from minicomputers to PCs, he worked as an administrator of Novell NetWare networks and as a PC support technician while operating a freelance desktop publishing business. After earning a Masters Degree in English and American Literature from NYU, Craig worked extensively on the integration of Windows NT into existing NetWare internetworks, and was employed as a technical writer, content provider, and Webmaster for the online services group of a large software company. Since devoting himself to writing and editing full-time, Craig has authored or contributed to a number of books on operating systems and networking topics, and has published articles with top industry publications including *Windows NT Magazine,* for which he is a contributing editor. He can be contacted at tcpip@zacker.com.

Preface

As computer networking advances toward the use of open standards that ensure interoperability between technologies, the TCP/IP protocol suite has become a ubiquitous fixture on business internetworks, from the Internet to private, corporate networks. Because it is based on freely available, public standards and supported by virtually every operating system used today, TCP/IP is seen as the logical choice for an all-purpose network protocol.

For these reasons, many networking professionals find themselves supporting TCP/IP systems without the benefit of a formal education on its foundations. The performance of practical maintenance tasks, such as TCP/IP-client configuration, can often be learned without a complete understanding of the system on which these tasks are based. This knowledge may be adequate for handling basic support issues, but when troubleshooting TCP/IP problems or explaining why something works becomes necessary, understanding the internal operation of the protocols is critical.

TCP/IP Theory

A primary function of this book is to explore the theoretical background of TCP/IP networking. This is accomplished by examining the various protocols that comprise the suite, the structure of the messages they use to communicate, and the way they work together to provide a full-featured internetworking solution.

Unlike many other networking systems (particularly proprietary ones), there is no shortage of easily obtainable documentation on the TCP/IP protocols. The standards are available, free of charge, from many different sites on the Internet, and also on the CD-ROM included with this book. In fact, you might say that the TCP/IP documentation offers an embarrassment of riches, as it consists of over 2,000 separate documents. While this book examines many aspects of TCP/IP communications – often in great detail – it cannot cover everything. You may find that, to solve a particular problem or learn more about a particular protocol, you need to consult these documents.

Another important element in any TCP/IP education is the fact that the protocol specifications are changing continuously. New documents are published on a regular basis that propose or define upgrades, additional features, or completely new protocols. Unlike many other networking standards, TCP/IP protocols are developed using a democratic model that invites the participation of all concerned users. Once you are familiar with the issues, you can become as involved in the standards-making process as you wish.

TCP/IP Implementations

Though the TCP/IP protocols were deployed as part of UNIX operating systems long before any PC networking platform, their adoption by Windows NT and

NetWare has made them as popular as they are on corporate networks. The massive growth of the Internet has been fueled by the use of TCP/IP on the other Windows client-operating systems. In addition to the theoretical material, this book covers the practical side of installing, configuring, and using the TCP/IP protocols on these platforms.

Computer networking does not take place in the pristine environment of the laboratory. While some networks are built using a single computing platform and operating system (OS), many others have evolved over the years into an amalgam of machines and OSs suitable for a particular task, at a particular time. There are many business networks that run both Windows NT and NetWare simultaneously, whether by choice or not. This book provides equal coverage of both by applying concepts learned from the TCP/IP standards to the specific implementations found in these OSs.

Part 1: Origins

The first three chapters cover the fundamentals of TCP/IP networking, such as the multilayer structure. This type of structure logically separates the functions of a computer's networking stack and the data-encapsulation process that enables various protocols to work together in providing network-communications services. You also learn about the naming and addressing conventions that identify systems on a TCP/IP network, and the process by which protocol standards are developed and published by the organizations responsible for the continued advancement of the TCP/IP technologies.

In this section, you begin to learn the particulars of the TCP/IP implementations in Windows NT and NetWare. When the TCP/IP protocols are integrated into an OS, they must be capable of communicating with existing programming structures through interfaces designed by the OS developers. Windows NT and NetWare use TCP/IP in distinctly different ways; here, you learn about the different programming interfaces they use to facilitate TCP/IP communications.

Part II: Protocols

Part II examines the protocols operating at each of the four layers in the TCP/IP reference model: the link layer, the internet layer, the transport layer, and the application layer. These protocols are found in all TCP/IP implementations and provide communications services, which are combined with those at the other layers. Together, these services achieve the overall degree of service required for a particular networking application. These chapters examine the protocols, in detail. Diagrams of the packet formats and explanations of the functions they provide are discussed in general terms that can be applied to any OS.

Part III: Servers

Part III examines the specific functionality of the TCP/IP protocols on Windows NT and NetWare servers. You learn how to install TCP/IP support on both platforms, and how the OSs and the protocols collaborate to provide basic services used by TCP/IP clients. Such basic services include the routing of data to systems on remote networks or the Internet, the automatic assignment of IP addresses and other configuration parameters to client workstations, and the use of friendly names (instead of IP addresses) to uniquely identify specific systems.

Part IV: Clients

Both Microsoft and Novell provide client TCP/IP implementations you can use on your network system. This section examines the capabilities of the various clients, and the processes by which you install and use them. You learn about specialized TCP/IP products, such as NetWare/IP, which enables NetWare's native IPX traffic to be carried by the TCP/IP protocols, and the IPX/IP Gateway, which provides IPX-only client systems access to TCP services.

Part V: Tools

TCP/IP implementations include an assortment of diagnostic tools you can use to test a computer's networking functions. This section examines the different types of TCP/IP tools, and the specific utilities included with the Microsoft and Novell TCP/IP clients and servers. Also included is coverage of the various TCP/IP applications that ship with the Windows NT and IntranetWare packages, including their respective FTP and World Wide Web servers. Finally, this section discusses the procedures for examining the TCP/IP traffic on your own network using NetXRay, a protocol-analyzer application supplied on the CD-ROM included with this book.

On the CD-ROM

The CD-ROM included with this book contains all of the current Requests for Comments (RFCs) published by the Internet Engineering Task Force (IETF). These documents are the standards on which the TCP/IP protocols and many other Internet technologies are based. Normally published as text or PostScript files, these documents are provided here in their original form (as well as in HTML and PDF formats that can be viewed using the Internet Explorer Web browser and the Adobe Acrobat Reader – also included on the CD-ROM). The disk also contains a selection of shareware, freeware, and demonstration versions of TCP/IP applications and utilities for your evaluation, and links to important TCP/IP-related sites on the World Wide Web.

Contents at a Glance

Table of Contents

Part 1

Origins

Chapter 1

Building a Network Standard

IN THIS CHAPTER

The TCP/IP protocols are based on a collection of open standards and informational documents developed by democratic committees and research groups. This chapter examines the processes by which these standards are developed, ratified, and published. The following topics are covered:

- ◆ Principles used to guide creation of the protocols

- ◆ Organizations involved in the standards-making process

- ◆ Formats and distribution methods for the publication of standards

THE TCP/IP PROTOCOLS WERE created in the 1960s in response to specific needs. Under the direction of the U.S. Defense Department, the Defense Advanced Research Projects Agency (DARPA) set out to build an experimental packet-switching network. This data communications infrastructure would resist enemy attack by its lack of a central nexus, or vulnerable point. A *packet-switching* network is one in which messages are broken up into pieces, called *packets*, for individual transmission over the network medium. Once the packets arrive at the destination, they are reassembled into their original form.

A *circuit-switching* network establishes a connection between the source and the destination before data is transmitted (see Figure 1-1). This connection remains in effect throughout the transmission, with all of the data taking the same route to the destination. On a packet-switching network, individual packets can take different routes to the destination, and even arrive in a different order. The easiest way to understand the difference between the two network types is to compare a telephone network, in which connections are established before communication begins, and a postal system, in which individual messages are sent in discrete envelopes.

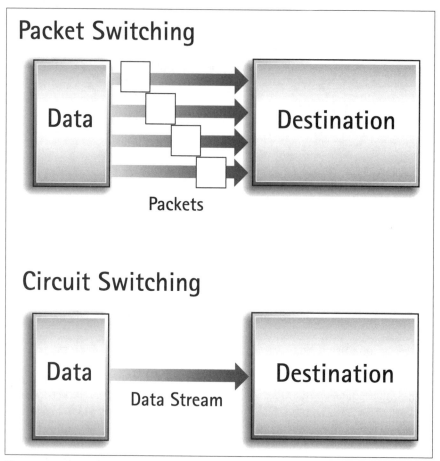

Figure 1-1: Packet-switching networks break a message down into pieces and transmit them separately, while a circuit-switching network transmits the entire message as a single, unbroken stream.

The new computer network developed by DARPA came to be known as the ARPANET. Comprised of computers located in governmental and educational institutions throughout the United States, ARPANET was conceived more than ten years before the first PCs. The use of local area networks (LANs) at business and commercial installations came about even later than PCs. Nevertheless, many of the development decisions made during the evolution of the ARPANET resulted in standards still used today – most notably those that define the TCP/IP protocols. As the ARPANET grew into what we now know as the Internet, the communications protocols were developed and refined using a democratic process that was unprecedented in the computing industry.

TCP/IP Design Principles

In the early 1970s, computing was much more of a single vendor-oriented industry than it is today. Proprietary systems forced institutions to choose one manufacturer for their hardware needs as interoperability between competing systems was virtually unknown. To be connected using the ARPANET, it was necessary to devise a networking infrastructure that enabled unlike systems to communicate.

The ARPANET quickly became a convenient and popular means of communication for its relatively limited academic user base. It wasn't until the ARPANET was officially declared an operational (rather than experimental) network in 1975 that work began on the protocols which ultimately became known as the TCP/IP suite. Named for two of the most commonly used protocols in the collection, the *Transmission Control Protocol* and the *Internet Protocol*, TCP/IP actually consists of over a dozen different protocols working together to provide a vendor-independent data communications solution.

The TCP/IP protocols became official standards in 1983, and were soon required equipment on all ARPANET systems. In the same year, the network was divided into two separate entities, called ARPANET and MILNET, which were referred to collectively as the Internet – literally, a network of networks. At this time, the TCP/IP protocols were first deployed as part of the Berkeley UNIX operating system.

Platform Independence

The ARPANET had been operational for several years by the time development of the TCP/IP protocols began. This experience provided the developers with valuable insight into the basic design principles to observe in the new protocol suite. Chief among these principles – and the guiding factor for the entire project – was that the protocols be completely independent of any particular vendor, computing platform, or hardware specification.

Platform independence means that a computer can connect to a TCP/IP network using any physical medium available, such as a leased phone line, an X.25 network, or a dial-up connection. As local area networking became more prevalent, and the ARPANET evolved into the Internet, physical-layer protocols such as Ethernet and Token Ring grew in popularity. These were also assimilated into the TCP/IP network.

Because of this adaptability to any hardware platform, the TCP/IP protocols effectively insulate the applications running on the networked computers from the physical aspect of the network. A client application on one Ethernet network may use the Internet to connect to a server on another Ethernet network, but the signal might pass through a dozen or more different network types during the journey.

Today, the TCP/IP protocols are supported by virtually every operating system and hardware platform used in network computing environments. They have become the protocols of choice when computers of different types must be connected to the same network – regardless of Internet involvement.

Creating platform-independent protocols led developers to other design principles, which became the hallmarks of TCP/IP protocols. An independent protocol suite meant that no assumptions could be made regarding the types of computers connected to the network. Requirements consisted only of some physical means to make the connection. The protocols had to provide all other elements necessary for computers to communicate with each other. These elements include the following:

◆ Each computer must have some means of uniquely identifying itself to the other systems on the network.

◆ Each system must create an interface between the new protocols and the physical medium used to connect to the network.

◆ Each computer must have a programming interface that enables the requests for network resources (issued by the system's applications) to be serviced using the new protocols.

◆ Growth potential for the network should not be limited by the new protocols.

◆ Standards defining the new protocols should be formatted to easily accommodate new computing platforms.

◆ New protocol standards should not limit use by trademarks, copyrights, or other publishing restrictions.

Addressability

A computer on a data communications network may be capable of generating the following three types of data transmissions:

◆ Broadcasts – the data is transmitted to every system on the network

◆ Multicasts – the data is transmitted to a group of systems

◆ Unicasts – the data is transmitted to a single system on the network

Broadcast transmissions are the easiest to implement because the data need only be circulated around the entire network. However, this is also the least efficient method when a transmission is actually intended for only one, or a few, other systems. The Internet would not be what it is today had it relied exclusively on broadcast transmissions.

The use of *unicast* and *multicast* transmissions introduces a critical problem. In order to transmit data to a single destination system, or group of systems, there must be a way of uniquely identifying it by using a name or an address. Many of the computing platforms used on the Internet already have an addressing system. Ethernet and Token Ring systems, for example, both have unique hardware addresses hardcoded into their network interface adapters. These would be quite serviceable for Internet use, except not every type of computer has them.

An older LAN protocol called ARCnet identifies systems with a numerical address between 1 and 256, which is assigned by the network administrator. This addressing system is fine for use on a private local network, but would hardly be distinguishable from 1,000 other networks when connected to the Internet.

ASSIGNING IP ADDRESSES

Due to the many different types of hardware addresses used on local networks, the TCP/IP protocols needed to have their own addressing system. A unique 32-bit binary number, called an IP address, was assigned to every computer on the network, in addition to any other hardware addressing system already in place. This address identifies both the network on which the computer is located, and the individual host system on that network. A host is defined as a computer containing at least one network interface adapter connected to a TCP/IP network. A host may, therefore, have more than one adapter – each of which has its own separate address.

Internet IP addresses are assigned according to classes defining how many hosts can be connected to a single network. You learn more about the structure and the use of IP addresses in Chapter 2, "TCP/IP Communications."

The IP address is used by TCP/IP protocols to identify and address the equivalent protocol driver running in another system on the network. In order to transmit data over the physical medium connecting the computers, the IP address must be converted. It must be transfigured into the native addressing system used, on each network the transmission passes through, on the way to its destination.

REGISTERING IP ADDRESSES

To ensure that every host on the Internet has a unique IP address, it is necessary to register the addresses with a central body. Even in the 1970s, it was obvious that the job of tracking the IP addresses of every individual system on the Internet would be a daunting one. On today's Internet, keeping up with the changes and the new addresses added each day would be a monumental task.

The TCP/IP working groups, therefore, decided that only networks would be registered. Unique host addresses would be assigned by administrators of each individual network. This arrangement demonstrates one of the most fundamental philosophies of the Internet and the TCP/IP protocols. By distributing onerous administration chores among the many networks that comprise the Internet, no one organization is excessively burdened. This distribution of labor makes the network highly scaleable – that is, it can grow to nearly unlimited size without collapsing under the weight of its own administrative needs.

The efficiency of the IP addressing system, as with many of TCP/IP's other features, is demonstrated by the explosive growth of the Internet in the mid to late 1990s. No one expected that the protocols would have to support a network containing millions of systems. The fact that it continues to function very well under the load is a testament to the designers. A problem that no one anticipated, however, is that all of the possible network addresses would be allocated. That situation is rapidly approaching and work is underway on standards that will provide additional address space for the new networks constantly being added to the Internet.

Modular Standards

From the beginning of the project, it was clear that no single, monolithic protocol would sufficiently support all the different computing platforms used on the Internet. Nor would one support the different types of communication required by these platforms. The new protocols had to work with the existing physical standards and accommodate all of the different physical media used by the networked computers – as well as any emerging, or future, physical standards. These protocols also needed to support different application programming interfaces (APIs), so programs running on different platforms could all request access to the same network resources.

All of these requirements resulted in a series of separate standards documents. These defined a collection of protocols functioning in four distinct operational layers. Separate protocols were defined for the various physical standards being used, and for the different APIs. This method of documenting the protocols provides several advantages to the development process:

◆ Separating the support for different physical media and APIs into discrete protocols. This allows development assignments to be delegated to people according to their areas of expertise. With two separate teams working on the standards for Ethernet and X.25 connections, for example, the individual protocols can be developed independently. Assembling a group of engineers familiar with both technologies is no longer necessary.

◆ Creating additional protocol standards to support new physical media and APIs can be accomplished without modifying the existing protocols.

◆ Scheduling the development of the protocols is accelerated by using independent teams to work simultaneously on separate areas of the project.

Defining standards in this manner provides the protocols with another form of scalability. In addition to supporting a steadily increasing number of systems, the protocols also support a growing number of system types. Through the creation of additional standards documents, these protocols adapt to emerging technologies.

Mutability is one of the basic tenets on which the Internet and the TCP/IP protocols are based. The computing and networking industries are constantly advancing, and technology is expected to change. The TCP/IP standards are acknowledged to be works-in-progress – with new versions of the documents regularly obsolescing older ones.

Public Standards

The standards documents defining the TCP/IP protocols are available to the public free of charge – with no limitations on their use, distribution, or republication. The average user can easily access source information used to create the TCP/IP implementations found in specific products and operating systems. The standards documents can be very valuable, both as learning and troubleshooting tools.

If you have ever attempted to obtain other standards documents – such as those published by the Institute of Electrical and Electronics Engineers (the IEEE) – you discovered that they charge exorbitant prices for their publications. The TCP/IP standards, on the other hand, are available as a free download from many different Internet sites.

ON THE CD The TCP/IP standards documents are also available on the CD-ROM included with this book.

Developing Internet Standards

Because the TCP/IP standards were intended for the fledgling Internet, they are developed and ratified as part of the Internet standardization process (even though they are now used on many private networks). In order to become an official Internet standard, a document defining a protocol, or other technical aspect of TCP/IP, must undergo an evaluation and ratification process. Anyone interested in contributing to the effort has the opportunity to test and comment on its contents. The standardization process is governed by a body called the *Internet Society* (ISOC), which is concerned with all aspects of the Internet's growth and evolution. ISOC is composed of several subgroups, including:

- ◆ The *Internet Architecture Board* (IAB) functions as technical advisor to ISOC, and is the highest-level committee involved in the standard-ratification process. Consisting of approximately 15 voluntary members, this board performs the final review of a potential standard document before its ratification.

- ◆ The *Internet Engineering Task Force* (IETF), which falls under the jurisdiction of the IAB, is most directly involved in the technological development and review of potential standards. The IETF is composed of eight areas: Applications, Internet, Network Management, Operational Requirements, Routing, Security, Transport, and User Services – each of which has one or more area directors. Each area is composed of working groups that investigate specific technical areas. The result may be the development of a standard document, or simply an effort to address a particular problem. Working groups are not permanent bodies; they are created with a specific goal in mind and are usually dissolved once that goal is achieved.

◆ The *Internet Engineering Steering Group* (IESG) is composed of the chairperson of the IETF, and the area directors of all of the working groups. The IESG is responsible for moving standards documents through the formal ratification process. The final ratification of an Internet standard comes from the IAB, and is based on recommendations submitted by the IESG.

◆ The *Internet Assigned Numbers Authority* (IANA) registers the numerical values used to uniquely identify protocol specifications – used by all implementations of a standard. For example, it is the IANA that assigns the standard port numbers for particular services and prevents those numbers from being duplicated. The IANA also assigns identifying numbers to MIBs (Management Information Bases), protocols, and other elements defined in Internet standards documents.

◆ The *Internet Research Task Force* (IRTF) performs long-term investigations of technological issues that are not necessarily involved in the standards ratification process. The issues may involve emerging technologies, which will eventually be passed to the IETF for development of a standard.

Most of the people working in these organizations are volunteers. Membership, particularly in the IETF, has a tendency to be rather amorphous. Any interested person can register for, and attend, one of the IETF meetings held three times annually. He or she may also participate in the discussions on the IETF's Internet mailing lists. Although many of the participants in the IETF are employed by important firms in the Internet industry, their involvement is strictly on an individual basis. They are not there as representatives of their employers, but simply as parties interested in the development and well-being of the Internet.

Actual activities of the IETF working groups consist of discussions – conducted by mailing lists and in person – that attempt to achieve the unofficial IETF motto: "rough consensus and running code." This means the group tries to reach a general agreement about how their goal should be achieved, and then tries to realize that goal in concrete terms, to prove it is a viable solution.

Subscribing to the IETF mailing lists is the easiest way to remain apprised of the ongoing standardization process. The address of the general IETF discussion list is ietf@cnri.reston.va.us. To subscribe to this list, send an e-mail message, with the single word "subscribe" as the subject, to ietf-request@ietf.org (not to the address of the list itself). There is also a second mailing list for announcements from the IETF concerning meetings and the progression of documents through the standardization process. Subscribe to this list by sending a message to ietf-announce-request@ietf.org.

The IETF has traditionally been responsible for all aspects of the process by which standards are conceived, originated, and developed in ISOC. The massive growth of the Internet in recent years, and its importance to the networking industry, have introduced an increasing number of nontechnical concerns to the process. Legal issues and liaisons with companies developing Internet technologies inevitably led the IETF away from its central function – the technical development of protocols and other standards.

In short, the IETF technicians are looking to absolve themselves of the nontechnical responsibilities that now seem an inevitable part of the standardization process. To do this, the Poised95 working group was created. This group would explicitly define the responsibilities of the IETF, and those of other organizations, such as ISOC. This reorganization is just one demonstration of how the standard-ratification process is constantly evolving – just like the standards themselves.

Requests for Comments (RFCs)

A series of documents, known as *Requests for Comments* (RFCs), is the published work of the IETF, IESG, IANA, and IAB. The name, alone, indicates the openness pervading the entire Internet standard-development process. In many ways, the RFCs document much of the Internet's history. The first document in the series, RFC0001, was published in April of 1969. There are now over 2,200 documents in the RFC series, and new ones are regularly added.

RFCs are available for viewing and downloading from many different Internet sites. All of the documents are in ASCII format, but some are also available as PostScript files to facilitate the inclusion of diagrams or other graphics. A file called RFC-INDEX.TXT contains the numbers, authors, and titles of the entire RFC series, and is updated whenever new documents are published. In many cases, RFCs are updated several times to reflect new developments. New versions of existing RFCs are always assigned a new number. RFC-INDEX.TXT contains notations indicating when a document is made obsolete, and when a new document replaces an old one.

The RFCs defining the TCP/IP protocol standards are the blueprints a software developer uses to develop and build a TCP/IP client or service software module. The document defines the structure of the data packets transmitted over the network and the nature of messages exchanged between client and server. A protocol standard defines the use of each field in the protocol's header, and how it interacts with the other protocols operating above and below it in the networking stack. The aim of a standard document is to provide software developers with sufficient information to create separate implementations of the protocol that are completely interoperable.

All of the official Internet standards are published as RFCs, but not all RFCs define Internet standards. Many of the documents are considered to be "on the Internet standards track" – that is, in the process of being developed for ratification as an official standard. Many other documents are not intended for the ratification process at all. Unlike most of the documents published by other standardization bodies, there are many RFCs which are quite comprehensible to the nonexpert user. Some, in fact, are specifically designed to introduce newcomers to certain aspects of the Internet. For instance, if you are interested in attending a meeting of the IETF, you should read RFC1718, "The Tao of IETF – A Guide for New Attendees of the Internet Engineering Task Force."

Throughout this book, you will see references to the RFCs that define the protocols or services being discussed, or that provide additional information on the current subject. All of the RFCs available at the time of publication are available on the accompanying CD-ROM.

The Standardization Process

Most of the RFCs defining the TCP/IP protocols are official Internet standards. Many of the documents being developed for standardization are published as RFCs several times during the process. By releasing the works-in-progress to the public, the greatest possible amount of feedback is received from concerned users. A major part of the standards-development process is "real-world" testing of the element being defined.

Before becoming RFCs, preliminary versions of standards documents may also be published in a special directory, called *INTERNET-DRAFTS*. This is a series of temporary documents – posted for a period of at least two weeks – being considered for advancement to the standards track. Internet-draft documents are removed from the directory once they are approved (by the IESG) for publication as RFCs, or after six months.

RFCs on the standards track undergo a series of revisions designed to provide adequate time for evaluation and testing – without interfering with the timeliness of the technology. An RFC document passes through at least three distinct stages of maturity on its way to becoming an official standard. The three stages are outlined as follows:

◆ **Proposed standard** – The elevation of a document to proposed-standard status by the IESG indicates that it is on the standards track, and that the technology defined is complete and generally stable. Usually, however, a proposed standard will not yet have been implemented or tested in the field. A document must remain a proposed standard for at least six months, and two implementations are required before it can be advanced to draft-standard status. Using software developed with proposed standards is recommended only in a lab environment, as significant changes in the technology may occur before it is advanced to the next stage.

◆ **Draft standard** – Before a proposed standard can be elevated to draft-standard status, it must have two implementations which include all features and options, and are completely interoperable. The technology should also have sufficient operational experience in the field. This demonstrates that it is mature and ready to become an Internet standard, with only a minimum of modification. Because changes should only be made to address specific problems, it is usually safe to develop production software based on a draft standard. A document must remain a draft standard for at least four months before it can be granted full Internet-standard status.

◆ **Internet standard** – Once a draft standard has had sufficient time to demonstrate its stability in extensive operational testing, it can be declared a fully ratified Internet standard. A ratified standard document is assigned another number, called an STD number, that is independent of the RFC number. This will remain with the document even when a new RFC updates the standard. The file is also copied to a separate directory which contains only standards. The RFC remains permanently in place, however, and the RFC-INDEX.TXT file is updated to show the STD number.

In addition, there are three states of maturity which can be applied to RFCs that are not on the standards track. These designations are not sequential, as are those of standards documents; rather, they are used to indicate a reason why particular documents are not being developed as standards. Following are the three states of maturity:

◆ **Informational** – An informational document is one that is not intended for the standards track at all. Rather, it is a document that is considered of general interest to the Internet community. It carries with it no implicit endorsement or recommendation from the IETF or any of its related bodies.

◆ **Experimental** – The experimental designation indicates that the document is the result of a research project (conducted by the IRTF or another body) that is not intended, or not yet ready, for development into a standard.

◆ **Historic** – A historic document is one that has been made obsolete by another specification and is now conceded to be of historical interest.

Informational and experimental documents may be the product of one of the Internet governing bodies, or they may come from outside sources of any type. Before an outside document is published as an informational or experimental RFC, it is reviewed by the RFC Editor and the IESG. This is done to prevent misuse of the RFC publishing process by those who want to introduce a document and make it appear to be a ratified Internet standard, when it is actually the product of an outside company or organization. If the document infringes upon work currently being done by the IETF, the editor may recommend that the specification be submitted to the appropriate working group for assimilation into their research (rather than being published as a separate document).

One of the best ways to track the progression of the standardization process is to consult an RFC called "Internet Official Protocol Standards." This document contains information concerning the current status of all of the RFC documents on the standards track. This RFC is updated frequently to reflect the latest changes. The current version, as of this document, is RFC2200.

Types of Standards

RFCs that are on the standards track fall into two general categories: technical specifications and applicability statements. A *technical specification* (or TS) describes a particular technology, such as a protocol or service, but not the requirements for use of that technology. An *applicability statement* (or AS) describes the circumstances under which one or more technical specifications are used to accomplish a networking task.

For example, there are many RFCs defining the individual protocols that are part of the TCP/IP suite. These TS documents do not, however, cover the way in which the protocols work together to provide network communications. A separate document, such as RFC1122, "Requirements for Internet Hosts – Communication Layers," describes the ways various protocols must interact on a host system where they have been implemented. An AS document like this contains references to the various TS documents involved, and may include corrections or clarifications for those documents.

The TS documents that are referenced by an AS must always be at the same stage in the standards-ratification process. An AS that is an official standard cannot reference TSs that are still in the draft-standard or proposed-standard stage.

Thus, proper implementation of the TCP/IP protocols in a software product must be based on the appropriate AS – along with the TSs that are cited within it, to varying degrees. When an AS document references TSs, it does so by clarifying the requirement level for each one, using the following terms:

- **Required** – The referenced TS is an essential part of the standard described in the AS, and must be implemented to conform to the standard. For example, the "Requirements for Internet Hosts" document specifies that the IP protocol (as documented in RFC791) is required in order to achieve the functionality described in the AS.

- **Recommended** – The referenced TS is not essential for conformance to the standard described in the AS. Operational experience has, however, led to the conclusion that the TS should be implemented, unless specific circumstances prevent it. For example, it may be recommended that a TCP/IP implementation include an FTP client, but it is not absolutely essential.

- **Elective** – The referenced TS is not essential for conformance to the standard described in the AS, but may be beneficial under certain circumstances. The implementation of the elective TS is left solely to the discretion of the software developer.

Often, these requirement levels are expressed in an AS using the terms "must" or "shall" to represent a required element, "should" to represent a recommended element, and "may" or "optional" to represent elective references. The use of these terms (and appropriate converses such as "must not," "shall not," and "should not") is carefully considered when creating the document, and should be taken as explicit instructions on the use of specific TSs. Some RFCs set the words MUST, SHALL, SHOULD, and MAY in uppercase letters when they are used in reference to TSs.

It is also possible for an AS document to reference TSs that are not on the standards track, or which have been deemed "historic." There are two alternative requirement levels that can be applied in these cases:

- **Not Recommended** – The referenced TS should not be used when implementing the standard described in the AS – either because the TS is obsolete or only intended for use in other situations.

- **Limited Use** – The referenced TS is recommended for use only in certain situations. This designation may be used to reference TSs that are experimental, in which case they should not be used except in a lab environment.

Summary

The TCP/IP protocols were designed for use on the multiplatform network which eventually became the Internet. The standards defining the protocols, and many other informational documents, are published in the public domain. They are published by organizations, comprised mainly of volunteers, whose primary concern is the development and the well-being of the Internet. The protocols were designed to be an independent network communications system, to be used on virtually any hardware or software platform.

In this chapter, you learned:

♦ How the TCP/IP protocols were designed

♦ How the continuing protocol development process is organized

♦ How the TCP/IP specifications are published and distributed to the public

The next chapter provides a basic overview of the TCP/IP protocol stack and the network-communications process.

Chapter 2

TCP/IP Communications

IN THIS CHAPTER
To better understand the complexities of network communications, the processes involved are broken down into distinct function-based layers. This chapter provides a basic overview of computer networking using the TCP/IP protocols. The following subjects are covered:

◆ The operational layers of a network implementation, known as a *protocol stack*

◆ The encapsulation process by which multiple protocols package data for transmission over a network

◆ The addressing system by which the TCP/IP protocols identify specific computers on an internetwork

◆ The domain-based system by which TCP/IP hosts are assigned familiar names

WHEN COMPUTERS COMMUNICATE USING the TCP/IP protocols, they follow the client/server model, even if the operating system (OS) provides peer-to-peer functionality, such as Windows NT. A *peer-to-peer* OS is simply one that contains both client and server components to be used simultaneously. At any given time, the computer can act as a server by providing access to its drives or application processes; or as a client, by accessing the resources of other systems.

On a system using TCP/IP, the networking protocols come into play when an application requests access to resources found elsewhere on the network. For transmittal over the network, this request must be packaged as a data structure suitable for the network medium, and delivered to the network interface adapter. In most cases, the adapter is a *network interface card* (NIC) in the computer, to which a network cable is attached. This packaging and delivery process is largely performed by a protocol suite, such as TCP/IP.

The Protocol Stack

The application generating the request for access to resources on the network is said to reside at the top of what is called a *protocol stack*. The bottom of the protocol stack is the interface to the network medium itself. The protocol stack is divided into several layers; each of which represents a protocol that performs some of the tasks necessary for effective communication with another system. The request generated by the application at the top of the stack is passed downwards. Each successive layer provides a service to the layer above, until the message reaches the network medium, which is usually a cable.

During its journey downwards through the stack, the request is transformed, from an Application Programming Interface (API) call – such as a word processor's *FileOpen* command – into a coded signal, suitable for network transmission. Depending on the network type, the signal may be an electric current, pulses of light, radio waves, or any other viable medium.

In order to process the request, the receiving computer must have an identical networking stack, representing the same protocols. The request is passed up through the layers where the same process is performed in reverse, until the decoded signal reaches the application at the top (see Figure 2-1). The receiving application – in this case, the file system of another computer – processes the request and generates a response that is transmitted back to the source.

The activities that occur in the protocol stack are the primary subject of this book. TCP/IP is one of several protocol suites that operating systems can use to process application requests for transmission over a network. Some operating systems, like UNIX, are completely dependent on TCP/IP, while others like Windows NT provide an open networking architecture that can use various different stacks – even simultaneously.

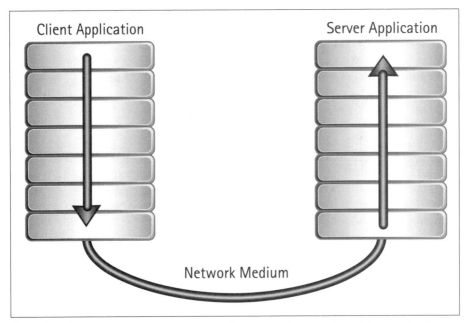

Figure 2-1: Client and server systems possess the same protocol stack, which can process incoming and outgoing data.

The OSI Reference Model

When seen at a very high level, the act of generating a request, transmitting it over a network, and receiving a response is deceptively simple. It might be likened to dropping a letter into a mailbox and receiving a response a few days later. However, the actual process of packaging the request and assuring its intact, timely delivery, is quite complex. The process is divided into layers to make it more manageable and comprehensible to both the designers of networking protocols and computer users.

In 1983, two standards bodies, the ISO (International Standards Organization) and the CCITT (which translates from the French as the International Telegraph and Telephone Consultative Committee), jointly published "The Basic Reference Model for Open Systems Interconnection." Based on research work performed by both bodies over the course of several years, this document, also called the *OSI reference model*, describes the network communications process. Using a seven-layer structure, the process has since become the standard reference and teaching tool for data networking.

The networking process within a computer's OS ranges from the application request (at the top of the protocol stack) to the network medium (at the bottom). The OSI reference model divides this functionality into seven discrete layers, as shown in Figure 2-2.

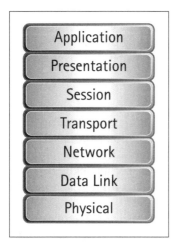

Figure 2-2: The OSI reference model contains seven layers that represent the entire networking functionality of the computer.

The seven layers of the OSI model perform the following operations:

- ◆ **Application** – Consists not of the actual application running on the computer (such as a word processor), but of the APIs providing the application with access to network resources.

- ◆ **Presentation** – Performs any syntax translations that are needed when computers of different types communicate using the same protocol stack.

- ◆ **Session** – Initiates and maintains the dialog between two communicating computers. It also creates checkpoints, allowing transactions to be rolled back to a previous state, in the event of an interruption in the communications process.

- ◆ **Transport** – Provides the end-to-end communication between two systems. This layer ensures that the appropriate quality of service is achieved for the type of transmission being used.

- ◆ **Network** – Routes transmissions across internetworks to destinations on other network segments. It may also provide end-to-end services such as flow control and error detection.

- ◆ **Data Link** – Packages the transmitted data into packets suitable for transmission over the network. This layer also controls access to the network medium, allowing multiple systems to utilize the same cable.

- ◆ **Physical** – Consists of the actual interface between the computer and the network medium. It is responsible for the final coding of information into the electrical impulses, or other signals, used to transmit data over the network.

Originally, the OSI model was intended to be the basis for a protocol stack. After many years of development, there is now an OSI stack, but it is not used in business LAN environments. When you examine TCP/IP, or any of the other stacks used in commercial networking products, you find that they do not exactly conform to the stratification of the OSI model. The model has, instead, become more of a tool for learning about the processes involved in computer networking, and not the implementations found in specific products.

The functionality of the OSI model's seven layers has become the vernacular of the networking industry. Presented here, it makes understanding which services are provided by the TCP/IP protocols much easier. Development of the TCP/IP protocols began in 1975, long before the documents defining the OSI reference model were published. In fact, the first official TCP/IP standards were published in 1983, the same year as the OSI documents.

The TCP/IP Stack

The TCP/IP protocols are also divided into layers representing some of the same processes (and using some of the same names) as their counterparts in the OSI model. The TCP/IP stack contains four layers, as shown in Figure 2-3.

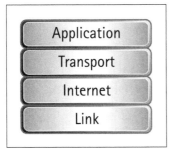

Figure 2-3: The TCP/IP protocol stack represents only part of a computer's networking system, and is designed to work with many other protocols.

The functions of the TCP/IP layers are as follows:

◆ **Application** – Some TCP/IP application-layer protocols are full-fledged user applications which generate network-service requests, such as TELNET and FTP. Other protocols provide support to applications in the form of services, such as the Domain Name System (DNS) and the Simple Network Management Protocol (SNMP).

◆ **Transport** – As in the OSI model, the transport layer provides end-to-end communications services in the form of two protocols: the Transmission Control Protocol (TCP) and the User Datagram Protocol (UDP).

◆ **Internet** – The internet layer contains IP (the Internet Protocol), which is responsible for the packaging, addressing, and routing of data to its destination. Also operating at this layer are the Internet Control Message Protocol (ICMP) and the Internet Group Management Protocol (IGMP).

◆ **Link** – The link layer contains protocols used to facilitate the transmission of IP data over the existing network medium. The TCP/IP standards do not define the functionality of the OSI data link and physical layers. Instead, the standards define protocols like the Address Resolution Protocol (ARP) that provide an interface between TCP/IP structures and the physical network as implemented by the OS.

The names of the four layers that comprise the TCP/IP protocol stack used here are those defined in RFC1122, "Requirements for Internet Hosts — Communication Layers." Many sources use alternative names, for instance, referring to the internet layer as the *network layer*. The link layer is sometimes called the *network interface layer* — or worse — the *data link layer*, giving rise to confusion with the OSI reference model layer of the same name. In this book, the link layer refers strictly to the protocols defined by the Internet standards. It does not include the functionality of OSI data link-layer protocols, such as Ethernet and Token Ring.

Each of the TCP/IP stack's layers and its protocols are examined at length in the individual chapters that comprise Part II of this book.

It is important to understand that the TCP/IP protocols do not provide all of the functionality found in the seven layers of the OSI model – nor can they be exactly equated to OSI equivalents. Roughly speaking, the two networking models can be compared as shown in Figure 2-4, in which the TCP/IP application layer is approximately equivalent to the application and presentation layers of the OSI model. The internet and transport layers of both stacks provide roughly the same functions, but the TCP/IP stack's link layer is a special case.

The link layer is special because the TCP/IP standards are designed for use on a wide range of hardware platforms and network types. The protocols controlling access to the network, and the actual signaling used on the medium, are found in the data link and physical layers of the OSI model. On today's business LANs, these are almost always Ethernet or Token Ring – which are the colloquial names assigned to the IEEE (Institute of Electrical and Electronics Engineers) 802.3 and 802.5 standards, respectively.

Obviously, Ethernet and Token Ring are not TCP/IP protocols, as they were developed by another standards body. Instead, these protocols are implemented by the network interface hardware and by device drivers installed into the OS. The TCP/IP standards do not define data link and physical protocols of this type. The TCP/IP protocols are designed to work with networking technologies like Ethernet and Token Ring, as well as many other lower-layer protocols used on Internet systems. Therefore, the TCP/IP link layer provides important functionality to the region of the OSI data link layer, but it doesn't necessarily replace it.

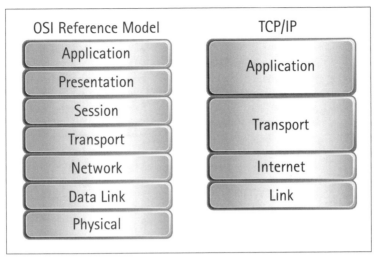

Figure 2-4: The layers of the TCP/IP stack do not correspond exactly to those of the OSI reference model.

Because the TCP/IP standards do not define physical and data link protocols, the four TCP/IP layers do not represent the entire network protocol stack, as does the OSI reference model. To see how the TCP/IP protocols fit into the NetWare and Windows NT protocol stacks, see Chapter 3, "TCP/IP and Operating Systems."

Protocol Symmetry

Another way to understand the use of layered protocols is to envision the protocol stacks of the sending and receiving systems side by side, as shown in Figure 2-5. Every protocol in use on the sending system must also be supported by the receiving system. In essence, each layer is directly communicating with its counterpart.

As a message travels down through the layers of the transmitting system, the various protocols apply their own specialized control data (this consists of mechanisms designed to provide the level of service required for transmission). When the message reaches the destination system and passes up through the protocol stack, the IP control data is read at the internet layer. The message is then passed up to the transport layer, where the TCP or UDP control data is read. Thus, the protocol operating at each layer of the sending system is capable of conducting a separate dialog with its equivalent in the receiving system.

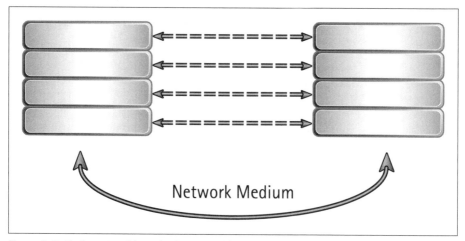

Figure 2-5: Each protocol layer in the networking stack communicates with its counterpart in the receiving system's stack.

Quality of Service

One of the primary benefits of using a stack of multiple protocols for network communications (as opposed to a single monolithic protocol) is that a transmission can be provided with the exact services needed to accomplish its appointed task. Whenever you transmit data across a network, you incur an additional measure of network traffic for control purposes. For example, you may download a 100K file from an Internet FTP site, but the total amount of data actually traversing the cable during the transmission process is substantially more than 100K. The additional traffic consists of control data needed to get the file to the correct location intact.

The ultimate goal in designing any networking protocol is to accomplish the required tasks with the least amount of additional control traffic. You could, for example, design a protocol that breaks every transmission down into 1K chunks, each of which is transmitted in a separate packet and requires a separate acknowledgment in return. This would get the job done, but would be wildly impractical because the amount of control data required would far exceed the size of the file being transmitted.

A protocol stack like TCP/IP is intended to service many different kinds of applications. The applications can also have different requirements of the protocol stack. A DNS transaction, for example, may consist of a very simple exchange. A workstation sends a single packet containing a host name to a DNS server, which then responds with a single packet containing the IP address that is the equivalent to that host name.

A transaction like this requires relatively little from the protocol stack. There is no need for the server to acknowledge the workstation's transmission because its response serves as an acknowledgment. If the workstation receives no response, it can simply resend the request — which would probably require less control traffic than an elaborate acknowledgment mechanism.

Transmitting a 100KB file from an FTP site requires considerably more from the protocol stack. Because the file must be broken up into multiple packets, it requires more elaborate mechanisms, such as packet acknowledgment, fragmentation, and flow control. The more services required, the greater the amount of control traffic.

The protocol stack in a TCP/IP system provides alternative protocols for exactly this reason. Although the protocols may operate individually, communicating with their counterparts on the destination system, they also work together to provide the overall quality of service required for the transmission. The *quality of service* is the aggregate sum of the features provided by all of the protocols used for a given transmission. The protocols at the various layers of the TCP/IP stack work together by providing the features required in the most efficient manner possible.

The IP protocol, for example, operates at the internet layer, and is used to carry the traffic of both transport-layer protocols, TCP and UDP. In order to minimize control traffic, IP provides only the services required by both of these upper-layer protocols. The extensive services required for an FTP transmission are implemented at the transport layer by TCP; UDP provides the simple basic service required for DNS transactions.

Each type of transmission receives the quality of service that it requires, and no more. A DNS exchange is not burdened with the additional control traffic incurred by services it doesn't need, and these same services are made available for FTP transfers, as needed. The TCP/IP protocols also factor other standards into the equation. Because data link-layer protocols like Ethernet and Token Ring both provide an error-checking mechanism for the entire contents of the packet, an equivalent service need not be implemented by TCP/IP.

Understanding Data Encapsulation

When a request is prepared for transmission over the network, each protocol in the stack applies its own control data through a process known as data encapsulation. *Data encapsulation* is the process by which each protocol in the stack takes the data handed down to it from the layer above and packages it by applying a header. A *header* consists of several additional bytes worth of information used to implement the particular features of that protocol. Headers vary in size depending on the features of the individual protocol.

Every network transmission requires a certain amount of control data, in addition to the information being sent to the destination. Again, think of the mail analogy: you cannot mail a letter without first putting it into an envelope and addressing it. The control data adds to the size of the transmission, just as the envelope adds to the overall weight of the letter. The more features needed to reliably transmit the request, the more control data is required.

At the top of the protocol stack, therefore, the data structure consists only of the original request generated by the application. It is a letter without an envelope. When the request is passed down to the TCP/IP application-layer protocol, a header is affixed (containing the control data needed by the same protocol at the receiving system). Once the header is applied, the original request becomes the *payload*, the baggage carried by the protocol. Just as the post office doesn't care what's in the envelope, a protocol doesn't care what it is carrying in its payload.

The protocol at application layer of the stack produces a structure, consisting of a header and a payload, which it passes down to the next layer (see Figure 2-6).

Figure 2-6: Networking protocols package the data to be transmitted by applying a header that functions as the "envelope" for the message.

The structure produced by the application-layer protocol is then passed down to the transport layer, where a second protocol applies its own header. Together, the application-layer header and payload become the payload of the transport-layer protocol (see Figure 2-7). The transport-layer protocol is unaware of the contents of the application-protocol header or the original request.

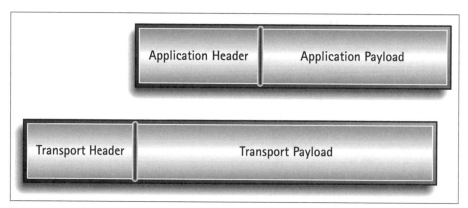

Figure 2-7: Each successive protocol in the stack packages the preceding layer's data structure as its own payload.

This process continues at each successive layer of the protocol stack, until a structure called a *packet* is created. The packet consists of four or more headers attached to the original message (see Figure 2-8). Each header contains control data, solely intended for a specific protocol on the receiving system. As the packet is passed up through the layers of the stack at the destination, each header is read, in turn, by the appropriate protocol. This process is known as *demultiplexing*. As in the transmitting system, each protocol is only concerned with the contents of the header intended for it, treating everything else as payload. This is how the protocols, at each layer, maintain a dialog with their equivalents on other systems.

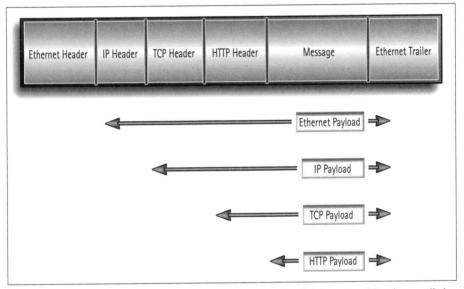

Figure 2-8: By the time a packet is transmitted, it has had multiple protocol headers applied to it.

The final header, added to the message before the originating system transmits it over the network, is the data link protocol—typically Ethernet or Token Ring. Unlike the TCP/IP protocols, this final step in message packaging contains a footer as well as a header. It encloses the data structure in an envelope suitable for transmission over the network medium to which the sending system is connected.

Naming Data Structures

One of the most confusing aspects of data encapsulation is the nomenclature used to refer to each data structure, as it is passed down through the layers of the protocol stack. In most cases, the original payload generated by an application that uses the UDP protocol is referred to as a *message*. If the application uses TCP, the data is called a *stream*.

Once it reaches the transport layer, the name given to the message again depends on the protocol used. TCP transmissions nearly always involve large amounts of data, even entire files, which are split up and sent as multiple segments. The segments that make up the transmission are collectively referred to as a *sequence.* The structures produced by the UDP protocol are called *packets.*

At the internet layer, the IP protocol is used to transmit both TCP segments and UDP packets within structures known as *datagrams.* Below the internet layer of the protocol stack, TCP/IP can use many different protocols, which may have different names for the structures they transmit. Ethernet and Token Ring networks refer to their individual transmissions as *frames* – which is now the most commonly used term. Thus, an Ethernet frame can contain an IP datagram which, in turn, contains a TCP segment of an application data stream, or a UDP packet with a message inside (see Figure 2-9).

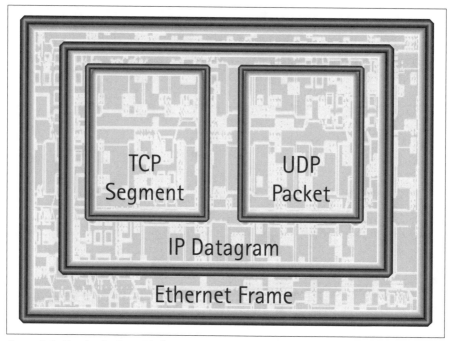

Figure 2-9: Nearly all of the TCP/IP protocols use a different name for the data structure formed by the protocol header and its payload.

Adding to the confusion of all of these terms is the fact that some of them are used interchangeably. Because all of the networks using TCP/IP can be defined as packet-switching networks, the term *packet* is often used generically when speaking of the fundamental unit transmitted across the network medium. This usage is not incorrect, even though this structure is more properly referred to as a frame in most cases. The term *datagram* is also used to refer to UDP structures because, like IP datagrams, they are independent transmissions, as opposed to TCP segments – which are part of a greater whole, composed of many frames.

Applying Protocol Headers

The header that each protocol applies to the payload (received from the layer above it) can vary greatly, depending on the features of the protocol. Each header consists of a number of discrete fields, of various sizes, that are used by the receiving protocol stack to implement the services required for the data being transmitted. The control data in the header fields can perform several tasks, including addressing, fragmenting, error checking, and flow control – all of which are outlined in the following sections.

ADDRESSING

One of the most important functions of the information in the protocol headers is to direct transmitted data to the exact place it must go in the destination system. When you mail a letter using a postal service, the address on the envelope describes the location of the intended recipient in increasingly specific terms. The letter is delivered first to the correct state, then to a city in that state, then to a street in that city, and finally to a house on that street.

In the same way an envelope bares an address, the destination of a TCP/IP transmission is specified by the information contained in the headers – which are provided by the successive protocol layers. Directing the data to the proper destination, however, consists of more than just locating the correct computer. Computers can be running many different processes simultaneously. As a result, data packets may arrive at a computer containing payloads intended for the TCP/IP protocol stack, or any one of several other possibilities. IP transmissions may be intended for either one of the two transport protocols, and TCP and UDP data can be directed to any one of several dozen application processes. This assortment of destinations within a single computer can be illustrated by a tree-like structure (see Figure 2-10).

For a transmission, directed at a specific application, to wend its way through this morass of protocols on the destination system, each layer of the stack must provide a sign to point the way. Each of the protocol headers contains a field dedicated to this purpose. A data link protocol, such as Ethernet, contains a code in its header that identifies the protocol stack for which the packet is intended. When a packet is passed to the internet layer of the TCP/IP stack, a field in the IP header specifies the protocol used at the transport layer. The transport-layer protocol header includes a port number that identifies the application process for which the message is intended.

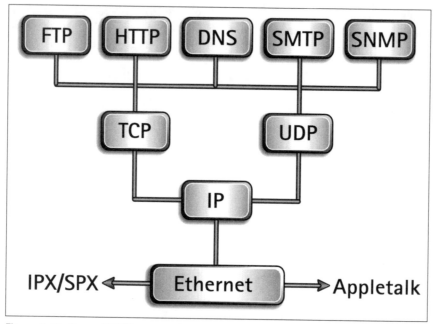

Figure 2-10: Once a TCP/IP message is transmitted to its destination, it must be directed to the proper protocol at each layer to arrive at the proper application process.

 The codes used by the TCP/IP stack to identify specific protocols and ports are defined in most operating systems by files called PROTOCOL and SERVICES, respectively. These are ASCII text files that contain lists of numerical codes and their equivalent protocols and ports. The values found in these files are published by the Internet Assigned Numbers Authority (IANA) in RFC1700, "Assigned Numbers."

FRAGMENTING

In many cases, a message that must be carried by a TCP/IP transmission is too large to be the payload of a single packet. TCP transmissions, for example, are designed to carry large amounts of data (such as FTP or HTTP file transfers) that must be split, or fragmented, into multiple segments. The IP protocol is also capable of fragmenting payloads that exceed the maximum packet size permitted on a given network segment. To execute transfers of large amounts of data, the protocol splits the payload into appropriately sized units, each of which is assigned a number and packaged for transmission in the usual manner. The number assigned to each fragment is stored in the protocol header and transmitted with the data.

Fragment numbers are needed because the packets that comprise the payload are transmitted individually. They may, conceivably, take different routes to the destination and arrive in a different order from that in which they were transmitted. At the receiving station, the numbers are used to reassemble the fragments in proper order (rather than relying solely on the sequence in which they are received).

The fragmentation process performed by IP and the segmenting of TCP transmissions are two entirely different mechanisms. However, they both rely on the data in their respective headers to provide the receiving system with the needed information to reassemble the pieces back into a whole.

ERROR CHECKING

A protocol stack uses several mechanisms to verify that the packets transmitted from a source to a destination have arrived undamaged. These mechanisms rely on the basic technique in which a value is calculated by the sending system, and stored in a protocol header field. When the destination system receives the transmission, it performs the same calculation and compares the results to the value provided in the header. If the values do not match, the data in that packet is assumed to be corrupted.

Error-checking mechanisms like these can be very simple and provide only marginal protection – such as when IP specifies the total length of the packet in its header. If the packet arriving at the destination is a different length, it is certainly damaged. Transmissions can, however, be damaged without their length being affected. A more thorough check is performed by the Ethernet protocol, which computes a *cyclical redundancy check* (CRC) value for its entire payload and delivers it in its header. When the CRC is recomputed at the destination, a different value results if even one bit of the payload is changed.

FLOW CONTROL

Flow control is the process by which a receiving system passes information to the transmitter regarding the speed at which it can receive data. This process is used in extended transmissions consisting of many packets (such as TCP sessions). Flow control is provided by a value in the header of each acknowledgment packet returned to the sender by the destination system. The value specifies the amount of data that the destination system is capable of receiving. If this value decreases during successive acknowledgments, the sender must decrease the rate at which it is transmitting data.

The functions of each field in the various protocol headers are examined in much greater detail in Part II of this book. They are discussed in the sections devoted to the individual TCP/IP protocols.

Diagramming Protocol Headers

The "Assigned Numbers" RFC (RFC1700) document defines a standard method for notating the headers and fields which make up a TCP/IP transmission. This book uses this method for diagramming the TCP/IP protocol headers examined in later chapters. The transmission is divided horizontally into 32-bit words, which are further divided into 8-bit bytes (see Figure 2-11). The most significant byte of each word is on the left side, and the least significant byte, on the right. This is known as *big-endian* order. The bytes of each word are transmitted from left to right, and the words from top to bottom.

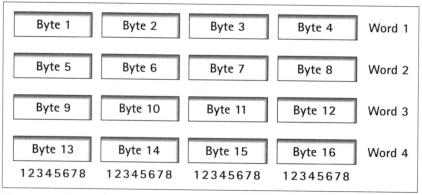

Figure 2-11: The TCP/IP standards diagram structures data by breaking it up into 8-bit bytes and 32-bit words.

Understanding IP Addressing

Once a TCP/IP packet leaves the transmitting workstation, it travels to its destination, whether the system is on the local network segment, a nearby segment of a private internetwork, or half a world away on the Internet. In order to reach the destination system, however, the packet must be properly addressed. On a typical PC LAN, this is not a problem. Data link protocol standards, such as Ethernet and Token Ring, have their own addressing systems based on hexadecimal addresses hardcoded into the network interface adapters.

The TCP/IP standards often use the term "internet" to refer to both private internetworks and the public network that grew out of the ARPANET. In this book, a capital "I" refers to the public Internet, and a lower case "i" is used to refer to a private internet or internetwork — that is, a network of networks.

Every Ethernet network interface card has a unique node address. Manufacturers are each assigned a prefix, to which they append sequential addresses for each device. The administrators of private networks are responsible for assigning a hexadecimal address to each network segment on an enterprise internetwork. The combination of the network address and the node address provides a unique identifier for each system – even on a huge internetwork containing thousands of nodes.

The TCP/IP protocols, however, were originally designed for use on the Internet. Following are two reasons this hardware-addressing system is unsuitable for the Internet environment:

1. Although individual network interface cards have unique addresses, there is no mechanism in place to prevent the duplication of network addresses, assigned by individual administrators.

2. While the hardware used in today's PC LANs supplies a robust addressing system, this was not always the case. The TCP/IP protocols were specifically designed to be independent of any particular hardware platform, at a time when the majority of the computers on the Internet did not use Ethernet or Token Ring at the physical layer.

It was, therefore, necessary for the TCP/IP standards to define an independent, self-contained addressing system that could be used with any hardware platform. In practice, TCP/IP uses a two-tiered system of network and node addresses just like Ethernet, but the network addresses are registered to avoid duplication. Thus, every computer on the Internet has a unique network and node identifier; the two are combined in a 32-bit IP address.

The header applied to packets by the IP protocol is the last one in the TCP/IP protocol stack, and is responsible for specifying the ultimate destination of the transmission. Every IP packet header contains fields holding the IP addresses of both the source and destination systems. TCP/IP packets may travel across dozens of networks as they traverse the Internet, and consequently, be packaged and repackaged in many different frames as they pass through Ethernet, FDDI, PPP, X.25, and untold other network types. Through all of this the IP header remains unchanged, providing a continuous reference to the packet's ultimate destination.

Network and Node Addresses

Using separate network and node addresses creates a system that packets to be more easily directed to a specific computer, on any network segment. On a large internetwork, a single list of thousands of node addresses would be most unmanageable, causing delays as routers repeatedly search the list for addresses. On the Internet, a node address list would contain millions of entries, bogging down the entire network with enormous router tables. Grouping the addresses by network simplifies the process by allowing routers to maintain lists of networks, instead of nodes. A router is only responsible for maintaining a list of the nodes on the networks to which it is directly connected.

Thus, a packet transmitted to a system on another network is sent first to the router responsible for that network. Then, the router consults its node list and directs the packet to the specific host. This is the internetworking equivalent to obtaining travel directions to a town, then asking someone there for directions to a specific street address.

IP Addresses

IP addresses are 32-bit binary addresses. They are usually expressed as four decimal numbers, representing 8 bits (or 1 byte) each, separated by periods. This is known as *dotted decimal* notation. An 8-bit binary number, when expressed in decimal form, can have a value from 0 to 255. Valid IP addresses, therefore, range from 0.0.0.0 to 255.255.255.255. Originally, the TCP/IP standards used the word *octet* to refer to each of these 8-bit values, and this term is occasionally still seen today. The more common word *byte* was avoided because some of the systems on which the protocols were developed (such as the DEC-10) did not use 8-bit bytes. Today, however, a byte is understood to be the equivalent of 8 bits on nearly every computer system made; it is the preferred term.

Thus, an IP address is 4 bytes long, and represents both the addresses of the network on which the computer is located, and the network interface within the computer itself. In TCP/IP parlance, a computer system is referred to as a *host*. A host can have more than one network interface in it, in which case, it must have multiple IP addresses. A host equipped with two or more network adapters is said to be *multihomed*. If a multihomed host is configured to pass traffic from one network to the other, it is said to be a *router*. Usually, a system must be specifically configured to act as a router, and can conceivably maintain connections to two separate networks without routing packets between them.

 In this book, the term "router" is used to describe any system propagating traffic between network segments — whether it is a dedicated hardware device or a PC on which routing is a software or OS function. The term "gateway" is often used in the RFC documents to refer to the same types of routing devices. Traditional networking terminology defines a gateway as a system that routes traffic between networks using different protocols.

IP ADDRESS CLASSES

Because an IP address identifies both the network and the host, there is always a dividing line between the network portion of the address and the host portion. Some of the 32 bits are used to represent the network, and the rest identify the individual host. The dividing line, however, is not located in the same place for all IP addresses. The TCP/IP standards identify several address classes that split the IP address in different ways to accommodate individual network sizes being serviced (see Figure 2-12). The address classes are identified as follows:

◆ **Class A** – In a class A IP address, the first bit is always 0. By default, the first 8 bits (or 1 byte) identify the network, and the remaining 24 bits identify the host.

◆ **Class B** – In a class B IP address, the first two bits are always 1 and 0. By default, the first 16 bits (or two bytes) identify the network, and the remaining 16 bits identify the host.

◆ **Class C** – In a class C IP address, the first three bits are always 1, 1, and 0. By default, the first 24 bits (or 3 bytes) identify the network, and the remaining 8 bits identify the host.

Classes A, B, and C are all used for *unicast* addresses – that is, addresses that identify a single host. Two additional classes, not officially used yet, are as follows:

◆ **Class D** – In a class D address, the first 4 bits are always 1, 1, 1, and 0. Class D addresses are not intended to identify individual hosts. Instead, they identify *multicast* groups – logical groups of computers receiving identical transmissions – not necessarily located on the same network.

◆ **Class E** – In a class E address, the first 4 bits are always 1, 1, 1, and 1. These addresses have been reserved for future use.

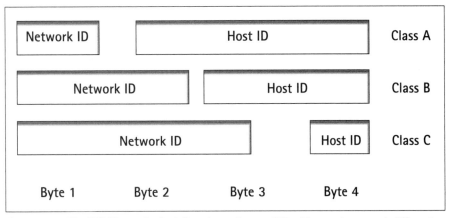

Figure 2-12: The TCP/IP standards define three classes of IP addresses to support different-sized networks.

These class definitions, because of the enforced values for their initial bits, impose limitations on the decimal values used to represent them. For example, the highest possible value for an 8-bit binary number beginning with 0 is 01111111, which in decimal form is 127. Thus, you can always recognize a class A IP address, because its first byte is 127 or less. In the same way, the division between the network address and the host address imposed by the class definitions specifies the maximum number of possible networks that can belong to a particular class, and the maximum number of hosts that can be addressed on a particular network. Because a class A IP address devotes 24 bits to the host address, there can be a maximum of 16,777,214 hosts on any one of 127 possible networks. Table 2-1 displays the number of networks and hosts available in each class.

TABLE 2-1 IP ADDRESS CLASSES

Class	First Byte	Number of Networks	Number of Hosts
A	0 - 127	127	16,777,214
B	128 - 191	16,384	65,534
C	192 - 223	2,097,151	254

Because of these class definitions, you can tell that an IP address of 201.72.101.47, for example, identifies a class C network with an address of 201.72.101. The remaining number, 47, identifies the host on that network. For clarity's sake, this network itself would be referred to as 201.72.101.0 in routing tables or other documents.

Different-sized IP address classes were developed primarily to facilitate the efficient routing of IP traffic while maximizing the number of addresses available for use. If all IP addresses split the network and host identifiers in the same place, there would always be a certain number of networks poorly served. If all IP addresses took the class C form, with three bytes devoted to the network address and one byte to the host, large organizations would be forced to maintain many different networks — each of which would require an entry in the routing tables on every system.

Conversely, if the class B division became the standard rule, with two bytes each devoted to the network and host addresses, a great many small organizations would be assigned a single network address supporting over 65,000 hosts (far more than would actually be used). Thus, any universal division of the IP address space into network and host segments would result either in excessively large routing tables, or a great many wasted host addresses.

At the time the class system was developed, the 32-bit IP address space seemed so vast, that routing efficiency was favored over conservation of host addresses. By now, virtually all of the class A and B addresses have been assigned and few, if any, of the organizations that own them are using all of their available host addresses. As the Internet approaches address saturation – the point at which all of the available IP network addresses have been registered – the IETF's Routing and Addressing (ROAD) working group is considering various strategies to remedy the problem, including classless addressing and the expansion of the 32-bit address space.

REGISTERING IP ADDRESSES

Because any computer on the Internet can send data to any other computer, it is vitally important that every system have a unique IP address. IP addresses cannot be assigned at the factory like those of Ethernet adapters because they are not associated with any particular hardware platform. In fact, there is no physical mechanism to stop users from specifying any IP address they wish in a workstation's TCP/IP configuration.

The developers of the TCP/IP protocols realized, early on, that in order to avoid duplication of IP addresses, there had to be an address registration system. This was a major problem as the thought of being the person whose phone would ring whenever a new system was added to the Internet was terrifying – even in 1983.

Using the same two-tiered network and node-addressing procedure found on the network provided the solution to this problem. The authorities delegated the responsibility for maintaining the IP addresses of networks all over the Internet to an organization called InterNIC (the Internet Network Information Center). By registering only the network addresses, InterNIC became responsible for a much more manageable collection of listings. Today, the list numbers in the thousands, rather than the millions of entries that would be required to list every node address.

Once an organization registers their network with InterNIC, the administrators of the network are responsible for assigning unique host addresses to each computer. This distributed management philosophy is one of the basic tenets of TCP/IP and the Internet. It is largely responsible for the scalability that has allowed the Internet to grow to enormous proportions. You will see it demonstrated again when you read about the Domain Name System (DNS) later in this chapter, that uses a similar method to maintain a distributed database of Internet host names.

The IP address class definitions are intended to allow organizations to register network addresses supporting varying numbers of hosts. A relatively small company could register a class C address that would support up to 254 computers, while large corporations might need class B or class A addresses.

This is not, however, exactly how the system works in practice. There is no single organization that has the 16 million nodes to justify a class A address. Nearly all of the class A and B addresses have already been registered by Internet service providers, who divide the network address into many different subnets and lease them to their clients.

PRIVATE NETWORK ADDRESSES

The IP address classification and registration systems are, of course, designed for use on the Internet. On a private TCP/IP network, addresses need not be registered and classifications can be ignored. As long as each system's host address is unique and located on the same subnet, the network will function properly.

Using unregistered IP addresses for computers on private networks is a practice that is being encouraged as the number of available IP addresses dwindles. The massive growth of the Internet in recent years has led to a situation that was not anticipated by the TCP/IP protocols' developers. There may soon come a time when all available addresses are exhausted. Authorities are trying to forestall this situation by urging network administrators to assign registered IP addresses only to the systems that require them.

There are two types of systems that do not require registered IP addresses: those that do not require access to other organizations' networks or the Internet, and those that connect to the Internet using a firewall or other application-layer gateway. In both cases, however, simply selecting IP addresses at random can later cause problems. A company merger or a connection to the Internet that was not planned when the network was designed can result in address conflicts requiring a huge administrative effort to resolve.

If, for example, you select 199.99.99 as the address for your private network, and designate your workstation as 199.99.99.3, you will have trouble connecting to an Internet site with a registered network address of 199.99.99.0. Renumbering every network and node on your network to remedy problems like this is no one's idea of a good time.

To avoid this situation, the IETF (Internet Engineering Task Force) designated three blocks of IP addresses for use on private networks. These addresses will not be assigned to any Internet network, thus avoiding the address conflicts that may result from routing between the private network and the Internet. These private network address blocks are outlined in Table 2-2.

TABLE 2-2 PRIVATE NETWORK ADDRESSES

Class	Addresses
Class A	10.0.0.0 through 10.255.255.255
Class B	172.16.0.0 through 172.31.255.255
Class C	192.168.0.0 through 192.168.255.255

SPECIAL IP ADDRESSES

Apart from the IP address blocks designated for use on private networks, there are other addresses that cannot be assigned to hosts because they have special uses, as shown in Table 2-3.

TABLE 2-3 RESERVED IP ADDRESSES

Address	Sample	Purpose
Host bits all zero	199.99.99.0	Used to identify a network
All bits one	255.255.255.255	Limited broadcast (to local network hosts only)
Host bits all one	199.99.99.255	Directed broadcast (to hosts on another network)
Network bits zero	0.0.99.75	Used to identify a specific host on the current network
All bits zero	0.0.0.0	Used to identify the current host on the current network
First byte 127	127.0.0.1	Internal host loopback address

In "Address Classes" earlier in this chapter, you learned that a TCP/IP network is referenced by using zeroes in place of the host portion of the IP address. Thus, there can be no individual host on a class C network with the address 199.99.99.0. This address identifies the network itself, and is used in router tables for this purpose.

In the same way, a host identifier of all 1's cannot be assigned to a network interface. This value is used as a broadcast address so a transmission can be sent to all of the hosts on a particular network. For example, on a class C network, you cannot create an IP address for a host in which the value of the last byte is 255.

To broadcast a transmission to all hosts on the local network, the address 255.255.255.255 is used. Transmissions using this address must not be propagated beyond the boundaries of the local network or subnet. For this reason, the 255.255.255.255 address is referred to as a *limited broadcast*.

To broadcast a transmission to all of the hosts on another network, only the host portion of the address is filled with ones. The 199.99.99.255 address would, therefore, be used to send a broadcast to all of the hosts on the class C network 199.99.99.0, from a location on another network. Because the transmission originates from a system on another network, this is called a *directed broadcast*. A directed broadcast can also be used to address the hosts on all of the subnets of a given network, by replacing the subnet portion of the address with ones. If a class B network with the address 162.14.0.0 uses the third byte of the IP address to identify multiple subnets, a broadcast address of 162.14.255.255 would cause identical transmissions to be sent to every host on every subnet.

Subnetting is the process of breaking down a registered class A, B, or C network address into multiple, smaller networks by designating additional bits from the host portion of the IP address as subnet identifiers. For more information, see "Subnetting" later in this chapter.

Because a TCP/IP transmission must emanate from a single system, it is obvious that this broadcast notation can only be used for destination addresses. IP packets must always include the address of the source (or sending) workstation as well. It is possible to form source IP addresses that identify a host on the current network by specifying 0's in place of the network portion of the address. A source address of 0.0.99.75, therefore, would represent the host possessing the address 99.75 on the class B network from which the transmission originated. The address 0.0.0.0 would represent the current host on the local network. These two address forms are only used by workstations that do not yet have an IP address, for obtaining address assignment from a server, using a protocol such as BOOTP.

Finally, any IP address with a value of 127 as its first byte (except those using the reserved values 0 and 255) can be used as the *internal host loopback address*. In other words, using a destination address of 127.0.0.1 is the equivalent of sending a message to yourself. Any system with a functioning TCP/IP protocol stack should be able to PING itself using the loopback address.

The problem with using the 127 address as a testing medium, however, is that loopback transmissions never leave the system; therefore, they do not test the operational capability of the network hardware. You can physically disconnect your system from the network by pulling the cable out of the wall, and still be able to successfully PING yourself using the loopback address.

The 127 address can be useful when testing and troubleshooting software. For example, if you are running a system that has both web server and web client software packages installed on it, you can use the client to connect to the server on the same system using the loopback address. This removes the physical network as a possible source of any problems being experienced.

Subnetting

When an organization registers a class A or B network address (even if it has the number of systems needed to use all of the host addresses provided), these systems are certainly not all located on a single network segment. Instead, the organization operates its own internetwork, consisting of many network segments, connected by routers. Even if this is the case, only the largest corporations could have internet-works that require all of the 65,534 hosts provided by a class B address.

More realistically, the A and B addresses have been registered by ISPs who are in the business of providing individuals or businesses with Internet connectivity and IP addresses. In either scenario, a class A or B network must be broken up into smaller units representing network segments or individual clients. These smaller units are called *subnets*.

Subnets are formed by "borrowing" some of the bits belonging to the host part of the address, and using them to identify the subnet. In its simplest form, this would be a matter of taking a class B address and using the third byte (originally intended to be part of the host address) and using it to identify the subnet (see Figure 2-13). This way, a class B network can be divided into as many as 254 sub-nets, each containing 254 hosts. Each subnet can be used to represent a network segment on a corporate internetwork, or be leased to a client at another location.

The number of possible subnets provided by an 8-bit subnet identifier is computed using the formula 2^8-2, in which two are subtracted to account for the subnet ID values of all 0's or all 1's, which normally are not used. NetWare's TCP/IP stack, however, allows the creation of subnets using a 0 address. It is recommended that you not use 0 for a subnet address unless you know your routers support this practice.

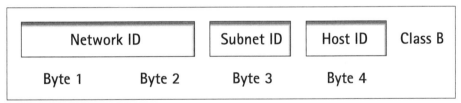

Figure 2-13: Subnetting involves taking some of the IP address bits allotted to the host identifier and using them to create a subnet identifier that functions as part of the network address.

Subnets are logical structures applied only within the bounds of the private internetwork. To the Internet, the borrowed bits are seen as the part of the host identifier that they originally were, just like any other address of that class. This is because the systems on the rest of the Internet need only be concerned with getting traffic to the router providing access to the private internetwork. From there, the borrowed bits are used by the network's internal routers to direct the traffic to the proper subnet, and then to the proper host.

A subnetted class B address enables Internet routers to maintain a record of that entire private internetwork with just one routing table entry. The alternative, which is a separate class C address for each network segment, would require Internet routers to maintain a routing table entry for each of those class C addresses. Multiply these additional routing table entries by the thousands of registered networks, and the result is an enormous additional burden on the Internet infrastructure.

Although it is not essential that IP addresses be subnetted to conform to the physical layout of an internetwork, it is beneficial to the routing process. If all of the systems on a large internetwork are assigned consecutive IP addresses irrespective of network segments (an arrangement called *transparent subnetting*), it becomes necessary to implement a system by which routers can determine the segment where a particular host is located.

Overall, the primary benefit to subnetting an internetwork is administrative. Individual host address assignments have to be made by the administrators of the registered network – and the assignments must be unique. Without subnets, the IP address list for an entire class B network would have to be maintained in one place. For an organization with many different offices, this would be most impractical. By creating subnets, individual branch offices or departments can be given the responsibility of maintaining their own individual IP address assignment lists.

SUBNET MASKING

This subnetting technique does present a problem. In previous sections, you read about IP address classes and the various ways to split the 32 bits of an IP address to identify a network and a host. Now, the logical question arises concerning how a computer determines where the dividing line between the network address and host address lies. The answer, when you are dealing with the standard address classes, is by the value of the first byte (128 to 191 representing class C networks, for example).

When you create subnets, however, this relationship is no longer reliable. A registered class B address can be subnetted using the third byte of the address as the subnet identifier. The addresses, therefore, function like class Cs, but the first byte still indicates class B. When subnetting was made a required feature of all TCP/IP hosts (in RFC950), a new mechanism was implemented to locate the dividing line between the network/subnet address and the host address. This mechanism is called a subnet mask. It is now a required element of all TCP/IP host configurations, along with the IP addresses. A subnet mask is simply a 32-bit binary figure that functions like a template for the IP address. Each bit with a value of 1 indicates that the bit is part of the network address. Bits with a value of 0 represent host address bits. Thus, the subnet mask for an ordinary, unsubnetted class B address is:

```
11111111 11111111 00000000 00000000
```

In decimal notation, this subnet mask is 255.255.0.0.

When you subnet the class B network, you can modify the mask by extending the network address to include the third byte, as follows:

```
11111111 11111111 11111111 00000000
```

The new subnet mask in decimal form is 255.255.255.0. This is the same mask that would be used for a naturally occurring class C address.

Technically, subnetted IP addresses can be said to be broken into three parts, instead of two. Those are a network address, a subnet address, and a host address, as shown in Figure 2-13. For masking and routing purposes, however, the network and subnet addresses are combined into a single explicit network address.

SUBNET MASK ORIENTATION

The previous example, of a class B address that is subnetted by using the third byte for a subnet identifier, demonstrates *byte-orient masking*. This is the simplest form of subnetting because masks are traditionally supplied in decimal form, and the binary figures 00000000 and 11111111 are easily converted into 0 and 255, respectively. You can, however, subnet any class of IP address by borrowing any number of bits from the host. When the boundary between the network and host addresses does not fall between bytes, however, the decimal values become much more difficult to understand. At these times, it is much simpler to think of the subnet mask in binary terms.

If, for example, you take a registered class C address and subnet it by borrowing 4 bits from the host address, your original subnet mask of:

```
11111111 11111111 11111111 00000000 or 255.255.255.0
```

becomes

```
11111111 11111111 11111111 11110000 or 255.255.255.240.
```

This mask allows you to create 14 subnets (2^4-2) containing 14 hosts each.

When a byte is used partly for a subnet identifier and partly for the host, you must also consider the binary values of the byte in assigning IP addresses to each workstation. The first subnet in the given example would have the binary value 0001, and the hosts would be numbered from 0001 to 1110 (the values 0000 and 1111 being invalid). This means that the hosts in that subnet would be assigned IP addresses with fourth-byte values ranging from 00010001 to 00011110, which translate into decimal form as 17 through 30.

The class C network 199.99.99.0 could, therefore, be subnetted as shown in Table 2-4.

TABLE 2-4 IP ADDRESS FOR A CLASS C NETWORK WITH A 4-BIT SUBNET ID

Subnet ID	Host IDs	IP Addresses
0001	0001 to 1110	199.99.99.17 to 199.99.99.30
0010	0001 to 1110	199.99.99.33 to 199.99.99.46
0011	0001 to 1110	199.99.99.49 to 199.99.99.62
0100	0001 to 1110	199.99.99.65 to 199.99.99.78
0101	0001 to 1110	199.99.99.81 to 199.99.99.94
0110	0001 to 1110	199.99.99.97 to 199.99.99.110
0111	0001 to 1110	199.99.99.113 to 199.99.99.26
1000	0001 to 1110	199.99.99.129 to 199.99.99.142
1001	0001 to 1110	199.99.99.145 to 199.99.99.158
1010	0001 to 1110	199.99.99.161 to 199.99.99.174
1011	0001 to 1110	199.99.99.177 to 199.99.99.190
1100	0001 to 1110	199.99.99.193 to 199.99.99.206
1101	0001 to 1110	199.99.99.209 to 199.99.99.222
1110	0001 to 1110	199.99.99.225 to 199.99.99.238

The Windows Calculator program, in its Scientific mode, provides an easy means of converting binary numbers to decimals.

VARIABLE-SIZE SUBNETTING

One of the problems that arises in the subnetting process is the difficulty in predicting the precise growth patterns of the network, in terms of how many hosts will be added to each subnet. As a result, administrators frequently waste IP addresses by planning for growth that never occurs, rather than risking modification of the entire subnetting strategy at a later date. NetWare supports a solution to this problem, defined in RFC1219, that calls for the creation of subnets of varying sizes.

Variable-sized subnets can be created by moving the dividing line between the subnet identifier and the host identifier. This results in hosts on different subnets with different subnet masks, depending on the number of host addresses needed for that subnet. Instead of borrowing a consistent number of bits from the host identifier and dividing a network address into a number of identical subnets (each containing the same number of hosts), the number of subnet bits is varied to allow as many host bits as are needed.

If a class B network address is to be subnetted, a subnet with a large number of hosts could have a mask in which the first four bits of the third byte form the subnet identifier. Following is an example:

```
11111111 11111111 11110000 00000000 or 255.255.240.0
```

Subnets containing a smaller number of hosts could use a standard byte-oriented mask in which the entire third byte identifies the subnet. An example of this looks like the following:

```
11111111 11111111 11111111 00000000 or 255.255.255.0
```

When you create variable-sized subnets, the subnet with the smaller number of hosts is a subset of the larger, and is sometimes referred to as a *stub network*. In order for the stub network to communicate properly with the rest of the host on the network, you must enable proxy ARP on the interface of the larger subnet. You do this by adding the *proxyarp=yes* parameter to the BIND command line, or by using the INETCFG.NLM utility in the NetWare implementation of TCP/IP. For more information, see "Proxy ARP" in Chapter 4.

In the latter case, the actual number of available subnets is limited. This is due to the last four bits of the third byte being used for host identifiers on the other subnet. These bits are being used to form IP addresses needed in the other, larger, subnet—rather than being squandered on another subnet with relatively few hosts.

A router connected to two network segments, one of which has many more workstations connected to it than the other, enables you to use different subnet masks for each interface. This accommodates the number of IP addresses needed for each.

This system of subnetting also provides a more flexible medium for network growth than the standard method. When administrators assign IP addresses, the values of the subnet and host identifiers are usually incremented from right to left, in binary notation. In other words, the progression of addresses (see Figure 2-14) shows the ones being added on the right and moving towards the left.

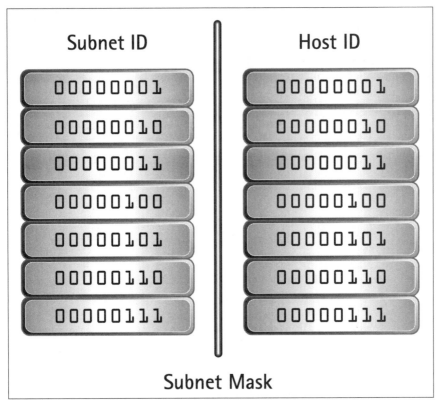

Figure 2-14: The numbering of subnets and hosts, when seen in binary notation, proceeds by adding 1 bit on the right side of the identifier, displacing the 0's on the left.

In this pattern, you can see that the "growth bits" – the bits you use for expansion purposes – appear on the left on both sides of the mask, forming the dividing line between the subnet and host identifiers. RFC1219 proposes that the growth bits for the subnet identifier be reversed. That way they appear on the right side, so the zero bits on both sides of the mask can be pooled, as shown in Figure 2-15.

With all of the growth bits pooled in between the subnet and host identifiers, you can move the subnet mask in either direction. This way, you can provide additional bits to either identifier depending on the needs of your growing network. To change the orientation of the growth bits, however, you must assign subnet identifiers using a binary counting process. This process is the mirror image of the traditional method, with ones entering on the left and moving towards the right.

Adopting this subnetting method obviously makes the administrator's task of assigning IP addresses and subnet masks more arduous, and more dependent on an understanding of binary IP-address values. Variable-sized subnets are not supported by dynamic routing protocols that don't carry subnet mask information – such as RIP – although the RIPII and OSPF protocols do carry subnet mask data.

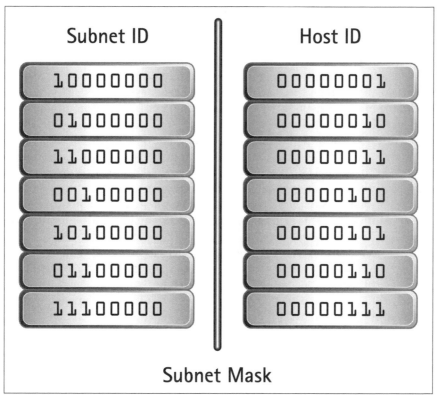

Figure 2-15: By reversing the order of the bits in the subnet identifier, the 0's (or "growth bits") of the address can be used by either the host or the subnet. This is done by simply moving the location of the mask.

 Before creating variable-sized subnets, be sure that all of the technologies on your network support their use — including routers and other operating systems' TCP/IP implementations.

Naming TCP/IP Systems

IP addresses are one of the primary strengths of the TCP/IP protocols. They enable any computer on a network to identify and communicate with any other computer, regardless of their hardware and software platforms. When it comes to human interaction with TCP/IP applications, however, IP addresses are difficult to remember and use. For this reason, standards were developed to assign names to TCP/IP hosts.

On the Internet, host names are assigned to IP addresses and maintained in a distributed database, called the *Domain Name System* (DNS). Internet host names consist of multiple words, separated by periods, that define the location of a particular host in a hierarchy of domains. Another naming convention used by TCP/IP systems is that of the NetBIOS programming interface. IBM developed this for the purpose of creating one of the first PC networking systems. The *NetBIOS* names assigned to computers are up to 16 characters long, and are used on private networks to identify specific computers.

The Microsoft Windows operating systems use NetBIOS names to identify networked systems (no matter what protocols are used to carry the transmissions). When the NetBIOS Over TCP/IP (or NetBT) standards are used for Windows networking, NetBIOS names are equated with IP addresses, just like Internet host names. Thus, a Windows 95 or Windows NT system on a corporate network must have an IP address, but it may also have a NetBIOS name and an Internet host name.

The TCP/IP protocols do not require (or even use) names to communicate with the other systems on a network. When a user supplies an Internet host, or NetBIOS, name in a TCP/IP client application (such as a Web browser), the client software immediately converts the host name into an IP address. It does this before any data is transmitted to the destination, through a process called *name resolution*. The IP protocol then uses only the address to identify the destination system. Names never appear in TCP/IP packet headers – only in the payload.

TCP/IP systems can use a number of different name-resolution mechanisms, depending on the size and complexity of the network. These mechanisms, and their relationships to the TCP/IP protocols and standards, are examined in detail in Chapter 11, "Name Registration and Resolution."

Hosts and Domains

An Internet host name, such as an IP address, is divided into two distinct parts. One part identifies the domain in which the host is located and the other identifies the host, itself. The host identifier is a single word, while the domain name consists of at least two words. For example, in a common host name allotted to a Web server, like *www.mycorp.com*, *www* identifies the host and *mycorp.com* the domain. Like IP addresses, Internet host names must be unique, and the responsibility for assigning and maintaining them is divided between the Internet authorities and the individual network administrators.

The multiple words of a domain name reflect the order formed by an Internet-naming hierarchy; this is used to implement the DNS. A *domain* is a logical identifier for a collection of hosts, which may or may not be located on the same TCP/IP network. Organizations register their domain names with an Internet authority like InterNIC, just as they do their IP network addresses (but the two are completely separate). You need not register one in order to use the other.

Internet domains are hierarchical, and can be displayed in a tree diagram, much like a directory structure. At the top of the hierarchy is the *root domain*, which consists of a collection of *root servers*. Beneath the root are the top-level domains, which have been established by the Internet authorities to provide basic categories for organizations using the Internet. There are two basic principles used in the creation of the top-level domains: geographical and organizational.

Most of the world outside the U.S. uses geographical domains. Based on the X.500 directory service structure, these top-level domains use two letter codes to represent countries. The domain name *uk* is used for the United Kingdom, for example, and *fr* for France. The domain name for Germany is *de*, for Deutschland, because the names are abbreviations of the country's name, in its native language. There is also a *us* domain name, which is coming into more popular use because of the serious depletion of effective names in the *com* domain.

Com is an organizational name, and is the prevalent system used in the U.S. There are six organizational top-level domain names, which are used by various bodies according to their primary function, as follows:

- **com** – used by commercial organizations

- **mil** – used by military organizations

- **gov** – used by government agencies

- **edu** – used by educational institutions

- **net** – used by network support organizations, such as ISPs

- **org** – used by nonprofit organizations, and other uncategorizable bodies

In addition, seven new generic top-level domains (gTLDs) have been approved by the Internet Ad Hoc Committee (IAHC). Currently in the process of being assigned official registrars, they are as follows:

- **firm** – used for businesses or firms

- **store** – used for businesses offering goods for purchase

- **web** – used for organizations emphasizing World Wide Web-related activities

- **arts** – used for organizations emphasizing cultural and entertainment activities

- **rec** – used for organizations emphasizing recreation/entertainment activities

- **info** – used for organizations providing information services

- **nom** – used for those wishing individual or personal nomenclature

The top-level domains are not registered or owned by particular organizations (as are those below the top level). A company, school, or other organization registers its selected name with the authority controlling the appropriate top-level domain. They are then assigned exclusive rights to that name. Domain names must be unique. In the past, failure to create unique names resulted in conflicts between companies seeking to obtain rights to the same name. As the primary contact mechanism used by Internet clients, domain names possess a marketing value that far extends any technical considerations (particularly in the commercial arena).

Having registered a domain name, an organization can assign host names to individual systems, or they can choose to create *subdomains*. Like subnetting IP addresses, the responsibility of creating subdomains lies exclusively with the organization's network administrators. The owners of the *mycorp.com* domain can create subdomains for each of their branch offices, such as *ny.mycorp.com* and *la.mycorp.com* — or use any organizational principle they wish, without consulting InterNIC or registering the names.

Host names are always written in the reverse order of IP addresses. The least significant word, the host identifier, comes first and each name in the domain hierarchy follows. The hierarchy culminates in the name of the top-level domain. The host identifier is also assigned by the network administrator, and must be unique within the domain (or subdomain). Systems are often named for the services they provide, such as *www* for Web servers and *ftp* for FTP servers. There is no official standard that controls host naming.

NetBIOS Names

NetBIOS is a software interface, developed by IBM in the early 1980s. It was created to be one of the first PC networking systems. NetBIOS provides unicast, multicast, and broadcast transmission capabilities using both *session* (connection-oriented) and *datagram* (connectionless) services. Originally designed for use with DOS operating systems, it is not based on any official standard. Other implementations were developed, based on IBM's documentation, that were not necessarily compatible with the original version.

The significance of NetBIOS in today's networking industry is that Microsoft used it as the foundation for the peer-to-peer networking functionality in its Windows NT, Windows 95, and Windows for Workgroups operating systems. The name that you assign to your computer when installing the networking modules in any of these OSs is, in fact, a NetBIOS name.

NetBIOS, therefore, provides a naming system but not a communications protocol. The Windows operating systems can use any one of several protocol standards with its NetBIOS interface. NetBEUI, the NetBIOS Extended User Interface, was the default protocol in the original Windows NT 3.1 release. NetBEUI strictly uses NetBIOS names to identify the other systems on the network. It does this by issuing name broadcasts and waiting for the appropriate system to respond. NetBEUI tends to flood networks with broadcasts; it also lacks a network layer and cannot be routed to other network segments. The TCP/IP protocols became the default in Windows NT 3.51, based on the RFC1001 and RFC1002 standards — which define a method for carrying NetBIOS data within normal TCP and UDP transmissions. Unlike NetBEUI, NetBIOS over TCP/IP (or NetBT), requires IP addresses for all communicating systems, just like any TCP/IP network. The standards, therefore, must define a means of resolving NetBIOS names into IP addresses (just as Internet host names are resolved into IP addresses by DNS). Because the NetBIOS interface, in the Windows OS, can use other networking protocols for its communication, NetBIOS names are a more integral part of the networking system than host names are to the Internet. It is quite possible to operate Internet services like Web or FTP clients and servers without ever using a host name or the DNS, but to perform standard Windows networking functions, you must provide a NetBIOS name for your computer.

TCP/IP Routing

The vast majority of TCP/IP packet transmissions are not destined for systems on the same local network segment. Instead, they are routed to another network; therein lies the essential difference between IP addresses and hardware addresses coded into network adapters. When a packet is transmitted over an Ethernet network, the destination address stored in an Ethernet header does not always identify the ultimate receiver of the packet. Instead, this header is designed only to get the packet to the next stop in its journey. When the next stop is a router providing access to another network segment, it changes the destination address in the Ethernet header to that of the next router in the journey.

If the router provides access to a different type of network, the Ethernet header is removed entirely and replaced with one appropriate for the new protocol. Through all of this, the destination address in the IP header identifies the system for which the packet's payload is intended. This does not change. In a TCP/IP transmission, the sending and receiving computers are referred to as *end systems*. All of the routers encountered during the journey are called *intermediate systems*.

In the OSI reference model, data link-layer protocols are not involved in the delivery of packets to their final destination. They are only involved with the next system down the line. The network-layer protocol handles the routing of packets through the internetwork to the destination system. In the TCP/IP protocol stack, the internet layer is the direct equivalent to the OSI network layer – which leaves the IP protocol responsible for internetwork routing.

When TCP/IP packets pass through intermediate systems on their way to a destination, they travel up the protocol stack. They do not, however, go any higher than the internet layer (see Figure 2-16). The IP protocol determines whether the destination system is located on the local network segment, or if the packets must be sent to another router. In the latter case, IP works in cooperation with ICMP, the system's internal routing tables, and specialized routing protocols like RIP (the Routing Information Protocol) to determine the most efficient route. Then, the hardware address of the next router is discovered and passed to the data link-layer protocol for transmission over the network medium.

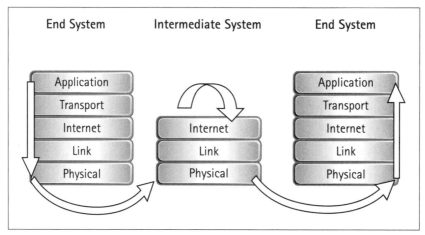

Figure 2-16: Incoming traffic travels no higher than the internet layer in an intermediate system.

On private internetworks, routing is a relatively limited exercise. The most commonly used data link protocol standards, Ethernet and Token Ring, impose strict limitations on the number of network segment packets that may pass through on the way to a destination. The Internet, however, uses many different data link-layer protocols, and imposes no such restrictions. It is not uncommon for packets to pass through up to 20 or more routers on their way to a destination. This phenomenon is easily demonstrated with a traceroute utility, like that found in UNIX and Windows operating systems.

Summary

This chapter described some basic structures and procedures involved in communicating over a network using the TCP/IP protocols.

In this chapter, you learned:

◆ How multilayered networking stacks are used to organize communications processes

◆ How the data generated by one protocol is encapsulated by another protocol for transmission

◆ How the IP addressing system is used to identify TCP/IP hosts

◆ How the domain naming system is used to create friendly names for Internet hosts

The next chapter examines the ways TCP/IP protocols are integrated into the Windows NT and IntranetWare products.

Chapter 3

TCP/IP and Operating Systems

IN THIS CHAPTER

The TCP/IP protocols are designed to operate in a modular fashion, for use in virtually any computing environment. Because the TCP/IP protocols don't comprise a complete networking stack, they must be integrated into an operating system's networking architecture. This means that the OS must provide interfaces to the networking hardware at the bottom of the stack, and to the applications at the top. This chapter examines the ways Windows NT and IntranetWare use the TCP/IP protocols, including the following topics:

- ◆ NDIS and ODI are multiprotocol interfaces used by Windows NT and IntranetWare. They enable communications between the TCP/IP stack and the networking hardware.

- ◆ Both operating systems support several different APIs that can use TCP/IP for their network communications, including Windows Sockets, NetBIOS, and others.

- ◆ Windows NT can use TCP/IP for all of its network communications, or the protocols can coexist with other sets of protocols.

- ◆ IntranetWare uses TCP/IP for its intranet and Internet services, but relies on the IPX protocols for its core networking functions. There are, however, several ways to carry the IPX traffic within IP datagrams, until Novell provides native TCP/IP support for the OS.

Network Interfaces

When a TCP/IP system is connected to a LAN, the functionality defined by the *Open Systems Interconnection* (OSI) reference model's data link and physical layers is not implemented by TCP/IP protocols. Instead, the OS must include a driver that acts as an interface to the network-layer protocol at the top, and the network adapter at the bottom (see Figure 3-1). In addition to passing data between the network and physical layers, the driver implements the data link-layer protocol by encapsulating IP datagrams and preparing them for transmission.

53

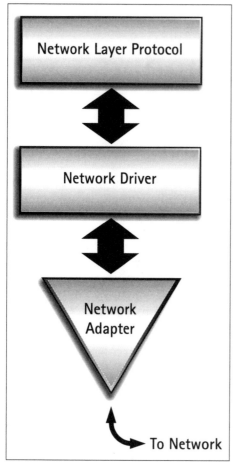

Figure 3-1: An operating system uses a network driver to process network-layer data and pass it to the network-interface adapter for transmission.

Originally, operating systems used dedicated LAN drivers called *monolithic* drivers. These were designed to operate with a specific protocol stack and a specific network card. NetWare clients, for example, required a network administrator to generate a LAN driver using a special program called WSGEN. This program bound the hardware configuration settings, for a particular network card, to the IPX protocol driver. If, at a later time, you wanted to change the hardware interrupt used by the adapter, you had to generate a completely new module.

This type of driver had other problems, as well. Monolithic drivers can only address a single protocol stack. To support both IPX and TCP/IP, for example, you had to use a specially designed driver (usually created by a third party using a proprietary design). Monolithic drivers also require more effort from the developer, because the drivers must use function calls that address the OS directly. In addition, the driver for each network adapter must contain what is, essentially, redundant code that is designed to perform tasks common to all drivers.

To address these and other shortcomings peculiar to each OS, both Novell and Microsoft designed modular interfaces to replace their monolithic drivers. Novell's is called the *Open Data-Link Interface* (ODI) and Microsoft's is the *Network Device Interface Specification* (NDIS). Both of these interfaces include a flexible-binding arrangement. This enables their respective operating systems to multiplex the data from two or more protocol stacks through multiple network interfaces. The following sections examine NDIS and ODI, and the services they provide to Windows NT and NetWare.

The Network Device Interface Specification (NDIS)

The Network Device Interface Specification (NDIS) was designed by Microsoft and 3Com in 1989. The purpose of this joint venture was to provide a standardized interface between the network layer and the physical layer. Windows NT 4.0 uses drivers written to version 4.00 of the NDIS standard, while NT 3.51 uses version 3.00 drivers.

Windows 95 uses NDIS network drivers, written to version 3.01 of the standard, that are not compatible with those written for Windows NT. The 3.01 drivers contain the same functions as the 3.00 versions, but are recompiled to include support for Windows 95 Plug and Play.

NDIS provides a library of function calls that LAN-driver developers can use instead of calls directly addressing the OS's kernel functions. Instead of addressing a network-layer protocol driver directly, a LAN calls an intermediate layer (called the NDIS wrapper) which, in turn, addresses the rest of the OS. Because the LAN driver is isolated from the protocol stack by the NDIS interface, protocols may be changed without modifying the adapter-hardware configuration.

NDIS makes it possible for a LAN driver to be easily ported to Windows NT's various processing platforms. Because the NDIS function calls are always the same, a driver designed for the Intel processor version of NT only needs to be recompiled for use on a DEC Alpha system. If the driver made its function calls directly to the OS kernel, extensive recoding would be necessary to accommodate the different platforms.

The IEEE 802 standards for data link-layer protocols divide that layer into the *Media Access Control* (MAC) and the *Logical Link Control* (LLC) sublayers. NDIS functions are divided in the same way, as shown in Figure 3-2. At the MAC sublayer, there are modules containing all of the hardware-specific routines needed to communicate with network adapters installed in the system. These modules are called *miniport drivers*. A miniport driver controls the actual communication with the network adapter, and provides the means to specify the hardware-configuration settings. Windows NT miniport drivers have a SYS extension, and may be provided by Microsoft or by the manufacturer of the network adapter.

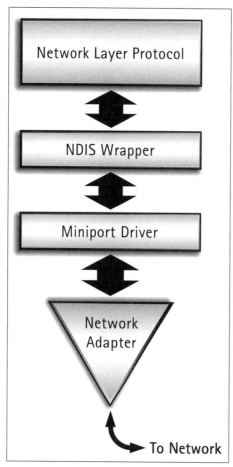

Figure 3-2: An NDIS implementation typically consists of one or more miniport drivers and the NDIS wrapper.

Above the miniport driver, at the LLC layer, is the *NDIS wrapper*. It is implemented in Windows NT as a module, called *Ndis.sys*. While a system runs a separate miniport driver for each network adapter in the machine, there is only one NDIS wrapper (which contains the functions common to all network adapters). Ndis.sys also controls the bindings of the network adapters to the protocol stacks.

The NDIS interface provides the capability to bind a single network adapter to multiple protocols, or a single protocol to multiple adapters. From Windows NT's Network Control Panel, you can control which protocol stacks are permitted to send and receive data using each network adapter. Theoretically, a Windows NT system can support an unlimited number of network adapters, and bind them to an unlimited number of protocol stacks.

INCOMING DATA

When data arrives at one of the network adapters in a Windows NT system (from a LAN), the hardware performs a filtering operation. It only permits the packets destined for that adapter (whether as a unicast, or part of a multicast or broadcast transmission) to pass up to the miniport driver. All other packets are discarded without processing by the system CPU. The miniport driver receives incoming packets from the network adapters, and passes them to the NDIS wrapper. The NDIS wrapper is responsible for demultiplexing the data to the appropriate protocol stacks.

Many network adapters can operate in a nonselective mode (sometimes called *promiscuous mode*). This mode disables the hardware filtering, which enables all packets to be passed to the miniport driver. The feature is typically used by protocol-analysis applications to examine all data traversing the network medium.

OUTGOING DATA

The NDIS wrapper also provides a generic interface to the protocol stacks operating at the network layer, and above. Data traveling down the stack, from an application, reaches the network layer and is passed to the NDIS wrapper. The wrapper then passes the data to the miniport driver that provides access to the network on which the destination system is located.

NDIS handles raw packets only — it can only transmit the data exactly as it is received from the network layer. NDIS does not build the data link-layer frame for outgoing transmissions. This task is performed by the protocol stack, surprisingly. Microsoft's TCP/IP implementation is capable of building frames for the following data link protocols:

◆ Ethernet II

◆ IEEE 802.3 with IEEE 802.2 LLC and SNAP

◆ Token Ring (IEEE 802.5)

◆ Fiber Distributed Data Interface (FDDI)

◆ ARCNET

◆ Point-to-Point Protocol (PPP)

INTERMEDIATE DRIVERS

In addition to the NDIS wrapper and the miniport drivers, NDIS supports another type of module called an *intermediate driver*. In the NDIS architecture, intermediate drivers fall in between miniport drivers and the transport protocol stacks – but they are still enveloped by the NDIS wrapper, as shown in Figure 3-3. Intermediate drivers enable Windows NT to use a link-layer protocol that is not supported by the protocol stack. To a protocol stack, the intermediate driver appears to be a miniport driver; to a miniport driver, it appears as a protocol stack.

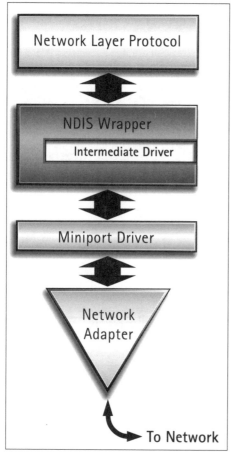

Figure 3-3: NDIS intermediate drivers provide media-translation services between protocol stacks and miniport drivers.

Windows NT uses intermediate drivers to support *Asynchronous Transfer Mode* (ATM) network adapters. Rather than modifying the protocol stack for every new data link-layer technology, an intermediate driver performs the translation between the new frame type and one supported by the stack.

WAN DRIVERS

NDIS miniport drivers are not limited to use with LAN adapters. In Windows NT, WAN connections using ISDN, X.25, and asynchronous links (such as dial-ups and dedicated telephone lines) are not configured as adapters, in the Network Control Panel, in the usual sense. There are, however, miniport drivers for WAN technologies, including those that use the interface provided by the system's standard serial ports. WAN miniports appear as adapters in Windows NT's Bindings screen (see Figure 3-4), where their relationships with protocols and services can be manipulated like those of other network adapters.

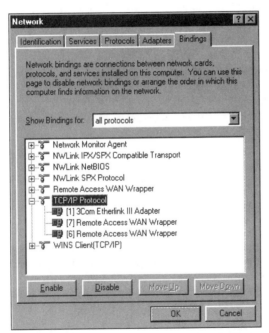

Figure 3-4: WAN miniport drivers can be selectively bound to protocols and services just like standard network interface adapters.

The PPP framing used in many WAN connections is supported by the Windows NT protocol stacks. WAN miniport drivers, however, can also function in a pass-through mode. This mode enables the networking interface hardware to perform PPP framing, encryption, and compression (when it is capable of doing so).

The Open Data-Link Interface (ODI)

The *Open Data-Link Interface* (ODI) specification was developed by Novell and Apple Computer. It was first published in 1989 — almost the same time as the first appearance of NDIS. ODI is similar to NDIS, in that it provides a modular interface between a system's protocol stacks and its network adapters, binding any network-layer protocol to any physical-layer protocol. ODI, however, isolates the two layers even more than NDIS by placing the entire data link-layer functionality in the ODI modules. Unlike NDIS, which relies on the protocol stack to create the data link-layer protocol frames, ODI drivers perform this task themselves. Thus, it is not necessary for the protocol stack implementation to support specific frame types.

Like NDIS, ODI separates the hardware-specific functions of the data link layer from the more general ones. ODI's LAN drivers are known as *Multiple Link Interface Drivers* (MLIDs), denoting their capability to send and receive packets containing different protocols. Each network adapter installed in the system requires an MLID.

Above the MLIDs is the *Link Support Layer* (LSL), which functions as the multiplexer/demultiplexer for the MLIDs and the protocol stacks. LSL processes the packets in the data stream and passes incoming data to the appropriate protocol, while passing outgoing data to the correct MLID. To exchange information with MLIDs and protocols, LSL writes the data to interim buffers, called *Event Control Blocks* (ECBs), that can be accessed from the layers above and below.

ODI COMMUNICATIONS

When a packet arrives at an ODI-equipped system, the network adapter strips off the preamble from the data link-protocol frame header. It performs the checksum computation needed to verify that the packet was received intact. The adapter then passes the packet to the MLID, which strips off the data link frame header and copies the information from the header fields to ECBs (see Figure 3-5). The ECBs are passed to the LSL, which uses a Protocol ID (PID) — contained in one of the ECBs — to determine which protocol stack should receive the data.

Outgoing data is processed in much the same way. The LSL receives data from a protocol stack and passes it, along with ECBs containing information received from the upper-layer protocols (such as the destination of the packet), to the appropriate MLID. The MLID receives the data from the LSL, and encapsulates it in a data link-layer frame using the information from the ECBs for the header fields.

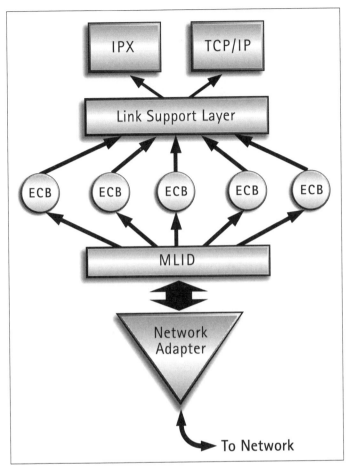

Figure 3-5: The ODI Link Support Layer uses ECBs to pass information to the MLIDs operating below it.

ODI DRIVERS

The ODI implementations used on NetWare servers, and clients running Novell's Client 32, are very similar. In fact, most of the MLID drivers designed for use with NetWare 4.1x can also be used on a Client 32 workstation. This is made possible by the NIOS.VXD module that forms the base for the entire Client 32 architecture. NIOS.VXD (named for the acronym Network Input/Output System) is based largely on the NetWare SERVER.EXE program. It permits 32-bit NetWare modules, such as NLMs and LAN drivers, to be executed on a DOS or Windows workstation.

To ease the development process for MLIDs, the functionality of the driver is subdivided into three separate modules, as follows:

◆ **Media Support Module (MSM)** – The MSM provides the generic initialization and runtime functions that enable the MLID to communicate with the LSL, and the rest of the OS. On a NetWare 4.1x server, this module is called MSM.NLM; on a Client 32 workstation, it is called CMSM.NLM.

◆ **Topology Support Module (TSM)** – The TSM controls all aspects of the MLID pertaining to the particular data link-layer protocol used by the network adapter (for example, the creation and manipulation of the protocol frame). Where appropriate (such as with Ethernet), the TSM provides all of the frame-type options supported by NetWare. NetWare server and Client 32 TSMs have names like ETHERTSM.NLM, TOKENTSM.NLM, and PPPTSM.NLM.

◆ **Hardware Support Module (HSM)** – The HSM provides all of the hardware-specific functions required for the MLID to communicate with the network interface adapter. The HSM is usually thought of as the LAN driver, a file with an LAN extension.

The 32-bit ODI modules designed for use on NetWare servers are assembly based, while Client 32 modules are based on the C language. In most cases, the assembly based LAN drivers, intended for servers, can be used on Client 32 workstations. Novell, however, is gradually moving towards the use of C for all of its LAN drivers. These same drivers will also function with the IntranetWare Client for Windows NT — even though this client is not based on the NIOS architecture as are the Client 32 releases.

While NetWare's Client 32 releases ship with 32-bit ODI drivers, they are capable of using almost any other adapter driver you may have installed on the system. This includes the 16-bit ODI drivers traditionally used with the NetWare DOS Requester (the VLM client), and in the Windows 95 client, the NDIS 3.1 drivers that ship with the OS.

The 16-bit ODI drivers are compiled as executable files with a COM extension, as they predate the workstation NIOS architecture introduced in Client 32. The 16-bit drivers do not use separate MSM and TSM components, either. All of the MLID functionality is supplied in a single module.

The 16-bit LSL implementation included with the NetWare DOS Requester is also an executable file, called LSL.COM. The 32-bit C-based version included with the Client 32 releases is called LSLC32.NLM.

Application Programming Interfaces (APIs)

To assimilate a protocol stack like TCP/IP into an OS, applications must issue the appropriate function calls to enable them to use the protocols. In a multiprotocol OS like Windows NT, an application may need to use one of several protocol stacks. Operating systems use *Application Programming Interfaces* (APIs) to provide a standard set of function calls for the network services provided by the system's protocol stacks. This eliminates the need for developers to modify their applications for each implementation of a protocol.

Windows Sockets

The Windows Sockets API is the most commonly used programming interface for TCP/IP applications. Nearly all TCP/IP client applications, such as Web browsers, news readers, FTP, mail clients, and standard utilities like PING, rely on Windows Sockets to access the TCP/IP protocol stack installed on the system. Based on the socket interface in the Berkeley UNIX OS, Windows Sockets is the result of a collaborative effort by more than 20 vendors of TCP/IP products.

In 1991, development of the API began. Developers of TCP/IP applications for the Windows platform had difficulty producing products that could function with the many different TCP/IP protocol stacks available for the Windows platform. At that time, the Windows platform consisted solely of the Windows 3.x product. The Windows NT and Windows 95 releases (which contain their own internal TCP/IP implementations) were still some years away, and users had to purchase a third-party solution to add TCP/IP to a Windows system.

Not surprisingly, the TCP/IP stacks designed by various vendors differed greatly. If a company produced an application that used TCP/IP's transport services, it had to accommodate the peculiarities of the various protocol stacks on the market. To do this, developers began creating their own interfaces to the protocols. These consisted of an *abstraction layer* that provided the generic function calls used by the application, and a collection of *providers* that addressed specific makers' TCP/IP protocol stacks.

This was not a satisfactory solution as developers had to update their providers, continually, to accommodate new and improved TCP/IP implementations. Thus, a committee was assembled to create an interface standard that would apply to applications and protocol stacks.

WINSOCK 1.1

The resulting standard is known as Windows Sockets version 1.1. It defines an interface like that of a Windows dynamic-link library, called *Winsock.dll*, as shown in Figure 3-6. To access the protocols' transport services, an application calls this DLL, regardless of which TCP/IP stack is running on the system. This provides application developers with a simple solution to the problem of multiple protocol stack vendors. Any Winsock-compliant program can run on any compliant TCP/IP stack.

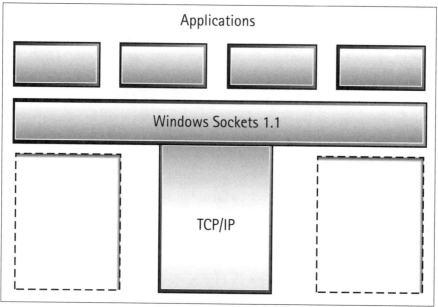

Figure 3-6: The Windows Sockets 1.1 standard requires a DLL to function as the interface to applications at the top of the TCP/IP protocol stack.

Winsock 1.1 provides two types of sockets for applications to request. A *stream socket* offers connection-oriented service, using the *Transmission Control Protocol* (TCP). A *datagram socket* uses the *User Datagram Protocol* (UDP) to provide connectionless service. The socket type, along with an IP address and a port number, identifies a socket on a particular TCP/IP system.

WINSOCK 2

The Winsock 1.1 standard defines a DLL that functions as a generic interface to TCP/IP applications, whereas the interface between the Winsock.dll module and the protocol stack is proprietary. Version 2 of the standard adds a *service provider interface* (SPI) between the DLL and the protocol stacks, which adds flexibility to the arrangement (see Figure 3-7).

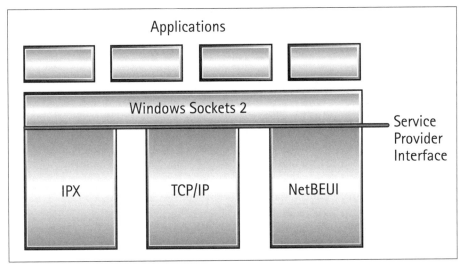

Figure 3-7: Version 2 of the Windows Sockets standard isolates the Winsock.dll from the application and protocol stack.

By isolating the Winsock DLL in this manner, applications can access multiple protocol stacks using the same interface. The multiple stacks can be implementations of the same protocols, such as multiple TCP/IP stacks, or various different protocols, such as TCP/IP and IPX. Winsock 2 also provides support for 32-bit applications, while remaining backwards-compatible with both 16-bit and Winsock 1.1 programs. As protocol stacks are initialized (typically during the system boot process), their capabilities are registered with the Winsock SPI interface and they become service providers for Winsock applications. Applications can then issue an API-function call to discover what protocols are available, as well as their properties and capabilities.

Because the Winsock 2 DLL is no longer associated with a particular protocol stack, it is more likely to be implemented as part of the OS. Windows 3.1 and Windows for Workgroups are probably the last Windows versions to lack an integrated TCP/IP implementation. Ironically, this all but eliminates the problem that Windows Sockets was intended to solve. With all Windows 95 and Windows NT systems using the same protocol stack, it is (theoretically) possible to write applications that address the protocol stacks directly. The use of Windows Sockets enables applications to access the protocols of any present or future Windows operating systems.

Windows NT 4.0 contains support for version 2 of the Windows Sockets standard and all previous versions, as will Windows 98. To support all existing Winsock applications, Windows NT includes the following libraries:

◆ **Ws2_32.dll** – provides support for 32-bit Windows Sockets 2.x applications

◆ **Wsock32.dll**–provides support for 32-bit Windows Sockets 1.1 applications

◆ **Winsock.dll**–provides support for 16-bit Windows Sockets 1.1 applications

NAME RESOLUTION

A basic function the Winsock library performs is resolving "friendly" names into the addresses needed for network communications. For the Winsock 1.1 standard, this is a relatively simple matter–the only protocol stack supported is TCP/IP, and a DNS request is the only requirement. Winsock 2, however, by supporting multiple protocol stacks, complicates the matter considerably.

Different protocol stacks have different addressing requirements and use different types of name spaces. A *name space* is a method by which a protocol associates the addresses it uses for network communications with friendly names. Winsock 2 can support many name spaces, which can be categorized using three different types:

◆ **Static**–A static name must be manually entered by an administrator into a database. DNS is an example of a static name space.

◆ **Dynamic**–A dynamic name space is capable of automatically registering the existence of a service, often using network broadcasts. The service must continually reiterate its broadcasts for the service to remain available to other systems. NetWare's Service Advertising Protocol is an example of a dynamic name space.

◆ **Persistent**–A persistent name space can automatically register services, and retains the information in permanent storage until it is expressly removed. X.500, NDS, and WINS are examples of persistent name spaces.

Winsock 2 uses software modules called *name space providers*. These provide the SPI with the necessary details for formulating queries and registering information with individual name spaces. This way, an application need not be aware of the name-resolution method employed by the protocol stack (or even of which protocol stack is being used for network communications services).

 For more information about name resolution, see Chapter 11, "Name Registration and Resolution."

NetBIOS

An API, called NetBIOS, was designed for use on PCs by IBM in 1984. Like Windows Sockets, NetBIOS is not a protocol; it is an interface that requires the services of a protocol stack for network communications. Unlike Windows Sockets, however, NetBIOS also includes a name space – which is the main reason the interface is still used today.

The NetBIOS interface was designed specifically for IBM's use, and there is no definitive document for the NetBIOS standard. Other companies developed their own implementations of the interface after IBM, resulting in significant incompatibilities. Today, the document commonly accepted as the NetBIOS standard is the "IBM PC Network Technical Reference Manual," published in 1984. In 1987, two RFCs (RFC1001 and RFC1002) were published by the IETF. These defined the use of the TCP/IP protocols as a transport mechanism for the NetBIOS service.

NetBIOS provides applications with both session and datagram services. A *session* is a connection-oriented, full-duplex, reliable link between two systems. The *datagram* service is a connectionless, unreliable message service. If NetBIOS is using the TCP/IP protocol stack for its communications, the session and datagram services correspond to the TCP and UDP protocols, respectively. NetBIOS can also use the IPX protocol stack or, on Windows NT, the NetBEUI protocol.

THE NETBIOS MODULES

Both Windows NT and NetWare support the NetBIOS API for use by applications. This includes a NetBIOS over TCP/IP alternative called *RFCNBIOS.EXE*, which is part of the NetWare/IP product. Windows NT supports NetBIOS applications with a dynamic-link library called *Netapi32.dll* that is accessed by the application, directly. The DLL, in turn, exchanges data with a NetBIOS emulator that passes the data to and from the appropriate protocol stack (see Figure 3-8).

NetBIOS applications, however, are relatively rare now, and Windows NT uses NetBIOS primarily for its name space. NT relies on NetBIOS names for its basic Windows-network communications. The computer name that you assign to a Windows (NT or 95 or Workgroups) system is actually a NetBIOS name. It is used to identify the system during all of its file- and printer-sharing activities. The first word of a Windows NT UNC name that describes a shared network resource is the system's NetBIOS name, as in \\server1\cdrive.

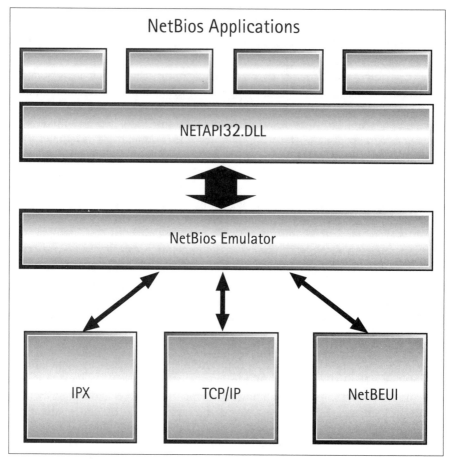

Figure 3-8: Windows NT enables NetBIOS applications to use any of the three primary protocol stacks supported by the OS.

NETBIOS NAMING

NetBIOS connections are established with names you can assign to individual systems, and groups of systems. NetBIOS uses a flat (as opposed to a hierarchical) name space, in which all names on the network must be unique. They can be up to 16 characters long, although Windows NT reserves the sixteenth character for use as a NetBIOS suffix that identifies the type of resource. The values used by Windows NT for the sixteenth character are shown in Table 3-1.

TABLE 3-1 WINDOWS NT NETBIOS SUFFIXES

Suffix (hex)	Name Type	Resource
00	Unique	Workstation Service
01	Unique	Messenger Service
01	Group	Master Browser
03	Unique	Messenger Service
06	Unique	RAS Server Service
1F	Unique	NetDDE Service
20	Unique	File Server Service
21	Unique	RAS Client Service
22	Unique	Microsoft Exchange Interchange(MSMail Connector)
23	Unique	Microsoft Exchange Store
24	Unique	Microsoft Exchange Directory
30	Unique	Modem Sharing Server Service
31	Unique	Modem Sharing Client Service
43	Unique	SMS Administrators Remote Control Tool
44	Unique	SMS Clients Remote Control
45	Unique	SMS Clients Remote Chat
46	Unique	SMS Clients Remote Transfer
4C	Unique	DEC Pathworks TCPIP service on Windows NT
52	Unique	DEC Pathworks TCPIP service on Windows NT
87	Unique	Microsoft Exchange MTA
6A	Unique	Microsoft Exchange IMC
BE	Unique	Network Monitor Agent
BF	Unique	Network Monitor Application
00	Group	Domain Name
1B	Unique	Domain Master Browser
1C	Group	Domain Controllers

continued

TABLE 3-1 WINDOWS NT NETBIOS SUFFIXES *(Continued)*

Suffix (hex)	Name Type	Resource
1D	Unique	Master Browser
1E	Group	Browser Service Elections
1C	Group	IIS
00	Unique	IIS

NetBIOS applications only deal with names. Nevertheless, a mechanism is usually required to resolve NetBIOS names into addresses for network communications. For example, the NetBIOS over TCP/IP documents describe two basic methods for resolving NetBIOS names into IP addresses. One is a broadcast method in which a system transmits a request containing the desired name and waits for a reply containing an address. The other is a NetBIOS name service that functions as a repository for NetBIOS names and their equivalent IP addresses. Windows NT relies primarily on TCP/IP for its NetBIOS services. The OS includes a NetBIOS name server called the Windows Internet Name Service (WINS), that solves many of the problems implicit in NetBIOS naming.

WINS and the NetBIOS name registration, and resolution, mechanisms used by Windows NT are discussed in detail in Chapter 11, "Name Registration and Resolution."

TCP/IP and the Windows NT Networking Architecture

The Windows NT OS uses a modular-networking architecture that provides flexibility in selecting protocols and technologies. Using the TCP/IP protocol with the OS figuratively slips the protocol stack into a space between two interfaces. NT's other supported protocols can also fit into this space.

The NDIS interface, as covered earlier in this chapter, lies just below the network layer of the OSI reference model. It provides access to the network-interface hardware that forms the physical layer. At the top of the transport layer is the *transport driver interface* (the TDI). As NDIS insulates the bottom of the protocol stacks from the network adapters, the TDI forms a boundary layer between the top of the stacks and the APIs (such as Windows Sockets, NetBIOS, and the Workstation and Server services – see Figure 3-9). This provides the client/server functionality used for sharing files and printer.

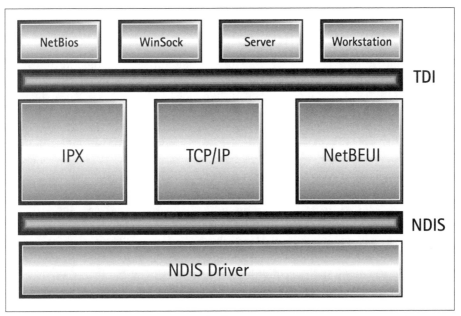

Figure 3-9: The transport driver interface (TDI) forms an abstraction layer between the protocol stacks and the application interfaces.

The Transport Driver Interface (TDI)

The TDI is not manifested as a separate software module, like NDIS. Instead, the TDI is an interface that the developers of protocol stacks use to define the upper boundary of the transport layer. This makes the protocols into service providers for the clients operating above the interface. These clients are the APIs that provide services to the actual applications that use them. The TDI provides its clients with a set of function calls that are used to map the primitive functions of the API requests to the various transport protocols.

Depending on the nature of the client API, the primitive functions may be sufficiently generic to enable the use of any protocol stack (or they may require the services of a specific transport protocol). The Windows Sockets 1.1 API, for example, can only address the TCP/IP protocol stack, and uses function calls that request particular TCP/IP services. Winsock 2, however, can use any protocol, and provides generic function calls which completely isolate the application from the transport protocol.

The TDI is extremely flexible, and supports all of the APIs implemented by Windows NT. It uses a collection of function calls that can be mixed and matched to any of the interfaces' service primitives. In addition, the TDI includes an extensible TDI_ACTION IOCTL request that maps calls for specific transport functions not defined by the interface. Transport protocols can also pass event notifications to programming interfaces through the TDI, without a client request.

NetBEUI, TCP/IP, and Streams

The first release of Windows NT, version 3.1, defaulted to using the NetBIOS Extended User Interface (NetBEUI) protocol. Designed for use on relatively small networks, NetBEUI is reasonably efficient, but it lacks features to make it suitable for today's expanding internetworks. Using the NetBIOS naming system, NetBEUI relies on broadcast transmissions to locate other systems on the network. This, and its lack of OSI network-layer functionality, restricts NetBEUI from being routed, and limits its use on multisegment networks.

This first version of Windows NT supported the TCP/IP and NWLINK (IPX) protocols, but only through an additional interface, known as Streams. Streams is a collection of modules that create a full duplex data conduit between the TDI and the NDIS interfaces. The Streams interface consists of a *stream head* (module that communicates with application interfaces above the TDI), a *stream end* (driver that communicates with the NDIS driver), and one or more additional modules that connect the two. Adapting the TCP/IP and NWLink protocols to the new Windows NT OS was greatly simplified by using the Streams interface, as shown in Figure 3-10.

Using Streams to implement a transport protocol stack imposes an additional layer of processing overhead on every protocol transaction. For an application to use TCP/IP services in Windows NT 3.1, it must issue a request to an API (such as Windows Sockets), which must then issue its own function call to Streams via the TDI. Streams then accesses the actual transport protocol driver.

In Windows NT 3.5, the shortcomings of the NetBEUI protocol in practical business networking became recognizable. Greater emphasis was then placed on routable, full-service protocols, such as TCP/IP and NWLink. As a result, these two protocols were fully assimilated into the Windows NT networking architecture without using Streams. This eliminated the unnecessary processing overhead imposed by the additional interface. Today, the TCP/IP protocols are more commonly used with Windows NT than NetBEUI. Windows NT offers greater expandability and many TCP/IP-based services are included with the OS, such as the DHCP, WINS, and DNS servers.

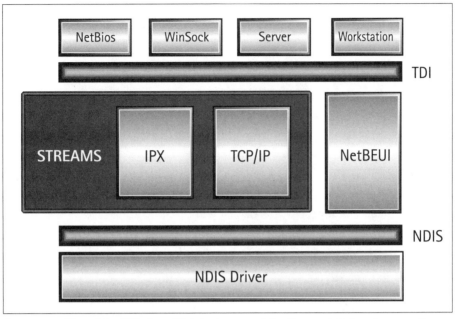

Figure 3-10: The original Windows NT 3.1 release used the Streams interface to access the TCP/IP and NWLink protocols.

NetBIOS over TCP/IP (NetBT)

A Windows NT system with the TCP/IP protocol stack installed can run NetBIOS applications using the message types defined in the NetBIOS over TCP/IP (NetBT) standards (RFC1001 and RFC1002). NetBT is, however, more commonly used for Windows NT's native file and printer-sharing operations. Windows NT's Server, Workstation, Browser, Messenger, and Netlogon services all use NetBT to communicate with other systems. These services do not send their requests through the NetBIOS emulator like standard NetBIOS applications. Instead, they address the TDI directly, to eliminate an extraneous layer of processing overhead.

NetBT messages fall into three basic service types:

 ◆ Name service – This service uses the UDP protocol and well-known port number 137. NetBT name service messages are used to resolve NetBIOS names into IP addresses by transmitting broadcasts, or unicast name-server requests.

 ◆ Session service – This service uses the TCP protocol and well-known port number 139. The NetBT session service transmits SMB traffic and exchange files and other data between peer systems on a Windows network.

◆ **Datagram service** – Using the UDP protocol and well-known port number 138, the NetBT datagram service is used to transmit brief messages to broadcast, multicast, and unicast addresses.

The following sections examine the various message types used by the NetBT session and datagram services. The name service message types are discussed in Chapter 11, "Name Registration and Resolution."

NETBT SESSION SERVICE MESSAGES

NetBT session service messages are carried within TCP data packets, after a standard TCP session is established with the target system. NetBT's own session-establishment procedure, when successful, causes the TCP session to transform into a NetBT session. Failure of the NetBT session-establishment procedure causes the TCP session to terminate.

All of the NetBT session service-message types, except for the SESSION MESSAGE and SESSION KEEP ALIVE messages, are devoted to the session establishment procedure. There are no explicit session-termination message types. NetBT sessions are terminated either by an elapsed timeout interval, or by a TCP termination (FIN) request. The format of the NetBT session service-messages types is shown in Figure 3-11.

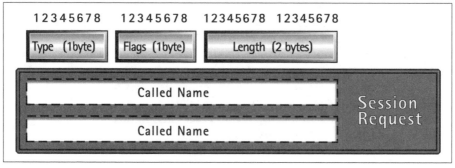

Figure 3-11: NetBT session service messages all contain the type, flags, and length fields, after which various other fields may follow, depending on the message type.

The functions of the fields found in the NetBT session service messages are as follows:

◆ **Type** (1 byte) – The type field contains a code that specifies the function of the NetBT message, as follows:

- 00 – SESSION MESSAGE – carries data during the steady-state phase of a NetBT session

- 81 – SESSION REQUEST – requests the opening of a session during the NetBT session-establishment phase

- 82 – POSITIVE SESSION RESPONSE – confirms the opening of a session during the NetBT session-establishment phase

- 83 – NEGATIVE SESSION RESPONSE – denies the opening of a session during the NetBT session-establishment phase

- 84 – RETARGET SESSION RESPONSE – refers a system, requesting the opening of a session, to another IP address and/or port number during the NetBT session-establishment phase

- 85 – SESSION KEEP ALIVE – maintains an open session during the NetBT steady-state phase when data is not actively being transferred

- **Flags** (1 byte) – the first seven bits of this field are unused and must contain a value of 0; the eighth bit is used as an additional high-order bit for the length field

- **Length** (2 bytes) – specifies the number of bytes in the message following the length field

- **Trailer** (variable) – contains different fields of various sizes for each possible session service-message type

The contents of the message-trailer fields for the different message types are as follows:

Session Message

- **User data** (variable) – contains a fragment of the data being transmitted to the destination

Session Request

- **Called name** (variable) – contains the NetBIOS name of the system that is the intended destination for the message

- **Calling name** (variable) – contains the NetBIOS name of the system transmitting the message

Positive Session Response

- contains no additional fields, and the value of the type field indicates the receiving system's acceptance of the SESSION REQUEST

Negative Session Response

- ◆ **Error code** (1 byte) – The Error code specifies the reason the receiving system denied the opening of a NetBT session, as follows:

  - ◆ 80 – **Not listening on called name** – The called name, specified in the SESSION REQUEST message, exists on the system with the designated IP address (taken from the TCP header's destination IP address field). There is, however, no process listening on the specified-port number.

  - ◆ 81 – **Not listening for calling name** – The called name, specified in the SESSION REQUEST message, exists on the system with the designated IP address. The system is not authorized to open a session with the sending system.

  - ◆ 82 – **Called name not present** – The called name, specified in the SESSION REQUEST message, does not exist on the system with the designated IP address.

  - ◆ 83 – **Called name present, but insufficient resources** – The called name, specified in the SESSION REQUEST message, exists on the system with the designated IP address. The system does not, however, have the memory available to initiate the session.

  - ◆ 8F – **Unspecified error**

Retarget Session Response

- ◆ **Retarget IP address** (4 bytes) – The retarget IP address field specifies the address of the system to which the SESSION REQUEST message should be sent.

- ◆ **Port** (2 bytes) – The port field specifies the port number on the system identified by the retarget IP address value, to which the SESSION REQUEST message should be sent.

Session Keep Alive

- ◆ The session keep alive message contains no additional fields, and no response is required. The value of the type field indicates (to the receiving system) that the NetBT session should not be permitted to time out. Because some TCP/IP implementations contain their own keep alive functions, the use of the NetBT keep alive may be configured to be optional.

NETBT DATAGRAM SERVICE MESSAGES

NetBT datagrams are carried within UDP packets, and may be sent as unicast, multicast, or broadcast transmissions, using separate message types. NetBIOS facilitates multicast communications by assigning NetBIOS names to groups of systems. Although it is used less often than the session service, the NetBT datagram service is supported by Windows NT. When you use the NET SEND command to transmit a message to a NetBIOS group name, or as a broadcast, Windows NT uses the NetBT datagram service.

Though NetBT name service messages are datagrams that use the UDP protocol for their transport services, they are not a part of the datagram service. They should be considered a service unto themselves.

NetBT datagram service messages can range from a minimum of 576 bytes to a maximum of 1,064 bytes, in length. Datagrams may, therefore, need to be fragmented and carried in two or more UDP packets. NetBT provides its own fragmentation mechanism, using the fields in the NetBT header. The layout of the header is shown in Figure 3-12.

The functions of the fields found in NetBT datagram service messages are as follows:

- **Msg type** (1 byte) – The msg_type field contains a code that specifies the nature or purpose of the datagram, as follows:

  - 10 – DIRECT_UNIQUE DATAGRAM – indicates that the datagram is a unicast

  - 11 – DIRECT_GROUP DATAGRAM – indicates that the datagram is a multicast

  - 12 – BROADCAST DATAGRAM – indicates that the datagram is a broadcast

  - 13 – DATAGRAM ERROR – indicates that a previously transmitted datagram was not successfully delivered

  - 14 – DATAGRAM QUERY REQUEST – queries a NetBIOS datagram delivery (NBDD) server to determine if a datagram can be relayed to a specified NetBIOS name

  - 15 – DATAGRAM POSITIVE QUERY RESPONSE – used by an NBDD server to indicate its capability to relay a datagram to the name specified in a DATAGRAM QUERY REQUEST

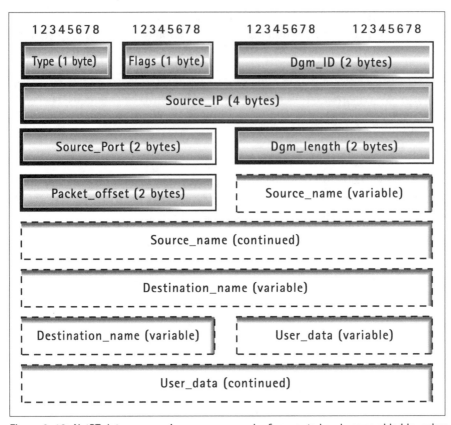

Figure 3-12: NetBT datagram service messages can be fragmented and reassembled by using its header fields.

◆ 16 – DATAGRAM NEGATIVE QUERY RESPONSE – used by an NBDD server to indicate its inability to relay a datagram to the name specified in a DATAGRAM QUERY REQUEST

◆ Flags (1 byte) – The individual bits of the flags field are numbered 0 to 7, and are used as follows:

   ◆ Bits 0 – 3 – These bits are unused, and must have a value of 0.

   ◆ Bits 4 and 5 – Source end-node type – This indicates the end-node type of the source system, where 00 = b-node, 01 = p-node, 10 = m-node, and 11 = NetBIOS Datagram Distribution (NBDD) server. The node type specifies the name-resolution mechanism(s) used by a particular system.

- ◆ **Bit 6 – First** – When activated, this bit indicates that it is the first packet in, what may be, a fragmented datagram.

- ◆ **Bit 7 – More** – When activated, this bit indicates that further fragments of the current datagram will follow.

- ◆ **Dgm_ID** (2 bytes) – The dgm_ID field contains a unique transaction-identifier value that is used to associate datagram fragments, requests with replies, and errors with a specific transmission.

- ◆ **Source IP** (4 bytes) – The source IP field contains the IP address of the transmitting system that the receiver uses to return error messages.

- ◆ **Source port** (2 bytes) – The source port field contains the port number of the process (on the transmitting system) that generated the datagram.

- ◆ **Data section** (variable) – The data section contains different fields, of varying sizes, for each of the possible datagram service-message types.

The contents of the data sections for the various message types, in the datagram service, are as follows:

Direct Unique Datagram, Direct Group Datagram, Broadcast Datagram

- ◆ **Dgm_length** (2 bytes) – The dgm_length field specifies the length of the NetBT datagram, minus the 14-byte header.

- ◆ **Packet offset** (2 bytes) – When a datagram is fragmented, the packet offset field specifies the number of bytes included in the data sections of all previous transmitted fragments. In the first fragment of a datagram, the value is 0.

- ◆ **Source name** (variable) – The source name field specifies the NetBIOS name of the sending system.

- ◆ **Destination name** (variable) – The destination name field specifies the NetBIOS name of the ultimate receiver of a datagram.

- ◆ **User_data** (variable) – The user_data field contains the message being delivered to the destination system.

Datagram Error

- ◆ **Error code** (1 byte) – The error code field contains a code that specifies the reason a datagram could not be delivered, as follows:

  - ◆ **82 – Destination name not present** – indicates that the NetBIOS name, specified in the destination name field, does not exist on the system specified by the UDP header's destination IP address field

- ◆ 83 – Invalid source name format – indicates that the NetBIOS name, specified in a datagram's source name field, does not conform to the second-level domain-system name format

- ◆ 84 – Invalid destination name format – indicates that the NetBIOS name, specified in a datagram's destination name field, does not conform to the second-level domain-system name format

Datagram Query Request, Datagram Positive Query Response, Datagram Negative Query Response

- ◆ **Destination name** (variable) – When querying a NetBIOS datagram destination server regarding its capability to deliver datagrams to a certain system, the destination name field contains the NetBIOS name of that system.

P-node and m-node systems are only capable of sending unicast transmissions. The NetBT standard, therefore, describes a *NetBIOS datagram delivery* (NBDD) server that these systems can use to relay their unicasts to NetBIOS group names, or to a broadcast address. The DATAGRAM QUERY REQUEST message, and its associated replies, are used by a source system to determine whether or not an NBDD server is capable of delivering a datagram to a specified NetBIOS name.

Server Message Blocks (SMB)

The *Server Message Blocks* (SMB) protocol is carried within NetBT session or datagram service messages. Windows NT redirector uses it to negotiate and control access to resources on other Windows network computers. All of the file and printer-sharing commands between Windows systems take the form of SMB messages. While the command to copy a file (for example, from a shared drive to a local drive) is transmitted in an SMB message, the actual file transfer does not use SMB. Instead, the data is carried inside a series of NetBT SESSION MESSAGE packets.

Following are the four basic types of SMB messages that Windows NT uses:

- ◆ **Session control** – Whenever the Workstation service on a Windows network computer connects to a network resource for the first time, the two systems negotiate a common dialect. After this, the client is authenticated to the Server service and connected to the appropriate share using the SMB protocol's NEGOTIATE, SESSION SETUP, and TREE CONNECT messages. Clients can terminate sessions using the TREE DISCONNECT and LOGOFF commands.

- ◆ **File access** – The SMB protocol includes a series of commands that a client uses to manipulate files on shared network drives, such as OPEN, CLOSE, READ, WRITE, RENAME, and DELETE.

◆ **Printer access** – Clients use the SMB protocol's OPEN PRINT FILE command to send a job to a print queue, on a server. The GET PRINT QUEUE command retrieves a listing of the queued print jobs from the server.

◆ **Message transport** – Applications use the SMB protocol's TRANSACTION commands to send messages to other systems on the network. Such messages might include notifying clients of printing problems, or messages created with the NET SEND command.

SMB message headers contain four identifiers that are used, under various conditions, to uniquely identify the session for which the message is intended. The significance of some identifiers varies depending on whether a server is configured for *share-level* or *user-level* security mode. In the share-level security mode, each shared resource is assigned its own passwords, which are stored on the server system. Any client possessing the password can access the share. User-level security requires the services of an external user directory, such as a Windows NT primary domain controller (PDC). The server's administrator selects specific users and groups that will be granted access to each share.

These identifiers used in SMB message headers are as follows:

◆ **Tree ID (TID)** – A TID value is assigned whenever a client is authenticated to a shared network resource, and is erased when the session is terminated. In share-level security mode, including the same TID value in a subsequent SMB message provides access to the share, without requiring reauthentication.

◆ **Process ID (PID)** – The PID value uniquely identifies a process created by a client system (such as accessing of a particular file), and associates all of the messages involved in that process. Clients begin a new process by generating an SMB message containing a new PID value.

◆ **User ID (UID)** – When a server operates in user-level security mode, the TID value identifies the network resource being shared. Continued access to the authenticated resource is provided by including the UID value assigned during the user-level authentication process.

◆ **Multiplex ID (MID)** – The MID value is used along with the PID to associate the requests and responses of specific tasks in what may be a multitasked series of messages.

Windows NT File Sharing

Most of the NetBT traffic used in Windows networking consists of session-service messages. Using the Windows NT Explorer program to access a shared drive on another Windows system causes the NT Workstation service to generate a file-system request that is sent to the system's I/O Manager. After recognizing that access to another computer's file system is required, the I/O Manager sends the request to the Windows network *redirector* (Rdr.sys). A redirector is a file-system driver (operating at the same level as the FAT and NTFS drivers used for local disk access), to which requests for files on remote systems are passed (see Figure 3-13). A Windows NT system configured to use its peer-to-peer networking capabilities *always* has the Rdr.sys module installed. Adding support for another file system, such as a NetWare client, installs another redirector module.

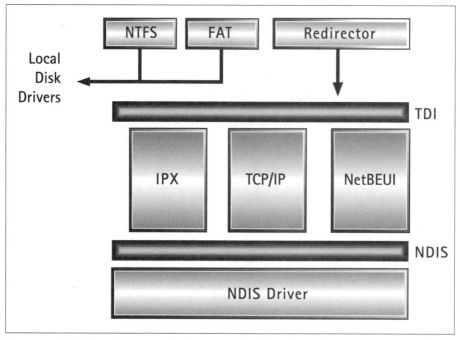

Figure 3-13: The Windows network redirector uses SMB and NetBT messages to provide access to file systems on remote computers.

 The system generating a request for access to a shared drive is functioning as the client, while the system receiving the request acts as the server. Windows networking operates using the peer-to-peer model, in which all machines can act as both clients and servers at the same time.

On the client system, the Windows network redirector initiates communications with the system where shared drive is located (the server) by executing the following procedures:

1. Before any unicast transmissions can be sent to a peer system, the sender must discover the IP address belonging to the target system's NetBIOS name. This is done by retrieving the address from an LMHOSTS file or internal cache, or by performing a NetBT name-service transaction. The nature of the name-service request depends on the NetBIOS name-resolution mechanisms that the system is configured to use.

2. Once it has obtained the IP address, the client system initiates a TCP connection with the server. It uses the standard three-way handshake procedure described in Chapter 6, "The Transport Layer."

3. With the TCP session established, the client initiates a NetBT session by transmitting a SESSION REQUEST message to port 139 on the server system. The server generates a POSITIVE SESSION RESPONSE message that is returned to the client, opening the NetBT session. If the server detects any other existing NetBT sessions with the same calling name at the client system (perhaps due to a client system reboot in which the session was not closed properly), they are terminated.

4. The client and server exchange SMB session-control messages using NetBT SESSION MESSAGE packets. They negotiate the dialect that will be used for communications between the two file systems, authenticate the client to the server share, and connect to a particular file-system tree.

5. Once access is granted to the appropriate network resource, the client generates SMB file-access messages to request specific file-system activities, such as the reading and writing of files on the shared server drive.

6. When actual file data must be transmitted to (or from) a server to satisfy a client's file-system request, the data is sent in NetBT SESSION MESSAGE packets. These are punctuated by periodic TCP acknowledgments returned by the receiver of data.

TCP/IP and IntranetWare

The IntranetWare product packages the NetWare 4.11 OS with a collection of TCP/IP applications. You can use it to develop and host intranet and Internet services on your NetWare network. These services run on a NetWare server, but use the TCP/IP protocols for their network communications rather than NetWare's native IPX protocol suite. NetWare's networking model permits multiple transport protocols to operate on the same server (thanks to the ODI architecture at the data link layer of the protocol stack).

Adding support for TCP/IP to a NetWare server has been assimilated into the OS installation procedure, or can be performed after installation using the INETCFG.NLM server-console utility. The TCP/IP stack must be added to the server-networking configuration for any product or service that involves the server in TCP/IP communications.

For more information about the INETCFG.NLM server-console utility, see Chapter 8, "Windows NT and IntranetWare."

TCP/IP and the NetWare Core Protocol (NCP)

While the release of IntranetWare has elevated the TCP/IP protocols to a more prominent position in the Novell networking architecture, they are not yet fully assimilated into the NetWare OS. By default, NetWare still relies on the IPX protocol suite that Novell developed specifically for use with their networking products. The IPX protocols were based, in part, on the TCP/IP standards. They are, however, primarily used on LANs and lack the extensibility and platform independence of TCP/IP. More importantly, the IPX protocols are proprietary and remain the exclusive property of Novell.

With the integration of Internet services into business networks, and the widespread adoption of TCP/IP on the UNIX and Windows NT platforms, NetWare remains an anachronism in terms of networking protocols. Most of today's networks that carry IPX traffic do so only to support NetWare, and many administrators are seeking to consolidate their networks by selecting a single protocol suite for all platforms.

On most NetWare networks, the majority of network traffic is devoted to file-sharing activities, which are conducted using the NetWare Core Protocol (NCP), and network printing, which uses the Sequenced Packet Exchange (SPX) protocol. Both of these transport protocols are carried within Internetwork Packet Exchange (IPX) packets. IPX is the network-layer protocol native to the NetWare OS – the equivalent of IP in the TCP/IP protocol suite.

At first glance, carrying NetWare's NCP traffic within IP datagrams (instead of IPX packets) may seem a relatively simple matter. This may be true, to some extent, but the larger problem lies in how the NetWare systems inform other network computers of their availability. All NetWare servers and IPX routers advertise their services by broadcasting Service Advertising Protocol (SAP) and Routing Information Protocol (RIP) messages every 60 seconds. This is an effective means of keeping a network's systems updated, but as networks grow larger, the amount of broadcast traffic generated by these messages can become excessive – especially over relatively slow WAN links.

Before NCP traffic can be ported to IP, the advertisement process must be addressed. Simply encapsulating RIP and SAP traffic into IP datagrams is one solution, but this does nothing to alleviate the excessive traffic. In addition, IP routers are not normally configured to propagate broadcast traffic to other network segments. This would prevent systems from seeing any NetWare servers other than those on the local network.

Over the years, Novell has provided several different mechanisms for carrying IPX traffic within IP datagrams. Some of the solutions are more effective than others, but none of them uses TCP/IP as a native carrier for NetWare traffic. In each case, the entire IPX data structure is carried within a UDP datagram, as shown in Figure 3-14. A true NetWare over TCP/IP implementation would eliminate the IPX header, entirely, and carry an NCP message directly within TCP or UDP.

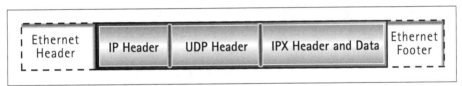

Figure 3-14: The TCP/IP solutions currently available for NetWare communications encapsulate an IPX packet, including the IPX header, within a UDP/IP data structure.

The following sections examine these various TCP/IP encapsulation solutions and how they address the problem of service advertisement.

IP TUNNELING

IP Tunneling was introduced with the NetWare 3.11 product, and has remained a part of the OS ever since. Taking the firm of a network-adapter driver, IPTUNNEL.LAN is a simple mechanism that enables two NetWare servers to communicate over an IP-only network. Usable only for point-to-point communications, IP tunneling is typically employed when servers must communicate on a network segment where IPX traffic is undesirable, such as an IP backbone. The tunneling driver takes all of the IPX traffic that a server intends for a particular destination, and encapsulates it within UDP datagrams. The datagrams are transmitted to the destination system using IP in the normal manner. There, the TCP/IP headers are stripped off and the IPX data is passed up the server's protocol stack. The upper-layer server processes are unaware of TCP/IP's participation in the communication process.

IP tunneling is not particularly suitable for use on WAN links, though it may seem otherwise. The tunneling driver encapsulates all of the IPX traffic intended for the target server in IP datagrams, including SAP and RIP messages. If the servers advertise a large number of services, the broadcast traffic generated by SAP and RIP can overwhelm a slower WAN connection.

To install the IP tunneling driver, use NetWare's IPCONFIG.NLM server-console utility, as if you were installing a standard network adapter. From the Boards menu, press the Insert key to add a new board, and select the IP Tunnel Driver from the list provided. This displays a Board Configuration screen like that shown in Figure 3-15. Supply a name that you will use to reference the driver, as well as the IP addresses of the local server, and the peer server at the other end of the point-to-point link. You can specify whether or not UDP checksums should be included, and the port number to use for the UDP communications – which defaults to 213, the well-known port number for IPX as listed in the "Assigned Numbers" RFC.

Figure 3-15: To implement IP tunneling, you install a board driver using NetWare's INETCFG utility and specify the IP addresses of the two servers.

IP tunneling is not a complete NetWare IP solution. It is designed only for communications between two servers, and does not affect client/server communications.

IP RELAY

IP relay is similar to IP tunneling in that it encapsulates the IPX traffic between specific NetWare servers within UDP packets, and installs as a LAN driver using the INETCFG utility. The difference between the two schemes is that IP relay supports point-to-point links between a collection of servers arranged in a star topology. One server functions as the hub of the star, and initiates the connections to the other servers, as shown in Figure 3-16.

The star topology reduces the amount of RIP traffic as each remote server communicates with only the hub (instead of every other server on the network). This makes IP relay preferable to IP tunneling for use on an IP backbone, and also for WAN connections between servers at remote locations. Like IP tunneling, IP relay involves the communications between servers, only. NetWare clients continue to use the IPX protocols in the normal manner.

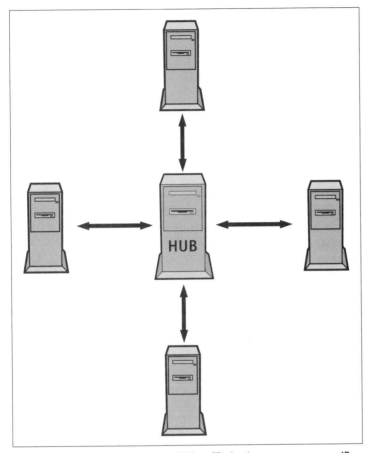

Figure 3-16: IP relay encapsulates IPX traffic in the same manner as IP tunneling, but uses a star topology, with one server functioning as the central hub.

IP relay is part of the MultiProtocol Router product that is included in the IntranetWare package. You must install MPR (using NetWare's INSTALL.NLM utility) before you can load the IPRELAY.LAN driver. To configure IP relay, use the INETCFG program to install the LAN driver on the server you intend to be the hub. To specify the IP addresses of the remote peer servers that must communicate with the hub, open INETCFG's IPX Protocol Configuration screen. On this screen, you can enable the Tunnel IPX through IP option, and then open the Tunnel Configuration screen, as shown in Figure 3-17.

Figure 3-17: You specify the IP addresses of the remote peer servers, with which an IP relay hub will communicate, in INETCFG's IPX Protocol Configuration screen.

NETWARE/IP

NetWare/IP is a comprehensive solution to the problem of using TCP/IP to carry NetWare traffic. Like IP tunneling and IP relay, NetWare/IP also encapsulates IPX traffic in UDP datagrams, but it is not limited to server communications. Clients can also communicate with NetWare servers using IP, but only if they have a NetWare/IP client installed. This requirement immediately escalates the implementation of NetWare/IP to a more complicated administrative project. Not only is it necessary to update the client software on all network workstations, you must also devise an IP-addressing strategy for your whole network – if you have not done so already – and not just selected servers.

Because NetWare/IP requires the use of TCP/IP on all of your NetWare clients and servers, the product integrates some of the standard TCP/IP elements into its architecture. When you install NetWare/IP, you create one or more domains on your network. A NetWare/IP domain is not the equivalent of a DNS domain; it is a subdomain of a DNS domain. For example, if your company has registered the *mycorp.com* domain name, the NetWare/IP domain could take the form *lan.mycorp.com*. All of the NetWare/IP systems on the network would then be configured to be part of the *lan.mycorp.com* domain. To facilitate the use of standard host names for NetWare/IP systems, the product includes a DNS server that runs on a NetWare server.

The current version of NetWare/IP included in the IntranetWare package is 2.2; the product is also available as a free download from Novell's online services. The NetWare/IP client modules are included in the NetWare DOS Requester, the Client 32 releases for DOS/Windows and Windows 95, and the IntranetWare Client for Windows NT. The NetWare/IP client is not a TCP/IP stack, itself. As with a server, the TCP/IP protocols must be installed and operational before you add NetWare/IP.

To install the server portion of the NetWare/IP product, you use NetWare's INSTALL.NLM utility at the server console prompt. When you select Product Options from the Installation Options screen, Install NetWare/IP is listed in the Other Installation Items/Products list, as shown in Figure 3-18.

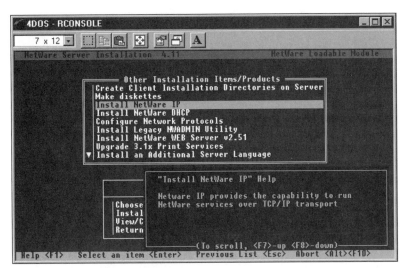

Figure 3-18: The NetWare/IP server modules are installed using NetWare's
INSTALL.NLM server-console utility.

Unlike NetWare's other IP-encapsulation technologies, NetWare/IP addresses the
problem of the SAP and RIP broadcasts used on IPX networks, by introducing an
alternative method. Instead of broadcasting RIP and SAP messages, or encapsulating them in datagrams, NetWare/IP includes a Domain SAP/RIP Server (or DSS)
module. This runs on a NetWare server, and maintains a database of the network's
router and service advertising information. Communications between NetWare/IP
servers and the DSS are conducted using straight UDP, without an encapsulated
IPX header. Rather than broadcast SAP/RIP information every 60 seconds, servers
send unicast transmissions directly to the DSS every five minutes. This results in a
dramatic reduction in SAP/RIP traffic, as shown in Figure 3-19. You can also modify the update interval to reduce traffic even further.

Every NetWare/IP domain must have a primary DSS server. For fault tolerance
and load balancing, you should create multiple secondary DSS servers on your network, especially at remote sites connected by WAN links. NetWare/IP systems
always send their SAP/RIP update requests to the nearest DSS server.

After NetWare/IP is installed to a server, you configure, manage, and start the
NetWare/IP, DSS, and DNS services using the UNICON.NLM program at the file-
server console. By selecting Manage Services from the Main Menu and choosing
NetWare/IP from the list of installed services, you see the NetWare/IP
Administration screen shown in Figure 3-20.

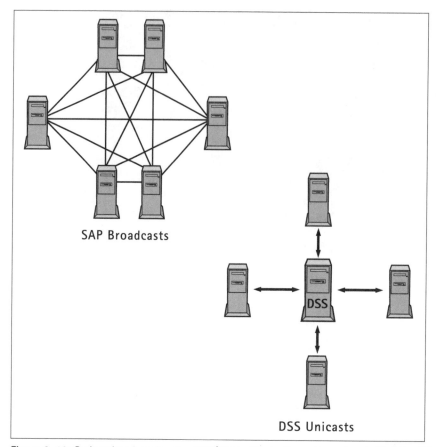

SAP Broadcasts

DSS

DSS Unicasts

Figure 3-19: Rather than broadcasting SAP/RIP traffic to the entire network, NetWare/IP sends unicast messages to central DSS servers.

Figure 3-20: Configuring NetWare/IP involves the address specification of systems running the DSS module that will provide the server with SAP/RIP information.

To configure NetWare/IP, specify the IP addresses of the DSS servers on your network, and then configure the DSS server, using screens like that shown in Figure 3-21. In most cases, the default values for Tunable Parameters screen are sufficient.

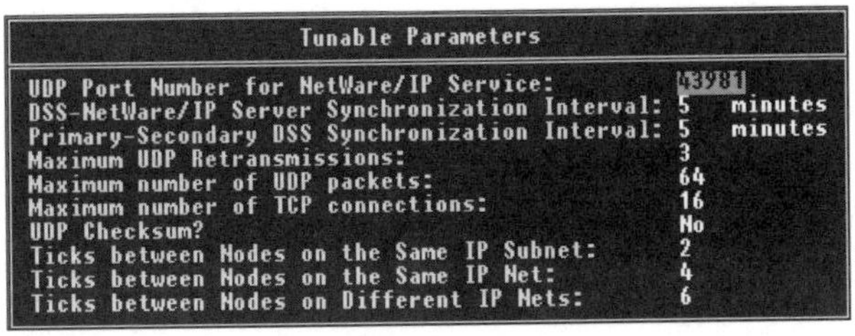

```
                      Tunable Parameters
 UDP Port Number for NetWare/IP Service:        43981
 DSS-NetWare/IP Server Synchronization Interval: 5    minutes
 Primary-Secondary DSS Synchronization Interval: 5    minutes
 Maximum UDP Retransmissions:                    3
 Maximum number of UDP packets:                  64
 Maximum number of TCP connections:              16
 UDP Checksum?                                   No
 Ticks between Nodes on the Same IP Subnet:      2
 Ticks between Nodes on the Same IP Net:         4
 Ticks between Nodes on Different IP Nets:       6
```

Figure 3-21: The DSS configuration screens enable you to specify time intervals when the NetWare/IP servers are updated, and primary and secondary DSSs are synchronized.

Upon configuring the services, you return to UNICON's Main Menu and select Start/Stop Services. Here, you can add NetWare/IP, DSS, and DNS to the Running Services list.

With NetWare/IP, you can eliminate IPX as a network-layer protocol on your network, while retaining compatibility with your applications. Strictly speaking, the IPX header is still present, as you will see by analyzing the IP packets traveling on the network. The IPX protocol stack is still present on NetWare/IP clients and servers; therefore, when traffic arrives at a system, the IP and UDP headers are removed and the IPX data is passed to the appropriate system process.

Moab

The next step in assimilating TCP/IP into the NetWare networking architecture is to remove the IPX header and protocol stack completely. This ensures that NCP and other data can be carried directly in TCP and UDP packets. The next version of IntranetWare, code-named *Moab* and scheduled for release in early 1998, provides you with the option to use IPX or TCP/IP (or both) as NetWare's native transport protocols. This is the feature NetWare users have been waiting years for, but it may cause unforeseen problems on some networks.

Though NetWare's services will be redesigned for use on IP-only networks, third-party NetWare applications are being used today for IPX networks – which may not function with IP. NetWare/IP's encapsulation is functionally invisible to applications; they receive normal IPX packets from the protocol stack and process them normally. Once that IPX header is eliminated from the packets, some applications may cease to function.

Moab no longer uses NetWare/IP's Domain SAP/RIP Servers to maintain information about network services. Instead, the OS uses the Service Location Protocol (SLP), a new protocol currently published as an Internet draft by the IETF (called draft-ietf-svrloc-protocol-17.txt). SLP employs *user agents* that an application uses to transmit queries. These queries are sent to *service agents* – on smaller networks – that provide information about a particular network service, or to *directory agents* – on large networks – that store information about all of a network's registered services. Client systems obtain the location of directory agents by manual configuration, or from a DHCP server.

In addition to native TCP/IP, Moab also supports upper-layer standards associated with TCP/IP, such as Windows Sockets 2, Secure Socket Layer (SSL) 3, and the Lightweight Directory Access Protocol (LDAP).

Summary

The TCP/IP protocols were designed to function in a wide range of computing environments. To effectively use the protocols, an OS must address the interfaces found at the top and bottom of the TCP/IP stack. This chapter examined some of the standard interfaces used to provide multiprotocol support to an OS, and the ways in which the TCP/IP protocols have been assimilated into the Windows NT and IntranetWare products.

In this chapter, you learned:

- How the NDIS interface enables Windows NT to multiplex data from several protocol stacks onto a single network adapter

- How ODI was designed to modularize NetWare's monolithic network drivers

- How Windows NT isolates the functions of its protocol stacks between the NDIS and TDI interfaces

- How NetWare is gradually assimilating the open TCP/IP standards into its long-standing proprietary networking architecture

The following chapter is the first of four that provide a detailed examination of each of the four TCP/IP protocol layers.

Part II

Protocols

Chapter 4

The Link Layer

IN THIS CHAPTER

The link layer is the bottom-most layer of the TCP/IP stack. Some TCP/IP link layer protocols function independently, while others work in conjunction with LAN protocols defined by other standards bodies. This chapter examines the various protocols operating at the link layer, and includes the following topics:

◆ Ethernet, the most commonly used LAN protocol in the world, and the variations of which that can be used with TCP/IP

◆ The Address Resolution Protocol and how it makes it possible for TCP/IP traffic to be carried in Ethernet frames

◆ The Serial Line Internet Protocol and the Point-to-Point Protocol and how they are used to connect two computers, as in a WAN or dial-up arrangement

THE LINK LAYER, THE BOTTOM layer of the TCP/IP protocol stack, possesses something of a dual personality because its functionality sometimes falls outside of the TCP/IP standards. Once network transmissions are packaged into IP datagrams at the internet layer, they are passed down the stack where another protocol encapsulates the datagrams and introduces them to the network medium.

Depending on the physical nature of the network, this protocol may or may not be defined by a TCP/IP standard. If a TCP/IP standard is used, it defines the protocol operating at the link layer. The data is then fed to a network interface defined by a physical-layer standard that lies outside the realm of TCP/IP. An example of this is a system connected to an Internet service provider (ISP) using an end-to-end protocol, such as the *Serial Line Internet Protocol* (SLIP) or the *Point-to-Point Protocol* (PPP), both of which are defined by TCP/IP link-layer standards.

In this arrangement, the only remaining element to the system's protocol stack is the physical network connection to the other computer. This usually takes the form of a telephone-type connection, such as a dial-up, leased line, or ISDN service. This connection is external to the computer (theoretically, if not physically), established by a modem, NT-1, or other device. The actual network interface in the computer is the serial port connection to the device, the properties of which are defined by the Electronic Industries Association (EIA) RS-232-E standard.

The protocols comprising the TCP/IP stack never define the entire network protocol stack for a computer system. There are always some elements provided by the operating system (OS) or the hardware platform. These elements are, however, included in the stack defined in the OSI reference model. It is possible to picture the end-to-end connection as a concatenation of the TCP/IP and OSI stacks, as shown in Figure 4-1.

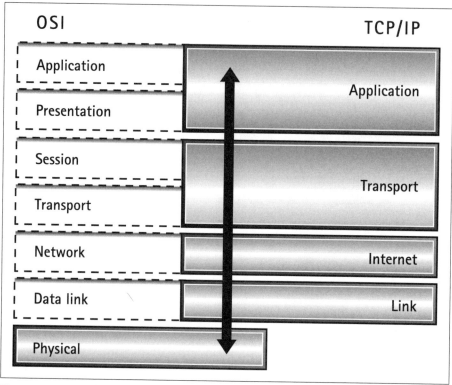

Figure 4–1: The TCP/IP protocol stack provides only part of the functionality defined by the OSI reference model.

The TCP/IP standards are responsible for the functionality of the system's application, transport, internet, and link layers. The RS-232-E interface is defined by an outside standard and represented by the OSI model's physical layer.

This type of end-to-end connection using PPP or SLIP is virtually the only case in which the entirety of the OSI data link layer's functionality is defined by TCP/IP standards. The alternative to this arrangement is when outside standards provide both data link and physical-layer functions. This is the case on local area networks (LANs), which today use the Ethernet and Token Ring protocols almost exclusively for their data link and physical layers.

The IEEE 802 family of protocols (which includes the 802.3 and 802.5 specifications, colloquially known as Ethernet and Token Ring) define both the data link and physical-layer functions, as laid out in the OSI model. In order for these protocols to carry IP datagrams, the IP address of the destination system must be converted into a hardware address useable in the Ethernet or Token Ring header.

To discover this hardware address, the TCP/IP standards define a link layer protocol called the *Address Resolution Protocol* (ARP). Another protocol, the *Reverse Address Resolution Protocol* (RARP), is used to discover an IP address based on a given hardware address. In this arrangement, the relationship of the TCP/IP stack and the overall networking system, represented by the OSI model, resembles that shown in Figure 4-2. The protocols of the OSI data link layer and the TCP/IP link layer work together to create an interface between IP and Ethernet or Token Ring. The IEEE standards provide the entire physical-layer functionality, which is realized in the network interface adapters and the wiring specifications used to build the network.

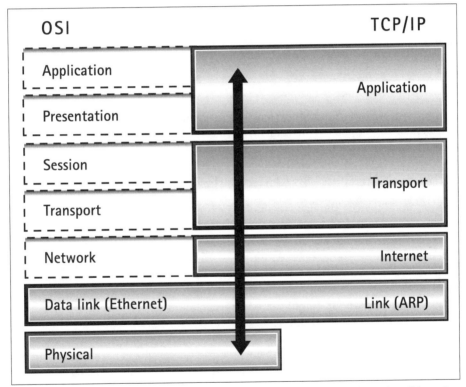

Figure 4–2: On a LAN, the TCP/IP protocol ARP works with other protocols, such as Ethernet, to transmit IP datagrams across the network.

Both the end-to-end and LAN link layer technologies are commonly found on corporate TCP/IP internetworks. SLIP or PPP are used to provide Internet or WAN connectivity, while Ethernet or Token Ring form the private network, itself. This chapter examines both arrangements: the TCP/IP protocols used to implement them, and the standards describing interaction between the TCP/IP and the IEEE protocols.

Using TCP/IP and Ethernet

Currently, the most common LAN infrastructure installed is 10BaseT Ethernet. *10BaseT* describes a network medium composed of copper-based telephone cable, wired in a star topology to centralized wiring *concentrators* or *hubs*. The actual network interface with each computer is an adapter that takes the form of an expansion card inserted into a PC, or a chipset mounted on the motherboard.

 Although 10BaseT Ethernet is wired in a star topology, the arrangement of circuitry within the hubs forms a logical bus network.

Technically speaking, this physical arrangement is not rightfully called Ethernet. It is actually an implementation of the IEEE 802.3 protocol, which has retained the Ethernet name from an earlier, similar networking standard.

Ethernet and IEEE Standards

The original Ethernet standard was published in 1980 by a committee of representatives from the Digital Equipment Corporation, Intel, and Xerox. Using the initials of these three companies, the document came to be known as the *DIX Ethernet* standard. Ethernet products based on this specification were produced by various manufacturers, but the DIX consortium eventually submitted the document to the IEEE for development as an industry standard.

In 1985, a revised version of the DIX specification (called *Ethernet II*) was published, as well as an IEEE document called "IEEE 802.3 Carrier Sense Multiple Access with Collision Detection (CSMA/CD) Access Method and Physical Layer Specifications." Although the IEEE version of the standard has been used for nearly all commercial hardware implementations, it is a small wonder the term Ethernet was informally retained.

All Ethernet standards consist of the following basic elements:

♦ a set of guidelines governing the nature and configuration of the physical medium used to connect a network's computers

♦ a mechanism enabling individual systems to fairly arbitrate access to the physical medium

♦ a protocol frame consisting of a header and footer used to package network-layer data for transmission over the network medium

The Ethernet and IEEE documents differ slightly in the configuration of their packet headers. The primary reason the IEEE specifications are used today for hardware is that their physical specifications for the network are continually updated to reflect new technologies. The original DIX Ethernet specification called for thick coaxial cable (or *thicknet*) as the network medium. Ethernet II added a thin variant (known as *thinnet*) as an alternative. The IEEE standards were, however, updated beyond this to include newer media, such as the unshielded twisted pair (10BaseT) and fiber optic cables prevalent today.

Ethernet Frame Types

Once a TCP/IP transmission travels down the protocol stack to the internet layer, it is packaged as an IP datagram — a structure that remains intact until the packet reaches the destination system. At the data link layer, the packet receives its final encapsulation before transmission. There are two separate TCP/IP documents that define standards for the encapsulation of IP data within Ethernet frames. One is for the DIX Ethernet specification (RFC894), and the other is for the IEEE 802 frame (RFC1042).

Although the vast majority of today's Ethernet network interface adapters are designed for use on 10BaseT networks, most Ethernet implementations can use the frame types defined in either the DIX Ethernet or the IEEE 802 committee specifications. The RFC standard defining the protocol-implementation guidelines for a TCP/IP host (RFC1122) states that:

♦ All TCP/IP hosts must be capable of sending and receiving packets using the Ethernet II frame type.

♦ All TCP/IP hosts should be capable of receiving IEEE 802 packets intermixed with Ethernet II packets.

♦ All TCP/IP hosts may be capable of sending packets using the IEEE 802 frame type.

When a host implementation provides the capability to support both frame types, it must include a configuration switch to select one of the two. The switch defaults to the DIX Ethernet II frame.

The use of the words "must," "should," and "may" in TCP/IP standards documents are strictly defined. "Must" indicates that a feature is required on all TCP/IP implementations. "Should" means that the inclusion of a feature is recommended, but not imperative. "May" indicates that a feature is optional.

DIX ETHERNET FRAMES

When used on a TCP/IP host system, the Ethernet encapsulation process functions very much like an extension of the TCP/IP protocol stack. Application-, transport-, and internet-layer protocol headers are applied to the payload data, leaving IP datagrams that are passed to the data link layer below. The Ethernet frame is then applied, with the datagram forming the payload of the packet, as shown in Figure 4-3.

Figure 4-3: Ethernet frames are used to encapsulate IP datagrams, just as the upper-layer protocols are encapsulated by IP.

The most obvious difference between the Ethernet frame and the upper-layer headers is that the Ethernet frame includes a trailer and a header, completely enclosing the payload data. The format of the frame defined by the DIX Ethernet standards is shown in Figure 4-4.

The function of each of the DIX Ethernet header fields is as follows:

◆ **Preamble** (8 bytes) – Before sending a packet, 8 bytes of alternating zeroes and ones are transmitted to inform the other systems on the network that a frame is about to be sent.

◆ **Destination address** (6 bytes) – This contains the 48-bit hardware address of the next system to receive the packet.

◆ **Source address** (6 bytes) – This address contains the 48-bit hardware address of the system transmitting the packet.

◆ **EtherType** (2 bytes) – EtherType contains a code, defined by the IEEE, that is used to identify the type of data being carried in the packet's payload. This field not only specifies that the packet is intended for the target system's TCP/IP stack, but also identifies the specific protocol carried in the payload. The hexadecimal codes used for TCP/IP packets are as follows:

  ◆ 0800 (2048 decimal) – IP datagram

  ◆ 0806 (2054 decimal) – ARP request/reply

  ◆ 8035 (32821 decimal) – RARP request/reply

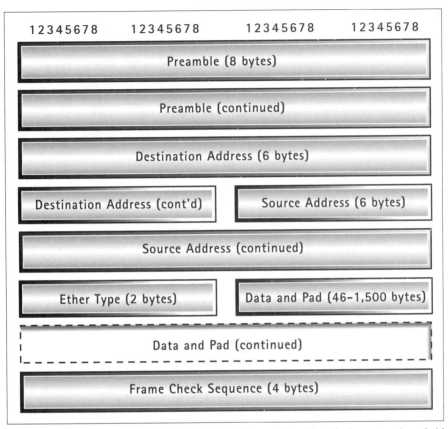

Figure 4-4: The DIX Ethernet frame uses an EtherType code to identify the protocol carried in the data field.

- ◆ **Data and Pad** (46 – 1,500 bytes) – Ethernet packets have a minimum and a maximum size for the data or payload carried within the frame. When the data being transmitted amounts to less than 46 bytes, the field is padded with null data to achieve the required size. Any packets that are too small on arrival to the destination are considered to be damaged, and are discarded.

- ◆ **Frame Check Sequence** (4 bytes) – This provides error-checking services to the protocol. The FCS field contains the results of a cyclic redundancy check (CRC) computation performed by the sending system on the entire Ethernet packet (including the header, the data, and the pad). The same computation is performed by the receiving system, and the results are compared to the value in this field to verify that the packet was not damaged in transit. Packets in which the values do not match are discarded.

IEEE 802 STANDARDS

Over the years, the IEEE 802 committee produced a series of standards documents that define several types of physical networks. Some of these are now obsolete or were never implemented commercially. The remaining documents include the following:

- ◆ 802.3 – defines a 10Mb/sec CSMA/CD network based on the original Ethernet standards

- ◆ 802.5 – defines a 4Mb/sec (and later 16Mb/sec) token-passing network using a ring topology

Thus, the 802.3 and 802.5 documents define the technologies usually referred to as Ethernet and Token Ring, in the networking industry. These documents define networking functions found in both the physical and the data link layers of the OSI reference model. The standards define the physical-layer specifications that must be used to construct the network. These specifications include the types of cable that may be used, and the limitations imposed on the network's physical configuration (such as cable-segment length, the number of workstations permitted on a segment, and the arrangement of the segments into an internetwork).

MEDIA ACCESS CONTROL   At the data link layer, the 802.3 and 802.5 documents each define a different media access control method. *Media access control* (MAC) is the mechanism that enables multiple computers to share a single baseband communications channel without interfering with each other. Ethernet (802.3) uses a MAC method called Carrier Sense Multiple Access with Collision Detection (CSMA/CD), which means that a system listens to the network to determine whether any other system is transmitting, then transmits its data, and effectively recovers from the natural packet collisions that occasionally occur when two systems transmit simultaneously.

Token Ring's MAC method involves a specialized packet called a token, that is circulated to each system on a cable ring. Only the workstation in possession of the token can transmit data, preventing collisions.

LOGICAL LINK CONTROL   Not all of the 802 standards define a complete physical layer technology. The MAC functionality defined in the standards documents is often placed in the OSI model as the bottommost of two sublayers. The sublayers are formed by splitting the data link layer in two, as shown in Figure 4-5. The uppermost data link sublayer is called the *Logical Link Control* (LLC) sublayer, as defined in the IEEE 802.2 document.

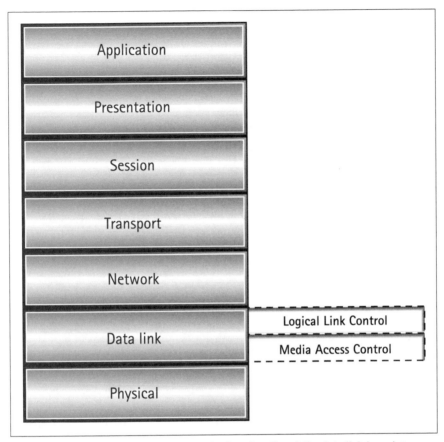

Figure 4–5: The IEEE 802 standards split the functionality of the data link layer into Logical Link Control and Media Access Control sublayers.

The LLC sublayer defined in the 802.2 document is applied, without modification, to whichever physical-layer standard is used (802.3 or 802.5). LLC is physically manifested as additional fields in the Ethernet header, which are used to provide what has been described as "a hole in the ceiling" of the data link layer. Codes in these fields inform the network-layer protocol, at the receiving system, of the location in memory where the packet's data can be found. This is particularly necessary when the same data link-layer protocol is being used to service multiple upper-layer protocol stacks simultaneously.

The 802.2 standard also defines a second frame element used for TCP/IP transport, called the Sub Network Access Protocol (SNAP). The SNAP header identifies the type of data carried within a particular packet – a function included in the DIX Ethernet II standard in the EtherType field, but omitted from the 802.3 specification. The SNAP fields are particularly important when Ethernet is used with TCP/IP, because they differentiate packets carrying ARP or RARP traffic from those carrying IP.

The LLC and SNAP fields are carried within the frame defined in the 802.3 standard. This sublayer is sometimes thought of as performing an encapsulation process of its own, and is referred to as the *LLC frame*, as shown in Figure 4-6.

Figure 4–6: The LLC and SNAP headers defined in the IEEE 802.2 standard are required for TCP/IP communications

IEEE 802 FRAMES

Using the frame format defined by the 802 standards to carry TCP/IP traffic, requires that a host include support for both the LLC and SNAP subheaders. Because the maximum size for an 802.3 packet is the same as that of a DIX Ethernet packet, the additional 8 bytes required for LLC and SNAP must be subtracted from the maximum size of the data field. The IEEE 802.2/802.3 frame format is shown in Figure 4-7.

The functions of the IEEE 802.2/802.3 frame's fields are as follows:

◆ **Preamble** (7 bytes) – Before sending a packet, 7 bytes of alternating zeroes and ones are transmitted to inform the other systems on the network that a frame is about to be sent.

◆ **Start of Frame Delimiter** (1 byte) – The final byte transmitted before the frame begins. The delimiter contains alternating bits as does the preamble, except that the final two bits of the field are consecutive.

◆ **Destination address** (6 bytes) – As in the Ethernet frame, this field contains the 48-bit hardware address of the next system to receive the packet.

◆ **Source address** (6 bytes) – As in the Ethernet frame, this field contains the 48-bit hardware address of the system transmitting the packet.

◆ **Length** (2 bytes) – Specifies the total number of bytes that follow in the packet, exclusive of any pad bytes and the FCS. This field can, therefore, be said to specify the length of the LLC frame.

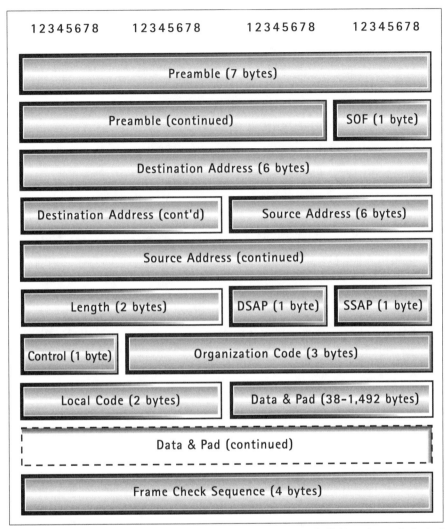

12345678   12345678   12345678   12345678

Preamble (7 bytes)

Preamble (continued)   SOF (1 byte)

Destination Address (6 bytes)

Destination Address (cont'd)   Source Address (6 bytes)

Source Address (continued)

Length (2 bytes)   DSAP (1 byte)   SSAP (1 byte)

Control (1 byte)   Organization Code (3 bytes)

Local Code (2 bytes)   Data & Pad (38–1,492 bytes)

Data & Pad (continued)

Frame Check Sequence (4 bytes)

Figure 4-7: The IEEE 802.2/802.3 frame uses the SNAP local code field as the equivalent of the EtherType field in the DIX Ethernet frame.

Following is a list of Logical Link Control (LLC) Fields:

◆ **Destination service access point** (1 byte) – This field contains a code, defined by the IEEE, that points to a location in memory where the upper-layer protocols on the receiving system can find the data enclosed in the packet. The DSAP value for all TCP/IP transmissions is the hexadecimal value *aa* (or 170, in decimal notation). Note that this value is not the one defined by the IEEE as representing the IP protocol (which is 6), but instead indicates that an EtherType value can be found in the SNAP fields.

♦ **Source service access point** (1 byte) – Containing the same value as the DSAP field, the SSAP field indicates the memory location in the sending system from which the packet data was taken.

♦ **Control** (1 byte) – This field is used to specify the type of LLC frame in the packet. In TCP/IP packets, its value is always *3*.

Following is a list of Sub Network Access Protocol (SNAP) Fields:

♦ **Organization Code** (3 bytes) – Also called a vendor code, this field contains all zeroes, indicating that the following two bytes contain an EtherType code.

♦ **Local Code** (2 bytes) – This field identifies the protocol being carried within the packet's data field (as does the EtherType field in the DIX Ethernet header) and uses the same codes.

♦ **Data and Pad** (38 to 1,492 bytes) – As in DIX Ethernet packets, the data field may be padded to achieve the minimum packet length. The possible values are 8 bytes less than those of the DIX Ethernet data field to account for the 8 bytes of the LLC and SNAP header fields.

♦ **Frame Check Sequence** (4 bytes) – Like the equivalent field in the DIX Ethernet frame, this field contains a CRC value that is used to provide error-detection services for all of the header fields, data, and padding in the packet.

In a DIX Ethernet packet, bytes 13-14 of the header contain an EtherType, while the 802.3 header uses this field to indicate the length of the data enclosed in the frame. Because the maximum size for the 802.3 data field is 1,500 bytes, and the EtherType codes (in decimal notation) are all greater than 1,500, there is no overlap of values. The field may then be used as a means of differentiating DIX Ethernet and IEEE 802 packets when both formats are used on the same network.

When you compare the DIX Ethernet frame format with that of the IEEE 802.2/802.3 frame, you can see that the latter is more complex. It contains 8 bytes more control data (and consequently, 8 bytes less payload) than the DIX Ethernet frame, and provides no additional functionality to the TCP/IP communications process. For these reasons, the DIX Ethernet II frame is used with the 10BaseT physical-layer specifications of IEEE 802.3, commonly found on TCP/IP LANs today.

Maximum Transmission Unit (MTU)

The maximum amount of data a data link-layer protocol can carry as payload is known as its *maximum transmission unit* (MTU). Data link protocols have widely varying MTUs. This is an important factor in transmitting TCP/IP data across internetworks composed of different network types. The IP protocol on a sending system packages the transport-layer data into datagrams and passes them to the data link layer. Before doing this, the protocol determines the MTU of the network interface and compares it to the size of the payload to be transmitted.

If the data is larger than the MTU, IP must perform a fragmentation process to generate multiple, smaller-sized packets. As the datagrams are transmitted across multiple network segments, they may have to be fragmented again, depending on the MTUs of the individual segments. The reassembly of fragments does not occur until all of the component datagrams arrive at the final destination.

Datagram fragmentation imposes additional processing overhead on all of the systems involved (as does the packaging of data into datagrams that are much smaller than the MTU). The optimum arrangement is to create the largest possible datagrams to be transmitted to the destination without fragmentation. To do this, a host must determine the smallest MTU found on any of the network segments en route to the destination. This is known as the *path MTU*.

The fragmentation and path MTU discovery processes are both performed by the internet-layer protocols. Both of these procedures (and, consequently, a significant aspect of the TCP/IP stack's efficiency) are highly dependent on the properties of the data link-layer protocols.

 All of the TCP/IP data structures used on Ethernet networks can be carried within the DIX Ethernet II or the IEEE 802.2/802.3 frame. Any discussion of EtherType values can refer to either the EtherType field of the Ethernet II header or the local code field in the 802.2 SNAP header.

ETHERNET IMPLEMENTATIONS

NetWare enables four possible frame types to be used with its Ethernet implementation — only two of which can be used for TCP/IP communications.

The four possible frame-type values are as follows:

◆ **Ethernet_802.3** – This specifies use of the frame defined in the IEEE 802.3 standard (without the additional LLC and SNAP header fields defined in IEEE 802.2). The frame can only be used on single protocol networks (typically NetWare's IPX/SPX), as it has no way to identify the protocol carried in the frame to the network layer.

◆ **Ethernet_802.2** – This specifies the use of the frame defined in the IEEE 802.3 standard, along with the LLC fields defined in IEEE 802.2 (but not the SNAP fields). The frame, by virtue of the SNAP fields in the LLC header, can be used with multiple protocols, such as IPX/SPX and AppleTalk, but not with TCP/IP.

◆ **Ethernet_II** – This value specifies the use of the frame defined in the DIX Ethernet II standard. This frame is commonly used for TCP/IP communications because it includes the EtherType field which is used to identify the protocol carried in the frame.

◆ **Ethernet_SNAP** – This specifies the use of the frame defined in the IEEE 802.3 standard, plus the LLC and SNAP fields defined in 802.2. Because the SNAP local code field is used to carry an EtherType value, this frame can also be used for TCP/IP communications.

The Ethernet implementation in Windows NT 4.0 defaults to the DIX Ethernet II frame to transmit TCP/IP data. You can change the frame type by modifying the *ArpUseEtherSNAP* REG_DWORD value in the Windows NT Registry, located in the following subkey:

```
HKEY_LOCAL_MACHINE
\System
        \CurrentControlSet
                \Services
                        \Tcpip
                                \Parameters
```

The default value of this key is 0. Changing the value to 1 causes the TCP/IP stack to transmit data using the IEEE 802.3/802.2 frame. The stack can receive TCP/IP data using either frame.

Ethernet Addressing

When IP datagrams are packaged as Ethernet frames, the encapsulation process seems much like an extension of the TCP/IP protocol stack, and, in many ways, it is. There is, however, a fundamental shift in emphasis that takes place during the process. IP, which provides the outermost TCP/IP header in the packet, is concerned with the addressing and routing of data to its final destination. With Ethernet, this is not the case.

On the host computer, Ethernet is implemented as a hardware device, the network adapter, and a device driver. As a software entity, Ethernet is quite separate from the TCP/IP stack, as is its function. The Ethernet software on a particular host is concerned only with local network communications; it is completely unaware of any systems other than those on its local network segment.

Like any protocols operating on adjacent layers of the OSI model, Ethernet provides a service to the protocol operating on the layer directly above it. The service that Ethernet provides to IP is delivering datagrams to other systems on the local network segment. If a TCP/IP host wants to transmit data to another host on the same segment, Ethernet takes care of the whole job. In most cases, the IP datagrams are destined for a system on another network segment. In this case, Ethernet can only carry the data on the first leg of the journey – that is, to a router that leads to another network segment.

The concept is similar to taking an airplane trip to a distant city. If you take a taxi to the airport in New York, fly to Los Angeles, and then take another taxi to your hotel, you don't ask the New York cab driver what heading the plane will take, or what the best route is to the hotel from the Los Angeles airport. You engage the taxi for its knowledge of the New York area roads, and the airline for its expertise in flying to Los Angeles. You are the only person concerned with the overall trip.

The Ethernet frame used to transmit IP data contains a source address and a destination address. These addresses differ from those in the IP header in two crucial ways:

♦ The IP destination address identifies the ultimate recipient of the transmission, whether it is on the local network segment or not. Ethernet can only transmit to systems on the same segment.

♦ Ethernet uses an addressing system completely different from that of IP.

Ethernet communications are based on *hardware addresses*, which are a property of Ethernet network interface adapters. Every Ethernet card and every Ethernet chipset installed on a PC motherboard has its own unique 48-bit hexadecimal address, sometimes called a MAC address. When an Ethernet system transmits a packet, every other system on the network segment receives it and reads the destination address in the Ethernet header. The system for which the packet is destined retains and processes the data; all of the other systems simply discard the packet.

Nearly all of today's new LANs use either Ethernet or Token Ring as their data link and physical layer protocols. Token Ring adapters have factory-applied hardware addresses, just like Ethernet devices. Other data link protocols, such as ARCnet, use addresses of different lengths that are assigned by the network's administrators.

Ethernet, in terms of the way that it is used by IP, is like a New York cabdriver. It must be given the address of a local destination, in terms it can understand. Since Ethernet cannot understand an IP address, IP must provide a hardware address. Furthermore, Ethernet cannot recognize a destination outside of the local network segment, so IP must supply the address of a router. This router functions as an intermediate system between the IP datagram's source and destination.

Working on the assumption that data is being sent to a destination on another network, the IP protocol coordinates all of TCP/IP's routing services. Ancillary protocols, such as ICMP and RIP, provide IP with information that helps it decide which is the most efficient route to the destination. On a sending host, these calculations result in the IP address of the router providing access to the next segment in the journey.

If a network segment has only one router on it, the decision is easy because the sending system is only responsible for the first hop. If there are several routers on the local segment, the sending system chooses the one offering the fewest hops between the source and the destination. The IP protocol in each intermediate system then chooses the next router in the journey.

The routing of TCP/IP traffic is a complex subject. It is examined in greater detail in Chapter 9, "Routing IP."

Once the IP protocol identifies the next system to receive a particular datagram, that system's IP address must be converted into a hardware address. This will be inserted into the destination address field in the Ethernet header. The responsibility for this task falls to the ARP, the Address Resolution Protocol.

The Address Resolution Protocol (ARP)

The *Address Resolution Protocol*, or ARP, is a link-layer protocol providing a service that lies between IP and Ethernet in the protocol stack. Based on RFC826, ARP is a required TCP/IP protocol whose primary function is to enable IP datagrams to be carried in Ethernet frames. ARP does this by translating IP addresses into the hardware addresses used by Ethernet. Though it is a link-layer protocol, ARP does not occupy that entire layer because it does not participate in the actual transmission of the datagrams. It performs its entire service before a datagram can be packaged into an Ethernet frame and transmitted over the network.

ARP also differs from nearly all of the other TCP/IP protocols as it is not transmitted within an IP datagram. All Ethernet packets must identify the network-layer protocol being carried within the frame, so that the receiving system knows how to process the data. The protocol is identified by the EtherType code found in the

Ethernet header. There are only three possible EtherType values for TCP/IP systems. These values represent IP, ARP, and another link-layer protocol, called RARP.

 Because ARP fails to use the IP protocol's datagram services for network transmissions, it is sometimes referred to as an internet-layer protocol. However, the TCP/IP standards place ARP at the link layer, which seems more appropriate, as the protocol exists only to provide a service to IP.

ARP COMMUNICATIONS

The ARP communications process is rather simple. A host that wants to transmit IP datagrams knows its own IP address as well as its own hardware address. The system also knows the IP address of the system to which the datagrams are being sent. The only thing it lacks is the hardware address of the destination system. ARP determines the hardware address of the destination system by broadcasting the destination IP address to the entire network segment. It then waits for the system holding that address to reply, as shown in Figure 4-8.

There are two types of ARP packets: requests and replies. The exchange of ARP packets proceeds as follows:

1. An *ARP request* packet contains the IP and hardware addresses of the sending host, and the IP address of the intended recipient. Because the hardware address of the recipient is unknown, the Ethernet packet containing the ARP request must be broadcast to the entire local network segment.

2. The ARP request is transmitted to every Ethernet host on the network segment, saying in essence, "If there is any system on this network with this particular IP address, please respond by sending your hardware address."

3. All of the systems on the local network segment, upon receiving the broadcast, read the EtherType field and pass the contents of the frame to the ARP protocol.

4. If a system fails to recognize its own IP address, the packet is discarded. The system possessing that IP address formulates an *ARP reply* packet that contains the hardware address corresponding to the IP address in the request.

5. The ARP reply packet is sent back to the original requester as a unicast transmission.

6. The hardware address received in the ARP reply is furnished to the Ethernet protocol. This is used as the destination address in the frame holding an IP datagram.

When an ARP request does not receive a reply, it is retransmitted at the intervals specified by the transport-layer protocol responsible for the transmission requiring ARP's services.

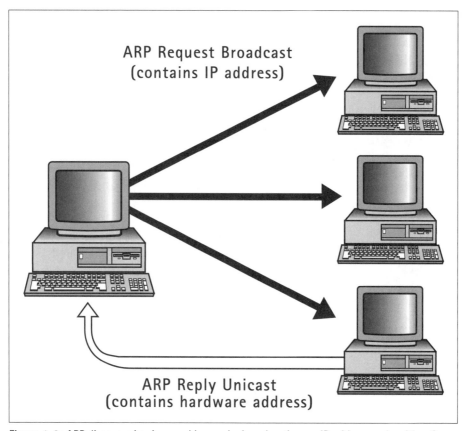

Figure 4-8: ARP discovers hardware addresses by broadcasting an IP address and waiting for the system using that address to respond.

ARP PACKET FORMAT

ARP requests and replies use the same packet format (see Figure 4-9). They are carried within standard Ethernet frames, using a hexadecimal value of *0806* as the EtherType. ARP request packets are transmitted using the standard Ethernet broadcast address, which contains all one bits. ARP replies are sent as unicast transmissions by way of the Ethernet source address found in the frame of the request packet.

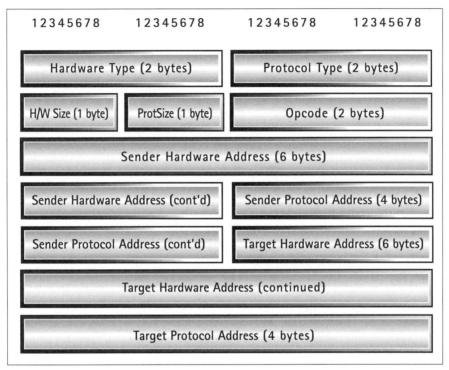

Figure 4-9: ARP and its opposite number, RARP, use the same packet format for all of their transmissions.

The functions of the fields in ARP request/reply packets are as follows:

◆ **Hardware Type** (2 bytes) – This identifies the type of hardware address carried in the other fields. The hardware type for Ethernet is 1.

◆ **Protocol Type** (2 bytes) – The Protocol Type field identifies the type of protocol address carried in the other fields. The protocol type for IP addresses is the hexadecimal value 0800 (this is also the EtherType value used to identify the IP protocol in Ethernet headers).

◆ **Hardware Size** (1 byte) – This field specifies the size (in bytes) of the hardware addresses carried in the other fields. The value for Ethernet hardware addresses is 6.

◆ **Protocol Size** (1 byte) – This field specifies the size in (bytes) of the protocol addresses carried in the other fields. The value for IP protocol addresses is 4.

- **Opcode** (2 bytes) – The Opcode field specifies the function of the packet, using the following values:

  - 1 – ARP request

  - 2 – ARP reply

  - 3 – RARP request

  - 4 – RARP reply

- **Sender Hardware Address** (6 bytes) – This field contains the hardware (for example, Ethernet) address of the system sending the packet (in both requests and replies).

- **Sender Protocol Address** (4 bytes) – This contains the protocol (for example, IP) address of the system sending the packet (in both requests and replies).

- **Target Hardware Address** (6 bytes) – This field is left blank in ARP requests; in replies, it contains the hardware (for example, Ethernet) address of the system to which the packet is being sent.

- **Target Protocol Address** (4 bytes) – This field contains the protocol (for example, IP) address of the system to which the packet is being sent in both requests and replies.

Although ARP was developed for use on Ethernet networks, the first four fields of the packet structure provide sufficient generalization for the protocol to be used with other data link and network-layer protocols. The only limiting requirement is that the data link protocol be capable of broadcasting transmissions to all of the systems on the local network.

When used to resolve IP addresses into Ethernet hardware addresses, the size of the ARP structure is 28 bytes. To be carried within an Ethernet frame, the ARP structure must be padded in order to achieve the minimum Ethernet packet size. When the IEEE 802.2/802.3 frame is used, 10 bytes of padding must be added; 18 bytes for the DIX Ethernet II frame.

In requests and replies, the values in the sender and target address fields of the ARP packet structure are reversed. A system generating an ARP request includes its own IP and hardware addresses in the sender fields. The IP address of the intended recipient is specified in the target protocol address field. The target hardware address field is left blank, as this is the information that is to be furnished by the recipient.

When the recipient of the ARP request creates an ARP reply packet, it takes the values of both sender address fields and moves them to the target address fields. The replying system's IP and hardware addresses are then inserted into the sender fields before transmission.

ARP CACHING

ARP can generate a significant amount of network traffic due to its use of broadcast transmissions. If an Ethernet network segment contains only one router, there are likely many ARP request broadcasts, all attempting to discover the hardware address of the same computer.

To prevent hosts from repeatedly generating ARP requests for the same target, the protocol standard calls for the implementation of a table containing IP/hardware address translations. This table, maintained in every TCP/IP host, is known as the *ARP cache*. The cache is automatically updated with the hardware address information contained in all of the ARP replies received by a host. The local cache is also consulted by every host before it generates an ARP request packet.

Entries in the ARP cache can be static or dynamic. *Dynamic entries* are those which are automatically added by TCP/IP stack. They are removed from the cache after a preset time limit, to provide for the possibility of changes in IP address assignments. *Static entries* are those that are added manually by a network administrator. They may or may not be purged from the cache, depending on the implementation.

ARP IMPLEMENTATIONS

Both Windows NT 4.0 and NetWare 4.11 support the use of ARP in their TCP/IP implementations, as required by the Internet Host Requirements document (RFC1122). Their implementations differ in some small configuration details and in the utilities used to manage the protocol.

ARP AND WINDOWS NT   Windows NT 4.0, by default, purges ARP cache entries after two minutes if they are not accessed for the purpose of sending additional IP datagrams. Cache entries that are being accessed are maintained for 10 minutes. An ARP cache entry can be purged at any time if it is the oldest entry in the table. ARP cache entries that are added manually using the Windows NT ARP utility are left in the cache permanently.

You can change the time periods for entry maintenance in the cache by modifying the *ArpCacheLife* REG_DWORD value in the Windows NT Registry. This is located in the following subkey:

```
HKEY_LOCAL_MACHINE
\System
      \CurrentControlSet
            \Services
                  \Tcpip
                        \Parameters
```

The default values are 600 seconds (10 minutes) for accessed entries and 120 seconds (2 minutes) for unaccessed entries.

Windows NT's ARP utility enables network administrators to view, add, and delete ARP cache entries from the command line. To learn more about using ARP, see chapter 14, "TCP/IP Utilities."

ARP AND NETWARE   NetWare 4.11 enables you to specify whether ARP should be used for TCP/IP communications when binding the TCP/IP protocol driver (TCPIP.NLM) to a LAN driver. It does this from the command line, or by using the INETCFG.NLM utility.

NetWare also includes a server utility called TCPCON.NLM. You can use this to view the contents of the ARP cache (here called the IP Address Translations Table), as well as add and delete entries. Manually configured entries to the cache can be designated as dynamic or static.

For more information on using the INETCFG.NLM and TCPCON.NLM utilities, see Chapter 14, "TCP/IP Utilities."

GRATUITOUS ARP

There is another use for ARP besides discovering the hardware addresses of other hosts. When a host system is booted, the TCP/IP stack can issue an ARP request containing its own IP address as the target. This is called a *gratuitous ARP* request, and it performs the following two functions:

◆ Broadcasts an ARP request for the host's own IP address to effectively test whether or not another system on the network segment is already using the address.

◆ Updates cache entries in other network systems if the hardware address of the host sending the ARP request has changed (for example, due to the installation of a new network adapter).

Windows NT systems running TCP/IP always broadcast a gratuitous ARP request when the system starts. If another system on the network segment responds, the TCP/IP stack on the requesting system is disabled and an error message is displayed on the screen, then added to the event log. The other system, which had first claim to the address, remains functional. If the other system is also running Windows NT, an informational message is displayed and logged, and the system then broadcasts its own ARP request to ensure that all of the ARP caches on the network list the correct hardware address for that system's entry.

When ARP broadcasts are received by host systems that do not possess the target IP address, the packets are not immediately discarded. Even though the information about the target host is incomplete (because no reply has been sent), the IP address and hardware address of the source system are available. In the event a system has to transmit data to that host in the near future, this information is added to the ARP caches of all of the hosts on the network segment.

PROXY ARP

Proxy ARP is when a router responds to ARP requests for the hardware address of a system located on an adjacent network. For example, if a router is connected to both network A and network B, and a host on network A issues an ARP request containing the IP address for a host on network B; the router can act as a proxy, responding for the host on network B.

Windows NT's Remote Access Service (RAS) server uses proxy ARP to respond to ARP requests sent by dial-up clients.

NetWare provides proxy ARP capabilities for use when the network contains devices that do not support subnetting. It, therefore, cannot recognize systems on other network segments that use the same IP network address. Proxy ARP is disabled by default, but NetWare can normally recognize the need for it and enable the feature by default. You can also force the use of proxy ARP through a setting found in the INETCFG.NLM utility, or from the BIND command line.

Proxy ARP is also required when you exercise NetWare's support for the creation of variable-sized subnets, as defined in RFC1219. In order for a stub network (that is, a logical subset of a larger subnet) to communicate with the other hosts on the network, you must force the use of proxy ARP on the router interface providing access to the larger subnet.

The Reverse Address Resolution Protocol (RARP)

Although it is no longer widely used, the Reverse Address Resolution Protocol (RARP) performs the opposite service of ARP. RARP is used to discover the IP address of a host system, based on its hardware address. Designed for use by diskless workstations, RARP enables a system with no capability to store configuration data to retrieve its IP address. It does this by broadcasting its own hardware address from a RARP server.

RARP uses the same communication procedures as ARP, with request packets sent as broadcasts, and replies as unicasts. The packet format is the same as well, except that the EtherType field in the Ethernet header has a hexadecimal value of *8035*, and the opcode field uses the values of *3* and *4* for requests and replies, respectively. A RARP request packet is attempting to discover information about itself, so the sender and target addresses in the RARP packet structure identify the same system.

Because the host does not yet know its IP address, the sender protocol address contains the value 0.0.0.0. This is a reserved address that refers to the local host on the local network. The target protocol address, as yet undiscovered in the request packet, is left blank. In a reply packet, both of the protocol address fields are filled with the IP address for the host provided by the RARP server.

RARP was the first of the protocols used to automatically assign IP addresses to TCP/IP systems. Compared to the later technologies BOOTP and DHCP, RARP provides a minimal amount of service, and has largely been abandoned. For a comparison of these three IP address allocation protocols, see Chapter 10, "DHCP and IP Address Management."

Using the TCP/IP End-to-End Protocols

Although the TCP/IP standards do not define LAN protocols, they do include protocols that provide complete link layer functionality. The TCP/IP end-to-end protocols, SLIP and PPP, create a link in the purest sense of the word: one computer is connected to another in order to exchange data. As with Ethernet and other LAN protocols, IP datagrams are encapsulated in a frame defined by the link-layer protocol standard.

The frame, however, is far simpler than that of the Ethernet standards. There is no need for a media access control mechanism or any sort of host addressing information in the frame header because there are only two computers involved in the physical connection. SLIP and PPP are both *connection-oriented* protocols — that is, the systems involved exchange identification and configuration information before any datagrams are transmitted.

SLIP and PPP are typically used to connect two networks or a host to a network when the distances between the two preclude the use of standard LAN protocols. The systems are often connected at the physical layer using a telephone link, such as a dial-up, leased line, or ISDN connection. Or they can be connected by another technology, such as frame relay, X.25, or ATM. Most of these protocols use the RS-232-E serial port that is all but ubiquitous in today's computers as the network interface. Other hardware devices, such as modems, use other protocols to achieve the data connection. These are entirely separate from the protocol stacks of the two computers, except for the limitations in transfer speed and other conditions they may impose on the connection.

The most common real-life scenarios in which the end-to-end protocols are employed are shown in Figures 4-10 through 4-13.

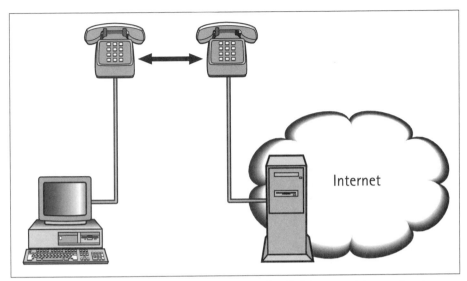

Figure 4-10: A host system uses an asynchronous modem link to connect to a router at a distant location, providing the remote user with access to a private internetwork or to the Internet.

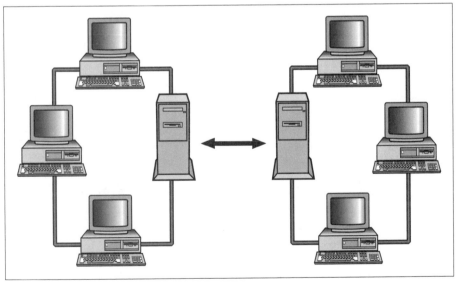

Figure 4-11: Routers on two networks at distant locations are connected to form a wide area network (WAN) to provide bidirectional access to users at both locations.

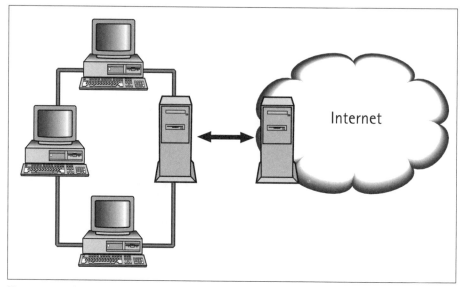

Figure 4-12: A router on a private network is connected to an ISP's router, in order to provide bidirectional access to the Internet.

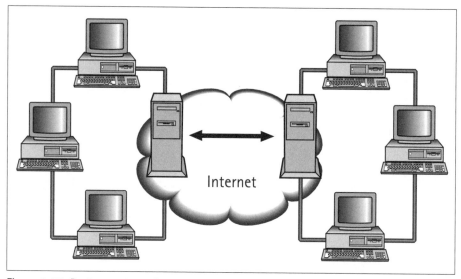

Figure 4-13: Routers on two private networks are connected to the Internet, and a specialized tunneling protocol is used to establish a virtual private network connection between the two. This provides WAN functionality without the need for a dedicated link.

Eliminating the complexities involved in local area networking removes much of the control overhead from the end-to-end protocols, but the environments where they are used present other significant problems. The document defining the SLIP protocol was published as an RFC in 1988, although the technology had been used as early as 1984. SLIP provides only the most basic data transfer functionality, and PPP was created to address many of its shortcomings.

Among other things, PPP provides support for the use of multiple network-layer protocols over a single link (including IP) and several different authentication protocols. These features make the protocol particularly suitable for remote networking and Internet connections. Windows NT supports both SLIP and PPP in its RAS and Dial-up Networking features. Novell's Multiprotocol Router product, included in the IntranetWare package, enables you to use PPP connections to provide NetWare networks with WAN and Internet access.

For more information on SLIP and PPP implementations, and on choosing the correct end-to-end protocol, see Chapter 8, "Windows NT and IntranetWare."

The Serial Line Internet Protocol (SLIP)

The Serial Line Internet Protocol (SLIP) was designed in the early 1980s as a quick and dirty solution to the problem of transmitting IP datagrams over serial links. As such, it consists of nothing more than framing characters that are used to package IP datagrams before transmission over the serial connection. SLIP has not been ratified as an Internet standard. Indeed, RFC1055 describes the protocol as "A Nonstandard for Transmission of IP Datagrams Over Serial Lines." This does not present much of a problem in terms of interoperability because the protocol is so simple, there is little to be standardized.

The list of features that SLIP is lacking (and which could make it a more useful protocol) is a long one. The major shortcomings follow:

◆ Host Addressing—SLIP has no means of informing the two connected systems of each other's IP addresses. Both hosts must be preconfigured with the identity of the other system.

◆ Protocol Type—SLIP has no equivalent of the EtherType field that identifies the contents of transmitted packets to the receiving host. As a result, SLIP is not a multiplexing protocol. Only one network-layer protocol (for example, IP) can be transmitted during a single session.

◆ **Error Detection and Correction** – SLIP provides no CRC error-checking mechanism to ensure the accurate transmission of data. This problem is not too severe because upper-layer protocols, such as TCP and IP, provide their own error detection (as do most of the modems used to establish the connection).

If you require any of these features in an end-to-end protocol, PPP is a better choice than SLIP because it provides all of them. There are, however, situations in which SLIP might be preferable. For example, if you want to create a private WAN by connecting routers in two offices using a leased phone line, SLIP could provide a viable solution with less control overhead than PPP.

If, however, you want to use multiple network-layer protocols over the connection, or secure the link with an automatic-authentication protocol, SLIP is inadequate. As recently as 1994, SLIP connections probably outnumbered those using PPP. The explosion of the dial-up ISP industry, however, has pushed PPP onto the vast majority of PCs because of the authentication and addressing services needed to regulate commercial Internet access accounts.

THE SLIP FRAME

The framing mechanism for a SLIP transmission is almost laughably simple. The protocol uses a 1-byte character called END as a frame delimiter. The END character has the hexadecimal value c0, and is transmitted after every IP datagram to identify the end of the packet. Many SLIP implementations also send an END character before each datagram begins. This way, if any line noise between packets is misinterpreted as data, the END character prevents the noise from being confused with the upcoming packet. The noise is treated as a packet unto itself, as shown in Figure 4-14. It is discarded by the upper-layer protocols when it is perceived to contain only garbage characters.

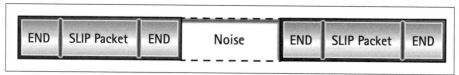

Figure 4-14: SLIP packets are delimited by an END character, which is also used to help prevent line noise from corrupting data.

There are two other special characters defined in the SLIP document for use when a byte within an IP datagram has the same value as the END character. To prevent the datagram from being wrongly delimited, the c0 byte is replaced with a *db* byte, followed by a *dc* byte. For SLIP's purposes, the *db* byte is known as the ESC character (not to be confused with the ASCII ESC character, which has a different value). If the ESC character appears as part of a datagram, it is replaced by a *db* byte, followed by a *dd* byte.

The main advantages of SLIP include adding very little overhead to TCP/IP transmissions, and being easy to implement.

THE COMPRESSED SLIP (CSLIP)

Serial connections are far slower than LAN connections. (A 10Mbps Ethernet connection is 347.2 times faster than a 28.8Kbps modem connection.) SLIP frames, themselves, add little overhead to a data transmission. The control data in the upper-layer headers of a packet are large enough to cause palpable delays when interactive programs (such as TELNET) are executed over serial links. File transfers are also significantly lengthened by the TCP and IP headers added to every packet.

When two hosts communicate over an end-to-end link, much of the data in the TCP and IP headers becomes redundant. The same fields are attached to hundreds or thousands of consecutive packets. In addition, some of the fields that do change for each packet are modified in a predictable manner, such as incrementing sequence numbers.

The Compressed SLIP (CSLIP) protocol defined in RFC1144 addresses the problem of this control traffic by compressing the TCP and IP headers in a packet from 40 bytes down to 5 bytes or less. CSLIP removes unneeded and redundant header information from TCP packets, and results in faster and more efficient SLIP data transfers. This same sort of header compression is also a feature of many PPP implementations, where it is referred to as Van Jacobson header compression, after the author of RFC1144.

The Point-to-Point Protocol (PPP)

The Point-to-Point Protocol (PPP) addresses all of SLIP's shortcomings, adding features and flexibility to serial-line transmissions. Of course, this added functionality comes at the cost of additional control overhead, but the PPP frame adds only 8 bytes (at most) to an IP datagram. This is less than half of the 18 or 26 bytes required by Ethernet. PPP has become the ideal protocol for host, or router, connections to the Internet due to its support of many features that facilitate the access-control procedures used by ISPs. PPP is also very useful for WAN connections because it supports the multiplexing of different packet types.

Windows NT's RAS defaults to using PPP because it enables a remote system to access a multiprotocol network through a dial-up connection. IntranetWare's Multiprotocol Router connects NetWare servers in the same way, forming a WAN on which TCP/IP and IPX/SPX traffic can share the same channel.

PPP, unlike SLIP, is an official Internet standard. It consists of several different elements that are defined in separate RFCs. The basic PPP components are as follows:

◆ A frame for encapsulating the data structures generated by multiple network-layer protocols. This enables them to be transmitted over a synchronous or asynchronous serial connection.

◆ A Link Control Protocol (LCP) that exchanges information with the other
  system to negotiate a common set of communications parameters.

◆ A collection of Network Control Protocols (NCPs) is designed to support
  the transmission of a different network-layer protocol.

The data encapsulation method, frame format, and the link-control protocol are
defined in RFC1661 and RFC1662. Each of the network-control protocols is defined
in a separate document. The NCP for IP, known as the Internet Protocol Control
Protocol (IPCP) is defined in RFC1332. The PPP connection sequence permits the
use of any one of several different authentication protocols during the process. The
authentication protocols are also defined separately. The most commonly used are
the *Challenge Handshake Authentication Protocol* (CHAP) and the *Password
Authentication Protocol* (PAP). These protocols are defined in RFC1334 and
RFC1994, respectively.

THE PPP FRAME

Despite its array of features, the PPP frame is quite small because much of the
header data found in the frame of a LAN protocol, such as Ethernet, is not needed
(see Figure 4-15). For example, Ethernet can be said to multiplex data in two ways:
it can carry the data generated by multiple network-layer protocols, and it can
carry the traffic generated by multiple computers, all over the same channel. The
protocol multiplexing is provided by the inclusion of the EtherType field, and the
workstation multiplexing by the source and destination addresses carried in every
packet.

PPP, like Ethernet, includes a means of identifying the transmitting system to
the recipient. Since there are only two computers involved (that is, no workstation
multiplexing), there is no need to include the addresses in every PPP frame. Instead,
an exchange of address information is performed when the PPP connection is
established. The parameters negotiated at this time remain in force throughout the
PPP session. This procedure, alone, reduces the PPP header on every packet by 12
bytes, when compared with the Ethernet header.

The PPP frame is based on that of the High-Level Data-Link Control (HDLC)
Protocol standard published by the ISO (the International Standards Organization).
The function of each of the PPP frame fields is as follows:

◆ Flag (1 byte) – The flag field, like SLIP's END character, functions as a
  packet delimiter, beginning and ending every PPP frame. The hexadecimal
  value of the flag byte is *7e*. When two packets are transmitted
  consecutively, only one flag is required (two constitute empty frames and
  are discarded).

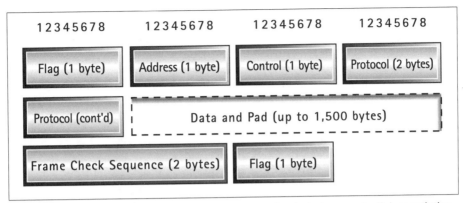

Figure 4-15: The Point-to-Point Protocol uses compression techniques and a link negotiation process to keep the size of its header to a minimum.

♦ **Address** (1 byte) – The address field is a single byte with the hexadecimal value *ff*. In binary notation, this is 11111111, indicating that the transmission is directed at all stations. Other values may be defined in future document revisions but, at present, frames containing other values should be discarded.

♦ **Control** (1 byte) – The control field contains a single byte with the hexadecimal value *03*. This is an *unnumbered information* packet, as defined in the HDLC standard. Other values may be defined in future document revisions but, at present, frames containing other values should be discarded.

♦ **Protocol** (2 bytes) – The protocol field, like the EtherType field in an Ethernet frame, identifies the information being carried in the packet's data field. The field can identify the network-layer protocol generating the data, the Link Control Protocol, one of the NCPs, or one of several optional protocols used during the PPP link-establishment process. The size of the field can be negotiated down to one byte during the link-establishment process. The values for the field are defined in the "Assigned Numbers" RFC (RFC1700). The most commonly used protocol values are:

♦ 0021 – IP Datagram

♦ 002b – Novell IPX

♦ 8021 – Internet Protocol Control Protocol (IPCP)

♦ 802b – Novell IPX Control Protocol

♦ c021 – Link Control Protocol (LCP)

◆ c023 – Password Authentication Protocol (PAP)

◆ c223 – Challenge Handshake Authentication Protocol (CHAP)

◆ **Data and Pad** (up to 1,500 bytes) – The data field contains the payload of the PPP frame. This defaults to a maximum length (also known as the Maximum Receive Unit, or MRU) of 1,500 bytes. Other values for the MRU may be negotiated by the two systems during the link-establishment process. The data field may also be padded with the number of bytes needed to reach the MRU.

◆ **Frame Check Sequence** (2 or 4 bytes) – The FCS field contains a CRC calculation for all of the data in the frame, exclusive of the flag bits and the FCS. Though it is normally 2 bytes, a 4-byte FCS may be negotiated during the link-establishment process.

◆ **Flag** (1 byte) – Identical to the flag field at the beginning of the frame.

Other data, apart from PPP frames, may be transmitted across a serial link, such as that generated by the physical layer. This includes the start-and-stop bits required for asynchronous communications, or the transparency bits used in synchronous communications. This data is considered separate from the PPP frame, and is included in FCS calculations.

Like the END character in the SLIP frame, the flag byte is escaped when it appears in the data field. This is done so it isn't mistaken for a packet delimiter. The hexadecimal character *7e* is, therefore, replaced by the escape character *7d*, followed by *5e*. The escape character *7d* is, itself, escaped with the sequence *7d 5d*. In addition, all bytes with a hexadecimal value less than *20* are also escaped. These are the codes corresponding to the ASCII control characters, which are used for special purposes by modems and serial port drivers. A data character with the hexadecimal value *01*, for example, is replaced with the sequence *7d 21*, the character *02* with *7d 22,* and so forth.

As part of the link-negotiation process, the communicating systems may agree to reduce the frame further by eliminating the address and control fields, and by reducing the protocol field to 1 byte. The presence of the address and control fields is tested by checking for the *ff 03* sequence. The standard does not permit the use of the *ff* character as the first byte of a protocol identifier, thus eliminating any chance of confusing the protocol field with the address field. This leaves a 5-byte PPP frame.

THE LCP FRAME

The Link Control Protocol (LCP) defines a data structure that is carried within a PPP frame, which is used to negotiate the creation of a connection with the target system. LCP packets are identified by the use of the hexadecimal character *c021* in the PPP header's protocol field, and use a packet structure, such as the one shown in Figure 4-16.

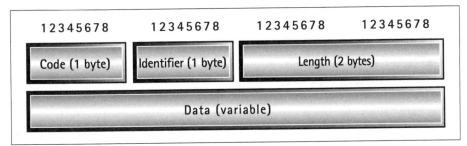

Figure 4-16: The Link Control Protocol is used to configure the properties of a PPP connection, before any network-layer data is transmitted.

The functions of the LCP packet fields are as follows:

◆ **Code** (1 byte) – The code field identifies the type of LCP packet contained in the frame. There are 11 LCP packet types, which fall into the following three categories:

Link Configuration Codes:

  ◆ 1 – Configure-Request

  ◆ 2 – Configure-Ack

  ◆ 3 – Configure-Nak

  ◆ 4 – Configure-Reject

Link Termination Codes:

  ◆ 5 – Terminate-Request

  ◆ 6 – Terminate-Ack

Link Maintenance Codes:

  ◆ 7 – Code-Reject

  ◆ 8 – Protocol-Reject

  ◆ 9 – Echo-Request

  ◆ 10 – Echo-Reply

  ◆ 11 – Discard-Request

◆ **Identifier** (1 byte) – The identifier field contains a unique code for each LCP packet exchange used to match requests with replies.

◆ **Length** (2 bytes) – The length field specifies the length of the LCP packet. This includes the code, identifier, length, and data fields, and is not to exceed the MRU of the PPP connection.

◆ **Data** (variable) – The data field varies in length and format, depending on the LCP packet type, as indicated by the code field.

The data field of the link configuration packets (code values 1 through 4) contain a series of configuration options, each of which consists of the following three fields:

◆ **Type** (1 byte) – The type field specifies the nature of the option being cited. It does this by using the following codes list in the "Assigned Numbers" RFC:

◆ 1 – Maximum-Receive-Unit

◆ 2 – Async-Control-Character-Map

◆ 3 – Authentication-Protocol

◆ 4 – Quality-Protocol

◆ 5 – Magic-Number

◆ 6 – Reserved

◆ 7 – Protocol-Field-Compression

◆ 8 – Address-and-Control-Field-Compression

◆ 9 – FCS-Alternatives

◆ 10 – Self-Describing-Pad

◆ 11 – Numbered-Mode

◆ 12 – Multilink-Procedure

◆ 13 – Callback

◆ 14 – Connect-Time

◆ 15 – Compound-Frames

◆ 16 – Nominal-Data-Encapsulation

◆ 17 – Multilink-MRRU

◆ 18 – Multilink-Short-Sequence-Number-Header-Format

◆ 19 – Multilink-Endpoint-Discriminator

◆ 20 – Proprietary

◆ 21 – DCE-Identifier

- ◆ **Length** (1 byte) – The length field indicates the length of this one configuration option, including the type, length, and data fields.

- ◆ **Data** (variable) – The data field is used to indicate the sending system's capabilities in regards to the option specified in the type field.

A Configure-Request packet contains individual option frames within an LCP frame, within a PPP frame, as shown in Figure 4-17.

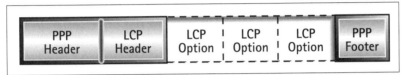

Figure 4-17: LCP link configuration packets contain a series of option frames that define the capabilities of a system's PPP implementation.

THE CHAP FRAME

When the Challenge Handshake Authentication Protocol (CHAP) is employed during the establishment of a PPP connection, a three-way handshake using specialized CHAP packets occurs. This is carried within PPP frames that have the hexadecimal value *c223* in the protocol field of the PPP header. The packet structure for CHAP is shown in Figure 4-18.

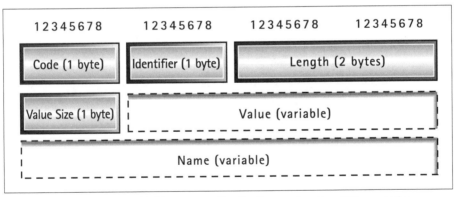

Figure 4-18: CHAP provides highly secure authentication services to a PPP connection.

CHAP is a highly secure authentication protocol that doesn't compromise account security by transmitting authentication data over the link. Each authentication exchange is disambiguated by transmitting a unique value to the destination, and an authentication "secret" is implemented on both systems using a third-party encryption algorithm. This makes it impossible for an intruder to gain access using data captured from a previous exchange. Once a successful CHAP authentication has occurred and access to the remote system has been granted, the authentication process is repeated at random intervals during the session. This limits the amount of time a successful intruder has access to the system.

The functions of the CHAP packet's fields are as follows:

- **Code** (1 byte) – The code field indicates the type of CHAP packet carried in the frame, using the following values:

  - 1 – Challenge
  - 2 – Response
  - 3 – Success
  - 4 – Failure

- **Identifier** (1 byte) – The identifier field contains a unique code for each CHAP packet exchange that is used to match requests with replies.

- **Length** (2 bytes) – The length field specifies the overall length of the CHAP frame, including the code, identifier, length, and data fields.

- **Data** (variable) – The contents of the data field are variable, depending on the value in the code field.

Challenge/Response

- **Value Size** (1 byte) – The value size field indicates the size of the value field.

- **Value** (variable) – The value field in a challenge packet contains a stream of bytes that must be unique to every challenge packet transmitted. In a response packet, the value field contains the result of a one-way hash calculation based on the values of the identifier field, the value field of the challenge packet, and an encryption "secret" common to the CHAP implementations on both systems. The length of the field is determined by the encryption algorithm used.

- **Name** (variable) – The name field contains a string identifying the sending system.

Success/Failure

- **Message** (variable) – The success and failure packets carry a text message indicating the success or failure of the authentication procedure. This is displayed to the user upon completion of the CHAP packet exchange.

THE PAP FRAME

The Password Authentication Protocol (PAP) is an alternative to CHAP, typically used when the communicating systems don't have support for other authentication protocols. PAP uses a relatively simple two-way handshake in which a user name and password are transmitted over the link in clear text. PAP uses packets carried within PPP frames containing the hexadecimal value *c023* in the header's protocol field. The PAP frame is similar in appearance to that used for CHAP transmissions. The functions of the packet fields are as follows:

- **Code** (1 byte) – The code field indicates the type of PAP packet carried in the frame, using the following values:

    - 1 – Authenticate-Request

    - 2 – Authenticate-Ack

    - 3 – Authenticate-Nak

- **Identifier** (1 byte) – The identifier field contains a unique code for each PAP packet exchange that is used to match requests with replies.

- **Length** (2 bytes) – The length field specifies the overall length of the PAP frame, including the code, identifier, length, and data fields.

- **Data** (variable) – The contents of the data field are variable, depending on the value in the code field.

Authenticate-Request

- **Peer-ID Length** (1 byte) – The peer-ID length field specifies the length of the peer-ID field.

- **Peer-ID** (variable) – The peer-ID field contains the account name that will identify the sending system during the authentication process.

- **Password Length** (1 byte) – The password-ID length field specifies the length of the password field.

- **Password** (variable) – The password field contains the password associated with the account name specified in the peer-ID field.

Authenticate-Ack/Authenticate-Nak

- **Message Length** (1 byte) – The message length field specifies the length of the value in the message field.

- **Message** (variable) – The ack and nak packets carry a text message indicating the success or failure of the authentication procedure. This is displayed to the user upon completion of the PAP packet exchange.

THE IPCP FRAME

Because PPP is capable of multiplexing network-layer protocols on a single connection, the properties of each protocol must be configured individually for their different requirements. These configurations are performed by Network Control Protocols (NCPs), which are defined by separate RFCs. The Internet Protocol Control Protocol (IPCP) is the NCP that is responsible for configuring IP communications over a PPP connection.

IPCP packets are carried in PPP frames that contain the value *8021* in the PPP header's protocol field. The protocol field values for the various NCPs are specified in the "Assigned Numbers" RFC. IPCP uses the same packet format as LCP, with some changes in the field values. The protocol enables only the link-configuration and link-termination values plus the code reject value (that is, 1 through 7) in the code field of the IPCP header. The use of the other link-maintenance values (8 through 11) cause the IPCP packet to be discarded.

IPCP packets also carry different options in the data field, using the same format as LCP options. The possible values for an option's type field include the following:

◆ **1 – IP-Addresses** – The IP-Addresses option has been supplanted by the IP-Address option. The former should not be used, except when the IP-Address option is added to the existing options in a Configure-Nak packet or included in a Configure-Reject packet.

◆ **2 – IP-Compression Protocol** – The IP-Compression Protocol option specifies the use of a particular protocol for the compression of IP headers (of which the only one available is Van Jacobson compression). Implementing Van Jacobson header compression causes alternative values to be used for the protocol field in the header PPP packets containing IP datagrams. These values are as follows:

   ◆ **0021 –** This value indicates that the packet contains normal, uncompressed IP datagrams.

   ◆ **002d –** This value indicates that the IP and TCP headers in the datagram have been compressed.

   ◆ **002f –** The 002f value indicates that the packet contains uncompressed TCP data, and that the PPP header's protocol-field value should be replaced by a slot identifier. This must specify the location where the state of a particular TCP connection is maintained.

◆ **3 – IP-Address** – The IP-Address option is used by the transmitting system to specify the IP address that it would like to use, or to request that the target system supply an address, by specifying the value 0.0.0.0.

Establishing a PPP Connection

Before any transmission of network-layer protocol data using PPP can begin, a link-layer connection must be established with the target system. Once the physical-layer connection is enabled using the handshake procedure of the modems (or other devices at both ends), the two systems exchange LCP packets. This provides information about their respective PPP capabilities. Once the two have agreed on a common set of communications parameters, an authentication process may follow. After that, individual NCP exchanges commence for each of the network-layer protocols to be used during the session. Once each NCP negotiation is completed, network-layer communications can begin. These proceed until LCP is again used to terminate the link.

A PPP connection passes through a series of distinct phases during the life of a connection, as shown in Figure 4-19. The following sections examine each of these phases.

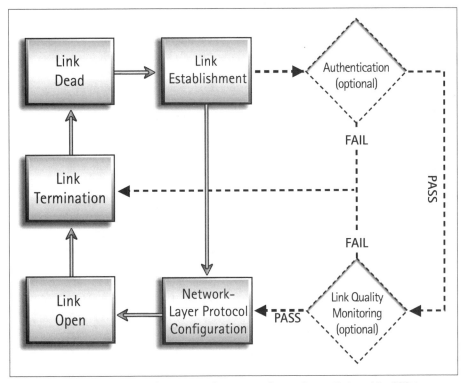

Figure 4-19: The complexity of its connection process is one factor that enables PPP to provide a full complement of features, while using a very small frame.

LINK DEAD

The *link dead* phase indicates that no physical-layer connection exists between the two computers. The link is dead both before a PPP connection is established and after one is terminated. The PPP implementation proceeds to the next phase after receiving an indication that a physical-layer connection has been established. This indication may be a modem's carrier detection or an explicit action like the loading of a software application.

LINK ESTABLISHMENT

The computer initiating the connection transmits an LCP Configure-Request packet which specifies the additional capabilities of the system it would like to implement. LCP is only used to configure PPP features that are not specific to a network-layer protocol.

A Configure-Request packet only contains options for values that differ from the sending system's default capabilities. A typical packet, for example, may include option type 3 to indicate that the system would like to use CHAP as an authentication protocol and option 8 to request the compression of the PPP frame's address and control fields.

If the system receiving the Configure-Request packet can support all of the specified optional features, it must return a Configure-Ack packet with the same identifier value as the request, and the same option values listed in the LCP data field. This completes the link-establishment procedure, enabling the connection process to proceed to the next phase.

If the system receiving the Configure-Request packet recognizes all of the options specified in the LCP data field, but doesn't support the value specified for one or more options, it must return a Configure-Nak packet with the same identifier value as the request. In the LCP data field of the Nak packet, the requested options that are supported by the receiving system are stripped away, leaving only the options requiring further negotiation. The receiving system specifies all of the values it can support for the given options, and may also add further options it would like to see added to the configuration. Once the Configure-Nak packet is received by the original sender, it generates a new Configure-Request packet containing revised option values for the other system's approval.

If the system receiving the Configure-Request packet fails to recognize one or more of the options in the LCP data field, it returns a Configure-Reject packet with the same identifier value as the request. The LCP data field of the Reject packet contains only the options that are not recognized by the receiving system. When the original sender generates a new Configure-Request packet, the options must not include those that were returned in the Configure-Reject packet.

Eventually, as shown in Figure 4-20, an acceptable Configure-Request is generated and acknowledged, and the connection process can proceed to the next phase.

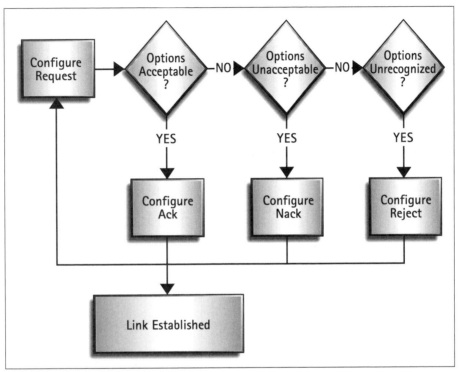

Figure 4-20: The LCP negotiation process enables a PPP connection to be established with the highest functionality supported by both systems.

AUTHENTICATION

Authentication is not a required phase of the PPP connection process, but it is frequently used, particularly for ISP connections. Authentication is performed using external protocols defined by other documents. Two of the most popular, PAP and CHAP, are supported by both Windows NT and IntranetWare, and are published as RFCs. Others may be based on documents published by other standards bodies (or by private companies such as SPAP, the Shiva Password Authentication Protocol) which is also supported by Windows NT (but not by IntranetWare).

CHAP is the most popular, and the most secure, authentication protocol used for PPP connections, today. Conversely, PAP is the least secure, as it transmits account names and passwords over the link with no encryption of any kind. In general, it is used as a last resort, when the two communicating systems have no other authentication protocols in common.

Using a particular authentication protocol during the establishment of a PPP link requires the inclusion of the Authentication Protocol option in the LCP Configure-Request packet. When a protocol is agreed on, by both systems, that protocol takes over the communication process, initiating the packet exchange defined in its specification. The authentication messages are carried as payload in

PPP frames. The values for the PPP header's protocol field, specifying the various authentication protocols, are published in the "Assigned Numbers" RFC.

CHAP, for example, sends a Challenge packet to the target system, which performs a computation based on data in the packet and an encryption key included in its own CHAP implementation. The target system then returns a Response packet to the sender that contains the computer value. Depending on whether or not the computations match, the sending system transmits a Success or Failure packet to the target.

PAP, on the other hand, uses a simple exchange in which an Authenticate-Request packet is sent to the target containing an account name and password. The target then responds with an Authenticate-Ack or Authenticate-Nak packet.

A successful authentication enables the connection process to proceed to the next phase. The systems' response to a failed authentication can vary, however, depending on the protocol and its implementation. Originally, the CHAP specification called for a failed authentication to force the PPP establishment process to immediately proceed to the Link Termination phase. Later revisions to the document allowed for other options, such as authentication retries and the granting of limited network-layer protocol access (for sending e-mail to the network administrator, for example).

LINK QUALITY MONITORING

Another optional element in the PPP connection process is the implementation of a link quality monitoring protocol. The use of such a protocol is negotiated using the Quality Protocol option during the LCP link establishment process. Only one such protocol is available (the Link Quality Report protocol) as defined in RFC1989. The protocol functions by generating packets at regular intervals, containing statistics on many aspects of the PPP connection. These aspects might include such things as the number of bytes, and packets transmitted and received by both systems.

Both of the computers involved in the PPP connection generate their own link quality reports. They transmit them to the other system within PPP frames that use the hexadecimal value *c025* in the PPP header's protocol field. They both compare their internally generated statistics with those received from the other system, in order to determine how many bytes and packets have been lost or damaged due to physical layer problems.

The Link Quality Report protocol document does not specify courses of action to take as a result of the link quality monitoring results. Responses are left to the individual PPP implementations.

NETWORK LAYER PROTOCOL CONFIGURATION

At this phase, all that remains to the PPP connection process is the configuration of the network-layer protocols used on the link. An individual NCP negotiation is required before any traffic using that protocol can be transmitted. NCP packet exchanges are very similar to those of LCP, except that the options reflect the unique requirements of each network-layer protocol. For TCP/IP communications, the IPCP protocol is used to specify the IP address of the transmitting system and (optionally) to implement compression of the IP and TCP headers, as discussed in "The IPCP Frame," earlier in this chapter. Other NCP exchanges may occur before or after the IPCP negotiation, until all of the desired network-layer protocols have been initialized. There are 21 NCPs listed in the "Assigned Numbers" RFC. Each one uses its own packet format, as identified by a code found in the protocol field of the PPP header. Any supported protocol can be initialized or terminated, using an NCP negotiation, at any time during a PPP session.

LINK OPEN

Once the NCP negotiations have been successfully completed, the PPP connection goes into the Link Open phase. This means that PPP packets containing traffic generated by LCP, NCP, or any properly initialized network-layer protocol, may be transmitted over the link.

LINK TERMINATION

A PPP connection can be terminated for a number of reasons, such as a physical-layer disconnection, an inactivity timeout, an authentication failure, a link-quality degradation, or a manual disconnection by the user of either system. In any of these cases, LCP packets are used to terminate the link.

The LCP Terminate-Request and Terminate-Ack packets contain no special options or parameters. There is only a code specifying the packet type and an identifier to associate the requests with the replies; one system sends a request, and the other responds with a reply.

NCPs can also use the Terminate-Request and Terminate-Ack packet types, but these are only used to terminate the use of a specific network-layer protocol. It is not necessary to individually terminate each protocol before the LCP termination request is issued, nor should the termination of all of the initialized network-layer protocols cause the entire PPP link to be terminated. Individual PPP implementations should signal the physical layer once the PPP connection is terminated, so that the physical connection can be closed.

Once the LCP termination has been successfully completed, the PPP connection returns to the Link Dead phase.

The Loopback Interface

The *TCP/IP loopback interface* operates at the link layer in a manner that appears (to the upper-layer protocols) no different from that of Ethernet, SLIP, or PPP. The TCP/IP standards require that the class A network address 127.0.0.0 be reserved for loopback purposes. The IP address 127.0.0.1 is typically used for this purpose, so a host can send TCP/IP transmissions to itself.

To the transport and internet layers, the loopback address appears the same as any other link-layer protocol. Outgoing IP datagrams, however, are diverted by the loopback interface back to the IP input queue. From there, they travel back up the protocol stack as if they arrived at a network interface.

In addition to IP datagrams addressed to 127.0.0.1, the loopback interface is used when a host transmits datagrams containing the broadcast address, or one of the host system's own IP addresses, as their destination. Broadcast transmissions are copied to the IP input queue and also transmitted over the normal network interface (because a broadcast by definition includes the sending system, itself, as part of the destination).

The loopback address is used for various types of system tests. For example, a TCP/IP client/server software product can be tested by running both applications on a single host, and then using the loopback address to provide the client access to the server. This form of testing eliminates any possible physical or data link-layer problems from the equation, because the upper-layer communications never leave the host system.

The loopback interface is useful for testing TCP/IP software implementations on a host system, but not for testing the performance of the network, itself. Even when a transmission is addressed to one of the host's IP addresses, the datagrams never reach the network interface or the network medium. You can PING your own system using 127.0.0.1, or its actual address, and receive a positive response even when the computer is not connected to the network.

Summary

The link layer of the TCP/IP protocol stack performs several different functions, depending on the network interface used at the physical layer.

In this chapter, you learned:

◆ How IP datagrams are encapsulated in LAN protocol frames

◆ How ARP uses IP addresses to discover the hardware address needed for LAN communications

◆ How end-to-end protocols, such as SLIP and PPP, connect two computers with a dedicated link

The following chapter examines the internet layer of the protocol stack. This is where IP, the central protocol of the TCP/IP suite, operates.

Chapter 5

The Internet Layer

IN THIS CHAPTER

The internet layer is the focal point of the entire TCP/IP protocol suite because the Internet Protocol operates there. Nearly all of the other TCP/IP protocols rely on IP for the basic services needed to carry data to a system on another network. This chapter examines the protocols that operate at the internet layer, and the services they provide, including the following:

◆ IP provides the fundamental TCP/IP "envelope" that carries data generated by the upper-layer protocols. It also addresses the envelope to its final destination.

◆ Two of the internet-layer processes are fragmentation and routing. These enable TCP/IP data to be transmitted across many different types of networks.

◆ The Internet Control Message Protocol also operates at the internet layer, and is used to transmit diagnostic and error information to other TCP/IP systems.

AS YOU MOVE UP through the layers of the TCP/IP networking stack, the protocols become increasingly responsible for the delivery of data to its final destination. Link-layer protocols are very limited in their vision; they are responsible only for delivering data to the next system in the journey. The Ethernet protocol, for example, can deliver data either to the destination system (if it is located on the local network segment) or to a router that provides access to another segment. The Ethernet implementation is told where to send the data; it makes no routing determinations of its own.

The protocols operating at the internet layer are the protocols responsible for specifying a destination to the Ethernet protocol. Chief among these is the Internet Protocol (IP), which is the primary internet-layer communications mechanism used by TCP/IP. The other major protocol that operates at the internet layer, the Internet Control Message Protocol (ICMP), is used to perform control tasks that aid IP in its duties. Although it is spoken of as operating at the same layer of the model, ICMP is not an alternative to IP (as TCP and UDP are alternatives to each other). ICMP messages are, in fact, carried within IP datagrams.

Apart from ICMP messages, the payload carried by the IP protocol consists of either TCP segments or UDP packets, as shown in Figure 5-1. Aside from identifying the protocol being carried within each datagram, IP treats the data generated by each of these protocols in exactly the same way. As with any data encapsulation process, the IP protocol is no more concerned with the payload carried within a datagram than postal workers care about the letters they carry.

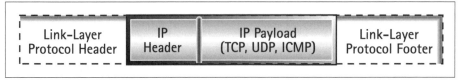

Figure 5-1: IP datagrams carry data generated by the transport-layer protocols TCP and UDP, as well as that of TCP/IP control protocols like ICMP.

The Internet Protocol (IP)

IP is the fundamental protocol on which TCP/IP networks are built, as it provides the data delivery service used by every other protocol operating at, and above, the internet layer. Its equivalent in the postal service is the standard business letter, a basic efficient carrier mechanism in which any kind of data can be inserted into the envelope.

IP Standards

The Internet Protocol standard currently used is version 4, as defined in RFC791. Additional documents define the encapsulation of IP within various link-layer protocols, such as the following:

- RFC894 – IP over Ethernet Networks

- RFC1042 – IP over IEEE 802 Networks

- RFC1188 – IP over FDDI Networks

- RFC1201 – IP over ARCNET Networks

Version 6 of the Internet Protocol is intended to address the many problems resulting from the enormous growth of the Internet in recent years. It is currently in the process of being ratified as an Internet standard. As of this writing, the first implementations of the new protocol are just arriving on the market.

Because it is used to carry many different types of data, IP is designed to provide only the minimum service required by all of the upper-layer protocols. The implementation of features, such as packet acknowledgment and flow control, are left to upper-layer protocols like TCP. Not all of the protocols that use the IP delivery service need these features. IP is, in essence, an inexpensive First Class Mail service to which additional options, such as Special Delivery and Certified Mail can be added if the contents of the envelope warrant such treatment. The price of these options is the additional control data overhead that is needed to implement the additional features.

Quality of Service

The service provided by IP is often thought to be connectionless and unreliable. As used here, *connectionless* and *unreliable* are technical terms that do not carry the stigma of inefficiency which pervades their general use. In fact, you can count on IP transmissions to reach their destination intact, in the vast majority of cases. A *connectionless* transmission occurs when a packet is sent without prior confirmation that the destination system exists and is ready to receive data. The opposite of this is a *connection-oriented* transmission (such as those provided by TCP) in which a handshake is performed between the source and destination systems before any application-layer data is transmitted.

An *unreliable* service is one in which no acknowledgment of a packet's successful receipt is expected from the destination system. IP makes its best effort to transmit data successfully. Additional services, used to guarantee the delivery of packets, must be implemented by upper-layer protocols if and when the data requires them.

The delegation of services, such as error correction and flow control, to various protocol layers is a critical aspect of TCP/IP's overall efficiency. The properties of the data being transmitted determine the required transport services and the protocols the client should use. For example, an FTP session transferring a large binary file requires a connection-oriented, reliable service (because the corruption of even one bit can render the file useless). By the time the FTP data reaches the internet layer, the file has been segmented into small pieces which are transmitted by IP as separate units called *datagrams*.

IP treats each of the datagrams it transmits as a separate entity. With no knowledge of the contents carried within its payload (or that the data contained in a group of datagrams will ultimately be combined to form a file), IP cannot judge the level of service needed by the data. The connection-oriented, reliable service needed for an FTP transmission is implemented higher up in the stack, by the TCP protocol.

At the same time, the relatively limited array of services provided by IP keeps the control traffic sent over the network to a minimum. As IP cannot assess the needs of the data it carries, it's possible to implement a greater number of features for all transmissions, for safety reasons. This, however, would result in a great deal of unnecessary data being transported over the network.

In the case of a DNS transaction, for example, the use of connection-oriented, reliable service at the internet layer would require the transmission of several additional packets. These would establish the connection, acknowledge the delivery of the data, and then break down the connection. In this case, the amount of control traffic for the transmission would be several times larger than the data, itself (which doesn't actually require any of these services).

For a DNS transaction, it is far more efficient to transmit the datagram, without establishing a connection, and wait for a response. If no response is received in a given amount of time, the datagram can be resent without even approaching the amount of data needed for a connection-oriented transmission.

The services provided by IP, at the internet layer, should be kept to a minimum. This enables the protocols operating higher in the stack (and closer to the data source) to determine the transmission requirements.

IP Functions

Despite the lack of connection-oriented service and guaranteed delivery, IP commands a lot of responsibility. In fact, IP performs some of the most complex operations involved in a TCP/IP transmission. The primary functions of the IP protocol are:

◆ packaging upper-layer data into datagrams

◆ addressing datagrams to their ultimate destination

◆ fragmenting datagrams for transmission over link-layer networks

◆ routing datagrams to their destinations on other networks

The datagram is the fundamental unit of transmission on a TCP/IP network. In the course of its journey, a datagram may be packaged in several different frames as it passes through various link-layer networks (see Figure 5-2). While link-layer frames can be applied and removed repeatedly, the datagram formed by IP remains intact throughout the entire journey (except for minor modifications made to the IP header during the trip).

IP is also responsible for identifying the destination of the transmitted data throughout its journey. The source and destination IP addresses, included in the IP header, identify the end systems for the TCP/IP transmission. Addresses specified in link-layer protocol headers refer only to the systems involved in a particular hop from one network segment to another.

As datagrams pass through different networks on the way to their destination, they may be subjected to different conditions. A datagram that originates at a system on an IEEE 802.5 token ring network, for example, can carry up to 4,464 bytes of data. When that datagram leaves the token ring network, it is likely to encounter link-layer protocols which require smaller packets. Once this happens, the IP implementation at the intermediate system acts as the gateway between the two networks.

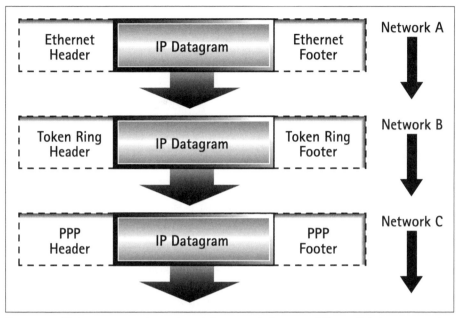

Figure 5-2: IP datagrams can be packaged for transmission over different link-layer network types many times in the course of their journey.

It is responsible for fragmenting the data into smaller pieces, each of which is transmitted as a separate datagram. The intermediate system must also provide sufficient information to ensure that the pieces can be reassembled properly, once they arrive at the destination.

A link-layer protocol is only concerned with delivering packets to the next system down the line, and a transport protocol is only involved with communications between the source and destination systems. IP, however, is responsible for the route the datagrams must take to their destination. In order to determine the most efficient route, the internet layer (at each intermediate system) communicates with the other routers on the same network segment. It then consults its own internal routing tables for information on what lies beyond the local network segment. As a result of this process, IP identifies the router to which a datagram will be sent and supplies this information to the link-layer protocol.

The IP Header

Like many of the TCP/IP protocols, the IP's functionality is largely implemented in the form of a header, which is applied to the data received from the layer above. In a typical transmission, data from the TCP or UDP transport-layer protocol is passed down to the internet layer. There it becomes the payload in a datagram when the IP header is applied, as shown in Figure 5-3.

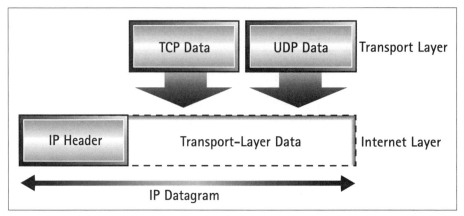

Figure 5-3: Transport-layer data is encapsulated at the internet layer by the application of the IP header.

The IP header is typically 20 bytes in length, except (in rare cases) when optional fields are included. The header can be displayed, like most TCP/IP headers, as a series of 32-bit (4-byte) words (see Figure 5-4). If optional fields are included, they are padded to fall on a 32-bit boundary.

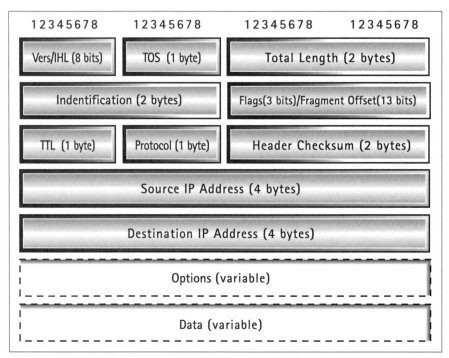

Figure 5-4: In most datagrams, the IP header consists of five 32-bit words which are added to the data received from the transport layer.

Each of the words that comprise an IP header are broken down into one or more fields, followed by the data. The functions of the datagram fields are as follows:

◆ **Version** – 4 bits – This field specifies the version of the IP protocol being used. The value of this field is always 4 (except in experimental implementations of IP version 6, which uses a header format completely different from that of version 4).

◆ **IHL (Internet Header Length)** – 4 bits – The IHL field specifies the length of the IP header, in 32-bit words, and is used to locate the beginning of the data field. The value of this field is typically 5, unless optional fields are present.

◆ **TOS (Type of Service)** – 1 byte – This field is composed of three precedence bits (that are no longer used) and four flags. The flags are activated by changing their values from 0 to 1, which indicate the service priority desired for the data carried in the packet. The eighth bit in the field always has a value of 0. The service types represented by the four flags are as follows:

  ◆ **0000** – Default

  ◆ **0001** – Minimize Monetary Cost

  ◆ **0010** – Maximize Reliability

  ◆ **0100** – Maximize Throughput

  ◆ **1000** – Minimize Delay

  ◆ **1111** – Maximize Security

◆ **Total Length** – 2 bytes – This field specifies the overall length (in bytes) of the datagram, including the header and the data. This setting is used to determine how much of a link-layer frame's payload is actually IP data. Some protocols (such as Ethernet) add padding bits to achieve a minimum size.

◆ **Identification** – 2 bytes – This field contains a unique value, incremented for each successive datagram. This value is used to reassemble data fragments in the proper order.

◆ **Flags** – 3 bits – This field contains bits that are used in the data fragmentation process, as follows:

  ◆ **Bit 1** – Not used

  ◆ **Bit 2** – **Don't fragment** – When set to a value of 1, this flag prevents a datagram from being fragmented under any circumstances.

◆ Bit 3 – More fragments – When set to a value of 1, this flag indicates that there are additional fragments of the current datagram still awaiting transmission. The flag is returned to a value of 0 when the final fragment is transmitted.

◆ **Fragment Offset** – 13 bits – This field indicates, in 8-byte (64-bit) units, where in the datagram this particular fragment belongs.

◆ **TTL (Time to Live)** – 1 byte – The TTL field specifies the maximum number of routers a datagram can pass through on the way to its destination. The number is decremented by each router as it processes the datagram. When the value reaches 0, the packet is discarded.

◆ **Protocol** – 1 byte – This field contains a code that identifies the protocol used to generate the data carried in the data field. The codes are specified in the "Assigned Numbers" RFC, some of which include the following:

   ◆ 1 – Internet Control Message Protocol (ICMP)

   ◆ 2 – Internet Group Management Protocol (IGMP)

   ◆ 3 – Gateway-to-Gateway Protocol (GGP)

   ◆ 6 – Transmission Control Protocol (TCP)

   ◆ 8 – Exterior Gateway Protocol (EGP)

   ◆ 17 – User Datagram Protocol (UDP)

◆ **Header Checksum** – 2 bytes – This field contains the result of a checksum computation performed on the IP header fields. The same computation is then performed at the receiving system, and the results are compared to check the accuracy of the transmission.

◆ **Source IP Address** – 4 bytes – The source IP address field contains the end system's address, where the datagram originated.

◆ **Destination IP Address** – 4 bytes – This field contains the address of the end system that will be the ultimate recipient of the datagram.

◆ **Options** – variable – The options field can contain entries for any of the 16 options defined in the "Assigned Numbers" RFC. Among these options are the following:

   ◆ **Loose source routing** – This is used to specify the IP addresses of routers that the datagram must pass through on the way to its destination. The datagram can pass through other routers aside from those listed in this field.

- ◆ **Strict source routing** – This option is used to specify the IP addresses of all of the routers the datagram must pass through on the way to its destination. The datagram can only pass through the routers specified in this field.

- ◆ **Record route** – Record route is used to store the IP addresses of each router the datagram passes through on the way to its destination

- ◆ **Internet timestamp** – This option stores the IP addresses of each router the datagram passes through on the way to its destination, and a record of the time when the router processed the datagram.

- ◆ **Data** – variable, up to the MTU (maximum transmission unit) – The data field contains the payload of the datagram, supplied by a transport-layer or another internet-layer protocol.

 In most TCP/IP implementations, the protocol field code numbers are listed in a text file called PROTOCOL. This file is found in a directory called ETC (pronounced *et'-see*) which, on NetWare servers, is found on the SYS volume. On Windows NT systems, the path to the directory is *windowsroot*\system32\-drivers\etc.

TYPE OF SERVICE

The IP header's type of service (TOS) field is used to differentiate the types of application-layer data carried within IP datagrams. For example, both FTP and TELNET use TCP at the transport layer and IP at the internet layer, but their functions are very different and so are the services they require from the lower-layer protocols. FTP is typically used for transfers of large files, which require long sequences of large TCP segments, while TELNET sends many small commands back and forth in order to interactively control a system from a remote location.

To accommodate the needs of these two applications, the TOS field can be modified by setting the maximize throughput flag for FTP, and the minimize delay flag for TELNET. These settings have no effect on the end systems involved in the transactions, but some IP router implementations assign precedence to certain data types based on the TOS settings.

The "Assigned Numbers" RFC specifies TOS settings for standard TCP/IP applications. For example, it recommends the maximize-reliability flag for SNMP and routing protocols, and the minimize monetary cost flag for the Network News Transfer Protocol (NNTP). Unlisted protocols utilize the default setting, which consists of 0 values for all four flags.

TIME TO LIVE

The time to live (TTL) field prevents IP datagrams from circulating endlessly in router loops. Typically set to a value of 32 or 64 by the system producing the datagram, the TTL field is one of the few IP header fields to be modified during the trip (from the source system to the destination). Other fields in the header are changed during the fragmentation process.

The "Assigned Numbers" RFC recommends that the TTL be set to a default value of 64, but most Microsoft clients use a value of 32, by default. Windows NT 4.0 clients, however, use a default TTL value of 128.

The routing specifications imposed by Ethernet and other LAN protocols limit a packet to three or four hops between the source and the destination. It is not, however, unusual for IP datagrams to pass through 20 or more routers as they are transmitted over the Internet. Each intermediate system a datagram passes through reduces the TTL value by at least one, ensuring that a packet cannot be passed endlessly from system to system by malfunctioning routers.

When a datagram's TTL value reaches 0, the packet is discarded by the last router, which returns an ICMP error message to the source system. There is a command line utility commonly found in UNIX and Microsoft TCP/IP clients called *traceroute* (or TRACERT.EXE by Microsoft). This utility employs the TTL field to display a listing of routers traversed by a datagram on the way to its destination.

The program transmits a series of datagrams to a given destination with progressively larger TTL values. This causes each packet to time out one hop further along on the journey. The ICMP messages, returned by the packets, identify each successive router. This defines the path the datagrams are taking to their destination.

For more information about the traceroute utility, see Chapter 14, "TCP/IP Utilities."

IP HEADER CHECKSUMS

The checksums, computed on an IP header, are an important factor in maintaining the data integrity of TCP/IP communications. IP computes its checksums only on the header fields because upper-layer protocols, such as TCP and UDP, have their own error-checking mechanisms for the data carried as payload, in an IP datagram.

Unlike TCP and UDP however, which are only concerned with end-to-end transmissions, IP checksum calculations are performed at every intermediate system along the datagram's destination path.

The IP checksum is computed on all of the IP header fields, including the checksum field, which is filled with 0's for this purpose. The header is then divided into 16-bit words and "one's complement" arithmetic is used to compute the sum of the entire header. Finally, the one's complement sum of this sum is placed in the header's checksum field, and the datagram is transmitted.

When the datagram is received by the next system on the path, a one's complement sum is again calculated on the entire IP header. Since the receiving system's computation is performed on the header (which contains the checksum computed by the sender), a value of all 1's indicates that all of the header bits have arrived undamaged.

IP has no mechanism for correcting the errors it detects. If the checksum calculations determine that the header has been damaged in transit, the datagram is silently discarded — no error message is returned to the source, no action is taken to retransmit the data. The upper-layer protocols are responsible for detecting the absence of information in the datagram, and resending it.

IP ADDRESSING

The IP protocol ensures that the data it receives from the transport layer is transmitted to the appropriate destination system. The source and destination IP addresses found in the IP header represent the end systems where the data originated and will ultimately be received. These addresses remain unchanged throughout the life of the datagram, which is in direct contrast to the hardware addresses found in the link-layer protocol header.

Link-layer protocols use the hardware addresses that are associated with particular network interface adapters. These are only responsible for communications within a particular network segment. As a packet travels on an internetwork, the hardware addresses are changed at every router to specify the next interim destination, or *hop*. The IP protocol determines which router should be the next intermediate system in the trip by consulting the routing tables stored in the system.

The IP addresses used at the internet layer are unique to the TCP/IP protocol stack. The structure of IP addresses and the subnetting techniques you use to define the boundaries of a TCP/IP internetwork are examined in Chapter 2, "TCP/IP Communications."

IP HEADER OPTIONS

The options field of the IP header is designed to hold various types of information. Some types are gathered as the datagram travels through the internetwork, and others govern the path the packets will take to the destination. The options field may contain multiple entries, each of which (with a few notable exceptions) consists of three fields, as follows:

- **Option type** – 1 byte – The option type field is composed of three subfields that are combined to form a single 8-bit value. The three subfields include the following:

  - **Copy flag** – 1 bit – If the datagram is fragmented, the copy flag indicates whether the option should be copied to each of the fragments. 0 = No, 1 = Yes.

  - **Option class** – 2 bits – The option class field contains a code that identifies the basic function of the option. Possible values are as follows:

    - 0 – Control
    - 1 – Reserved
    - 2 – Debugging and measurement
    - 3 – Reserved

  - **Option number** – 5 bits – The option number field contains a unique identifier for the particular option, as specified in the "Assigned Numbers" RFC.

- **Option length** – 1 byte – The option length field specifies the overall length of a particular option, including the type, length, and data fields.

- **Option data** – variable – The option data field contains the information particular to a given option.

The options that don't include length and data fields are used to delimit the various options included in the datagram. They also signal the end of the option list, as follows:

- **No operation** – When multiple entries are included in the options field, option type 1 (containing the binary value 00000001) is placed between the entries to ensure that they are not confused.

- **End of option list** – Option type 0 (containing the binary value 00000000) is used to signal the end of the entries contained in the options field.

The IP header's options field always ends at a 32-bit boundary and is, therefore, padded with 0's to complete a partially filled word.

IP options are generally not required for normal communications, but can be implemented for special situations, such as the debugging of new TCP/IP host implementations or environments that require increased data security measures. Many of the available options can be activated using the command line parameters built into the PING program. For more information on using PING to specify IP options, see Chapter 14, "TCP/IP Utilities."

As the name implies, these *options* may or may not be included in IP headers as needed. The capability to send and receive packets containing these options is, itself, not optional. This capability is a requirement for all TCP/IP hosts and routers.

Fragmenting Datagrams

IP datagrams can be carried by many different link-layer protocols on the way to their destination. These protocols can have widely divergent properties and limitations. When you use a Web browser to connect to a site on the Internet, for example, your system is aware of the link-layer protocol used on your local network. In some cases, it may know the protocol used at the destination network, but will not be conscious of the properties of the networks that lie between the source and the destination.

The most important property of each link-layer network type, for the purposes of transmitting IP datagrams, is the maximum transmission unit (MTU). The MTU specifies the largest possible frame that can be transmitted on that network type. When a datagram encounters a network with an MTU that is smaller than the datagram's size, it must be split into segments that are small enough to transmit over that network. This process, performed by the IP protocol, is called *fragmentation*.

The MTUs of some of the most commonly used link-layer networks are as follows:

Network	MTU (in bytes)
Maximum MTU	65,535
Token Ring (IBM 16MB/sec)	17,914
Token Ring (IEEE 802.5 4MB/sec)	4,464
FDDI	4,352

Network	MTU (in bytes)
Ethernet	1,500
IEEE 802.3/802.2	1,492
Point-to-point	1,500
SLIP	1,006
Point-to-point (low delay)	296
Minimum MTU	68

When a datagram is fragmented, its payload is divided into several segments—each of which is transmitted as a separate packet with its own IP header. Datagrams can be fragmented at the end system where the packet originates, or at any intermediate system during the journey. Sometimes datagrams must be fragmented more than once in the course of a transmission. If a fragment encounters a network with a smaller MTU, it is divided into even smaller segments.

No matter what fragmentation takes place during the transmission process, the reassembly of fragments takes place only at the internet layer of the datagram's destination system. Strictly speaking, the term *datagram* refers to the entire data structure possessing a specific value in the IP header's identification field. Thus, a series of fragments can be collectively referred to as a datagram, even though each is transmitted in a separate IP packet.

THE FRAGMENTATION PROCESS

Fragmentation typically takes place when a datagram arrives at an intermediate system, and the internet-layer protocol queries the network interface (over which the packet is to be transmitted to determine its MTU). If the datagram is larger than the MTU, the fragmentation process begins.

Three fields of the IP header are used during the fragmentation process to:

◆ ensure that the fragments of a particular datagram can be associated at the destination

◆ specify the order in which the fragments should be reassembled

◆ identify the last of the fragments composing the datagram

When a datagram is split into fragments, new IP packets (containing the same value in the identification field) are created. At the destination system, this value is used to identify the fragments that will be reassembled into a particular datagram. As the packet containing each fragment is created, the data field is filled from the payload of the original datagram, until the MTU for the new network is reached (to the nearest 8 bytes).

When a datagram, that originated on an FDDI network, is fragmented for transmission over an Ethernet network, only 1,500 bytes can be carried in each Ethernet frame. Since the MTU for the Ethernet protocol includes the internet-layer header, only the first 1,480 bytes of the datagram's payload can be carried in the first fragment. This allots 20 bytes for the IP header, as shown in Figure 5-5.

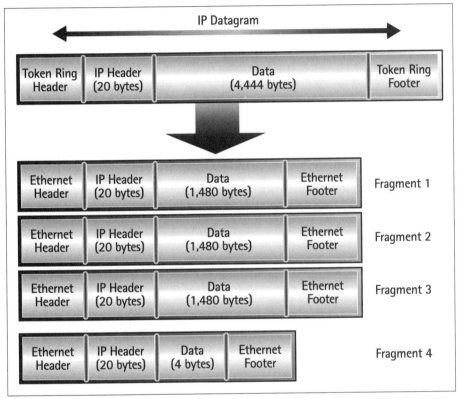

Figure 5-5: Each fragment of a datagram carries as much of the original data field as possible in the link-layer frame of the new network type.

 In this example, the maximum amount of data that can fit into the Ethernet frame is 1,480 bytes, which happens to be a multiple of 8. When the arithmetic does not work out this evenly, the data field of a fragment is rounded off to the nearest 8-byte (or 64-bit) unit that can fit in the MTU.

Before the first fragment is transmitted, the IP header's total length field is modified to reflect the size of the fragment (instead of the size of the entire datagram).

The fragment offset field is set to 0 (indicating that this is the first fragment of the datagram), and bit 3 of the flags field – the *more fragments* flag – is set to a value of 1.

The header of the datagram's second fragment is almost identical to the first. The only difference is that the fragment offset field is set to 1,480 to indicate the amount of data already transmitted in previous fragments. This is a crucial element of the fragmentation process because the datagram fragments are transmitted like any other IP packets. The fragments may take different routes to the destination and arrive in a different order from that in which they were sent. The fragment offset field enables the destination system to sort the incoming fragments into the proper order before they are reassembled.

 IP implementations use different strategies to determine the size of the fragments to be created. In some cases, the first fragment is the size of the MTU and the rest of the data is divided into fragments of equal size. Other implementations divide the data into fragments of 576 bytes, which is the default path MTU used by many routers. The intention, in this case, is to create smaller packets during the initial fragmentation so they are less likely to be fragmented again during the rest of the journey.

The final fragment of a datagram contains the last of the original data. This is true regardless of whether or not it is a multiple of 8 bytes. The more-fragments flag is set to 0, indicating that no further fragments of this datagram should be expected.

WHEN FRAGMENTATION OCCURS

Fragmentation is a necessary, if undesirable, part of the IP communications process. Apart from the additional processing overhead involved in constructing the IP packets containing fragments, there is no mechanism for retransmitting a single fragment of a datagram. If one fragment fails to reach the destination, the entire datagram must be refragmented and each fragment, re-sent. The system that originally transmitted the datagram has no knowledge of the fragmentation processes performed by the intermediate routers along the way.

In addition, IP has no time-out facility. Datagrams with missing fragments are never passed to the transport layer of the receiving system. The upper-layer protocol is responsible for detecting their absence and correcting the error.

Datagrams containing either TCP or UDP data can be fragmented; however, UDP fragmentation is more prevalent. The TCP communications process involves establishing a virtual connection between the source and destination systems (this includes MTU information for the networks on which the two end systems are located). The TCP protocol performs its own form of fragmentation at the transport layer. It divides the application-layer data into segments suitable for transmission, and the exchange of MTU information is used to determine the size of the segments. TCP transmissions may encounter networks with smaller MTUs during the course of their travels. In this case, the datagrams containing the TCP segments are fragmented by the IP protocol in the same way as UDP datagrams.

PATH MTU DISCOVERY

A method that involves the discovery of the path MTU can be used to minimize IP fragmentation. The *path MTU* is the smallest MTU of all the networks on the datagrams' path (from the source to the destination). Most TCP/IP stacks estimate the path MTU by using the MTU of the local network, or 576 bytes – whichever is smaller. Often, this results in smaller IP packets than are necessary (and consequently more of them), as many Internet segments support packets larger than 576 bytes.

The default path MTU is 576 because the "Requirements for Internet Hosts" (RFC1122) specifies that all TCP/IP hosts must be capable of receiving packets up to 576 bytes in size.

A method for determining the true path MTU of a given route is specified in RFC1191. Few TCP/IP implementations support this feature during normal TCP or UDP communications. You can, however, use the PING utility to determine the path MTU of a particular route. This is done by setting the second bit in the IP header's flags field, the *don't-fragment* bit, to a value of 1 (using PING's *-f* parameter).

Setting the don't-fragment flag prevents a datagram from being fragmented by IP, under any circumstances. If a datagram reaches a router that connects to a network with an MTU smaller than the datagram, the packet is discarded. An ICMP "destination unreachable" message is returned to the source, specifying that fragmentation is required, but the don't-fragment bit has been set. By sending successively smaller PING packets with the don't-fragment bit set, you can determine the largest permissible packet size to reach the destination (see Figure 5-6).

For more information on using PING for path MTU discovery, see Chapter 14, "TCP/IP Utilities."

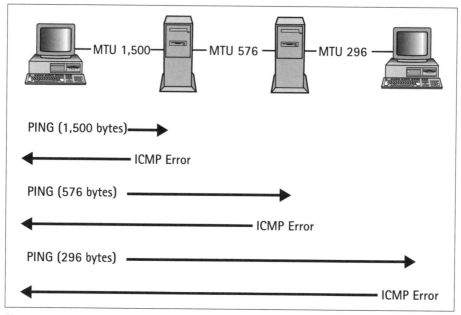

Figure 5-6: By transmitting packets with the don't-fragment flag set, you can use a trial-and-error process to determine the path MTU for a particular source and destination.

The path MTU discovery method, outlined in RFC1191, requires that routers return the MTU of the next-hop network in the ICMP destination unreachable message. In many cases, determining the path MTU is a process of trial and error. At this time, Solaris 2.x is the only major operating system to support this method of path MTU discovery, using it to modify the size of the IP packets that it sends.

IP Routing

Routing is one of IP's primary functions. When TCP/IP was developed for use on the Internet, certain scalability requirements were imposed. These requirements were, in large part, responsible for improving the efficiency of today's routing methods. Routing information, such as IP addressing and DNS data, is distributed throughout the Internet to limit the burden placed on individual systems. Each router is responsible for directing IP traffic to the host systems found on its local network. A router must also be able to forward packets to other routers in an intelligent manner, so that transmissions can take the shortest possible route to their destination.

The efficiency of an internetwork route is gauged by the number of *hops* between the source and destination systems. Each router between the two end systems is one hop — regardless of the physical distance between the systems.

Routing is a process that is accomplished one hop at a time. When an end system transmits an IP packet over the Internet, it does not determine what route the packet will take to its destination, nor do any of the intermediate systems. Each router involved in the process recognizes only the systems on the local networks (that is, those to which it is directly attached). It must take incoming packets and transmit them to the next router along the journey. Each router must make an informed decision as to which of the other routers on its local network provides the shortest path to the destination (see Figure 5-7).

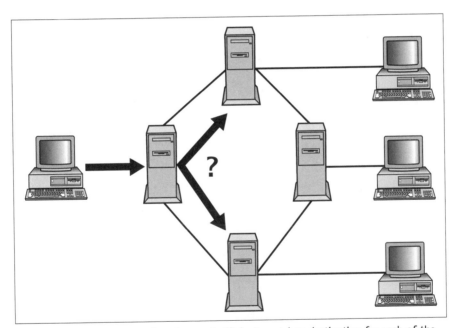

Figure 5-7: A router must select the most efficient next-hop destination for each of the datagrams it forwards.

The IP specifies the address of the local network system, to which the link-layer protocol should send each of the datagrams which are passed downwards from the internet layer. In most cases, this address is not the destination IP address carried in the IP header. In order to determine the address that should be furnished to the link-layer protocol, IP consults the routing table stored in the system's memory.

The internet layer always furnishes a packet's link-layer destination in the form of an IP address. When the packet is transmitted using a LAN protocol, such as Ethernet or Token Ring, ARP is used at the link layer to convert the IP address to a hardware address.

In TCP/IP parlance, a *router* is a system with multiple interfaces that is connected to two or more network segments. It is configured to receive packets on one interface and forwards them out one of the others. A router can be a dedicated hardware device, or simply a computer fitted with two or more network cards, that runs software providing routing capabilities.

A *multihomed host* is a computer with multiple network interfaces that does not function as a router. If, for example, you have a system connected to a LAN, that you also use to connect to the Internet with a dial-up point-to-point (PPP) connection, you have a multihomed host. It is not functioning as a router unless you are providing other systems on the same LAN with Internet access through your modem connection.

All TCP/IP systems have a routing table (even if they do not function as a router) because selecting the correct next-hop destination is a part of every IP transmission process. The routing table can be populated with information received from several different sources, including the protocol stack's configuration parameters, ICMP messages from other routers, and data gathered by dynamic routing protocols, such as the Routing Information Protocol (RIP).

The routing table in a TCP/IP system is not designed to provide a complete path to a destination system, or even a destination network. Its only purpose is to specify the address of the router, on the system's local network, to provide the shortest route to the destination. In Figure 5-8, data traveling from the source to the destination can take one path through routers A, B, and C; but a shorter path is available through routers A and C.

Each time data arrives at the internet layer (either from the transport layer above or the link layer below), the routing process proceeds as follows:

1. IP searches the routing table for an entry that exactly matches both the network identifier and the host identifier, found in the header's destination IP address. This indicates that the destination system is located either on one of the local networks to which the system is attached, or is accessible through an end-to-end link (such as a PPP or SLIP connection). If it finds such an entry, the destination address specified by the routing table entry is passed to the link-layer protocol.

2. If an exact match to the datagram's destination IP address cannot be found in the routing table, IP searches for an entry with the same network identifier (using the system's subnet mask). Such an entry will specify the address of a router on one of the local networks, to which the system is attached, that can be used to access the network where the destination system is located. The router specified in the table entry is not necessarily located on the network where the destination system is located. It is just the router on the local network that provides the best possible access to the destination.

3. If no matching entry is found for the full destination IP address or the destination network address, IP searches for the default gateway specified in the TCP/IP protocol stack configuration. It then passes its address to the link layer.

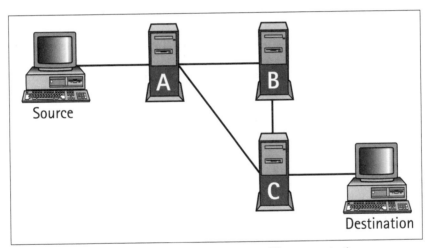

Figure 5-8: When a network has multiple routers providing access to the same destination network, the routing table specifies the most efficient path.

In the majority of cases, especially on the Internet, datagrams are transmitted to a destination system on the local network, or to the default gateway. The other entries in the routing table are created as the result of previous routing efforts and by routing protocols.

The IP routing process, including the structure of routing tables and the use of dynamic-routing protocols, is covered in greater detail in Chapter 9, "Routing IP."

The Internet Control Message Protocol (ICMP)

Although it is not used to carry the data generated by the upper-layer protocols, ICMP is an important part of the TCP/IP protocol stack. ICMP is always positioned as an internet-layer protocol, even though its messages are carried within IP datagrams. The primary function of ICMP is to return error messages to a transmitting host when datagrams encounter problems during the journey to their destination. These messages cause IP, or sometimes the transport-layer protocol, to modify its transmission parameters or take other action to alleviate or bypass the reported problem.

ICMP is often used as a general-purpose messenger to inform transmitting systems of problems that have occurred during the course of a transmission, or to carry requests for information to specific hosts and returns their replies. The protocol, the basic structure of which is defined in RFC792, is a required element of every TCP/IP host and gateway implementation. ICMP messages perform many different functions, and new tasks are added regularly. While RFC792 defines the original functions for which the protocol was intended, many of the newer applications are defined in other documents, in the sections specifically devoted to those functions.

ICMP Packet Structure

The general structure of an ICMP message is quite simple (see Figure 5-9). The IP header specifies a value of 1 in the protocol field, and the type of service is 0. The ICMP message, itself—the payload of the datagram—consists of two 1-byte fields. These fields identify the function of the message, a 2-byte checksum, and a variable length data field that takes different forms for the various message types.

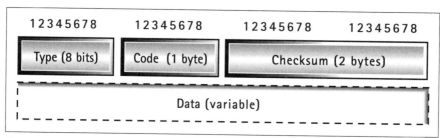

Figure 5-9: ICMP messages are carried within IP datagrams, and take different forms, depending on their function.

The functions of the ICMP message fields are as follows:

♦ **Type** – 1 byte – This field contains a code that identifies the message as conforming to one of the basic ICMP functions.

♦ **Code** – 1 byte – This field is used as a subidentifier, to differentiate the various messages that can be carried in ICMP packets of the same type. When a type has only one variant, the value of the code field is 0.

♦ **Checksum** – 2 bytes – This field contains the result of a checksum computation performed on the entire ICMP message, including the type, code, checksum, and all data fields. The algorithm used is the same as that for IP header checksums.

♦ **Data** – variable – After the three preceding fields, which are present in all ICMP packets, the format of the rest of the message varies according to the message type and code.

Apart from error messages, ICMP is also used to send query-type messages, such as the echo requests and replies that form the basis for the PING utility. These two types of messages, queries and errors, take different forms and are subject to different rules of usage. Table 5-1 contains all of the currently allotted ICMP types and codes listed in the "Assigned Numbers" RFC. It also specifies whether each one is a query or an error message.

TABLE 5-1 ICMP MESSAGE TYPES AND CODES

Type	Code	Query/Error	Name
0	0	Q	Echo Reply
3			Destination Unreachable
3	0	E	Net Unreachable
3	1	E	Host Unreachable
3	2	E	Protocol Unreachable
3	3	E	Port Unreachable
3	4	E	Fragmentation Needed and Don't Fragment was Set
3	5	E	Source Route Failed
3	6	E	Destination Network Unknown
3	7	E	Destination Host Unknown

continued

TABLE 5-1 ICMP MESSAGE TYPES AND CODES *(Continued)*

Type	Code	Query/Error	Name
3			**Destination Unreachable**
3	8	E	Source Host Isolated
3	9	E	Communication with Destination Network is Administratively Prohibited
3	10	E	Communication with Destination Host is Administratively Prohibited
3	11	E	Destination Network Unreachable for Type of Service
3	12	E	Destination Host Unreachable for Type of Service
4	0	E	Source Quench
5			**Redirect**
5	0	E	Redirect Datagram for the Network (or subnet)
5	1	E	Redirect Datagram for the Host
5	2	E	Redirect Datagram for the Type of Service and Network
5	3	E	Redirect Datagram for the Type of Service and Host
8	0	Q	Echo Request
9	0	Q	Router Advertisement
10	0	Q	Router Solicitation
11			**Time Exceeded**
11	0	E	Time to Live Exceeded in Transit
11	1	E	Fragment Reassembly Time Exceeded
12			**Parameter Problem**
12	0	E	Pointer Indicates the Error
12	1	E	Missing a Required Option
12	2	E	Bad Length
13	0	Q	Timestamp

continued

Type	Code	Query/Error	Name
12			Parameter Problem
14	0	Q	Timestamp Reply
15	0	Q	Information Request
16	0	Q	Information Reply
17	0	Q	Address Mask Request
18	0	Q	Address Mask Reply
30	0	Q	Traceroute
31	0	E	Datagram Conversion Error
32	0	E	Mobile Host Redirect
33	0	Q	IPv6 Where-Are-You
34	0	Q	IPv6 I-Am-Here
35	0	Q	Mobile Registration Request
36	0	Q	Mobile Registration Reply

The ICMP message-type values over 18 have been assigned to functions that are part of new technologies. Some of these are documented in Internet Draft specifications, while others have not yet reached that early stage of development. These functions have not yet been implemented in any but the most experimental fashion, and should not be considered as anything other than works-in-progress.

ICMP Error Messages

When IP datagrams leave the end system, from which they are transmitted, acknowledgments of successful delivery are not returned at the internet layer. Even in the case of a connection-oriented transport-layer transmission, such as TCP, acknowledgment messages are not returned by intermediate systems. ICMP functions as a monitor of internetwork communications at the internet level, by returning error messages when datagrams cannot be forwarded by a router or processed by the destination system.

In most cases, the datagrams that encounter a problem are discarded by the system generating the ICMP error message. It should be noted that ICMP does not function as an error-correction system, per se. Detecting the packet loss and arranging for the retransmission of data is left to the upper-layer protocols. There are many different reasons why a packet may not reach its destination, and ICMP error messages are used only to inform the sender of the nature of the difficulty. This way the communication environment can be modified to ensure that subsequent transmissions don't fall prey to the same problem.

One of the most common of the ICMP error messages is the type 3 "Destination Unreachable" message. There are 13 different codes, for this message type, that serve to isolate the exact location of the problem. Thus, type 3 ICMP errors may be returned by routers when the destination network or system cannot be located. They can also be returned by the destination system when the protocol specified in the IP header, or the port number specified in the transport-layer protocol header, is not found.

The circumstances under which ICMP error messages are transmitted are limited to prevent the generation of unduly large amounts of ICMP traffic. These circumstances include the following:

◆ ICMP error messages are never generated in response to other ICMP error messages. This is done to prevent the "ping-pong" effect in which systems continuously bounce error messages back and forth from each other. It is possible, however, for an ICMP error to be returned in response to an ICMP query message.

◆ When IP datagrams are fragmented, ICMP errors can only be returned in response to the transmission of the first fragment.

◆ ICMP error messages are never generated in response to broadcast or multicast transmissions, or transmissions with a source IP address of 0, or a loopback address.

Each of these conditions could result in the generation of many identical ICMP messages, if restrictions were not imposed.

Although the data portion of the ICMP packet differs for the various message types, ICMP error messages always include the 20-byte IP header of the datagram experiencing the problem (plus the first 8 bytes of the datagram's own data field). For TCP and UDP packets, these 8 bytes include the source and destination port fields and, in TCP packets, the sequence number field as well. This information enables the system receiving the error message to identify the exact transmission that resulted in the error, and the exact place where the problem occurred.

RFC792, published in 1981, states that ICMP error messages must include the first 28 bytes of the IP datagram. Later developments, however, such as IP-in-IP tunneling, have created the need for more of the IP datagram in the ICMP message. The RFC that defines the requirements for IP routers states that routers *should* include as much of the datagram in ICMP error messages as possible in a packet of 576 bytes. This is a recommendation, however, and not a requirement. The host requirements RFC is less forceful, stating that a host may include more than 28 bytes of the datagram.

DESTINATION UNREACHABLE MESSAGES

An ICMP destination unreachable message can be generated by either a router or a destination system, when a resource to which data is directed is unavailable. The various values for the code field identify the resource that is unreachable, or further identify the nature of the problem.

When a router receives a datagram that it can't deliver to its intended destination, it discards the packet and returns a *host unreachable* ICMP message. If the destination IP address is on the local network, this message is a type 3, code 1. If the packet cannot be forwarded to the next router, a type 3, code 0 message communicates a *network unreachable* message. In the same way, a packet may actually arrive at the destination system, and the transport-layer protocol, or application service, for which the data is intended is unavailable. The system would then return a *protocol unreachable* (type 3, code 2) or *port unreachable* (type 3, code 3) message to the sender.

ICMP error messages stating that hosts or networks are unreachable aren't necessarily indications of a permanent condition. TCP/IP host implementations should, therefore, not interpret them as such. These messages mean that a particular datagram was undeliverable at a particular time. These messages may be the result of a transient situation that has since been addressed, or has corrected itself.

Other destination unreachable messages are used when IP options prevent datagrams from being delivered to their destination. If the don't-fragment flag is set on a datagram, and the packet is too large for transmission over an intermediate network, the packet is dropped. A specialized ICMP message (type 3, code 4) is returned, stating that fragmentation is required but can't be performed because of the flag.

The IP source routing option is another feature that imposes communications restrictions on IP traffic. Source routing occurs when the IP addresses of the routers, to be used during the datagram's journey, are specified in the IP header. If the destination cannot be accessed using the specified routers, a *source route failed* message (type 3, code 5) is generated by the last router in the datagram's path.

These six destination unreachable codes are the only ones defined in the original ICMP standard, but additional codes have been defined in other documents over the years. Code values 6 through 12 were defined in the Internet host requirements (RFC1122) and router requirements (RFC1812) documents, as follows:

◆ **7 – Destination Host Unknown** – This message is used when a router determines, from link-layer protocol communications, that a specified host does not exist on a destination network.

◆ **11 – Network Unreachable for Type Of Service** – This code is used when a router can't forward a datagram to the next router using the requested (or default) type of service identifier in the IP header.

◆ **12 – Host Unreachable for Type Of Service** – This code is used when a router can't forward a datagram to the destination system on the local network using the requested (or default) type of service identifier in the IP header.

◆ **13 – Communication Administratively Prohibited** – This code is used when datagrams can't be transmitted because administrative filters are in place (such as those applied by encryption or other security systems).

◆ **14 – Host Precedence Violation** – This code is used when a datagram can't be transmitted because a validation filter has been implemented to block IP traffic of a specific precedence.

◆ **15 – Precedence Cutoff in Effect** – This code is used when a datagram can't be transmitted because a network has a minimum precedence level that is higher than the datagram's precedence.

Other codes defined in these documents are now obsolete, such as the following:

◆ **6 – Destination Network Unknown** – This code was used to indicate a router's discovery that a destination network doesn't exist. The standard *network unreachable message* (code 0) should now be used in place of this code.

◆ **8 – Source Host Isolated** – This code should no longer be used; *the network unreachable* (code 0) or *host unreachable* (code 1) message should be used instead.

- ◆ 9 – Communication with Destination Network Administratively Prohibited – This code should no longer be used; the *Communication Administratively Prohibited message* (code 13) should be used instead.

- ◆ 10 – Communication with Destination Host Administratively Prohibited – This code should no longer be used; the *Communication Administratively Prohibited* message (code 13) should be used instead.

SOURCE QUENCH MESSAGES

The *source quench message* is used to provide basic flow-control services to the upper-layer protocols. If a router or a host is receiving datagrams so quickly that its memory buffers are full (or nearly full), it may return an ICMP source quench message (type 4, code 0) to the sender, for each packet received. Source quench messages do not necessarily indicate that datagrams have been discarded due to traffic congestion. Systems are permitted to generate them when the situation approaches this condition, so that data loss may be avoided, preemptively.

When a system receives source quench messages, it should slow down its transmission rate until it no longer receives errors. After the errors cease, it can gradually increase speed again.

 TIP Source quench messages are an elementary flow-control device. They are more suitable for use by host systems than by routers, because of the demands they make on bandwidth and router CPU time. It is recommended that router implementations be equipped with more advanced flow-control mechanisms, and that source quench messages be avoided.

REDIRECT MESSAGES

ICMP *redirect messages* are an integral part of the IP-routing process. They help hosts and gateways learn more efficient routes to a particular destination. When a router receives a datagram and determines that the next destination (to which the packet will be sent) is also directly accessible by the original sender, the router sends a redirect message to that sender, informing it of the more efficient route. The packet is then transmitted normally, and the original sender updates its routing table with the new information.

To illustrate the use of redirect messages, consult Figure 5-10 and assume that the host on Network 1 is sending a datagram to the host on Network 2, and selects Router A as its first hop. Router A determines that the next intermediate hop for the datagram should be to Router B, but also realizes that Router B is on the same network as the source host. Router A transmits the datagram to Router B, but it also sends an ICMP *redirect-for-network* message (type 5, code 0) back to the sender. This informs the host that a hop can be eliminated from the journey by transmitting its datagrams directly to Router B. The source receives the message and updates its routing table accordingly. After this, all future traffic to the Network 2 host is sent to Router B.

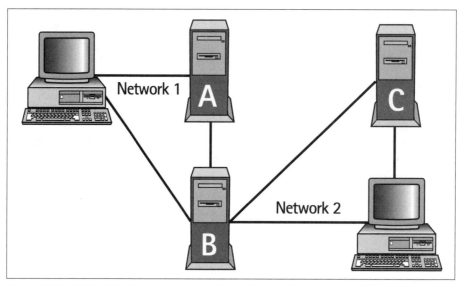

Figure 5-10: ICMP redirect messages are used to inform senders of more efficient routes to a particular network or host.

Like all ICMP error messages, redirects contain the IP header and the beginning of the IP data field. This is used, by the message recipient, to determine which datagram should be rerouted as the result of the message. Another field, in which the address of the recommended router is carried, is also included. This results in a packet format like that shown in Figure 5-11.

Redirect messages are only generated by routers (not by hosts), and can have the following four codes:

Code	Definition
0	Redirect datagrams for the network
1	Redirect datagrams for the host
2	Redirect datagrams for the type of service and network
3	Redirect datagrams for the type of service and host

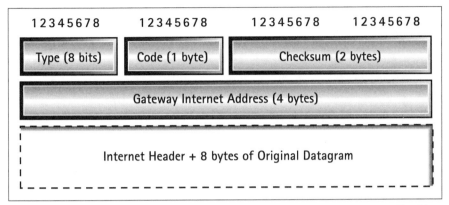

Figure 5-11: ICMP redirect messages contain an additional field used to store the IP address of the router or host providing a more efficient path for the recipient's datagrams.

The codes specify whether or not the router address provides more efficient access to an entire network or to a specific host (with or without the datagram's type of service applied). The code used by the sending system determines the format of the entry made in the recipient's routing table.

TIME EXCEEDED MESSAGES

ICMP *time exceeded messages* are used in two situations, as defined by the following two codes available for the message type:

Code	Definition
0	Time-to-live exceeded in transit
1	Fragment reassembly time exceeded

Code 0 messages are used when a router receives a datagram in which the time-to-live value specified in the IP header has reached 0. A router is, in this case, required to discard the packet and return an ICMP message to the source system.

Code 1 messages are sent by destination host systems when they are trying to reassemble incoming fragments into a datagram, and one or more of the required fragments has not been received in the amount of time allotted by the host. If fragment 0 of a particular datagram is not received, no ICMP message is sent at all (because ICMP errors can only be generated by the first fragment of a datagram). In either case, the fragments received are discarded, and the entire datagram must be retransmitted.

PARAMETER PROBLEM MESSAGES

An ICMP *parameter problem message* is used by routers or hosts to inform a sending system that a datagram has a problem, in its IP header, that prevents it from being processed. Such a problem might occur with an improperly formatted option, or an undefined value for a particular field. This message type is used when the datagram's problem is not specifically defined by another ICMP message type.

There are three codes for parameter problem messages, as follows:

Code	Definition
0	IP header bad
1	Required option is missing
2	Bad length

The *code 1* message was added to the original definition of the message type to accommodate military applications. It became necessary to inform a sending host that a required security option was missing from its datagram's IP headers. *Code 2* indicates improper length for the IP header.

The parameter problem message is only used when the header problem is so severe it causes the datagram to be discarded. This contains an additional field (as shown in the packet diagram in Figure 5-12) that specifies the byte number in the IP header, where the problem is located.

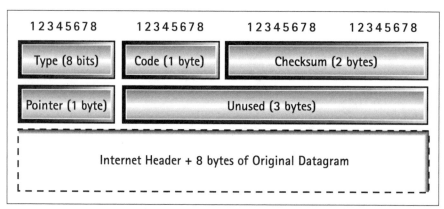

Figure 5-12: The ICMP parameter problem message specifies the IP header byte of a datagram that is incorrectly formatted.

ICMP Query Messages

Aside from error messages, ICMP is used to send queries to other systems, and to return the responses. *Query messages* are used to request a particular type of information or service from another system. They are not transmitted in response to an outside activity, as are error messages. Instead, they are typically used in a request/response pattern to form their own independent transactions between source and destination systems.

For this reason, query messages do not carry references to other IP transmissions, such as the datagram header information found in all error messages. Query packets have the type, code, and checksum fields common to all ICMP messages, but the format of the data field for the different message types varies more widely than that of error message packets.

ECHO REQUESTS/REPLIES

The ICMP echo request (type 8, code 0) and echo reply (type 0, code 0) messages are used to determine if a particular TCP/IP system on a network is operational, and capable of responding to a request. As such, these message types form the basis for the PING utility that is implemented in some form in every TCP/IP stack. The echo request and reply packets are formatted as shown in Figure 5-13.

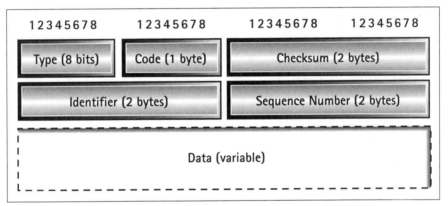

Figure 5-13: ICMP echo request and reply packets are used by the PING utility to test the operational status of TCP/IP implementation.

The identifier and sequence number fields are used to associate particular requests and replies. The data field contains padding, used to create a datagram of the size specified by the PING program.

When a system receives an echo request message, it formulates a reply by reversing the source and destination IP address fields. This changes the ICMP type field from 8 to 0, and recomputes the checksum. All of the other fields in the ICMP message must remain unchanged.

Using the PING program, and a discussion of how its parameters affect the structure of the ICMP request and reply messages, is covered in Chapter 14, "TCP/IP Utilities."

ROUTER SOLICITATIONS/ADVERTISEMENTS

ICMP router solicitations and advertisements enable a host to self-configure a default gateway setting, in its routing tables by processing the advertisement messages it receives from the routers on the local network. These messages do not comprise a routing protocol in the strictest sense of the term, because they don't furnish information concerning which router provides the best path to a given destination. The messages simply enable systems to identify the routers available to them.

The router discovery process begins when a host broadcasts (or multicasts) a simple router solicitation message (type 10, code 0), that takes the form shown in Figure 5-14.

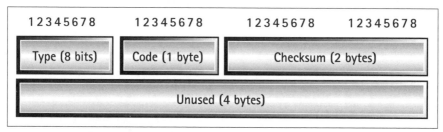

Figure 5-14: An ICMP router solicitation message is a request for routers to identify themselves to the host.

Routers, on receiving the request, formulate router advertisement messages, as shown in Figure 5-15. Host systems update their routing tables with the information in the advertisement packets. They select a default gateway for their transmissions based on the new data. Advertisements are later repeated at regular intervals (typically 7 to 10 minutes, by default) to inform hosts of the routers' continued availability.

The initial type, code, and checksum fields are common to every ICMP message. Functions of the router advertisement packet's fields are as follows:

- **Number of addresses** – 1 byte – Router advertisement messages can contain multiple router addresses, and the number of addresses field specifies how many are included in this packet. There are separate router address and preference level fields included in the message for each address.

- **Address entry size** – 1 byte – The address entry size field specifies the number of 32-bit words devoted to each of the router addresses contained in the message. The value is always 2.

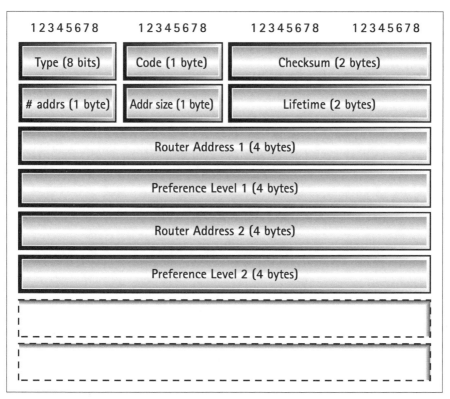

Figure 5-15: ICMP router advertisements inform hosts of a router's availability.

- **Lifetime** – 2 bytes – The lifetime field specifies the maximum amount of time (in seconds) that can elapse between advertisements, before a host assumes that an advertised router is no longer available. The default value is typically 1,800 seconds (30 minutes).

- **Router address** – 4 bytes – The router address field contains the IP address of the router transmitting the message.

- **Preference level** – 4 bytes – The preference level field contains a value that is used by a host to determine which router it should use as a default gateway. When more than one advertised router provides access to the same network, the host chooses the one with the higher preference level. Network administrators can specify a preference level in a router's configuration to control whether it should be used by hosts as their default gateway.

For more information on the use of ICMP router solicitation and advertisement messages as a router discovery option, see Chapter 9, "Routing IP."

TIMESTAMP REQUESTS/REPLIES

The ICMP timestamp messages enable a system to query another system for the
current time, or determine the amount of time elapsed between the transmission of
a packet to a particular destination, and its receipt. The time is provided as the
number of milliseconds since the previous midnight; there is no provision for furnishing the date using this protocol.

The timestamp request (type 13, code 0) and reply (type 14, code 0) packets are
formatted as shown in Figure 5-16.

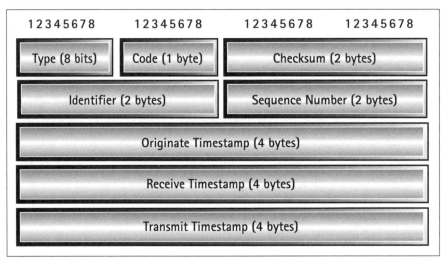

Figure 5-16: ICMP timestamp messages are used to exchange timing information between
systems.

The identifier and sequence number fields are used to associate requests and
replies. The three 4-byte timestamp fields are used as follows:

◆ **Originate timestamp** – 4 bytes – specifies the time that the request packet
last processed the packet before transmitting it

◆ **Receive timestamp** – 4 bytes – specifies the time that the request packet is
received at the destination

◆ Transmit timestamp – 4 bytes – specifies the time that the reply packet is transmitted by the (original) destination system

INFORMATION REQUESTS/REPLIES

The ICMP information request and reply messages were designed to enable self-configuring systems (such as diskless workstations) to ascertain the address of the network to which they are attached. Since the introduction of configuration protocols, such as RARP, BOOTP, and now DHCP, these message types are no longer used.

ADDRESS MASK REQUESTS/REPLIES

The ICMP address mask request (type 17, code 0) and reply (type 18, code 0) messages are used by self-configuring hosts to ascertain the value for their TCP/IP protocol stack's subnet mask parameter. Diskless workstations using RARP to obtain an IP address have no means of obtaining a subnet mask from a RARP server, so a mechanism like these ICMP messages is used instead. These message types are rarely used today, however, because the RARP protocol is virtually obsolete. Its replacements, BOOTP and DHCP, can both supply a subnet mask to a client, along with the IP address.

Summary

The internet layer of the TCP/IP protocol stack is a crucial part of the network communication process.

In this chapter, you learned:

◆ How the IP protocol is used to carry the data generated by the upper-layer protocols

◆ How IP datagrams are fragmented for transmission across networks with different packet-size limits

◆ How the IP protocol routes datagrams across various networks to reach distant destinations

◆ How ICMP query messages are used by TCP/IP utilities, such as PING

◆ How ICMP error messages are used to inform transmitting systems of conditions on the path to the destination

The following chapter examines the transport layer of the TCP/IP protocol stack, where the TCP and UDP protocols provide different levels of service for network applications.

Chapter 6

The Transport Layer

IN THIS CHAPTER

The TCP/IP transport-layer protocols provide additional communication services to applications, based on need. This chapter examines the transport-layer protocols and the services they provide, including the following:

◆ Transport-layer protocols are encapsulated within IP datagrams, and work with the other layers to provide the quality of service required by an application.

◆ The User Datagram Protocol is a simple, basic transport service that carries data while adding very little control overhead to the transmission.

◆ The Transmission Control Protocol provides a full array of services that guarantee the accurate delivery of data to its destination.

THE TCP/IP PROTOCOL STACK'S transport layer provides different levels of end-to-end communications service to the application-layer protocols operating above it. There are many different TCP/IP applications and services that have widely divergent needs when it comes to network communications. An FTP session may require the transfer of large amounts of data that must arrive at the destination in bit-perfect condition (even the slightest amount of corruption can render a program file unusable). On the other hand, a user browsing the Web can require frequent Internet name resolutions, each of which requires a brief transaction with a DNS server.

No single protocol can efficiently accommodate the requirements of these two scenarios. The control overhead incurred by the FTP session would be wasteful for the DNS transactions, consuming time, bandwidth, and processor-clock cycles. Conversely, the basic service used for the DNS transactions does not provide the reliability needed for an FTP file transfer.

As a result, the transport layer provides two protocols, either of which may be used by an application process. The Transmission Control Protocol (TCP), is a connection-oriented, reliable service intended for use by application protocols that require guaranteed delivery of relatively large amounts of data, such as FTP. The User Datagram Protocol (UDP), is the direct opposite. It is a connectionless, unreliable service that sends datagrams to a destination with a minimum of overhead (thus, leaving any other service-oriented tasks to the application layer).

Transport Layer Demultiplexing

Transport-layer protocols only deal with end systems – they are completely ignorant of the IP-routing process and other processes that occur during the journey.
When TCP/IP traffic passes through an intermediate system, it travels up the protocol stack only as high as the internet layer. There, IP determines the next-hop destination, and passes the packet down again to the link layer (see Figure 6-1). The
TCP and UDP data (carried in the data field of IP datagrams) remain untouched and
unchanged until the datagram reaches its ultimate destination.

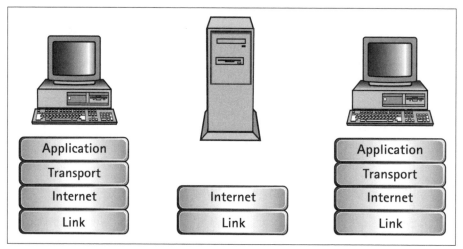

Figure 6-1: Transport-layer protocols are only involved in communications between source
and destination systems.

The IP protocol deals with routing datagrams to the proper system, as identified
by an IP address. Once packets arrive at their destination, IP passes the data contained in the payload to the appropriate transport-layer protocol, as identified in
the protocol field of the IP header (see Figure 6-2). This process is known as
demultiplexing. A decimal value of 6 in the IP protocol field indicates that TCP data
is being carried within the datagram (17 indicates UDP).

The transport-layer protocols affix a header to data received from the application layer before passing it down through the protocol stack. The IP header specifies the transport-layer protocol used to create the payload data, while TCP and
UDP headers both identify a *port number* (the application-layer service where the
payload data originated). TCP/IP then combines the communications output of
multiple applications into one data stream for transmission over the network
medium. This process is known as *multiplexing* (see Figure 6-3).

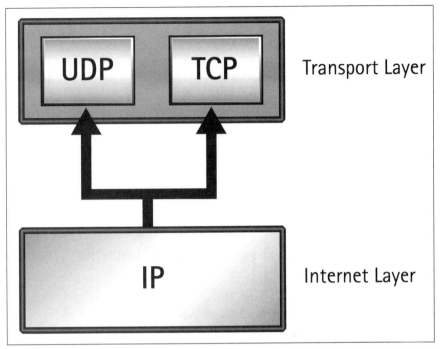

Figure 6-2: The IP header specifies the transport-layer protocol that was used to generate the information carried in the packet's data field.

Computers can run several applications and services at the same time. Simply directing network traffic to a specific system is not sufficient to ensure that it goes where it needs to. The same computer can be functioning as an FTP server, a Web server, and a DNS server. A means of identifying the nature of the data carried within an IP packet is necessary. Just as an IP address identifies a network interface in a particular system, a port number identifies a particular process running on that system.

An IP address combined with a port number is sometimes used to identify a more specific destination for a TCP/IP transmission. This combination is called a *socket*; it is written by appending the port number to the IP address, separated by a colon. Following is an example:

```
123.45.67.89:80
```

All of the standard TCP/IP applications have default port numbers (sometimes called *well-known port numbers*) allotted to them in the "Assigned Numbers" RFC. Since the transport-layer protocol is defined in a packet's IP header, the port number in no way specifies whether TCP or UDP is being used. This means that the two protocols can have their own independent lists of port numbers, and use the same values for different applications. In practice, however, most applications have the same port number assigned to them for both TCP and UDP – even when the application only uses one of the two protocols.

 In most TCP/IP implementations, the well-known port numbers are listed in a text file, located in the ETC directory, called SERVICES. On NetWare servers, the ETC directory is found on the SYS volume. On Windows NT systems, the path to the directory is \windowsroot\system32\drivers\ and so on.

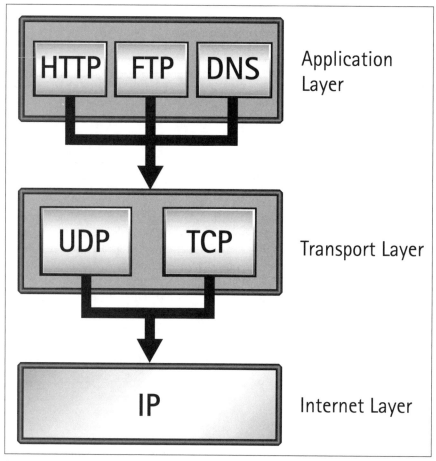

Figure 6-3: Each of the transport-layer protocols can receive data from several application-layer protocols, simultaneously. The data is combined into a single stream of packets, which are identified using port numbers.

Some of the most commonly used port numbers follow:

Application	Port
FTP	21
FTP-data	20
Telnet	23
SMTP	25
DNS	53
HTTP	80
POP3	110
NNTP	119
HTTPS	443

The port number assignments published in the RFC are recommendations, not requirements. Many implementations of TCP/IP services enable you to specify a different port number – to hide the service from general use. Client programs typically default to the use of the published port numbers. Web browsers, for example, use port 80 for a URL with the HTTP prefix; but you can specify a different port number to connect to a custom-configured server.

The transport-layer protocols have both source and destination port number fields in their headers. The port numbers assigned to TCP/IP servers (which are the typical destinations) are permanent. This ensures that processes are always in the same place, but clients can use any port number that does not conflict with the other processes running on the system. The Internet Assigned Numbers Authority (IANA) is responsible for port numbers from 1 to 1,023. Most TCP/IP client implementations choose a port number between 1,024 and 5,000, which remains in use only for the duration of the current transaction. These randomly chosen, short-term assignments are known as *ephemeral ports*.

The transport-layer protocols are responsible for the demultiplexing of incoming traffic, according to the port numbers provided. Therefore, they must deal with packets containing destination port numbers that do not exist, or are nonfunctional. In a case like this, the transport protocol discards the offending packet, and generates an ICMP port unreachable message. This is passed down to the internet layer for transmission back to the source.

The rest of the TCP and UDP header fields provide the additional services required by the application-layer data. Since TCP provides guaranteed delivery of packets and connection-oriented service, its header is 20 bytes long — much longer than that of UDP, which is only 8 bytes.

The User Datagram Protocol (UDP)

The User Datagram Protocol is very simple, providing the barest minimum service to application-layer protocols. UDP multiplexes the data passed down from multiple application-layer protocols, and provides an end-to-end checksum verification of the UDP header and data. For all other services, UDP functions as a pass-through protocol, providing applications with direct access to the internet-layer functions.

A *pass-through protocol* is one that provides no function of its own, but simply acts as a conduit between the layer above and the layer below. For example, an application transmits data using UDP. During the journey, a datagram encounters a problem that causes the return of an ICMP destination unreachable error. UDP takes no action on its own as a result of the error. It must, however, pass the ICMP message up to the application layer.

In this manner, all UDP implementations must pass IP option information between the application and internet layers — in both directions. Other IP information from incoming datagrams must be passed through to the application layer, as well. At times, an application must ascertain the source IP address of an incoming packet to address its replies correctly. This can only occur if UDP makes this information available. For data moving downwards through the stack, the UDP implementation must pass values (for the type-of-service and time-to-live fields of the IP header) from the application layer to the internet layer.

UDP provides only a datagram-based service to the application-layer protocols. This means that, unlike TCP, every UDP message is packaged as a single datagram and passed down to the internet layer. IP may have to fragment the datagram at some point during the transmission, but this process is invisible to the transport layer. UDP implementations must, however, provide a method for an application to determine the path MTU used by IP. This circumvents the need for IP fragmentation by adjusting the amount of data passed to the transport layer (for transmission as a single datagram).

UDP is also described as being connectionless and unreliable. This means data is transmitted without recognition of the destination system's status or condition. No acknowledgment of delivery is returned to the sender. UDP transmissions are not any less likely to reach their destinations intact. These additional services are not provided because UDP-based applications do not require them.

UDP Applications

UDP is traditionally used for TCP/IP control applications, as opposed to applications that carry actual user data. These control applications provide some form of support service for TCP/IP clients, or for the network itself. Chief among these on client systems is the Domain Name System (DNS), which provides name resolution services for many other TCP/IP applications. The automatic client-configuration protocols, BOOTP and DHCP, also use UDP. This is due largely to their reliance on broadcast transmissions to perform their functions.

 TCP is a host-to-host protocol that establishes a connection between two systems before any application data is transmitted. TCP is, therefore, incapable of sending broadcast and multicast transmissions. All TCP/IP applications that require broadcasts or multicasts must use the UDP protocol to function.

Another protocol that is traditionally associated with BOOTP is called the *Trivial File Transfer Protocol* (TFTP). Like the TCP-based FTP, TFTP is designed to transmit binary files across the network. It was designed specifically for use with diskless workstations during the boot process. After BOOTP supplies a workstation with an IP address and other TCP/IP client configuration settings, TFTP transfers an executable OS boot file to the workstation. TFTP is something of an anomaly in the TCP/IP protocol suite, as TCP would be more suitable for the task. For this particular purpose, a stripped-down version of the protocol stack must be stored in a diskless workstation's ROM — and UDP provides the lowest possible overhead.

UDP is also used for network-oriented services, such as the Routing Information Protocol (RIP) and the Simple Network Management Protocol (SNMP). These protocols are used to exchange routing and diagnostic information between TCP/IP systems. Both are well suited to UDP because they retransmit information on a regular basis. In cases where the receipt of a particular message is more critical, a request/reply system with a timeout is usually implemented.

In recent years, the burgeoning popularity of the Internet has led to a new area of application development where UDP is an important element. The desire to supply multimedia content for Web sites has led to the development of many applications that attempt to deliver audio and video to Internet clients in real time. Videoconferencing applications are also growing in their capabilities, and in popularity. Bandwidth limitations make the transmission of audio and video content difficult. This is particularly true when the applications use a transport protocol with much control overhead, such as TCP.

Many of these applications have, therefore, turned to UDP for the transport of these data types. Streaming audio and video requires the transfer of a large amount of data — a task normally allotted to TCP — but the nature of the data makes UDP a particularly suitable choice. Apart from its low control overhead, UDP's potential for lost packets does not affect the application's performance.

Losing a few bytes here doesn't render the rest of the data unusable, as it would in transferring a file containing binary programming code or textual data. An audio or video clip played on a client system in real time, using UDP transmissions, may experience a momentary drop in quality when a packet is discarded. The display continues, though, absorbing the data loss without the need for retransmission. TCP is less suitable for tasks like these for two reasons. One, it has a slower transfer rate due to increased control traffic, and two, its retransmission of lost packets which is useless to an application that is displaying data in real time.

UDP Transactions

The main reason for using a lightweight transport protocol, such as UDP, is that certain TCP/IP applications simply do not need the full services provided by TCP. This is because the application, itself, provides the equivalent of these services, and using TCP would create much unnecessary overhead. To better understand the benefits of using UDP, it helps to examine a typical transaction, such as a DNS name resolution.

DNS transactions are used whenever a TCP/IP client application permits a user to specify an Internet host name for a target service. The IP protocol relies completely on IP addresses when transmitting data. When given a host name, a client program (such as a Web browser) resolves that name into an IP address. It does this by sending it to a DNS server and waiting for a reply.

DNS exchanges are a perfect example of the UDP protocol's benefits. First, the amount of data sent to the DNS server is very small, consisting only of the host name. The only thing expected in return is a 4-byte IP address. Thus, there is no need (at the transport or internet layers) for the use of multiple packets to send the message. This eliminates the need for mechanisms, such as flow control and segmentation, which are used to transmit large amounts of data to a destination.

Second, the entire purpose of the transaction is to send a query to a server and receive a reply in return. The reply, containing the IP address, functions as an acknowledgment of the query's receipt, thus making the transaction reliable without the need for a separate acknowledgment message. The idea of a DNS server receiving a query, transmitting an acknowledgment message, and then transmitting the reply to the query, does seem ridiculous.

The small size of the packets involved, and the expectation of an immediate reply eliminates the need for a connection-oriented service. The entire transaction usually consists of one request packet and one reply. It is hardly worthwhile to double or triple the amount of data transmitted to establish and then terminate a connection. Instead, the client transmits its DNS request and if no reply is received in a given amount of time, repeats the request. After a specified number of retries, the client may send its query to an alternate server specified in the TCP/IP client configuration.

Certain TCP/IP applications have sufficient communications logic built into them to make the use of a simple protocol, such as UDP, feasible. It is often said that the services UDP lacks are provided by the application-layer protocol, and to a certain extent, this statement is true. This does not mean that the application has an internal system explicitly designed to provide error correction, flow control, or connection-oriented service. Instead, it usually means that the natural functions of the application are designed to make these services unnecessary or redundant.

The use of UDP is only practical for certain kinds of applications. By eliminating the connection, termination, and acknowledgment packets, and by reducing the size of the transport-layer protocol header, UDP transactions are faster and use bandwidth more efficiently than their TCP counterparts.

UDP Servers

UDP server implementations tend to accommodate the brief transactions that are typical of UDP applications. TCP/IP application servers fall into two categories: iterative and concurrent. An *iterative* server is one that processes each client request individually and sequentially. A *concurrent* server spawns a new process (or task, or thread) for each request, enabling it to serve multiple clients simultaneously. In most cases, UDP servers are iterative, while TCP servers are concurrent.

Obviously, iterative servers are best suited for brief transactions. Requests arriving at a UDP server, that cannot be processed immediately, are temporarily stored in an input queue. If the queue should outgrow the buffer space allotted to it, the oldest datagrams are discarded. Delays incurred by extended transactions would, therefore, be more likely to cause data loss than the brief exchange of services, such as DNS.

 When packets are discarded as a result of an overfilled input queue, returning ICMP source quench messages to senders is optional. This means that packets can be lost without any notification being sent to the client.

The UDP Header

UDP applies a small header (only 8 bytes) to the data it receives from the application-layer protocol. This small size is in keeping with the streamlined nature of the protocol. UDP packets, like IP packets, are sometimes (confusingly) called datagrams. They are carried in IP's data field as shown in Figure 6-4. The format of the UDP packet is shown in Figure 6-5.

Figure 6-4: UDP packets are encapsulated in IP datagrams before transmission.

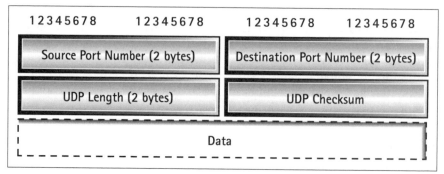

Figure 6-5: The UDP header is small and simple, containing only four fields and no options.

The functions of the UDP packet fields are as follows:

♦ **Source port number** – 2 bytes – The source port number identifies the process (in the transmitting system) that has generated the UDP data. This field usually contains an ephemeral port number that is selected by the client for each UDP transaction.

♦ **Destination port number** – 2 bytes – The destination port number identifies the process in the receiving system for which the UDP data is intended. When the destination is a standard TCP/IP application running on a server, this field contains a well-known port number as defined in the "Assigned Numbers" RFC. A response to a UDP query uses the source port number specified in the request packet as its destination.

♦ **UDP length** – 2 bytes – The UDP length field contains the length of the UDP header and data fields, in bytes. This value can also be determined, from the IP header, by subtracting the internet header length field from the total length field.

♦ **UDP checksum** – 2 bytes – The UDP checksum field contains a checksum computed from the UDP header and data, plus a pseudoheader consisting of selected IP header fields.

♦ **Data** – variable, up to 65,507 bytes – The data field contains the information passed down from the application-layer protocol. Although it rarely even approaches the maximum, the largest possible data field is determined by the maximum IP datagram size minus the size of the IP and UDP headers (65,535 – 28 = 65,507).

Most standard TCP/IP applications using UDP restrict the size of their largest packets to achieve IP datagrams smaller than 576 bytes. This is done to accommodate the default maximum datagram size specified in the Internet standards.

The UDP Checksum

The checksum carried in the UDP header has become a controversial issue due to Internet standards. These state that including the checksum in the UDP data generated by an application is optional (although it must be included when a control is provided). All TCP/IP hosts must be capable of processing the UDP checksums of incoming packets, but a transmitting system can opt to fill the checksum field with 0's and avoid the entire checksum computation process.

The checksum in the IP protocol header is computed only on the header itself, and not the data. The IP header is modified by each router as a datagram travels across an internetwork, and it is necessary to verify the accuracy of the header at each hop. Because the contents of the IP data field remain unchanged throughout the transmission, there is no need to perform checksums on the data at the internet layer.

The UDP checksum includes the data field in its computation and, like all transport-layer communications, involves only the source and destination systems. The checksum is defined as optional because many of the LAN-based link-layer protocols (such as Ethernet and Token Ring) verify the accuracy of the entire frame at each hop. This doesn't provide a full end-to-end check, however, because a link-layer checksum verifies only that a frame transmitted by one system is received correctly by the next system (see Figure 6-6). If one or more of the networks traversed does not provide a checksum (such as a SLIP or PPP connection), then any data corruption occurring while the packet travels across that network is not detected during subsequent checks.

Mathematically, the UDP checksum is computed in the same manner as the IP header. The source system generates a checksum value that is carried to the destination in the UDP header's checksum field. The destination system recomputes the value and if an error is detected, discards the packet silently.

The major difference in the UDP checksum is that the computation is performed not only on the UDP header and data, but also on additional fields from the IP header. These additional fields are referred to as a *pseudoheader* because, although the fields are not actually copied to the UDP header, the checksum computation is performed as though they were.

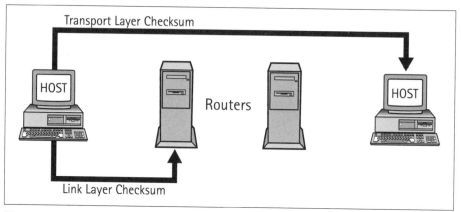

Figure 6-6: Some link-layer protocols include a checksum verification of the entire frame, but this does not guarantee an error-free end-to-end transmission as does a UDP checksum.

The UDP pseudoheader includes the source and destination IP addresses, the protocol field from the IP header, and the UDP length. These additional fields ensure that the datagrams reaching the UDP implementation have not been delivered to the wrong destination system, or the wrong protocol in that system by IP. The UDP checksum is computed in the transmitting system at the same time as the first IP header checksum. The IP header is modified and its checksum recomputed by every router during the journey across the internetwork. The UDP header and its checksum, on the other hand, remain undisturbed until the datagram reaches the destination.

In addition to the pseudoheader, a single byte of padding is appended to the UDP data field (if necessary) to achieve an even number of bytes. This is done because the checksum computation is based on 16-bit words. The virtual data structure that is used during the UDP checksum computations is shown in Figure 6-7.

The question of whether or not applications using UDP should include checksums has been widely debated. Studies have shown that substantial numbers of UDP data errors are often detected during internetwork transmissions. For this reason, most of today's applications do include checksums in their UDP transmissions.

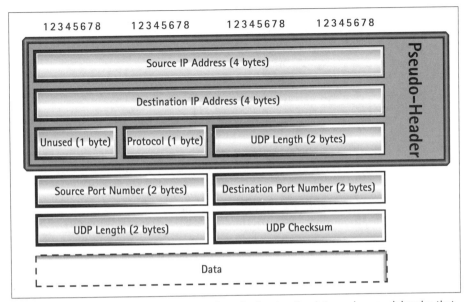

Figure 6-7: The UDP checksum is computed on the header, the data, and a pseudoheader that is comprised of fields from the IP header.

The Transmission Control Protocol (TCP)

Compared to UDP, TCP is a much more comprehensive transport-layer protocol that provides a full range of services to the applications operating above it. TCP is typically used to deliver data requested by TCP/IP clients, such as Web browsers, news readers, and FTP clients. This is the data the client actually presents to the user, as opposed to the "behind-the-scenes" control data often carried by UDP.

The nature of the data carried by TCP imposes a different set of requirements on the transport protocol. TCP often transfers larger amounts of data in a single transaction than UDP. FTP transfers can be many megabytes in size, and even a modestly sized HTTP Web page is larger than can be carried in a single datagram. TCP, therefore, expects a larger amount of data from the application layer and has its own mechanism for splitting the data into small pieces for transmission over the internetwork (see Figure 6-8).

Each of these pieces is called a *segment*, and the segments making up a single application-layer data structure are collectively referred to as a *sequence*. When discussing TCP communications, the term *transaction* indicates the transmission of an entire sequence (not just a single segment or datagram).

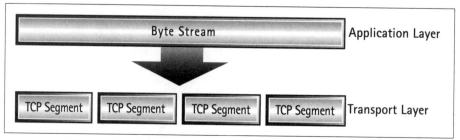

Figure 6-8: TCP is capable of transmitting large amounts of data by dividing a byte stream into segments.

There are also TCP applications that perform many transfers of small amounts of data, in both directions. These are the interactive applications, such as Telnet, that require a rapid-response time because the client is waiting to display results from each action to the user. While these requirements may seem to conflict, both types of applications have a common need for strict reliability in the transfer of data – this is the primary goal of TCP.

Applications using TCP produce data as a stream of bytes. The transport layer is responsible for ensuring that all of the data arrives at the destination, intact. As with all of the layers in the protocol stack, the application layer remains completely ignorant of the transport layer's method of transmitting the data. The application doesn't receive information as to how many segments are created, or by what processes they are reassembled at the destination. As long as the receiving system's transport layer passes the incoming data to the target application in the same form, that's all that matters. This is known as *byte stream* service.

In the same way, the internet layer must package and address the segments it receives from the transport layer, before passing them down to the link layer for transmission. The IP protocol is unaware of its datagram's contents, or that they are parts of a larger whole. TCP, therefore, is entirely responsible for ensuring that all segments reach the destination, on time, intact, and that they can be reassembled into the proper sequence.

Most of the services provided by the TCP protocol, as defined in RFC793, contribute to the achievement of this goal. These services are as follows:

♦ **Connection-oriented service** – Before any application-layer data is transmitted, TCP executes a handshake with the destination system to determine if it is operational and ready to receive data. This handshake initiates a virtual connection between the two systems that remains in force until the transaction is completed.

♦ **Packet acknowledgment** – As segments are transmitted to the destination, the receiving system returns periodic acknowledgments to inform the sender of which packets have been successfully received.

- ◆ **Error detection** – Like UDP, TCP performs a checksum verification of both the header and the data. Packets found to contain errors are discarded.

- ◆ **Packet retransmission** – Segments that fail to arrive at the destination, or that are discarded by the error detection process, are retransmitted by the sender. This assures the complete and accurate transfer of a data sequence.

- ◆ **Packet sequencing** – TCP segments are transmitted within IP datagrams, and like all IP datagrams, they can travel to the destination by different routes and arrive out of sequence. Once all segments are received, TCP reorders them into the original sequence before passing any data to the application layer.

- ◆ **Flow control** – TCP/IP systems allocate a certain number of memory buffers to hold incoming TCP segments until an entire sequence is assembled. To prevent the loss of data while the buffers are all filled, a receiving system can instruct the sender to slow down its transmission rate until the buffers are cleared.

TCP Multiplexing

TCP, like UDP, is capable of multiplexing the data generated by several different application-layer processes. Once the data is segmented, the individual packets can be passed down to the internet layer in any order. Each TCP connection is uniquely identified by the sockets (that is, the IP addresses and the port numbers) of the two systems involved.

When a system receives TCP data, it uses all four of these fields – the source IP address, the source port number, the destination IP address, and the destination port number – to demultiplex the segments to the correct processes. The source address and port number are needed because most TCP servers operate concurrently – that is, they spawn a new process for each client connection.

A concurrent server can maintain several connections with the same system as it processes multiple connections at once. With a multitasking operating system, such as Windows NT or Windows 95, you can open multiple DOS sessions and use each one to initiate an FTP connection with the same server. Each connection has the same destination IP address and port number, and also the same source IP address. Examining the source port number field is the only way the server can direct incoming packets to the correct application process. This field contains an ephemeral port number that is unique to the client system. Because TCP communications require a connection between two systems, the protocol cannot be used for broadcast or multicast transmissions. TCP does, however, provide full duplex service between the two systems involved in the connection. If the application permits, TCP can also send data in both directions, using a single connection.

TCP Applications

It is important to understand how applications use TCP connections within the network-communications environment. When a LAN user logs on to a file server, a connection (often called a session) is established between the two systems. The connection remains in force until the user logs out. This is distinctly different from a TCP connection, which is generally of shorter duration, and consists of a single data exchange.

When you use a browser to connect to a Web site on the Internet, you initiate a TCP connection between your workstation and the Web server for the purpose of transferring HTTP data. The client system opens a connection and requests an HTTP file from the server. The server then returns the requested file to the client using the same connection, and the connection is terminated, as shown in Figure 6-9. If the HTTP contains links to graphic files that are integrated into the Web page, then a separate TCP session must be established for each file. In the same way, each time you click on a Web hyperlink, a new TCP connection to the target server is created.

Applications can use the services provided by TCP in different ways. FTP, for example, uses simultaneous TCP connections. A control connection is established when a client logs in to the FTP server, and remains open until the user logs out. Additional data connections are opened and closed for each file transfer. The point is that the establishment and termination of TCP connections isn't necessarily tied to an activity that is visible from the client (such as user authentication or access to a particular server).

The TCP Header

In order to provide all of its services, TCP obviously requires a substantially larger and more complex header than UDP. For all of its functionality, however, the header ends up being only 20 bytes long. As data is received from the application layer, TCP creates appropriately sized segments and affixes a header to each one before passing it to the internet layer. The entire TCP data structure is carried within a standard IP datagram, as shown in Figure 6-10.

The layout of the TCP packet is shown in Figure 6-11. Because TCP is a connection-oriented protocol, the receiving system is an active participant in the data transmission process and communications between the source and the destination travel in both directions. TCP uses the same header for all of its packet exchanges, with the values of different fields being modified by either system.

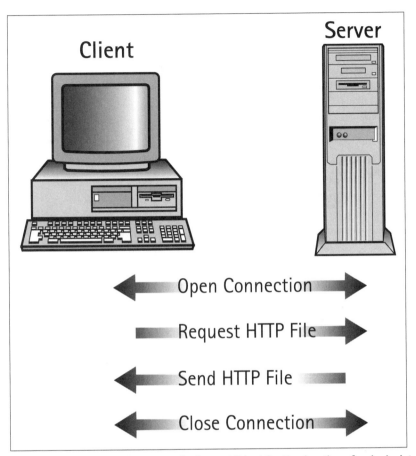

Figure 6-9: TCP connections are typically established for the duration of a single data exchange, which can be bidirectional.

Ethernet Header	IP Header	TCP Header	TCP Data	Ethernet Footer

Figure 6-10: TCP segments are encapsulated by the IP protocol for transmission. At the destination, they are reassembled into their original sequence.

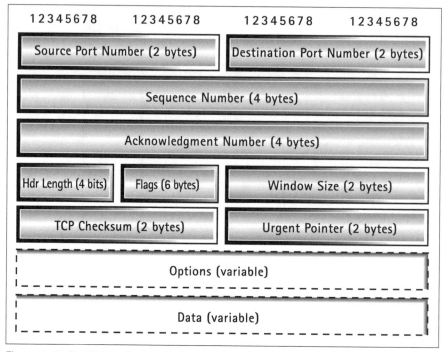

Figure 6-11: The TCP header is 20 bytes long (without options) and provides a wide array of functions and services.

The functions of the TCP packet fields are as follows:

◆ **Source port number** – 2 bytes – This source port number identifies the process in the transmitting system that has generated the TCP data. This field usually contains an ephemeral port number that is selected by the client for each TCP transaction.

◆ **Destination port number** – 2 bytes – The destination port number identifies the process in the receiving system for which the TCP data is intended. When the destination is a standard TCP/IP application running on a server, this field contains a well-known port number, as defined in the "Assigned Numbers" RFC. Reverse-TCP traffic uses the source port number, specified by the sender, as its destination.

◆ **Sequence number** – 4 bytes – The sequence number field identifies the first byte in this packet's data field in relation to the entire data sequence. This value is used to ensure that the segments are reassembled in the proper order at their destination.

◆ **Acknowledgment number** – 4 bytes – The acknowledgment number field is used to specify the next sequence number an acknowledging system receives from the sender. This field is active only when the ACK flag is set.

◆ **Header length** – 4 bits – The header length field identifies the beginning of the data field by specifying the length of the TCP header, in 32-bit words. This field is needed because options can extend the header from 20 to up to 60 bytes (in 4-byte increments).

◆ **Reserved** – 6 bits – Unused bits.

◆ **Flags** – 6 bits – The flags field consists of six binary 1-bit flags that may be individually activated (by setting the value to 1) as needed. The functions of the flags are as follows:

   ◆ **URG** – The URG flag indicates to the recipient that urgent data is being transmitted and causes the urgent pointer field to be activated, in order to identify the sequence number of the urgent data.

   ◆ **ACK** – The ACK flag specifies that this packet functions as an acknowledgment and activates the acknowledgment number field.

   ◆ **PSH** – The PSH flag instructs the receiving system to push all data in the current sequence that has already been delivered to the application process, represented by the destination port number.

   ◆ **RST** – The RST flag orders the receiving system to reset the TCP connection, thus discarding all of the previously delivered segments.

   ◆ **SYN** – The SYN flag is used to synchronize the sequence numbers between the source and destination systems, initiating a TCP connection.

   ◆ **FIN** – The FIN flag is used to inform the receiving system that all data has been sent and the connection is to be terminated.

◆ **Window size** – 2 bytes – The window size field is used to specify the number of bytes the receiving system can accept, thus providing the flow-control mechanism for the TCP connection.

◆ **TCP checksum** – 2 bytes – The TCP checksum field contains a computation that covers the TCP header, the data, and a pseudoheader comprised of fields from the IP header.

◆ **Urgent pointer** – 2 bytes – The urgent pointer field is used in combination with the URG flag to specify the data in the sequence that the receiving system should treat as urgent.

♦ **Options and Padding** – variable – The options field contains additional information used to govern a TCP connection, padded with zeroes to reach a 32-bit boundary. The possible options are as follows:

  ♦ **Maximum segment size** – The maximum segment size option is used to specify the size of the largest TCP segments that the sending system expects to receive from the destination.

  ♦ **Window scale factor** – The window scale factor option is used to expand the functionality of the TCP window size field from 16 to 32 bits. This creates larger window sizes at receiving systems.

  ♦ **Timestamp** – The timestamp option is designed to carry timestamps in transmitted packets that are returned in the acknowledgments for those packets. Using this data, a system can determine the round trip time measurement (RTTM) for a TCP connection.

♦ **Data** – variable – The data field contains a part of the information passed down to the transport layer from an application-layer protocol. The data field may be left empty in packets used to control the TCP connection, such as SYN, FIN, and ACK messages.

Of the TCP options listed, only the MSS option (defined in RFC793) is commonly used. The others have been implemented in only a few systems, and are defined in RFC1393, along with others that remain experimental. The format of options which can be included in the TCP header is much like that of the IP options described in Chapter 5, "The Internet Layer." This includes the 1-byte "no operation" and "end of option list options" that are used to delimit multiple options and indicate the end of the last option in the header.

Anatomy of a TCP Session

Additional network traffic overhead, incurred by a TCP transmission, is not solely due to the increased header size. In the course of a TCP session, the two systems involved also exchange packets that exist only for control purposes (such as receipt acknowledgments and messages used to establish and terminate a connection) and that do not contain data. The best way to fully understand the TCP communications process and the functions of the header fields is to examine what goes on in the course of a TCP session. The following sections track a typical TCP connection between a Web browser and a Web server, from its inception to its termination. They also explains how the protocol functions at each step of the process.

ESTABLISHING THE CONNECTION

TCP requires that a connection be established between the source and destination systems before any application-layer data can be transmitted. Establishing the connection initializes the packet sequencing process and enables the systems to exchange the information used to create data segments of the proper size for transmission.

Although a TCP connection between two systems functions like a true circuit-switched connection (in which a path from the source to the destination is maintained throughout the transaction), the connection is actually a virtual one between the transport layers of the two systems involved. TCP segments are packaged and transmitted within standard IP datagrams and are, therefore, subject to the same routing peculiarities as other IP transmissions. Datagrams can take different routes to the destination, be lost or fragmented in transit, or arrive in a different order than they were sent. Many of TCP's features are specifically designed to overcome these aspects of the IP service.

The typical TCP communications scenario involves a client requesting data from a server. Depending on the application, however, these roles may not be immediately obvious. All Windows NT systems, for example, are capable of functioning as both servers and clients. This is the nature of a peer-to-peer operating system. Whenever a TCP/IP system requests a service from another system, it is functioning as a client, while the system responding to the request is functioning as a server.

When one system seeks to establish a TCP connection with another, the first part of the procedure is an exchange of control messages known as a *three-way hand-shake*. The handshake proceeds as follows:

1. The client sends a SYN packet containing its initial sequence number to the server.

2. The server replies with a packet that acknowledges the client's SYN and sends a SYN of its own.

3. The client sends an acknowledgment of the server's SYN.

At this point, the connection is established, and the transmission of application data can begin. This exchange seems simple, but it sets the stage for all of the packet exchanges to follow.

STEP 1   The client system first generates a packet in which the TCP header's source, and destination port number, fields contain an ephemeral port number and the well-known port number for a Web server (that is, the HTTP port 80), respectively. In addition, the packet's SYN flag is set and an *initial sequence number* (ISN) is specified in the sequence number field, as shown in Figure 6-12. The exchange of SYN packets by the client and server always indicates the opening of a connection, just as the use of the FIN flag signals its termination. The system that sends the first SYN packet is referred to as performing an *active open*, while the system that replies with its own SYN performs a *passive open*.

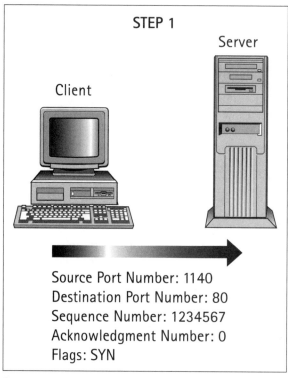

Figure 6-12: The client initiates the TCP connection process by transmitting a SYN packet containing an initial sequence number.

 The TCP standard also describes a rarely used simultaneous open procedure. In this procedure, two systems perform an active open to a well-known port on the other system (at approximately the same time). A simultaneous open requires four packets for connection establishment — (two SYNs and two ACKs) — and results in a single connection.

The sequence number in an IP packet is used to reorder the data segments at the destination system. Each byte in a data sequence is consecutively numbered, beginning with the value chosen by the sending system for its ISN. The SYN packet occupies the first number of the sequence, with the first data segment having the sequence number ISN+1.

The ISN, specified by a TCP/IP system for each connection, is controlled by an algorithm built into the operating system. This continuously increments the ISN assigned when an application requests a TCP connection. The TCP standard recommends that the ISN be incremented every 4 microseconds, meaning that the 32-bit number runs through a complete cycle every 4.55 hours.

The point of maintaining this cycle is to ensure that no two connections between the same sockets that are active on the network at any one time are using the same sequence numbers. If a user establishes a TCP connection to a server and the client application crashes, that user may restart the program and establish a new connection to the same server. Because the source and destination sockets are the same for both connections, only the difference in sequence numbers distinguishes the packets generated by the two connections.

STEP 2   When the server receives the client's SYN packet, it responds with a packet of its own. This reply packet performs two functions:

1. It acknowledges the client's SYN message by setting the ACK flag.

2. It initializes its own sequence by setting the SYN flag and specifying an ISN.

The ACK flag notifies the client that the application process (on the server represented by the destination port number) is operating and ready to receive data. The server also sets the SYN flag (see Figure 6-13) because TCP is a full-duplex protocol and the server must supply its own ISN when transmitting data back to the client.

The concept of full-duplex communications applies to TCP in that both systems can transmit application-layer data using the same connection. If one system transmitted application data and the other replied with control packets, there would be no need for an ISN from both sides. For some applications, this may be the case, but TCP always initializes a sequence in both directions, assuming that a typical transaction involves a request and a reply.

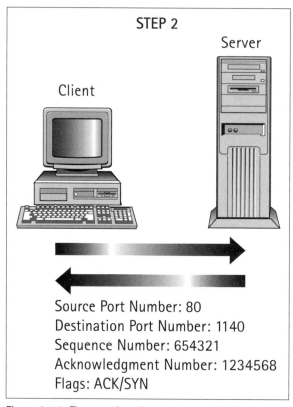

STEP 2

Server

Client

Source Port Number: 80
Destination Port Number: 1140
Sequence Number: 654321
Acknowledgment Number: 1234568
Flags: ACK/SYN

Figure 6–13: The server's reply to the client functions both as an acknowledgment of the client's SYN, and as an initialization of the server's own sequence.

The ISN supplied by the server is completely different from that of the client. Both systems must keep track of their own sequence numbers, in addition to those of the other system. This is demonstrated by the acknowledgment-number value specified in the server's ACK/SYN packet. In reply to the client's sequence number 1234567, the server includes the value 1234568 in its acknowledgment-number field. This is the value that appears in the sequence number field of the client's next packet. A packet arriving with any other sequence number is not accepted as belonging to the current connection.

STEP 3   After receiving the server's ACK/SYN packet, the client transmits an ACK packet of its own (see Figure 6-14). It uses the sequence number 1234568, which is expected by the server. The packet acknowledges the server's ISN and includes the value 654322 in its acknowledgment-number field. This is the server's ISN+1.

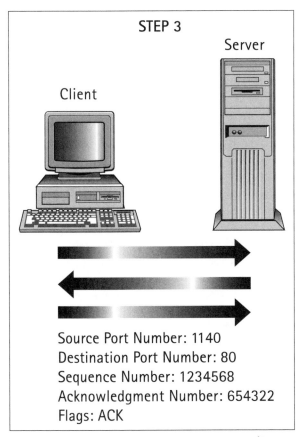

STEP 3

Server

Client

Source Port Number: 1140
Destination Port Number: 80
Sequence Number: 1234568
Acknowledgment Number: 654322
Flags: ACK

Figure 6-14: The client responds to the servers ACK/SYN packet with an acknowledgment of its own, completing the connection handshake sequence.

When the server receives the client's ACK packet, the connection is established and the application-layer protocol data can be transferred. After each system acknowledges the other's sequence, it knows what packet to expect in the next transmission.

The next message can originate from either one of the connected systems, depending on the nature of the application. In an HTTP transaction, the next packet originates at the client, which transmits a URL request to the server. Other applications, however, may proceed with a message transmitted by the server. FTP, for example, sends a "server ready" message to the client as the first data packet.

Packets containing the SYN flag occupy sequence number space, but those containing only the ACK flag do not. When the client sends its first data packet after the connection is established, the packet's sequence number is 1234568 — the same as the acknowledgment packet transmitted by the client in Step 3.

SEGMENTING DATA

Besides initializing the sequences, the exchange of SYN packets between the client and server systems has another function. In most TCP implementations, SYN packets contain an option field that the sending system uses to announce its maximum segment size (MSS) to the other system. The MSS specifies the largest segment the system expects to receive from the other system. The MSS option adds an additional four bytes to the TCP header in three fields, as shown in Figure 6-15.

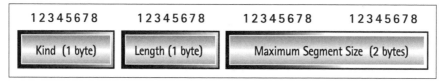

Figure 6-15: The MSS option is the most commonly used TCP header option.

The functions of the MSS option fields are as follows:

♦ **Kind** – 1 byte – The kind field contains a code that specifies the function of the option. For the MSS option, the value is 2.

♦ **Length** – 1 byte – The length field specifies the length of the entire option, in bytes. For the MSS option, the value is 4.

♦ **Maximum segment size** – 2 bytes – The maximum segment size field specifies the size of the largest segment that the sending system expects to receive from the destination.

After a TCP implementation receives data from an application-layer protocol (for transmission to another system), it initiates the connection-establishment process. This occurs before the data is prepared for transmission because the MSS received from the other system dictates the size of the data segments. A system determines its MSS based on the capabilities of its network interfaces. The largest possible value for the MSS is the MTU of the network interface transmitting the data, minus the size of the IP and TCP headers. On a network using Ethernet II frames, the MSS can be no larger than 1,460 bytes $(1,500 - 20 - 20 = 1,460)$.

Windows NT and the Maximum Segment Size

Windows NT systems exchange MSS values during the establishment of a TCP connection. The smaller of the two values is selected as the segment size for the connection. When the systems are on different networks, however, the client uses the path MTU discovery method described in RFC1191 to modify the MSS.

Once the connection is established, the first data segments are transmitted with the selected segment size. The packets are also transmitted with the don't-fragment flag activated in the IP header, causing them to be discarded if they encounter a network segment with a smaller MTU. When this happens, an ICMP destination unreachable message is returned to the sender (usually containing the MTU of the offending segment in its header). The sending system dynamically adjusts its segment size, for all subsequent transmissions, to that of the MTU received (minus 40 bytes for the IP and TCP headers).

This process can be repeated several times, if packets encounter successively smaller MTUs en route from the source to the destination. The path MTU discovery mechanism may also fail if a router returns an incorrect MTU in its ICMP messages, or returns no ICMP messages at all. This is known as a "black hole" router.

Two registry settings enable you to modify TCP's behavior, in this respect. Both settings are located at: HKEY_LOCAL_MACHINE\SYSTEM\CurrentControlSet\Services\-tcpip\parameters. Activating the **EnablePMTUBHDetect** key (by setting the REG_DWORD value to 1) modifies the path MTU discovery mechanism to attempt to detect "black hole" routers on the data path. Disabling the **EnablePMTUDiscovery** key (by setting the REG_DWORD value to 0) turns the path MTU discovery mechanism off entirely. This causes Windows NT to use a maximum segment size of 536 for all internetwork TCP connections.

When a TCP implementation sends no MSS in its SYN packets, the receiving system defaults to an MSS value of 536 bytes (the 576-byte default datagram size minus 40 bytes for the headers). Some systems also specify this value for their MSS whenever TCP is used to connect to a system on another network segment.

TCP/IP systems attempt to use the largest possible MSS for their TCP transmissions. Larger data segments mean fewer packets are needed to transmit the sequence. Fewer packets mean fewer headers, less control traffic, and greater network efficiency. When the transmitted segments become large enough to require IP fragmentation, however, network efficiency degenerates, rapidly. Determining a proper segment size for a TCP connection is a tradeoff between these factors.

TCP determines the size of the segments it creates based on the capabilities of the network. This does not mean that the datagram containing TCP segments are exempt from fragmentation by the IP protocol. The route datagrams take to their destination is not always predictable, and segments may be fragmented at the internet layer during the internetwork-transmission process. The fragments are then reassembled at the destination before any data is passed up to the transport layer — making the entire process invisible to TCP.

ERROR CHECKING

The TCP header includes a checksum field, which provides end-to-end error detection for the entire TCP segment — both header and data. The checksum is computed as it is for UDP, except the inclusion of a checksum in every packet is mandatory for the TCP protocol.

Like UDP, the TCP checksum computation includes a pseudoheader that contains fields from the IP header (see Figure 6-16). Using the pseudoheader, the transport layer verifies that the packets being passed upwards, from the internet layer, are actually addressed to that system and intended for the TCP protocol.

The checksum is included in the TCP header strictly for error detection purposes; it doesn't correct the errors that it finds. The receiving system silently discards any packets that fail the checksum comparison. TCP's retransmission mechanism then treats them as if they never arrived at the destination.

ACKNOWLEDGING TRANSMISSIONS

When application-layer data is transferred, the receiving system uses the header's acknowledgment number field to inform the sender that data has been received intact. A data packet's sequence number is incremented to identify bytes from the application data stream that are contained in this segment. If the packet is received in a timely manner and passes the checksum test, the receiving system can return a packet with the ACK flag set and an acknowledgment number that specifies the next byte that it expects to receive.

The acknowledgment number derives from the sequence number of the last packet received, plus the number of bytes in that packet's data field (as calculated by subtracting the header length value from the IP header's total length value), plus one. This is called a *positive acknowledgment*, because the receiver informs the sender of intact segments received. In Figure 6-17, the first data packet sent from the client to the server has a sequence number of 1234568. Assuming the packet's data field is filled and the MSS for the connection is 536 bytes, the server must return an ACK packet with an acknowledgment number of 1235105 (1234568 + 536 + 1).

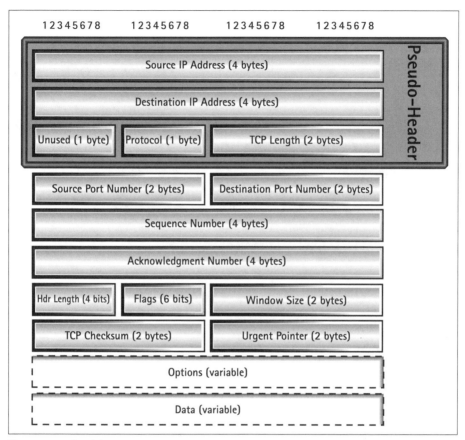

Figure 6-16: The TCP checksum computation includes a pseudoheader containing the source and destination IP addresses, and the protocol field from the packet's IP header.

This acknowledgment number informs the client that 536 bytes have been received correctly. It also specifies that the next segment should have a sequence number of 1235105 (meaning that the data should begin with the 537th byte in the stream). If the first segment fails to arrive, or is discarded because of a checksum error, the server sends its ACK packet (after a timeout period) with an acknowledgment number of 1234568. This number indicates that it still expects to receive byte 1 in the stream.

TCP does not require an acknowledgment for each data packet. Using a timer built into the TCP/IP implementation, the destination system periodically returns ACK packets specifying the amount of sequence data received. One acknowledgment may be sent for two or three segments worth of data, thus reducing TCP's control traffic while exposing a distinct shortcoming in the acknowledgment process.

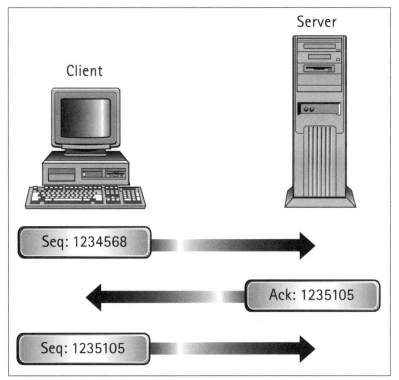

Figure 6-17: The receiving system acknowledges the receipt of data by returning ACK packets to the sender. These packets also specify the next byte to be transmitted.

If a destination system receives segments 4, 5, and 6 in a particular sequence and discards segment 4 due to a checksum error, an ACK packet is returned to the sender. This packet must contain the acknowledgment number that represents the first byte in segment 4's data field, even though segments 5 and 6 were received correctly. All three segments must be retransmitted because *negative acknowledgments* (requesting retransmission of segment 4) or *selective acknowledgments* (informing that only segments 5 and 6 were received correctly) are not possible.

TCP uses a system of *delayed acknowledgments* to determine when ACK packets must be sent. A system typically runs a cyclical delay timer of 200 milliseconds; when packets arrive, ACK generation is delayed until the timer cycles, as shown in Figure 6-18. This is done so other segments arrive, or so data transmits in the other direction; a single packet then serves more than one purpose. (When data travels in both directions on a TCP connection, such as in a Telnet session, an acknowledgment can be piggybacked onto a data segment traveling in the opposite direction, thus reducing the overall number of packets generated.)

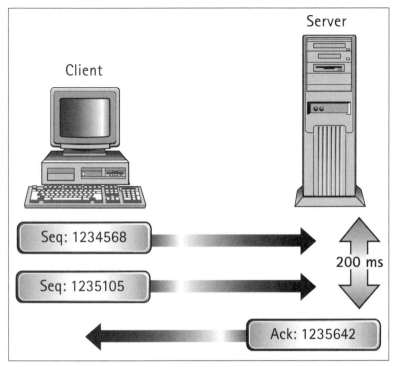

Figure 6-18: TCP uses a delay mechanism to avoid the traffic overhead incurred when acknowledgments are sent for every segment.

Some implementations incorporate an "every other packet" philosophy into the mechanism. Windows NT, for example, immediately generates an ACK packet when the preceding segment was not acknowledged. It then waits 200 milliseconds when no other segments are waiting to be ACKed.

Theoretically, it would be possible to delay acknowledgments for longer periods, but the delay cycles are kept short deliberately. This provides quick response for interactive applications, and prevents unnecessary segment retransmission (resulting from the lack of a selective acknowledgment mechanism or the expiration of the sender's retransmission timeout).

RETRANSMITTING PACKETS

TCP's error-correction mechanism is known as *positive acknowledgment with retransmission*. This means the receiving system only acknowledges the segments received intact, and the sender is responsible for retransmitting all others. The sender maintains a retransmission queue with copies of every segment transmitted. As ACKs are received from the destination, the sender deletes the acknowledged segments from the queue. After a designated timeout period, the unacknowledged segments are retransmitted.

The retransmission timeout is one of the more complex aspects of a TCP implementation. A transmitting system starts a timer countdown for each segment as it's passed down to the internet layer. The packet is automatically retransmitted if no acknowledgment arrives for that segment, by the time the countdown expires. Computing the length of the countdown, however, is difficult.

The time elapsed between a segment's transmission and receipt of its acknowledgment is known as the *round trip time* (RTT). The different environments in which TCP is used can result in a wide variation of RTT values. A transmission to a system on the same local Ethernet network has a much smaller RTT than an Internet transmission. Due to routing changes and other network conditions, RTT values can also vary considerably during the course of a single connection. It is, therefore, necessary for the retransmission timers to be dynamically calculated for each TCP connection.

The algorithm, by which a system determines the timeout value for a connection, is based on the calculation of a *smoothed round trip time* (SRTT) from the RTTs of the previously transmitted segments. RFC793 describes a basic method for computing the SRTT, but this method is incapable of dealing with large variations in the RTT. The standard was later revised (in RFC1122), requiring the implementation of two newer algorithms created by Phil Karn and Van Jacobson.

The Karn and Jacobson algorithms are defined in two articles originally presented at the SIGCOMM conference in 1987 and 1988, respectively. The articles are called "Estimating Round Trip Times in Reliable Transport Protocols" by P. Karn and C. Partridge, and "Congestion Avoidance and Control" by Van Jacobson and Michael J Karels. These articles are available from the Lawrence Berkeley National Laboratory Network Research Group's Web site at http://www-nrg.ee.lbl.gov.

NetWare's TCP implementation uses the Jacobson algorithm to calculate minimum and maximum retransmission timeout values (which can be displayed using the TCPCON utility). Windows NT sets the timeout value to 3 seconds at the beginning of a connection, and adjusts it dynamically using the SRTT calculation from RFC793. Each time a segment is retransmitted, the timer value is doubled for that particular segment. Windows NT retransmits up to 5 times by default, which can be modified by adding the **TcpMaxDataRetransmissions** key to the Registry at HKEY_LOCAL_MACHINE\SYSTEM\CurrentControlSet\Services\tcpip\parameters and assigning it a REG_DWORD value ranging from 0 to FFFFFFFF (hex).

FLOW CONTROL

Segments encounter vastly different network conditions along their journey; therefore, a transmitting system must be capable of controlling the rate at which it sends data. A receiving system has a finite amount of buffer space to store incoming segments, and must discard packets when those buffers are full. To prevent this, TCP uses a technique called a *sliding window* to control its transmission speed.

To understand the sliding window technique, picture the segments of a TCP data transfer as a single horizontal line, with those on the left being transmitted first. The *offered window* is the group of segments the receiver permits the sender to transmit, as shown in Figure 6-19. The size of the window is dictated by the receiving system in the window size field of every acknowledgment packet.

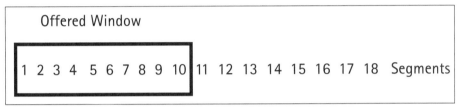

Figure 6-19: A receiving system specifies its available buffer space in the window size field of the TCP header.

The window size value is based on the receiving system's available buffer space. It is always applied in relation to the sequence number, acknowledged in the same packet. If the acknowledgment number in a segment is 1235105 and the window size is 4096, then the sender has permission to transmit the bytes, with the sequence numbers 1235105 to 1239201.

Segments transmitted by the sender are placed in the receiver's buffers, awaiting acknowledgment. At this point, the sending system may continue to transmit by computing the usable window available to it. The *usable window* consists of the number of bytes in the last acknowledgment's window size field minus the number of bytes transmitted without acknowledgment.

As the incoming segments are acknowledged by the receiving system, they pass out of the window, causing its left edge to move to the right. As acknowledged bytes are passed up to the application-layer protocol, buffers are cleared, causing the right edge of the window to move to the right. In this way, the window is said to slide from left to right along the data sequence, as shown in Figure 6-20.

SLOW START   The sliding window mechanism implements flow-control services from the receiving end of the TCP connection. In many cases, however, network traffic congestion occurs before data ever reaches the destination. Routers must also buffer packets and can lose data when they are overwhelmed. The slow start mechanism is a flow-control method originating from the sending system. It is designed to prevent TCP from transmitting a large number of segments (up to the window size) at the beginning of a transfer.

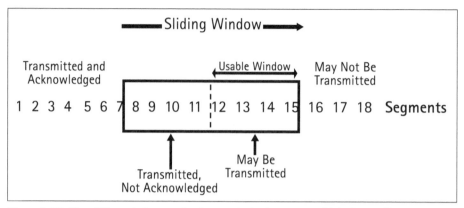

Figure 6-20: The sliding window mechanism controls the rate at which the sending system transmits data.

Slow start involves creating a *congestion window* at the sending system to limit the amount of data it transmits. Upon connection, the sender creates a congestion window the same size as a single segment. Each time the sender receives an acknowledgment, it doubles the size of the window until it equals the size of the receiver's sliding window. The sender's transmission starts with a single packet. Afterward, the rate gradually increases until a router is forced to discard packets, or the receiver's window is filled.

If the transmission rate reaches the point where packet loss is detected, the sender uses a *congestion avoidance* algorithm. This algorithm cuts the transmission rate in half, gradually increasing by a factor of one over the congestion window size, or one segment at a time (whichever is larger). Transmission speed increases more gradually, until it reaches the fastest rate possible for the network connection.

THE PUSH FLAG   The PSH flag in the TCP header enables the sending application-layer process to instruct the receiver to pass the current segment's data (plus all of the acknowledged data waiting in the TCP buffers) up to the application layer, immediately. When it is suitable for the application, using the PSH flag enables the incoming data to be processed more quickly, and clears space in the TCP buffers for more incoming data. Many of the commonly used TCP/IP applications, such as Web and FTP servers, routinely set the PSH flag when transmitting data. This ensures that the information reaches the client application as quickly as possible.

URGENT MODE   The URG flag in the TCP header is used by a transmitting system to signal the receiver that high priority data is on the way. The urgent mode feature is used by interactive applications, such as Telnet and FTP, to interrupt a running process. The data stream, containing the interrupt command, can take precedence over any other traffic. To do this, the sending system must set the URG flag and use the urgent pointer field to identify the last byte of the urgent data (in relation to the packet's sequence number).

The TCP standard specifies that only the receiving system may pass the urgent mode information to the appropriate application-layer process. It does not, however, define the action that the destination system should take upon receipt of the URG flag.

TERMINATING THE CONNECTION

To close a TCP connection, each system must transmit a packet containing the FIN flag and receive an acknowledgment, as shown in Figure 6-21. Because TCP is a full-duplex protocol, the connection traveling in each direction must be terminated individually. Although rarely done, a system can terminate the connection in one direction and leave the other active. This is called a *half close*.

As with the connection-establishment process, the first system to transmit a FIN packet is said to perform an *active close*. The other system then performs a *passive close*.

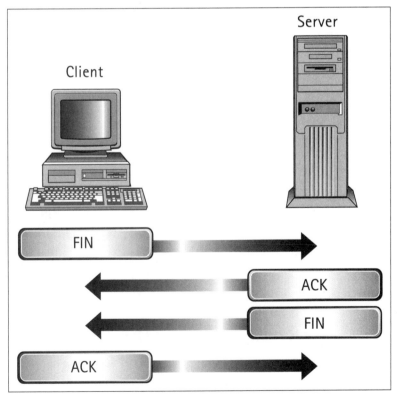

Figure 6-21: To terminate a TCP connection, both systems must transmit a packet containing the FIN flag.

Summary

The transport layer of the TCP/IP protocol stack must achieve the quality of service required by an application. Depending on its own capabilities, a program can be designed to use the minimal service provided by UDP, or the comprehensive array of features built into the TCP protocol.

In this chapter, you learned:

◆ How transport-layer protocols are carried within IP datagrams

◆ How UDP carries application data with a minimum of control overhead

◆ How a TCP connection between source and destination systems is established

◆ How TCP provides error-detection and flow control services

The following chapter examines the application layer of the TCP/IP protocol stack, where TCP/IP programs generate messages that are exchanged between clients and servers.

Chapter 7

The Application Layer

When you reach the application layer of the TCP/IP protocol stack, you arrive at a level that transcends the mechanics of network communications. The application protocol provides an interface to user processes and to communicate with a counterpart program operating on a different system. The applications do not move data across the network; they are totally reliant on the services provided by the lower-layer protocols to get the messages to the appropriate destination.

This chapter examines some of the most commonly used application protocols, defined in the RFCs. The focus is on the services they provide to the user or to other applications, such as the following:

◆ On TCP/IP systems, many different application-layer services use the transport- and internet-layer protocols by multiplexing data.

◆ Application-layer protocols using UDP for their transport services typically follow a request/response format. They often exchange control information, rather than user data.

◆ Applications using TCP transport transmit large amounts of user data that must reach the destination undamaged.

As with all of the protocols in the stack, application-layer protocols don't recognize the operational details of the other layers. The transport layer provides two distinct services, UDP and TCP. An application-layer protocol using TCP as its transport protocol, for example, can distinguish the services it provides (including guaranteed delivery and error checking), but it doesn't necessarily know how these services are implemented.

TCP/IP Application Architecture

Application-layer functions take many different forms. Consider any process that uses the services provided by the lower layers of an application protocol. The RFCs define the standard application protocols found in virtually all TCP/IP implementations. Some are executable programs with a standardized user interface, such as FTP and Telnet. Others, like SMTP and LDAP, provide services that include a user interface for third-party programs. Still others are support protocols, such as DNS and RIP, that provide services required by other TCP/IP protocols.

The TCP/IP protocols provide network communications services to commercial applications and operating systems. Windows NT uses NetBIOS, and other application interfaces, with TCP/IP to provide peer-to-peer file system services for Microsoft Windows networks. Novell's NetWare/IP product uses TCP/IP to carry NetWare's native IPX protocols. Many other third-party applications and services use TCP/IP services through a variety of application programming interfaces (APIs).

The application layer is the upper boundary of the TCP/IP stack, and functions as an interface to the more proprietary aspects of a system's architecture. Internet standards impose some interoperability on TCP/IP systems, but implementing and integrating protocols into an operating system can vary widely among vendors. TCP/IP protocols provide well-defined services, however, the way an application uses those services is up to the developer.

Client/Server Communications

Most application-layer protocols are designed using the client/server model. A server running on one system waits in "listen" mode for requests to arrive from clients (see Figure 7-1). The client usually initiates a session by requesting data from the server, which is returned as a reply. To the lower-layer protocols, these roles are not particularly relevant. Data is transmitted and received, traveling in one or both directions, while the contents of the payload remain inconsequential.

At the application layer, this is not the case. Being the top layer of the stack, this is the ultimate source (or destination) of data that is repeatedly encapsulated at the lower layers. Application-layer standards define the syntax that clients and servers must use when generating their requests and replies. Because these are more clearly defined roles, application-layer protocols tend not to be symmetrical like those at the lower layers.

Transport-, internet-, and link-layer protocol implementations often operate as transmitters and receivers, providing the same functions in either direction. You can, for example, use the same Windows NT system to run a Web server and a Web client browser (the operation of the lower-layer protocols will be the same for each one). The client and server application modules, however, are not interchangeable. Both use HTTP at the application layer, but that protocol defines the different roles for the client and the server.

Application Layer Multiplexing

As you reach the application layer of the TCP/IP stack, a "tree" displays the protocols. Multiplexing capabilities blossom enormously, as shown in Figure 7-2. The transport layer offers two protocols for network data transfers, while the internet layer only provides one. The application layer contains dozens of protocols, many of which can be operating on a single system at the same time.

Similar to the internet and transport layers, application-layer protocols make use of the services provided by the layer beneath. Data from many different application processes is passed down to each of the transport-layer protocols. TCP or UDP data arriving at the system is passed up to the application-layer process that is identified by the destination port number.

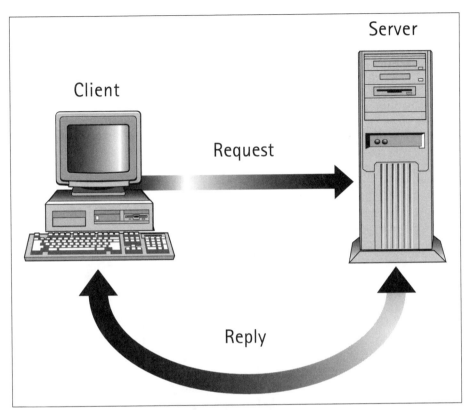

Figure 7-1: Application-layer protocols typically contain clearly defined roles for clients and servers.

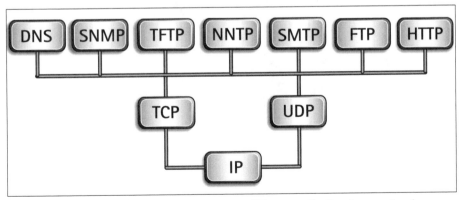

Figure 7-2: A typical TCP/IP system can run many different application-layer protocols simultaneously, all of which avail themselves of the lower-layer services.

The Transport/Application Interface

For applications to use the lower-layer services effectively, there must be an interface that enables the application to specify parameters for data transmissions and receive the results, as shown in Figure 7-3. This interface must provide access to the transport-layer protocols, as well as the internet layer.

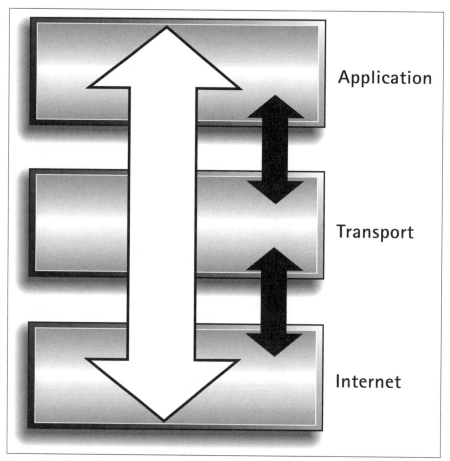

Figure 7-3: The application layer's interface enables programs to send and receive information from protocols operating at the transport and internet layers.

When an application transmits data, it must indicate a destination. This destination consists of a port number (for the transport protocol) and an IP address, as well as a source IP address, in the case of a multihomed system. In addition, the application must specify the use of push and urgent mode options for TCP transmissions, and IP's time-to-live, type of service, and option values.

The interface also supplies the application with feedback concerning the data transmitted. ICMP error messages are passed from the internet layer, through the transport layer, and to the application layer. The program addresses the specified problem by providing an alternative destination, or modifying the way the data is prepared for transmission.

UDP applications must be informed of the maximum possible datagram size for a particular source, destination, and type of service. TCP applications must be informed of situations where the maximum number of segment retransmissions is reached. The action an application takes as a result of this information is left to the developers. The Internet standards only specify the information that a TCP/IP implementation must provide to the application layer.

UDP Applications

To the average user, many of the application protocols using UDP for their network data transmissions operate invisibly. They provide support services to other applications and protocols. The diverse functions performed by the protocols range from file transfers to request/response exchanges to file system operations.

The Trivial File Transfer Protocol (TFTP)

The Trivial File Transfer Protocol (TFTP), as defined in RFC1350, is designed to transmit files between a client and server with the minimum possible overhead. The protocol delivers an executable file to a diskless workstation during the boot process. When the protocol is used, the client system has an IP address and other TCP/IP configuration settings (assigned by BOOTP) which also launches the TFTP session.

TFTP is a UDP-based counterpart to FTP. UDP is not well-suited to file transfers, but one of its design requirements specified that the networking stack be loaded into the client's memory, from ROM, at boot time. Using UDP reduces the implementation's storage and memory requirements greatly, thus allowing the transfer to occur within the workstation environment.

Diskless workstations are less common today than they used to be, especially on NetWare and Windows NT networks. Consequently, TFTP is rarely used. To understand how the application layer defines client and server roles (and provide functions that might otherwise fall to a transport-layer protocol, such as TCP), an examination of the protocol is helpful.

TFTP MESSAGES
When designing a protocol to deliver a file to a client with UDP, the most evident problem involves the file not being small enough to fit inside a single datagram. Because UDP does not have a segmentation mechanism like that of TCP, the application layer must divide the requested file into pieces and reassemble them at the

destination. The protocol uses a small enough amount of system memory to load from the client system's ROM at boot time; simply reproducing TCP's functionality at the application layer was not a viable option. The solution involved sacrificing speed to provide the necessary functionality. TFTP was intended only for limited use and did not have to be an all-purpose file-transfer protocol. The complexity of TCP's packet sequencing, delayed acknowledgment, user authentication, and sliding-window flow control mechanisms was eliminated. Instead, TFTP uses a *stop and wait* system, in which a single data packet is transmitted and no further action taken until an acknowledgment is received. This technique is slower, but it provides error detection (using the UDP checksum), eliminates the problem of overflowing receive buffers, and ensures that packets arrive in the order in which they were sent – all with a minimum of control overhead.

The TFTP standard defines five message types, each of which is carried in the data field of a UDP packet. Each type is identified by a 2-byte *opcode* field at the beginning of the message. The five message types and their *opcode* values are as follows

1 – **RRQ** – Read request

2 – **WRQ** – Write request

3 – **Data** – Contains the file being transferred

4 – **ACK** – Acknowledgment

5 – **Error** – Contains an error message to return to the sender

READ/WRITE REQUESTS   A TFTP client can request only two functions of a server: to transmit a particular file and to receive a particular file. Unlike FTP, there is no facility for browsing the server's directories – the client must know the name and the exact location of the file to be transferred. On a diskless workstation, this information is specified in the BOOTP configuration data delivered to the client.

The TFP read and write requests use the same structure, shown in Figure 7-4. The message begins with the 2-byte opcode, then specifies the name of the file to be transferred, followed by a mode indicator. The *mode* field contains one of the two values specifying the nature of the requested file: *netascii* (for straight text files) or *octet* (for binary files).

Figure 7-4: TFTP read and write requests only specify a filename and a description of the file type, or mode.

DATA PACKETS   The TFTP application generates data packets (see Figure 7-5) to transmit a requested file. Each packet contains an opcode field with a value of 3, followed by a 2-byte block number and a data field. The transmitting system divides the requested file into 512-byte blocks (except for the last block, which can go up to 511 bytes), each of which is carried in a separate packet.

The first packet containing data in a file transfer is assigned block number 1, which is incremented for each packet. When a client sends an RRQ message, the server responds with the first data packet (block 1). If the client sends a WRQ, the server responds with an acknowledgment containing the block number 0, after which the client transmits block 1. The receiver recognizes receipt of the last block in the file transfer when it receives a data packet containing less than 512 bytes.

Figure 7-5: TFTP divides files into 512-byte blocks that are numbered for transmission.

ACKNOWLEDGMENTS   An ACK message contains only an opcode of 4 and the 2-byte block number of the data packet being acknowledged, as shown in Figure 7-6. Every TFTP packet must be acknowledged by the receiver before the next packet is transmitted.

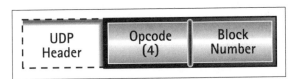

Figure 7-6: The receiving TFTP system generates an acknowledgment packet for each incoming message.

ERROR MESSAGES   TFTP error messages can be sent in lieu of an acknowledgment message, to indicate that a request cannot be fulfilled or that a data read/write error has occurred. The error message contains an opcode value of 5, a 2-byte error number field, and an error message string that is displayed to the receiving user (see Figure 7-7).

Figure 7-7: TFTP error messages are sent to the client to indicate a server's failure to complete a requested operation.

The possible values of the error number field are as follows:

0 – Not defined, see error message (if any)

1 – File not found

2 – Access violation

3 – Disk full or allocation exceeded

4 – Illegal TFTP operation

5 – Unknown transfer ID

6 – File already exists

7 – No such user

In most cases, an error message indicates the termination of a TFTP transmission. It is, however, possible for a data transfer to recover from a single packet loss, because the sender retains one packet for retransmission. Because UDP cannot detect lost packets and retransmit them, a mechanism is implemented at the application layer. After a timeout period elapses, the receiving system returns the last packet to the source. The sender then retransmits the next packet, and continues from there.

BOOTP and DHCP

The Bootstrap Protocol (BOOTP) is an automatic client-configuration protocol that delivers TCP/IP parameters to network clients. BOOTP can also be configured to initiate TFTP transfers on diskless workstations. The Dynamic Host Configuration Protocol (DHCP) has supplanted BOOTP because it's capable of assigning IP addresses dynamically, and reclaiming them when they are no longer being used.

Both of these application-layer protocols are based on UDP, because they rely on broadcast transmissions. A client awaiting an assigned IP address can only communicate with DHCP or BOOTP servers by broadcasting messages to the entire local network. The ensuing message exchanges comprise a series of requests and replies, functioning as their own acknowledgments.

The message types and client/server exchanges used by BOOTP and DHCP are covered in Chapter 10, "DHCP and IP Address Management."

The Domain Name System (DNS)

The Domain Name System (DNS) is one of the fundamental technologies of the Internet. DNS functions as an authoritative database of all systems on the network, and yet the data is distributed among thousands of computers all over the world. The way all of these computers work together to form a unified whole is examined more fully in Chapter 11, "Name Registration and Resolution." In its simplest form, DNS consists of a client (called a *resolver*) sending a query that contains a system's Internet host name to a server and receiving the equivalent IP address as a reply.

As an application protocol, DNS supports all other applications that allow clients to specify host names as targets of an operation or request. Because the traffic generated by a client application is carried in IP datagrams, the system must know the IP address of the intended recipient before any requests can be transmitted. TCP/IP client programs, therefore, perform a rapid DNS exchange to resolve the host names (supplied by the user) into IP addresses before the actual client traffic is generated (see Figure 7-8).

DNS is unusual among application-layer protocols in that it is capable of using TCP (although it primarily uses UDP for its transport-layer services). Port number 53 is assigned to DNS for both TCP and UDP in the "Assigned Numbers" RFC. While many applications have the same port number for both transport protocols assigned to them, few of them actually use both.

DNS primarily uses UDP for many of the reasons already discussed. TCP requires too much overhead for what produces an exchange of a small amount of data. In many Web browsers, it is possible to see the amount of time elapsing during the name resolution process. When specifying a URL that contains an Internet host name in the Internet Explorer browser, you see the rapid change of information in the status bar at the bottom of the screen. This occurs as the DNS transaction causes the target indicator to change from the host name to the IP address. If the browser performed all of the steps to establish and break down a TCP connection, the response would be much slower.

DNS communications involve exchanges between servers as frequently as they do between client/server transactions. There is, however, only one message type used for both queries and replies. The size of the message varies, as a single packet contains multiple responses (called *resource records)* to a single query. When DNS uses UDP as its transport protocol (which is usually the case for client/server queries), the message is limited to 512 bytes and a timeout/retransmission mechanism is provided at the application layer.

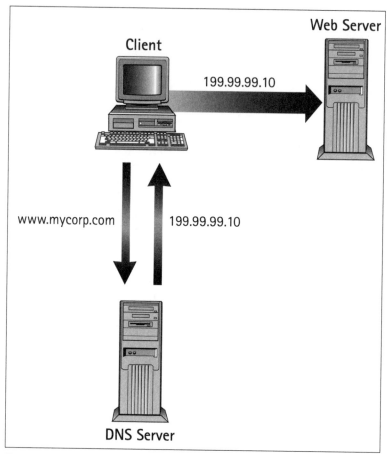

Figure 7-8: DNS provides services that convert host names to IP addresses for
many other TCP/IP applications.

In a basic query/reply exchange between a DNS client and server, the resolver
sends a packet containing the query to the server. In the course of satisfying the
query, the server adds response information to the same packet and returns it to the
sender. If the added information causes the message to exceed 512 bytes, it is truncated before transmission, and a flag is activated to inform the sender. Upon receipt
of a truncated reply packet, the resolver generates a new request using TCP, which
can handle the larger amount of data by segmenting it. DNS also uses TCP for its
zone transfers, which replicate the DNS data from primary to secondary servers.
DNS transactions that use TCP employ the same message format as UDP transactions (except for a 2-byte length field that specifies the number of bytes in the rest
of the message).

Dynamic Routing Protocols

The service a protocol (such as DNS) provides to a TCP/IP client may be fleeting, but it is perceivable to the user. Other application-layer protocols provide vital services to a TCP/IP network without ever reaching a host system. Routing IP datagrams to destinations on other networks intelligently involves exchanging information about the networks to which the routers are attached. Routers insert this information into their routing tables, which they consult when a packet arrives and is destined for another network.

This routing information is transmitted using specialized application-layer protocols called *dynamic routing protocols*. These protocols automate a process that network administrators can perform by manually creating static routes. Dynamic routing, however, enables a network to compensate automatically for changes in the network infrastructure. Possible changes include malfunctioning systems and physical-layer breakdowns.

Dynamic routing protocols are not directly involved in the IP routing process. A support protocol, such as DNS, is called by another client process when needed, but routing protocols are not. Instead, they transmit their data at regular intervals so routing tables all over the network can be updated continually.

The routing of IP datagrams and the mechanics of static and dynamic routing are examined in Chapter 9, "Routing IP."

THE ROUTING INFORMATION PROTOCOL (RIP)

The Routing Information Protocol (RIP) was one of the first dynamic routing protocols to come into general use. The Berkeley 4.3 UNIX operating system first included it, and it is still one of the most commonly used, to this day. Almost all TCP/IP router or gateway products include a version of RIP (including NetWare and Windows NT). There have, however, been interoperability problems between different implementations because RIP was implemented in many different products before it was standardized. RFC1058 (published in 1988) was not the origin of RIP, but rather an attempt to create a standard implementation to decrease the chance of future conflicts.

Routers transmit RIP messages in UDP datagrams using port number 520. A RIP packet contains information on up to 25 routes, each of which requires 20 bytes. The rest of the message is 4 bytes, making the maximum size of a RIP message 504 bytes—small enough to fit in a single UDP datagram.

RIP is referred to as a *distance vector* routing protocol, because it measures the efficiency of routes in terms of hop counts (the number of routers a packet must pass through on the way to a particular destination). Approximately every 30 seconds, routers transmit update packets using either broadcasts (on LANs) or unicasts to the other end of a point-to-point link.

THE OPEN SHORTEST PATH FIRST PROTOCOL (OSPF)

Although RIP is used widely, it is criticized for the amount of broadcast traffic it generates, its inability to recognize subnet masks, and the convergence delays (occurring when the protocol must adapt to a change in the routing environment due to equipment failure). The Open Shortest Path First Protocol (OSPF) is a new protocol, developed to address the shortcomings of RIP.

OSPF is distinctly different from RIP in that it doesn't measure the efficiency routes in hop numbers. OSPF in a *link state* protocol, meaning that a router running OSPF tests its link with each of the other routers on the network, and transmits the results of all of the tests. Link state protocols converge (that is, update other routers) faster when the network's routing environment changes. OSPF also uses multicast transmissions instead of broadcasts, which it sends to a special class IP address (224.0.0.5) – designated the *AllSPFRouters* address. This reduces the bandwidth required to keep routers updated.

OSPF is unusual in that it uses no transport-layer protocol, but is encapsulated directly into IP datagrams instead. OSPF packets contain the protocol number 89 in the IP header's protocol field. The OSPF application makes an effort to keep its packet size below 576 bytes, so a message can fit into a single datagram. The protocol, however, is capable of creating packets up to 65,535 bytes (the largest possible datagram size), relying on IP fragmentation when necessary.

THE BORDER GATEWAY PROTOCOL (BGP)

RIP and OSPF are designed for use on a single, autonomous system. An *autonomous system* (AS) is a collection of networks falling under a single point of administrative control. A corporate internetwork, for example, would likely comprise a single AS. The administrators of the network select a single dynamic routing protocol, such as RIP or OSPF, and use it on all of the network's routers.

Assuming that the corporate internetwork is connected to the Internet, routing information must also be exchanged between autonomous systems. The Border Gateway Protocol (BGP) is a distance vector routing protocol. It specifies the path of ASs that traffic must move through to reach a specific Internet destination. This routing information is more detailed and more useful than the simple hop count used by RIP.

BGP uses TCP connections to exchange information with other routers. Periodic updates and keepalive messages ensure that the connections remain active. While dynamic routing protocols perform similar application-layer functions, at the lower layers, developers can use the services provided in very different ways to support the specific requirements of the application.

The Simple Network Management Protocol (SNMP)

As private networks grow, administration becomes more difficult due to the number of machines involved and the distance between them. The SNMP protocol enables network management products to transfer status and configuration information between a central management console and agents running on systems all over the network.

The network agent is the client side of the process, that runs as an application on many network devices. The agent gathers information about the system on which it runs, and makes it available to the management console (i.e. the server) using SNMP messages carried in UDP datagrams. The console process stores the information, from all network agents, in a management information base (MIB). It then collates the information into statistical displays for the network administrator. In most network management products, the console executes a specific task in response to information received from an agent (such as generate an e-mail message or page an administrator).

SNMP communications can travel in both directions using five message types, three of which are generated by the management console, and two by agents. The message types are referred to as PDUs (*protocol data units* – a term sometimes used more generically to refer to the payload of any TCP or UDP packet) and are assigned a PDU type value that is carried in the SNMP message. The five messages and their PDU type values are as follows:

0 – Get-request – Network management consoles send get-request messages to agents to gather specific pieces of information as necessary.

1 – Get-next-request – The get-next-request is used by the console to request the next in a list of statistics maintained by an agent.

2 – Set-request – The set-request message enables the console to specify a value for a particular variable on an agent system.

3 – Get-response – The get-response message is transmitted by the agent, to the console, in response to any of the three previous message types.

4 – Trap – The trap message is sent by an agent, to the console, informing it of a particular occurrence (such as a malfunction). Management consoles transmit PDU types 0 through 2 to UDP port 161, on agent systems. A separate port number, 162, is set aside for the trap messages that agents send to the console. This ensures that a single system can run both client and server modules, simultaneously.

The SNMP specifications that are published as RFCs do not define every aspect of the network management application. Rather, they are intended as a framework on which third-party developers can construct applications of their own. Apart from the SNMP protocol, the RFCs describe the format of the MIB, and a means of identifying and referencing specific elements stored there. Developers must decide how the application uses the information gathered from the network agents.

The Network File System (NFS)

The Network File System (NFS) is a client/server application developed by Sun Microsystems. It was designed to provide file system access to remote computers running different operating systems on different hardware platforms. File system access is very different from the file transfer services provided by protocols, such as FTP and TFTP. An NFS client can access the files on a server in a manner that is completely transparent to any application running on the client system. Instead of being transferred to a local drive, remote files (or parts of files) are read into memory directly from their original locations.

NFS relies on an application-layer protocol developed by Sun Microsystems, called Remote Procedure Calls (RPC), to convey its messages between clients and servers. The NFS client calls a function of the NFS server, but is not involved in the communications aspect of the transaction. RPC emulates the server's function call on the client system using what is known as a *client stub*. The client stub packages the request in an RPC message and transmits it (usually in a UDP datagram) to the server. An RPC server stub runs on the receiving system, and passes the original function call to the actual NFS server process (see Figure 7-9). The NFS server's response is returned to the client in the same manner.

Sun Microsystems originally developed NFS and RPC, but specifications for both were released to the public domain and published as RFCs. As a result, other developers have created implementations of both technologies for various products running on many platforms. Both NetWare and Windows NT support RPC and can run NFS applications to provide their clients with access to the file systems of UNIX workstations.

NFS operates using a client/server model, in which the client is granted access to the file system of the server. These functions are integrated into the OS so well that computers can run both the client and server modules to achieve full peer-to-peer access between systems.

NFS was designed, originally, for use only on local networks with UDP as its transport protocol. Some later implementations, however, were designed to operate over wide-area links, as well. Because WANs are more prone to packet loss caused by congestion and transmission errors, a more reliable transfer protocol is needed, and TCP is used.

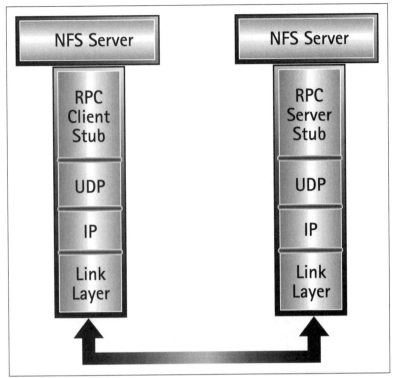

Figure 7-9: NFS is an application that uses RPC to manage its client/server communications.

NFS and RPC demonstrate how application-layer protocols can be assimilated so completely into an operating system that users don't know they're accessing network resources. Even computers of radically different types can communicate, as long as they have a TCP/IP protocol stack in common.

TCP Applications

Many services that are familiar to Internet users employ the TCP protocol at the transport layer. These services deliver files, or other data, to clients intact and in a timely manner. As with UDP-based services, the application protocols using TCP can provide various levels of functionality, and can be implemented in different ways by developers.

The File Transfer Protocol (FTP)

The File Transfer Protocol (FTP) provides file transfer services, which should be distinguished from the file system access provided by applications, such as NFS. The primary purpose of FTP is to copy files between clients and servers, not to access them in place on a remote system. Towards this end, FTP provides additional services to facilitate the file-transfer process, such as the capability to navigate the server's directory tree and list the files in a directory. The lack of these features severely limits the functionality of TFTP, the UDP-based file transfer protocol. The capability to browse through a server's directories has made FTP one of the most useful TCP/IP applications.

Some FTP clients implement these additional functions, making them seem a part of the computer's local file system, but this should not be confused with true file system access. FTP enables clients to copy files, but not open them.

 FTP was designed with the character-based client interface found in most client operating systems supporting TCP/IP, including Windows 95 and Windows NT. In recent years, the popularity of graphical user interfaces has resulted in a large number of third-party client programs that provide point-and-click access to FTP server directories. Some clients emulate the appearance of operating system utilities, such as Windows 95 Explorer. These clients do not represent a change in the FTP protocol, or the client/server command syntax; they are graphical programs that automate transmission of the appropriate text commands to the server.

FTP CONNECTIONS

FTP is unusual among TCP-based applications, in that every session uses two different TCP connections, simultaneously. FTP was assigned two well-known port numbers by the "Assigned Numbers" RFC. Port number 21 is the control port. When an FTP server module is loaded on a TCP/IP system, the program performs a passive open on port 21, placing the server in listen mode.

When an FTP client addresses a server, it establishes a connection to port 21 that will remain active throughout the FTP session. Through this interactive connection, the client is authenticated to the server, and issues the commands that control all future activities. When the client issues a command to the server requesting a file transfer (and a directory listing is considered a transfer of an ASCII file), a second connection, using port 20, is opened. When the transfer is complete, the connection is closed again.

The different functions of these two connections lead the FTP protocol to request different type-of-service values in the IP header. The control connection, involving interactive exchanges between the user and server, uses IP packets with a "minimize delay" TOS, while data connections use specify "maximize throughput" in the TOS field. This is a good example of how application-layer protocols can dictate the conditions used at the internet layer. Normally, a protocol can only communicate with processes in adjacent layers of the stack, but TCP passes certain information from the application layer through to the internet layer.

FTP COMMANDS

FTP clients and servers communicate over the control connection by exchanging commands between the user-protocol interpreter (in the client program) and the server-protocol interpreter, as shown in Figure 7-10. Unlike many application protocols that use message packets with coded field values for communications, FTP uses text-based commands and arguments. The commands are 3- or 4-byte uppercase ASCII strings, some of which carry additional arguments.

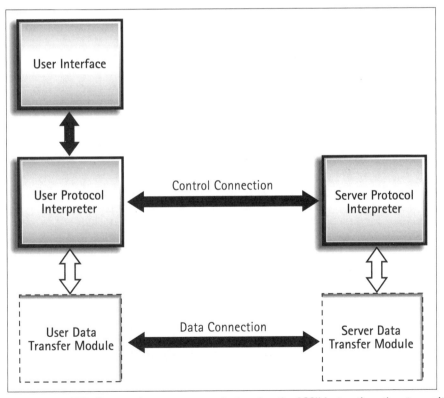

Figure 7-10: FTP clients and servers communicate using the ASCII instructions they transmit over the control connection.

FTP's use of ASCII text for its command language can impose a serious lack of security on the protocol. Although it is possible to secure an FTP server by requiring authenticated access, clients transmit user names and passwords in clear text. This data is easily intercepted by a network-monitoring utility configured to capture packets on the network.

The protocol interpreters (PIs), in both client and server sides of an FTP connection, communicate using a command syntax that isn't necessarily the same as the one presented to the user at the client system. The FTP standard defines the commands used by the PIs, but the design of the user interface is left to the application's developer. The client program converts the user's commands into the proper syntax for transmission to the server, and then interprets the responses the same way. A one-to-one correspondence between commands of the user interface, and those of the user PI, is not necessary. A single instruction entered at the keyboard can result in several commands transmitted to the server. The commands used by the client and server protocol interpreters are listed in Table 7-1.

TABLE 7-1 FTP PROTOCOL INTERPRETER COMMANDS

Command	Function
USER *username*	Specifies the user's name for authentication to the server file system; usually the first command transmitted by the client.
PASS *password*	Specifies the password associated with a user name for authentication purposes.
ACCT *account*	Specifies an account used to access the server file system. Unlike the USER command, ACCT may be issued at any time during the session.
TYPE *type-code*	Specifies the type of file to transfer over a data connection. Options currently used include: *A* (for ASCII), indicating a plain text file, and *I* (for IMAGE), indicating a binary file. Two other options, EBCDIC and LOCAL, are no longer used. Three additional print format control options are defined for the ASCII and EBCDIC values. The default value is *N* (for NONPRINT). Two other values, *T* (for Telnet format control) and *F* (for Fortran carriage control), are no longer used.

continued

Command	Function
STRU *structure-code*	Specifies the structure of a file to be transferred. The default setting is *F* (for FILE), indicating that the file is a contiguous byte stream. Two other options, RECORD and PAGE, are no longer used. MODE *mode-code* specifies the transfer mode for a data connection. The default option is S (for STREAM), indicating that the file will be transferred as a byte stream. Two other options, BLOCK and COMPRESSED, are no longer used. CWD *pathname* changes the working directory in the server file system to that specified by pathname.
CDUP	Shifts the working directory in the server file system up one level in the tree hierarchy.
SMNT *pathname*	Mounts a different file system on the server, as specified by pathname.
QUIT	Terminates the session begun with the USER command and closes the control connection.
REIN	Terminates the session begun with the USER command, leaving the control connection open. A new USER command is expected to follow.
PORT *host/port*	Enables the client to notify the server of the IP address and ephemeral port number where it expects a data connection to open. The host/port variable takes the form of six integers, separated by commas. The first four of these integers contain the four bytes of the IP address, followed by two 8-bit values specifying the port number.
PASV	Instructs the server to select the port number where it will await a data connection from the client. The reply from the server includes a host/port variable like that for the PORT command.
RETR *filename*	Instructs the server to transfer the file specified by filename to the client.
STOR *filename*	Instructs the server to receive the file, specified by filename from the client, overwriting a file with the same name in the server directory.

continued

TABLE 7-1 FTP PROTOCOL INTERPRETER COMMANDS *(Continued)*

Command	Function
STOU	Instructs the server to receive the file transferred by the client, assigning it a unique name in the server directory. The reply to this command must contain the chosen file name.
APPE *pathname*	Instructs the server to receive the file specified by filename from the client, appending the incoming data to the file (of the same name) already stored in the server directory. If no file of the same name exists, a new file is created.
ALLO *bytes*	Allocates the number of bytes (specified by bytes on the server) prior to the actual transmission of data by the client.
REST *marker*	Specifies the point within a file where a file transfer is to be restarted.
RNFR *filename*	Specifies the name of a file that must be renamed; this must be followed by a RNTO command.
RNTO *filename*	Specifies the new name of the file previously referenced in an RNFR command.
ABOR	Instructs the server to abort execution of the command in progress. Any data connections open when this command is received are closed.
DELE *filename*	Instructs the server to delete the file specified by filename.
RMD *pathname*	Instructs the server to remove the directory specified by pathname.
MKD *pathname*	Instructs the server to create a new directory, using the name specified in pathname.
PWD	Instructs the server to return the name of the current working directory.
LIST *pathname*	Instructs the server to transmit an ASCII file containing a full listing of the directory's contents, specified by pathname (or the current working directory, if no argument is provided).
NLST *pathname*	Instructs the server to transmit an ASCII file containing a filename listing of the directory's contents, specified by pathname (or the current working directory, if no argument is provided). Unlike the LIST command, which includes file attributes, NLST requests only include a listing of file names.
SITE *string*	Carrries specialized, nonstandard commands to a particular server implementation.

continued

Command	Function
SYST	Instructs the server to return the name of the operating system running (using the system names specified in the "Assigned Numbers" RFC).
STAT *filename*	Instructs the server to return an indicator of the operation's status over the control connection (when issued during a file transfer). Instructs the server to return information for the file over the control connection normally included in a response to the LIST command (when issued with a filename argument).
HELP *string*	Instructs the server to return information regarding details of its implementation. A string may be included to request more specific information on a particular topic.
NOOP	Instructs the server to return an "OK" response. The command performs no other actions.

FTP REPLIES

Every command an FTP client sends to a server must result in at least one reply from the server. The replies that servers return to clients consist of a three-digit numerical code and a text string. The text is presented to the user, while the client program interprets the code to determine its next action.

The server constructs reply codes based on specified definitions for the individual values of the three digits. Given the variable *xyz*, representing the three digits of the code, the possible values for the first digit, x, are as follows:

- ◆ 1yz – **Positive preliminary reply** – indicates that the previously requested action has begun, and that the client should wait for another reply message before sending any further commands.

- ◆ 2yz – **Positive completion reply** – indicates completion of the previously requested action, and the server's readiness to receive a new command.

- ◆ 3yz – **Positive intermediate reply** – indicates the server's acceptance of the previous command, and the delay of execution pending additional information from the client.

- ◆ 4yz – **Transient negative completion reply** – indicates the server's denial of the previous command due to a temporary condition. The command (or command sequence) should be re-sent.

- ◆ 5yz – **Permanent negative completion reply** – indicates the server's denial of the previous command due to a permanent condition. The command (or command sequence) should not be re-sent.

While the first digit of the reply code provides the client with general information regarding the next action to take, the second digit provides more specific information on the type of message contained in the reply. The possible values for the second digit, y, are as follows:

♦ x0z – Syntax – indicates that a command does not conform to any recognizable syntax structure acceptable to the server.

♦ x1z – Information – indicates that the reply is sent in response to a client's request for information.

♦ x2z – Connections – indicates that the reply concerns the condition of FTP control or data connection.

♦ x3z – Authentication and accounting – indicates that the reply concerns the login procedure or the account process.

♦ x4z – Unused.

♦ x5z – File system – indicates that the reply concerns the status of the file system on the server.

The third digit of the reply code provides more specific information, within the guidelines specified by the first two digits. The specific code numbers defined in the FTP standard must be implemented by all FTP servers (the text accompanying each code may vary). The possible values for FTP reply codes are as follows:

♦ 110 – Restart marker reply (MARK *yyyy* = *mmmm*, where *yyyy* is the user-process' data stream marker, and *mmmm* is the server's equivalent marker).

♦ 120 – Service ready in nnn minutes.

♦ 125 – Data connection already open; transfer starting.

♦ 150 – File status okay; about to open data connection.

♦ 200 – Command okay.

♦ 202 – Command not implemented; superfluous at this site.

♦ 211 – System status, or system help reply.

♦ 212 – Directory status.

♦ 213 – File status.

♦ 214 – Help message.

♦ 215 – NAME system type (where NAME is an official system name from the list in the "Assigned Numbers" RFC).

◆ 220 – Service ready for new user.

◆ 221 – Service closing control connection.

◆ 225 – Data connection open; no transfer in progress.

◆ 226 – Closing data connection. Requested file action successful.

◆ 227 – Entering Passive Mode (h1,h2,h3,h4,p1,p2).

◆ 230 – User logged in, proceed.

◆ 250 – Requested file action okay completed.

◆ 257 – "PATHNAME" created.

◆ 331 – User name okay, need password.

◆ 332 – Need account for login.

◆ 350 – Requested file action pending further information.

◆ 421 – Service not available closing control connection.

◆ 425 – Can't open data connection.

◆ 426 – Connection closed; transfer aborted.

◆ 450 – Requested file action not taken; file unavailable.

◆ 451 – Requested action aborted; local error in processing.

◆ 452 – Requested action not taken; insufficient storage space in system.

◆ 500 – Syntax error command unrecognized.

◆ 501 – Syntax error in parameters or arguments.

◆ 502 – Command not implemented.

◆ 503 – Bad sequence of commands.

◆ 504 – Command not implemented for that parameter.

◆ 530 – Not logged in.

◆ 532 – Need account for storing files.

◆ 550 – Requested action not taken; file unavailable.

◆ 551 – Requested action aborted; page type unknown.

◆ 552 – Requested file action aborted; exceeded storage allocation.

◆ 553 – Requested action not taken; file name not allowed.

The Hypertext Transfer Protocol (HTTP)

The Hypertext Transfer Protocol (HTTP) is the primary application-layer protocol used for World Wide Web communications – now responsible for a significant amount of the traffic on the Internet. The Web is actually a simple service, as far as the network communications are concerned. A Web client browser establishes a TCP connection to a Web server, and uses HTTP to request that the server transmit a specific file. The protocol consists of little more than requests and replies, and the server program is responsible only for transmitting existing files to clients.

By far, the most complex part of the Web service is the client. A typical Web page consists of an ASCII text file written in HTML (Hypertext Markup Language), and possibly some separate graphic image files. An HTML file contains the text to be displayed to the client user, plus tags dictating how that text must be displayed and how the graphics are must be integrated into the page layout. To the server and the protocol, however, these are just text and image files. The browser is responsible for the way HTML display options appear on the user's screen.

The browser also interprets the HTML tags to establish what parts of display text should function as hyperlinks. A *hyperlink* is a block of text, triggered by the user, to activate a link to another file on the same (or different) server. The browser processes a hyperlink by generating a new HTTP request to the server specified in the HTML file. Hyperlinks can point to other HTML files, graphics, or applications, and specify use of different application protocols for connecting to other services, such as FTP or Telnet.

The contents of a Web page seem complex, as they appear in the browser, but this is usually the result of the concatenation of different files into the same display. To the Web server, each file requested, and delivered, using HTTP requires a separate TCP connection. This is necessary regardless of whether the files contain text, graphics, or binary code.

Graphic-intensive Web sites can slow down a browser's response time. This occurs from the large amount of bandwidth needed to transmit image files, and also the additional overhead incurred by opening and closing many different TCP sessions between the same two systems. One of the major flaws in Web communications, the increasing popularity of the Web is responsible for a monstrous amount of wasted Internet bandwidth.

The HTTP protocol consists of two basic message types: *requests* and *replies.* An exchange between an HTTP client and a server is always commenced by the client, which opens a TCP connection (usually to well-known port 80) and transmits its request. The server returns a reply on the same connection, usually containing the file requested by the client, and signals the end of the response by closing the TCP connection.

HTTP REQUESTS

As with FTP, the messages exchanged by HTTP clients and servers are based on ASCII text strings rather than coded fields. A typical request message consists of a request line and a series of headers, terminated by a blank line (a CR/LF code). The request line consists of three variables on a single line, separated by spaces, as follows:

```
requesttype requestURI HTTPversion
```

The `requesttype` variable specifies one of three possible requests, as follows:

◆ GET – Requests that a server transmit a file (specified by the requestURI variable) to the client.

◆ HEAD – Requests that the server send only its header information, and not the requested file, itself. This tests the specified target for availability and modifications since the last access.

◆ POST – Sends data from the client to a server. This is the only request that includes a body after the blank line signaling the end of the headers.

The `requestURI` variable specifies the name of the file or directory being requested by the client. A Uniform Resource Identifier (URI) is a text string that identifies the uniqueness of a particular network resource. URIs, defined in RFC1630, are a comprehensive naming system for network resources, sufficiently extensible for use with new Web protocols and technologies as they develop. For the purposes of HTTP message exchanges, the more commonly known term URL (Uniform Resource Locator) is the functional equivalent. An HTTP request can specify the full path to a specific file, a relative path name, or a directory path – in which case, the server accesses its configured default file name (usually index.htm, index.html, or default.htm).

The `HTTPversion` variable specifies the version of the HTTP protocol implemented by the client. Version 1.0 of the HTTP standard, published in May 1996 as RFC1945, is implemented by most of the mainstream client and server products marketed today. Version 1.1 was published in January 1997 as RFC2068. Both of these versions require that implementations be backwards-compatible with versions of the standard going back to HTTP 0.9.

When a user enters an Internet host name into a Web browser to contact a server at a specific site, the HTTP request line (sent by the client to the server) looks something like the following:

```
GET / HTTP/1.0
```

The three variables of the request line are delimited by spaces. The slash used for the `requestURI` value represents the default file located in the root directory of the Web server. This is usually the organization's main home. The `requestURI` variable transmitted to the server does not need to include the entire URI of the Web site. The browser has already processed the scheme (that is, the prefix to the URI specifying the protocol to be used, such as HTTP://), the host name (which is resolved to an IP address using a DNS transaction), and the port number. The HTTP request must include only the path and filename information that follows the port number in an absolute URI.

 Most Web browsers enable users to reduce keystrokes by defaulting to HTTP, as the scheme, and 80, as the port number. For example, entering the host name www.mycorp.com in a browser is the equivalent of the URL HTTP://www.mycorp.com:80. For more information on Web browsers and the structure of URLs, see Chapter 15, "TCP/IP Applications."

HTTP HEADERS

After the request line, the HTTP client includes a series of 0 or more headers. The term header, in this case, does not refer to the protocol encapsulation process. An HTTP header consists of a field name followed by a colon, a space, and a field value, as follows:

`fieldname: fieldvalue`

HTTP messages use headers to provide the other system with information about the protocol implementation, system configuration, data in the body of the message (if any), and many other aspects of the HTTP environment. The server receiving a request message uses the header information to control the format of the response.

All of the HTTP headers are optional, as is the receiving system's capability to use the information contained in the headers. Some implementations insert proprietary information in the header for use when clients connect to servers manufactured by the same vendor (but these are not defined in the Internet standards).

The basic field names used in HTTP version 1.0 headers are as follows:

- ◆ **Allow** – Allow is used in messages containing a body to specify the *requesttypes* or *responsetypes* that can be used with the resource specified by the requestURI variable.

- ◆ **Authorization** – This is used by a client to deliver authorization information to a server.

- ◆ **Content-encoding** – This is used in messages containing a body to specify the type of encoding performed on the resource specified in the requestURI, and the decoding needed to produce the media type specified in the content-type field.

◆ **Content-length** – This name specifies the length of the body enclosed in the message (or in the case of a HEAD request, the body that would be enclosed in the message) in bytes.

◆ **Content-type** – This is used in messages containing a body to specify the media type of the resource specified in the requestURI variable (for example: text/html).

◆ **Date** – This name is used to specify the date and time that the message was generated.

◆ **Expires** – This is used in messages containing a body to specify the date and time the resource specified in the requestURI variable should be considered.

◆ **From** – From is used in request messages to specify the e-mail address of the user generating the client request.

◆ **If-modified-since** – This is used in GET messages to specify the date and time the file identified by the requestURI variable was last saved in the client cache. If the server determines that the file has not changed since the specified date, it does not transmit the file, returning instead a response code that the client interprets as an instruction to load the file from the cache.

◆ **Last-modified** – This name used in messages containing a body to specify the date and time that the resource specified in the requestURI variable was last modified.

◆ **Location** – This is used in messages containing a body to specify the exact location of the resource specified in the requestURI variable.

◆ **Pragma** – Pragma is used in request and response messages to specify directives that are specific to the implementation.

◆ **Referer** – Referer is used in request messages to specify the resource from which the requestURI reference was obtained.

◆ **Server** – This is used in response messages to identify the Web server product.

◆ **User-agent** – This is used in request messages to specify the properties of the client implementation, such as screen resolution, color depth, operating system, and processor type.

◆ **WWW-authenticate** – This name is used in response messages to inform the client that authentication is required to access the resource specified in the requestURI variable.

Version 1.1 of the HTTP standard contains many more header field names (some of which are currently used by client and server implementations that claim to conform to version 1.0). Version control in the marketplace has never been precise, as far as the HTTP standard is concerned.

HTTP RESPONSES

Response messages generated by HTTP servers are similar, in formation, to requests. There is only a single form for a response, and it begins with a status line. The status line contains the HTTP version running on the server, a status code, and a status phrase, in the following format:

HTTPversion StatusCode StatusPhrase

Following the status line is an optional series of headers, formatted exactly like those included in request messages. They follow a blank line, the body of the message, and contain the contents of the file specified in the `requestURI` field, of the request message.

As in FTP, the `StatusCode` field contains a three-digit numerical code. The first digit specifies the general nature of the response, as follows:

◆ 1yz – **Informational** – not used

◆ 2yz – **Success** – the request has been accepted by the server

◆ 3yz – **Redirection** – additional action is required by the client

◆ 4yz – **Client error** – problems with the request prevented its execution

◆ 5yz – **Server error** – a valid request could not be executed by the server

The `StatusPhrase` field contains a text string for display at the client-user interface (again, like FTP). Exact messages displayed for the status codes may be modified in specific implementations, but the codes, themselves, must be supported. The response messages defined in the HTTP 1.0 standard are as follows:

◆ 200 – OK

◆ 201 – Created

◆ 202 – Accepted

◆ 204 – No Content

◆ 301 – Moved Permanently

- ◆ 302 – Moved Temporarily
- ◆ 304 – Not Modified
- ◆ 400 – Bad Request
- ◆ 401 – Unauthorized
- ◆ 403 – Forbidden
- ◆ 404 – Not Found
- ◆ 500 – Internal Server Error
- ◆ 501 – Not Implemented
- ◆ 502 – Bad Gateway
- ◆ 503 – Service Unavailable

The Simple Mail Transfer Protocol (SMTP)

The Simple Mail Transfer Protocol (SMTP) is another ASCII-based messaging protocol, used to transmit e-mail messages over TCP/IP networks. SMTP is not implemented by e-mail clients (also known as user agents). Instead, the protocol is used by mail transfer agents (MTAs) that insulate the user from the application-layer process, as shown in Figure 7-11.

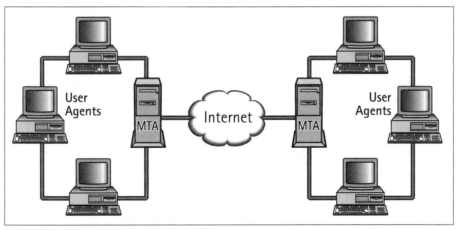

Figure 7-11: SMTP communications are conducted between e-mail servers only – not between the clients, themselves.

In practice, both the sender and the receiver of the e-mail message interact with a client program, and e-mail clients are not defined by any Internet standard.

Instead, the client sends its e-mail messages to an MTA using a communications method devised by the application's designer. The MTA can be any mail server application that is suitable to the environment in which it is used. On UNIX systems, sendmail is the most commonly used MTA. Microsoft's Exchange Server and Novell's GroupWise also function as MTAs. A PC that is networked only by a dial-up connection to an Internet service provider, details of the MTA implementation, may be unknown to the user (except as a host name or IP address). A typical exchange between MTAs using SMTP appears similar to the communications between FTP protocol interpreters. The client (that is, the MTA sending the mail message) transmits messages, consisting of four-letter command strings plus arguments, to the server's TCP port 25. The server replies with three-digit numerical response codes.

SMTP COMMANDS

The commands used in SMTP exchanges are as follows:

- ◆ HELO *domainname* — This command enables the client to identify itself to the server by specifying the full domain name of the sending MTA.

- ◆ MAIL *sender* — This initiates a mail transaction by specifying the e-mail address of the user sending the message.

- ◆ RCPT *receiver* — This command specifies the intended recipient of the mail message. Multiple recipients require separate RCPT commands.

- ◆ DATA *message* — This transmits the multiline contents of the mail message. The command is terminated by the transmission of a line containing only a period.

- ◆ RSET — RSET aborts the current mail transaction, causing all saved and buffered information to be deleted.

- ◆ VRFY *address* — This command tests the operational validity of a specified e-mail address without actually sending a message.

- ◆ EXPN *listname* — This instructs the server to return the contents of a specified mailing list.

- ◆ HELP — HELP instructs the server to return help screens to the client.

- ◆ NOOP — NOOP instructs the server to return an "OK" response without performing any other action.

- ◆ QUIT — QUIT instructs the server to return an "OK" message and then close the TCP connection.

Three other commands, SEND, SOML, and SAML, essentially duplicate the functionality of the MAIL command, and are rarely used.

E-MAIL PACKAGING

The overall structure of an e-mail message, as transmitted using SMTP, consists of the *envelope*, the *headers*, and the *body*. The envelope contains the information specified in the MAIL and RCPT command. These are the "To" and "From" addresses needed for every form of mail. The headers are informational fields structured like those in the HTTP protocol. Header lines can be added to an e-mail message by both the user agent and the MTA, and are transmitted with the body text using the DATA command. They specify detailed information about the generation of the e-mail message (such as the time and the sender's e-mail address) and its processing by the MTA.

Headers often add a significant amount of data to a small e-mail message. Some user agents suppress the header information when they display messages, and others give you the option to view the headers. SMTP headers provide valuable information for network administrators in the detective work that is sometimes necessary to trace an e-mail problem to its origin.

SMTP RESPONSES

The reply codes returned by an SMTP server are constructed much like those of FTP, using the same values for the first of the three digits, as follows:

- ◆ 1yz – Positive preliminary reply
- ◆ 2yz – Positive completion reply
- ◆ 3yz – Positive intermediate reply
- ◆ 4yz – Transient negative completion reply
- ◆ 5yz – Permanent negative completion reply

The values for the second digit are slightly different from those of FTP, as follows:

- ◆ x0z – Syntax
- ◆ x1z – Information
- ◆ x2z – Connections
- ◆ x3z – Unspecified
- ◆ x4z – Unspecified
- ◆ x5z – Mail system

The reply codes defined in the SMTP standard (RFC821) are as follows:

- ◆ 211 – System status, or system help reply
- ◆ 214 – Help message
- ◆ 220 – <domain> Service ready
- ◆ 221 – <domain> Service closing transmission channel
- ◆ 250 – Requested mail action okay; completed
- ◆ 251 – User not local; will forward to <forward-path>
- ◆ 354 – Start mail input; end with <CRLF>.<CRLF>
- ◆ 421 – <domain> Service not available closing transmission channel
- ◆ 450 – Requested mail action not taken; mailbox unavailable
- ◆ 451 – Requested action aborted; local error in processing
- ◆ 452 – Requested action not taken; insufficient system storage
- ◆ 500 – Syntax error command unrecognized
- ◆ 501 – Syntax error in parameters or arguments
- ◆ 502 – Command not implemented
- ◆ 503 – Bad sequence of commands
- ◆ 504 – Command parameter not implemented
- ◆ 550 – Requested action not taken; mailbox unavailable
- ◆ 551 – User not local; please try <forward-path>
- ◆ 552 – Requested mail action aborted; exceeded storage allocation
- ◆ 553 – Requested action not taken; mailbox name not allowed
- ◆ 554 – Transaction failed

The Network News Transfer Protocol (NNTP)

The Network News Transfer Protocol (NNTP), defined in RFC977, is the application-layer protocol that binds a virtual network of servers supporting *newsgroups*. Newsgroups are public (and sometimes private) news-posting services that are to e-mail what a party-line telephone is to a private line. The news network, often referred to as USENET, consists of thousands of separate newsgroups dedicated to every subject under the sun. Users post messages to a particular newsgroup; these messages are then read, and replied to, by other users in a free-form society that has existed since the early days of the ARPANET. The amount of data involved in USENET communications is enormous. Operating a server that takes a full news feed from approximately 20,000 newsgroups, today, requires several gigabytes of disk space a day. This is obviously quite a bit more than a dial-up Internet connection.

USENET, like DNS, is a distributed network service for which there is no central point of administration. Thousands of Internet sites operate news servers that receive and transmit data. A server often provides comprehensive newsgroup access to users by receiving incoming data from other servers. It may also host a handful of its own newsgroups, which it disseminates to others.

NNTP is the protocol that news servers use to communicate with each other, and that news clients (called news readers) use to communicate with news servers, using TCP port 119. Like many of the other TCP-based Internet protocols, NNTP clients transmit commands as ASCII text and receive three-digit numerical reply codes. The commands enable news clients to navigate specific newsgroups and retrieve articles posted there. Other commands enable news servers to set up a relationship with other servers, in which all incoming data is automatically passed on, thus keeping all of the servers updated with the latest postings.

The Telecommunications Network Protocol (Telnet)

The Telecommunications Network Protocol (Telnet) is one of the oldest of the TCP/IP application-layer protocols. It was designed to enable a client user to log in to another system running a Telnet server, and to control it from a remote location. The two computers need not run the same operating system or use the same hardware platform. At the beginning of a Telnet session, the two systems perform an option negotiation procedure through which they agree on a common format.

Telnet does not employ a client-user interface that is distinguishable from the protocol, as do FTP or SMTP. Instead, Telnet functions by delivering the keystrokes, entered at the client, to the server and returning their results to the client. The effect is one of remote control, as though the client user were actually working at the server. Any commands entered by the client user are executed on the server system, using the server's resources.

Telnet was designed for use on character-based UNIX systems, which is where its functionality still lies. Client operating systems like Windows 95 and Windows NT include Telnet client implementations, but neither NetWare nor Windows NT includes a Telnet server (except for a module included with the NetWare/IP product that enables X-Windows terminals to access the NetWare server console using Telnet).

Summary

Many protocols operating at the application layer of the TCP/IP stack use the services provided by the lower layers. They also provide services of their own to client and server applications. Unlike the transport and internet layers, the application-layer interface is more amorphous, as the protocols are implemented in very different ways.

In this chapter, you learned:

◆ How application-layer protocols enable systems to communicate using the services provided by the lower layers

◆ How UDP applications provide network-control services to TCP/IP hosts and routers

◆ How TCP applications transmit files and application data with guaranteed reliability

Applications, such as FTP and Telnet, are accessed directly by users, while others operate invisibly to clients. Some of the support protocols, such as DNS and SMTP, provide a service to client/server applications, while the dynamic routing protocols are essential to the operations of TCP/IP internetworks – and never reach client workstations.

The application layer, being at the top of the stack, must provide the interface to the rest of the operating system. Various APIs supported by operating systems, such as NetWare and Windows NT, enable developers to use the TCP/IP application protocols for their own devices, or create their own protocols that use the lower-layer services.

The following chapter examines the process of installing TCP/IP support on NetWare and Windows NT servers.

Part III

Servers

Chapter 8

Windows NT and IntranetWare

IN THIS CHAPTER

To provide TCP/IP services of any kind to network clients, a server must be running a TCP/IP protocol stack. Although NetWare and Windows NT servers use the protocols in different ways, both ship with a TCP/IP stack that conforms to the Internet standards. This chapter examines the processes by which you install TCP/IP support in NetWare and Windows NT, including the following:

◆ The process of manually loading the modules required for TCP/IP communications, and binding them to your network-adapter drivers (as NetWare originally required). This is still a valuable skill, especially if you must work with older versions of NetWare.

◆ A server console utility called INETCFG.NLM (which NetWare 4.1*x* includes) offering an interface with a menu to the server's networking modules.

◆ The Network Control Panel (a tabbed dialog box that contains all of the parameters for the networking modules) in which Windows NT's networking support is configured.

INSTALLATION OF THE TCP/IP STACK is optional, however. Both Windows NT and IntranetWare include applications that require the protocols, and the inclusion of the stack in the installation process is recommended by the manufacturers.

Both operating systems can use TCP/IP for their LAN file and print services, as well as for Internet and intranet services. Windows NT now defaults to TCP/IP protocols, but IntranetWare requires the installation of the NetWare/IP product that enables the default IPX protocols to be carried within IP datagrams. The next version of IntranetWare is expected to use TCP/IP as its native protocol.

This chapter covers the installation and configuration of the TCP/IP protocol stack on Windows NT and NetWare servers. In both cases, you can install TCP/IP during the OS installation process, or onto an existing system. Both products also include automated protocol installation tools, as well as manual alternatives.

Installing TCP/IP on NetWare 4.11

The TCP/IP protocol stack on a NetWare server is based on the following modules:

* **TCPIP.NLM** – implements the TCP/IP protocol stack

* **SNMP.NLM** – provides support for the Simple Network Management Protocol

* **SNMPLOG.NLM** – SNMP event logger

* **TCPCON.NLM** – TCP/IP console utility

* **IPCONFIG.NLM** – IP-static route configuration utility

* **PING.NLM** – ICMP echo utility

* **TPING.NLM** – TCP echo utility

* **BOOTPFWD.NLM** – provides BOOTP forwarding capabilities

* **IPFLT.NLM** – provides IP-filter support

* **IPTUNNEL.LAN** – provides IP-tunneling support

* **IPTRACE.NLM** – ICMP traceroute utility (TCPIP.NLM 4.00 only)

* **HOSTS** – sample host-name database file

* **NETWORKS** – sample network-number database file

* **PROTOCOL** – sample protocol-code database file

* **SERVICES** – sample port-number database file

If you choose to perform a custom installation of NetWare 4.11, the program gives you the option of installing the TCP/IP protocol stack with NetWare's default IPX protocols. This option provides only minimal configuration capabilities. You are prompted to supply an IP address and subnet mask for each of the network interface adapters in the server – and nothing more.

In some cases, these basic options are sufficient for a TCP/IP installation. Setting any other configuration parameters, such as IP routing or additional IP addresses for your TCP/IP services, requires use of NetWare's INETCFG.NLM utility, or manual editing of the LOAD and BIND statements in the server's AUTOEXEC.NCF file. INETCFG provides menu-driven configuration of all NetWare's networking components from the server console. At the end of the installation process, you have the option to Configure Network Protocols, which loads the INETCFG program for you.

Configuring TCP/IP Manually

The INETCFG utility provides a front end for the configuration of NetWare's networking modules. Actually, it does nothing more than automate the creation of commands that would normally be found in NetWare's AUTOEXEC.NCF file. INETCFG ensures that the commands are executed in the proper order during the server-boot process, and that they are correct, syntactically.

The INETGFG utility is a convenient addition to NetWare, especially for the old-timers who remember when there was no choice beyond manual configuration of the protocol and LAN drivers. It is, however, a good idea to understand what is happening beneath the surface of a utility, such as INETCFG. At some point, you may need to troubleshoot a TCP/IP installation, or update one of the drivers or protocol-support modules involved in the TCP/IP communications process, and familiarity with the components is helpful.

Following are three basic steps to activate the TCP/IP protocol stack on a NetWare server:

1. Load the TCPIP.NLM module.

2. Load the appropriate drivers for the network-interface adapters installed in the server.

3. Bind the TCPIP module to the network drivers.

The following sections cover each of these steps in detail, including options you can add to the LOAD and BIND commands. You can perform the entire TCP/IP-configuration process, interactively, from the server-console prompt, or you can insert the same commands into the server's AUTOEXEC.NCF file. AUTOEXEC.NCF is located in the server's SYS:SYSTEM directory and can be edited with a standard text editor, or the INSTALL.NLM utility, as shown in Figure 8-1.

Figure 8-1: NetWare's INSTALL utility provides editorial access to the AUTOEXEC.NCF and STARTUP.NCF files that control the server boot sequence.

The LOAD command is a staple of the NetWare server-console interface. You use LOAD to execute programs that run on a NetWare server (such as NetWare Loadable Modules — NLMs) and various device drivers (LANs, DSKs, HAMs, and CDMs).

LOADING TCPIP.NLM

The TCPIP.NLM module implements the TCP/IP protocols on a NetWare server. This provides the transport- and internet-layer functionality needed to support applications included in the IntranetWare product. Before TCP/IP communications can begin, however, a link-layer protocol is required. The link-layer protocol is implemented by a device driver specifically designed to work with the network-interface hardware installed in the computer.

TCPIP.NLM can only be loaded once, and yet it provides protocol services for all of the server's network adapters. The module also controls routing and other functions of the TCP/IP protocol stack. By loading TCPIP.NLM with the appropriate command-line parameters, you can control whether or not your server functions as an IP router, and how its routing table is compiled.

The syntax for loading TCPIP.NLM is as follows:

```
LOAD TCPIP [forward=yes|no] [rip=yes|no] [static=yes|no]
     [trap=ipaddress]
```

- ◆ **Forward=no|yes** – The forward parameter specifies whether the NetWare server should route IP packets to other network segments, or function as an end node, only. When disabled, the server may be connected to multiple network segments, but packets entering through one interface are not forwarded out through another. When enabled, the server consults its routing table to determine if incoming packets should be forwarded to another network. By default, packet forwarding is disabled unless the Novell Multiprotocol Router product is installed on the server (in which case, it is enabled).

NetWare's IP-routing feature is completely separate from its capability to route the IPX protocol. IPX routing by a multihomed NetWare server is enabled by default, while IP must be enabled explicitly.

◆ RIP=yes|no – The `RIP` parameter specifies whether or not a NetWare server should use the Routing Information Protocol to update its internal routing table. If the server is configured to function as a router (forward=yes), enabling the RIP option causes the server to advertise its routing services by transmitting RIP packets. If the server only functions as an end node (forward=no), the RIP option permits the server to read incoming RIP packets, but not to transmit them. RIP is enabled by default.

◆ Static=yes|no – The `static` parameter specifies whether a NetWare server (configured to function as an IP router) should load the entries from the static-routing database into the server's routing table, when the protocol stack is initialized. When disabled, static-routing entries are not loaded, even if they are present in the database. You create static-routing entries using either the INETCFG.NLM or TCPCON.NLM utility. Static routing is disabled by default.

◆ Trap=*ipaddress* – The `trap` parameter identifies the system to receive the SNMP trap messages generated by the server. If you use an SNMP-based network management product on your network, the IP address specified should be that of the network management console. By default, trap messages are directed to the internal-loopback address (127.0.0.1).

NetWare's TCP/IP support has evolved significantly since the days when it was necessary to install the protocol stack manually. The parameters for the TCPIP.NLM command line, shown here, provide access to the most basic TCP/IP options. To take advantage of the module's more-advanced options, use the INETCFG.NLM utility to configure the protocol stack, as discussed later in this chapter in "Configuring TCP/IP with INETCFG.NLM."

The TCPIP.NLM module included in the IntranetWare package is version 3.05. Since that release, Novell has upgraded its Web Server product to version 3.1, which requires a new version of TCPIP.NLM. This version is 4.00, available from Novell's online services, in an archive called TCPN03.EXE. This release includes the following improvements:

◆ Common TCP/IP modules for versions of NetWare 3.12 and above

◆ Support for path-MTU determination

◆ A DNS-aware version of PING.NLM

◆ Support for IP multicasting

◆ A NetWare version of the UNIX-traceroute program, called IPTRACE.NLM

◆ Support for the automatic assignment of IP addresses over PPP connections

◆ A new version of TCPCON, capable of flushing routes in the routing table

LOADING LAN DRIVERS

Every network-interface adapter installed in a NetWare server requires a device driver (which typically has a LAN extension in NetWare). This is true even when the adapter is not used to connect to a LAN — as with a modem or other type of point-to-point connection. The LAN driver provides the link-layer protocol support that is appropriate to the hardware, be it Ethernet, Token Ring, PPP, or any other protocol.

NetWare LAN drivers are written to the Open Data-Link Interface (ODI), which permits the same driver to be used with a particular network adapter — no matter what protocol stacks are running. Therefore, if you installed a server that is already running IPX, you can add TCP/IP without loading additional drivers. The LAN driver can function as a network interface for multiple protocol stacks, as shown in Figure 8-2.

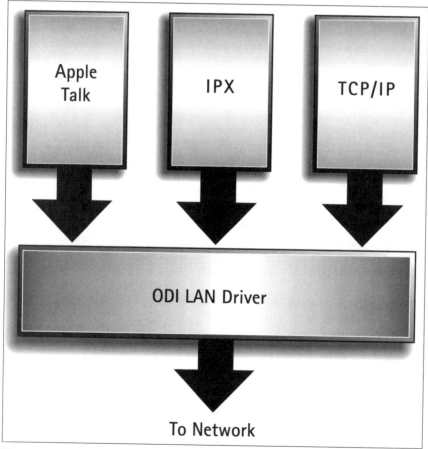

Figure 8-2: The LAN device driver provides link-layer services for all of the protocol stacks running on a NetWare server.

For more information on ODI and its Windows NT counterpart (NDIS), see Chapter 3, "TCP/IP and Operating Systems."

NetWare 4.11's installation program identifies the LAN adapters installed in a server, and loads the appropriate device drivers. As with TCPIP.NLM, you can choose to load a driver manually, or modify the command line in the AUTOEXEC.NCF file, if necessary.

LAN drivers for most of the popular network-interface adapters on the market are included in the IntranetWare package. The manufacturer of a hardware device is almost always the best source for the latest, and greatest, drivers. LAN-driver incompatibilities are a frequent cause of communications problems on NetWare networks, and should be one of the first elements tested in the troubleshooting process. As with many software products, however, fixing one problem often creates another. You should upgrade the LAN drivers on a NetWare server only when there is a specific issue to be addressed – and not just for the sake of running the latest version.

The syntax for loading a LAN driver is as follows:

```
LOAD landriver [slot=w] [int=x] [port=y] [mem=z] [frame=frametype]
[name=netname]
```

- Slot=*w* – The slot parameter identifies the location of a network-interface adapter on a PCI or EISA system.

- Int=*x* – The int parameter identifies the hardware interrupt used by a network adapter in an ISA system.

- Port=*y* – The port parameter identifies the I/O port used by a network adapter in an ISA system.

- Mem=*z* – The mem parameter identifies the memory address used by a network adapter in an ISA system.

- Frame=*frametype* – The frametype parameter identifies the format of the link-layer protocol header used by the network adapter.

- Name=*net* – The name parameter assigns a unique name to each instance of a re-entrantly loaded LAN driver.

The first function of the parameters on a LAN driver's command line is to specify the location of the network-interface hardware. Selecting parameters for this purpose depends on the type of network interface used, and the bus type of the computer. More than one adapter (of the same type, installed in the system) requires that the driver be loaded with a separate command line for each device. Most drivers are capable of loading re-entrantly, meaning that the same code can address two separate iterations of the driver with different parameters.

In addition to the hardware parameters, the command line often must identify the frame type for TCP/IP communications. On a LAN, the frame type specifies the format of the link-layer protocol header. If you are adding support for TCP/IP to a NetWare server with LAN drivers installed, you may need to modify the frame type on the driver command lines to one that supports multiple protocols.

NetWare has four frame-type options for Ethernet networks, as follows:

◆ **Ethernet_802.3** – Also known as "raw" Ethernet, the Ethernet 802.3 frame header only includes the fields defined in the IEEE 802.3 standard.

◆ **Ethernet_802.2** – The default frame type for NetWare 4.11, the Ethernet_802.2 frame header includes the fields from the IEEE 802.3 specification, plus the Logical Link Control fields from the 802.2 document.

◆ **Ethernet_SNAP** – The Ethernet_SNAP frame header includes the fields from the IEEE 802.3 specification, plus the Logical Link Control and SNAP fields from the 802.2 document.

◆ **Ethernet_II** – The Ethernet_II frame header includes the fields defined in the DIX Ethernet II specification.

Only the Ethernet_II and Ethernet_SNAP frames contain an Ethertype field that identifies the protocol carried within the link-layer frame. For this reason, only these two options can support TCP/IP on a network also running IPX. The other frame types do not provide the information needed to demultiplex incoming data packets to multiple protocol stacks. The following frame types support the use of the TCP/IP stack for the most commonly used LAN protocols:

Protocol	Frame Types
Ethernet	ETHERNET_II, ETHERNET_SNAP
Token Ring	TOKEN-RING_SNAP
FDDI	FDDI_SNAP
PCN	IBM_PCN2_SNAP
Arcnet	NOVELL_RX-NET

For more information on the NetWare frame types for Ethernet networks, see Chapter 4, "The Link Layer."

You can load a LAN driver re-entrantly with multiple frame types, in the same way you specify multiple hardware options. With the name parameter, you assign a unique name to each iteration of the driver that is used to reference it later in a BIND command. Without a name-parameter value, it is necessary to specify the hardware, and frame-type parameters from the LAN driver command line (in the BIND command) to identify the driver being bound.

BINDING LAN DRIVERS TO THE TCP/IP PROTOCOL STACK

The TCP/IP support module and the LAN drivers can be loaded in any order, but they must be bound together in order for IP communications to proceed. The binding process connects the internet layer of the protocol stack with the link layer, and provides the NetWare networking architecture with much flexibility. Each iteration of every LAN driver loaded on the server can be bound individually to any, or all, of the installed protocol stacks.

Many different scenarios result from this capability. You can build a NetWare server with two network adapters (one of which is connected to an IPX LAN for file and print services, and the other to an ISP using a point-to-point link). This permits the same server to host a web site on the Internet. You can also bind the same LAN driver to more than one protocol stack, providing network users with both IPX file and print, and TCP/IP intranet access.

Aside from specifying the network interfaces that will use the TCP/IP protocols, the BIND command configures the basic parameters needed by any TCP/IP interface. In many cases, a driver being bound to IP will only need an IP address, a subnet mask, and perhaps a default gateway – but there are many other IP parameters that you can set.

The syntax of the BIND command is as follows:

```
BIND IP TO LANdriver addr=ipaddress [mask=subnetmask] [gate=gateway]
```

- *LANdriver* – The LANdriver variable specifies the driver to which IP should be bound. It uses the name of the driver itself, or a vale assigned in the name parameter of the driver's command line.

- Addr=*IPaddress* – The addr parameter specifies the IP address to be assigned to the network interface (in dotted decimal or hexadecimal notation).

♦ **Mask=***subnetmask* — The `mask` parameter specifies the subnet mask to be applied to the network interface's IP address (in dotted decimal or hexadecimal notation).

♦ **Gate=***gateway* — The `gate` parameter specifies the IP address of the router to be used as the default gateway for packets transmitted over the network interface. These packets travel to destinations on other networks, in dotted decimal or hexadecimal notation. If no value for the gate parameter is supplied, default gateway information is obtained using the RIP-routing protocol.

♦ **Bcast=***broadcast* — The `bcast` parameter specifies the IP address to use when transmitting broadcasts over the network interface (in dotted decimal or hexadecimal notation). The default value is 255.255.255.255, and need only be changed to accommodate some early routers using 0.0.0.0 as the broadcast address.

♦ **Defroute=yes|no** — If the `defroute` parameter is set to yes, the server advertises the network interface as the default gateway for the local network, using RIP. The default value is no.

♦ **Arp=yes|no** — If the `arp` parameter is set to yes, the ARP protocol resolves IP addresses into hardware addresses on the attached network. The default value is yes.

♦ **Cost=***integer* — The `cost` parameter specifies a preference value to be assigned to the network interface. This value is used in routing decisions to determine the interface to use, when there are multiple routes available to a specified destination. Possible values range from 1 to 15, with higher values making the interface less likely to be chosen. The default value is 1.

♦ **Poison=yes|no** — The `poison` parameter specifies whether RIP should use its "poison reverse" feature when routing IP packets. The default value is no, which enables the "simple split horizon" method.

When you construct the BIND command line, you use the name parameter that you specified previously while loading the LAN driver. If you only have a single adapter in the server, the name parameter is not necessary. You can use the name of the LAN driver, itself (without the LAN extension), for the LAN driver variable in the BIND command.

Implementing TCP/IP in AUTOEXEC.NCF

Using steps from the preceding three sections, the portion of an AUTOEXEC.NCF file modified to implement TCP/IP would look something like the following:

```
LOAD TCPIP rip=yes static=yes forward=yes
LOAD SMC8000 port=240 mem=C8000 name=SMC8000_E82
 frame=ETHERNET_802.2
LOAD SMC8000 port=240 mem=C8000 name=SMC8000_EII frame=ETHERNET_II
LOAD AIOCOMX port=3F8 int=4 name=MODEM
BIND IP SMC8000_EII addr=199.99.99.10 mask=255.255.255.0
 gate=199.99.99.12 arp=yes
BIND IP MODEM addr=199.99.98.1 mask=255.255.255.0
BIND IPX SMC8000_E82 net=1
```

The TCPIP.NLM command line indicates that the server will function as a router, using both static and dynamic (RIP) routing. There are two network interfaces installed in the server, one of which is an Ethernet card and the other a dial-up connection to an Internet service provider (ISP). The driver for the Ethernet card is loaded re-entrantly, to support two frame types.

Assuming the adapter was installed in the machine using the Ethernet_802.2 frame type for standard IPX connectivity, it is preferable to load the driver the same way a second time, than change the frame type on the original command line to Ethernet_II. Though it cannot support multiple protocols on the same network, Ethernet_802.2 frame type is already used by client workstations. Furthermore, configuring the server to support both frame types is easier than modifying all of the workstation configurations.

The second driver, AIOCOMX.LAN, activates the serial port (located at the specified hardware interrupt) and I/O port for use by a modem. By using Novell's Multiprotocol Router product, you can configure a dial-up connection to an ISP that functions like any other network interface. Both drivers are then bound to the TCP/IP protocol stack, and each is assigned its own IP address. The third BIND command is for the previously existing IPX protocol stack, using the Ethernet_802.2 frame.

This sample code illustrates a basic scenario for providing a NetWare IPX network with TCP/IP-based Internet access, as shown in Figure 8-3. The NetWare server still fulfills its original role on the LAN, but also functions as a router between the local network and the Internet. In addition, you can host web sites and other IP services on the NetWare server, and publish documents to both intranet and Internet users.

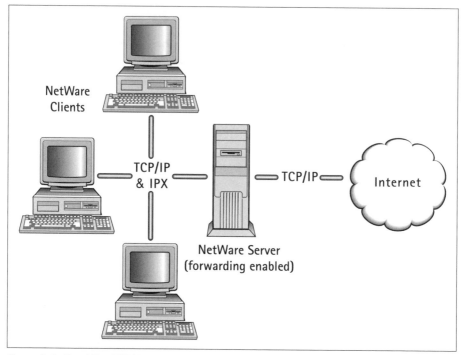

Figure 8-3: By adding TCP/IP support to an existing NetWare server, you can provide LAN users with access to the Internet.

Assigning additional IP addresses to a specific interface is also possible. This can be done directly from the server console prompt, or the AUTOEXEC.NCF file. To host web sites for a number of different clients on the same server, you might want to assign each site its own IP address. Novell's Web Server product is capable of doing this, but first you must make those IP addresses available to the web server software. Following is the syntax for adding an IP address to an interface that is already loaded and bound:

```
ADD SECONDARY IPADDRESS IPaddress TO LANdriver
```

The command can be repeated as often as necessary to provide the requisite number of IP addresses. As in a BIND command, IPaddress can be in dotted decimal or hexadecimal form, and the LANdriver variable can be the driver name, or the value of the driver's name parameter.

Configuring TCP/IP with INETCFG.NLM

While manual configuration is suitable for basic TCP/IP installations, the INETCFG.NLM utility is a more practical alternative. The INETCFG.NLM utility

provides access to all available networking options through a menu-driven inter-
face. INETCFG is a NetWare server-console utility that uses the standard interface
found in all of NetWare's character-based menu utilities. When you select
Configure Network Protocols (during the NetWare installation process or from the
Product Options screen) in NetWare's INSTALL.NLM utility, the program launches
INETCFG.

The NetWare operating system includes the INETCFG.NLM utility, version 3.10.
This contains all of the functionality needed to load LAN drivers, configure the
supported protocol stacks, and bind the two together. The IntranetWare product,
however, includes Novell's Multiprotocol Router, and when you install this package
on a NetWare server, INETCFG is upgraded to version 3.30. Its functionality is then
expanded to include WAN configuration capabilities.

TIP The Novell Multiprotocol Router product is incorporated into the Novell
Internet Access Server (found on disk 3 of the IntranetWare release). The set-
tings and screens in the following sections are based on version 3.30 of the
INETCFG.NLM utility.

When launching INETCFG.NLM for the first time, the program searches the
server's AUTOEXEC.NCF file for the LOAD and BIND commands involved in the
protocol stack, and LAN-driver initialization processes. After disabling these commands in AUTOEXEC.NCF, INETCFG transfers them to its own data files (after
prompting you for confirmation). These files are located in the server's SYS:ETC
directory and, depending on the options configured, may include any of the
following:

◆ INITSYS.NCF

◆ NETINFO.CFG

◆ TCPIP.CGF

◆ NLSP.CFG

◆ IPXSPX.CFG

◆ AURP.CFG

The format of the LOAD and BIND command lines found in these files is similar
to those you create in AUTOEXEC.NCF. You can view these files to examine the
commands, but be careful not to modify them in any way, as this can render them
unusable by INETCFG.

The procedure for installing TCP/IP on a NetWare server using INETCFG is identical to performing the task manually; the program simply provides a front end for

the individual steps. Working from INETCFG's Internetworking Configuration menu (see Figure 8-4), add LAN drivers by selecting Boards, activate and configure the TCP/IP stack from the Protocols screen, and bind protocols to drivers by selecting Bindings. The following sections examine each of these screens and the options provided by INETCFG.

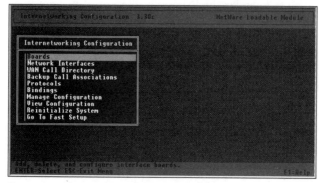

Figure 8-4: The NetWare INETCFG.NLM utility provides
menu-driven access to the server's TCP/IP configuration process.

CONFIGURING A NETWORK BOARD

Selecting Boards from INETCFG's Internetworking Configuration menu displays a list of the network-interface drivers currently installed on the server, as shown in Figure 8-5. The Configured Boards list displays a summary of the hardware parameters for each device, and its current status. When you choose a driver from the list and press Enter, a Board Configuration screen appears, containing a more detailed description of the device's properties.

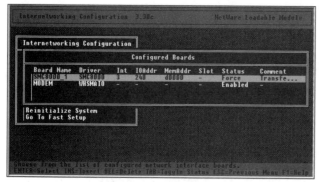

Figure 8-5: The Configured Boards screen displays a list of the
LAN drivers to be loaded on the server.

The term *board,* which is used repeatedly in INETCFG's various screens, can be something of a misnomer. INETCFG is capable of loading and configuring drivers for several different types of network interfaces that are not boards. Among these are modems and other types of communication interfaces. The Board Configuration screens for these drivers contain parameters that are appropriate for the medium.

The Board Configuration screen is concerned primarily with the hardware parameters needed to locate the physical device, as shown in Figure 8-6. Unlike the manual configuration process, the frame type is specified elsewhere. The options on the screen, as well as the text in the Driver Info field, vary depending on the type of device being supported by the driver. Where applicable, the hardware settings contain menus that let you select from among the allowed values for the parameter. INETCFG derives this information from an LDI file included with each of the LAN drivers in the NetWare package. For a driver without an LDI file, you must manually supply the values for each parameter.

Figure 8-6: Each Board Configuration screen contains the hardware settings that are applicable for the network-adapter type.

When INETCFG transfers LAN-driver command lines from the AUTOEXEC.NCF file, it notes this fact in the Comment field. You can also use this field to store any text string up to 50 characters long. The other fields in the Board Configuration screen contain a user-configurable Board Name. This corresponds to the name parameter in a driver command line, and an indicator of the board's current status. Possible values for the Board Status field are:

◆ Enabled – The Enabled setting indicates that the device driver is loaded and operational.

◆ Disabled – The Disabled setting indicates that there are no LOAD or BIND commands in INETCFG's data files,for this device-driver iteration. You can disable a particular device at will (for troubleshooting purposes, for example) by changing a driver's status to this setting.

◆ Force – The Force setting causes the driver to be loaded with all possible frame types. This is usually not necessary because INETCFG's binding process loads the required frame types as needed.

 As with any device-configuration process, the physical settings of the hardware must match those configured in the software driver. Understand that specifying hardware parameters in a Board Configuration screen does nothing but modify the commands stored in INETCFG's data files. At this point, the program cannot stop you from selecting an incorrect value for a hardware parameter because the new commands are not executed until you reinitialize the system. It is, therefore, possible to install a driver for a board that does not physically exist in the server. The absence of the hardware is detected until the driver loads and attempts to locate the board.

ADDING A NEW BOARD

When installing a new network adapter, you can choose from a list of NetWare's LAN drivers, or use the INSTALL.NLM program's hardware-detection capabilities. To add a new board driver manually, you press the Insert key from INETCFG's Configured Boards screen to display the list shown in Figure 8-7. Selecting a driver opens a Board Configuration screen, in which, you must configure the hardware parameters.

When adding a driver manually, you are responsible for selecting the correct parameters to match the hardware configuration. If two adapters of the same type are installed in the server, the same driver can be loaded twice. INETCFG does, however, detect when two drivers are configured to use the same hardware resource. The program displays an error message, and then adds the driver command line as configured. This allows you to create multiple entries for the same device, in order to test out a new driver or for any other reason. As long as one of the entries remains disabled, no problems will result.

Figure 8-7: The Select A Driver screen displays the names and descriptions of the LAN drivers included with the NetWare operating system.

If the driver for your hardware is not listed in the Select A Driver screen, or if you're installing a new (or updated) driver from the hardware manufacturer, press the Insert screen. This displays a New Driver window in which you may type the path and file name of the driver. INETCFG copies the new driver to the SYS:SYSTEM directory, and the configuration process can proceed.

Rather than select a driver manually, you can prompt NetWare to attempt to locate the hardware installed in your server, To do this, load the INSTALL.NLM program and select Configure Network Drivers from the Driver Options screen. Selecting Discover and Load Additional Drivers from the screen (see Figure 8-8) begins the detection process. This identifies the device, and then loads the appropriate driver with the proper parameters.

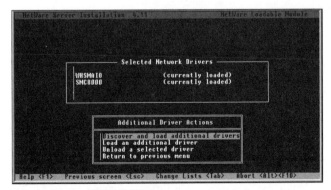

Figure 8-8: The INSTALL.NLM program contains the hardware-detection routines you use to identify the proper settings for an installed network adapter.

You can also manually select and configure a new driver from the INSTALL utility – but these processes do not cooperate with INETCFG. INSTALL operates by actually loading the selected drivers at the server-command prompt. Only when the server-configuration process is completed does the program generate AUTOEXEC.NCF and STARTUP.NCF files, from the server's command history. If the networking-configuration commands are transferred to the control of INETCFG, INSTALL is only useful in ascertaining the hardware parameters of a device already installed in the server. Once the driver is loaded, you can examine the command line to discover the parameters to set for the driver in INETCFG.

CONFIGURING THE TCP/IP PROTOCOL STACK

Selecting Protocols from INETCFG's main screen displays a list of the protocol stacks supported by NetWare, as well as their current status. When you select TCP/IP from the list, you see a protocol-configuration screen like that shown in Figure 8-9. In the simplest of environments (such as adding TCP/IP support to run the Novell Web Server on your intranet), you need only enable the protocol and proceed to the binding phase.

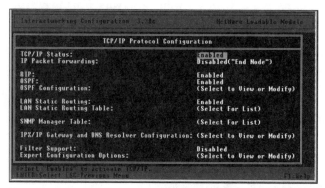

Figure 8-9: The TCP/IP Protocol Configuration screen provides access to a large number of settings and parameters.

The other options on this screen concern IP-routing issues and other specialized TCP/IP services. INETCFG activates many of these options by adding parameters to the TCPIP.NLM command line. The TCP/IP configuration parameters are as follows:

   ◆ **TCP/IP Status** – This specifies whether the TCPIP.NLM module should be loaded to enable the protocol stack. Disabling the stack with this setting unloads the module, but other parameters configured in this screen are retained.

   ◆ **IP Packet Forwarding** – This specifies whether a multihomed NetWare server should function as an IP router or an end node. The default value is disabled, unless the Multiprotocol Router product is installed on the server.

◆ RIP – RIP specifies whether the Routing Information Protocol should be used on the server for dynamic routing. When this setting is enabled and the server is configured to forward IP packets, RIP messages are transmitted and received (when functioning as an end node, RIP packets are received, only). The default value is enabled.

◆ OSPF – OSPF specifies whether the Open Shortest Path First Protocol should be used, on the server, for dynamic routing. The default value is disabled, and should only be enabled when other routers on the network are also configured to use this protocol.

OSPF Configuration

◆ Router ID – This specifies the IP address of the router within the autonomous system. When no value is supplied, INETCFG uses the first IP address bound to a network interface.

◆ Autonomous System Boundary Router – This specifies whether or not OSPF will be permitted to use routing information learned from other protocols, or static routes. The default value is disabled.

◆ Area Configuration – The area configuration provides the capability to create multiple OSPF areas within an autonomous system.

◆ Virtual Link Configuration – This provides the capability to create virtual links between OSPF areas that are not directly connected to the backbone area.

◆ IP Load Sharing – IP load sharing specifies whether OSPF should divide IP traffic among routes of equal cost. The default value is disabled.

◆ LAN Static Routing – This specifies whether or not NetWare should use manually configured routing information. The default value is disabled.

◆ LAN Static Routing Table – The LAN static routing table enables the the creation of new entries in the static routing table.

◆ SNMP Manager Table – This specifies the IP addresses of the network management systems to which NetWare should send SNMP trap messages.

IPX/IP Gateway and DNS Resolver Configuration

◆ IPX/IP Gateway – This specifies whether the Novell IPX/IP Gateway should be enabled, permitting NetWare clients to access TCP services using an IPX client.

The default value is disabled. Enabling this feature activates the following three settings:

◆ **Client Logging** – Client logging specifies whether or not client access to services through the gateway should be logged. When enabled, a file called IPXGSTAT.LOG is created at the root of the SYS: volume (here the client, the service, and the time of access are logged).

◆ **Console Messages** – This specifies the amount of information displayed on the gateway screen at the server console, and logged to the SYS:IPXGW.LOG file. The three possible values are: Errors Only, Warnings and Errors, and Informational Warnings and Errors.

◆ **Access Control** – Access control specifies whether or not access to the gateway should be restricted to specified users. The default value is enabled. Disabling this feature permits all users to access the gateway.

◆ **DNS Resolver Configuration** – This specifies the name of the domain containing this server and the IP addresses of up to three DNS servers (used for resolving host names).

◆ **Filter Options** – This specifies whether or not TCP/IP should use the packet forwarding and routing information filters, created with the FILTCFG.NLM utility. The default value is disabled.

Expert Configuration Options

◆ **Directed Broadcast Forwarding** – This specifies whether or not broadcast messages should be forwarded to a particular subnet. The default value is disabled.

◆ **Forward Source Route Packets** – This parameter specifies whether IP source route packets should be forwarded. The default value is enabled.

◆ **BOOTP Forwarding Configuration** – This specifies whether the server should function as a BOOTP relay agent, permits the specification of the IP addresses of target BOOTP servers, and the configuration of logging options.

◆ **EGP** – EGP specifies whether the Exterior Gateway Protocol should be used to transfer routing information between autonomous systems.

◆ **EGP Configuration** – This specifies the number of the AS to which this server belongs, the number of EGP neighbors with which the server can exchange information, and the IP addresses and autonomous-system numbers of those neighbors.

The dynamic routing protocols supported by NetWare, such as RIP, OSPF, and EGP, and other routing issues, are examined in Chapter 7, "The Application Layer," and Chapter 9, "Routing IP." For more information on the Novell IPX/IP Gateway, see Chapter 13, "IntranetWare TCP/IP Clients." BOOTP is examined in Chapter 10, "DHCP and IP Address Management."

BINDING DRIVERS TO PROTOCOLS

As in a manual configuration, you must select the network interfaces to be bound to the protocol stacks installed on the server. With INETCFG, you do this by selecting Bindings from the Internetwork Configuration menu, which displays a list of the Protocol to Interface/Group Bindings, as shown in Figure 8-10. Each protocol must be bound, individually, to every network interface over which it will be used. You can bind different protocols to a single network interface, and multiple interfaces to a single protocol. It is even possible to create multiple bindings of IP and the same network interface to bind the interface to multiple subnets sharing the same physical network.

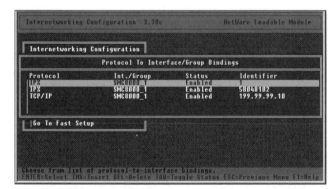

Figure 8-10: INETCFG's Bindings screen configures the BIND commands to be executed whenever the server is initialized.

INETCFG simplifies the process of creating new bindings by creating menus from the configured boards and protocols. When you press the Insert key to create a new binding, you must select one of the protocol stacks you've activated and configured in the Protocols screen, and then one of the network interfaces you've configured in the Boards screen. Once you select these basic parameters for the binding, INETCFG displays a screen like that shown in Figure 8-11, from which you can configure bind options.

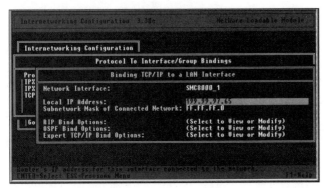

Figure 8-11: Binding TCP/IP to a LAN Interface screen provides access to the options that appear on the BIND command line.

The available options are as follows:

◆ **Local IP address** – This option specifies the IP address to be assigned to the selected network interface, in dotted decimal or hexadecimal notation. The IP address must contain the same network identifier as the network to which it is attached.

◆ **Subnetwork mask of connected network** – This specifies the subnet mask to be applied to the specified IP address, in dotted decimal or hexadecimal notation knowledgebase.

RIP Bind Options

◆ **Status** – The status option specifies whether the Routing Information Protocol is being used on this network.

◆ **Cost of Interface** – The cost of interface option specifies a preference value to be assigned to the network interface. This value is used in routing decisions to determine which interface to use when there are multiple routes available to a specified destination. Possible values range from 1 to 15, with higher values making the interface less likely to be chosen. The default value is 1.

◆ **Originate default route** – When enabled, RIP is used to advertise only the local server as the default router for the network. The default is disabled.

◆ **Poison reverse** – This option specifies whether the poison-reverse technique should be used in dynamic routing with RIP. The default value is disabled.

♦ **Split horizon** – This specifies whether the split-horizon technique should be used in dynamic routing with RIP. The default value is enabled.

♦ **Update time** – The update time option specifies the time interval (in seconds) at which RIP should transmit update messages. The default value is 30 seconds; possible values are 30 to 10,922.

♦ **Expire time** – This option specifies the time interval (in seconds) when a route (which has not been updated) should be deleted from the routing table. The default value is six times the update value; possible values are six times the update value to 65,535.

♦ **Garbage time** – The garbage time option specifies the time interval (in seconds) that a route remains in the routing table after going down. The default value is four times the update time; possible values are four times the update time to 65,535.

♦ **RIP version** – RIP version specifies whether the server is to support RIP version I or II, or both. The default value is RIPI. Selecting RIPII or RIPI & RIPII activates the RIPII options fields. In these fields, you can enable authentication between routers and specify an authentication password.

♦ **RIP mode** – This option specifies whether RIP should operate in normal, send-only, or receive-only mode. The default value is normal.

OSPF Bind Options

♦ **Status** – This specifies whether the Open Shortest Path First Protocol should be used on this network interface, overriding the general setting in the TCP/IP Protocol Configuration screen. The default value is enabled, but is ignored if the general OSPF setting is disabled.

♦ **Cost of interface** – The cost of interface option specifies the precedence to assign to this network for use by the OSPF protocol. The default value is 1; possible values are 1 to 65,535.

♦ **Area ID** – This option identifies the area with which the network is associated using dotted decimal notation. The ID for the backbone area is 0.0.0.0.

♦ **Priority** – Priority specifies the precedence for this router when multiple routers attempt to be the designated router for the network. The default value is 1; possible values are 1 to 255.

♦ **Authentication password** – The authentication password specifies the 8-byte string used when authentication is enabled for the area containing this network.

◆ **Hello interval** – This specifies the time interval (in seconds) between the transmission of hello packets on this network. The default value is 10 seconds; possible values are 1 to 65,535.

◆ **Router dead interval** – This option specifies the time interval between hello packets after which the router's neighbor should declare the router dead. The default value is 40 seconds; possible values are 1 to 7FFFFFFF (hex) seconds.

◆ **Neighbor list** – This option is used to specify the IP addresses of OSPF neighbors.

Expert TCP/IP Bind Options

◆ **Frame type** – Frame type specifies the link-layer protocol header format to be used on the selected network interface. The menu containing the possible values only displays the frame types that support TCP/IP with the link-layer protocol.

◆ **Use of ARP** – This option specifies whether the Address Resolution Protocol is used on this network. The default value is enabled.

◆ **Broadcast address** – This option specifies the IP address to be used when transmitting broadcast messages on this network. The default value is 255.255.255.255.

◆ **Multicast override IP address** – This specifies an IP address to which all multicast transmissions for this network should be sent (overriding the standard multicast transmitting technique).

◆ **Force proxy ARP** – The force proxy ARP specifies whether proxy ARP should be used on the network. The default is disabled.

◆ **Router discovery options** – This specifies whether router discovery should be enabled on the network, and whether discovery packets should be sent as broadcast or multicast transmissions. If IP packet forwarding is enabled, router discovery causes the server to advertise itself as a router; if forwarding is disabled, the server sends discovery requests to locate a router. Default values are for router discovery to be disabled, and for discovery packets to be sent using multicast transmissions.

USING FAST SETUP

NetWare provides a wealth of options in its TCP/IP implementation, as you have seen, but in most cases, the actual configuration of the protocol stack is quite simple. INETCFG also includes a Fast Setup option that enables you to configure only the base parameters needed to activate a network interface. Using a different setup paradigm from the procedure documented in the previous sections, Fast Setup lets you add a new LAN driver, or reconfigure an existing one, by interactively guiding you through the parts of the procedure. The many different options available in the other INETCFG screens are omitted here; only the essential elements remain.

Choosing Go to Fast Setup from INETCFG's main screen produces a summary of the current networking environment, as shown in Figure 8-12. By pressing Enter, you can select one of the listed boards, or choose to add a new one – which you select from the same list available in the Boards screen. Once the board is identified, the program leads you through a short series of dialogs, enabling you to configure essential parameters along the way. Once you have completed these few steps, the configuration is complete.

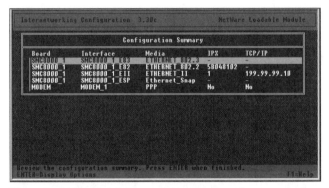

Figure 8-12: The Fast Setup option streamlines the process of configuring a new network adapter by eliminating all but the essential configuration parameters.

The screens of the Fast Setup process proceed as follows:

1. **Board configuration** – enables you to specify hardware-configuration parameters needed to locate the device installed in the server

2. **IPX configuration** – enables you to specify the frame types and IPX network numbers

3. **Run TCP/IP?** – asks whether or not the TCP/IP stack should be bound to the board driver

4. **IP Address** (if TCP/IP is to be used)

5. **Subnet Mask** (if TCP/IP is to be used)

REINITIALIZING THE SERVER

In the previous sections, the INETCFG procedures modified the parameters of the LOAD and BIND commands (executed by the server during the boot process). None of these procedures affect the active network configuration until the server is rebooted, or the networking stack reinitialized. When you select Reinitialize System from INETCFG's Internet Configuration menu, all of the networking modules currently in memory are unloaded. They are then reloaded with the new parameters, incorporating all of your changes.

When one of the LOAD or BIND commands results in an error (due to an incorrect parameter, or even a hardware failure), INETCFG switches to the server console screen, so you can view the results of the command.

Installing TCP/IP on Windows NT 4.0

Unlike NetWare, Windows NT 4.0 defaults to using TCP/IP as its primary protocol stack. The OS is capable of using any of three stacks for its basic networking service, while NetWare relies on its native IPX protocols. You are, therefore, more likely to have TCP/IP installed, along with the Windows NT OS, than with NetWare.

Installing TCP/IP on a Windows NT server follows the same basic steps as a NetWare installation. The interface provides the primary differences. You must select a driver for each network-interface adapter in the system, install and configure the TCP/IP protocol module, and then bind the two together. The protocol and adapter driver provide the transport-, internet-, and link-layer functionality that Windows NT services use for network communications.

In Windows NT, "service" is a technical term that describes an application process. This process launches whenever the OS is started, and runs continuously in the background. Many of Windows NT's TCP/IP applications (including the DNS, DHCP, and Internet Information Server) run as services. The Server, Workstation, and Browser modules that provide NT's core Windows networking functions (such as file and printer access) also run as services. These modules, however, can use the NetBEUI or NWLink protocol stacks as easily as TCP/IP, as shown in Figure 8-13.

 Because Windows NT is a peer-to-peer OS, every machine (whether running NT Server or Workstation) functions as both a client a and server. This, and the more complete integration of TCP/IP into NT's core networking architecture, makes the protocol-installation process on a server similar to that of a workstation. The primary differences between the two products are the additional programs and services included with Windows NT server, which are installed separately.

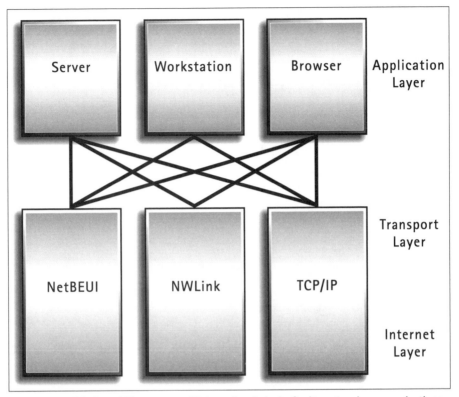

Figure 8-13: Windows NT can use multiple protocol stacks for its network communications, but TCP/IP is the default.

All of Windows NT's networking functions are configured from the Network Control Panel, shown in Figure 8-14. This dialog box contains tabbed pages in which you can install and configure different networking components, and control their interaction.

Installing a Network Adapter

Like NetWare, Windows NT uses device drivers to address your server's network-interface hardware. These drivers can be used with any of the protocol stacks supported by the OS. Instead of ODI, Windows NT uses the Network Device Interface Specification (NDIS) as the basis for its adapter drivers. NDIS functions as a universal interface between the network and data link layers (which, in TCP/IP parlance, are the internet and link layers). It directs the data, traveling down the networking stack to the appropriate network interface, no matter which protocol is used.

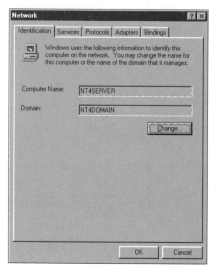

Figure 8-14: The Network Control Panel is
the central administration point for the
entire Windows NT networking architecture.

The Windows NT 4.0 OS installation process, while not supporting the Plug and
Play standards, can identify most network adapters and install the correct drivers.
When you must install an additional adapter driver, open the Adapters page of the
Network Control Panel and click the Add button. After selecting the appropriate
driver for your device (see Figure 8-15), a configuration dialog box appears. This
contains hardware settings suited to the adapter type, like the one shown in
Figure 8-16. To add an unlisted device, click the Have Disk button and navigate to
the location of the INF file included with the device driver.

 Windows NT 4.0 requires network-adapter drivers that are written to the
NDIS 4.0 specification. These are different from the drivers used by Windows
NT 3.5x, which are written to NDIS version 3.0, and Windows 95 (NDIS 3.1).

Once the adapter driver is installed and configured, it is automatically bound to
all of the protocol stacks installed in the system. Unlike NetWare, Windows NT's
default assumes that all of the networking modules should be configured to work
with each other. If TCP/IP is installed when you add a new adapter, you are
prompted to specify an IP address and subnet mask for the new interface. You must
specify that an adapter not be bound to a specific protocol to limit the network
traffic that can use a particular interface.

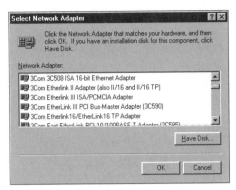

Figure 8-15: Windows NT includes drivers for most of the popular network adapters on the market today.

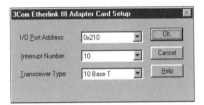

Figure 8-16: Each NDIS adapter driver includes a customized configuration dialog box with the appropriate settings for the hardware.

Installing the TCP/IP Protocol

The Network Control Panel refers to TCP/IP as a protocol, when it is a suite of protocols. (The RFCs supported by Windows NT's TCP/IP implementation are listed in Appendix A, "RFCs Supported by Windows NT and IntranetWare.") You install the basic TCP/IP transport- and internet-layer services from the Protocols page of the Network Control Panel. Simply click the Add button and select the TCP/IP module from the list provided. This module also contains client support for application-layer protocols like DNS, DHCP, and WINS, the Windows NT NetBIOS name server.

As with an adapter installation, adding the TCP/IP protocols causes the stack to bind to all the network interfaces installed in the system. The Network Control Panel also recognizes the relationships between the networking modules — automatically installing the elements needed to support the services, protocols, or adapters that you select. For example, if you add the TCP/IP protocol and there are no adapters installed, you are prompted to select one. In the same way, if you install a service that requires TCP/IP, NT automatically adds the protocol.

Once the TCP/IP module is added to the networking configuration (whether by the operating systems SETUP program, a manual addition, or the installation of a related module), you must configure it using the Microsoft TCP/IP Properties dialog box, shown in Figure 8-17. This dialog box consists of tabbed pages containing the TCP/IP client-configuration parameters for each of the network interfaces in the system. The following sections cover the parameters on these pages, and their functions.

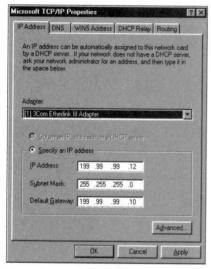

Figure 8-17: The TCP/IP Properties dialog box contains all of Windows NT's TCP/IP client configuration settings.

CONFIGURING IP ADDRESSES

The IP Address page of the TCP/IP Properties dialog box contains the parameters that are essential to the protocol stack's operation. The Adapter selector lets you choose the network interface that you want to configure, from the adapter drivers installed in the system. The parameters on the IP Address page are as follows:

◆ **IP Address** – This parameter specifies the unique 32-bit IP address to be assigned to the network interface, which appears in the Adapter field (in dotted decimal notation).

◆ **Subnet mask** – This specifies the proper subnet mask to apply to the specified IP address. This determines which of the address' bits identify the network to which the adapter is connected, and which bits identify the host.

◆ **Default gateway** – This parameter specifies the IP address of the system to be the default router for the IP packets, transmitted out through the selected interface, that are destined for other networks.

Each interface, on a multihomed system, must have its own IP address and subnet mask. A default gateway is not required because the network may consist of only a single segment.

ACTIVATING THE DHCP CLIENT   Selecting the Obtain an IP Address from a DHCP Server radio button activates Windows NT's DHCP client, causing it to broadcast requests to DHCP servers on the network. A properly configured DHCP server can supply a Windows NT system with all the client-configuration information necessary for TCP/IP communications. This eliminates the need to set any parameters in the TCP/IP Properties dialog box.

If your network uses DHCP, any values left in the TCP/IP Properties dialog box, when the DHCP client is activated, will override the settings supplied by the server. It is not possible for the same system to be both a DHCP client and a DHCP server. If you plan to run Windows NT's DHCP-server service on the system, you must configure the TCP/IP client manually.

For more information on DHCP and automatic TCP/IP client configuration, see Chapter 10,"DHCP and IP Address Management."

CONFIGURING ADVANCED IP ADDRESS OPTIONS   When you click the Advanced button on the IP Address page, you see the Advanced IP Addressing dialog box, shown in Figure 8-18. You can specify additional IP addresses to assign to each network interface, as well as additional default gateway addresses. This dialog box is a superset of the IP Address page. Any IP address, subnet mask, and default gateway settings configured there also appear in this box.

By assigning multiple IP addresses to a single interface, the networks on which different subnets share the same physical-network segment are supported. Multiple addresses may be necessary when you want to host independent web sites on the same server.

Specifying the IP addresses of additional gateways is intended as a fault-tolerance mechanism for the TCP/IP client (when there are multiple gateways on the network segment, to which the adapter is attached). If the first gateway listed goes down, IP packets are sent to the second router in the list. You can specify up to five gateways for each installed adapter.

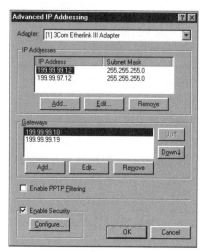

Figure 8-18: The Advanced IP Addressing
dialog box enables you to specify multiple
addresses and gateways for each installed
adapter.

PACKET FILTERING   The Enable PPTP Filtering checkbox (on the Advanced IP
Addressing dialog box) prevents all traffic, not using the Point-to-Point Tunneling
Protocol, from entering the system through the specified interface. You can create
a *virtual private network* (VPN) with a Windows NT system by connecting to the
Internet and implementing PPTP. This provides secure, encrypted network commu-
nications to remote users or networks.

Essentially, a VPN replaces the leased lines normally used for wide area networking with the Internet. Two systems connect to a different local ISP and communicate by transmitting their normal WAN traffic over the Internet – which is
secured by the use of PPTP. Windows NT's PPTP filtering feature prevents intruders
from using the Internet connection to gain unauthorized access to your network.

You can also filter out other types of TCP/IP traffic by enabling security from
the Advanced IP Addressing dialog box. The security feature lets your NT server
function as a rudimentary firewall by allowing only traffic using specific ports
and/or protocols to enter and exit the system. In the TCP/IP Security dialog box
(see Figure 8-19), you control the traffic passing through the interface. Simply
select the TCP and UDP port numbers, and the IP protocol-code numbers that
TCP/IP packets must use to access the device specified in the Adapter field.

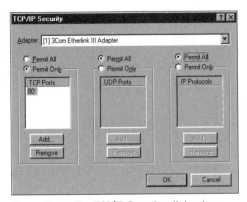

Figure 8-19: The TCP/IP Security dialog box provides filters that restrict network access to traffic destined for specific protocols and ports.

CONFIGURING DNS OPTIONS

On the DNS page of the TCP/IP properties dialog box (see Figure 8-20), you specify the IP addresses of the DNS servers the system should use to resolve Internet host names into IP addresses. Unlike the parameters in the IP Address page, the DNS settings are applied to the whole system – and not to a specified adapter. Configuring the DNS settings is not required for the operation of the TCP/IP stack. If the Windows NT system is not connected to the Internet, DNS is rarely needed as host names are probably not used. Also, if the system connects to the Internet using Windows NT's Dial-up Networking feature, you specify the DNS servers used elsewhere on that connection (or obtain them from your ISP).

In the Host Name and Domain fields, you insert the name assigned to your system and the domain in which it resides. The host name need not be the same as the NetBIOS name (assigned to the system during the Windows NT installation process), although administrators often use the same name for the sake of convenience. In fact, these two fields have no direct bearing on the communications process, and can be omitted without ill effects. When the host name field is left blank, the system defaults to the NetBIOS name for the host.

In the DNS Service Search Order field, you specify the addresses of the DNS servers that the system should use. These servers can be located anywhere on your internetwork, or if you are connected to the Internet, on any accessible network. If your organization does not host its own Internet services, it won't need to run a DNS server (it can use the services of your ISP, instead). Because DNS is a distributed-database system, you can resolve any registered host name using any DNS server on the Internet. Of course, having a DNS server on the premises will speed up the name-resolution process.

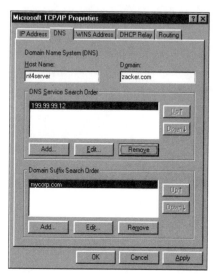

Figure 8-20: The DNS page of the TCP/IP
Properties dialog box specifies the addresses
of resolvers. These are used to discover the
IP addresses of destination systems.

The Windows NT system sends name-resolution requests to the alternate DNS servers on the list when the first server cannot be reached. You can modify the order of the addresses in the list using the Up and Down buttons.

The Domain Suffix Search Order field hosts commonly used domain-name suffixes that are appended to host names, when no domain is supplied. If, for example, you must access the web server at *www.mycorp.com* several times each day, you can add *mycorp.com* to the suffix list. Then, if you simply type *www* in your web browser, the *mycorp.com* suffix is automatically added to the host name. You can specify up to five suffixes in the list, and adjust the order with the Up and Down buttons, as needed.

CONFIGURING WINS ADDRESS OPTIONS

WINS is the Windows Internet Naming Service, a name-resolution service included with Windows NT Server. It performs the same function for NetBIOS names that DNS does for host names. A system's NetBIOS name is the computer name assigned to it during system installation. Windows NT uses NetBIOS names for all its resource-sharing activities. A shared drive, for example, is identified on the network using a Universal Naming Convention (UNC) – a name consisting of the NetBIOS name and the share name, such as *\\nt4server\cdrive*.

WINS is not an alternative to DNS, but a complement to it. DNS is used on the Internet, and WINS is used on private internetworks. For more information about DNS and WINS name resolution in Windows NT and IntranetWare, see Chapter 11, "Name Registration and Resolution."

If your network uses WINS, you use the WINS Address page of the TCP/IP Properties dialog box to identify WINS servers for the system to use in resolving NetBIOS names (see Figure 8-21). Unlike the DNS page, you specify WINS servers, individually, for the installed adapters. The system only accesses the secondary server when the primary is unreachable.

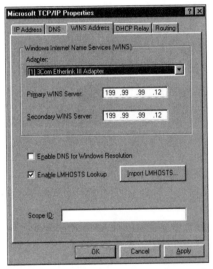

Figure 8-21: You specify the addresses of WINS servers that will resolve NetBIOS names into IP addresses, for TCP/IP communications.

By checking the Enable DNS for Windows Resolution checkbox, you may use Internet host names in place of NetBIOS names, in UNC paths. Referring to a share as \\nt4server.mycorp.com\cdrive would use DNS to resolve the server name, instead of WINS. This option also enables NT to use DNS servers and the HOSTS file to resolve NetBIOS names (should the standard NetBIOS name resolution methods fail).

The LMHOSTS file is the NetBIOS equivalent to the HOSTS file that was the original host name resolution method. Like HOSTS, it is a text file containing names and their equivalent IP addresses. Normally, LMHOSTS must be maintained on each individual system, but the Enable LMHOSTS Lookup feature permits you to import a file from a central location on a network server.

The Scope ID is a rarely used NetBIOS feature. It enables you to define a group of systems that can only communicate with each other. A system can have only one scope ID, no matter how many adapters are installed.

CONFIGURING DHCP RELAY OPTIONS

Windows NT Server can function as a DHCP or BOOTP relay agent, forwarding the DHCP broadcasts (generated by clients on the local network) to selected DHCP servers on other networks. Broadcast transmissions cannot pass through routers to other networks, so the relay agent sends them as unicasts to specific servers. You must list these servers in the DHCP Relay page of the TCP/IP Properties dialog box, shown in Figure 8-22. This way, a DHCP server can assign client-configuration settings to clients on other networks, eliminating the need for a server on every segment.

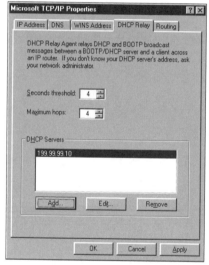

Figure 8-22: DHCP relay agents enable a single DHCP server to provide for clients on many different network segments.

The Seconds Threshold and Maximum Hops parameters control the distance over which the relay agent can send messages. In the DHCP Servers field, you enter the IP addresses of the servers on other networks that you want to service the DHCP clients, on the local network.

Apart from these configuration parameters, the DHCP relay agent requires the installation of a TCP/IP service (which is included in the NT Server package). If you add IP addresses to the DHCP Servers field, Control Panel will attempt to install the service when you close or apply changes to the dialog box.

WINDOWS NT ROUTING

The Routing page of the TCP/IP Properties dialog box contains only a single check-box. By checking it, you enable IP forwarding between multiple adapters. When unchecked, the server functions as a multihomed end host, connected to multiple networks. The other elements of Windows NT's routing capabilities are implemented as separate modules. RIP, for example, must be installed separately, as a network service, although it is included with the OS. Microsoft released an upgrade to the routing functionality of Windows NT 4.0, called the *Routing and Remote Access Service Update for Windows NT*. It is available as a free download from the Microsoft web site at http://www.microsoft.com/ntserver/info/routing&ras.htm.

Unlike NetWare, the drivers for dial-up, X.25, and other types of WAN connections don't appear in the adapters listing of the TCP/IP Properties dialog box. Instead, you configure them by using Windows NT's Dial-up Networking feature. These connections function just like network interfaces, in terms of routing and binding.

Binding Networking Modules

In Windows NT, binding is a more complex process than in NetWare – which defines the relationship between protocols and LAN drivers. The Bindings page in the Network Control Panel displays the relationships between all services, protocols, and adapters installed on the system. In this three-tiered architecture, protocols provide transport for services, and adapters provide network access to protocols. The Bindings page lets you sort the often-complex relationships between these elements. The page enables you to view a list of all services, all protocols, or all adapters, and to expand each entry to display its related modules (see Figure 8-23).

By default, all networking components installed on the system are bound together – that is, all of the installed adapters are configured to use all of the installed protocols. Some services are designed for a specific protocol, such as the Windows NT DHCP server, which must use TCP/IP. Others, however, can use various protocols, and are bound to each of the stacks that support the service.

You can fine-tune the networking environment on the NT system by unbinding certain modules, or modifying the order in which they are bound. For example, you can unbind the TCP/IP protocol (from an adapter that is attached to an IPX-only network) by highlighting the connection and clicking the Disable button. This permits you to disable specific modules, for troubleshooting purposes, without removing them entirely and losing your configuration parameters.

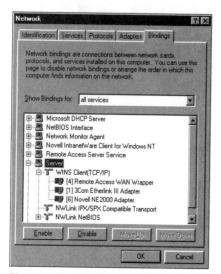

Figure 8-23: The Bindings screen enables you to view and modify the relationships between Windows NT's networking module.

The order in which modules are bound to each other is also significant to your network's performance. For example, NT's resource-sharing communications can use any of the operating system's supported protocols. If you have NWLink installed for IPX access to NetWare servers, as well as the TCP/IP protocol stack, the Server and Workstation services will use whichever of the two protocols they are bound to, for their communications needs. If, in the Bindings page, NWLink appears first in the bindings to these services, and you want to use TCP/IP as your primary networking protocol, you can change the configuration by dragging and dropping the TCP/IP protocol above NWLink.

Summary

Both Windows NT 4.0 and IntranetWare provide server TCP/IP protocol stacks that are easily implemented. They also provide a wealth of options for advanced networking configurations.

In this chapter, you learned:

◆ How to manually implement TCP/IP on a NetWare server using the LOAD and BIND commands

◆ How to use NetWare's INETCFG.NLM utility as a front end to the TCP/IP configuration process

◆ How to configure Windows NT's TCP/IP stack from the Network Control Panel

The following chapter examines the process by which TCP/IP traffic is routed to systems on remote networks. In it, you find information on the specialized routing protocols and manually configured static routes that make the process possible.

Chapter 9

Routing IP

IN THIS CHAPTER

Routing traffic between networks is one of the primary functions of TCP/IP. The protocols were designed for use on an internetwork far larger than that of any private organization. Compared to an Ethernet LAN, on which packets may pass through three or four routers on their way to a destination, Internet traffic is routed through 15 or more networks. The sheer number of networks on the Internet stretches the routing capabilities of the protocols to their limits. It is a fine reflection on TCP/IP's developers that their designs continue to function on an internetwork that has grown to enormous proportions.

This chapter examines the process by which TCP/IP systems determine the route for each IP datagram, including the following:

◆ How TCP/IP systems use a table of routing information to determine the next destination for every IP packet transmitted by the system

◆ How you can add entries to a system's routing table, manually, to customize your network communications

◆ How routing tables are dynamically updated using ICMP messages and specialized routing protocols

◆ How to configure the routing capabilities of Windows NT and IntranetWare

The Routing Process

When TCP/IP data is passed down a system's protocol stack, for transmission over a network, an important decision must be made as the packet passes from the IP protocol (at the internet layer) to the data link-layer protocol. IP datagrams are always addressed to the system that is the ultimate destination for the data. This destination system may be a machine on the same subnet as the sender, or on a network half a world away.

The data link-layer protocol can only transmit to systems located on the same network segment. IP must specify the system on the local network to which the data link-layer protocol should transmit the datagram (so that it can be routed to its final destination). For example, when a computer on an Ethernet LAN attempts to connect to a Web site on the Internet, the packets generated by the IP protocol contain the address of the Web server (the destination) located on another network, somewhere on the Internet. IP must supply a destination on the local network for the Ethernet driver, and select the address of a system that functions as a router, or gateway, between the local LAN and the Internet (see Figure 9-1).

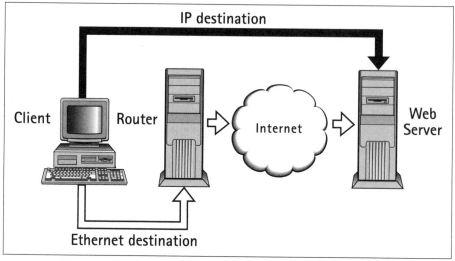

Figure 9–1: IP specifies the address of the system on the local network to which the data link-layer protocol should transmit each frame.

 In traditional networking parlance, the term *gateway* refers to a system that routes data between two networks, while translating between two network-layer protocols. The terminology in the TCP/IP standards, and in this chapter, uses the term *gateway* as a synonym for *router*. It is a system that forwards the packets received through one interface out through another interface.

When the data reaches the specified router, the same process begins again. The packets are transmitted to another router, which, in turn, provides access to another network. Eventually, the data wends its way to a router connected to the network, on which the Web server is located, and the packets are transmitted to their destination. Considering the Internet consists of thousands of networks merged with a vast, tangled maze of connections, and this routing process can occur over 20 times for every TCP/IP packet transmitted, you can see the enormity of the task.

The fundamental problem with the routing process is that a TCP/IP system has a choice of two or more routers on the local subnet, to which it can send its packets.

The system may have a choice between a router that provides access to the destination system and one that doesn't. Or it may be that both routers provide a path to the destination, but one provides a more efficient path. A system must have a mechanism for intelligently determining which router is the best choice for a transmission to a particular destination. This mechanism takes the form of a list of network addresses and associated gateway systems called a *routing table*.

Routing Tables

Every TCP/IP system uses the routing table to store information needed to make routing decisions. The table consists of entries that tell the IP protocol which router to use to ensure that the packets reach a particular host or network. Routing tables are not only found on systems that function as routers. Even a host system with a single network interface must select the proper router for its data transmissions.

On a Windows system configured as a TCP/IP client, you can display the routing table's contents by issuing the ROUTE PRINT command at the DOS prompt. This command produces a display similar to the following:

```
Network Address          Netmask  Gateway Address       Interface  Metric
        0.0.0.0          0.0.0.0   211.52.54.144   211.52.54.146      1
      127.0.0.0        255.0.0.0       127.0.0.1       127.0.0.1      1
     211.52.54.0    255.255.255.0   211.52.54.146   211.52.54.146      1
   211.52.54.146  255.255.255.255       127.0.0.1       127.0.0.1      1
   211.52.54.255  255.255.255.255   211.52.54.146   211.52.54.146      1
        224.0.0.0        224.0.0.0   211.52.54.146   211.52.54.146      1
  255.255.255.255  255.255.255.255   211.52.54.146         0.0.0.0      1
```

This display was generated on a system with a single network interface, with the IP address 211.52.54.146. Each table entry contains the following information:

◆ Network address – This entry specifies the host or network address for which routing information is to be provided.

◆ Netmask – The netmask entry specifies the subnetwork mask to be applied to the network address. This identifies which bits are the network, the subnet, and the host.

◆ Gateway address – This entry specifies the IP address of the router (or gateway) that the system should use to transmit data to the specified network address. When the network address field contains a local network destination, the gateway address field specifies the IP address of the local system's interface.

◆ Interface – This entry specifies the IP address of the network interface in the local system that should be used to transmit data to the specified gateway address.

♦ Metric – The metric entry specifies the number of hops needed to reach the destination identified by the network address.

In a routing table entry, the network address column identifies either a host system or a network, depending on the value in the netmask column. When a TCP/IP-application process generates data for transmission to another system, the IP protocol examines the destination IP address for each packet. It then searches the routing table for an entry matching all, or part, of that address. This procedure occurs in the following four stages:

1. IP searches the routing table for a host address that matches the destination IP address of each packet, exactly.

2. If the routing table does not contain a matching host address, IP searches for an address that matches the destination network and subnet identifiers.

3. If the routing table does not contain a matching network address, IP searches for the entry defining the default gateway address.

4. If the routing table does not define a default gateway address, a *destination unreachable* error message is returned to the application process that generated the data.

THE DEFAULT GATEWAY

On a simple TCP/IP client system with a single network interface, the majority of IP packets are transmitted to the default gateway system on the local network. In the preceding (sample) routing table, the default gateway is defined by the entry with a network address and netmask of 0.0.0.0. The entry instructs IP to send all packets with destinations that are not identified in the table to the gateway system with the IP address 211.52.54.144. Because the client system has only one network adapter, the interface value must be the IP address of that adapter. A metric value of 1 indicates that the specified gateway is located on the same network segment as the transmitting system.

IP then passes the datagram to the data link-layer protocol (in this case, Ethernet). The IP header, as always, contains the IP address of the datagram's final destination, but the IP protocol also furnishes the data link layer with the IP address of the default gateway system specified in the routing table. The gateway system's IP address is then resolved into a hardware address by an ARP transaction, and the datagram is encapsulated within an Ethernet frame (which specifies the gateway system as the destination). This is known as an *indirect route* because the IP destination differs from the Ethernet destination. When the packet reaches the gateway system, the Ethernet frame is stripped away, and the entire process begins again – the system reads the destination IP address and searches its own routing table.

DIRECT ROUTES

When a TCP/IP system is connected to a LAN, it communicates with other systems located on the same network segment, at times. To do this, the IP protocol finds a network address that matches the local subnet in the routing table. In the sample, the table entry with the network address 211.52.54.0 is used whenever the system transmits datagrams with a destination IP address containing the same network identifier (211.52.54). This entry instructs IP to transmit the packets using the gateway address 211.52.54.146 – the local network interface.

In this case, the destination furnished to the data link layer is the same as that in the IP header because the target system is located on the local network. Again, the system uses ARP to discover the target system's hardware address, and the Ethernet frame can be transmitted to its final destination, directly. Because the Ethernet frame's destination address identifies the same system as the IP header's destination address (see Figure 9-2), this is called a *direct route*.

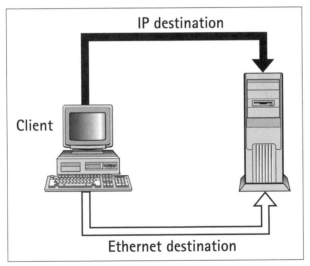

Figure 9-2: When IP locates the address of the local network in the routing table, it supplies the data link–layer protocol with the IP address of the destination system, called a direct route.

HOST ROUTES

Although it is rare, it is possible for IP to find the exact host address of the destination system during its first search of the routing table. If, for example, a system on the local network functions as a gateway to a remote server connected by a point-to-point link, there might be a routing table entry similar to the following:

```
Network Address          Netmask  Gateway Address      Interface  Metric
 206.119.87.199      255.255.255.0   211.52.54.149     211.52.54.146      1
```

This entry informs the IP protocol that it must use an indirect route – through the gateway on the local network with the address 211.52.54.149 – to reach the remote system with the IP address 206.119.87.199.

Two of the other entries in the routing table are used when the system addresses IP datagrams to itself. The system's own IP address is listed, as well as the standard loopback network address, 127.0.0.0. In each case, the table entry instructs the IP protocol to use the system's loopback interface, 127.0.0.1, for these transmissions. This ensures that the data is passed directly to the IP input queue, rather than exiting the system.

BROADCASTS AND MULTICASTS

The remaining entries in the sample routing table process broadcast and multicast transmissions. All of the class D IP addresses, ranging from 224.0.0.0 to 239.255.255.255, are reserved for multicast identifiers. The group addresses, that have been formally registered in the "Assigned Numbers" RFC, fall under the 224.0.0.0 network address. This is why a 224.0.0.0 entry is always added to a Windows system's routing table. In addition, the standard 255.255.255.255 broadcast address, and the broadcast address for the local network (211.52.54.255, in this case), are also entered in the table. All of these entries require the system's network interface to act as the gateway because all transmissions are directed to systems on the local network.

IP Routers

The role of a system functioning as an IP router is a good deal more complex than that of a single-host client system, but the basic principles remain. A router has interfaces to two or more TCP/IP networks, and is responsible for receiving datagrams through one interface and transmitting them out through another (a process known as *IP forwarding*). An IP router can be a specialized hardware device dedicated entirely to forwarding network traffic, or it can be a standard PC running a network OS like NetWare or Windows NT. No matter what hardware configuration is used, however, a router still bases its forwarding decisions on the contents in its routing table.

The routing table in a router is usually more complex than that of the routing table in a host system. Not only are there more entries, but the Interface column takes on a greater significance, as the router has a choice of network interfaces to transmit data. The complexity of IP forwarding, however, involves the mechanisms by which routing information is added to the table – rather than the actual data receipt and transmission processes.

The nature of the networks to which a router is connected determines the amount of information that is needed in its routing table. For example, when a private internetwork is connected to the Internet, the router between the two has a relatively simple job. A default gateway entry in the routing table forwards all of the incoming traffic to the Internet (except for the packets addressed to systems using the registered network address of the private organization). This type of router is not heavily burdened because it only has to watch for a single network address and send everything else to the default gateway. The router has no real information about the network on which the destination system is located; it simply "passes the buck" to the next router up the line.

Somewhere, however, the buck has to stop. Datagrams cannot reach their destinations on a network as complex as the Internet by using default gateway addresses at every router along the journey. The truly complex IP routing is performed by systems, at the top-level routing domains, that form the backbones of the Internet. These systems have huge tables that contain routing information for most of the networks on the Internet. They are capable of making intelligent forwarding decisions for the data that passes through them.

The difference in capabilities of Internet routers is easily demonstrated by using a traceroute program like TRACERT.EXE (which is included with all of the Windows network OSs). TRACERT uses ICMP transmissions to identify the routers forwarding datagrams, on their way to a specific destination. If you run the TRACERT program with an IP address that does not exist on the Internet, you see results like the following:

```
Tracing route to 194.183.19.1 over a maximum of 30 hops

  1     1 ms    <10 ms     1 ms   211.52.54.144
  2     *        *          *     Request timed out.
  3   138 ms   134 ms    132 ms   core1-ether0.garde.NY.isp.net [204.70.83.50]
  4   139 ms   137 ms    133 ms   core3-serial1.newyo.NY.isp.net [204.70.54.121]
  5   138 ms   137 ms    133 ms   core1-ether0.newyo.NY.isp.net [204.70.74.1]
  6   171 ms   153 ms    148 ms   core1-serial0.bedfo.MA.isp.net [204.70.54.101]
  7   152 ms   183 ms    144 ms   core-fddi4-0.bedfo.MA.isp.net [179.60.185.1]
  8   157 ms   151 ms    144 ms   903.Hssi3-0.GW1.BOS1.ALTER.NET [137.39.135.113]
903.Hssi3-0.GW1.BOS1.ALTER.NET [137.39.135.113]  reports: Destination host
  unreachable.
Trace complete.
```

Although the requested IP address is invalid, the datagrams had to complete nine hops to reach the router containing information necessary to reject the address and generate a host unreachable message. All of the previous routers relied on default gateway addresses to pass the data to a gateway with sufficient information to forward the packets intelligently.

For more information on traceroute programs and how they work, see Chapter 14, "TCP/IP Utilities."

Routing and ICMP

The *Internet Control Message Protocol* (ICMP) is a critical element in the IP routing process. Routers generate ICMP messages to inform source systems of various errors encountered during the routing process. They also furnish updated routing information to both host systems and to other routers. Systems receiving the ICMP messages can react by passing the error information up the protocol stack where the application can generate an error message to the user, or by updating their routing tables to avoid repeating the same action.

For more information on the structure and formation of ICMP messages, see Chapter 5, "The Internet Layer."

ROUTING ERRORS

When an IP router forwards datagrams from one network to another, the network traffic does not go beyond the network layer in the system's protocol stack. The router remains unaware of the data carried within the datagrams and makes no assumptions regarding the upper-layer protocols' reliability. Routers, therefore, are responsible for notifying the system where a datagram originated when packets cannot be forwarded. These notifications take the form of ICMP error messages, which are transmitted directly back to the source system.

ICMP error messages are generated by routers under the following conditions:

◆ **Network unreachable (type 3/code 0)** – This message occurs when the routing table contains no default gateway entry, or entry with a network or host address matching the datagram's destination IP address.

◆ **Network unreachable for TOS (type 3/code 11)** – This message occurs when the routing table contains no default gateway entry, or entry with a network or host address matching the datagram's destination IP address (specifying the same type-of-service as the datagram, or the default type-of-service).

♦ **Host unreachable (type 3/code 1)** – This message occurs when the router determines there is no valid path to a destination address on a network directly connected to that router. Usually, the router makes this determination after transmitting ARP request packets to the destination address and receiving no replies.

♦ **Host unreachable for TOS (type 3/code12)** – This occurs when the router determines there is no valid path to a destination address on a network directly connected to the router with the same type-of-service as the datagram (or the default type-of-service).

♦ **Time exceeded (type 11/code 0)** – The time exceeded message occurs when a datagram, awaiting forwarding, arrives at the router with a value of one in the time-to-live field of the IP header.

♦ **Fragmentation needed but don't fragment bit set (type 3/code 4)** – This message occurs when a datagram arrives at the router, but is too large to be forwarded to a particular network without fragmentation. In this case, the Don't Fragment bit is set in its IP header.

♦ **Source quench (type 4/code 0)** – This message occurs when incoming traffic arrives at a router at an overwhelming rate, and it causes the system to discard packets.

The Internet standards state that routers should not generate ICMP source quench messages, but they do not prohibit them. When a router implementation requires this flow-control method, the rate at which the system generates the messages must be configurable to limit the network bandwidth, and the processing cycles used by them.

REDIRECT ERRORS

Most ICMP error messages are generated by routers when IP datagrams must be discarded due to a lack of routing information, a system outage, or a configuration problem. One exception to this occurs when the router returns an ICMP message to the sender while successfully forwarding the datagram. The ICMP redirect messages inform a sending system of a more efficient route to a particular destination than the one being employed.

While there are many complex methods, and protocols, used by TCP/IP systems to exchange routing information, the ICMP redirect message is actually rather simple. The message is generated when a router receives a datagram through one of its network interfaces and, after consulting its routing table, forwards the datagram to another gateway (or host). It uses the same interface (see Figure 9-3) router where

A informs the client that its transmission should be sent to router B, instead. In other words, router A determines that it has functioned as an unnecessary middle-man, and that the sender could have transmitted the packet directly to router B, eliminating one hop from the trip.

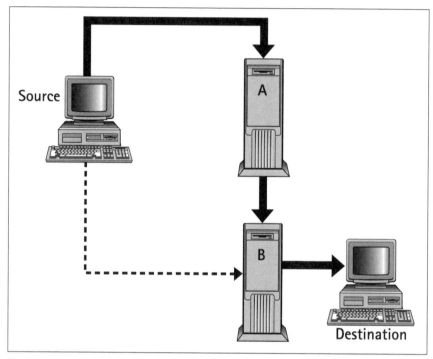

Figure 9-3: Routers use ICMP redirect messages to instruct host systems to update their routing tables.

The router forwards the datagram in the normal manner, but also sends an ICMP redirect message back to the sending system. This contains the IP address of the gateway that the sender should use when transmitting to that destination. A router cannot generate a redirect message unless all of the following conditions are met:

◆ The router forwards the datagram using the same network interface through which it arrived.

◆ The system that originally transmitted the datagram is located on the same network as the gateway system to which it is being routed.

◆ The recipient of the redirect message is located on the same subnet as the router generating the message.

◆ The IP header of the datagram does not contain a source route option.

The ICMP standard defines the redirect message as having a value of 5 in its type field, and one of the following values in its code field:

- ◆ **0 – Redirect datagrams for the network** – This value indicates that the gateway address (specified in the redirect message) should be used for transmissions to all hosts on the network (specified in the destination IP address of the original datagram).

- ◆ **1 – Redirect datagrams for the host** – This value indicates that the gateway address (specified in the redirect message) should be used for all transmissions to the host (specified in the destination IP address of the original datagram).

- ◆ **2 – Redirect for type-of-service and network** – This value indicates that the gateway address (specified in the redirect message) should be used for transmissions to all hosts on the network (specified in the original datagram's destination IP address) that use the same, or the default, type-of-service value in the IP header.

- ◆ **3 – Redirect for type-of-service and host** – This indicates that the gateway address (specified in the redirect message) should be used for all transmissions to the host (specified in the destination IP address of the original datagram) that use the same, or the default, type-of-service value in the IP header.

Routers are prohibited from generating ICMP redirect messages with the code types 0 and 2 by RFC1812, the "Requirements for IP Version 4 Routers" document. This is due to the ambiguity imposed by the subnetting process on the gateway address contained in the redirect message. Without a sure indication of the subnet mask to be applied to the gateway address, the recipient of the message cannot ascertain the network address with any certainty.

The host system receiving the ICMP redirect message uses the information contained in the packet to update its routing table with the new gateway address supplied by the router. Like all ICMP errors, the redirect message contains the beginning of the datagram that caused the error in its data field. By reading the destination IP address from the original datagram's IP header, the host determines whether an existing entry in its routing table must be modified, or whether a new entry must be added.

A host implementation may also perform a series of checks before updating its routing table. This is done to ensure that the information supplied by the router is valid and correct. For example, the host may read the source IP address from the redirect message's IP header (the router's address), and consult the routing table to verify that the entry for the original datagram's destination specifies that router in the gateway address field.

In most cases, ICMP redirect messages are generated in response to host transmissions using a default gateway address. These messages only occur when the host has multiple routers to choose from on the local subnet. The process enables host systems to build a more efficient routing table over time, without using a dynamic-routing protocol. ICMP redirects are not intended for transmission to other routers, as it is assumed that routers already use another (more efficient) method of obtaining routing information. If a router is not configured to use another method, however, it may use redirect messages.

ROUTER DISCOVERY MESSAGES

RFC1256 defines another method for updating static routes using extensions to the ICMP standard. These extensions take the form of two additional message types used to advertise the routers on the local network, and to request advertisements from routers. A TCP/IP client supporting this method would multicast, or broadcast, a router solicitation message (ICMP type 10) to the local network upon restart. All routers on the subnet that receive the message transmit their own router advertisement messages (type 9). The client uses the information in the advertisement message to create a default gateway entry in its routing table.

The router solicitation message contains no special fields; the message type defines its entire purpose. Figure 9-4 illustrates how the router advertisement message is formatted.

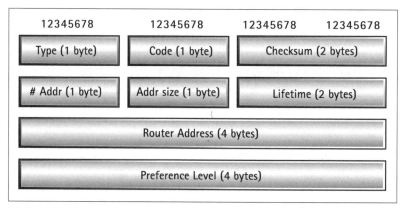

Figure 9-4: Routers supporting RFC1256 broadcast, or multicast, router advertisement messages at regular intervals containing the IP addresses of their network interfaces.

The functions of the fields in the router advertisement message are as follows:

◆ **Type (1 byte)** – The type field specifies the function of the ICMP message. For router advertisement, the value is always 10.

◆ **Code (1 byte)** – The code field is used as a message type subclassifier. There is only one router advertisement message format, so the code value is always 0.

◆ **Checksum (2 bytes)** – The checksum field contains the result of a checksum computation performed on the entire ICMP message, including the type, code, checksum, and all data fields to use for error-correction purposes.

◆ **Number of addresses (1 byte)** – The number of addresses field indicates how many router address/preference level pairs are included in the message.

◆ **Address entry size (1 byte)** – The address entry size field specifies the total size of each router address entry in the message, in 32-bit words. An entry is comprised of a 4-byte router address field and a 4-byte preference level field, resulting in a value that is always 2.

◆ **Lifetime (2 bytes)** – The lifetime field specifies the amount of time (in seconds) that the message's router addresses should be considered valid by the recipients, in the absence of subsequent advertisements. The default value is 1,800 seconds (30 minutes).

◆ **Router address (4 bytes)** – The router address field specifies the IP address of one of the network interfaces in the router generating the message. A single router advertisement message can contain as many router addresses as specified in the number of addresses field (each of which must be accompanied by a preference level field).

◆ **Preference level (4 bytes)** – The preference level field contains a 32-bit integer that the message recipients use to determine which router address to use as the default gateway, on the local subnet. The value of this field has significance only in comparison to the preference-level values of other router addresses on the same subnet. Administrators can assign any values they wish to this field, to establish a hierarchy of preferred gateway addresses on a given subnet. A client system uses the router address with the highest preference-level value as its default gateway. A hexadecimal value of 80000000 indicates that clients should not use the associated router address as a default gateway, under any circumstances.

In addition to responding to router solicitation messages, routers continue to transmit advertisements every 7 to 10 minutes while active. The repeat interval is randomized so routers do not become synchronized and flood the network with advertisements at regular intervals. These ICMP messages do not constitute a routing protocol because the advertisements provide no information regarding the efficiency of various routes available to a client.

The messages have a mechanism to provide hosts with information regarding changes in the availability of gateway systems. This can occur by default, when a router stops transmitting advertisements, and hosts remove the gateway address from their routing tables after the lifetime interval expires. Or, a router implementation can transmit an advertisement message with a lifetime value of 0, forcing the immediate removal of the gateway address.

Static Routing

To properly route datagrams, a TCP/IP system must be capable of adding information to its routing table. The mechanisms the system uses to build and update its routing table depends on the size and complexity of the networks to which the system is attached. The most basic method used to create routing tables is to add entries during the initialization of the TCP/IP protocol stack, or other system software. Other methods include the use of ICMP redirect messages generated by routers, and the manual addition of table entries with a routing utility like Microsoft's ROUTE.EXE.

All three of these methods are called *static routing* mechanisms because they explicitly define the gateway to use when transmitting to a particular destination. On a small, simple network, static routing is adequate. When the configuration of the network changes, administrators can modify the routing tables in gateway systems, manually, to achieve maximum efficiency. On nondedicated routers, running Windows NT or IntranetWare, you make routing table changes using a utility included with the OS.

Using ROUTE.EXE

Microsoft's ROUTE.EXE program is a DOS command-line utility that is included with all Windows network OSs. Windows NT is the only Windows OS that routes IP traffic, but Windows 95 and Windows for Workgroups systems (with the TCP/IP-32 protocol stack installed) use routing tables as well. The ROUTE utility's functionality is the same on all of the platforms.

To use the ROUTE utility, you execute the program with one of the following four root commands:

- ◆ **Print** – displays the contents of the routing table

- ◆ **Add** – creates a new entry in the routing table

- ◆ **Delete** – removes an entry from the routing table

- ◆ **Change** – modifies an entry in the routing table

The syntax for the use of these commands is as follows:

```
ROUTE PRINT [-p] [netaddress ]
ROUTE ADD [-f] [-p] [netaddress] [MASK netmask] [gateway] [METRIC
 hops]
ROUTE DELETE [netaddress]
ROUTE CHANGE [netaddress] [MASK netmask] [gateway] [METRIC hops]
```

The functions of the ROUTE command-line parameters are as follows:

- ◆ **–f** – When used without one of the root commands, the –f parameter deletes all of the entries from the routing table. When used with the ADD command, –f clears the routing table before adding the new entry.

- ◆ **–p** – When used with the ADD command, the –p parameter makes the new entry a persistent route that remains in the table permanently, even if the system is rebooted. When used with the PRINT command, –p displays only the persistent routes in the routing table.

- ◆ *netaddress* – The *netaddress* parameter identifies the host, or network IP address, that appears in the Network Address column of the routing table. When used with the PRINT, DELETE, and CHANGE commands, only the table entry for the *netaddress* value is affected.

- ◆ MASK *netmask* – The MASK parameter indicates that the *netmask* variable immediately following contains the subnet mask to apply to the IP address, represented by the netaddress variable. When used with the CHANGE command, the MASK parameter modifies the existing *netmask* value for the routing table entry identified by the *netaddress* variable.

- ◆ *gateway* – The *gateway* parameter specifies the IP address one network interface in the router that the system should use to access the host (or network) identified by the *netaddress* variable. When used with the CHANGE command, the value of the gateway variable replaces the existing gateway address for the routing table entry identified by the *netaddress* variable.

- ◆ METRIC *hops* – The METRIC parameter specifies the number of hops between the local system and the network (or host) specified by the netaddress variable. For a destination located on the same subnet as the local system, the value of the *hops* variable should be 1.

On a Windows host system with a single network interface, it isn't always necessary to modify the routing table manually. The default gateway entry is created by specifying a router address in the TCP/IP configuration, or by obtaining the address from a DHCP server. If the system is located on a network segment with two or more routers, ICMP redirect messages update the routing table to maximize the use of the nondefault gateways.

If you are statically routing IP with a Windows NT system, however, it may be necessary to create routing table entries manually (especially if you are using NT's Remote Access Server to connect to a remote network, such as that of an ISP).

Using TCPCON.NLM

When you install support for the TCP/IP protocol on a NetWare server, and configure it using the TCP/IP Protocol Configuration screen in the INETCFG utility, you can enable static routing on the server. A NetWare server has a routing table like that of any other TCP/IP system, and enabling static routing lets you create entries in the table manually.

For more information on the other uses of TCPCON, see Chapter 14, "TCP/IP Utilities."

You can create static routes using the INETCFG program, but to view and manage all of the routing table entries on a NetWare server, you use the TCPCON.NLM utility at the server console. This program provides a number of other traffic and control-utility functions, in addition to its routing capabilities.

When you load TCPCON at the NetWare server console and select IP Routing Table from the Available Options menu, you see a Route Selection Options screen, like that shown in Figure 9-5. On this screen, you can highlight the Proceed field and press Enter to display the entire routing table. You may also use other fields on the page to create filters that only display selected table entries.

```
┌──────────────────────────────────────────────────────────────┐
│         Routing Table - Route Selection Options              │
│  Proceed:          <Enter> when done                         │
│  Mask:             <Enter> to see list                       │
│  Next Hop:         *                          '*' for all n ...│
│  Protocol:         All                        'All' for all ...│
│  Cost:             All                        'All' for all ...│
│  Interface:        <Select to View or Modify>                │
│  Flush All Routes: <Enter>                                   │
└──────────────────────────────────────────────────────────────┘
```

Figure 9-5: TCPCON enables you to view the entire server routing table, or create a custom-configured selection of table entries.

The fields on the TCPCON Route Selection Options screen are as follows:

♦ Proceed – This applies the filter options specified in the other fields on this screen, and displays the resulting subset of the routing table. By default, the entire contents of the routing table are displayed.

♦ Mask – This option enables you to filter the routing-table display on the basis of the entries' subnet masks. By selecting this option, you can add one or more masks to the list and limit the routing-table display to the entries containing those masks.

♦ Next hop – The TCPCON utility refers to the gateway address of a routing table entry as the "next hop." By specifying an IP address in this field, you force TCPCON to display only the routing table entries that direct traffic to this gateway address.

♦ Protocol – When you select this option, you are presented with a list of routing protocols. By selecting a specific protocol, you limit the routing-table display to the entries obtained using that protocol.

♦ Cost – The cost of a route, in the NetWare routing table, is the equivalent of the metric in a Windows table – the number of hops between the local machine and the destination network, or host system. You can filter the routing table display, based on the cost of the route, by selecting an operator and a value for this field. The available operators are < (less than), > (greater than), and = (equals).

♦ Interface – When you select this option, you are presented with a list of network interfaces installed in the NetWare server. Using the Tab key, you can limit the routing table display to show entries associated with the selected interfaces, only.

When you display the contents of the routing table, you see a screen like that shown in Figure 9-6.

```
                  IP Routing Table (3 Routes)
 Destination          Next Hop          Type     Cost     Interface
 default              209.61.45.144     remote   1        1
 192.168.98.0         192.168.98.99     direct   1        2
 209.61.45.0          ny-library        direct   1        1
 <End of Table>
```

Figure 9-6: The TCPCON utility can display all of the routing table entries on a NetWare server.

Unlike Windows systems, the standard TCP/IP configuration settings for a NetWare server do not include a default gateway address. If you are not using a dynamic-routing protocol, you must rely on ICMP router-advertisement messages to create a default gateway entry in the routing table, or create one manually.

To create a routing table entry with TCPCON, manually, press the Insert key from the IP Routing Table, to display the screen shown in Figure 9-7. Edit the fields by inserting the proper information, as follows:

◆ **Destination** – The destination field specifies the IP address, or the simple DNS name, of the network or host for which a route is being specified. By pressing the Insert key, you can select from the network addresses listed in the server's SYS:\ETC\NETWORKS file.

◆ **Mask** – The mask field specifies the subnet mask to apply to the IP address specified in the destination field. For a default gateway address, the value should be 0.0.0.0; for a destination specifying a host address, the value should be 255.255.255.255.

◆ **Next hop** – The next hop field specifies the network interface's IP address (in the gateway system) to use to reach the network or host specified in the destination field. By pressing the Insert key, you can select a system from those listed in the server's SYS:\ETC\HOSTS file.

◆ **Type** – The type field specifies whether the system specified in the next hop field is on the same network as the destination system (a direct route), or on a different network (a remote, or indirect, route).

◆ **Interface** – The interface field contains an index number, identifying the network interface in the local system, that should be used to access the system specified in the next hop field. The index numbers of the installed interfaces are shown in TCPCON's Interfaces screen.

◆ **Protocol** – The protocol field specifies the routing protocol that was used to create the table entry. When manually creating a static route, the value of this field is *netmgmt* (which cannot be edited).

◆ **Age** – The age field specifies the time elapsed since the routing table entry was last updated.

◆ **Cost** – The cost field specifies the routing metric, or the number of hops needed to reach the destination network or host.

◆ **Metric 2 through Metric 5** – The additional metrics fields are used by dynamic-routing protocols to specify the costs of alternative routes to the destination. When they are not used, as in the creation of static routes, they contain a value of –1.

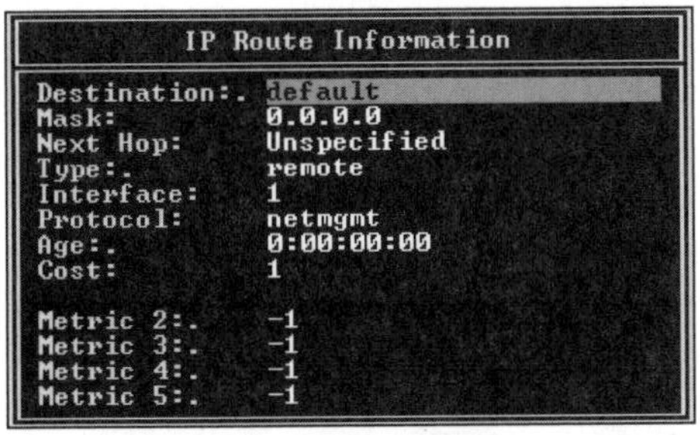

```
┌─────────────────────────────────────┐
│         IP Route Information         │
├─────────────────────────────────────┤
│ Destination:. default                │
│ Mask:         0.0.0.0                │
│ Next Hop:     Unspecified            │
│ Type:.        remote                 │
│ Interface:    1                      │
│ Protocol:     netmgmt                │
│ Age:.         0:00:00:00             │
│ Cost:         1                      │
│                                      │
│ Metric 2:.    -1                     │
│ Metric 3:.    -1                     │
│ Metric 4:.    -1                     │
│ Metric 5:.    -1                     │
└─────────────────────────────────────┘
```

Figure 9-7: The IP Route Information screen is used to display and edit the properties of a routing table entry.

Dynamic Routing

On the Internet, or even on large private internetworks, the use of static routing is not practical. Even if there was sufficient manpower to manually configure the routing tables of the thousands of gateways on the Internet, the network is so volatile, it would be virtually impossible to keep up with the constant changes in network-traffic patterns and system status. Large networks, therefore, use *dynamic routing*. This takes the form of protocols that systems use to exchange routing information, automatically.

Dynamic-routing protocols provide information on existing routes to a particular destination, as well as the data enabling a system to select the most efficient route. By transmitting updates at regular intervals, systems using routing protocols can modify their routing tables to compensate for changes in the network, as they occur. When a particular route to a destination becomes invalid, a system can discover an alternative route using the information delivered by the routing protocol. This compensation process is known as *convergence*.

This dynamic-routing process is the reason protocols, such as TCP and IP, can split messages into segments, or fragments, and apply sequence numbers to each part of a message to facilitate the reassembly process. Because routes can be changed during the course of a transmission, packets may follow different paths to their destination, and arrive out of sequence.

Using dynamic routing on an internetwork does not affect the *routing mechanism* employed by TCP/IP systems. Routing-table searches are performed in the same way as with static routing. The only change, provided by the dynamic protocols in the *routing policy*, is the way information is added to (and removed from) the routing table.

Routing Protocols

Many routing protocols are used on the Internet that – for administrative purposes – can be placed into two categories: *interior gateway protocols* (IGPs) and *exterior gateway protocols* (EGPs). A protocol, by definition, is a common language, or vocabulary, used during the communication of two or more entities. Administrators of private internetworks must make their own decisions regarding preferable routing protocols (as they must with much of the Internet infrastructure). For routing purposes, a collection of connected networks, falling under the control of a single administrative body, is referred to as an *autonomous system* (AS). The administrators of an AS choose an IGP to be used on the routers within the AS.

The most commonly used IGPs are the *Routing Information Protocol* (RIP) and the *Open Shortest Path First* (OSPF) protocol. These must be supported by all routers capable of using dynamic-routing protocols. Other IGPs are designed by router hardware manufacturers, or based on open standards. To function on the Internet, autonomous systems must exchange routing information with other autonomous systems – providing another example of the Internet's two-tiered administrative hierarchy.

Inter-AS routing is done using an *exterior gateway protocol*, as shown in Figure 9-8. This term can be confusing because, while used generically to refer to the category of Inter-AS routing protocols, one of the most commonly used protocols of this type (defined in RFC904) is also called the *Exterior Gateway Protocol*. In recent years, however, the Border Gateway Protocol (defined in RFC1267) has risen in popularity because it addresses some of the limitations of the Exterior Gateway Protocol.

The Routing Information Protocol (RIP)

RIP is the most commonly implemented and used interior gateway protocol, but it has been the target of harsh criticism. RIP has limitations that make it unsuitable for very large internetworks, but its ready availability and easy implementation still make it popular among many network administrators. RIP was originally devised for use with the Berkeley UNIX variant, in the form of a daemon called *routed* (pronounced *route-dee*). Other implementations were later developed, and in 1988, RFC1058 was published. This consolidated the differences between various RIP implementations into a single standard. Since then, documents defining a second version of the protocol were published, retaining the basic design of the first version while attempting to address some of its shortcomings.

Windows NT and IntranetWare support both RIP versions for the routing of the IP and IPX protocols – as do most of the dedicated-router products on the market. You can, therefore, build a small- to medium-sized internetwork using both OSs as routers, and ensure that they will be capable of exchanging routing information.

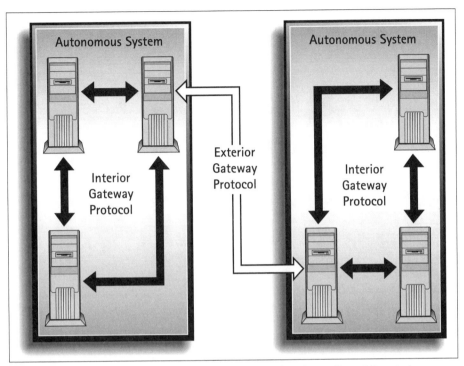

Figure 9-8: Interior gateway protocols are used for intradomain routing, while exterior gateway protocols are used for interdomain routing, between autonomous systems.

A router using RIP relies on UDP broadcast transmissions, to the well-known port 520, to exchange routing information with the other RIP-enabled systems on attached networks. Most RIP traffic uses two message types: requests and replies. When a router initializes, it broadcasts a RIP-request message over each of its network interfaces. The request messages cause the other routers on local networks to transmit their routing tables' entire contents using reply messages. Ensuing RIP transactions can take the form of a system requesting information on specific routes, or a router transmitting updates at periodic intervals, when the metric of a specific route changes.

RIP VERSION 1

A RIP message using version 1 of the protocol uses the format shown in Figure 9-9. A single message can contain up to 25 routes, each of which adds 20 bytes to the packet. Depending on the size of the internetwork and the number of routers, multiple packets may be required to transmit the entire contents of a system's routing table.

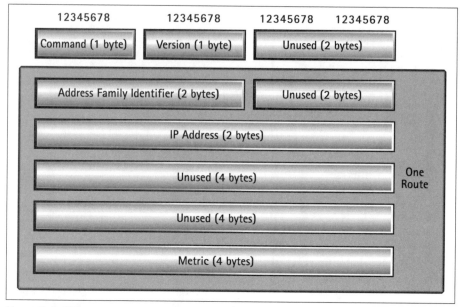

Figure 9-9: RIP messages are carried within UDP datagrams that are broadcasted on the system's local networks.

The fields in the header portion of a RIP message function as follows:

◆ **Command** (1 byte) – This specifies the function of the message, using the following codes:

  ◆ **1 – Request** – This field is used to request transmission of routing table information on specific routes, or entire routing tables.

  ◆ **2 – Reply** – Reply is used to transmit routing table information, either in response to a request or as an update.

  ◆ **3 – Traceon** – Traceon is obsolete; ignored by all RIP implementations.

  ◆ **4 – Traceoff** – Traceoff is also obsolete; ignored by all RIP implementations.

  ◆ **5 – Poll** – Poll is undocumented; used by some utilities for testing and troubleshooting.

  ◆ **6 – Poll-entry** – Poll-entry is also undocumented; used by some utilities for testing and troubleshooting.

◆ **Version** (1 byte) – The version field specifies the version of the RIP-packet format used to create the message; possible values are 1 and 2.

♦ **Unused** (2 bytes).

Each 20-byte route in a RIP message consists of the following fields:

♦ **Address family identifier** (2 bytes) – The RIP-message format
accommodates routing information for other protocols besides IP; the
address family-identifier field contains a code that identifies the protocol
(the value for IP is 2).

♦ **Unused** (2 bytes).

♦ **IP address** (4 bytes) – This field identifies a network or host that is
accessed by routing traffic through the gateway system generating the RIP
message.

♦ **Unused** (4 bytes).

♦ **Unused** (4 bytes).

♦ **Metric** (4 bytes) – This field specifies the number of hops required for
traffic to reach the destination indicated in the IP address field (through
the gateway generating the RIP message); the maximum number of hops
supported by RIP is 15 (a value of 16 in this field indicates that the
gateway has no route to the destination network or host specified in the
IP address field).

When a new router, connected to networks A and B, receives the routing table
from a system connected to networks B and C, it assimilates the information into
its own routing table, as shown in Figure 9-10.

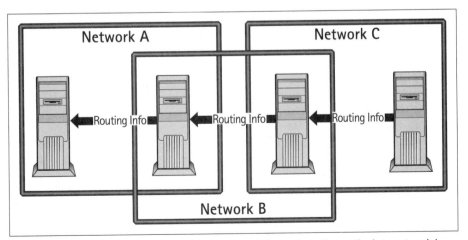

Figure 9-10: RIP transmissions disseminate routing information all over the internetwork by
relaying it from system to system.

The information received by the new router concerns not only the systems on network C, but also information passed from routers on networks D, E, and so on. By relaying information to systems on adjacent networks in this manner, routers can build a table of information about the systems on all segments of the internetwork.

On most internetworks, however, routers are not arranged on network segments in a daisy-chain fashion, as shown in the figure. Instead, there may be several routers on various network segments, resulting in a choice of routes to a particular destination. RIP transmissions containing routing-table information include a metric for each table entry (specifying the number of hops needed to reach a particular destination). As table entries are passed from router to router, the metric is incremented so each system can compare the relative efficiency of alternative routes. When a system receives a RIP-reply message, it compares the metric for each route with the table entries received, for the same destination, from other sources. Only the entry with the smallest hop count is added to the system's routing table. This is known as *distance vector routing*.

After the initialization process, RIP routers retransmit all, or part, of their routing tables every 30 seconds. This refreshes the information on the network's other routers, continually. If a routing table entry is not refreshed at least once every three minutes (that is, six times the update frequency), its metric value is changed to 16. This prevents its use and removes it from the table 60 seconds later. While these updates keep the network's routing tables current, they can also generate a good deal of broadcast traffic — which is one of the criticisms of the RIP protocol.

While RIP propagates basic routing information among an internetwork's gateways, it suffers from several fundamental drawbacks, preventing it from being more functional. The most obvious shortcoming of the protocol is the 15-hop limit of the metric field. This invalidates the protocol's use on large internetworks that require more hops to reach a destination.

RIP VERSION 2

Another serious problem with version 1 of the RIP protocol is its failure to include subnet masks for the IP addresses, specified in its routes. RIP implementations usually apply the subnet mask of the interface, through which the RIP message arrived, to each of the IP addresses in the packet — but this is not necessarily accurate. There is no sure way for the router to determine whether an IP address (with some of its nonnetwork bits set) identifies a host system, or a network address, with a subnet identifier.

Version 2 of the RIP protocol addresses some of the shortcomings of version 1 by including additional data in each of a RIP message's routes. The packet format of a RIP-2 message is the same as that of RIP 1, except that it uses the unused fields, as shown in Figure 9-11. Since the message format is unchanged, systems only supporting RIP-1 can process RIP-2 messages in the normal manner, ignoring the additional data in the "unused" fields. RIP-2 also addresses the problem of RIP-1's excessive broadcast traffic by enabling the use of multicast transmissions (preventing non-RIP systems from having to process routing messages).

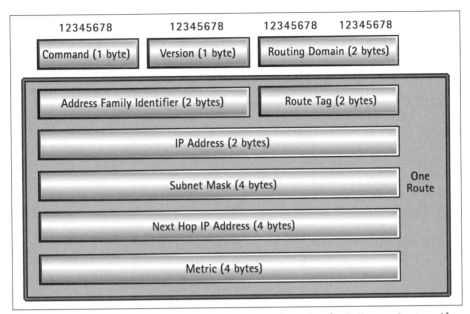

Figure 9-11: Version 2 of the RIP protocol adds more information (including a subnet mask) to each route.

In a RIP-2 message, the existing fields from the RIP-1 message retain their original values, except for the version field which now has a value of 2. Following are the functions of the new RIP-2 fields that replace the unused fields of the RIP-1 message:

◆ **Routing domain** (2 bytes) – The routing domain field contains a value that identifies the routing process to which this message contributes. By using different routing domains, administrators can create multiple, separate RIP "clouds." A system receiving a RIP message with a routing-domain value different than its own silently discards the packet. The default value is 0.

◆ **Route tag** (2 bytes) – The route tag field carries an autonomous-system number that enables RIP to interact with exterior gateway protocols, such as EGP and BGP.

◆ **Subnet mask** (4 bytes) – The subnet mask is applied to the contents of the IP address field to enable the receiving system to identify subnet (and/or host bits) in the address.

◆ **Next hop IP address** (4 bytes) – The next hop IP address field identifies the gateway interface to which traffic (destined for the system specified in the IP address field) should be sent. In most instances, the next hop address is the same as that from which the RIP message packet was received. In this case, the value of this field can be 0.0.0.0. This field may seem redundant, but it is valuable when RIP is used on intranetworks also running other routing protocols. A single router supporting both RIP-2 and OSPF, for example, can propagate routing information that was gathered by using OSPF to other RIP routers. This is done by specifying the gateway addresses of the OSPF routers in the next hop IP address field.

RIP-2 also contains an option that forces routing messages to be authenticated by receiving systems before they are processed. The authentication mechanism takes the place of the first route in a RIP-2 packet. When the address family field has a hexadecimal value of FFFF, the remaining 18 bytes of the route are used for authentication purposes, as follows:

◆ **Authentication type** (2 bytes) – The authentication type field specifies the nature of the password included in the packet. A simple, clear-text password is type 2.

◆ **Password** (16 bytes) – The password field contains an unencrypted password that is padded with 0's to reach the full size of 16 bytes.

The Open Shortest Path First (OSPF) Protocol

Another problem with both versions of RIP is in the fundamental concept of distance vector routing. Calculating the efficiency of a route based on the number of hops, alone, can be wildly inaccurate. A single hop from one network to another can involve two Ethernet segments, a slower point-to-point link, or any other networking technology. Traffic might traverse several hops across lightly used Ethernet networks in the time it takes for a single hop across a congested point-to-point link.

To address this problem, there is a different type of IP routing, called *link state routing*. With this method, routers actually test their connections to other routers, saving the link state information to a database that is propagated around the internetwork. The most popular IGP using this method is the *Open Shortest Path First* (OSPF) protocol. OSPF routers on an internetwork all maintain an identical database, which describes the topology of the network and updates it regularly by testing the links to each of the other routers.

When the link state information is transmitted to the other routers, the shortest path to a given destination can be determined, based on empirical data (rather than the network architecture). Each router then constructs its routing table based on the collated information in its database. One of the primary advantages of OSPF over RIP is its capability to converge more quickly if there's a change in the network infrastructure, such as the failure of a router or connection.

Other advanced features of OSPF are as follows:

♦ **Load balancing** – When two or more different routes to the same destination have identical metrics, OSPF splits outgoing traffic among the routes to prevent excess traffic on any one path.

♦ **Authentication** – All OSPF messages are authenticated, by default, before being processed by the recipient. An authentication type field in the message header defines the type of authentication to be used. Current options use a simple, clear-text password or no authentication at all, but the protocol is designed so additional authentication types may be added.

♦ **Subnetting** – OSPF includes a subnet mask for the IP address of every route it advertises. This enables the receiving system to identify routes to host systems and variable-length subnets.

♦ **OSPF areas** – An autonomous system can contain subsets of networks, called OSPF areas. These are treated as routing domains, separate from the rest of the AS. Routers in an OSPF area maintain their own, separate topological database that is invisible to the rest of the AS. These routers transmit their routing messages only to the other routers in the area (thus reducing the routing traffic on the rest of the network). Routers that connect areas to other areas, or the rest of the AS, are known as *area border routers*. Each OSPF area can have its own authentication type, thus providing different levels of protection.

♦ **External routing information** – OSPF can assimilate routing information obtained from external sources, such as static routes and exterior gateway protocols. External routing data is propagated to other OSPF routers without modification.

♦ **TOS-based routing** – OSPF databases can maintain separate routing information for each type of service specified in the IP header, resulting in separate routing table entries for each TOS value.

OSPF messages are carried directly within IP datagrams with no intervening transport-layer protocol, using an IP-protocol field value of 89.

Routing IP with Windows NT

Windows NT 4.0 is capable of routing IP traffic between LANs using multiple network interface cards, or between a LAN and a remote network using modems or an ISDN or X.25 connection. This enables you to create a variety of networking scenarios, such as the following:

◆ Connect two LANs using the same or different data link-layer protocols or topologies, such as Ethernet-to-Ethernet, Ethernet-to-Token Ring, or 10BaseT-to-Thinnet. This enables clients, on each network, to access resources on the other.

◆ Connect to an office Windows NT system from a home or portable computer using a modem, and gain access to all network resources normally available at work.

◆ Connect to an ISP from your office workstation and provide Internet access to other users on your local network.

Both Windows NT Server and Workstation include Multiprotocol Router 1. This is capable of forwarding IP, IPX, and/or NetBEUI traffic using static routes, but NT Server includes support for dynamic routing with the RIP protocol. In addition, NT Server can support up to 256 dial-up network clients, while Workstation can handle only one. The operating systems are designed to provide routing services for relatively small internetworks and branch offices. For more heavy-duty use, Microsoft released an update to Windows NT Server called the Routing and Remote Access Service (formerly code-named Steelhead) that adds support for more advanced routing features, such as the OSPF protocol, virtual private networking, and demand-dial WAN routing.

Static LAN Routing

Once you understand the function and formation of the routing table, it is simple to set up a Windows NT system as a gateway between two LANs using static routes. After installing and properly configuring the two network interface adapters, you must enable IP routing by filling the appropriate checkbox in the Microsoft TCP/IP Properties dialog box. The appropriate static route entries are automatically added to the routing table.

The static routes instruct the system to direct all IP traffic destined for one network to a specific interface. All traffic destined for the other network is transmitted through the other interface, as in the following example:

```
Network Address          Netmask  Gateway Address       Interface  Metric
     198.96.65.0   255.255.255.0      198.96.65.1   198.96.65.1        1
     198.96.68.0   255.255.255.0      198.96.68.1   198.96.68.1        1
```

The two network adapters in the Windows NT system use the IP addresses 198.96.67.1 and 198.96.68.1. Each workstation (on the 198.96.67.0 network) uses the 198.96.67.1 interface on the Windows NT system as its default gateway, while the other network's workstations use 198.96.68.1.

This arrangement is simple because you are dealing with two networks, only —
both of which are known to the NT system (shown in Figure 9-12). If one of the
networks has another gateway on it, providing access to another network, you must
add an indirect route to the routing table for the other network address. The
Windows NT gateway system can route traffic between networks A and B, but it
has no direct knowledge of network C, as shown in Figure 9-13.

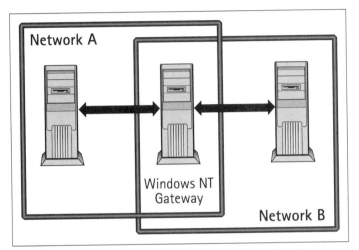

Figure 9-12: Static routing between two networks requires two
additional entries to the gateway system's routing table.

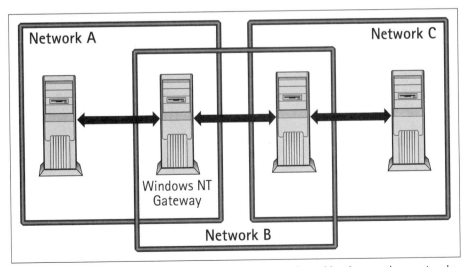

Figure 9-13: You must add new entries to the system's routing table when you have networks
that aren't directly connected to a Windows NT gateway system.

The new entry should appear as follows:

```
Network Address          Netmask  Gateway Address      Interface  Metric
    198.96.66.0    255.255.255.0      198.96.65.2    198.96.65.1      1
```

This entry causes the NT system to transmit all IP traffic, destined for the 198.96.66.0 network, out the 198.95.65.1 interface. It travels to another gateway system with one adapter, using the address 198.96.65.2, and another adapter connected to the 198.96.66.0 network. With only one other gateway system on the 198.96.65.0 network, you can achieve the same effect by specifying that system's IP address as the default gateway for the 198.96.65.1 adapter, in the Microsoft TCP/IP Properties dialog box. This creates an entry in the routing table like the following:

```
Network Address          Netmask  Gateway Address      Interface  Metric
        0.0.0.0          0.0.0.0      198.96.65.2    198.96.65.1      1
```

If you also assign a default gateway address to the other network adapter in the system, two default gateway entries are added to the routing table. Only the entry corresponding to the adapter, listed first in the Bindings screen of the Network Control Panel dialog box, is used. You can modify the order of bindings, but it is easier to specify a default gateway address for the adapter requiring one, only.

As your internetwork grows, each additional network requires a new entry in the routing table of every gateway system not directly connected to it. Once your network grows to include more than a handful of gateway systems, static routing becomes an increasingly confusing task.

Dial-Up Network Routing

By using Windows NT's Dial-Up Networking feature to connect to a remote internetwork, you can route IP traffic from the Point-to-Point Protocol (PPP) connection to your LAN. This provides your LAN clients access to remote network resources. The feature is most often used to connect to an ISP, and can provide basic Internet access to local network users. For greater bandwidth than a standard asynchronous modem connection, Windows NT includes support for multiple modem, ISDN, and X.25 connections.

There are several tricks to routing IP through a Windows NT Dial-up Networking connection—most of these make sense, but one does not. As with a LAN-to-LAN connection, the network adapter must be configured properly, in the Network Control Panel. You must assign it an appropriate IP address and enable IP forwarding. Do not, however, enter a default gateway address for the network adapter connected to the LAN.

As mentioned in the previous section, only one default gateway address is permitted on a system. When you are connecting a LAN to the Internet, you must have the network traffic default to the Internet side. Otherwise, you have no way of identifying the thousands of possible network addresses your clients may access.

The odd part of the routing-configuration process comes when you try to set up the default gateway address you need for routed Internet access. When you configure the parameters for the protocols, used on the Dial-Up Networking connection, you use the PPP TCP/IP Settings dialog box to specify the IP address and name servers used by the modem connection (see Figure 9-14).

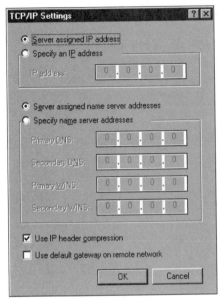

Figure 9-14: To route IP traffic over a dial-up connection successfully, you must disable the Use Default Gateway on Remote Network feature.

This dialog box has a Use Default Gateway on Remote Network checkbox. When enabled, this automatically creates the default gateway entry in the routing table, like the following:

```
Network Address          Netmask  Gateway Address     Interface  Metric
       0.0.0.0           0.0.0.0  208.197.87.24    208.197.87.24      1
```

TIP When you enable this feature, the system inexplicably fails to route traffic to, or from, the Internet (despite a properly configured routing table). IP traffic can be forwarded successfully by clearing the checkbox and manually creating the same default gateway entry in the routing table, using the ROUTE utility.

Using the Routing and Remote Access Service

The standard Windows NT 4.0 Server product includes a network service that provides support for RIP. If you require dynamic routing for your internetwork, you should install the Routing and Remote Access upgrade for Windows NT Server. This package provides OSPF support, as well as RIP, and includes a graphical utility for configuring the system's routing parameters.

To install the update, your server must be running Windows NT Service Pack 3 (the update does not run on Windows NT Workstation). The installation process also removes the existing Remote Access and RIP services (if installed), and enables you to select one of the following components for installation:

- **Remote access service** – provides dial-in and dial-out network access using modems, ISDN, or X.25

- **LAN routing** – provides routing between local networks

- **Demand dial routing** – provides routing support for remote WAN and dial-up network connections

The greatest benefit of the Routing and Remote Access Service is the Routing and RAS Admin utility (see Figure 9-15). This is a graphical utility that can monitor and manage the routing activities of all NT servers on your internetwork. Some of the functions provided by this utility include the following:

- Create, configure, and activate remote access connections to ISPs or WANs

- View and edit the server's routing table using a graphical interface (see Figure 9-16), including both static and dynamic routes

- Install, configure, and view the routing data gathered by dynamic-routing protocols, such as RIP and OSPF

- Monitor traffic passing through a particular network interface

- Create IP packet filters to limit the types of traffic permitted to pass through the router

- Create virtual private networks (VPNs) using the point-to-point tunneling protocol (PPTP)

The functionality of the Routing and Remote Access Service for Windows NT is not limited to IP routing. The product is a multiprotocol router that provides similar monitoring and management capabilities for IPX and NetBEUI routing.

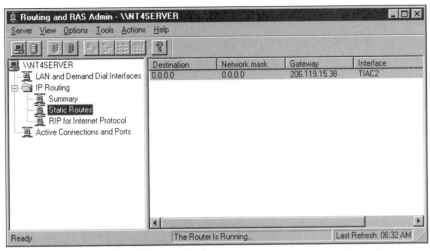

Figure 9-15: The Routing and RAS Admin utility provides a single administration interface for all the routing activities of a server.

Destination	Network mask	Gateway	Interface	Metric	Protocol
127.0.0.0	255.0.0.0	127.0.0.1	Internal Loopback Interface	1	Local
209.61.45.0	255.255.255.0	209.61.45.144	[1] 3Com Etherlink III Adapter	1	Local
209.61.45.144	255.255.255.255	127.0.0.1	Internal Loopback Interface	1	Local
209.61.45.255	255.255.255.255	209.61.45.144	[1] 3Com Etherlink III Adapter	1	Local
224.0.0.0	224.0.0.0	209.61.45.144	[1] 3Com Etherlink III Adapter	1	Local
255.255.255.255	255.255.255.255	209.61.45.144	[1] 3Com Etherlink III Adapter	1	Local

Figure 9-16: The Routing and RAS Admin utility provides a graphical interface to the routing table, eliminating the need to use the character-based ROUTE utility.

Routing IP with IntranetWare

The IntranetWare product includes Novell's Multiprotocol Router 3.1, which provides routing services similar to those of Windows NT (including support for the RIP and OSPF routing protocols). Installing MPR adds new screens to the INETCFG.NLM utility, which enable you to configure the protocols' properties and create static routes.

As with any other system that functions as an IP router, you must install two or more network interfaces and configure them to use TCP/IP. MPR provides the capability to route between LAN, WAN, and dial-up connections. Once the interfaces are active, you must enable IP Packet Forwarding in INETCFG's TCP/IP Protocol

Configuration screen, as shown in Figure 9-17. From this screen, you can also enable MPR's various routing policies, including RIP, OSPF, and static routing. By selecting the LAN Static Routing Table field, you may view and modify the static routes in the table.

Unlike the TCPCON utility, INETCFG displays only the static routes in the routing table. TCPCON also enables you to view the routes created by dynamic-routing protocols.

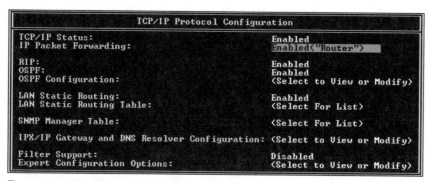

```
                  TCP/IP Protocol Configuration

  TCP/IP Status:                           Enabled
  IP Packet Forwarding:                    Enabled("Router")

  RIP:                                     Enabled
  OSPF:                                    Enabled
  OSPF Configuration:                      <Select to View or Modify>

  LAN Static Routing:                      Enabled
  LAN Static Routing Table:                <Select For List>

  SNMP Manager Table:                      <Select For List>

  IPX/IP Gateway and DNS Resolver Configuration: <Select to View or Modify>

  Filter Support:                          Disabled
  Expert Configuration Options:            <Select to View or Modify>
```

Figure 9-17: The INETCFG.NLM utility provides the administrative interface to a NetWare server's routing capabilities.

Configuring OSPF

INETCFG splits the OSPF-configuration parameters between two different screens. The OSPF Configuration screen is accessed from the TCP/IP Protocol Configuration screen, and contains the following fields:

◆ **Router ID** – The router ID field specifies the IP address used to identify the router to the rest of the autonomous system. By default, the system uses the first IP address bound to a network adapter during the TCP/IP initialization process.

◆ **Autonomous system boundary router** – When activated, the autonomous system boundary router feature enables OSPF to propagate routing information (gathered from other sources, such as RIP, exterior gateway protocols, and static routes). By default, this option is disabled.

◆ **Area configuration** – The area configuration field provides access to a list of additional OSPF areas in your autonomous system. By default, the list includes the backbone (or default) area, identified by the address 0.0.0.0.

◆ **Virtual link configuration** – Virtual links connect the area border routers of an autonomous system's backbone area to those of other areas with no direct connection to the backbone. This option provides access to a list that enables you to create new virtual links. This is done by specifying the router ID of the border router in the remote area, and the address of an area between the remote and backbone area.

◆ **IP load sharing** – The IP load sharing option enables MPR to split IP traffic between as many as four routes, with the same metric. By default, this option is disabled.

When you use INETCFG's Bindings screen to bind a network interface to the TCP/IP protocol stack; there is an OSPF Bind Options screen for each interface, that contains the following fields:

◆ **Status** – When you enable OSPF in the TCP/IP Protocol Configuration screen, support for the protocol is automatically enabled for all interfaces bound to the TCP/IP stack. With this option, you can disable OSPF for a selected interface, thereby preventing the exchange of routing information with OSPF gateways on the attached network.

◆ **Cost of Interface** – The cost of interface field contains the metric associated with the network interface. Possible values range from 1 to 65,535; this field is not editable.

◆ **Area ID** – The area ID field identifies the OSPF area to which the network interface belongs. By pressing the Insert key, you can select from the areas already created in the OSPF Configuration screen.

◆ **Priority** – When there is more than one OSPF router on a network, the priority field contains a value that determines which router should be the designated router for that network. The default value is 1; possible values range from 0 to 255.

◆ **Authentication password** – The authentication password field holds an 8-byte password that must be shared by all OSPF routers in the area, when authentication is enabled.

◆ **Hello interval** – The hello interval field specifies the length of time (in seconds) between transmissions of OSPF hello messages over the network interface. The default value is 10 seconds; possible values range from 1 to 65,535. All OSPF routers on a given network must have the same value for this parameter.

◆ **Router dead interval** – The router dead interval field specifies the amount of time (in seconds) that must elapse between hello message transmissions (before an OSPF router is considered nonfunctional). The default value is 40 seconds; possible values range from 1 to (hexadecimal) 7FFFFFFF seconds. As with the hello interval, all OSPF routers on a network must have the same value for this parameter.

◆ Neighbor list – The neighbor list contains the IP addresses of other OSPF routers on the same network, for use on nonbroadcast networks that can't identify the other routers by other means.

Configuring RIP

To use RIP with TCP/IP, you must enable the protocol in INETCFG's TCP/IP Protocol Configuration screen. The RIP support for each network interface is configured from the Bindings screen. The RIP Bind Options screen, shown in Figure 9-18, contains the following options:

◆ Status – In the status field, you can enable or disable the RIP protocol for a particular network interface. You can use RIP on a NetWare server whether it functions as a router or not. When a host system uses RIP, it functions in "listen-only" mode.

◆ Cost of interface – The cost of interface field contains the metric to be associated with use of the network interface. The default value is 1; possible values range from 1 to 15. You can edit this value, if desired, to decrease the likelihood that the network interface will be used for routing.

◆ Originate default route – When enabled, the originate default route feature causes RIP to transmit messages containing routing information for the local system, only. By default, this option is disabled.

◆ Poison reverse – When enabled, the poison reverse option causes the router to include routing information (obtained from a particular gateway) in the messages addressed to that gateway, with a metric value of 16. This helps to prevent routing loops, at the cost of a moderate increase in RIP-traffic volume. By default, this option is disabled.

```
╔══════════════════════════════════════════════════════════╗
║                    RIP Bind Options                      ║
╠══════════════════════════════════════════════════════════╣
║ Network Interface:       SMC8000_1                       ║
║ Interface Group:                                         ║
║                                                          ║
║ Status:                  Enabled                         ║
║ Cost of Interface:       1                               ║
║ Originate Default Route: Disable: Present Normal Routes  ║
║ Poison Reverse:          Disabled                        ║
║ Split Horizon:           Enabled                         ║
║ Update Time:             30      (Seconds)               ║
║ Expire Time:             180     (Seconds)               ║
║ Garbage Time:            120     (Seconds)               ║
║ RIP Version:             RIPI & RIPII                    ║
║ RIP Mode:                Normal                          ║
║ RIPII Options:           (Select to View or Modify)      ║
╚══════════════════════════════════════════════════════════╝
```

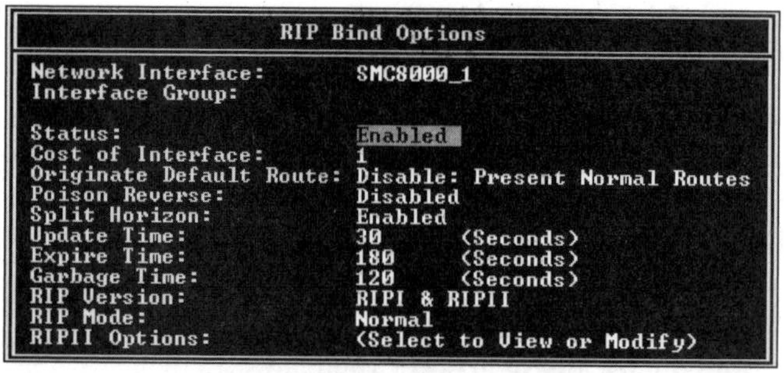

Figure 9-18: IntranetWare's Multiprotocol Router supports RIP versions 1 and 2, which is configured for each network interface in the server.

- **Split horizon** – When enabled, the split horizon option prevents the router from including any routing information (obtained from a particular gateway) in RIP messages transmitted to that gateway. By default, this option is enabled.

- **Update time** – The update time field specifies the interval (in seconds) between RIP update transmissions. The default value is 30 seconds; possible values range from 30 to 10,922.

- **Expire time** – The expire time field specifies the amount of time (in seconds) that a routing-table entry is used without an update. When the expire-time interval elapses, the metric of the table entry is changed to 16, preventing its use. The default value is six times the update time value; possible values range from six times the update time value to 65,535.

- **Garbage time** – The garbage time field specifies the amount of time (in seconds) that an expired route remains in the routing table before being purged. The default value is four times the expire-time value; possible values range from four times the expire-time value to 65,535.

- **RIP version** – The RIP version field is used to specify the packet format used by the router. The default value is RIP-1; possible values are RIP-1, RIP-2, or RIP-1 and RIP-2.

- **RIP mode** – The RIP mode option specifies whether the router should send RIP messages only, receive them only, or both (which is the Normal setting). The default value is Normal.

- **RIP II options** – When the RIP version option is set to RIP-2, or RIP-1 and RIP-2, two additional options are activated, as follows:

  - **Authentication** – The authentication field specifies whether RIP-2 packets should be generated with the first route, in the message, configured to carry authentication information. To process the messages, each router receiving them must also be configured to use RIP-2 with authentication activated, and must possess the same password. By default, authentication is disabled.

  - **Authentication password** – The authentication password field contains a password of up to 16 bytes that must be shared by all other RIP-2 routers with authentication enabled.

Summary

The process of routing IP datagrams to a distant destination is relatively simple. Each system along the path is responsible only for passing the data to the next system. The most difficult aspect of the process is furnishing routers with information regarding what lies beyond the networks to which they are attached. The bulk of the routing process involves gathering information, which is stored in the routing table of each system on a TCP/IP network.

In this chapter, you learned about some basic techniques for passing routing information to various gateway systems on an internetwork, including the following:

◆ How static routing can be used on small networks to provide gateway systems with information about other networks

◆ How to create static routes on Windows NT systems and NetWare servers

◆ How dynamic-routing protocols can disseminate routing information, automatically, to all gateway systems on an internetwork

◆ How to implement the Routing Information Protocol and the Open Shortest Path First protocol on Windows NT and NetWare systems

Chapter 10

DHCP and IP Address Management

IN THIS CHAPTER

DHCP is a system for automatically configuring TCP/IP network-client parameters, such as IP addresses and subnet masks. This chapter examines the following aspects of DHCP:

◆ The origins of DHCP in two early configuration protocols called BOOTP and RARP

◆ The DHCP message types and client/server communications procedures

◆ The Microsoft DHCP Server

◆ The IntranetWare DHCP Server

TCP/IP'S SELF-CONTAINED ADDRESSING system is one of its major strengths, but this system has become an administrative nightmare. When the protocols were originally envisioned, no one expected to see hundreds (or thousands) of desktop computers connected to a TCP/IP network at a single location. Registering network IP addresses, and having network administrators assign host addresses decentralized IP address assignment tasks, reduced the size of Internet routing tables.

Assigning unique IP addresses to every computer system is now a continuous burden, due to large, private internetworks. Available network addresses are being consumed rapidly by organizations seeking Internet access. It is necessary to see that host addresses are not squandered due to administrative oversights.

Since the early 1980s, we have needed a mechanism for assigning IP addresses to hosts from a centralized location. Nearly a decade passed, however, before a document was published to define such a system. The system described, known as the *Dynamic Host Configuration Protocol* (DHCP), performs all of the IP-address assignment and TCP/IP client-configuration tasks needed for a large internetwork. It is supported by IntranetWare and Windows NT, with either implementation capable of providing a comprehensive solution for an entire enterprise network.

The Problem

On a small network, client configuration is not much of a burden on network administrators. Working on each workstation, individually, usually requires less time than implementing an automated solution. When configuring TCP/IP client systems, however, administrators must be careful to assign unique IP addresses to each host, and to configure all other parameters needed to initialize a TCP/IP stack, correctly.

Duplicate IP addresses are one of the most common problems on TCP/IP networks. They often cause mysterious system outages that come and go according to the usage patterns of the computers involved. Traditionally, network administrators have relied on spreadsheets and paper records to track the addresses assigned to particular computer systems. Even with this approach, mistakes are common and users have a way of foiling the most carefully planned administration strategies.

On a large internetwork (especially one on which TCP/IP is being added to an existing infrastructure), configuring hundreds, or thousands, of network clients can be monumental – and assigning unique IP addresses complicates matters further. Accomplishing this task requires either a concerted effort by a team of network administrators (often augmented with temporary help), or the development of complete documentation that is simple enough for users to follow to configure their own systems. Both of these alternatives are time-consuming and expensive, and don't necessarily provide a foolproof solution. Organizational, or even typographical, errors can result in duplicate IP addresses and nonfunctioning clients.

Microsoft discovered these facts while evaluating the TCP/IP protocols for use on their own 35,000-node worldwide intranetwork, in the early 1990s. The logistics of delegating groups of host addresses to administrators in facilities located in 50 different countries was daunting. As a result of testing, Microsoft set about developing a system to configure TCP/IP systems, automatically, and to store its IP addresses (and other settings) in a centrally located database.

At that time, Microsoft decided to address other problems inherent in the client-configuration process. Many networks use portable computers, either in the form of laptops or in-house demonstration systems, that may be connected to different subnets on a regular basis. Rather than delegate multiple IP addresses to a single machine, of which only one would be used at a time, a system was needed to allocate an address and then reclaim it after it was used.

This idea of dynamic address allocation led to another problem: name resolution. If the IP address of a system changed automatically, name servers would need the changed information, to circumvent manual modifications when an address was reassigned. Microsoft considered all of these factors while developing the systems known as DHCP and the *Windows Internet Naming Service* (WINS).

The impact of DHCP and WINS on name resolution is covered in Chapter 11, "Name Registration and Resolution."

The Origins of DHCP

DHCP was not the first system designed to assign IP addresses from a central location. In fact, DCHP was built on the designs for the *Bootstrap Protocol* (BOOTP) – an earlier Internet standard providing some of the same basic functionality. Even before BOOTP, however, was the *Reverse Address Resolution Protocol* (RARP), published as Internet standard RFC903.

RARP

When TCP/IP clients are used on Ethernet networks or other LAN types, they rely on the *Address Resolution Protocol* (ARP). This protocol enables them to discover the hardware addresses of the systems to which they will transmit. The clients do this by broadcasting the IP address of the desired host and requesting that it reply with its hardware address. RARP performs the opposite function; it ascertains a computer system's IP address by broadcasting a hardware address.

RARP was designed for use on diskless workstations without any means of storing TCP/IP configuration data, such as the system's own IP address. These workstations recognize their own hardware addresses, as this information is hardcoded into the network interface adapter. When a RARP client broadcasts its own hardware address, a RARP server can respond by sending an IP address that the workstation uses in its own TCP/IP client configuration (see Figure 10-1). Although designed for diskless clients, this service could easily be used by TCP/IP clients running on systems with hard disks, as well.

For more information on the packet structure and the communications procedures used by the RARP protocol, see Chapter 4, "The Link Layer."

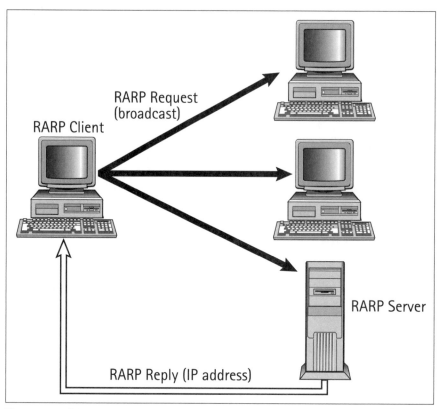

Figure 10-1: RARP clients obtain their IP addresses by broadcasting their hardware addresses to RARP servers.

Unlike ARP, which treats all host systems equally, RARP relies on a client/server relationship. A RARP server functions as a repository for the IP addresses of all diskless TCP/IP workstations on the network. These are manually entered, by the network administrator, into a reference table stored in a file called /etc/ethers. RARP, therefore, does nothing to prevent IP-addressing problems caused by administrative errors.

As an administrative tool, RARP also has other shortcomings. First, it is limited to supplying IP addresses only. Today's TCP/IP clients require numerous other parameter settings, such as subnet masks, default gateways, and DNS client configuration. The second shortcoming is that RARP clients rely on broadcasts to communicate with the server. Because the diskless workstation has no configuration data of its own when issuing a RARP request, it can only broadcast the packet to the entire network.

Broadcast transmissions, however, are limited to the local network segment. This means that a RARP server must be on every segment of an internetwork, and each must be configured with IP addresses for the systems located on that segment. Thus, RARP can conceivably save network administrators some time traveling to individual machines, but it still leaves many of the requirements for a full-featured administration tool unaddressed.

BOOTP

The Bootstrap Protocol (as defined in RFC951, and with extensions published as RFC1533 and RFC1542) was also developed in the 1980s for use with diskless workstations. This protocol provides sufficient functionality and is still used today, while RARP is all but obsolete. To use RARP, client systems must be capable of sending and receiving the packets generated by a specialized link-layer protocol. BOOTP, however, is based on UDP/IP communications, which must be supported by all TCP/IP implementations – enabling its use on a wider array of client hardware platforms.

When used on diskless workstations, BOOTP also provides client systems with the capability to download an executable boot file from a server. This function is performed using a *Trivial File Transfer Protocol* (TFTP) transfer. Diskless work-stations are seldom used today, so this feature is rarely implemented.

Two of RARP's most important shortcomings (which are addressed by BOOTP) are the limitations imposed by the use of broadcasts, and the type of information supplied to the client by the protocol. Because the protocol was developed for client systems that cannot store TCP/IP configuration settings, clients must use broad-casts to contact the BOOTP server. With RARP, this factor imposes the need for a server on every network segment, but BOOTP overcomes this limitation by defining a software feature for routers or hosts, called a *BOOTP relay agent*.

A BOOTP relay agent propagates BOOTP-client broadcasts to servers located on another network segment. This enables a single BOOTP server to support clients on multiple network segments. Many of today's routers support BOOTP relay as an optional feature, and Windows NT includes a relay agent that runs on a host sys-tem. Because DHCP uses the same basic communications procedures as BOOTP, the same relay agents function with both systems.

BOOTP is also capable of delivering more than just an IP address to a client. RFC2132 defines a series of optional TCP/IP configuration parameters that can be provided to clients using either BOOTP or DHCP – including the subnet mask and the default gateway.

Though BOOTP improves on RARP in several important ways, it remains a mechanism for storing configuration data and delivering it to clients on demand. Network administrators must manually enter and maintain the clients' IP addresses and other settings at the BOOTP server. This is not an insignificant achievement, as BOOTP can save administrators the time and effort needed to travel to each system, but they still must assign addresses individually. They are also subject to the same errors as any other manual configuration process.

Understanding DHCP

DHCP builds on the capabilities of BOOTP, but takes the concept of automatic client configuration to a higher level. Rather than simply storing IP-address assignments that have been manually entered by administrators, DHCP automatically assigns addresses to clients from a pool, as needed. The addresses are then reclaimed when they are no longer in use. When Microsoft set about developing its own client-configuration system, its goals were more comprehensive than those used to create BOOTP or RARP. Microsoft's concern was not for booting diskless workstations, but for creating a service that would completely automate the TCP/IP-client configuration process.

The goals for the design of the DHCP service follow:

◆ A DHCP client should not require manual configuration of the TCP/IP client. All of the required settings should be obtainable through the DHCP-communications process.

◆ IP addresses should be assigned and maintained to eliminate the possibility of address duplication among DHCP clients.

◆ A DHCP server should service clients located on multiple subnets, using BOOTP relay agents to pass through routers.

◆ The DHCP system should coexist with clients that have been configured manually. It should also assign permanent IP addresses to specific clients, as needed.

◆ DHCP clients should, whenever possible, retain their TCP/IP-configuration settings, despite a reboot of the client or the DHCP server.

To achieve these goals, the DHCP specification defines two elements developers can use to build a system that automatically configures TCP/IP hosts. The two elements are as follows:

◆ A service that allocates IP addresses and other configuration parameters to clients

◆ A protocol used to deliver TCP/IP-client configuration data from DHCP servers to DHCP clients

Assigning IP Addresses

TCP/IP networks and systems can have different IP-address requirements. DHCP attempts to account for them all by providing the following three address-allocation strategies:

◆ **Manual allocation** – Like the BOOTP and RARP services, manual allocation occurs when a network administrator assigns a specific IP address to a client. The DHCP server is responsible only for delivering the address.

◆ **Automatic allocation** – Automatic allocation occurs when a DHCP client is assigned an IP address, from a pool, when it is configured for the first time. The client retains the address permanently, or until it is manually removed at the client workstation.

◆ **Dynamic allocation** – Dynamic allocation occurs when a DHCP client is assigned an IP address, from a pool, on a leased-time basis. If the client stops using the address for a set period of time, the lease expires and the address is returned to the pool for reallocation.

In certain situations, it is necessary for a TCP/IP system to have a specific IP address. For example, systems hosting Internet services, such as FTP and Web servers, should not be subjected to the random address assignments used by the automatic- and dynamic-allocation methods. These services are typically accessed by client applications using Internet host names. At present, there is no way to update DNS entries, automatically, when a system's IP address changes due to a DHCP transaction. It would be possible to configure the IP addresses of such systems by hand, but using DHCP's manual allocation capability maintains all IP-address assignments in one place. It also ensures that no other system is assigned the same address.

Running a network that contains a mixture of DHCP and individually configured clients often results in a lot of confusion. You should use DHCP for all (or none) of your TCP/IP clients. Systems running the DHCP server software are the sole exception to this rule, as they cannot obtain their own IP addresses using a DHCP client.

The question of whether to use automatic- or dynamic-address assignment depends on the volatility of your network's design. If your network configuration rarely changes, or if systems are installed in one location and not moved often, dynamic-address allocation is probably not needed. If, however, you have laptop users attaching to the network from different locations, or if you find systems or departments, must be moved on a regular basis, dynamic allocation may be recommended.

Another use for dynamic allocation is when you have a limited number of IP addresses available and clients that occasionally need TCP/IP access. Leasing addresses enables you to service users on demand with a relatively small block of addresses.

In any case, the only cost of using dynamic, over automatic, allocation is the additional network traffic incurred by the lease negotiation and renewal process. You can adjust the length of time an address is leased for, to optimize the amount of DHCP traffic on your network.

Assigning Client-Configuration Parameters

Apart from IP addresses, you can use DHCP to assign values to a large number of TCP/IP client-configuration options. A goal of the DHCP's designers was to enable a workstation's TCP/IP client to be configured using data retrieved from the DHCP server. If a network administrator must travel to a workstation to manually complete the client-configuration process, a major part of the service's functionality is compromised.

To achieve this goal, the IntranetWare and Microsoft DHCP servers include a large number of options provided with the IP address. Microsoft's server, for example, lists over 50 client parameters, nearly all of which are defined in the DHCP specification.

 The specifications for DHCP are divided among several RFCs. RFC2131 is the base document that defines the packet structure for the protocol, and the lease-negotiation process. RFC1542 contains material on the BOOTP relay agents that DHCP also uses for the propagation of its packets across network-segment boundaries. The additional configuration parameters, which can be used by both DHCP and BOOTP systems, are defined in RFC2132. Many of these options are classified as "vendor extensions" — options submitted, by partisan authors, for inclusion in the document. Vendor extensions undergo the same IETF standards-ratification process as other DHCP specifications.

Most DHCP clients, however, require only a small subset of available options to create a fully functional TCP/IP configuration. Some of the most commonly used client options can be set using either the Microsoft or Novell DHCP server are as follows:

♦ **IP address** – the 32-bit address that TCP/IP uses to identify a specific host on a specific IP network

♦ **Subnet mask** – the 32-bit dotted-decimal value specifies which IP address bits are used to identify the network, and which identify the host

♦ **Router** – the IP address of the router on the local network segment that a host should use, by default, to access remote networks

- ◆ **DNS servers** – the IP addresses of systems running a DNS name server (accessed in the order they are listed)

- ◆ **Domain name** – the name of the Internet domain in which the host system belongs

- ◆ **NetBIOS over TCP/IP Name Server addresses** – the IP addresses of name servers (usually Windows NT WINS servers) used for NetBIOS name resolution on a private internetwork

- ◆ **NetBIOS over TCP/IP Node Type** – a code that indicates which NetBIOS name-resolution mechanisms a client system should use (and the order in which they should be used)

- ◆ **NetBIOS over TCP/IP Scope** – a name assigned to a group of systems which can be identified using a single NetBIOS name

- ◆ **Ethernet Encapsulation** – specifies the type of Ethernet frame to use in order to encapsulate IP datagrams on the host system

- ◆ **IP Address Lease Time** – the length of time a dynamically allocated IP address can be used by a client, without renewal

- ◆ **Renewal (T1) Time Value** – the length of time that a leased IP address can operate before it passes into the renewal state

- ◆ **Rebinding (T2) Time Value** – the length of time a leased IP address can operate before it passes into the rebinding state

Microsoft's DHCP server adheres more closely to the RFC specifications, providing many options that are never used by Windows TCP/IP clients, but are called for in the documents. The set of options found in Novell's DHCP server is not as complete, but it does contain all of the settings commonly used by the Microsoft clients, such as the NetBIOS name server options required on a Windows NT network running WINS. Novell's implementation also includes a collection of nonstandard options used for NetWare/IP clients.

 Both Microsoft and Novell DHCP servers provide TCP/IP-configuration options for the Windows operating systems that comprise most of the DHCP clients found on private internetworks. There are only two scenarios in which the available configuration options should affect your decision as to which DHCP implementation to use. If you are running NetWare/IP DHCP clients, the Novell server is preferable. If you are running UNIX (or other) client platforms, you may require the additional RFC-standard options provided by the Microsoft version.

The DHCP Packet Structure

DHCP uses a complex communications process between clients and servers that employs seven different message types. All of these messages use the same packet structure, however, as illustrated in Figure 10-2. DHCP messages are carried by the UDP protocol, using port 67 at the server and port 68 at the client.

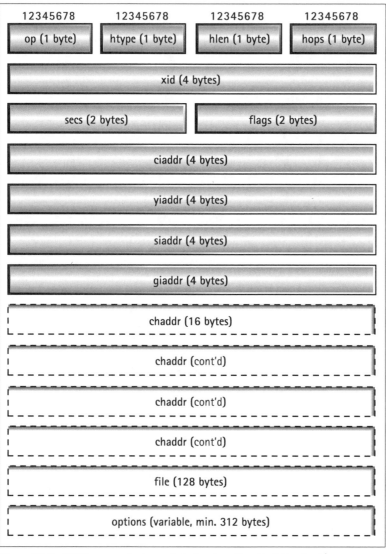

Figure 10-2: DHCP uses a single-packet structure for all of its client/server communications.

The functions of each of the fields in a DHCP packet are as follows:

◆ **op** (1 byte) – The op field contains a code that specifies the origin of the packet transmission, as follows:

   ◆ 1 – BOOTREQUEST – client-to-server transmission

   ◆ 2 – BOOTREPLY – server-to-client transmission

◆ **htype** (1 byte) – This field contains a code that specifies the type of hardware address in the chaddr field, using values from the ARP section of the "Assigned Numbers" RFC:

   ◆ 1 – 10Mb Ethernet

◆ **hlen** (1 byte) – The hlen field indicates the length of the hardware address found in the chaddr field, in bytes. (For 10Mb Ethernet, the value is 6.)

◆ **hops** (1 byte) – This field is set to 0 by the client and incremented by each relay agent encountered during the packet's journey to the server. This tracks the number of interim network segments.

◆ **xid** (4 bytes) – The xid field contains a transaction identifier, chosen at random by the client, that is used to associate the requests and responses of a DHCP transaction.

◆ **secs** (2 bytes) – The secs field specifies the number of seconds that have elapsed since the beginning of an address allocation or lease-renewal process. This distinguishes messages of the same type that might be transmitted during a particular DHCP transaction.

◆ **flags** (2 bytes) – The first bit of the flags field is known as the *broadcast bit*. When set to a value of 1, this bit specifies that DHCP servers and relay agents should use broadcast (not unicast) transmissions to send packets to this client. All of the other bits are currently unused, and must be set to a value of 0.

◆ **ciaddr** (4 bytes) – This field contains the workstation's IP address when the client is in the bound, renewal, or rebinding state (and is negotiating for continued use of the address with a DHCPREQUEST message). At all other times, its value must be 0.

◆ **yiaddr** (4 bytes) – This field contains the IP address a server offers, or assigns, to a client by in a DHCPOFFER or DHCPACK message. At all other times, its value must be 0.

◆ **siaddr** (4 bytes) – This field contains the IP address of the next server to be used in a bootstrap sequence. A server supplies this information, in a

DHCPOFFER or DHCPACK message, when DHCP supplies an executable boot file to a client, and the boot files for different machine types are stored on different servers.

◆ **giaddr** (4 bytes) – This field contains the relay agent's IP address to which a server should send replies, when located on a different network segment than the client. When the client and server are located on the same network, its value should be 0.

◆ **chaddr** (16 bytes) – This field contains the client's hardware address, as defined by the htype and hlen fields. The chaddr value is transmitted to the server in DHCPDISCOVER and DHCPREQUEST messages. The server uses this value to address unicast replies to the client.

◆ **sname** (64 bytes) – The sname field contains the (optional) host name of the DHCP server. It may also be used to hold overflow data from the options field.

◆ **file** (128 bytes) – The file field contains the name of an executable boot file for diskless workstations. In a DHCPDISCOVER message, the field may contain a generic filename; in a DHCPOFFER, a full path and file name is specified. The field may also be used to hold overflow data from the options field.

◆ **options** (variable, 312 bytes minimum) – This field is composed of substructures containing any of the DHCP options defined in RFC2132. These options may include any additional TCP/IP configuration parameters that DHCP can furnish to a client. The DHCP message-type option defines the function of this particular packet, and the magic cookie defines how the rest of the data in the field should be interpreted.

By definition, some IP communications must occur before a DHCP client is assigned an IP address. Most TCP/IP implementations will accept incoming datagrams that are delivered to the system's hardware address using unicast transmissions. They will pass them upwards for processing at the network layer, even if the client has no IP address. The broadcast bit, found in the flags field, is for those implementations that do not support these incoming unicasts.

The options field of the DHCP packet always begins with the 4-byte magic cookie (which contains the byte values 99, 130, 83, and 99, in decimal notation). This field always concludes with the End option, one byte with the decimal value 255. In between, there may be any number of valid options – in any order. Options usually consist of three fields of their own, as follows:

◆ **Code** (1 byte) – The code (or tag) field contains a value that uniquely identifies the function of the option. The code values are defined in RFC2132.

◆ **Length** (1 byte) – The length field indicates the length of the upcoming data field (in bytes), and is used to delimit each option in the packet.

◆ **Data** (variable) – The data field contains information specific to the option, such as a value that must be supplied for a particular client-configuration parameter. The size of this field is defined by the value in the length field.

Most of the available options are used to carry configuration values, but some are used to configure the operation of DHCP, itself. While the op field indicates whether a DHCP packet has originated at a client or server, a required entry in the options field (called DHCP Message Type) indicates the actual function of the message, using the following values:

◆ **1 – DHCPDISCOVER** – clients use this to locate DHCP servers and request an IP address assignment

◆ **2 – DHCPOFFER** – servers use this to offer IP addresses to clients

◆ **3 – DHCPREQUEST** – clients use this to request or renew a specific IP address assignment

◆ **4 – DHCPDECLINE** – clients use this to reject an offered IP address assignment

◆ **5 – DHCPACK** – servers use this to acknowledge a client's acceptance of a client's IP-address assignment

◆ **6 – DHCPNAK** – servers use this to reject a client's acceptance of an IP-address assignment

◆ **7 – DHCPRELEASE** – clients use this to terminate the lease of an IP address

◆ **8 – DHCPINFORM** – clients that already possess an IP address use this to obtain other client-configuration parameters from a server

These various message types are used during packet exchanges. Through such exchanges, a DHCP client obtains its configuration parameters from a server.

The DHCPINFORM message type was added to the DHCP specifications in the March 1997 revision (RFC2131 and RFC2132). DHCPINFORM is used when a TCP/IP client has already been manually configured with an IP address, but still requires other settings to be fully activated. It has not yet been implemented in the Windows NT, or Novell IntranetWare DHCP server modules (which are based on the previous versions of specifications: RFC1533, RFC1541, and RFC1542).

When a DHCP message contains a large number of options, they may spill out of the options field. In this case, they may be stored in the packet's sname and file fields. These two fields are optional and rarely used. They can carry 192 additional bytes of option data, if needed. The message must include the Option Overload option, with a value appropriate to the desired configuration, to use these two fields.

DHCP Communications

When a DHCP client implementation is activated for the first time, it exchanges messages with the DHCP servers on the network to negotiate an IP-address assignment. This same exchange may occur in other circumstances, for example, when a system's lease on its IP address has expired, when the client has explicitly released its address, or when the system is moved to another subnet – rendering its current address invalid.

This part of the communications process is the same, whether dynamic-, auto-matic-, or manual-address allocation is being used. If the server allocates addresses dynamically, further DHCP client/server exchanges occur at regular intervals so the clients can renew their IP address leases.

When a TCP/IP system is multihomed (that is, when it contains multiple host adapters), each adapter is configured, individually, to be a DHCP client. When DHCP is used to configure more than one adapter on a system, separate IP-address assignment and lease-negotiation exchanges with the server are required.

NEGOTIATING AN IP ADDRESS ASSIGNMENT

When a DHCP client first initializes, it does not recognize the DHCP servers on the network, and operates without an IP address of its own. This is known as being in the *init* state. The only communications it is capable of are network broadcasts. To begin the client-configuration process, the workstation begins broadcasting DHCPDISCOVER messages to the local network segment at regular intervals (see Figure 10-3). These messages contain the hardware address from the system's network-interface adapter in the chaddr field (as defined by the values in the htype and hlen fields). Other information regarding the client's requirements may also be included, such as preferred IP address, and the lease-time duration. These are spec-ified using the Requested IP Address and the IP Address Lease Time options.

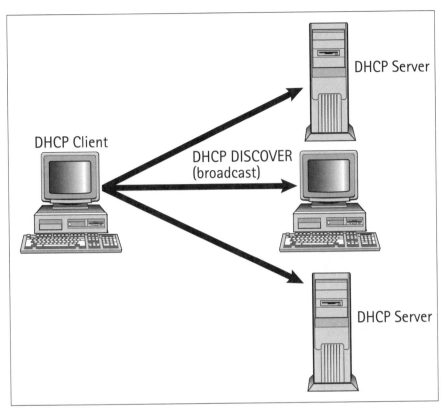

Figure 10-3: A DHCP client begins the process of acquiring an IP address by broadcasting DHCPDISCOVER messages to the network.

Any relay agents located on the local network segment must propagate the DHCPDISCOVER messages to the other segments to which they are connected. Though relay agents enable one DHCP server to service clients on multiple network segments, many sites maintain multiple servers for load balancing purposes. Each DHCP server operates independently, and is responsible for responding to every DHCPDISCOVER broadcast message it receives – as long as it has IP addresses available for allocation.

On receiving a DHCPDISCOVER message, a DHCP server generates a DHCPOFFER message containing an IP address in the yiaddr field. It also contains the other client options that the server is configured to supply, as shown in Figure 10-4. The DHCPOFFER message is sent as a unicast transmission, addressed to the hardware address found in the DHCPDISCOVER message. If, however, the broadcast bit is set to 1, the message is sent as a broadcast. The general rule for DHCP clients and servers is to minimize the amount of network traffic they generate by keeping broadcasts to a minimum.

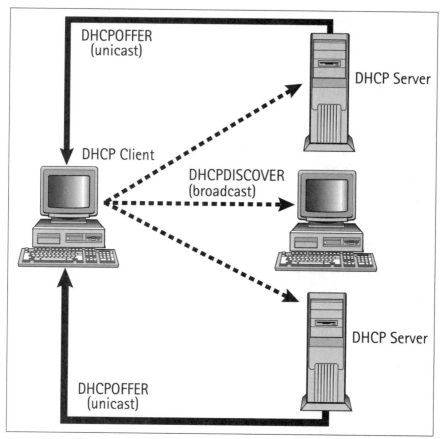

Figure 10-4: DHCP servers respond to clients' broadcasts with DHCPOFFER messages containing proposed IP address assignments.

As a result of its DHCPDISCOVER broadcasts, a client may receive DHCPOFFER messages from several servers (each containing a different IP address). The client must accept one of the offers before the IP address is reserved for the client's use. In the meantime, if addresses are scarce, a server may offer the same address to another client, simultaneously.

Once a preset timeout interval expires, the DHCP client stops broadcasting DHCPDISCOVER messages and selects one of the addresses it has been offered. The client then generates a DHCPREQUEST message. This contains the IP address of the selected server in the Server Identifier option, and the offered IP address (from the yiaddr field) in the Requested IP Address option (see Figure 10-5). The message may also contain options requesting values for additional configuration parameters from the server. If no offers have been received, the client times out, generates an error message, and begins the discovery process again.

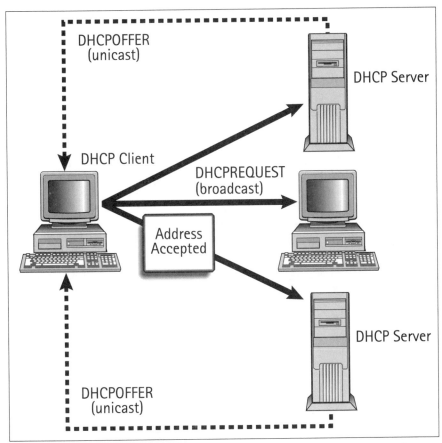

Figure 10-5: A client accepts one of the offered IP addresses and rejects all others by broadcasting a DHCPREQUEST message to the network.

Among the perceived shortcomings of DHCP is that servers cannot allocate IP addresses from a common pool. Each one must be configured with its own block of addresses that are not duplicated on other servers. This prevents the use of multiple servers as a fault-tolerance solution for the network. When a DHCP server goes down, the addresses in its pool are not available for reallocation once their leases expire. When IP addresses are in short supply, this can cause clients to lose their TCP/IP access until the server is repaired.

Although it's impossible to unicast the DHCPREQUEST to the selected server, the client transmits this packet as a broadcast, instead. This message informs the selected server that its offer is being accepted, and all other servers that their offers are being declined. To ensure that the packet passes through all the same relay agents, and reaches all of the servers involved, the DHCPREQUEST message must contain the same value in the secs field as the original DHCPDISCOVER message. It must also be transmitted to the same broadcast address.

The server commits the offered IP address (and other configuration settings) to its database, in association with this particular client, on receipt of the DHCPREQUEST. Combining the client's hardware address (from the chaddr field) and its new IP address (from the yiaddr field) creates a unique identifier for this lease, and appears in all subsequent DHCP communications between client and server. This combination of addresses is sometimes referred to as the *lease identification cookie*. To confirm the address assignment, the server sends a DHCPACK message to the client as a unicast (see Figure 10-6).

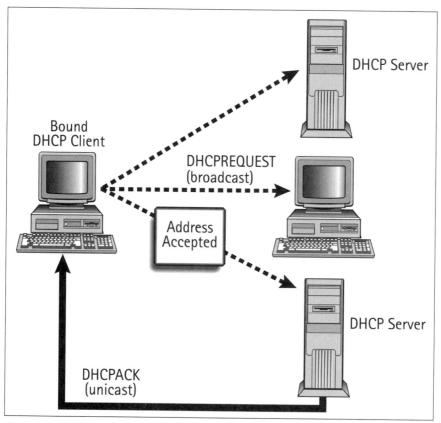

Figure 10-6: On receipt of a DHCPACK message, a client enters the bound state, and uses the IP address and other configuration settings supplied by the server.

If the server is unable to complete the address assignment (because that address has been bound to another client, for example), it transmits a DHCPNAK message to the client, and the entire negotiation is nullified. The client must begin the entire process again by generating new DHCPDISCOVER broadcasts.

Once a DHCPACK is received, the client uses ARP to ensure that the assigned IP address is not already being used on the network. If there is no response to the ARP broadcasts, the client is configured and referred to as being *bound*. If ARP detects that the address is already being used, the client returns a DHCPDECLINE message to the server and the entire negotiation process must begin again.

RELEASING AN IP ADDRESS

At any time after it is bound, the DHCP client may choose to relinquish its lease on the IP address. It does this by transmitting a DHCPRELEASE message to the server, containing its client identifier (the lease identification cookie). The client is then returned to the unbound state, and the address is returned to the server's address pool for reallocation.

REUSING AN ASSIGNED ADDRESS

Each time a DHCP client system is rebooted, or the client reinitialized, it must negotiate the reuse of its assigned IP address. This involves an abbreviated form of the initial address-negotiation procedure, in which the DHCPDISCOVER and DHCPOFFER messages are eliminated. The client begins in the *rebooting* state by broadcasting a DHCPREQUEST message. This message contains its previously assigned IP address in the Requested IP Address option, and no values in the ciaddr field or in the Server Identifier option.

Upon receipt of the DHCPREQUEST message, the server that originally negotiated the address assignment responds with a DHCPACK or DHCPNAK message (as in the original negotiation). This transaction tests whether the client system has been moved to a different subnet, in which case, it cannot use its previously assigned IP address. When the DHCP server detects this condition, it returns a DHCPNAK message to the client, which must begin a new negotiation with DHCPDISCOVER broadcasts.

Upon receiving a DHCPACK, the client tests the address with ARP broadcasts, as before, and either enters the bound state or transmits a DHCPDECLINE message. If the client is bound, it continues to use its original address, the lease for which is renewed at the time the DHCPREQUEST was first transmitted.

If the client system receives no response to its DHCPREQUEST broadcast after ten retries, it begins the negotiation process again with DHCPDISCOVER broadcasts. If the DHCP server still does not respond, the client returns to the previous settings, and uses the originally assigned IP address until the lease expires.

IMPLEMENTING LEASE RENEWAL

The capability to lease IP addresses and reclaim them when they are no longer being used is DHCP's primary advantage over BOOTP. When a DHCP server is configured to dynamically assign IP addresses, there are three client-configuration options to specify the lease duration and the client's communications activities during the lease-renewal process:

- ◆ **IP Address Lease Time** – This specifies the period of time (in seconds) that the client may continue using the assigned IP address without renewing the lease.

- ◆ **Renewal (T1) Time Value** – This value specifies the period of time (in seconds) that the client may use the assigned IP address before it passes into the renewing state. In this state, it begins the process of trying to renew its existing lease. The value defaults to 50 percent of the IP Address Lease Time.

- ◆ **Rebinding (T2) Time Value** – This value specifies the period of time (in seconds) that the client may use the assigned IP address before it passes into the rebinding state. In this state, it begins the process of trying to obtain a new lease from any available server. The value defaults to 87.5 percent of the IP Address Lease Time.

Once it is successfully assigned an IP address, a client remains in the bound state until the lease reaches the T1 point (which usually consumes half of the total lease time). When it reaches this point, a client enters the *renewing* state, and attempts to contact its DHCP server to renew the lease (see Figure 10-7). Both the Microsoft and Novell DHCP servers default to a lease period of three days – which means clients make their first attempts to renew the lease after 36 hours of continuous operation.

When network users shut down their workstations at night, their leases are renewed each time they boot their systems. This and the default 50 percent T1 value make lease expirations a rare occurrence on most networks (unless the DHCP servers are inoperative).

When a client enters the renewing state, it begins transmitting DHCPREQUEST messages to the server that holds its lease. The messages contain the client's IP address in the ciaddr field and no value in the Server Identifier option. Unlike the DHCPREQUEST messages sent while the client is in the init or rebooting state, however, these messages are sent as unicast transmissions.

If the server holding the client's lease responds with a DHCPACK in the usual manner, the client returns to the bound state and the lease timer is reset. A DHCPNAK reply from the server terminates the lease and forces the client to begin a new negotiation process with DHCPDISCOVER broadcasts.

If no response is received from the DHCP server, the DHCPREQUEST unicast is repeated whenever half of the remaining time until the T2 point has expired. If the T2 point arrives with no response from the server holding the lease, then the client enters the *rebinding* state and the DHCPREQUEST messages are transmitted as broadcasts. At this point, a new lease is solicited from any available DHCP server. Broadcasts are repeated again whenever half of the remaining time (until the expiration of the lease) has elapsed.

If no server responds with a DHCPACK or DHCPNAK message and the client remains in the rebinding state until the lease expires, its IP address is returned to its address pool. The client then returns to the *unbound* state, and all TCP/IP communications cease, except for the DHCPDISCOVER packets needed to negotiate a new lease.

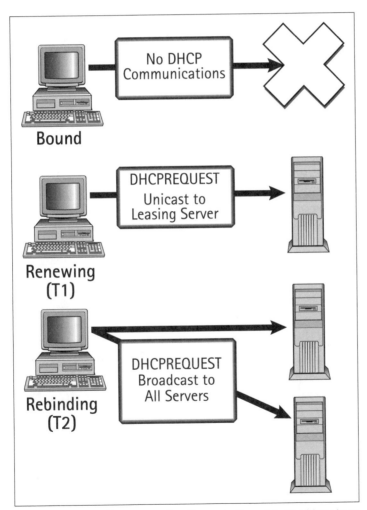

Figure 10-7: As a client approaches the expiration of its IP address lease, it increases its efforts to contact a DHCP server for a lease renewal.

Using DHCP

Despite this complex array of communications procedures, implementing DHCP on an internetwork is a relatively simple task. The first step is to consider how many DHCP servers you need and where they will be located. In most cases, a single DHCP server can service all of the clients on your network. Microsoft's product can manage 10,000 IP addresses. Network traffic conditions, load balancing, and fault tolerance should all play a part in your decision.

When planning a DHCP deployment on an internetwork, your first consideration should be routing. If your routers support the BOOTP relay agent behavior defined in RFC1542 (sometimes called BOOTP forwarding), you can use a single DHCP server to configure clients on multiple network segments. Both Windows NT and IntranetWare servers can function as routers to support BOOTP forwarding. On a NetWare server, you must load the BOOTPFWD.NLM program, while Windows NT includes a DHCP relay agent module that installs as a network service.

Before you install the DHCP software on a server, you must first install and configure the operating system's TCP/IP stack. A DHCP server cannot be a DHCP client, itself. You must assign a static IP address to the system, along with all of the other necessary configuration parameters. These procedures are discussed in Chapter 8, "Windows NT and IntranetWare."

The next factors to consider are the needs of your clients. You must decide what type of address allocation to use, which systems require permanent address assignments, and what other options your clients require. All of these decisions dictate the way you will configure the pools of IP addresses that your DHCP servers assign to clients. Windows NT refers to these address pools as *scopes*, while NetWare calls them *subnetwork profiles*.

Using Multiple DHCP Servers

Despite the capabilities of the DHCP server software, a single system should not be used to service a large internetwork. This practice would concentrate all DHCP traffic onto a single segment, and provide a single point of failure for the entire TCP/IP network. Once you come to rely on DHCP, you should always have backup servers available in case of a system failure. Both the IntranetWare and Windows NT DHCP servers are included with the OS and do not require a dedicated computer. This makes it easy to install and configure a backup copy of the software on another machine and leave it dormant, in case of an emergency.

The Microsoft DHCP Server

Microsoft's DHCP server ships as part of the Windows NT Server 4.0 package. The software installs as a network service from the Network Control Panel, and contains a Windows-based administration program called DHCP Manager (DHCPADMN.EXE). With this program, you can manage all of the Microsoft DHCP servers on your network from a single location.

INSTALLING THE MICROSOFT DHCP SERVER

The only prerequisite for the Microsoft DHCP server is a functioning TCP/IP client with its own static IP address on a Windows NT server system. To install the DHCP service, you launch the Network Control Panel and display the Services screen. When you add a new service and select DHCP Server from the list (see Figure 10-8) you are prompted to insert the Windows NT installation CD-ROM (if the source files are not available already).

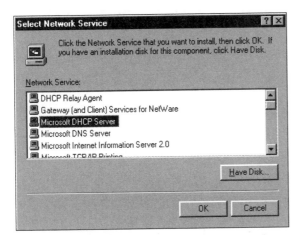

Figure 10-8: Microsoft's DHCP server installs from the Network Control Panel as a standard network service.

 From the same Services screen, you can also install the Windows NT DHCP Relay Agent. This enables the system to route DHCP broadcasts to network segments other than the one where the DHCP server resides.

The installation process copies the files needed to run the DHCP service and the DHCP Administrator to your server's hard drive. The installation also creates the DHCP database, which is where all of the server's IP address assignments, and other configuration data, are stored. The database consists of the following files, stored in the *systemroot*\System32\Dhcp directory:

- ◆ DHCP.MDB
- ◆ DHCP.TMP
- ◆ J50.LOG
- ◆ J50#####.LOG
- ◆ J50.CHK

Windows NT 4.0 uses the Exchange Server database engine to store the DHCP information, which is a substantial improvement over the database used in previous NT versions. If you upgrade a Windows NT server to version 4.0 from any previous version that has DHCP installed, the existing database is converted to the new format using a utility called JETCONV.EXE. The old versions of the database files are saved to a subdirectory created beneath the existing DHCP directory.

The entries in the DHCP database are automatically backed up every 15 minutes, by default. You can change this interval by modifying the following Registry value, located in the following subkey:

```
SYSTEM
  \current
      \currentcontrolset
          \services
              \DHCPServer
                  \Parameters
                      BackupInterval
```

When the installation process is complete, you can start and stop the service, and specify whether the service should start when the system boots from the Services Control Panel. You can also use the NET START DHCP and NET STOP DHCP commands at the system prompt to manually operate the service.

CONFIGURING THE DHCP SERVER

Once the DHCP service is operational, you must create one or more scopes before it can be used by clients. A *scope* is a series of IP addresses on a particular subnet that will be allocated to clients. You can only create one scope on a subnet, but this scope can consist of any number of IP addresses. To create a scope, you launch the DHCP Manager utility from the Windows NT system's Start menu. You can also run the application from any other Windows NT system (Server or Workstation) by accessing the DHCP server's C: drive and launching DHCPADMN.EXE from the *systemroot*\System32 directory.

When you launch DHCP Manager from the DHCP server, you see the screen shown in Figure 10-9. If you launch the program from another system, the DHCP

Servers column is blank, and you must choose Add from the Server menu and specify the IP address of a DHCP Server. You can build a list of all of the DHCP servers on your network this way, and manage them from one location.

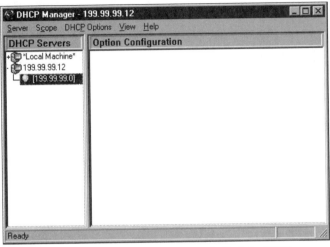

Figure 10-9: The DHCP Manager can control all of the DHCP servers on your network from any Windows NT system.

CREATING A SCOPE   When you select Create from the DHCP Manager's Scope menu, you see the Create Scope dialog box. Here, you specify the most basic elements of a DHCP configuration: the IP addresses to be assigned, the subnet mask for those addresses, and the duration of the address leases. This dialog box enables you to specify any group of IP addresses by creating a range, and excluding specific addresses within that range.

For example, you can see in Figure 10-10 that the address range is set to start with 199.99.98.10 and end with 199.99.98.50. The addresses 199.99.98.35 to 199.99.99.38, however, are excluded from that range, perhaps because they are already assigned to other systems. You can create as many exclusions as you wish, and exclude single addresses by specifying the same value for both the Start and End Address fields.

The Lease Duration box enables you to change the default IP Address Lease Time from three days to whatever time you wish. You may also specify unlimited leases, which switches this scope from dynamic- to automatic-address allocation. Different lease times may be configured for each scope, depending on the needs of your users.

After creating the scope, DHCP Manager prompts you to confirm its activation. Clients cannot be allocated addresses from the scope until it is activated. You can also activate and deactivate scopes, at will, from the Scope menu.

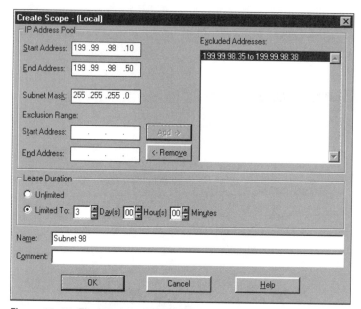

Figure 10-10: The Windows NT DHCP server calls a pool of IP addresses
that will be allocated to clients as a scope.

You can manually create IP address leases by selecting Add Reservations from
the Scope menu (see Figure 10-11). This is the Windows NT DHCP server's implementation of manual allocation. Here, you may specify the IP address that you
want assigned to a specific client, as well as the client system's Unique Identifier
(that is, its hardware address). A Client Name is also required, for reference
purposes.

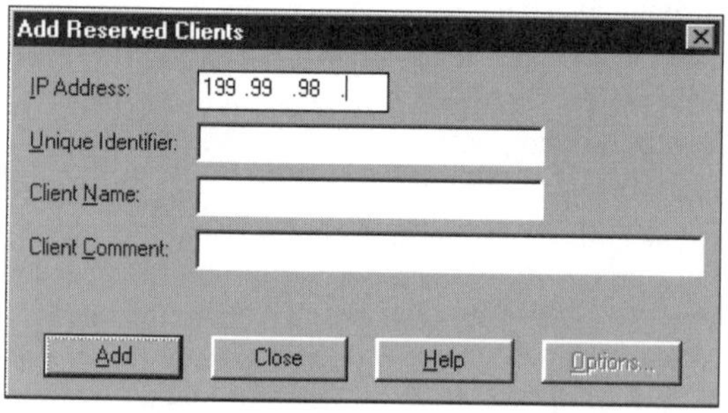

Figure 10-11: You can allocate IP addresses, manually,
by creating a reservation that consists of the client's
hardware address and its intended IP address.

When you select Active Leases from the scope menu, you see a statistics screen, like that in Figure 10-12. This displays all of the currently leased addresses, including the reservations that you have created manually.

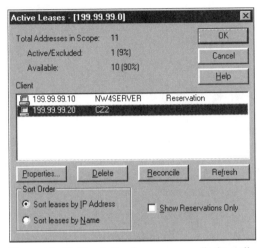

Figure 10-12: The Active Leases screen displays all of the currently allocated IP addresses, and information about the clients that are using them.

CONFIGURING CLIENT OPTIONS   After creating scopes that provide the most basic TCP/IP-configuration settings, you may configure additional options for your clients. The DHCP Manager program enables you to specify option values in the following three ways:

◆ **Default values** – These values enable you to specify the default value for any of the predefined options. When the option is selected for inclusion with a client configuration, the default value is applied unless another value is specified.

◆ **Global options** – Global options enable you to specify configuration options that are applied to all IP address assignments, regardless of scope.

◆ **Scope options** – Score options enable you to specify configuration options that are applied to all of the IP-address assignments, within a particular scope.

While it is possible to create all of your options for each individual scope, default values and global options can save you effort. These options permit you to define options that apply to all of your clients, once. For example, all of your clients are likely to use the same DNS servers and the same domain name.

Configuring these as global options prevents you from having to select them from every scope.

To configure a default value for a particular option, you select Defaults from the DHCP Options menu to display the dialog box (see Figure 10-13). When you make a selection in the Option Name field, the contents of the Value box change to reflect the nature of the information being stored. When you click Edit Array, you can supply a value for that option that is automatically applied when you select it as a global or scope option.

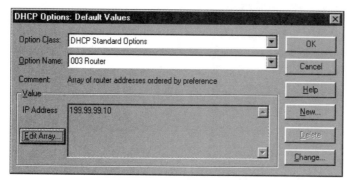

Figure 10-13: You can assign your own default values for any of the DHCP server's predefined options.

You can also use this dialog box to create new options. If your DHCP clients can use options that aren't predefined in the Microsoft server, or if the DHCP specifications are modified to all new options, you can create them yourself. First, click the New button and fill in the appropriate information in the dialog box provided.

Creating new options in the DHCP server does not mean they will be of use to a client. This feature is intended as a hedge against the obsolescence of the server software. As the features of DHCP clients change, the server can be updated to accommodate them.

Selecting Global or Scope from the DHCP Options menu produces dialog boxes that are virtually identical (see Figure 10-14). Global options are applied to all DHCP clients automatically, but you must select a scope from the DHCP Servers column before defining scope options. In each case, the dialog box contains a column of Unused Options on the left side that you can add to the Active Options column on the right. By clicking the Value button, the dialog box expands to display the default value of the selected option and an Edit Array button that you can use to change the value.

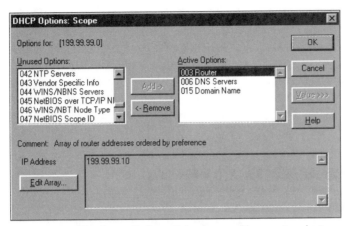

Figure 10-14: The Scope Options dialog box enables you to select any of the options, defined in the DHCP specifications, for delivery to clients. The Global Options dialog box uses the same format.

 For more information on the most commonly used DHCP options, see "Assigning Client Configuration Parameters," earlier in this chapter.

The NetWare DHCP Server

Novell's DHCP server is included in the IntranetWare product and runs as an NLM on a NetWare server (as does the configuration utility, DHCP Server Console). Novell's DHCP server supports Microsoft Windows clients. It includes options like those for NetBIOS name resolution, that are typically used to reference Windows NT WINS servers. Novell also provides additional options to support its own NetWare/IP clients, which use TCP/IP to carry the IPX communications that are the NetWare default.

INSTALLING THE NETWARE DHCP SERVER

As with Windows NT, a NetWare server must have a functional TCP/IP stack before you can install the DHCP server. To begin the installation, load the INSTALL.NLM utility at a NetWare server console and select Product Options. In the Other Installation Items/Products box at the top of the screen, select Install NetWare DHCP and provide the correct path to the IntranetWare installation CD-ROM (disk 1). After INSTALL.NLM copies the installation files, it launches a Product Installation program.

In this program, you select the names of the NetWare servers on which you want to install the DHCP software. You may install multiple DHCP servers at one time, and then configure them all from a single workstation using the RCONSOLE utility.

Once the installation is complete, you must reboot the server and load the DHCP server modules: DHCPIO.NLM and DHCPSRVR.NLM. To load the DHCP server with its default settings, you simply issue the LOAD DHCPSRVR command from the server console prompt. Both of these modules, however, have optional command line parameters, as follows:

```
LOAD DHCPIO [-mmode]
```

where *mode* is replaced with one of the following options:

- **DeleteDuplicate** – causes an old IP-address assignment to be deleted immediately if a bound client system is moved to another subnet and assigned a new IP address

- **YesDuplicate** – causes new IP addresses to be assigned to bound client systems that have moved to another subnet, without deleting the old address assignments

- **NoDuplicate** – prevents new IP addresses from being assigned to client systems that are bound to an address on another subnet:

  ```
  LOAD DHCPSRVR [-v] [-q] [-t time] [-a time] [-h]
  ```

- **–v** – causes DHCP transaction messages to be displayed on the server console

- **–q** – prevents activities from being noted in the DHCP log file (SYS:ETC\DHCP.LOG)

- **–t** *time* – modifies the time interval that elapses between checks of the DHCP database file (SYS:ETC\DHCPTAB) – the default value is 60 seconds

- **–a time** – modifies the time interval that elapses between checks for elapsed client IP-address leases – the default value is 10 minutes

- **–h** – displays a help screen

When the server is loaded, a DHCP Server screen is added to the server console. This displays the status and the activities of the program.

CONFIGURING SUBNETWORK PROFILES

As with the Windows NT DHCP server, you must define the pools of available IP addresses before clients can access the service. In the NetWare DHCP Server, these pools are called subnetwork profiles, and are created using the DHCP Server Console program (DHCPCFG.NLM). See Figure 10-15.

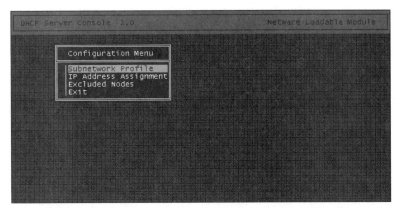

Figure 10-15: Use the DHCP Server Console program to create the subnetwork profiles defining the configuration options that will be supplied to clients.

By launching DHCP Server Console for the first time, and selecting Subnetwork Profiles, the default profiles are created for all subnets of which the server is aware. To create new profiles for other subnets, press the Insert key, following the standard keystroke assignments for NetWare server console utilities.

The default profiles created during the DHCP installation process are designed for the static assignment of IP addresses. You can change a profile to assign addresses automatically, and to add client configuration options, by selecting the profile (which displays the screen shown in Figure 10-16).

Figure 10-16: The subnetwork profile screen provides access to all optional settings provided by the Novell DHCP server.

The subnet profile screen is rather bare when first displayed, but additional options appear as needed. For example, when you change the Automatic IP Address Assignment option to Yes, the Assign All Subnet IP Addresses option appears. This enables you to allocate all of the addresses in that subnetwork using DHCP. If you say no to this option, the Start Address and End Address fields appear. Unlike the

Microsoft DHCP server, you cannot define exceptions to the range of automatically assigned addresses. You can, however, define individual, static address assignments for addresses in the range that will be assigned to particular systems, permanently.

 Novell uses different terminology than the DHCP specifications when referring to its IP address assignment capabilities. In NetWare, manual addressing is known as static addressing, and automatic addressing refers to what the RFCs call dynamic addressing. No support is provided for the permanent assignment of addresses from a pool — which the RFCs refer to as automatic allocation.

When you activate automatic address assignment, all addresses are leased for a default period of three days, unless you specify a different value for the Lease Time option. The T1 and T2 intervals default to 50 percent and 87 percent, respectively, conforming (approximately) to the defaults found in the DHCP specifications.

The number of options supported by the NetWare DHCP Server is limited in comparison to the Microsoft version; however, the essential items for the configuration of a Windows or NetWare/IP TCP/IP stack are provided. To configure the NetBIOS options needed to access Windows NT WINS servers, select the NetBIOS Parameters option. This displays the screen shown in Figure 10-17. In this screen, you can specify the IP addresses of up to three NetBIOS name servers (for example, WINS servers), and the node type specifying which NetBIOS name-resolution method the client should use.

Figure 10-17: The NetWare DHCP Server accommodates the needs of Windows DHCP clients by providing the NetBIOS options needed to use WINS, a Windows NT NetBIOS name server.

 The computer name assigned to every Windows 95 and Windows NT system is a NetBIOS name. When TCP/IP is used to carry NetBIOS traffic, these names must be resolved into IP addresses (just like Internet host names). Windows NT Server includes WINS, a name server for NetBIOS that performs these name-resolution tasks. For more information on WINS and name resolution, see Chapter 11, "Name Registration and Resolution."

You can also define NetWare/IP options in a subnetwork profile by entering Yes in the NetWare/IP Configuration option. This displays the screen shown in Figure 10-18. Here, you specify a NetWare/IP domain name, the addresses of up to five DSS (Domain SAP/RIP Service) and NetWare/IP servers, and other NetWare/IP parameters.

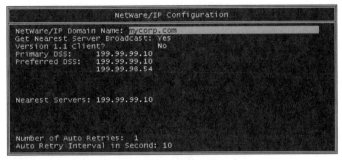

Figure 10-18: Novell's DHCP server supports NetWare/IP clients by providing separate screens containing the required options.

CREATING IP-ADDRESS ASSIGNMENTS   By selecting IP Address Assignment from DHCP Server Console's Configuration Menu, the program displays a list of IP addresses that are currently assigned (including those that were automatically assigned). When you select an automatically assigned address from this screen, you can view the client's hardware address, and the time remaining in the current lease.

This screen enables you to create static IP-address assignments for specific workstations. By pressing the Insert key, a screen like that shown in Figure 10-19 appears. In this screen, you enter an identifying name for the system, the desired IP address, and the computer's hardware address. The hardware address should be notated as six hexadecimal values, separated by colons. When you create a static assignment, the Lease Time fields are inaccessible. The zero values that appear as defaults indicate that the address has been assigned to that workstation, permanently.

Figure 10-19: You create static IP-address assignments by specifying the hardware and IP addresses that will be associated in the DHCP database, permanently.

EXCLUDING NODES

NetWare's DHCP server enables you to specify the hardware addresses of network systems that are to be denied DHCP services, even when they request them. Some routers have been known to issue erroneous DHCP requests, and this feature prevents them from monopolizing your available IP addresses.

By selecting Excluded Nodes from the Configuration Menu, you can add entries to the list. This is done by pressing Insert and specifying a hardware address in the Physical Address box provided. For Ethernet and Token Ring systems, this value consists of six hexadecimal figures separated by colons — just like the hardware addresses in the IP-Address Assignments listing.

You can use the asterisk character as a wildcard in an excluded hardware-address entry. For example, because the first three figures in a hardware address identify the device's maker, the value 00:23:ac:*, prevents all network adapters, of a particular manufacturer, from receiving automatic-address assignments.

Summary

The Dynamic Host Configuration Protocol is an invaluable tool for the network administrator. Dynamically assigning IP addresses, and automatically configuring the TCP/IP stacks of client workstations, can save hundreds of man hours. They also drastically reduce the incidence of communications problems from faulty configurations and user error. Both Novell IntranetWare and Microsoft Windows NT include DHCP software products that can run on existing servers that are used for other tasks. IP address assignments are stored in a database that prevents duplication, and absolves administrators of maintaining assignment records, manually.

In this chapter, you learned:

◆ How DHCP developed from earlier protocols to address specific client-configuration problems

◆ How DHCP clients and servers communicate

◆ How to implement the Microsoft DHCP server

◆ How to implement the IntranetWare DHCP server

The next chapter examines the processes by which Internet host names are converted into the IP addresses needed for TCP/IP communications.

Chapter 11

Name Registration and Resolution

IN THIS CHAPTER

This chapter examines the various ways names are assigned to IP addresses, a process called *name registration*. The assigned names are then converted back to addresses as needed; the conversion is called *name resolution*. The topics covered in this chapter are as follows:

- ◆ The structure of various types of names representing IP addresses

- ◆ The NetBIOS names that Windows NT network communications use, and various methods of registering and resolving them

- ◆ Installing and using Windows NT's Windows Internet Name Service (WINS) to manage NetBIOS names

- ◆ Understanding DNS names and using the NetWare and Windows NT Domain Name System servers

THE IP ADDRESSING SYSTEM is one of the greatest strengths of the TCP/IP protocols, providing Internet systems around the world with a unique identity. Many veteran TCP/IP network administrators can rattle off the IP addresses of their routers and other key systems from memory, but most users find it difficult to identify systems by their addresses. To remedy this problem, naming systems were devised. These systems enable users to replace IP-address references, in their applications, with alphabetical names that are much easier to type and remember.

The TCP/IP protocols, themselves, do not use "friendly" names for their communications processes. Names exist only for the users' convenience; therefore, when supplied as a destination within an application interface, the names must be converted into IP addresses before the communication process, with the target system, can begin. Thus, when you type the name of a desired site, such as *www.mycorp.com*, into your Web browser, it immediately initiates a name-resolution process that is independent of the application's other activities. Once the browser discovers the IP address of the system hosting the *www.mycorp.com* Web site, it opens a TCP session with that system that delivers the site's files to your desktop.

Host Names and NetBIOS Names

The need for friendly names was recognized by TCP/IP's designers early in the development of the protocols. They also recognized that administering the names was at least as complex as registering IP addresses. The first naming system was designed for use on the Internet, which raised a number of problems. Systems on the Internet must have a unique name, just as they require a unique IP address, and someone has to ensure that no duplication of names occurs. As with IP addresses, however, maintaining a single database of all systems on the Internet (and their host names) was an enormous task, even in the 1970s.

Eventually, the same two-tiered system used to register IP addresses was implemented as a solution. With IP addresses, only the network identifier needs to be registered. Administrators of individual networks must assign the host-identifier portion of the IP address to each network interface. With Internet host names, a system of domains was devised to function in the same way. Administrators register a domain name, such as *mycorp.com*, and then assign the individual host names within the domain (see Figure 11-1). Thus, an Internet host name of *www.mycorp.com* represents a system called *www* within a domain called *mycorp.com*.

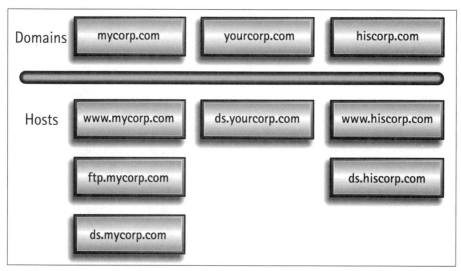

Figure 11-1: An Internet host name is formed by taking a registered domain name and adding a unique name for the specific host.

A typical organization using the Internet registers both an IP network address and a domain name, but the two aren't necessarily associated. You can, for example, register several different class C IP addresses and assign all of the machines using those addresses names in the same domain. You can even assign a name in your domain to a system using someone else's IP address. If you outsource your Web site to another company, they can host the site on their system and still use a name in your domain.

There are two methods used to resolve Internet host names into their equivalent IP addresses. One is a *HOSTS file*, an ASCII text file stored on each individual system that contains a simple table of host names and their equivalent IP addresses. The other method is the *Domain Name System* (DNS), which is a database containing the same information as a HOSTS file, but for the entire Internet. The DNS database is distributed on systems all over the world, arranged in a hierarchical tree fashion. Clients generate name-resolution requests and send them to a DNS server. The DNS server then passes the requests up the tree until the system containing the required information is found.

Internet host names are not the only friendly names used to represent IP addresses. The TCP/IP protocols are now used on a great many private internetworks, and these too require friendly names for their systems. UNIX networks traditionally use domain-based naming and DNS servers, even when the network is not connected to the Internet. NetWare networks that use TCP/IP can use DNS also, but their name-resolution needs are limited to servers. As a true client/server network OS, NetWare clients do not require names because they only communicate with servers, and not with other clients.

Windows NT is a peer-to-peer network OS, in which any computer must be capable of communicating with any other computer. What's more, the OS is designed to use any one of three protocol stacks for its core file- and printer-sharing activities. As a result, Windows NT systems are identified first by name, and networks using TCP/IP have been adapted to use IP addresses to represent those names.

Windows networks use the NetBIOS naming system to identify each of the systems on the network – whether running Windows NT, Windows 95, or Windows for Workgroups. NetBIOS names are designed for use on private networks, only. Each system must have a unique name, but registering these names, outside of the organization hosting the network, is not necessary. Because of this limited environment, the name registration and resolution methods for NetBIOS names are more varied and automated than those for Internet host names.

Unlike Internet host names, the NetBIOS name space is flat (as opposed to hierarchical). During installation, each system is assigned a 15-character name that must be unique on the network. When a Windows network uses TCP/IP as its primary transport protocol, each system is also assigned an IP address, in the usual manner. In March of 1987, the IETF published two documents (in RFC1001 and RFC1002) defining the standard for the use of NetBIOS over TCP/IP, commonly called *NetBT*. Windows NT's NetBT functionality is provided by a module called NETBT.SYS.

Systems using NetBT must resolve NetBIOS names into IP addresses in order to communicate – as do systems using Internet host names. Windows networks have name-resolution methods equal to those used by Internet systems. The LMHOSTS file functions much the same as the HOSTS file, and the Windows NT Server package includes the Windows Internet Name System (or WINS), that maintains a database of NetBIOS names and their associated IP addresses. A third method emerges from the fact that the NetBIOS naming system is limited to use on a private network. A system can discover the IP address for a NetBIOS name by broadcasting a request containing that name to the entire network. The system using that name then responds with a message containing its IP address.

The following sections examine these naming concepts in greater detail, and describe how to implement them on your network.

NetBIOS Naming

When you install a client for the Windows network on a system running Windows NT, Windows 95, or Windows for Workgroups, you must supply a name for the computer. Although not identified as such, this is the NetBIOS name that will identify that system on the network (no matter what protocol stack you elect to use). All shared-system resources on a Windows network are identified using a combination of the NetBIOS name and a name assigned to the specific share. These names are notated using the *Universal Naming Convention* (UNC) format, in which the NetBIOS name always appears first, after the double slash, as follows:

```
\\NetBIOSname\sharename
```

The NetBIOS-name space requires the use of 16 character names, which cannot begin with an asterisk ("*") because that character is used as a wildcard. The Windows network, however, uses only 15 characters for its computer names. The sixteenth character of the NetBIOS name is reserved for a suffix, which is used as a resource identifier. This character identifies the function of the system in the context of the current communications session. For example, when you use Windows NT to access a shared drive on another system, your computer is identified by its computer name, plus a sixteenth character with a hexadecimal value of 00.

00 is the resource identifier for Windows NT's Workstation service, which is the client module used to access shared resources on other Windows systems. Thus, the NetBIOS name is specified by using the computer name assigned during the OS installation, plus the appropriate number of spaces to pad the name out to 15 characters, followed by the resource identifier.

For a list of the suffixes that Windows NT uses to identify the resource type associated with a NetBIOS name, see Table 3-1 in Chapter 3, "TCP/IP and Operating Systems."

When the Windows network uses the TCP/IP protocols, a computer's NetBIOS name is associated with the IP address assigned to its network adapter. The Windows NT Browser service advertises the NetBIOS names of the computers configured to share their resources with other networked systems. Before you can access a shared resource, however, your system must resolve the remote computer's NetBIOS name into its IP address. Only then can IP datagrams be addressed to the other system, directly.

Name-Resolution Methods

Windows NT provides several mechanisms for resolving NetBIOS names, but they all rely on the same basic resource: a look-up table of NetBIOS names with their equivalent IP addresses. The differences between various NetBIOS name-resolution mechanisms are based on the answers to the following questions:

◆ How is the look-up table compiled?

◆ Where is the look-up table stored?

◆ How do clients access the look-up table?

LMHOSTS FILE

The easiest way for a system to resolve NetBIOS names is to use a look-up table stored on its local drive. On Windows systems, the table takes the form of an ASCII file called *LMHOSTS*. The use of an LMHOSTS file is not mentioned in the NetBT documents because its use does not involve any network communications. When a user wants to access a share on another system, the computer accesses the LMHOSTS file and searches for the name supplied by the user. The entry for the name specifies its equivalent IP address, and the computer can initiate IP communications with the destination system, as shown in Figure 11-2.

The advantages of the LMHOSTS file are obvious. Because it is stored on a local drive, it is fast, and adds no additional communications traffic to the network. The disadvantages, however, are equally obvious. For the LMHOSTS file to function, someone must keep it updated with all of the names and addresses currently being used on the network. Once the network grows beyond a handful of workstations, updating the files on each individual computer becomes increasingly difficult. Windows NT provides an option by which a single, centralized LMHOSTS file is accessed from a network drive. On a large network, however, manually updating even a single file is unwieldy.

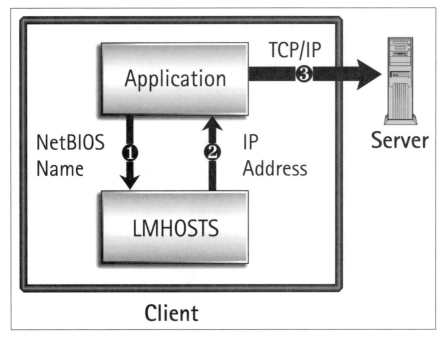

Figure 11-2: An LMHOSTS file is an ASCII look-up table of NetBIOS names and IP addresses, stored on the local drive of each network system.

BROADCASTS

The second mechanism NT provides for NetBIOS name resolution is the *broadcast* method. When a system wants to communicate with another computer on the network, it transmits a broadcast message, containing the NetBIOS name, requesting the computer using that name to generate a reply. On receiving the broadcast, the system holding the requested name transmits a unicast message to the sender, containing its IP address, as shown in Figure 11-3. The original system can then initiate its own unicast transmission to the other computer.

The broadcast method dynamically constructs a look-up table in each system that employs it. Once a system resolves a NetBIOS name, it is stored in a local cache along with its related IP address. The cache is volatile, which means it is erased whenever the system is restarted. The advantage of using broadcasts is that it isn't necessary to manually update the look-up table. Changes to the network are registered, automatically, in the cache whenever a new broadcast resolution is performed.

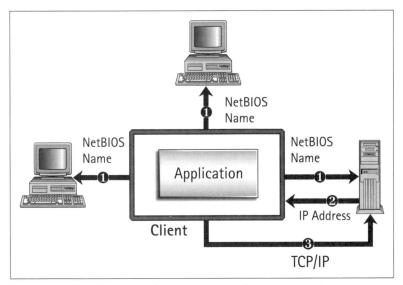

Figure 11-3: Broadcast transmissions may be used to request that a computer supply potential clients with its own IP address.

Broadcast name resolution suffers from two major drawbacks, however. First, the method generates a large amount of extraneous network traffic. Broadcast messages are received by every computer on the network. To the lower-layer protocols on each system, the messages are properly addressed to that system and must be passed up to the higher layers. Only when the message reaches the NetBIOS interface, above the transport driver interface (TDI), is the requested name read. If the system is not the name holder, it silently discards the message – but not before expending the processor cycles needed to receive the packet and pass it up the protocol stack. On a network with many systems generating name-resolution broadcasts, this can result in a waste of network bandwidth and system resources.

The second drawback of the broadcast name-resolution method is that it's usually limited to the local network segment. If you have a multisegment network, broadcasts are not capable of resolving the names of systems located on other segments. While it is possible to configure IP routers to propagate broadcasts to other networks, this practice further exacerbates the traffic problem mentioned earlier. The broadcast method is, therefore, recommended only for use on small networks, preferably those comprised of a single segment.

NETBIOS NAME SERVER (NBNS)

The third name-resolution mechanism used on Windows networks is an application called a *NetBIOS name server* (NBNS), as defined in the NetBT standards. Windows NT Server includes an NBNS, called Windows Internet Name Service (WINS), that stores a dynamically created look-up table of names and addresses for an entire internetwork. To use WINS, a client system is configured with the IP addresses of primary and secondary WINS servers on the network. Whenever the system is restarted, it transmits a unicast message to the WINS server, containing its NetBIOS name and IP address. The server maintains the information in a database, which can be replicated to other WINS servers on the network for fault-tolerance and load-balancing purposes.

When a system has to resolve a NetBIOS name, it sends a query to its designated WINS server. It then receives a reply containing the needed IP address information, as shown in Figure 11-4. Like the broadcast method, WINS requires no manual updating of the look-up table. The primary advantage of WINS is that it uses only unicast transmissions for its name registration and resolution transactions. As a result, it is not limited to use on a single network segment. WINS servers can service clients anywhere on an internetwork, using continually updated information as clients log in and out of the network.

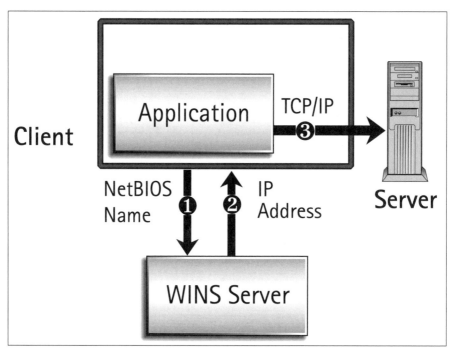

Figure 11-4: WINS is a NetBIOS name server that stores the names and IP addresses for all systems on an internetwork, and replies to the name-resolution requests received from its clients.

If WINS has any drawbacks, they involve the administration needed to implement the service. The installation of the WINS server program on a Windows NT server is easy; however, each client system on the network must be configured with the addresses of the WINS servers it will use. You can automate this configuration process using Windows NT's DHCP server, which is designed to work together with WINS. When using DHCP to assign TCP/IP-configuration settings to a client, you must include the client's WINS server addresses as part of the configuration. The DHCP server then automatically registers the IP address it assigns to the client, in the WINS database.

NetBIOS Node Types

Because Windows NT provides a number of different name-resolution methods, there must be a way for a particular system to select the proper mechanism to use. Fortunately, these methods are not mutually exclusive. The NetBT standard defines several node types, specifying various combinations of name-resolution methods and the order in which they should be used. When one method fails, others are attempted until the requested name is successfully resolved. The node types defined in the NetBT standard are as follows:

◆ **Broadcast node (b-node)** – A b-node system uses the broadcast method for name registration and resolution.

◆ **Point-to-point node (p-node)** – A p-node system uses unicast transmissions to NetBIOS name servers (such as WINS) for name registration and resolution.

◆ **Mixed mode node (m-node)** – An m-node uses the broadcast method for name registration. For name resolution, an m-node first uses broadcasts, but if no reply is received, it switches to unicast transmissions directed at a NetBIOS name server.

The mixed mode-node type is designed for use on networks composed of more than one segment (but where a typical workstation's communications are mostly limited to the local segment). The NetBIOS name server is reserved for occasional use when a connection to a system on another network is required. This arrangement is not used by Windows NT because WINS provides name-resolution services for an entire enterprise network, completely replacing the broadcast method. Instead, Windows NT defines two additional node types that are better suited to the name-resolution mechanisms provided with the OS. The Windows NT node types are as follows:

◆ **Modified b-node** – A Windows NT system, which is not a WINS client, can be configured as a b-node that differs slightly from the NetBT standard definition. If the client fails to resolve a name using broadcast queries, it consults the LMHOSTS file on the system's local drive.

◆ **Hybrid node (h-node)** – An h-node uses unicast transmissions to a NetBIOS name (WINS) server for name registration and resolution. If the system is unable to contact a WINS server, it switches to broadcast name resolution, but only until a WINS server is available, at which time it reverts back to unicast transmissions.

♦ **Microsoft-enhanced** – Windows NT provides options that enable a system to supplement the standard-node types with LMHOSTS name resolution, and standard Windows Sockets calls to a DNS server and a HOSTS file.

Windows NT systems that are configured to use WINS become h-nodes, by default. Because they use broadcast name resolution as a backup for the NetBIOS name server, h-nodes can continue to resolve names on the local network segment (even if their WINS servers are not available). When it isn't configured to use WINS, a Windows NT system functions as a modified b-node. You can also specify the node type to be assigned to a client system (including p-nodes and m-nodes) using a DHCP server.

Two additional options in the Microsoft TCP/IP-client configuration let you Enable DNS for Windows Name Resolution and to Enable LMHOSTS Look-up. The DNS option provides name look-ups in the HOSTS file, on the system's local drive, and calls to the DNS servers specified in the TCP/IP-client configuration. With this option enabled, you can use a system's DNS name as part of a UNC path, instead of the NetBIOS name. Should both the WINS and broadcast methods fail, the LMHOSTS option causes the system to perform a NetBIOS name look-up, in the LMHOSTS file stored on the local drive.

On an h-node system, with all of the Windows NT options enabled, the NetBIOS name-resolution process begins (see Figure 11-5) using the following steps:

1. If the name to be resolved consists of more than 15 characters, it is assumed a DNS name. The client system then uses a DNS call as the first name-resolution method.

2. If the name to be resolved is 15 characters or less, or if the DNS name-resolution attempt fails, the client system checks for the name in the NetBIOS name cache.

3. If the NetBIOS name cache does not contain the name to be resolved, the client system sends a name-query request. This is sent as a unicast to the primary WINS server specified in the TCP/IP-client configuration. If the primary WINS server fails to respond, the system sends a query request to the secondary server.

4. If both WINS servers fail to respond to the unicast queries, the client system begins broadcasting name-query requests.

5. If the client system does not receive any replies to the broadcast requests, it performs a name look-up in the LMHOSTS file on the local drive.

6. If the name to be resolved is not listed in the LMHOSTS file (and the name is 15 characters or less), the client system transmits DNS requests to the servers specified in the TCP/IP configuration.

7. If the DNS cannot be contacted, or fails to resolve the NetBIOS name, the name-resolution process is declared a failure and an error message displays on the client system.

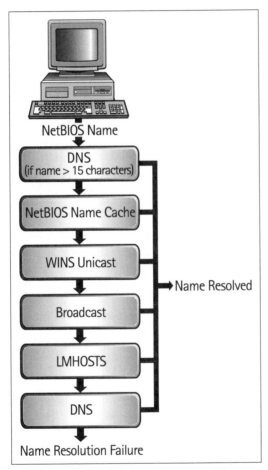

Figure 11-5: Windows NT provides many different name-resolution mechanisms, all of which must be exhausted for a resolution to fail.

NetBIOS Name Registration

Name registration is the process by which a system claims a NetBIOS name for its own use. The process may include the addition of the NetBIOS name, and its equivalent IP address, to the look-up table used by a particular name-resolution mechanism. The name-registration process ensures that all of the NetBIOS names on the network are being used by one system, only.

LMHOSTS FILE

When you use an LMHOSTS file for NetBIOS name resolution, the name is registered when you create the entry in the file specifying the NetBIOS name and its IP address. Nothing can prevent the same name from being listed in the file with two different IP addresses. When the LMHOSTS file is parsed during the name-resolution process, the system always uses the first entry that contains the desired name. All subsequent entries containing that name are ignored.

BROADCASTS

The broadcast method does not use a look-up table, except for the NetBIOS name cache on each system. The name-registration process occurs during the initialization of the TCP/IP client. The system broadcasts a NAME REGISTRATION REQUEST message to the local network and awaits any responses. The NAME REGISTRATION REQUEST message is a NetBIOS name-service message, packaged within a UDP datagram, that contains the name the client system is attempting to register.

The broadcast is repeated three times, at 250-millisecond intervals. If another b-node (or m-node) system on the network is already using the same NetBIOS name, it transmits a NEGATIVE NAME REGISTRATION RESPONSE message as a unicast to the original client. This causes registration to be denied, forcing the user to select a different computer name, and begin the process again. If the client receives no responses for one second after each of its broadcasts, it takes ownership of the name, and broadcasts a NAME OVERWRITE DEMAND message to declare its possession (see Figure 11-6). A *demand* message is a single transmission that the receiving system is expected to obey unconditionally; no response is required or expected.

Because m-node systems use broadcasts, as well as name-server queries for name resolution, they must register their NetBIOS names using both broadcasts and name-server unicasts. An m-node system cannot use a NetBIOS name until it successfully completes both registrations. Once a b-node or m-node system claims ownership of a NetBIOS name, it must respond to any requests for that name's equivalent IP address, and challenge any attempts (by other systems) to use the same name.

When a b-node system is shut down, it broadcasts a NAME RELEASE DEMAND message that informs the other b-nodes on the network that the system is relinquishing the hold on its NetBIOS name. This allows the other systems to remove the entry from their NetBIOS name caches, so they don't send transmissions to the system in error.

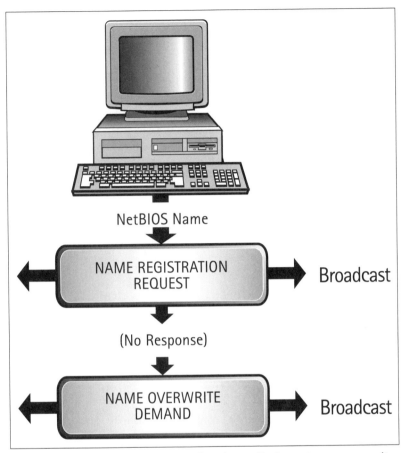

Figure 11-6: In the broadcast name-registration method, a system announces its claim to a particular NetBIOS name and, if no other system objects, is granted the use of the name.

P-node and h-node systems, using unicast transmissions to a NetBIOS name server for their name registration and resolution services, do not respond to NAME REGISTRATION REQUEST broadcasts—even if they possess the same name as the broadcaster. Also, NAME REGISTRATION REQUEST broadcasts are limited to the local network segment, like any other broadcasts. These conditions enable two systems to be registered in the same name, on the same internetwork. You should select one node type for all systems on your network, and avoid duplication when assigning names on other segments.

WINS

A p-node or h-node client system that uses a NetBIOS name server for its name-resolution services must first register its name with that service. The NAME REGISTRATION REQUEST message that a Windows NT system sends to the WINS server (specified in its TCP/IP-client configuration) differs from those used in the broadcast-registration method. The difference lies in a few minor field values, and in the fact that the request is sent as a unicast transmission, instead of a broadcast.

When the WINS server receives a NAME REGISTRATION REQUEST, it checks its database to see if any other system has registered the requested name, already. If no entry for the name exists, the server creates a new record containing the new NetBIOS name and the client's IP address. It then transmits a unicast POSITIVE NAME REGISTRATION RESPONSE back to the client system, as shown in Figure 11-7. The response message contains a *time-to-live* (TTL) value that specifies how long the name registration will persist without renewal.

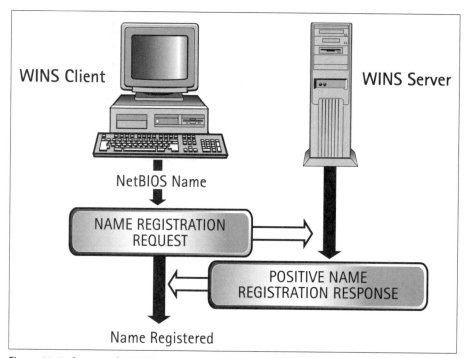

Figure 11-7: A successful WINS name registration consists of a single exchange of unicast transmissions.

If the WINS server determines that another client already holds a registration for the requested name, it performs a name challenge by transmitting a NAME QUERY REQUEST unicast message to the system currently using the name. The WINS server sends up to three requests, 500 milliseconds apart, to each of the system's registered IP addresses. If the challenged system is operational, it must return a POSITIVE NAME QUERY RESPONSE to the WINS server, thereby defending the name. The WINS server then transmits a NEGATIVE NAME REGISTRATION RESPONSE to the original challenger, denying the registration and forcing the system to change its NetBIOS name, as shown in Figure 11-8.

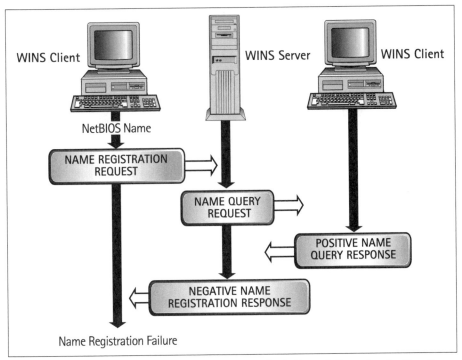

Figure 11-8: When a WINS name-registration request is challenged, the system holding the name must defend its right to continue using it.

If the WINS server receives no response to its NAME QUERY REQUEST messages, or if the challenged system returns a NEGATIVE NAME QUERY RESPONSE (indicating that it is not using the name specified in the query), the existing entry is purged from the WINS database. The name is, consequently, reassigned to the new registrant.

REFRESHING WINS NAMES   The TTL value, assigned to each WINS client during the name-registration process, ensures that systems do not retain claims to NetBIOS names they no longer use. Each time a WINS client is restarted, it re-registers its NetBIOS name, resetting the TTL counter to its original value (six days, by default) and extending the registration. If the WINS client remains logged in to the network until half of the TTL period has expired, the system begins attempts to renew the registration.

 The TTL value, found in NetBIOS name-service messages, is in no way related to the field of the same name in the Internet Protocol header. The latter is used by routers to prevent packets from endlessly circulating around a network, while the former is used by WINS to remove expired NetBIOS names from its database.

To renew its name registration, the client transmits a NAME RENEWAL REQUEST message to the WINS server, which responds with a POSITIVE or NEGATIVE NAME RENEWAL RESPONSE message. A positive response contains a new TTL value for the name registration; a negative response forces the registration of a new name. If the client receives no response from the server, it retransmits its requests at two-minute intervals until half of the remaining TTL time has expired.

At this time, the client begins to send its requests to the secondary WINS server specified in the TCP/IP-client configuration. Once again, the client repeats its requests until half of the remaining TTL time has expired, and then reverts back to the primary server. The process continues until the client receives a response from either server, or the TTL expires. A failure to contact either one of the configured WINS servers causes the client system to revert to the broadcast method of name registration and resolution. If the TTL time period expires without a renewal attempt from the client, the server releases the NetBIOS name.

RELEASING WINS NAMES   When a WINS client is shut down in a controlled manner, it transmits a NAME RELEASE REQUEST message to the WINS server. The client awaits a POSITIVE or NEGATIVE NAME RELEASE RESPONSE from the server before releasing the name, and continuing the shut-down process. The client, however, ignores the contents of the response message and releases the name regardless of the response message it receives. The WINS server only returns NEGATIVE NAME RELEASE RESPONSE messages to the client when the IP address registered (in the server database) for that NetBIOS name doesn't match that of the client requesting the release, or when the server experiences a database error.

Once a NetBIOS name is released, the WINS server can reassign it to another system without performing the challenge process, first. When a client system is shut down improperly (due to a system crash or power interruption, for example), its name is not released, and the server challenges any attempt to register the name. After a name remains in the released state for a designated period of time, it is declared extinct, and eventually removed from the database.

NetBIOS Name Resolution

The NetBIOS name-resolution process occurs on a Windows system running TCP/IP whenever a client uses another system's name in an application (either in a UNC path name or by selecting it in a graphical interface). When using Windows Explorer to access files on another Windows system, you select its NetBIOS name from the tree display. To browse the files on the shared drives, however, your computer must first establish a NetBT session with the other system, using the TCP protocol. Before this process can begin, your system must discover the IP address of the other computer, which it does by resolving the system's NetBIOS name.

Because NetBIOS names are resolved into IP addresses, you can also use them in Web browsers, and other TCP/IP applications, to access intranet services as you would Internet host names. The following sections examine the various name-resolution mechanisms available to Windows NT systems.

THE NETBIOS NAME CACHE

Whenever a Windows NT system resolves a NetBIOS name by any other means, the name and its equivalent IP address are stored in memory in a NetBIOS name cache. Because it is stored in memory and requires no network communications, the cache is the fastest resolution method available. It is also the first resource checked when the IP address of a NetBIOS name is needed. This prevents the system from having to resolve the same names, repeatedly.

The NetBIOS name cache, because it is maintained in volatile memory, is erased whenever the system is restarted. This ensures that the information in the cache remains up-to-date. You can view the contents of the cache using the *nbtstat* command from the Windows NT (or Windows 95) command line with the *-c* switch, as follows:

```
c:\>nbtstat -c
  Node IpAddress: [141.1.21.45] Scope Id: []
            NetBIOS Remote Cache Name Table
      Name            Type       Host Address      Life [sec]
  --------------------------------------------------------------
  NT4SERVER    <03>  UNIQUE     141.1.29.61          -1
  NT4SERVER    <00>  UNIQUE     141.1.29.61          -1
  NT4SERVER    <20>  UNIQUE     141.1.29.61          -1
  CZ1          <03>  UNIQUE     141.1.25.30          -1
  CZ1          <00>  UNIQUE     141.1.25.30          -1
  CZ1          <20>  UNIQUE     141.1.25.30          -1
  CZ5          <03>  UNIQUE     141.1.25.109         -1
  CZ5          <00>  UNIQUE     141.1.25.109         -1
  CZ5          <20>  UNIQUE     141.1.25.109         -1
```

The various services on a Windows NT system cause different values to be used for the sixteenth character of the NetBIOS name (shown in hexadecimal form within angle brackets). As far as the NetBIOS service is concerned, these are different names and are, therefore, listed separately in the nbtstat display.

For more information on using the nbtstat utility and the data it displays, see Chapter 14, "TCP/IP Utilities."

If you access particular Windows systems on a regular basis, you can preload their NetBIOS names and IP addresses into the NetBIOS name cache. This is done by using entries in the LMHOSTS file that contain the #PRE tag. The LMHOSTS file is scanned for #PRE entries during the system-boot sequence, providing almost instantaneous memory-based resolution for the names it finds.

USING AN LMHOSTS FILE

The LMHOSTS file is the NetBIOS equivalent of the HOSTS file used for resolution of Internet host names. Consisting only of ASCII text, LMHOSTS is a look-up table of NetBIOS names and IP addresses, stored on each system's local hard drive. On Windows NT systems, the file is located in the *systemroot*\system32\drivers\etc directory. Because it is on a local drive, the LMHOSTS file is an efficient method of name resolution, but maintaining the files for dozens, or hundreds, of machines makes administration tasks formidable.

The difficulty in keeping a network's LMHOSTS files current makes them an impractical choice for a primary name-resolution mechanism. LMHOSTS entries, however, can be used to store the names and addresses of frequently accessed systems. They can also be used to store information about selected systems located on other network segments (as in the case of b-nodes).

LMHOSTS name resolution can be an optional addition to the standard b-node or h-node name-resolution strategies. This is activated from the WINS Address page of the Microsoft TCP/IP Properties dialog box, by filling the Enable LMHOSTS Lookup checkbox (see Figure 11-9). The Import LMHOSTS button displays a standard file-selection dialog box that enables you to copy an LMHOSTS file from another system to your own.

The LMHOSTS file is formatted as a list of IP addresses and their related NetBIOS names. Separated by a least one space, each name/address pair is on a separate line, as follows:

```
141.1.29.61    NT4SERVER
141.1.25.30    CZ1
141.1.25.38    CZ5
```

LMHOSTS files generally use the 15-character NetBIOS name employed in the Windows NT interface. The resource-type code that forms the sixteenth character need not be included.

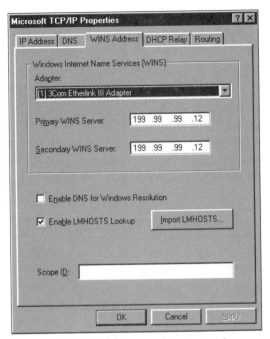

Figure 11-9: LMHOSTS name resolution can be enabled from the WINS Address page of the Microsoft TCP/IP Properties dialog box, regardless of whether or not WINS is enabled.

LMHOSTS files also provide for the use of tags on individual entries. These simplify the administration of files and streamline your system's name-resolution strategy. You include most of the tags on the same line as a name address entry, separated by at least one space, as shown:

```
141.1.29.61    NT4SERVER          #DOM:nt4domain
141.1.25.30    CZ1                #PRE
```

The functions of the various tags you can use in an LMHOSTS file are as follows:

- ◆ **#PRE** — The addition of the #PRE tag causes an LMHOSTS entry to be preloaded into the NetBIOS name cache, each time that the system is booted. This provides the fastest possible name-resolution service for frequently accessed systems. The commands in the LMHOSTS file are parsed in the order that they appear. Whenever it is used during a name-resolution sequence, you should place preloaded entries at the end of the file to avoid repeated, unnecessary delays incurred when they are processed at the beginning of each file access.

◆ **#DOM:***domainname* – The #DOM tag is used to identify systems on the network that function as Windows NT domain controllers. Identifying the controllers this way adds them to the system's domain name cache, which is accessed whenever the system issues a domain request (such as a network logon). After, the system can send domain requests as unicasts directly to controllers on other subnets, rather than have them be limited to the local network segment. Adding #DOM entries for all of the domain controllers located on other subnets enables a non-WINS system to browse all of the computers in its domain, despite the existence of intervening routers. #DOM entries should be preloaded by using the #DOM tag in combination with the #PRE tag, as follows:

```
141.1.29.61    NT4SERVER      #PRE#DOM:nt4domain
```

◆ **#MH** – The #MH tag is used to create LMHOSTS entries for multihomed systems with more than one IP address. You can specify up to 25 addresses for a single, unique NetBIOS name by creating separate entries for each address, as follows:

```
141.1.29.61    NT4SERVER      #MH
141.1.29.62    NT4SERVER      #MH
```

◆ **#SG:***groupname* – The #SG tag is used to create a special group of systems, or devices, that can be addressed using a single unique NetBIOS name. In Windows NT, it uses a sixteenth character value of <20>. A group can consist of up to 25 members, each of which must have its own entry in the LMHOSTS file. You specify the NetBIOS name for the group immediately following the #SG tag, as follows:

```
141.1.25.30    CZ1            #SG:ntgroup
141.1.25.38    CZ5            #SG:ntgroup
```

◆ **\0x##** – The \0x## tag is used, in most cases, to specify a nonprinting character in a NetBIOS name. To use the tag, you must enclose the entire NetBIOS name in quotation marks, and use \0x## in place of a single character, where ## is replaced by the hexadecimal value for the desired character. The quotation marks also make the entire NetBIOS name case sensitive. Note that the \0x## tag replaces only a single character of the NetBIOS name, and the quotation marks cause the name to be read exactly as specified. If you use the tag to specify a sixteenth character value for a name, you must pad out the first fifteen characters with spaces so the tag begins at the sixteenth character of the name, as follows:

```
141.1.29.61    "NT4SERVER      \0x20"
```

◆ **#INCLUDE** *filename* – The #INCLUDE tag is used to specify the location of an LMHOSTS file on a network drive. This enables network administrators to update only a single copy of the LMHOSTS file on a centrally located drive. During the name-resolution process, the tag causes the system to access the specified file as if it was present on the local drive. This practice, however, slows down the LMHOSTS name-resolution process by introducing network communications into the equation. To use the #INCLUDE tag, place the tag on a line of its own in the LMHOSTS file, followed by a fully qualified UNC path name to the location of the remote file. If the UNC path uses the NetBIOS name of the remote server, include a separate LMHOSTS entry providing the IP address of that server, that contains the #PRE tag. A typical #INCLUDE entry appears as follows:

```
#INCLUDE \\NT4SERVER\CDRIVE\WINNT\SYSTEM32\DRIVERS\ETC\
   LMHOSTS
```

◆ **#BEGIN_ALTERNATE/#END_ALTERNATE** — The #BEGIN_ALTERNATE tag signals the beginning of a subroutine containing multiple #INCLUDE commands, for fault-tolerance purposes. When you place a #BEGIN_ALTERNATE tag in an LMHOSTS file on a line of its own, followed by two or more properly formatted #INCLUDE commands, the system attempts to access each of the specified remote LMHOSTS files, until one is located. This enables network administrators to place copies of the same LMHOSTS file on different servers, in case one server should become unreachable. As soon as the system successfully accesses one of the specified LMHOSTS files, it skips the following commands until it reaches an #END_ALTERNATE command, which signals the end of the subroutine. Parsing of the file then proceeds with the command following the #END_ALTERNATE tag, if needed. A typical subroutine appears as follows:

```
#BEGIN_ALTERNATE

#INCLUDE \\NT4SERVER\CDRIVE\WINNT\SYSTEM32\DRIVERS\ETC\
   LMHOSTS
#INCLUDE \\CZ1\CDRIVE\WINNT\SYSTEM32\DRIVERS\ETC\LMHOSTS
#INCLUDE \\CZ5\CDRIVE\WINNT\SYSTEM32\DRIVERS\ETC\LMHOSTS
#END_ALTERNATE
```

BROADCAST NAME RESOLUTION

When a b-node or m-node system must resolve a NetBIOS name, it first consults the NetBIOS name cache to determine if the name was resolved during a previous transaction. If the name is not in the cache, the system transmits NAME QUERY REQUEST messages as broadcasts to the local network. The requests are NetBIOS name-service messages, packaged within a UDP datagram, that contain the name to be resolved.

Other b-node and m-node systems on the network receive the broadcasts and process them to see if the NetBIOS name within is registered to them. (Systems configured to use WINS neither transmit nor listen to NetBIOS name-service broadcasts.) The system possessing the name specified in the broadcasts must respond by transmitting a POSITIVE NAME QUERY RESPONSE packet back to the sender as a unicast, using the address in the IP header's source IP address field. The response packet contains the name

holder's own IP address, which the broadcaster can then use to transmit unicast IP datagrams to the destination.

WINS NAME RESOLUTION

By default, Windows NT designates a system that is configured to use WINS for name resolution, an h-node. As with all node types, the NetBIOS name resolution begins with a search of the NetBIOS name cache. If the desired name is not found, the system transmits a NAME QUERY REQUEST message, as a unicast, to the primary WINS server specified in the WINS Address page of the Microsoft TCP/IP Properties dialog box. As with the NAME REGISTRATION REQUEST messages, the difference between a broadcast and a unicast NAME QUERY REQUEST packet is only a few bytes, dedicated to flags specifying the nature of the message.

On receiving the request, the WINS server must respond to the client. It must send either a POSITIVE NAME QUERY RESPONSE containing the IP address of the requested NetBIOS name, or a NEGATIVE NAME QUERY RESPONSE containing one of the following error codes:

- ◆ FMT_ERR – indicates that the request was improperly formatted

- ◆ SRV_ERR – indicates that the NetBIOS name server cannot resolve the name due to a server error or malfunction

- ◆ NAM_ERR – indicates that the NetBIOS name specified in the request does not exist in the NetBIOS name server's database

- ◆ IMP_ERR – indicates that the NetBIOS name server does not include support for the transmitted request type

- ◆ RFS_ERR – indicates that the NetBIOS name server has refused to process the request for policy reasons

If the client receives no response from the primary WINS server after repeated requests, it switches to the secondary server. If neither WINS server responds to the requests, an h-node switches to broadcast NAME QUERY REQUEST transmissions. The client continues to poll for the WINS servers and when one returns to service, reverts back to unicast name resolution.

Using the Windows Internet Name Service (WINS)

The *Windows Internet Name Service* (WINS) is a network database service, based on the Exchange Server Storage engine, that is included with the Windows NT Server product. You install WINS from the Network Control Panel by selecting the Services tab, clicking the Add button, and selecting Windows Internet Name Service from the list of modules displayed. Windows NT then installs and activates the service, as well as the WINS Manager application you use to administer your WINS servers.

The default settings of the WINS server are sufficient for clients to begin using its services once it's installed. You can modify the operational parameters of your WINS servers and monitor their activities using the WINS Manager utility. Implementing WINS on an enterprise network usually involves deploying several servers and configuring them to replicate their information to each other. You can create these relationships and manage all of your network's WINS servers from any Windows NT system.

The WINS Manager program ships only with the Windows NT Server package. You can, however, run it on an NT Workstation by creating a shortcut to the Winsadmn.exe file in the \WINNT\SYSTEM32 directory of any server with WINS installed. Launching the WINS Manager displays a screen like that shown in Figure 11-10. The IP address of the local WINS server is shown in the left pane of the screen. You can add the addresses of other servers on the network to this by selecting Add WINS Server, from the Server menu. Selecting a server in the list displays its current statistics on the right side of the screen, such as the number of successful and failed name-resolution queries. Selecting Detailed Information from the Server menu displays additional statistics.

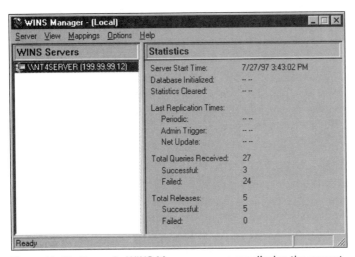

Figure 11-10: The main WINS Manager screen can display the current statistics for all of the WINS servers on your internetwork.

> **TIP**
> You can view the contents of the WINS database at any time by selecting Show Database from the Mappings menu. The display enables you to sort the database and display only the entries gathered by a specific WINS server, as shown in Figure 11-11.

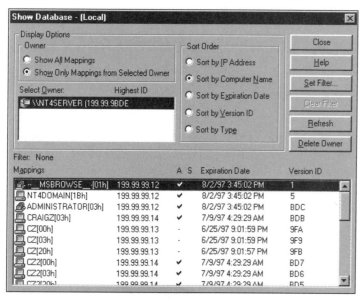

Figure 11-11: The WINS Manager's Show Database screen displays the NetBIOS names and IP addresses of all registered clients. It also shows the expiration date and time for each name registration.

SETTING WINS NAME REGISTRATION PARAMETERS

For most networks, the standard name-registration parameters set by WINS are sufficient. By default, a registered name expires in six days, is declared extinct after six more days, and removed from the database after another six days. The WINS Server Configuration dialog box (displayed by selecting Configuration from the Server menu, in Figure 11-12) enables network administrators to modify these intervals. If you run a network, on which the NetBIOS names associated with specific IP addresses rarely change, you can save a small amount of network bandwidth by extending the Release Interval. On the other hand, if the NetBIOS names on your network change frequently, such as in a lab or classroom setting, you can reduce the interval. The time settings in the WINS Server Configuration dialog box are applied to all entries in the WINS database, except for static mappings.

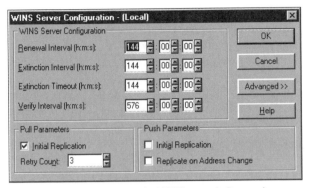

Figure 11-12: By adjusting the WINS server's Renewal
Interval, you can force clients to reregister their NetBIOS
names as often, or as seldom, as needed.

CREATING STATIC DATABASE MAPPINGS

Activating a WINS client causes its NetBIOS name to be dynamically registered in
the WINS database, but it's possible to create a static name to address mappings for
systems that aren't WINS clients, or for groups of systems. Static mappings are not
challenged by the WINS server, nor are they subject to the renewal and extinction
intervals imposed on dynamic mappings. A manually configured database entry
remains active until explicitly removed from the database, by the administrator.

To view, add, delete, modify, or import database entries, select Static Mappings
from the WINS Manager's Mappings menu. After specifying a NetBIOS name and
an IP address, you can designate the mapped name as one of the following:

◆ **Unique** – indicates a standard NetBIOS name mapping to a single IP
   address

◆ **Group** – used to map an IP address to a NetBIOS group name

◆ **Domain** – indicates that the mapped system is a domain controller; applies
   the hexadecimal value 1c to the sixteenth character of the NetBIOS name

◆ **Internet group** – used to map an IP address to an Internet group of
   network resources (such as printers); applies the hexadecimal value 20 to
   the sixteenth character of the NetBIOS name

◆ **Multihomed** – used to map multiple IP addresses to a single NetBIOS
   name for systems with two or more network interface adapters

REPLICATING WINS DATABASES

A single WINS server performs up to 1,500 name registrations and 4,500 name
resolutions per minute. Even if your network does not generate this much WINS
traffic, there are several reasons to run multiple WINS servers. On a network with

multiple segments, WINS provides internetwork browsing and other services your users may rely on. The failure of a network's lone WINS server can, therefore, interrupt productivity. Installing a secondary server is a good idea. You should also install multiple WINS servers at remote network locations to minimize WINS traffic across slow WAN connections.

To maintain consistent, up-to-date information on all of your WINS servers, you can configure them to replicate their database information at scheduled intervals. WINS servers use separate push and pull relationships with other servers, enabling you to create a replication ring (or any other configuration) connecting any number of servers (see Figure 11-13). Each server retrieves updated information from one machine and passes its own information to another. You can schedule the replication activities of each server to accommodate the needs of your network. For example, you can schedule the replication traffic that must cross WAN links to occur during the night, when traffic is low.

You configure a WINS server's replication behavior by selecting Replication Partners from the Server menu. This displays the dialog box shown in Figure 11-14. Here, you can add other WINS servers on your network to the display and designate them as push partners, pull partners, or both. By clicking the Configure buttons in the Replication Options box, you can schedule the replication activities for each server partnership. You can also start unscheduled replications using the Replicate Now button and the controls in the Send Replication Trigger Now box.

USING WINS PROXIES

If you have both WINS clients and b-node systems on your internetwork, you can configure a Windows NT computer to function as a WINS proxy. This enables the b-node systems to take advantage of WINS name-resolution services. A WINS proxy system listens for NAME QUERY REQUEST broadcasts on the network, and satisfies them by searching its own NetBIOS name cache. If necessary, it queries its own configured WINS server for the IP address corresponding to the broadcasted name (see Figure 11-15). The proxy system then passes the information to the b-node, and caches the data for later use.

A WINS proxy system, therefore, violates the dictates of the NetBT standard by listening and responding to NetBIOS name-service broadcasts while using unicasts to communicate with WINS servers. The mechanism does, however, provide a useful function on networks containing mixed node types, as it enables b-nodes to resolve the NetBIOS names of systems on other networks.

To configure a Windows NT system as a WINS proxy, you must edit the NT registry by setting the REG_DWORD value for the *EnableProxy* parameter to 1. This parameter is located in the following registry key:

```
HKEY_LOCAL_MACHINE\SYSTEM\CurrentControlSet\Services\Netbt\Parameters
```

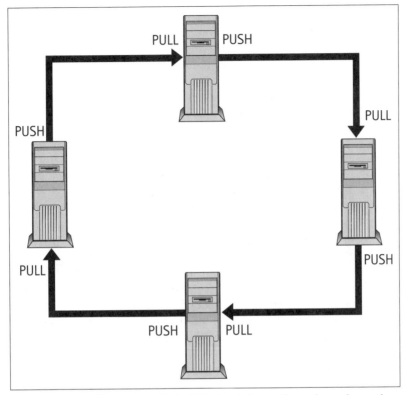

Figure 11-13: WINS servers replicate their data between themselves using push and pull relationships

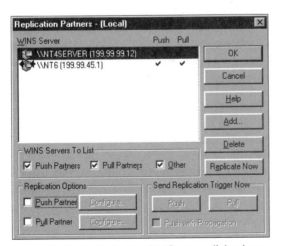

Figure 11-14: In the Replication Partners dialog box, you can configure the relationships between the WINS servers on your network.

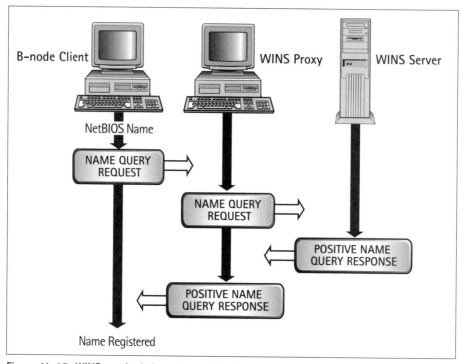

NetBIOS Name

Name Registered

Figure 11-15: WINS proxies help systems using broadcast name resolution to discover the IP addresses of computers on other networks.

Domain Naming

The system of domain-based naming, designed for use on the Internet, is much more complex than the flat-naming system used by NetBIOS. An Internet-naming system must support thousands of networks and millions of computers, and be administered, practically. The system of domains used to organize and categorize the names assigned to Internet systems makes managing the names assigned to organizations possible, without expending an inordinate amount of administrative resources. In much the same way, the Domain Name System (DNS) technology, which was developed to provide users with access to those names, distributes the burden of database processing among systems located all over the Internet.

Originally, the ARPANET was so small that a simple text file was sufficient to provide name-resolution services for the entire network. Users e-mailed name changes to a central agency (the Stanford Research Institute's Network Information Center) and periodically downloaded an updated a file, called HOSTS.TXT. This is how the HOSTS file, still used for name resolution to this day, originated.

As the network grew, the maintenance of the HOSTS.TXT file became increasingly impractical, in the volume of changes to be made, and in the bandwidth necessary for every system to download updated files on a regular basis. This was a perfect example of a system outgrowing its resources, and an object lesson to the creators of the new naming system. The Internet standards for the Domain Name System (RFC1034 and RFC1035), that were first published in 1984, define the name space, the functionality of the DNS clients and servers, and the application-layer protocol they use to communicate.

The Domain Hierarchy

Because unique names are needed for many computers, DNS uses a hierarchical-tree structure to construct names for Internet systems. These names are composed of one or more domain names preceded by a host name. A *domain* is an organizational unit in the DNS tree that can contain subdomains, as well as hosts, much like a directory in a file-system tree. Administration of the tree is distributed by assigning the responsibility for certain domains to various bodies. A *fully qualified domain name* (FQDN) is constructed by taking the name of the host and adding the names of each domain above it, separated by periods, all the way to the root of the tree. Each name can be up to 63 characters in length, and the tree can extend to 127 levels, although a name this long would hardly be a friendly alternative to an IP address.

Do not confuse the concept of the domain, as defined by the DNS standards, with the domains used by Windows NT or other networking systems. Both can be defined as a group of networked computers, but they are based on entirely different organizational paradigms.

For example, a simple name, such as *www.mycorp.com,* indicates that the system with the host name *www* can be found in the *mycorp* domain, which is part of the *com* domain (see Figure 11-16). Technically, the root of the tree is represented by a null character, but it is referred to with a dot, if anything. In most cases, Internet hosts names omit the trailing period.

A hierarchical system makes it possible to assign unique names to every computer on the Internet. Assigning single names, like those used by NetBIOS, would soon result in duplication or random alphabetical combinations that would be difficult to remember. Once a particular organization is assigned a domain name, their only concern is to assign unique names to the hosts within that domain. This way, systems all over the Internet can have the same host name, such as *www,* as long as they are in different domains.

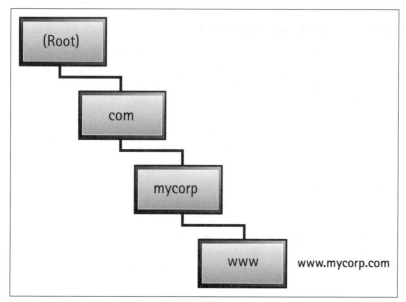

Figure 11-16: An Internet host name is composed of a host and one or more domains, tracing the location of the system from the root of the DNS tree.

TOP-LEVEL DOMAINS

The administration of the DNS tree is divided according to the domain level — that is, the distance from the root. Just below the root of the tree are the *top-level domains*, which contain all of the lower-level domains. The top-level domains organize the structure of the tree according to geographic or functional principles. Originally, the DNS standards defined the following eight top-level domains:

- ◆ **com** – used for commercial organizations

- ◆ **edu** – used for educational organizations

- ◆ **gov** – used for U.S. government organizations

- ◆ **mil** – used for U.S. military organizations

- ◆ **net** – used for networking organizations

- ◆ **org** – used for noncommercial organizations

- ◆ **int** – used for international organizations

- ◆ **arpa** – used for address-to-name DNS mapping

International Top-Level Domains

As the Internet continued to grow into a worldwide network, the obvious American predilection, in the composition of the top-level domains, became more of a problem. Not only would there be a significant language barrier involved in the registration of international domains by American organizations, the use of the existing top-level domains would provide no way to identify the location of a particular site. Despite a client's ability to contact any server on the Internet (anywhere in the world), practicality dictates that accessing a local server is preferable to using a transoceanic link whenever possible.

To better serve Internet users outside of North America, 236 additional top-level domains were created using the two-letter abbreviations for country names listed in the ISO 3166 standard. The administration of these domains was delegated to various responsible organizations, such as government departments and universities. For example, the top-level domain *uk* is used in the United Kingdom and administered by the Department of Computer Science at University College, London.

The top-level domains are not owned by private individuals or organizations, but are intended to represent the infrastructure of the Internet, itself. Most of the original top-level domains (com, edu, gov, org, net, plus the root) are administered by InterNIC, the same organization that registers network IP addresses. The mil domain, obviously, is administered by the U.S. armed forces, and individual country domains, by organizations delegated by those countries.

In recent years, the explosive growth of commercial interests on the Internet has led to a paucity of effective domain names, as well as conflicts between similarly named companies, particularly in the com domain. As a result, the addition of seven new *generic top-level domains* (gLTDs) has been approved, with registration to begin as soon as administrators are selected. These new domains are as follows:

- **firm** – used for businesses or firms

- **store** – used for businesses offering goods for purchase

- **Web** – used for organizations emphasizing World Wide Web-related activities

- **arts** – used for organizations emphasizing cultural and entertainment activities

- **rec** – used for organizations emphasizing recreation/entertainment activities

- **info** – used for organizations providing information services

- **nom** – used for those wishing individual or personal nomenclature

SECOND-LEVEL DOMAINS

The main function of administrative bodies, such as InterNIC, is to control the registration of second-level domains by companies, schools, and other institutions. At the second level, the widest distribution of DNS administration and database processing occurs. Every organization that registers a second-level domain name, such as *mycorp.com*, is responsible for managing the branch of the DNS tree falling within that domain.

The administrators of *mycorp.com* can create any structure of subdomains, and hosts, they wish – as long as all names contained within any one domain, or subdomain, are unique. For example, if they are a small company, *mycorp.com* can simply assign host names to their systems within the second-level domain (such as *www.mycorp.com* and *ftp.mycorp.com*). A larger company, however, might create subdomains to represent their different offices, such as *newyork.mycorp.com* and *paris.mycorp.com*, and then assign host names within those subdomains, as shown in Figure 11-17. Additional levels of subdomain names are possible, but each new level adds to the length of a system's fully qualified name – making it more difficult to remember and to type.

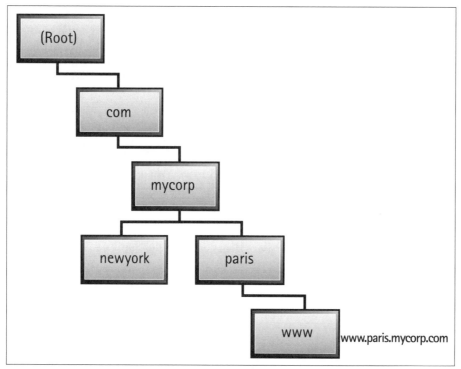

Figure 11-17: Once an organization registers a second-level domain name, it is responsible for assigning and managing subdomain and host names within that domain.

The hierarchy of subdomains and hosts, created within a second-level domain, need not have any relationship with the registered organization's subnetting strategy, its geographical layout, or its physical network infrastructure. The DNS tree is a completely independent organizational medium, related to TCP/IP's network structure only in that certain host names are equated with certain IP addresses. A company can register several domain names and divide its computers among them, or register several network IP addresses and assign the systems on all three networks names in a single domain.

Domain Name Servers

In the Domain Name System, a name server is a software module that stores information about the computers in a *zone*. A zone contains all of the information for a particular domain, except for subdomain information, which is stored elsewhere. For example, the top-level domain *com* includes all of the thousands of second-level domains beneath it, as well as their subdomains and hosts. The name servers associated with *com,* however, don't contain the name and address information about the host systems contained within the second-level domains; they only contain information about the actual systems in the second level. While the *com* domain contains all of the subdomains and hosts stretching to the bottom of the tree, the *com* zone only contains the systems on the level directly beneath *com*, as shown in Figure 11-18.

In many cases, a zone is no different from a domain. Most second level-domain name servers contain information about all of the hosts and subdomains found within the domain. There would only be a second zone within the domain if administrators delegated the name-server responsibilities for a subdomain to a different computer.

Domain name servers perform Internet host name-resolution tasks for their clients by accessing an internal table. This table consists of the host names assigned to all computers in the zone and their IP addresses. When an organization registers a second-level domain name, it must maintain two domain name servers that are accessible to Internet users. Because the administrators of the domain are responsible for assigning unique host names to their own computers, they are also responsible for ensuring that their DNS servers are updated with the required information about those names.

These servers are referred to as the *authoritative servers* for that particular zone, as they are the ultimate source of information about that zone. Whenever another computer, anywhere on the Internet, attempts to resolve a host name in that zone, the IP address information comes from one of those servers (whether directly or indirectly). A single DNS server can be the authoritative server for many different zones, if necessary, and need not be located in the zone or domain that it serves. Many ISPs, for example, provide DNS services for their clients using computers that function as authoritative name servers for dozens of different zones.

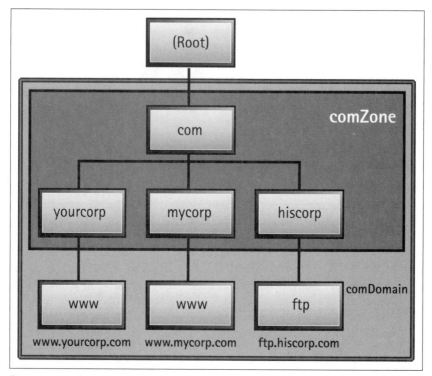

Figure 11-18: Domain name servers contain the host name and IP address information for systems in a particular zone, which may or may not be the equivalent of a domain.

The two authoritative name servers for a particular zone are referred to as the *primary master* and the *secondary master*. The difference between the two is that the primary master server gets its information from its own internal database files, which are created and maintained by the network administrators. The secondary master server gets its information by periodically downloading the data from the primary master, using a process called a *zone transfer*. Two servers are required for each zone in a registered Internet domain (for reasons of fault tolerance and load balancing). The zone-transfer process ensures that both servers contain the same information and eliminates the need for administrators to apply the same updates to two different systems.

Essentially, DNS is an enormous look-up table of names and addresses, broken into pieces and distributed on name servers throughout the Internet. There is no single server, network, or organization that contains all of the Internet's DNS data in one place. The thousands of DNS name servers must work together to provide clients access to information about any host, in any domain, anywhere on the Internet.

The Domain Name System is not restricted to use on Internet systems. For years, DNS has been the standard name-resolution mechanism for many UNIX OSs — regardless of whether the networks are connected to the Internet. When used on a private network, however, DNS functions as little more than a centralized look-up table of names and addresses.

Resolvers

A *resolver* is the client portion of the Domain Name System. It usually takes the form of a function call built into an application, or into an API, such as Windows Sockets. When a user types the DNS name of an Internet system into an application, such as a Web browser, the application (or the API) issues a function call. This call generates a query-request packet containing the host name specified by the user. The system then transmits the packet to the IP address of the DNS server, specified in the computer's TCP/IP-client configuration. Due to the distributed nature of the DNS data, a client's designated DNS server rarely possesses the information needed to resolve the requested host name. The server can, however, pass the request onto an authoritative server containing the information. This way, a client can be configured to access any DNS server on the Internet, and resolve a name in any domain.

On receiving a response to its DNS request, the resolver (in the client system) passes the newly discovered IP address back to the application, which begins its normal TCP/IP-communications process. The resolver is a simple element of the DNS architecture, and is completely unaware of the distributed nature of the DNS database. The name server, itself, is responsible for locating (and retrieving) the information required by the client.

Internet Host Name Registration

Unlike NetBIOS names, which can be automatically registered on the network using broadcast transmissions or unicasts to a WINS server, registering Internet host names is a strictly manual process. Both HOSTS files and DNS servers rely on static name and address entries that must be added, manually, by the system user or the network administrator.

A HOSTS file is an ASCII text file containing a list of IP addresses and their equivalent DNS names, stored on a local drive. On a Windows NT system, HOSTS is located in the *systemroot*\system32\drivers\etc directory, just like the NetBIOS LMHOSTS file. On a Windows 95 system, the file is located in the \Windows directory.

Unlike an LMHOSTS file, there are no special tags or other additional features in a HOSTS file. You simply enter each address and name combination on a separate line, separated by at east one space, as follows:

```
127.0.0.1              localhost
141.1.29.61            www.mycorp.com
```

HOSTS files usually begin with the *localhost* entry, which is a standard generic name for the 127.0.0.1 loopback address.

The DNS server-software products traditionally found on UNIX systems also use text files to store their data. You register new host names, or modify existing ones, by editing the files with a standard text editor. The DNS servers included with both Windows NT and IntranetWare provide a menu-driven interface for the server-configuration and data-entry functions. The IntranetWare DNS server uses the UNICON.NLM server-console utility, and Windows NT uses the DNS Manager program.

Internet Host Name Resolution

The process of resolving a DNS name into an IP address is much simpler than that of a NetBIOS name – from a client standpoint. Typically, DNS names are used in TCP/IP applications designed for them, specifically. The NetBIOS-naming system, on the other hand, is completely integrated into the Windows-networking architecture. Most standard TCP/IP applications use the Windows Sockets API to interact with the OS. Winsock contains a function, called *gethostbyname,* which begins the resolution process for the host names supplied by an application.

USING A HOSTS FILE
In the DNS name-resolution process, the HOSTS file is always checked before a call is issued to a DNS server. In contrast to the LMHOSTS file, this is used as a backup for other name-resolution methods. Naturally, a HOSTS file-name resolution is faster than a DNS call, because the file is stored on a local drive. You can, therefore, accelerate the name-process for commonly accessed sites by adding their names and IP addresses to the HOSTS file on your system.

Internet sites that receive large amounts of incoming traffic often employ multiple servers to share the load. Distributing clients among the servers may be accomplished by having DNS servers resolve the site's name to the IP addresses of the various servers in rotation. Placing one of the server IP addresses in your HOSTS file may prevent you from accessing the site because that one server is overloaded or out of service (when other servers are fully operational).

UNDERSTANDING DNS COMMUNICATIONS
When the HOSTS file cannot satisfy a name-resolution request, the client system's resolver generates a query-request message. This message contains the name to be resolved, which it transmits to the DNS server specified in the system's TCP/IP-client configuration. DNS can support both the TCP and UDP transport protocols.

Most resolver queries, however, use UDP (addressed to the well-known port number 53) as specified in the "Assigned Numbers" RFC. TCP (which also uses port 53) is used primarily for zone transfers, in which larger amounts of data must be transferred.

When the DNS server receives a name-resolution request, it checks to see if the ame is in the zone where the server contains authoritative information. If so, the server accesses its tables to locate the IP address for the requested name. It then inserts the data into the request message and returns it to the resolver. This is the simplest form of DNS-name resolution, and in the case of Internet systems, the rarest. In most cases, a client's DNS server does not possess the information required to resolve a request. It must consult other servers to locate the authoritative source for the requested name.

Every DNS name on the Internet has an entry in an authoritative server for the zone in which it is located. To resolve a name, a DNS server must locate the authoritative server for the correct zone. The server then returns to the top of the DNS tree and works its way down through the hierarchy to the appropriate server. This works because the name servers, for every domain, can specify the authoritative servers for the subdomains on the next lower level.

ROOT-NAME SERVERS   A series of root-name servers, containing information about all top-level domains, resides at the top of the DNS tree. These machines, themselves, are the authoritative servers for most of the original U.S. top-level domains. They can also identify the authoritative servers for all other top-level domains in the world. The root servers are critical to the entire Domain Name System because every DNS server on the Internet is configured to refer its requests to them.

When a client's DNS server cannot resolve a name using its internal resources, it begins the referral process at the root. It locates the authoritative server for each domain level in the name, from right to left. The client server begins by forwarding the request to one of the root-name servers, which responds by identifying the authoritative server for the name's top-level domain, as shown in Figure 11-19.

When a DNS server attempts to discover the IP address of the system using the name *www.mycorp.com*, it sends a request to a root-name server, which refers it to the authoritative server for the *com* domain. This directs the request down the branch of the DNS tree that eventually will lead to the server containing the IP address for *www.mycorp.com*.

In this example, the root-name server and the authoritative server, for the *com* domain, are probably different zones running on the same computer. The referral process remains the same if the top-level domain server is located on another system.

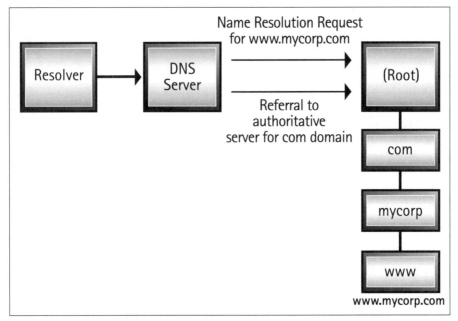

Figure 11-19: A DNS client's name server begins the name-resolution process by passing the client's request to a root-name server.

The root-name server's response is known as a *referral*, because it does not supply a resolution for the name. Instead, it provides the location of a name server that's one level closer to satisfying the request. The client's name server then transmits the request to the authoritative server for the top-level domain, as identified by the root server.

All DNS servers begin the name-resolution process with a call to one of the root-name servers. These machines must be capable of handling enormous amounts of traffic, as they must process thousands of requests every minute.

TOP-LEVEL DNS SERVERS   The primary function of a top-level domain-name server is to identify the authoritative servers for its second-level domains. In other words, the DNS server processing the request will receive another referral, instead of a name resolution. Every organization registering a domain name must supply the IP addresses of its primary-master and secondary-master DNS servers. These are stored in the top-level domain's name servers. When the top-level server receives the request from the client's name server, it responds with a referral to the authoritative servers (for the requested name's second-level domain), as shown in Figure 11-20.

The authoritative servers for the *com* domain can identify the DNS servers specified by the registrants of *mycorp.com*. They can do the same for every other registered subdomain contained within the *com* domain.

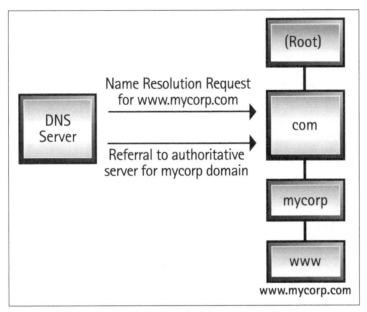

Figure 11-20: Each successive referral of the name-resolution request takes the client's DNS server one step closer to resolving the name.

SECOND-LEVEL DNS SERVERS   The name servers at the second level of the DNS tree perform most of the actual name resolutions on the Internet. For example, when the authoritative server for the *com* domain refers a request to the *mycorp.com* name servers, these machines actually contain the IP address of www.mycorp.com. Thus, the response returned to the client's original DNS server contains a resolved name, which the server can pass back to the resolver that initially generated the request (see Figure 11-21).

The resolution process can continue to travel down through lower levels in the tree. If administrators of the mycorp.com domain created subdomains with their own name servers, another referral would need to be returned to the requesting server, and the process would continue.

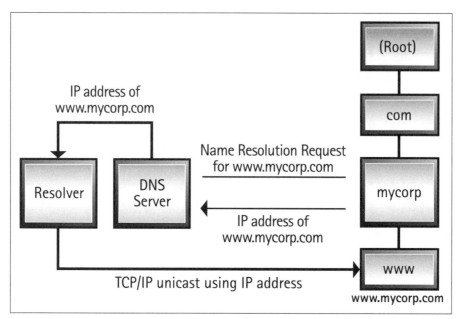

Figure 11-21: Most DNS names are resolved by the authoritative server for a second-level domain.

RECURSIVE VS. ITERATIVE REQUESTS

The DNS server that receives the original request from the resolver is responsible for managing the name-resolution process. This system must retransmit the name resolution request to a different server for each domain in the DNS name. The burden on the original DNS server results from the resolver, in the client system, issuing what is known as a recursive request.

A *recursive request* is designed to put the lightest possible burden on the resolver in the client. The DNS server receiving the request can return a response containing a successfully resolved name, or an error message explaining its inability to resolve the name. The server is, therefore, responsible for processing all referrals from the upper-level servers until it finds one that can resolve the name.

Most DNS clients issue recursive requests, but another type, called an *iterative request,* requires greater effort from the resolver. When a DNS server receives an iterative request, it returns only the information already in its possession to the requester, without performing any additional queries. If the server has no specific information concerning any of the domains specified in the requested name, it can at least supply the address of one of the root-name servers. The client is then responsible for retransmitting its request to the server specified in the response.

These request types do not only apply to the resolvers found in DNS client systems. When a DNS server sends a request to another DNS server, it, too, is functioning as a client, and can be configured to send either type of request. In resolving *www.mycorp.com*, the original DNS server receives a recursive request from the client, but issues iterative requests to the other servers. If the server sends a recursive request to a root-name server, for example, it passes the name-resolution responsibility to that root server. The root server must then transmit repeated requests to the lower-level domain servers until the name is resolved. If all DNS servers did this, the additional burden on the root-name servers would bring the entire Domain Name System to a screeching halt.

ADDRESS-TO-NAME MAPPING

The original purpose of the DNS was to resolve names into IP addresses, but many applications require the opposite service at times, and IP addresses must be resolved into DNS names. This presents a problem, as the DNS name space is keyed to names, not addresses. Locating a particular name involves a progression from server to server representing each successive domain name. Finding a specific IP address without knowing the equivalent name would require a search of every domain-name server on the Internet – clearly an impractical proposition.

The DNS addresses this problem by using *in-addr.arpa* (a special domain in which names and IP addresses are reversed). In this domain, the IP addresses are stored in the name space, with each byte of the dotted-decimal address functioning as a domain name. The actual DNS name of each system is stored in each record's IP address field. In other words, the top-level domain, *arpa*, contains the second-level domain, *in-addr*, which, in turn, contains 256 possible third-level subdomains. This represents all possible first-byte values for an IP address. Each of the 256 third-level subdomains contains 256 fourth-level subdomains, and so on, down to the sixth level. This creates a name space that can hold a database record for every possible IP address, as shown in Figure 11-22. IP addresses can then be resolved into DNS names using the same procedure in which names are resolved into addresses.

The least significant byte of an IP address (written last in the standard IP address notation) functions as the host name portion of a fully qualified domain name in the *in-addr.arpa* domain. Because IP addresses are notated with the least significant bit on the right, and DNS names place the least significant name on the left, an IP address of 141.1.29.61 (stored in the *in-addr.arpa* domain) would be written as *61.29.1.141.in-addr.arpa*.

DNS CACHING

As a DNS server resolves the names requested by its clients, it gathers information about the DNS name space that may be useful in later transactions. To increase the efficiency of the system, the server caches this information and reuses it as needed. If, while resolving the name *www.mycorp.com*, the server learns the IP addresses of the authoritative servers for the *mycorp.com* domain, it later sends its first request to one of those servers when asked to resolve *ftp.mycorp.com*. Querying the top-level domain-name server again is not necessary because the information is already in the cache.

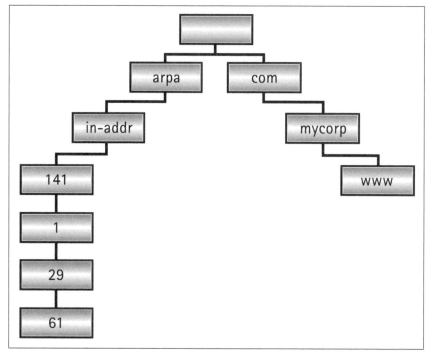

Figure 11-22: The in-addr.arpa domain forms a name space for DNS records named for IP address values.

Cached DNS information can become dated, however, and cannot be stored indefinitely. Every DNS server on the Internet assigns a TTL value to the information it supplies to other systems. After this expires, the data must be deleted from all caches in which it is stored. This places the control over DNS-data volatility in the hands of those who administer its source. If the IP-address assignments for the systems in the *mycorp.com* domain rarely change, a longer TTL value saves network bandwidth, eases the burden on the DNS servers at every domain level, and speeds up the name-resolution process for clients.

Installing a DNS Server

The DNS server modules that ship with the Windows NT and IntranetWare products are designed to simplify a complicated task in administering a TCP/IP network. Traditional UNIX-based DNS servers are short on documentation, and use configuration files that administrators must edit using precise formatting guidelines (without them, the server will not perform properly). The Microsoft and Novell DNS servers automate this formatting process by providing data-entry screens with context-sensitive help, thus, enabling you to add new information to the DNS configuration files.

In both products, the basic installation and initialization procedures result in a DNS server that is preconfigured and ready for clients to use in resolving Internet names. The addresses of the root-name servers are already added. Requests can, therefore, be forwarded to begin the authoritative server-discovery process for top-level and second-level domains.

If your network is connected to the Internet, you might want to run a DNS server (even if you haven't registered a domain name, and don't need to advertise your systems to other networks). For Internet clients, accessing a DNS server on the local network is almost always faster than using one on the Internet. It also enables you to conserve bandwidth on the link to your ISP. In this case, you may not have to perform any custom-configuration tasks on the DNS server; the default configuration should serve you well.

If you are using your own domain name, however, you must add resource records to the DNS for your various systems. A resource record is an entry in the DNS database (usually consisting of a system's DNS name and its IP address) and, in some cases, other information. The major resource-record types, which are the same for all DNS-server implementations, are as follows:

◆ **Start of Authority (SOA)** – The *start of authority* record is the first entry in all DNS-database files. It indicates that the name server is the authoritative source for information about this domain. The record contains the name of the domain, the FQDN of the name server, and the e-mail address for the domain's administrator (in which the "@" character is replaced with a period). Other fields in the resource record control the default TTL value assigned to the server data, and the parameters controlling the zone-transfer process. Only one SOA record can be in each database file, and both the Novell and Microsoft DNS servers create the resource record, automatically.

◆ **Name Server (NS)** – Individual *name server* records are used to identify each of the DNS servers in the domain. An NS entry contains the name of the domain, and the FQDN of the name server.

◆ **Address (A)** – *Address* records contain the name-to-address mappings for systems in the domain, which are the primary informational resource of the DNS. An address record contains the FQDN of a system and its equivalent IP address. For a multihomed system, a separate address record (containing a duplicate FQDN) is required for the IP address of each network-interface adapter installed in the system. (A response to a DNS name-resolution request can contain multiple IP addresses. If the name server is on the same network as the requester, it may attempt to sort the IP addresses so the one nearest to that network appears first in the response. If the name server and requester are on different networks, the name server may be capable of rotating the IP addresses in each successive response to balance the load on the interfaces.)

◆ **Canonical Name (CNAME)** – A *canonical name* record is used to create an alias, or an alternative DNS name, for a system already registered with an A record. CNAME records contain a new alias name (also called a synonymous name) and the system's original (or canonical) name. Aliases are used to assign multiple names to a single system, for example, when the same computer hosts both Web and FTP servers. When the alias name is resolved, all of the addresses mapped to the canonical name are returned to the client.

◆ **Pointer (PTR)** – *Pointer* records are used to create the address-to-name mappings found in the in-addr.arpa domain. Each record contains an IP address in the form of a fully qualified domain name (for example, *61.29.1.141.in-addr.arpa* for the address 141.1.29.61) and the actual canonical name mapped to the IP address. There should only be one PTR record for any particular IP address.

◆ **Mail Exchange (MX)** – *Mail exchange* records identify a host that is responsible for delivering, or forwarding, e-mail addressed to a particular DNS name. The record contains the FQDN of the addressee, the DNS name of the mail server, and a 16-bit preference value (used to establish priorities when there are multiple records specifying different mail servers for the same address). The preference value in an MX record has no implicit significance in itself, it is simply compared to the values in the other records. Lower values take precedence over higher ones.

◆ **Responsible Person (RP)** – A *responsible person* record is used to designate the individual responsible for the administration of a particular host or domain. The record contains the name of the host, or domain, to be referenced. It also includes two optional arguments an e-mail address for the responsible person (in which the "@" character is replaced with a period, as in an SOA record), and a DNS name, for which there is a TXT record in the same file containing additional information. One or both of these arguments can be replaced with a period, representing the root of the tree, as a placeholder.

◆ **Text (TXT)** – A *text* record contains a DNS name and a text string up to 256 characters long (in quotation marks) containing information to be associated with the name. Used in conjunction with an RP record, for example, a TXT record can contain the full name and telephone number for the responsible person.

◆ **Well Known Services (WKS)** – *Well known services* records are used to specify the services provided by a particular protocol, on a particular network interface. Applications can use WKS records to determine if a system provides support for a service before it actually sends traffic to the port associated with that service. A WKS record contains the DNS name of the host, the IP address of a network interface on that host, a protocol name (which is usually TCP or UDP, but can be any protocol found in the system's PROTOCOLS file), and the name of a service using a port number below 256, as specified in the system's SERVICES file.

 The fully qualified domain names used in DNS resource records include a trailing period to represent the root of the DNS tree (for example, *cz1.mycorp.com.*).

USING THE MICROSOFT DNS SERVER

Microsoft's DNS server is included with the Windows NT Server 4.0 product, and installs as a service from the Network Control Panel. The system running the service must be configured to use the TCP/IP protocols. It should also have its host and domain names entered in the appropriate fields, on the DNS page of the Microsoft TCP/IP Properties dialog box. The DNS server includes the DNS Manager utility, a Windows program that enables you to configure and administer Microsoft DNS servers anywhere on your network.

You can run the DNS Manager from any Windows NT system, using a shortcut to execute the Dnsadmin.exe file, on the system where the service is installed. The left pane of the DNS Manager screen, that is displayed when you launch the utility, lists the DNS service on the local machine (if you are running the program on that same machine). To administer Microsoft DNS services on other computers, you must select New Server from the DNS menu and specify the IP address or host name of the desired system.

Assuming the network is connected to the Internet, the default configuration of the DNS service is capable of resolving Internet DNS names for network clients, immediately. This is called a *caching-only server*, because it is not the authoritative source for any part of the DNS name space. To support your own domain, however, you must create zones on the server and add resource records to the DNS databases.

ADDING ZONES   To properly service your domain, you should create at least two zones (a primary and a secondary) on each of the DNS servers. One zone is for your domain's name-to-address mappings, and one is for reverse look-ups in the in-addr.arpa domain. To create a zone, right-click a server in the DNS Manager's main screen and select New Zone from the context menu displayed. You are then prompted to specify whether the zone is to be a primary master or a secondary master. Enter the name of your domain, and confirm the name to be used for the zone's data file.

When adding a zone to a server, the DNS service automatically adds the zone to the server list display, creates the appropriate data file, and adds the required SOA and NS resource records to it. It also adds an A record for the server's own host name and IP address. Once created, you can modify the operating characteristics of a zone by right-clicking it, and opening the Zone Properties dialog box, as shown in Figure 11-23. Here, you can change a zone from a primary to a secondary, and modify the properties of the SOA record, such as the Minimum Default TTL value that is applied to all data supplied by the server to clients.

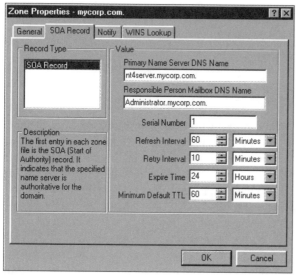

Figure 11-23: The Zone Properties dialog box enables you to modify the settings in the SOA record, as well as other parameters.

After creating the zones for your domain, you can customize the settings used to affect the zone transfer of data from the primary server to the secondary (or secondaries). You identify the secondary servers on the Notify page of the Zone Properties dialog box, while the time-interval settings are found on the SOA Record page.

You should create the zone for your reverse look-up *in-addr.arpa* domain at the same time as your primary and secondary zones – before you create any additional resource records. The Microsoft DNS server includes a feature that automatically creates a PTR record, in the *in-addr.arpa* zone, for every A record you create in the primary zone.

ADDING RESOURCE RECORDS   After creating your zones, you can begin to add resource records by right-clicking a zone name and selecting either New Host or New Record from the context menu. The New Host dialog box (see Figure 11-24) speeds up the process of creating A records (and optional PTR records) by providing a simple interface that only contains fields for the Host Name and the Host IP Address.

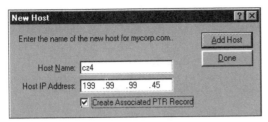

Figure 11-24: You use the New Host dialog box to create name-to-address mappings for the systems on your network.

The New Resource Record dialog box (see Figure 11-25) enables you to create any of the record types supported by the DNS server, including the A records that can be added with the New Host dialog box. When you select a record type, the fields in the Value box are modified to accommodate the specific properties of the chosen record.

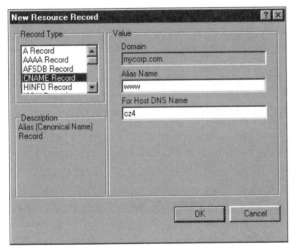

Figure 11-25: The New Resource Record dialog box can create and properly format any type of resource record in the DNS server database.

USING THE NOVELL DNS SERVER

Novell's DNS server takes the form of an application that runs on a NetWare server. The DNS server module is included as part of the NetWare/IP product that ships in the IntranetWare package, but you don't have to use NetWare/IP's services to run the DNS server. After installing NetWare/IP using the INSTALL.NLM utility, you configure and manage the DNS server using the UNICON.NLM program at the server console.

After loading UNICON, select Manage Services from the Main Menu and choose DNS from the list of services that display the DNS screen shown in Figure 11-26. The first step in configuring the DNS server is to select Initialize DNS Master Database. This prompts you for the name of your domain, creates the zone and the database files for that domain, and activates the DNS service. The initialization process also automatically creates the SOA, NS, and A records for the server.

Figure 11-26: You manage the Novell DNS server using the UNICON server-console utility.

After initializing the DNS databases, select Administer DNS to display DNS Server Administration screen. From this screen, you can access the following functions:

- **Manage Master Database** – This option enables you to create and modify resource records in the DNS database, and create subzones.

- **Manage Replica Databases** – This option enables you to specify the IP addresses of DNS servers that will function as replicas (or secondaries) to the current server's master (or primary) database.

- **Link to Existing DNS Hierarchy** – This option enables you to register your DNS server as the authoritative source for information about your domain (assuming you control the name servers operating at the next higher level in the DNS tree). By default, the names and addresses of the root-name servers are preconfigured as the sources for information about your domain.

- **Query Remote Name Server** – This option enables you to transmit a specific query to another DNS server, to determine whether it is functioning properly.

- **Disable DNS Service** – This option enables you to disable the master database on this server.

To create new resource records in the DNS database, select Manage Master Database from the DNS Server Administration menu, and then Manage Data from the Manage Master Database menu. This displays the contents of the database, as shown in Figure 11-27.

```
                        Contents of Database

  Domain                       Type    Data
▲ lb.zacker.com.                cname   loopback.zacker.com.
  localhost.zacker.com.         cname   loopback.zacker.com.
  localhost.zacker.com.         cname   loopback.zacker.com.
  loopback.zacker.com.          a       127.0.0.1
  loopback.zacker.com.          a       127.0.0.1
  ny-library.zacker.com.        a       209.61.45.147
  osd-frog.zacker.com.          a       130.57.6.40
  osd-frog.zacker.com.          a       130.57.6.40
  sj-in1.zacker.com.            a       192.67.172.71
  sj-in1.zacker.com.            a       192.67.172.71
  sj-in5.zacker.com.            a       130.57.6.144
  sj-in5.zacker.com.            a       130.57.6.144
  zacker.com.                   ns      ny-library.zacker.com.
  zacker.com.                   soa     ny-library.zacker.com.
```

Figure 11-27: UNICON enables you to view, add, and modify the resource records in the DNS database.

 From the Contents of Database screen, you can access any existing resource record in the database. This includes the SOA record, in which you modify the zone transfer, and TTL (called caching, here) parameters. To insert a new record, press the Insert key to display a list of the DNS-resource record types. Selecting a record type displays a window containing the fields required for that type, into which you enter the appropriate values.

Summary

The use of friendly names to represent TCP/IP systems is almost as old as the protocols, themselves. For the names to be associated with IP addresses, a mechanism external to the TCP/IP protocol stack is required. This chapter examined various methods by which IP addresses are registered to use specific names, and the systems that resolve those names back into IP addresses, as needed.

In this chapter, you learned:

♦ How Windows NT uses NetBIOS names for its peer-to-peer networking tasks

♦ How a variety of name registration and resolution strategies can be used to associate IP addresses with NetBIOS names

♦ How the hierarchical Domain Name System was devised to provide name-resolution services for the Internet

♦ How to install and operate the DNS-server products included with Windows NT and IntranetWare

The following chapter examines the installation and configuration of the TCP/IP clients released by Microsoft for use in their Windows operating systems.

Part IV

Clients

Chapter 12

Microsoft TCP/IP Clients

IN THIS CHAPTER

To take advantage of TCP/IP applications and services, client systems must be configured to support the protocols (just as a server must use them to provide a service). Not long ago, a TCP/IP stack was an optional element in a client-workstation configuration. The explosive growth of the Internet caused a rise in TCP/IP-based intranet services in corporate environments, and the use of Internet e-mail became universal. Because of this, TCP/IP-client support is a virtual necessity in today's business-computing environment. In this chapter, you learn:

◆ How to install and configure the TCP/IP client in the Windows 95 and Windows NT OSs

◆ How to add the Microsoft TCP/IP-32 client to a Windows for Workgroups 3.11 System

◆ How to connect a Windows client to a TCP/IP LAN

◆ How to connect to a remote TCP/IP network or the Internet using a dial-up connection

Windows 3.1x and TCP/IP

The Windows 3.1x and Windows for Workgroups operating systems were designed before "Internet" became a household word, and before a TCP/IP stack became essential to an OS. Support for the TCP/IP protocols were not included with either product.

 For the sake of convenience, Windows 3.1x and Windows for Workgroups are referred to here as OSs, even though they actually run on top of DOS, and include no boot files of their own.

In fact, Windows 3.1x does not include network-client software of any kind. To connect the system to a network, you must install and load an external client, such as the NetWare DOS Requester, from the DOS prompt before launching Windows.

The NetWare DOS Requester uses Open Data-Link Interface (ODI) drivers, which support multiple-protocol stacks, but NetWare uses the IPX protocols, and no TCP/IP support is included in the standard client.

Windows for Workgroups includes a network client that connects the system to a Windows peer-to-peer network (composed of other Windows for Workgroups or Windows NT systems). When Windows for Workgroups was released, the default protocol used for networking Windows machines was NetBEUI. To implement the TCP/IP protocols, you had to use a third-party product. Due to the huge, installed userbase running Window 3.1x and Windows for Workgroups, the market for TCP/IP products grew quickly as users clambered for Internet access.

Third-Party TCP/IP Products

Third-party TCP/IP packages typically included a TCP/IP protocol stack, a Windows Sockets module (Winsock.dll) and a collection of applications, and the modules necessary for connecting to a TCP/IP network, with a LAN or a dial-up connection. Designers created these packages primarily for Internet access, as the concept of the intranet had not yet been invented. They included programs, such as FTP and e-mail clients, Web browsers, and news readers; and were intended to be an all-purpose connectivity solution.

Gradually, Netscape Navigator and Internet Explorer took over the Web browser market, and there was less demand for commercial applications, when equivalent or superior products were available as free downloads. Network administrators needed only the connectivity modules to add TCP/IP support to Windows client workstations. In addition, the access software distributed by major online services often contained its own Winsock implementation, complete with a dial-up client.

Once Windows NT adopted TCP/IP as its default networking protocols, and when Windows 95 was released (also with a built-in TCP/IP stack), the need for third-party TCP/IP support decreased. Users and administrators became comfortable with the idea of not paying extra for a protocol stack.

Today, there are still commercial TCP/IP packages for Windows 3.1x and Windows for Workgroups on the market. Solutions providing systems with TCP/IP access can be found on the Internet for free, however. Novell's Client 32 for DOS/Windows 3.1, for example, includes a TCP/IP stack that uses a standard Winsock.dll file, which provides general-purpose access to all TCP/IP services.

Novell's Client 32 for DOS/Windows 3.1 is available from Novell's online services as a free download, but the license agreement for the product states that it can be used "solely for their intended purpose of supporting legally obtained, commercially available Novell operating system software."

For more information on installing and using the TCP/IP support in Client 32, see Chapter 13, "IntranetWare TCP/IP Clients."

TCP/IP and Windows for Workgroups

The TCP/IP support provided to Windows 3.1x, by external protocol stacks, is used primarily for running Winsock applications. These applications are used most often to connect to Internet services. Eventually, TCP/IP became the protocol of choice for Windows networking, largely due to the development of the *Dynamic Host Configuration Protocol* (DHCP) and the *Windows Internet Naming Service* (WINS). Both of these simplified the configuration of TCP/IP clients, and reduced the amount of broadcast traffic needed for network communications. To keep the Windows for Workgroups platform current with the rest of the Windows network OSs, Microsoft released an update, called TCP/IP-32 for Windows for Workgroups 3.11.

TCP/IP-32 is designed to connect a Windows for Workgroups system to a LAN using the TCP/IP protocols. The networking support included in the standard Windows for Workgroups product could use only NetBEUI and/or Microsoft's IPX-compatible protocol, called NWLink. Adding TCP/IP enables the workstation to share its drives with network users, to access resources shared by other systems, and to log on to a Windows NT domain (just as it could using the other protocols). TCP/IP-32, however, includes DHCP and WINS client capabilities, as well as a Winsock module that provides access to Internet and intranet services.

Networking support in Windows for Workgroups is provided by three software components, which include the following:

♦ **Adapter drivers** – The default drivers for the network interface adapters, used in Windows networking, are based on the Network Device Interface Specification (NDIS) standard. Windows for Workgroups supports both enhanced mode and real mode NDIS drivers. You can also use Novell ODI drivers, which are required if you intend to connect to NetWare, and/or Windows network systems. You can only install one driver per adapter, but Windows for Workgroups supports multihomed systems.

♦ **Protocols** – Both NDIS and ODI drivers can multiplex two or more protocols through a single network adapter. This enables you to add the TCP/IP-32 protocol support module to the networking configuration, whether running IPX, NetBEUI, or both. If other systems on your Windows network don't use TCP/IP, or if you don't use Windows networking at all, you can still use TCP/IP-32's Winsock support to access Internet or intranet services.

◆ Clients – Windows for Workgroups ships with the Windows networking client, and supports a second client (such as Novell NetWare or Banyan VINES). Microsoft doesn't provide the client software for these other network OSs, but Windows for Workgroups enables you to identify the other network type, and use it alongside the Windows network functionality.

Before installing TCP/IP-32 for Windows for Workgroups, you must be running Workgroups version 3.11, and apply the upgraded networking files found on Microsoft's Web site at http://www.microsoft.com/kb/softlib/-mslfiles/WFWFILES.EXE. The TCP/IP-32 for Windows for Workgroups 3.11 software can be downloaded from http://www.microsoft.com/kb/softlib/-mslfiles/TCP32B.EXE.

In addition to the protocol stack and Winsock support, TCP/IP-32 includes character-based FTP and Telnet clients. It also contains a selection of utilities that are typically associated with TCP/IP networking on the Windows platform, such as the following:

◆ Ping – used to send echo-request messages to other TCP/IP systems

◆ Arp – used to view and manage the contents of the system's Address Resolution Protocol cache

◆ Route – used to view and manage the contents of the system's routing table

◆ Tracert – used to determine the exact route IP packets must take to a specific destination

◆ Nbtstat – used to display statistics concerning the current NetBIOS over TCP/IP (NetBT) sessions

◆ Netstat – used to display protocol and TCP/IP-connection statistics

◆ Ipconfig – used to display the system's network adapter and TCP/IP client-configuration settings

Find more information on using these programs in Chapter 14, "TCP/IP Utilities."

Installing TCP/IP-32

To display the networking modules installed on a Windows for Workgroups system, launch the Windows Setup program from the Main program group, and select Change Network Settings, from the Options menu. This displays the Network Setup dialog box shown in Figure 12-1. If you have not selected a network client, click the Networks button and select the Install Microsoft Windows Network radio button.

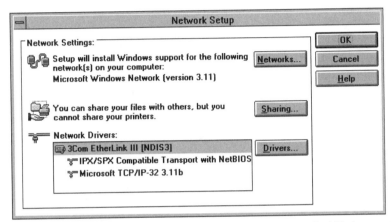

Figure 12-1: The Network Setup dialog box provides access to the Windows for Workgroups networking modules.

Click the Drivers button in the Network Setup dialog box to display the Network Drivers dialog box shown in Figure 12-2. Here, you can add, remove, and configure the adapter and protocol drivers installed in the system. If you don't already have an adapter driver installed, you can click the Add Adapter button to select a driver from those provided with Windows for Workgroups (see Figure 12-3). You may also select Unlisted or Updated Network Adapter to supply an NDIS or ODI driver, obtained from the hardware manufacturer. By clicking the Detect button, the system will attempt to identify the network-interface hardware already installed in the system.

Windows for Workgroups ships with NDIS drivers for many network adapters that were popular when the product was released, in the early 1990s. If using a new model network card, you may need to use a driver supplied by the manufacturer.

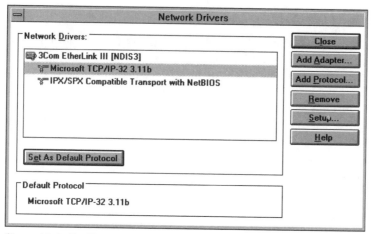

Figure 12-2: The Network Drivers dialog box enables you to select the adapter and protocol drivers used on your system.

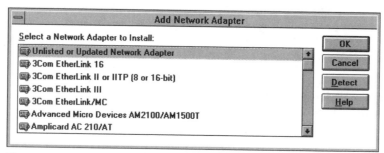

Figure 12-3: The Add Network Adapter dialog box lists NDIS drivers for many popular network interface cards.

Once an adapter driver is installed, you must add a protocol driver so the client can communicate with the network interface. When you click the Add Protocol button in the Network Drivers dialog box, you are presented with the Add Network Protocol list shown in Figure 12-4. Here, you may select from the Windows for Workgroup's internal protocols. To add the TCP/IP-32 protocol driver, however, you must select Unlisted or Updated Protocol and navigate to the directory with the TCP/IP-32 install files.

TIP Before installing TCP/IP-32, remove any other TCP/IP stack that may be installed on the system, including previous versions of the Microsoft TCP/IP protocol stack.

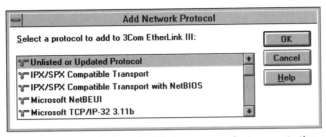

Figure 12-4: The Windows for Workgroups product supports the Microsoft NetBEUI and IPX/SPX Compatible Transport protocols, with or without support for NetBIOS applications.

If you downloaded TCP/IP-32 from one of Microsoft's online services, you retrieved a self-extracting archive file. This should be placed in an empty directory and executed in order to expand the installation files. Among these is a file called Oemsetup.inf, that Windows uses to create a new entry in a pick list. When you select the directory where the TCP/IP-32 Oemsetup.inf file is located, you may add the Microsoft TCP/IP-21 3.11b protocol to the networking configuration, as shown in the Network Drivers list. This process copies the required files to the \WINDOWS and \WINDOWS\SYSTEM directories, and creates a Microsoft TCP/IP-32 program group containing icons for the FTP and Telnet clients.

Configuring TCP/IP-32

Before using the newly installed TCP/IP stack, you must configure it by assigning an IP address to the system's network interface adapter(s). The configuration screens, for any installed adapter or protocol driver, can be accessed by highlighting the module in the Network Drivers dialog box, and clicking the Setup button. When you select an adapter driver, you can configure any of the hardware parameters required by that particular adapter. By selecting the TCP/IP-32 protocol, you will see the Microsoft TCP/IP Configuration dialog box shown in Figure 12-5.

TCP/IP-32 AND DHCP

If you use the Dynamic Host Configuration Protocol (DHCP) to configure the TCP/IP clients on your network, you need only check the Enable Automatic DHCP Configuration checkbox. TCP/IP-32 then retrieves a client configuration. The DHCP client capabilities, built into the TCP/IP-32 protocol stack, recognize only a limited number of the configuration parameters that DHCP servers can deliver. Any unsupported parameters included in a DHCP message are ignored. The parameters recognized by TCP/IP-32 are as follows:

◆ IP Address

◆ Subnet Mask

- Default Router

- DNS Servers

- NetBIOS over TCP/IP Name Server (that is, WINS) Addresses

- NetBIOS Node Type

- NetBIOS Scope ID

- DHCP message type

- IP Address Lease Time

- Renewal (T1) Time Value

- Rebinding (T2) Time Value

TCP/IP-32 does not support DHCP options carried as overflow, in the sname and file fields of a DHCP message. The maximum size for the options field, in a message directed to a system using TCP/IP-32, is 336 bytes. In configuring your DHCP servers to include options that exceed the maximum size, you must be sure the options recognized by the TCP/IP-32 client are located in the first 336 bytes of the field.

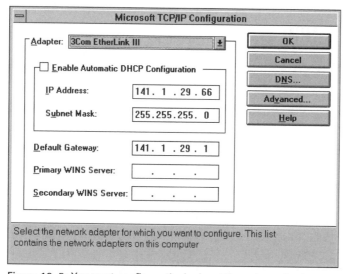

Figure 12-5: You must configure the basic settings shown in the Microsoft TCP/IP Configuration dialog box before your system can communicate using the TCP/IP protocols.

You can use any DHCP server with TCP/IP-32; you are not limited to using the Microsoft DHCP server included with the Windows NT Server product. The server must, however, conform to the Internet standards defining the protocol's packet formation and message exchanges, and must observe the limitations of the TCP/IP-32 DHCP client.

For more information on the DHCP protocol and setting up DHCP servers on your network, see Chapter 10, "DHCP and IP Address Management."

MANUAL CONFIGURATION

If your network does not use DHCP, you must supply values for the fields in the Microsoft TCP/IP Configuration dialog box, which follow:

♦ **IP Address** – The IP address uniquely identifies both the network interface in your system and the network to which the system is connected.

♦ **Subnet Mask** – The subnet mask specifies which bits of the IP address are used to identify the network and which bits identify the host (or network interface).

♦ **Default Gateway** – The default gateway field contains the IP address of the router the system must use to access systems on other subnets (or network segments).

♦ **Primary WINS Server** – The Windows Internet Naming Service (WINS) determines the IP address of another system on a Windows network based on the computer (NetBIOS) name. This setting is optional.

♦ **Secondary WINS Server** – The secondary WINS server is used when the primary server is unavailable. This setting is optional.

The administrators of a TCP/IP network must develop an IP-addressing strategy to organize the network, and provide a unique identifier for each machine. When manually configuring a TCP/IP client, it is important to use IP addresses and other configuration settings that conform to the network plan. Randomly selecting an IP address may enable your system to function properly, but you may be preventing someone else's system from working by using their address. Duplicate addresses can be difficult to trace, and if the address you're using happens to belong to your boss, updating your resume might be a good idea.

For more information on developing an IP addressing and subnetting strategy for your network, see Chapter 2, "TCP/IP Communications."

If your system has more than one network interface adapter installed, you must supply a separate set of configuration values for each adapter that will use the TCP/IP protocols. An Adapter pull-down list in the Microsoft TCP/IP Configuration dialog box enables you to select from the adapter drivers you previously installed. TCP/IP-32 only supports multiple network adapters when you use NDIS drivers, however. If you use ODI drivers, you are limited to a single adapter.

NAME RESOLUTION   As discussed in Chapter 11, Windows network communications are based on the computer names (which are actually NetBIOS names) assigned to each system on the network. If you've used your Windows for Workgroups system to communicate with other Windows systems using a different protocol, you are familiar with the process of accessing network resources, based on their computer names and the names assigned to network shares.

The computer name assigned to your machine, and the name of the workgroup to which it belongs, is specified in the Network applet of the Windows Control Panel, as shown in Figure 12-6.

Microsoft Windows Network		
Computer Name: CZ2		OK
Workgroup: WORKGROUP		Cancel
Comment: Craig Zacker		Help

Logon Status
Currently logged on as CRAIGZ

Default Logon Name: CRAIGZ

Log Off

Options:

Startup   Password   Event Log

Figure 12-6: The computer name assigned to your Windows for Workgroups machine enables other computers on the network to identify your system.

TCP/IP communications are based on IP addresses, not computer names. To access a shared network resource, a TCP/IP system must be capable of converting a computer name into an IP address. As discussed in Chapter 11, name resolution is the primary function of WINS, which runs on Windows NT. WINS maintains a database containing the computer names and IP addresses of all systems on your company's internetwork.

When configuring the TCP/IP-32 client with the IP addresses of WINS servers on your network, your system sends a request to the WINS server each time you attempt to access a shared resource on the Windows network. The request contains the name of the system sharing the resource, and the WINS server responds with that computer's IP address. Your system can then initiate communications with the other system, using the TCP/IP protocols.

WINS is not the only method TCP/IP-32 uses to resolve computer names. If your network does not use WINS, your system can still communicate using the TCP/IP protocols. It does this by employing other name-resolution methods, such as network broadcasts or an LMHOSTS file. The mechanisms a system uses to resolve NetBIOS names are specified by the computer's node type, which you can specify using DHCP. For example, a b-node system uses network broadcasts to resolve NetBIOS names, while a p-node uses a NetBIOS name server, such as WINS.

A system can have only a single node type – even if it is multihomed. You can, however, have multiple network adapters use different resolution methods. To do this, you must designate the system as a b-node, and then specify the IP addresses of WINS servers in the configuration dialog box, for only one of the adapters. The WINS settings override the broadcast-name resolution method specified by the b-node assignment.

For more information about the different name-resolution methods, see Chapter 11,"Name Registration and Resolution."

DNS CONFIGURATION   By clicking the *Domain Name System* (DNS) button on the Microsoft TCP/IP Configuration dialog box, you see the Microsoft TCP/IP – Connectivity Configuration dialog box, as shown in Figure 12-7. The Domain Name System is another name-resolution mechanism used on TCP/IP networks, but DNS is used primarily on the Internet, rather than private internetworks.

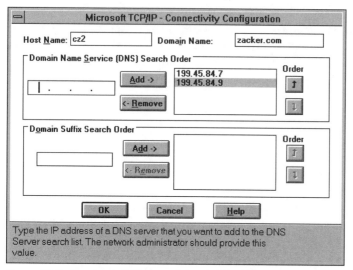

Figure 12–7: A system's DNS name uniquely identifies it on the Internet, while DNS servers resolve DNS names into IP addresses.

DNS is based on a different naming system than the Windows network. By combining the Host and Domain Names in the Connectivity Configuration dialog box, you specify a DNS name that uniquely identifies the system on the Internet. The domain name identifies your company (or other organization), and the host name identifies your system within that domain. On a Windows system, the host name need not be the same as the computer name, but often is, for the sake of convenience.

Although a Windows for Workgroups system can have multiple network interface adapters and multiple IP addresses, it has only one DNS configuration page.

To use a DNS name on the Internet, it must be registered in a DNS server, by a network administrator. In the DNS Search Order box, you specify the IP addresses of the servers your system will use to resolve the DNS names of other computers on the Internet. As with computer names, a DNS name must be converted to an IP address before TCP/IP communications can commence. Whenever you specify the DNS name of a desired destination (like TCP/IP-32's FTP client), your system sends a name-resolution request to its DNS server, and receives an IP address in return. You can specify the addresses of multiple DNS servers, as a fault-tolerance mechanism. If the first server listed is not available, every server is accessed until one is contacted.

In the Domain Suffix Search Order box, you specify domain names that will be appended to host names you specify in an application, automatically. This enables you to contact systems on frequently accessed domains by typing a host name, rather than a full DNS name. If, for example, you add *mycorp.com* to the list, and specify the name *www* in your Web browser, the application will connect to the system with the name *www.mycorp.com*. You can add multiple domains to the list, which are then searched in the order you specify.

TCP/IP-32 also includes the capability to resolve DNS names using a HOSTS file (an ASCII text file containing DNS names and their equivalent IP addresses), which is stored on the system's local drive. Microsoft's TCP/IP stack always searches the HOSTS file before sending a name-resolution request to a DNS server.

For more information on the Domain Name System and other name-resolution mechanisms used in Windows networking, see Chapter 11, "Name Registration and Resolution."

ADVANCED SETTINGS   When you click the Advanced button in the Microsoft TCP/IP Configuration dialog box, you see the dialog box shown in Figure 12-8. Each installed network adapter has its own Advanced Microsoft TCP/IP Configuration dialog box, in which you specify multiple IP addresses, default gateways, and other settings.

TCP/IP networks can be divided into subnets, which are logical divisions based on IP-address assignments. On most internetworks, the subnets are created according to the arrangement of physical-network segments. Some networks, however, may have two or more subnets sharing the same physical segment. A computer with a single network adapter can, therefore, be connected to one physical network and two TCP/IP subnets. In this case, the network adapter needs two IP addresses – one on each subnet – so the system can communicate with systems on both IP networks.

The advanced configuration dialog box enables you to specify up to five pairs of IP address and subnet masks, and add them to the configuration. All addresses in the list remain active, simultaneously. You can also specify up to five default gateway addresses, but these are only used as a fall-back mechanism, should the first gateway in the list be unreachable.

In the Windows Networking Parameters box, you can activate two additional mechanisms to resolve Windows computer names into IP addresses. The Enable DNS for Windows Name Resolution checkbox lets you use a system's DNS name, instead of its computer name, when accessing shared resources on a Windows network. The Enable LMHOSTS Lookup checkbox causes the system to check the contents of an ASCII-text file on the local drive (called LMHOSTS) if the other computer's name-resolution methods fail.

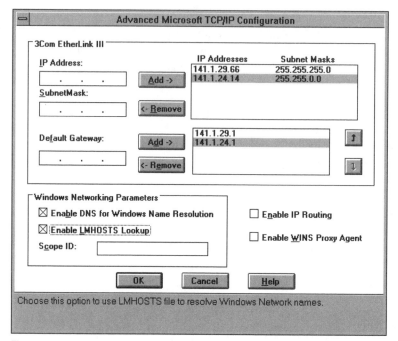

Figure 12-8: The advanced configuration options for TCP/IP-32 include multiple IP addresses, default gateways, and alternative name-resolution methods.

Learn more about formatting LMHOSTS files in Chapter 11, "Name Registration and Resolution."

A *NetBIOS Scope ID* is a name that identifies a group of systems, permitted to communicate with each other, only. This capability is seldom used in Windows networking, but you can specify a scope ID in the appropriate field, if necessary.

If your system has two or more IP addresses, assigned to one or more network adapters, the Enable IP Routing checkbox is activated. This enables the system to pass incoming IP traffic from one address, out through another.

By filling the Enable WINS Proxy Agent checkbox, your Windows for Workgroups system can use WINS servers on other network segments. This satisfies the NetBIOS name-resolution requests broadcasted by other computers on the local network.

Windows 95 and TCP/IP

When Windows 95 was released, the product contained a built-in TCP/IP stack which enabled users to connect to a Windows network, an ISP, or both. Windows NT had, by this time, adopted the TCP/IP protocols as its defaults. The less capable NetBEUI was replaced, providing support for large internetworks of Windows systems. Since TCP/IP support is included with the OS, you can install the protocol stack along with the other networking components.

Windows 95 Networking

The Windows 95 networking architecture is based on four types of modules. Combined, they form an effective stack connecting the networking hardware to the system's applications. The four module types are as follows:

◆ **Clients** – A client module provides the session-layer services needed by a Windows 95 system to connect to a particular type of network. Windows 95 includes 32-bit protected mode-client modules for Windows and NetWare networks. It also includes support for third-party networks, such as Banyan VINES, NFS, and Novell's own NetWare client software.

◆ **Services** – A network service is a form of application that runs continuously in the background, and provides some utility to other system applications. Microsoft's own services include modules that enable you to share your system's files and printers with Windows or NetWare networks, add support for Novell Directory Services, or host Web pages with a Personal Web Server (OEM Service Release 2 only). The Windows 95 product also includes services produced by other companies that facilitate system backup and printer control functions, and support external service modules.

◆ **Protocols** – Windows 95 can support multiple protocol stacks, including TCP/IP, NetBEUI, and IPX, simultaneously. The Windows network client can function with any of these. If all three protocols are installed, you must modify the bindings of the client and protocols to determine which should be used by default.

◆ **Adapter drivers** – Windows 95 uses NDIS 3.1 enhanced drivers for network adapters, by default. It also supports real mode NDIS drivers and Novell 32-bit ODI drivers. Real mode NDIS drivers are included with the OS to provide networking support while operating in DOS mode. If you boot Windows 95 to a DOS prompt and connect to the network, using the NET BASIC or NET WORKSTATION command, you are using a real mode driver.

Because TCP/IP is based on open standards, interoperability problems between different manufacturers' products are rare. For example, Windows 95 provides support for different implementations of the IPX-protocol suite. IPX is a collection of proprietary protocols, developed by Novell, for use with NetWare. Microsoft developed its own IPX-compatible protocol for use with the Windows network, and with its own NetWare client. When you use IPX to connect to other Windows systems and load a NetWare client for Windows 95 (such as Novell's Client 32), your system actually runs two separate IPX protocol drivers.

The TCP/IP protocol stack included with Windows 95 has effectively destroyed the market for other Windows 95 TCP/IP implementations. There is no persuasive reason for a third-party Windows 95 product to include its own TCP/IP stack; indeed, most products requiring TCP/IP transport services rely on the internal stack.

Installing TCP/IP LAN Support

Opening the Windows 95 Network Control Panel displays a list of the networking modules currently installed on the system, as shown in Figure 12-9. If you upgrade a system to Windows 95 from DOS, Windows 3.1x, or Windows for Workgroups, the Setup program installs networking support (based on the system's environment when the upgrade begins). By installing the Windows 95 equivalents to the pre-existing network-client software, the same level of network service is maintained after the upgrade process is completed.

This does not mean that Windows 95 can recognize every existing network client. Existing Windows network, or NetWare, clients are recognized and upgraded (usually). If, however, you've been using a third-party TCP/IP stack, chances are Windows 95 will not recognize it. If this happens, you may have to add the TCP/IP protocol driver manually, and possibly other modules.

 When upgrading a large number of systems to Windows 95, you can modify the OS's installation parameters to recognize third-party networking products, and take a specific course of action.

The basic procedure for adding a networking module to Windows 95 is a simple one. By clicking the Add button on the Configuration page of the Network Control Panel, you select one of the four module types (see Figure 12-10), and the system displays lists of the available modules. Each of these lists contain a Have Disk button, which you can use to supply a driver that you've obtained from another source, such as a hardware manufacturer. Once the component is installed, you can highlight it in the display and click the Properties button to display a configuration dialog box.

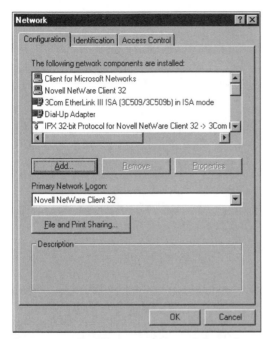

Figure 12-9: The Windows 95 Network Control
Panel is the central point of administration for all
networking activities of the OS.

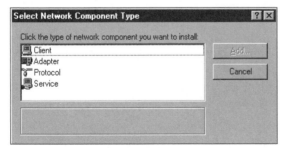

Figure 12-10: To add a component to the Windows 95
networking environment, select the type of module you
want to install first.

In Windows 95, you can install multiple clients, protocols, and adapters in
almost any combination and expect them to work together. Both clients and
adapters are capable of supporting multiple-protocol stacks, simultaneously. By
default, the OS binds all of the installed components together, so every possible
configuration is supported. For example, if you install the Microsoft IPX-
compatible protocol and both the Windows and NetWare network clients, IP is

bound to both automatically. If you want to avoid using IPX for Windows network communications, you must explicitly unbind the protocol from the client.

Windows 95 also recognizes the capabilities of each of the networking modules and the relationships between them. It will not, for example, try to bind the NetBEUI protocol to the NetWare client because NetWare doesn't support NetBEUI. Similarly, if you add the NetWare client, the system automatically installs the IPX-compatible protocol, which is required to communicate with NetWare servers.

The same theory holds true for adapter drivers. When you add the TCP/IP protocol stack, it is automatically bound to all of the adapters installed in the system (including the Microsoft dial-up adapter that enables you to connect to a remote network, using a modem).

ADDING AN ADAPTER

No matter what the previous networking configuration of the computer, if you install Windows 95 with a network adapter in the machine, it will likely be recognized – and an adapter driver will be installed, automatically. Although you can add an adapter driver from the Network Control Panel, manually, it is preferable to use the Add New Hardware wizard (also accessible from the Control Panel). When you launch the wizard, you may choose to let it detect your hardware automatically, or you may select a driver from a list. Whichever method you choose, this procedure not only installs the adapter driver, but also recognizes the hardware settings of the device and configures the driver accordingly.

After installing the adapter driver, you can open its Properties dialog box and select the Bindings tab to see the protocol stacks to which the driver is bound (see Figure 12-11). To prevent an adapter from carrying a particular protocol, simply clear the appropriate checkbox.

ADDING A CLIENT

Protocols are bound to adapters in the Windows 95 networking architecture, as well as to clients. You must install a client to use the TCP/IP protocols, to complete the networking stack that links the system's applications with its network hardware. A Windows 95 client is a file-system driver that redirects application calls to files located on other systems, down the network stack.

The client module most often used with TCP/IP is the Client for Microsoft Networks, which takes the form of a module called Vredir.vxd. With this client, you can access shared resources on Windows NT, Windows for Workgroups, and other Windows 95 systems. If you plan to share the files on your own system with Windows network users, you must install the File and Printer Sharing for Microsoft Networks service, Vserver.vxd. If you are not connected to a Windows network, and only intend to use TCP/IP to access the Internet through a dial-up connection, the client module must still be present, and is installed with the protocol driver.

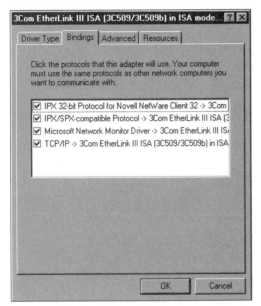

Figure 12-11: The Bindings page of an adapter's Properties dialog box displays the protocols that are using that adapter.

To use the Windows 95 Client for Microsoft Networks to log on to a Windows NT domain, open the Client for Microsoft Networks Properties dialog box, fill the appropriate checkbox, and specify the name of the domain.

ADDING TCP/IP

When you choose Protocol from the Select Network Component Type dialog box and select Microsoft TCP/IP, Windows 95 installs the Vtcp.vxd module. It then adds a new TCP/IP entry to the network component list for each adapter installed in the system, as shown in Figure 12-12. As with any TCP/IP implementation, each network interface must have its own IP address and other configuration settings. You must configure each interface separately, by highlighting it in the component list and clicking the Properties button.

Like all Microsoft TCP/IP implementations, the easiest way to configure a Windows 95 TCP/IP client is to use a DHCP server. You can use this to assign IP addresses and other parameters. To select the Obtain an IP address automatically radio button, on the IP Address page of the Properties dialog box, simply click the OK button (see Figure 12-13). All of the required configuration parameters can be assigned using DHCP.

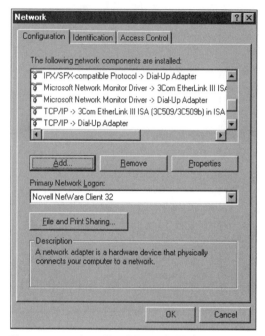

Figure 12-12: Installing Microsoft TCP/IP
automatically binds the protocol stack to each
of the network interfaces installed in the system.

 If you activate the Windows 95 DHCP client after configuring some (or all) of the parameters in the TCP/IP Properties dialog box, the values left in the dialog box override those provided by the DHCP server. Be sure to clear any existing values that you don't want, before enabling DHCP.

If your network does not use DHCP, you must configure the TCP/IP client, manually. This is done by supplying values for parameters found on various pages of the TCP/IP Properties dialog box. These parameters are as follows:

IP Address Page

- ◆ **IP Address** – The IP address uniquely identifies the system's network interface, as well as the TCP/IP network to which the system is attached. The IP address and the subnet mask are the only two parameters absolutely necessary for TCP/IP communications.

- ◆ **Subnet Mask** – The subnet mask is used to indicate which of the IP address bits identify the network, and which identify the host.

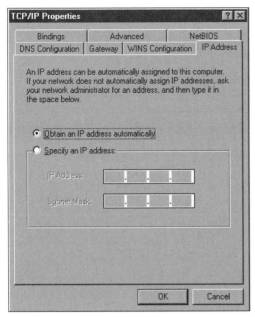

Figure 12-13: Windows 95's DHCP client can obtain all necessary TCP/IP-configuration settings from a Windows NT (or other) system running DHCP server software.

For more information on subnetting and masks, see Chapter 2, "TCP/IP Communications."

Gateway Page

◆ **Default Gateway** — When a TCP/IP system is attached to an internetwork, the default gateway parameter identifies the router that the system should use to communicate with computers on other networks. Windows 95 permits you to specify the IP addresses of up to eight default gateways. Additional routers can only be accessed when the previously specified system is unreachable. If your network only consists of a single segment, or subnet (and has no routed Internet access), a default gateway is not needed.

WINS Configuration Page

♦ **Primary WINS Server** – WINS is a standards-based NetBIOS name server that runs on Windows NT. It is used to resolve Windows computer names into the IP addresses needed for TCP/IP communications. The use of WINS is optional, but specifying the IP address of a Windows NT system running WINS decreases the amount of broadcast traffic on your network. The reason for this lies in the absence of WINS. When WINS is absent, systems must broadcast the name of the computer they're trying to contact, and wait for a reply containing the IP address.

 For more information, see "Name Resolution" earlier in this chapter, or Chapter 11,"Name Registration and Resolution."

♦ **Secondary WINS Server** – A Windows 95 system only accesses the secondary WINS server when the primary one cannot be contacted. If both servers fail, the system reverts to the broadcast name-resolution method.

♦ **Scope ID** – The scope ID is a seldom-used NetBIOS convention that permits a group of systems to be identified by a single name. The computers in the group communicate only with each other and are isolated from the rest of the network.

DNS Configuration Page

♦ **Enable/Disable DNS** – DNS is the standard name-resolution service for the Internet. You cannot specify friendly DNS names for Internet sites in an application (such as *www.mycorp.com*) unless you use DNS servers for name resolution. If your system and network aren't connected to the Internet, you can disable the DNS client (unless your network uses it to resolve internal network names).

♦ **Host Name** – The host name is the part of a DNS name that uniquely identifies a system within a particular domain. If this field is left blank, the system's computer name is also used as its DNS host name.

♦ **Domain Name** – The domain name identifies an organization with a presence on the Internet in the Domain Name System (DNS) hierarchy. When you append the domain name to the host name, you have a DNS name (such as *www.mycorp.com*), which functions as a unique identifier for one particular computer on the Internet.

◆ **DNS Server Search Order** – DNS servers resolve DNS names into IP addresses, just as WINS servers resolve NetBIOS names. In this field, you can specify the IP addresses of up to three DNS servers your system will use for this purpose. The second and third servers listed are accessed only when the first server is unavailable.

◆ **Domain Suffix Search Order** – You can simplify the process of entering the DNS names of systems in commonly used domains by adding up to six domain suffixes in this field. For example, adding *mycorp.com* to the list causes the name *www* to be parsed in an application as *www.mycorp.com*.

TCP/IP and Windows 95 Dial-Up Networking

The Windows 95 networking architecture is not just designed for connecting to a LAN. The OS's Dial-Up Networking feature enables you to use a modem for connecting to a remote network, as well. You can use this feature to connect to your office computer from home, access the LAN in another office, or connect to an ISP. Despite the use of a modem instead of a network interface card, Windows 95 treats a dial-up connection like any other networking environment, and requires the same types of components.

Windows 95 includes a Dial-Up Adapter driver (called Pppmac.vxd) that lets a modem function as the interface to the physical network, like a normal network adapter. You can use any of the standard Windows 95 protocols and clients with the dial-up adapter, enabling you to connect to a remote site using NetBEUI, IPX, TCP/IP, or any combination of the three. When you configure your system to use Dial-Up Networking, the components list in the Network Control Panel displays entries for the dial-up adapter driver and the protocols to which it is bound (see Figure 12-14).

Your Windows 95 system can connect to a wide variety of remote network servers, regardless of whether you are connected to a LAN simultaneously. Windows NT, for example, includes Remote Access Server (RAS) capabilities that enable you to access Windows network resources at another location. You can also connect to any server offering dial-up access, using the *Serial Line Internet Protocol* (SLIP) or the *Point-to-Point Protocol* (PPP). The Serial Line Internet Protocol and the Point-to-Point Protocol are based on TCP/IP link-layer standards, and are designed to connect one computer directly to another. Nearly all ISPs use one (or both) of these protocols, so you can use Windows 95 to connect to the Internet whether their dial-up servers are running UNIX, Windows NT, or any other OS.

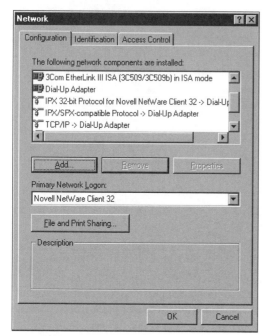

Figure 12-14: Dial-Up Networking uses the same architectural components as Windows 95's LAN networking.

For more information on the SLIP and PPP protocols, see Chapter 4, "The Link Layer."

Windows 95 can also function as a dial-up networking server, to which other Windows network clients can connect and access the computer's local resources. Windows 95 is also capable of providing remote users access to other systems on the network, using the IPX and NetBEUI protocols. A Windows 95 system, however, cannot function as an IP router. This means that a remote user dialing into your Windows 95 system cannot access other computers on your local network, using the TCP/IP protocols. It also means that you cannot connect to an ISP with a Windows 95 system and provide other systems on the LAN with Internet access. Windows NT, on the other hand, is capable of both these things.

SETTING UP THE DIAL-UP NETWORKING CLIENT

Although the components of the dial-up networking client are the same as those for a LAN connection, you don't configure the service by manipulating the modules in the Network Control Panel. Instead, you select Dial-Up Networking from the Start Menu's Accessories group and activate the Make New Connection wizard. To do this, you must have installed and configured your modem for use with Windows 95.

When you start the wizard, you're prompted to specify a name for the connection, select the modem you intend to use (from those installed in the system), and supply the telephone number of the server to which you will connect. Once you complete this process, a new icon appears in the Dial-Up Networking window, with the name you supplied for the connection. Depending on the configuration of the server you're dialing, you may be able to proceed using the default configuration. In many cases, you must configure the networking parameters for the connection by right-clicking the icon and selecting Properties from the context menu. This displays the dialog box shown in Figure 12-15.

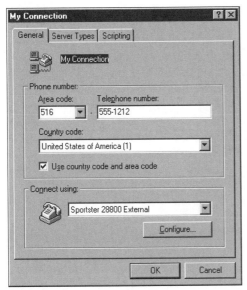

Figure 12-15: Each connection you create in the Dial-Up Networking window has its own Properties dialog box, which you can use to configure its TCP/IP parameters.

 When you create your first connection in the Dial-Up Networking window, the system checks to see whether or not the Dial-Up Adapter is installed in the Network Control Panel. If it's not, the wizard installs it for you automatically and binds it to all of the currently installed protocols.

CONFIGURING A DIAL-UP NETWORKING CONNECTION

The General page of the dialog box contains the modem selection and telephone number that you supplied to the wizard. You can modify these settings, if necessary, and click the Configure button to access the modem's Properties dialog box. In addition to the functionality of the modem itself, two settings (found on the Options screen of this dialog box) can be helpful when you establish a dial-up networking connection. You can display a terminal window before, or after, the modem dial (or both). The terminal window lets you send typed AT commands directly to the modem (before dialing), or to the connected server (after dialing). For example, using this terminal access, you can interactively perform a logon to the dial-up server, as shown in Figure 12-16.

Figure 12-16: You can configure a dial-up connection to open a terminal window before, or after, the dialing process.

SERVER TYPES   On the Server Types page of a connection's Properties dialog box (see Figure 12-17), you select the Type of Dial-Up Server to which you will connect. The server types supported by Windows 95 include the following:

◆ **NRN: NetWare Connect** – NetWare Connect is a product that enables remote users to dial directly into a NetWare server and access its resources (and to those of the other NetWare servers on the network). To use the NetWare Connect option, you must also install the Microsoft Client for NetWare Networks and the IPX/SPX-compatible protocol in the Network Control Panel.

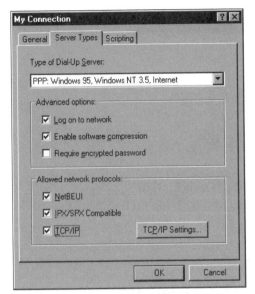

Figure 12-17: On the Server Types page, you specify the options that are supported by the system, to which the Windows 95 computer will connect.

◆ **PPP: Windows 95, Windows NT 3.5, Internet** — The dial-up server capabilities of Windows 95 and Windows NT (versions 3.5, 3.51, and 4.0) are based on the Point-to-Point Protocol, as are most ISP-server implementations. PPP is the default value for the Type of Dial-Up Server field, and is used in the majority of Windows 95 Dial-Up Networking connections.

◆ **SLIP: UNIX Connection** — SLIP is a precursor to PPP that is used primarily on UNIX systems, but it has largely been replaced by the newer protocol. SLIP provides only the most basic encapsulation of IP datagrams for delivery to a remote system, while PPP provides many additional features, such as support for multiple transport protocols, authentication services, and error detection.

◆ **CSLIP: UNIX Connection with IP Header Compression** — CSLIP is a variation of the SLIP protocol, in which the TCP and IP headers within the datagrams to be transmitted are compressed by the removal of redundant data.

◆ **Windows for Workgroups and Windows NT 3.1** — These OSs can only support remote clients using a proprietary RAS protocol that carries NetBEUI traffic; they cannot support TCP/IP or IPX. You must select this option when connecting to either of these OSs, but it will also function when connecting to a Windows 95 server or to Windows NT version 3.5 or higher.

ADVANCED OPTIONS   The Advanced Options on the Server Types page of a connection's Properties dialog box include the following:

◆ **Log on to network** – When this option is enabled, Windows 95 attempts to log you in to the remote network, after a connection is established. It does this using the name and password that you supplied during your local Windows 95 logon. If you use a terminal window or a script to perform a nonstandard logon to the remote network, you can disable this automatic logon. This option is enabled by default for all Dial-Up Networking connections.

◆ **Enable software compression** – When enabled, this option causes the system to attempt using software compression in its communications with the server. The use of compression is negotiated with the server during the Link Control Protocol (LCP) exchanges, which occur during the establishment of a PPP connection. The feature is used only if both systems support compression. This option is enabled by default for all Dial-Up Networking connections using the PPP protocol, and unavailable for any server types other than PPP.

◆ **Require encrypted password** – This option causes the Windows 95 system to negotiate the use of encrypted passwords with the connected server. When it is enabled, and both systems support the feature, no passwords are exchanged between the systems using clear text. This option is disabled by default for all Dial-Up Networking connections using the PPP protocol, and unavailable for any server types other than PPP.

SELECTING PROTOCOLS   In the Allowed Network Protocols box, you select the protocols that can be sent or received using the dial-up connection. PPP is the only link-layer protocol, supported by Windows 95, that can multiplex different protocols. It is, therefore, the only server type in which all three of the protocol checkboxes are enabled. For the other server types, only the protocols that they support are activated.

The settings on this page do not affect the bindings of the networking components as they are displayed in the Network Control Panel. You can disable one or more of the protocols and find that they are still bound to the Dial-Up Adapter, although the traffic over the connection is effectively suppressed. The opposite is not true, however. You can enable a protocol on this page, but unless the equivalent module is installed in the Control Panel, communications do not occur.

By default, all three of the available protocols (NetBEUI, IPX/SPX Compatible, and TCP/IP) are enabled when you create a connection using the PPP server type. During the PPP connection-establishment process, each protocol must be initialized using a separate Network Control Protocol (NCP) negotiation process. It is, therefore, recommended that you disable the protocols you don't intend to use on that connection. For example, when you connect to an ISP, you need only TCP/IP, and when you connect to a Windows network system, you probably need TCP/IP or NetBEUI – but not both.

CONFIGURING TCP/IP   When Dial-Up Networking installs the Dial-Up Adapter module into the components list of the Network Control Panel, it binds each protocol installed on the system to the adapter. You don't use the Control Panel's TCP/IP Properties dialog box to configure the parameters used during a dial-up connection, however. Instead, you click the TCP/IP Setting buttons on the Server Types page of a connection's Properties dialog box, as shown in Figure 12-18. This way, you can specify different configuration values for each of the connections you create.

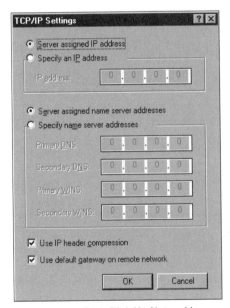

Figure 12-18: Each Dial-Up Networking connection has its own TCP/IP Settings dialog box.

By default, a Dial-Up Networking connection assumes that the server will dynamically assign values for the IP address, and name-server fields to the client. Depending on the nature of the service you're accessing, however, you may need to specify values for these parameters, yourself. If the administrators of the remote network have allocated a specific IP address for use by your system, you should enter it in the IP Address field. When you do this, the client system specifies the address during the establishment of the PPP connection, when the IP protocol is initialized.

The IP address that is assigned to the Dial-Up Networking client, either by the server or the client, is associated with the Dial-Up Adapter—effectively creating a multihomed system. Once the remote connection is established, you can simultaneously access resources on both of the networks to which the system is attached.

The DNS and WINS servers addresses (on the remote network your system should use for name resolution) can also be assigned by the remote server, or by manually configuring them here. DNS and WINS are not required for TCP/IP communications, but clients almost always use DNS servers when connecting to the Internet, and WINS servers when connecting to a remote Windows network.

When enabled, the Use IP Header Compression feature causes the client to negotiate the use of the Van Jacobson header compression algorithm, during the PPP connection-establishment process. When it is supported by both client and server, this algorithm can reduce the TCP and IP headers in a datagram from a total of forty bytes to as little as five bytes. By default, this option is enabled and need not be changed, because data compression is never performed unless both systems agree to its use.

When you fill the Use Default Gateway on Remote Network checkbox, a new entry is automatically added to your system's routing table. This causes all traffic to be routed out of the system using the IP address assigned to the dial-up adapter, by default. If your computer is also attached to a LAN, there is another entry in the table that causes all traffic (destined for the local network) to be transmitted by the system's local network interface adapter. This option is enabled by default.

SCRIPTING   When connecting to a server that uses a nonstandard logon procedure, you can either open a terminal window to manually perform an interactive logon, or use a script to automate the process. A typical example of a nonstandard logon occurs when an ISP uses character-based menus during the connection-establishment process. This enables you to select a link-layer protocol, or other client features.

On the Scripting page of the connection's Properties dialog box, you can browse for one of the existing scripts supplied with the OS, or one that you create. Once you have specified the script to use when the connection is established, you can click the Edit button to open the file in the Windows 95 Notepad utility, and activate the Step Through Script feature to pause the processing of the script after each command. This makes it easier to debug scripts that you are customizing for a particular logon procedure. Once you determine that the script is functioning properly, fill the Start Terminal Screen Minimized checkbox to execute the script invisibly whenever you connect to that server.

TIP Support for Dial-Up Networking scripts was not included in the original Windows 95 release, though it is available in Microsoft Plus! For Windows 95, as well as the OEM Service Release 2, as shown here. The scripting module is also available in Windows 95 Service Pack 1 and can be downloaded separately from Microsoft's Web site at *http://www.microsoft.com/kb/softlib/-mslfiles/SCRIPT.EXE.*

The dial-up scripts are ASCII text files with an SCP extension. Windows 95 includes scripts for use with the CompuServe online service (which uses a unique logon sequence) and for SLIP and PPP servers that use menus. You can easily modify these scripts to accommodate the procedures required for your servers. The commands are based primarily on the recognition of specific keywords, received from the server, and the transmission of variables in response. For example, the Pppmenu.scr script causes the Windows 95 system to respond to a prompt of *username:* by transmitting the contents of the $USERID variable. If you are logging on to a server that uses *hostname:* as its prompt instead of *username:*, it is easy to modify the script accordingly.

Windows NT and TCP/IP

Although the underlying code is quite different, Windows NT uses a networking architecture that appears similar to that of Windows 95. Network access is provided by modules called services, protocols, and adapters, that are bound together to form a stack connecting the network hardware to the APIs supported by the OS. The modules themselves are quite different, though. Windows NT uses adapter drivers written to the NDIS 3.0 standard, instead of the NDIS 3.1 drivers used by Windows 95. Windows NT does not use networking modules that have been implemented as VxDs, the 32-bit protected-mode virtual device drivers used by Windows 95.

You install and configure Windows NT's networking components using the Network Control Panel, as in Windows 95. NT, however, integrates its networking support more completely into the OS. You do not explicitly install a client for Windows networking. Instead, Windows NT's basic networking architecture always includes the Workstation, Server, Browser, Messenger, and Network Logon services. These enable the system to access shared network resources, and share its own. Clients for other network OSs are implemented as services, as well.

Adding Network Components

Windows NT includes many different network services that implement optional protocols and applications, which you can add as needed. The optional services related to Windows NT's TCP/IP functionality include the following:

- **Dynamic Host Configuration Protocol (DHCP)** – DHCP is a service that automatically configures Windows network clients. It does this by assigning IP addresses from a pool, as well as values for other parameters.

- **Windows Internet Name Service (WINS)** – WINS is a NetBIOS name server that Windows network clients can use to resolve the computer names of LAN systems into the IP addresses needed for TCP/IP communications.

- **Domain Name System (DNS)** – DNS is a name server used to resolve the host names, used by Internet systems, into IP addresses. It does this by accessing the data distributed in other DNS servers located all over the Internet.

- **Remote Access Service (RAS)** – RAS is the service that provides remote client systems with the capability to access Windows networks using a dial-up connection.

- **Microsoft Peer Web Services/Internet Information Server** – PWS and IIS are the NT Workstation and Server versions of the World Wide Web, FTP, and Gopher services.

- **Simple TCP/IP Services** – The Simple TCP/IP Services enable Windows NT to function as a server for the Character Generator, Daytime, Discard, Echo, and Quote of the Day protocols, as defined in the Internet standards.

- **Point-to-Point Tunneling Protocol (PPTP)** – PPTP enables computers at remote sites to communicate using an encrypted point-to-point connection with the Internet as a carrier medium.

- **Microsoft TCP/IP Printing** – The TCP/IP printing service enables a Windows NT system to transmit print jobs to the line printer daemon (lpd) on another computer, using the line printer (lpr) protocol.

- **Simple Network Management Protocol (SNMP)** – The SNMP service implements a protocol that computers can use to send statistics and informative messages about the system's operational status to a central network management console.

To add a service, you open the Services page in the Network Control Panel (as shown in Figure 12-19) and click the Add button to choose one of the services included with the OS. Some of the services include a Properties dialog box containing configuration parameters for that service, which you can access by clicking the appropriate button.

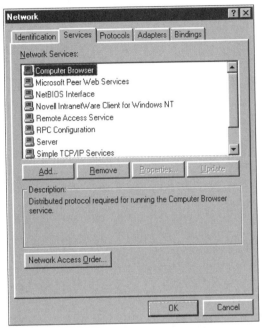

Figure 12-19: Windows NT includes a wide assortment of network services that you can add to the system as needed.

 Windows NT services are designed to run continuously, providing a resource that can be used by applications running on the local, or on remote systems. As with all software modules, services occupy system resources all the time they are running. You should, therefore, install only the services you require for your computing environment, and disable those that aren't actually being used. (You can start, stop, and pause services using the Windows NT Services Control Panel.)

As with Windows 95, NT supports the NetBEUI, IPX, and TCP/IP protocols, all of which can be multiplexed over a single network adapter, if needed. Because NT is a peer-to-peer OS, the process of configuring TCP/IP support for a LAN client is the same as that for an NT server.

See Chapter 8, "Windows NT and IntranetWare" for a detailed discussion of the configuration process.

TCP/IP and Windows NT Dial-Up Networking

Windows NT includes the Remote Access Service (RAS) to host remote users and connect to a network using a dial-up connection. When you use an NT 4.0 system to dial into a remote server, RAS is known as Dial-Up Networking for the sake of consistency with the Windows 95 interface. RAS NT, however, includes greater functionality for incoming client traffic. Although Windows NT Workstation can host only a single dial-up user (like Windows 95), NT Server can host up to 256 users and provide them with network access.

Windows NT is also capable of functioning as an IP router—Windows 95 cannot. You can, therefore, use an NT system to establish a dial-up connection to an ISP and provide other users on your LAN with Internet access, by using the NT computer as a gateway. For more information on routing with Windows NT, see Chapter 9, "Routing IP."

INSTALLING RAS

The modules involved in implementing Windows NT's RAS feature differ from those used in Windows 95. You must first install the Remote Access Service by adding it to the Services page in the Network Control Panel. Once you have installed the service, you highlight it and click Properties to display the Remote Access Setup dialog box. This dialog box displays a list of the ports on your system, for which a modem has been configured. By selecting a port and clicking Configure, you can configure each individual port to dial-out to remote servers, receive incoming calls from clients—or both.

Once you configure a port, you can click the Network button to configure its client/server parameters. When you restrict a port to dial-out services only, the Network Configuration dialog box consists only of Dial out Protocols checkboxes (see Figure 12-20). From these, you select the protocols that can be transmitted over the dial-up connection. If you elect to receive calls, the Server Settings parameters are displayed, as shown in Figure 12-21. With these, you can control the incoming network traffic.

Another way that Windows NT RAS differs from Windows 95 is that NT does not require you to install a Dial-Up Adapter driver. When you display the Adapters page in the Network Control Panel, you see only drivers for the network adapters installed in the system. Once you install and configure RAS, however, additional adapter icons are added to the Network Control Panel's Bindings screen, as shown in Figure 12-22. Adapter icons labeled Remote Access WAN Wrapper represent the connections made through RAS, even though you haven't explicitly loaded a driver for them.

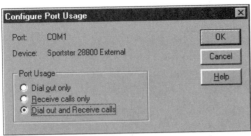

Figure 12-20: The settings displayed in the Network Configuration dialog box for a particular port depend on whether you enable incoming or outgoing traffic, or both.

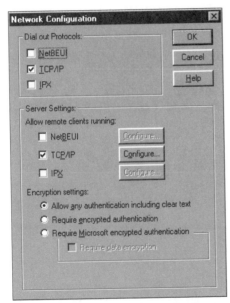

Figure 12-21: When you elect to receive incoming calls from RAS clients, you can configure the server parameters for each protocol, individually.

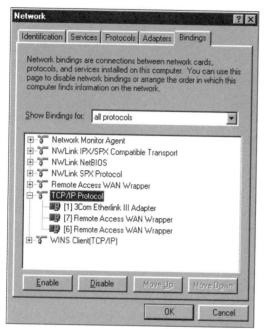

Figure 12-22: The Network Control Panel's Bindings
screen displays the relationships between NT's
networking components.

USING TCP/IP ON A RAS SERVER

In configuring RAS to receive incoming TCP/IP traffic from remote clients, you can click the Configure button, in the Network Configuration screen, to display the RAS Server TCP/IP Configuration dialog box (see Figure 12-23). Here, you specify whether you want only remote clients to be capable of accessing this computer, or the entire network. This setting can prevent incoming RAS IP traffic from being routed to the other network adapters installed in the system, but it doesn't configure the system to route IP, itself. You must configure the TCP/IP protocol to route by enabling IP forwarding in the Microsoft TCP/IP Properties dialog box, and by installing a routing protocol or configuring static routes.

The RAS server also specifies how a dial-up client should obtain the IP address that it will use to communicate with the network. The RAS Server TCP/IP Configuration dialog box provides the following three alternative methods:

◆ **Use DHCP to assign remote TCP/IP client addresses** – When you use DHCP for RAS client-address assignment, the RAS server acts as a proxy. It leases a group of addresses from the DHCP server and allocates them to clients during the PPP link-establishment process. As far as the DHCP server is concerned, the addresses are leased to the computer functioning as the RAS server.

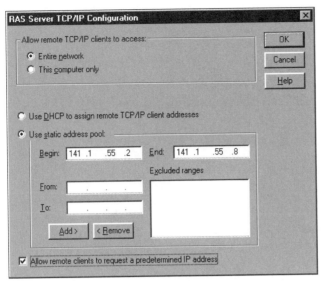

Figure 12-23: The RAS Server TCP/IP Configuration dialog box
controls RAS client access to the system and the network.

♦ **Use static address pool** — This option enables you to specify a group of IP
addresses to assign to RAS clients, without using DHCP. In the Begin and
End fields, you define a range of IP addresses. You can then exclude
specific addresses within that range by entering them in the From and To
fields and adding them to the Excluded Ranges list. (To exclude a single
address, enter the same value in both the From and To fields.)

♦ **Allow remote clients to request a predetermined IP address** — This
option enables the RAS client to specify the address it will use when it
connects to the server.

CONFIGURING A RAS TCP/IP CLIENT

To configure a Windows NT system to be a RAS client, you access Dial-Up
Networking from the Accessories group in the Start Menu (as in Windows 95). NT
uses a different dialog box to create and configure RAS connections, however, as
shown in Figure 12-24. When you click the New button, you see the New
Phonebook Entry dialog box. After creating an entry, you can edit its parameters at
any time by selecting Edit Entry and Modem Properties from the More menu.

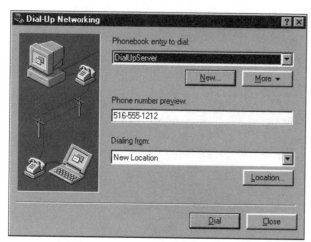

Figure 12-24: You use the Dial-Up Networking dialog box to create and configure RAS client connections.

On the Basic page of the dialog box, you enter a name for the RAS connection, the port containing the modem you wish to use, and the telephone number of the remote server. You can also specify alternate phone numbers to be dialed in sequence when the primary number is busy or unresponsive. On the Server page (see Figure 12-25), you select the type of server you will connect to, and the protocols you will use to communicate with the remote network. The RAS client supports the PPP, SLIP, and Windows NT 3.1 RAS clients, as described in the "Server Types" section, earlier in this chapter. From this page, you can enable data compression at the software level (replacing the hardware-based compression supplied by most modems) and permit the client to use the latest protocol extensions during the PPP link-negotiation process.

You access the PPP TCP/IP Configuration settings dialog box by clicking the TCP/IP Settings button. In this dialog box, you specify whether an IP address (and the addresses of the DNS and WINS servers on the remote network) are furnished for the client, or permit the server to assign the addresses to the client, automatically.

As with Windows 95, you can configure the RAS client to open a terminal window once the connection is established. This enables you to log on manually, or use a script to automate the logon process. Windows NT 4.0 supports the same scripting language used by Windows 95, as well as a script format of its own that is described in the Switch.inf file configured as the default script.

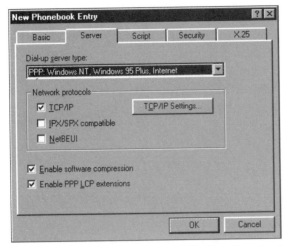

Figure 12-25: On the Server page of the New Phonebook Entry dialog box, you specify the type of server at the other end of the connection, and the protocols to be used.

Summary

The Windows operating systems are all capable of functioning as TCP/IP clients, both on LANs and using a dial-up connection.

In this chapter, you learned:

◆ How to add the Microsoft TCP/IP-32 stack to a Windows for Workgroups system

◆ How to install the Windows 95 TCP/IP stack

◆ How to configure Windows 95 Dial-Up Networking connection to a remote TCP/IP system

◆ How to set up Windows NT to be a TCP/IP client

The following chapter examines the TCP/IP capabilities of Novell's IntranetWare clients, as well as NetWare/IP and the IPX/IP Gateway.

Chapter 13

IntranetWare TCP/IP Clients

IN THIS CHAPTER
Although NetWare still uses the IPX protocols for its primary network-transport services, the IntranetWare product elevates TCP/IP to a much more prominent position in the network architecture. The Internet/intranet services included in the IntranetWare package are accessible by standard Winsock TCP/IP clients. Such clients include those found in the Windows 95 and Windows NT OSs, and those provided by third-party companies for Windows 3.1x. You can also use TCP/IP to carry the IPX traffic generated by NetWare's native file and print services using the NetWare/IP product, included with IntranetWare.

The IntranetWare clients for Windows 95 and Windows NT rely on the protocol stacks built into those OSs for TCP/IP transport, but include additional modules to support NetWare/IP data encapsulation. The clients for DOS and Windows 3.1x, however, supply a TCP/IP stack of their own, which provides access to IntranetWare; as well as general TCP/IP services. Novell also provides an alternative means of providing IPX clients with access to TCP/IP services, in the form of an IPX/IP gateway that runs on a NetWare server.

This chapter examines the various types of TCP/IP support provided by the IntranetWare clients, such as the following:

- Using the VLM/IP Client

- Using Client 32 for DOS/Windows 3.1 for TCP/IP services

- Using NetWare/IP with Windows 95 and Windows NT clients

- Using the Novell IPX/IP Gateway

NetWare Clients and TCP/IP

IntranetWare includes client software for all of the Windows OSs, but provides a TCP/IP stack only with the software for DOS and Windows 3.1x. IntranetWare clients use TCP/IP for two primary purposes: to support Windows Sockets applications, such as Web and FTP clients, and to encapsulate IPX packets containing *NetWare Core Protocol* (NCP) data for transport to and from NetWare/IP servers.

Novell's Windows 95 and Windows NT clients don't need to supply Winsock support or the TCP/IP protocol stack, because they can use the OSs' own TCP/IP implementation. The clients do include a protocol driver for NetWare/IP support that must be added to the network-client configuration. The following sections examine the TCP/IP support provided in each of the IntranetWare clients.

Using the VLM/IP Client

For several years, the NetWare DOS Requester, also known as the *VLM client*, was the standard NetWare client for DOS and Windows workstations. The Client 32 releases far surpass the VLMs in functionality and convenience, but there are still a great many systems running the older client. The original NetWare DOS Requester is still included as part of the IntranetWare product, but there is also a second version of the software included. This version is designed to support the use of NetWare/IP and the Novell TCP/IP services.

The *VLM/IP client* is virtually identical to the original NetWare DOS Requester, except that it includes a TCP/IP stack and a WINSOCK.DLL file. It also includes a few rudimentary TCP/IP utilities, including PING, a desktop SNMP client, and LWPCON.EXE, the Novell LAN Workplace console. The TCP/IP stack takes the form of an executable file, called TCPIP.EXE, and NetWare/IP functionality is provided by a module, called NWIP.EXE.

When a workstation executes these two programs in addition to the standard VLM-client components, all NCP traffic is encapsulated within UDP datagrams. These are transmitted to NetWare/IP servers, including the IPX header information. This process is known as *IP tunneling*. In addition, TCPIP.EXE provides support for the following APIs:

◆ Network File System (NFS)

◆ Streams

◆ BSD UNIX 4.3 sockets

◆ NetBIOS over TCP/IP (b-node)

◆ Windows Sockets 1.1

WINDOWS SOCKETS

Windows Sockets, implemented as a dynamic-link library called WINSOCK.DLL, is the most common API. The WINSOCK.DLL file is used by many TCP/IP client applications (such as the Netscape Web browser included with IntranetWare) to connect to intranet or Internet services, such as the Novell Web Server. When a Windows Sockets application launches, it searches for the WINSOCK.DLL file to initialize the network-communications process. Any WINSOCK.DLL file supporting the Windows Sockets standard can be used with any application also written to the standard. This makes the VLM/IP client suitable as a general-purpose TCP/IP stack for use with DOS, Windows 3.1, or Windows for Workgroups.

Although any standards-based WINSOCK.DLL module can support Windows Sockets applications, this doesn't mean that the Winsock files themselves are interchangeable. Each TCP/IP product designs a Winsock module to communicate with its own protocol stack. Because you may have various TCP/IP-software products installed on a single system, it's easy for the WINSOCK.DLL files to be confused. The VLM/IP client installs the module to the \NET\BIN directory by default, and adds that directory to the end of the PATH command in the AUTOEXEC.BAT file.

Other products may observe different policies, when it comes to placing the WINSOCK.DLL file, that can affect the performance of the client. For example, if another software package installs its own WINSOCK.DLL in the \WINDOWS directory, the VLM/IP client is likely to access the wrong module because \WINDOWS probably precedes \NET\BIN in the PATH statement. In a case like this, the TCP/IP protocol stack functions properly, but Windows Sockets applications fail to initialize. Thus, if you can PING a Web site, but you can't connect to it with a browser, a Winsock incompatibility is likely to be the problem.

INSTALLING THE VLM/IP CLIENT

The INSTALL.EXE program, for the VLM/IP client, integrates the added TCP/IP and NetWare/IP functionality into the standard VLM-installation routine. Apart from the installation, however, the TCP/IP modules are distinctly separate from the VLMs. By default, the NetWare DOS Requester files are installed to a directory called \NWCLIENT, and configuration parameters are stored in a NET.CFG file. TCPIP.EXE and WINSOCK.EXE, and their ancillary files and utilities, are installed to a \NET\BIN directory. There is also a separate configuration file for DNS parameters, called RESOLV.CFG. You can disable the TCP/IP functions of the client simply by removing or remarking the commands that execute TCPIP.EXE and NWIP.EXE from STARTNET.BAT – the batch file that loads the client modules.

To display additional information about the servers contacted during the NetWare/IP initialization process, modify the STARTNET.BAT file to execute NWIP.EXE with the /V parameter.

The VLM/IP-client software is located on disk 1 of the IntranetWare package. You can use the NetWare INSTALL.NLM utility to copy clients to subdirectories below the SYS:\PUBLIC\CLIENT directory of your NetWare server. When you launch the INSTALL.EXE program for the VLM/IP client, you begin by supplying the basic information needed for any VLM-client installation, such as the target directory for the client software, the location of the Windows home directory, and the network adapter driver to load. You must then configure the TCP/IP stack by supplying values for the configuration parameters, shown in Figure 13-1.

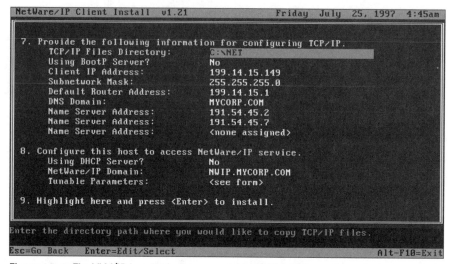

Figure 13-1: The VLM/IP installation program includes the basic configuration parameters for the TCP/IP client.

The functions of the parameters are as follows:

◆ **TCP/IP files directory** – The directory where the TCP/IP support files will be installed. The default directory is C:\NET.

◆ **Using BOOTP Server?** – This parameter is used to specify whether you want to use a DHCP or BOOTP server to obtain an IP address, and other TCP/IP-configuration parameters for the system. If "yes," the Client IP address and subnetwork mask fields are removed from the configuration form.

◆ **Client IP Address** – This is used to specify the IP address for the network adapter selected in the installation procedure.

◆ **Subnetwork mask** – This is used to specify the mask that should be applied to the specified IP address to determine which bits identify the network and which identify the host.

◆ **Default router address** – This is used to specify the IP address of a gateway system, on the local subnet, that provides access to systems located on other networks.

◆ **DNS domain** – This parameter is used to specify the name of the DNS domain where the system is located.

◆ **Name server addresses** – This is used to specify the IP addresses of up to three DNS servers that will resolve DNS names into IP addresses for TCP/IP applications.

All of the TCP/IP-configuration data from these fields is entered in the same NET.CFG file that contains the other VLM-client parameters. The only exceptions are the DNS domain and name-server addresses (which go in the RESOLV.CFG file). The data is placed in a section of the file with the heading *Protocol TCPIP*, that appears as follows:

```
Protocol TCPIP
PATH TCP_CFG   C:\NET\TCP
ip_address     199.14.15.149
ip_netmask     255.255.255.0
ip_router      199.14.15.1
```

You can edit the NET.CFG file, directly, to modify any of these parameters at a later time. If you plan to use NetWare/IP for the system's NetWare communications, you must also configure the following parameters during the installation process:

- ◆ **Using DHCP server?** — This parameter is used to specify whether or not you are using a DHCP server to assign NetWare/IP configuration values to the workstation. If "yes," the NetWare/IP domain field is disabled. The NetWare/IP options are not defined in the DHCP standards, but they have been added to Novell's DHCP server implementation. They are not provided in Microsoft's DHCP server.

- ◆ **NetWare/IP domain** — This is used to specify the fully qualified name of the domain that contains your NetWare/IP servers. This domain name must be different from your DNS domain name. Usually, the NetWare/IP systems are placed in a subdomain of the DNS name, such as NWIP.MYCORP.COM. An FQDN includes a trailing period, to represent the root of the DNS tree.

- ◆ **Tunable Parameters**

    - ◆ **DSS preferences** — This parameter is used to identify up to three Domain SAP/RIP Servers in the NetWare/IP domain, using either host names, IP addresses, or network addresses.

    - ◆ **Nearest server preferences** — This is used to identify up to three servers running the NetWare/IP server in the domain, using either host names, IP addresses, or network addresses.

The NetWare/IP parameters are stored in the NET.CFG file, in a section called *NWIP*, which is formatted as follows:

```
NWIP
NWIP_DOMAIN_NAME        NWIP.MYCORP.COM
NSQ_BROADCAST           ON
```

```
NWIP1_1 COMPATIBILITY        OFF
AUTORETRIES                  1
AUTORETRY SECS               10
PREFERRED DSS                199.14.15.76
NEAREST NWIP SERVER          199.14.15.34
```

Some NetWare/IP parameters are not configured in the installation program, and can only be configured by editing the NET.CFG file. These parameters are as follows:

- ◆ AUTORETRIES – This specifies the number of times the client attempts to contact the specified DSS during the system-startup process. The default is 1; possible values range from 0 to 50.

- ◆ AUTORETRY SECS – This parameter specifies the number of seconds between the automatic DSS contact retries. The default value is 10 seconds; possible values range from 5 to 100 seconds.

- ◆ NSQ_BROADCAST – This specifies whether or not the client should use Nearest Server Query broadcast transmissions to locate the nearest server on the network. The default value is ON. If there are no NetWare/IP servers on the same subnet as the client, set the value of this parameter to OFF to prevent delays incurred by repeated broadcasts.

- ◆ NWIP1_1 COMPATIBILITY – This specifies whether or not the client should be capable of communicating with servers running NetWare/IP 1.1. The default value is OFF.

Once the INSTALL.EXE program copies the client files to the appropriate locations and modifies the configuration files, you must reboot the system to load the client. In addition to the normal VLM modules, the TCPIP.EXE and NWIP.EXE programs display their basic configurations as they load, as follows:

```
Novell TCP/IP Transport v5.0 (960123)
(C) Copyright 1992-1995 Novell, Inc.  All Rights Reserved.

Network Name:  IP_NET              Bind: 3C5X9
IP Address: 199.14.15.149             Board Number: 2
Subnet Mask: 255.255.255.0            Board Instance: 1
Default Router: 199.14.15.1           Frame: ETHERNET_II

NetWare/IP IPX Far Call Interface Emulator v2.20b (960523)
(C) Copyright 1990-1995 Novell, Inc.  All Rights Reserved.

NWIP Domain Name: NWIP.MYCORP.COM
Configuration: Node Address: 199.14.15.147
```

VLM/IP MEMORY REQUIREMENTS

The VLM/IP client provides basic TCP/IP functionality and can easily be added to an existing VLM-client workstation. Adding the TCP/IP and NetWare/IP modules, however, exacerbates what is already a major problem. The standard NetWare DOS Requester installation requires 90KB of memory or more, and TCPIP.EXE and NWIP.EXE need an additional 28KB and 20KB, respectively.

Even with aggressive memory management, this is a large percentage of a DOS system's resources to devote to a network client. Memory handling is one of the reasons Novell has replaced the NetWare DOS Requester with Client 32 for DOS and Windows 3.1.

Using Client 32 for DOS/Windows 3.1

Novell's Client 32 for DOS and Windows 3.1 represents a significant improvement in NetWare client capabilities and resource management. Like the VLM/IP client, Client 32 provides DOS and Windows 3.1 systems with TCP/IP and NetWare/IP services, but it does so using a 32-bit protected mode architecture that provides increased performance while virtually eliminating the conventional memory problem of the VLM-based clients.

Client 32 is based on a single executable file, called NIOS.EXE (the NetWare I/O Subsystem), which functions as a platform on which other modules can be loaded. Launching NIOS.EXE creates a 32-bit environment that switches the system processor into protected mode. Here, the processor can access all of the system's extended memory (that is, the memory over 1MB) as a single range of addresses. The NetWare DOS Requester, by contrast, runs the processor in real mode and requires conventional memory.

The idea of running a 32-bit client on a 16-bit OS may seem contradictory. NIOS.EXE, however, provides the hooks that enable protected mode modules to perform real mode operations, and access real mode system interrupts, when necessary.

After NIOS.EXE has been launched, it's possible to load other 32-bit modules on the system. Modules, such as NLMs and LAN drivers, can be loaded using the LOAD command, very much like a NetWare server. In fact, NIOS.EXE resembles the NetWare SERVER.EXE file in many ways. The ultimate result is that Client 32 requires only 4KB of conventional memory, which can be loaded high using memory-management software. All other required memory is allocated from the protected-mode memory address pool.

Client 32 uses many of the same modules as the NetWare DOS Requester, except that they've been converted from executable COMs to NLMs and LANs. The TCP/IP stack and the NetWare/IP functionality are provided by the TCPIP.NLM and

NWIP.NLM modules, respectively. By default, Client 32 uses 32-bit ODI drivers for network adapters, that have a LAN extension like those used on servers. The Client 32 drivers are written in C, but the client can also use most of the assembly based LAN drivers written for NetWare 4.x servers, or the 16-bit ODI drivers from the real mode clients.

Like VLM/IP, Client 32 includes a WINSOCK.DLL module that provides general purpose TCP/IP support for Internet and intranet applications. The client also includes a PING program, and a ROUTE utility, that enables you to define static routes for IP traffic.

 For more information on using the PING and ROUTE programs, see Chapter 14, "TCP/IP Utilities."

INSTALLING CLIENT 32 FOR DOS/WINDOWS 3.1

Client 32 includes two installation programs, as it supports both DOS and Windows 3.1. INSTALL.EXE is used with DOS, while SETUP.EXE is used with Windows 3.1. Both programs are capable of installing both DOS- and Windows-client support. When you execute either program, you select the modules you want to install, as shown in Figures 13-2 and 13-3. The modular architecture of the client implements TCP/IP and NetWare/IP by loading the appropriate NLMs, using commands in the STARTNET.BAT file.

```
Install 2.01                              Friday  July  25, 1997  04:50am


       Select the products you want to install on your workstation
                                                        .

                  [X]  NetWare Client 32 for DOS
                  [X]  NetWare Client 32 for Windows
                  [X]  NetWare TCP/IP protocol stack
                       [X]  NetWare IP (TCP/IP Required)
                  [ ]  Desktop SNMP
                       [ ]  HOSTMIB for SNMP (SNMP Required)
                  [ ]  NetWare TSA for SMS



       Select products you want with the <SPACE BAR>. Press <ENTER> or <F10> when
       you are finished.


Install will copy the files necessary to run the NetWare client from DOS.
Esc=Go Back                                                    Alt-F10=Exit
```

Figure 13-2: Client 32's DOS-based INSTALL.EXE program enables you to specify the installation of client support for Windows 3.1 on the system.

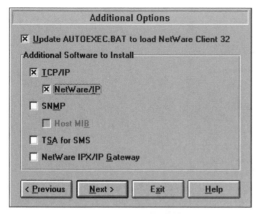

Figure 13-3: The Client 32 SETUP.EXE program installs client support for both DOS and Windows 3.1.

When you elect to install the TCP/IP stack, the installation program displays a TCP/IP Configuration dialog box like that shown in Figure 13-4. Here, you enter the basic TCP/IP client-configuration parameters, such as the system's IP address, subnetwork mask, and default router address. These are entered in the client's NET.CFG file, using the same format as the VLM/IP client.

TCP/IP Configuration	
Client IP Address:	199.45.15.199
Default Router Address:	199.45.15.1
Subnetwork Mask:	255.255.255.0
DNS Domain Name:	ZACKER.COM
Domain Name Server Address:	199.45.15.47

< Previous   Next >   Exit   Help

Figure 13-4: The TCP/IP Configuration screen provides an interface for the basic protocol settings of the NET.CFG file.

In the same manner, a NetWare/IP Configuration dialog box (see Figure 13-5) enables you to specify the NetWare/IP domain name, and IP addresses, of the DSS and NetWare/IP servers on your network. You can also add the same NET.CFG parameters for the NWIP section, which are defined in the "Installing the VLM/IP Client" section, earlier in this chapter.

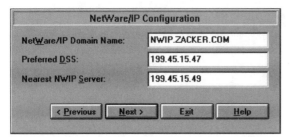

Figure 13-5: The NetWare/IP Configuration dialog box configures Client 32 to encapsulate its IPX traffic in UDP datagrams.

ADVANCED TCP/IP CONFIGURATION OPTIONS

When compared to VLM/IP, Client 32 provides greater control over the TCP/IP stack. It does this through the additional parameters you can manually add to the *Protocol TCPIP* section of the NET.CFG file. These parameters are as follows:

◆ ARP_AGING_TIMEOUT *seconds* – This specifies the amount of time a remote system's hardware address is retained in the client's ARP cache, after discovery. If your network systems are not often moved to different subnets and you do not use DHCP, you can safely increase this value to marginally reduce network traffic. The default value is 300 seconds; possible values range from 1 to 7,200 seconds.

◆ ARP_CACHE_MAX *number* – This parameter specifies the maximum number of entries that can be stored in the client's ARP cache. The default value is 64 entries; possible values range from 8 to 256. If a client is likely to access more than 64 different TCP/IP systems on the local network segment, within the interval defined by the ARP_AGING_TIMEOUT parameter, you can increase this value to reduce redundant ARP transactions.

◆ ARP_TIMEOUT *seconds* – This specifies the amount of time a client waits for a reply to a transmitted ARP request message. The default value is 5 seconds; possible values range from 1 to 120 seconds. Because ARP messages are transmitted only to systems on the local network segment, it's unlikely a value greater than the default would be needed on a properly functioning network.

◆ IP_CONFIGURATION *configtype* – This parameter specifies the method by which the client obtains its IP address and other TCP/IP-configuration settings. The default value is static; possible values are as follows:

- ◆ **static** – The static value indicates that the TCP/IP-configuration settings are provided through the use of additional entries in the NET.CFG file, such as IP_ADDRESS, IP_ROUTER, and IP_NETMASK.

- ◆ **dhcp** – The dhcp value indicates that the TCP/IP client-configuration settings are all obtained from a DHCP server.

- ◆ **bootp** – The bootp value indicates that the TCP/IP client-configuration settings are all obtained from a BOOTP server.

- ◆ **rarp** – The rarp value indicates that the client's IP address is obtained from a RARP server, while all other parameters are configured using additional entries in the NET.CFG file.

◆ **IP_ADDRESS** *address* – This parameter specifies the IP address for the network interface. Client 32 supports only one IP address per interface.

◆ **IP_BROADCAST** *address* – This parameter specifies the address for broadcast transmissions to the local network segment. The default value is 0.0.0.0. You can use this parameter to specify an alternate broadcast address (such as 255.255.255.255) if your network does not support the default.

◆ **IP_NETMASK** *mask* – This specifies the subnetwork mask value that should be applied to the interface's IP address.

◆ **IP_REASSEMBLY_TIMEOUT** *seconds* – This specifies the amount of time the client should wait for the arrival of all pieces of an IP packet (that has been fragmented at the network layer before discarding the datagram). The default value is 15 seconds; possible values are 1 to 120 seconds. Except in unusual situations, such as when you frequently connect to systems that are very distant or use low bandwidth connections, 15 seconds should be sufficient time for all of a datagram's fragments to arrive.

◆ **IP_RIP** *yes|no* – This parameter specifies whether the client should use the Routing Information Protocol to build its routing table. The default value is no. RIP is not needed for workstation routing, except on a complex network segment with multiple routers.

◆ **IP_ROUTER** *address* – This specifies the IP address of the router on the local network segment, to which the client should send the traffic destined for systems on other networks (when no explicit routing table entry exists for that network). You can add up to three IP_ROUTER entries for each network interface. The second and third entries are accessed in the order in which they appear, but only in the event that the first router specified is unreachable.

◆ IP_RTSW_TRIGGER *retries* – This enables TCP "dead gateway" detection by specifying the number of times the client should attempt to retransmit TCP packets to a specific router. When this number is exhausted, the client declares it unreachable and switches to another router. The default value is 3 retries; possible values range from 1 to the value of the TCP_RXMIT_LIMIT parameter, plus one.

◆ IP_TTL *hops* – This parameter specifies the default time-to-live (TTL) value for an IP transmission. The TTL is the number of routers the packet can pass through (also called hops) on the way to its destination. The default value is 128 hops; possible values range from 1 to 255. The value for this parameter should be at least double the number of hops an IP packet might actually make. The default value should be more than sufficient, as IP transmissions to even the most remote locations rarely require more than 30 hops.

◆ TCP_CONNECT_RETRY *retries* – This specifies the number of times the client should retransmit a TCP connection-request message before declaring the destination unreachable. The default value is 5 retries; possible values range from 1 to 256. You can raise this value to increase the chances of connecting to marginal systems, but this is no guarantee that communications with the destination will fail once the connection is established.

◆ TCP_KEEPALIVE *yes|no* – This specifies whether or not the client should transmit TCP "keep alive" packets to prevent a connection from timing out. The default value is yes. Keep alive packets are generated only when no other traffic is being transmitted over the TCP connection.

◆ TCP_KEEPALIVE_INTERVAL *seconds* – This specifies the time that should elapse between the transmission of keep alive messages, when no other traffic traverses the connection. The default value is 7,200 seconds; possible values range from 1 to 14,400. You can raise or lower this value to accommodate the properties of the systems, to which the client connects.

◆ TCP_RCV_WINDOWSZ *bytes* – This parameter specifies the size of the largest receive window the client can create during a TCP connection. The default value is 16,384 bytes; possible values range from 1 to 65,535.

◆ TCP_RELEASE_WAIT_TIME *seconds* – This specifies the maximum amount of time the client should wait after transmitting an acknowledgment to a termination request, before releasing the socket used by the connection. The default value is 120 seconds; possible values range from 1 to 600.

◆ TCP_RXMIT_LIMIT *retries* – This specifies the number of times the client should retransmit the same TCP packet before closing the connection to the destination system. The default value is 12 retries; possible values range from 1 to 24. Raising this value increases the fault tolerance of the client system, particularly on high-traffic networks.

◆ TCP_RXMIT_MAXTIME *milliseconds* – This parameter specifies the maximum amount of time that can elapse between TCP packet retransmissions. The default value is 120,000 milliseconds; possible values range from the value of the TCP_RXMIT_MINTIME parameter, plus one, to 240,000.

◆ TCP_RXMIT_MINTIME *milliseconds* – This specifies the minimum amount of time that can elapse between TCP-packet retransmissions. The default value is 110 milliseconds; possible values range from 2 to the value of the TCP_RXMIT_MAXTIME parameter, minus 1.

◆ UDP_CHECKSUM *yes|no* – This specifies whether checksums should be included in the headers of UDP packets generated by the client. The default value is yes. UDP checksums should always be enabled, for reasons explained in Chapter 6, "The Transport Layer."

Using NetWare/IP with Windows 95 and NT

The networking architectures of Windows 95 and Windows NT include a more clearly defined barrier between the protocol stack tops installed on the system, and the APIs above them, than that of Windows 3.1x. This barrier is called the *transport driver interface* (TDI). The combination of the TDI above, and the NDIS interface below, the stacks effectively isolates the functionality of the protocols. Furthermore, it provides any module written to those interfaces with access to their services.

Novell's Client 32 for Windows 95 and IntranetWare Client for Windows NT can both use any TCP/IP protocol stack written to the TDI interface. Because the OSs both include their own TCP/IP stacks, the inclusion of TCP/IP support in the client software would be pointless and redundant. These two clients, therefore, are designed to use the services of the Microsoft TCP/IP stack, but they can also operate with any TDI-compliant that may be installed on the system.

 The Client for Windows NT treats its IPX communications in the same way as TCP/IP. The client includes no IPX protocol stack of its own, but instead uses Microsoft's IPX-compatible protocol, NWLink. This is in contrast to Client 32 for Windows 95, which includes its own IPX 32-bit protocol for the client's exclusive use.

Despite the fact that it possesses many of the same capabilities, the IntranetWare Client for Windows NT was not given the name Client 32 like the Windows 95 software. Client 32, whatever OS it is designed for, is defined by the use of a NIOS platform, which enables the client to load networking modules, such as NLMs, into a specially constructed environment. In Client 32 for Windows 95, the NIOS module takes the form of a VxD (a virtual device driver), while its DOS/Windows 3.1 counterpart is an executable file, NIOS.EXE.

Client 32 functions as a "shell," something like the old NETX client, by intercepting calls for network resources before they reach the Windows 95 *Installable File System* (IFS) Manager. The Client for Windows NT, however, is not based on the NIOS platform. Rather, it takes the form of a redirector/file system driver, the primary module for which is called NWFS.SYS. The redirector functions as a part of the Windows NT I/O Manager. It assesses applications' file-system requests and passes them to the appropriate resource for fulfillment – whether that is a local storage device, or a network protocol stack.

While both clients can use the TCP/IP protocols provided by the OS, Microsoft obviously does not provide NetWare/IP support. NetWare/IP is implemented as a separate module that you install along with the TCP/IP stack.

NETWARE/IP AND WINDOWS 95

The Client 32 for Windows 95 software includes NetWare/IP support in the form of a protocol you install from the Network Control Panel. Once you install Client 32, the Novell NetWare/IP Protocol appears in the Select Network Protocol dialog box. The NetWare/IP module, called NWIP95.NLM, operates along with the Microsoft TCP/IP protocol stack. It replaces the functions of the IPX 32-bit Protocol for Novell NetWare Client 32, which is installed with the client by default (see Figure 13-6).

All NetWare/IP client implementations support communications through one network interface. You can connect to NetWare/IP servers on either a local network, or on a remote network accessed through a dial-up connection. Whichever interface you first use for NetWare/IP is the only one that will function.

The NWIP95.NLM module is responsible for encapsulating the workstation's IPX traffic. All NetWare/IP client implementations appear, to applications, as normal IPX services. Once the application data is packaged within an IPX header, it's passed to NetWare/IP, which operates between the network layer and the data-link layer. NWIP95 then sends the IPX data to the top of the TCP/IP protocol stack (see Figure 13-7), where it's packaged in a UDP/IP datagram. Only then is the packet sent to the adapter driver, either NDIS or ODI, for transmission over the network.

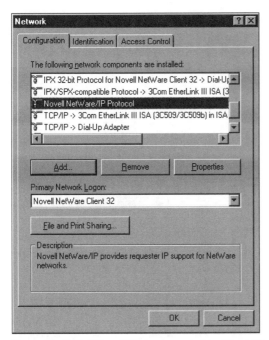

Figure 13-6: NetWare/IP is implemented in Client 32
for Windows 95 as an additional protocol module.

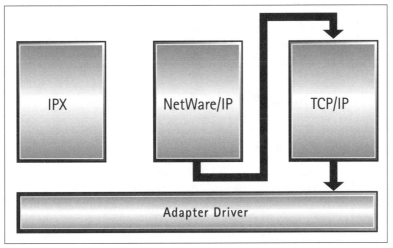

Figure 13-7: In Windows 95, NetWare/IP intercepts the output from the IPX
protocol stack and sends it to the TCP/IP client.

NETWARE/IP AND WINDOWS NT

The IntranetWare Client for Windows NT implements NetWare/IP as a service you add in the Network Control Panel. The module providing the NetWare/IP support, however, is not a service at all (or a protocol, as in Windows 95). NWIP.SYS is an NDIS device driver that intercepts the NetWare NWLink traffic and redirects it to the top of the TCP/IP protocol stack for encapsulation, as shown in Figure 13-8.

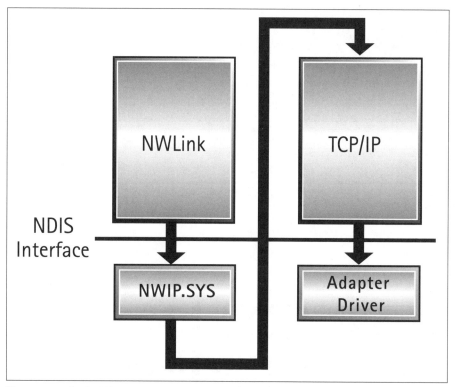

Figure 13-8: In the Windows NT client, NetWare/IP is implemented as an NDIS driver that passes data between the bottom of the NWLink protocol stack and the top of the TCP/IP stack.

This arrangement is necessary because the IntranetWare client uses the Microsoft IPX-protocol implementation, instead of its own stack. Windows NT protocol stacks are bounded by the transport device interface (TDI) at the top, and the NDIS interface at the bottom. It is more practical to capture the NWLink traffic through a documented interface, such as NDIS, than to try to reverse engineer the protocol stack, itself.

NetWare/IP is not supported on the Windows NT Server product — only on Windows NT Workstation. Also, if your Windows NT 4.0 system has multiple processors, you should install the Microsoft Windows NT Service Pack 2 (or greater). This corrects problems in the original OS release that denigrate NetWare/IP performance.

CONFIGURING NETWARE/IP

Once you install the appropriate component in the Network Control Panel, the process of configuring the NetWare/IP client is virtually the same for Windows 95 and Windows NT. When you highlight the NetWare/IP protocol, or service, and click the Properties button, you see the dialog boxes shown in Figures 13-9 and 13-10.

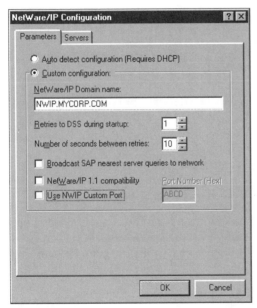

Figure 13-9: The IntranetWare Client for Windows NT provides NetWare/IP support in the form of a network service.

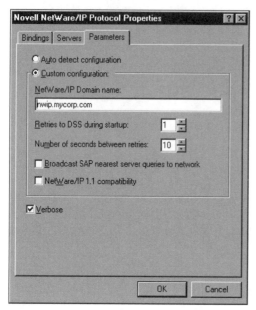

Figure 13-10: NetWare/IP takes the form of a protocol driver in Client 32 for Windows 95.

The settings in the Parameters page of the NetWare/IP Configuration dialog box (in Windows NT) and the Novell NetWare/IP Protocol Properties dialog box (in Windows 95) are as follows:

◆ **Auto detect configuration** – This indicates that the client will obtain its NetWare/IP parameter settings from a DHCP server on the network. Only the Novell DHCP server provides preconfigured NetWare/IP options.

◆ **NetWare/IP Domain name** – This setting specifies the name of the domain that contains the network's NetWare/IP clients and servers. The NetWare/IP domain name cannot be the same as the DNS domain name.

◆ **Retries to DSS during startup** – This specifies the number of times the client should repeat its attempts to contact a DSS server, during the NetWare/IP initialization process. The default value is 1 retry; possible values range from 0 to 10.

◆ **Number of seconds between retries** – This setting specifies the time interval between DSS retries, in seconds. The default value is 1 second; possible values range from 5 to 60.

◆ **Broadcast SAP nearest server queries to network** – This specifies whether or not the client should use Service Advertising Protocol (SAP) messages to locate the nearest NetWare/IP server on the network. When disabled, the client discovers the nearest server by transmitting unicast queries to a DSS.

◆ **NetWare/IP 1.1 compatibility** – This setting provides the client with the capability to communicate with servers and DSSs running NetWare/IP 1.1. This feature is intended for use as an interim measure until all of the systems can be upgraded to NetWare/IP 2.2.

◆ **Verbose** (Windows 95 only) – This enables more detailed logging of NetWare/IP activities to the \Novell\Client32\Nwip.log file on the client workstation.

◆ **Use NWIP Custom Port** (Windows NT only) – This setting specifies a NetWare/IP port other than the default, which has a hexadecimal value of ABCD.

In the Servers screen of the dialog boxes, you can identify up to five NetWare/IP servers and five DSSs, using DNS names, IP host addresses, or IP network addresses. Identifying servers in this way isn't required, but can eliminate the delays and network traffic incurred by the client's server-discovery process.

Using the IPX/IP Gateway

The IntranetWare product is designed to promote more widespread use of the TCP/IP protocols on NetWare networks. The product includes TCP/IP-based services, such as the Novell Web and FTP servers, which network administrators can use to publish information to network clients, and build applications that enhance their computing environment. The bulk of this chapter concerns the packaging of IPX traffic for transmission on a TCP/IP-only network, but on many NetWare networks, the problem is the exact opposite.

The process of rolling out TCP/IP client support on a NetWare IPX network can be long and complex, requiring a great deal of planning and administrative effort. IntranetWare, however, includes a product, called the *Novell Internet Access Server* (NIAS), that facilitates the connection of a NetWare network to the Internet. NIAS provides routing services between a local network and an ISP using various types of WAN connections, such as dial-ups, ISDN, and frame relay.

NIAS can also enable a NetWare server to function as a gateway between an IPX and a TCP/IP network. In TCP/IP parlance, the term *gateway* is often used as a synonym for *router*, but the general network vocabulary defines a gateway as a link between two networks that translates one protocol to another. Novell's IPX/IP gateway enables IPX clients to access TCP/IP services by packaging TCP data in IPX packets.

A client system on the IPX network can run a TCP/IP application, such as a Web browser or an FTP client, and request a connection to an Internet or intranet service. The request is passed to the gateway server, which opens the TCP connection to the desired destination, retrieves the requested data, and returns it to the client in IPX packets (see Figure 13-11).

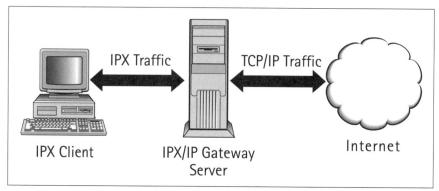

Figure 13-11: Novell's IPX/IP Gateway Server functions as a proxy for IPX clients by retrieving data from TCP services and relaying it back to the workstation.

IPX/IP Gateway Architecture

The IPX/IP Gateway consists of both client and server elements. A gateway client consists of an additional protocol that you install on a Client 32 for Windows 95, or DOS/Windows 3.1, system. The protocol includes a Winsock.dll module for the system, but there is no TCP/IP stack or IP address needed. This specialized Winsock enables the client system to run standard TCP/IP applications, but sends the client requests to the gateway server instead of the destination specified by the user.

The IPX/IP Gateway protocol does not provide client systems with full TCP/IP capabilities. The Winsock module is designed to access TCP-based services, such as Web servers, but it does not support UDP communications of any kind.

Normally, a TCP/IP client processes an application request by making a call to the Winsock.dll module. This resolves the DNS name of the destination into an IP address (if necessary) before opening a TCP connection. Because the IPX/IP Gateway Winsock module does not support the UDP communications used for DNS transactions, it sends the basic application data to the gateway server. This server uses its DNS-client capabilities to resolve the name and generate the request message.

The gateway is installed as part of the NIAS product, which includes the NetWare Multiprotocol Router, the WAN extensions for the router, and the Netscape Navigator Web browser. Installing NIAS adds functionality to the INETCFG.NLM utility, enabling you to configure the server to route traffic between your local network and another router connected by a wide-area link. NIAS facilitates the connection of NetWare networks to an ISP, but you can also use it to build a WAN by linking LANs at remote locations.

To function as a gateway, the server must be connected to at least one TCP/IP network, and configured with its own IP address and other configuration settings, like any other TCP/IP system. When the server receives TCP requests from clients, it behaves like a client and connects to the requested resource in the normal manner. When the server receives a response from the destination system, it repackages the TCP data into IPX packets. It then returns them to the IPX client, which demultiplexes them and passes the TCP data to the application.

As far as the client application is concerned, the system has issued a request and received a response. The application is completely unaware of the TCP/IP stack's absence, as well as the use of IPX. To the system providing the TCP/IP service, it has received a request from the gateway server, and has returned a response. What the gateway does with the data is its own business.

IPX/IP Gateway Security

Because an IPX/IP Gateway client has no IP address or TCP/IP protocol stack, it is naturally immune to outside intrusion. By acting as a proxy server, the gateway also functions as a firewall between the client system and the Internet. Potential intruders can't get beyond the gateway server because they have no way of identifying, or contacting, IPX systems from the Internet.

The gateway server also functions as an administration point for internal network users. When you enable the gateway, INETCFG extends the *Novell Directory Services* (NDS) schema by adding two new screens to the Details dialog box of every User, Organization, Organizational Unit, and Group object in the NDS tree. From the IPX/IP Gateway Service Restrictions screen, the network administrator can restrict or deny users' access to the IPX/IP gateway. Restrictions are placed according to the time of day, the application protocol or port number used by the service, or a combination of these criteria, as shown in Figure 13-12. You can, for example, limit your users' Internet access to nonbusiness hours, grant Internet access to selected users or groups of users only, or specify the services users can access.

In this manner, you can use the IPX/IP Gateway Host Restrictions screen to specify the IP addresses of TCP/IP systems. You can permit a user access to the services hosted by that system during certain hours of the day, only, or deny them access, completely.

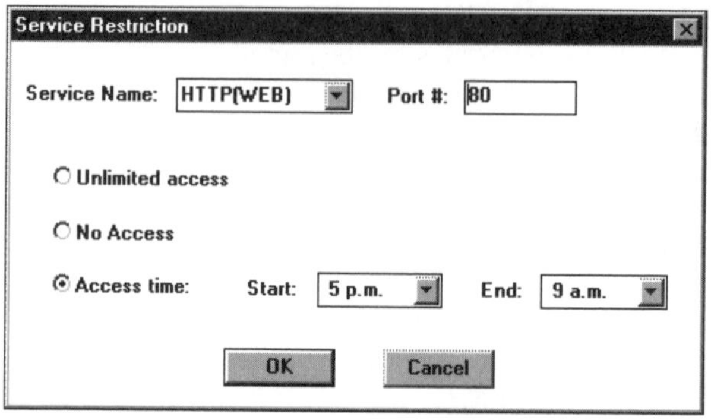

Figure 13-12: You can configure the IPX/IP Gateway to permit clients access to specific TCP/IP services at specific times, only.

Because the host and service restrictions are stored in the NDS database, they are keyed to the account that is used to log the workstation in to the network – not the computer, itself. You can apply these access-control measures to specific user objects, or to the container objects where users are located, so the restrictions are inherited by the users.

Installing the IPX/IP Gateway Server

Once you install the NetWare Internet Access Server, you must configure the NetWare server to function as a router between your IPX LAN and a TCP/IP network, using either a local or wide-area connection. The server must support standard logins from IPX clients on the LAN, and PING hosts on the TCP/IP network. Once support for both protocols is provided, you enable the IPX/IP Gateway (from the TCP/IP Protocol Configuration screen in the NetWare server's INETCFG utility) by selecting IPX/IP Gateway Configuration, as shown in Figure 13-13.

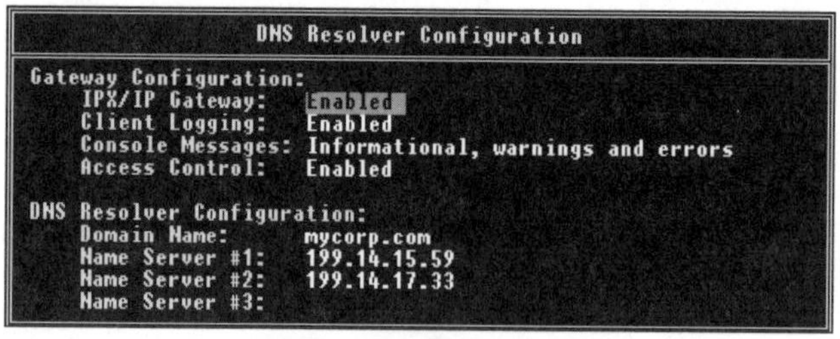

Figure 13-13: On INETCFG's DNS Resolver Configuration screen, you can enable various features of the IPX/IP gateway and specify the DNS servers to use when processing client requests.

The following are gateway parameters that appear on the configuration screen:

◆ **IPX/IP Gateway** – This feature enables or disables the gateway functionality for this server. Enabling the gateway loads the IPXGW.NLM module and modifies the schema of the NDS database.

◆ **Client Logging** – When enabled, this feature logs all client accesses to TCP services, through the gateway, in a file called GW_AUDIT.LOG. This file is stored in the root directory of the server's SYS volume. The log file identifies the client, the service requested, and the time interval of the service connection.

◆ **Console Messages** – This feature specifies the types of messages (generated by the gateway software) that should be displayed on the server console. These messages are also logged to the GW_INFO.LOG file, which is stored in the root directory of the server's SYS volume. The possible values are as follows:

   ◆ **Errors only**

   ◆ **Warnings and errors**

   ◆ **Informational, warnings, and errors**

◆ **Access Control** – When enabled, this feature grants you control of clients' access to TCP services through the gateway. It modifies the properties of NDS user, and container, objects. Disabling this feature provides all clients with unrestricted use of the gateway.

◆ **Domain Name** – This feature specifies the name of the DNS domain, in which the server resides.

◆ **Name Server** – This specifies the IP addresses of up to three DNS name servers the gateway will use to resolve the DNS names supplied in client requests.

The INETCFG utility does not modify the server's networking parameters in real time. Instead, the program makes changes to the configuration files that control the server's startup commands. Once you configure the settings for the IPX/IP Gateway, you must restart the server, or select Reinitialize System from INETCFG's main menu, to reload the server's networking modules with the new settings.

The first time you enable the gateway, you must provide the NDS user name and password for an account with supervisor object rights to the [Root] of the NDS tree. This is done so the program can extend the NDS schema to create a gateway-server object, and add access-control screens to existing NDS objects. The gateway-server object is given the same name as the server with -GW appended to it.

Installing the IPX/IP Gateway Client

For a client workstation to use the IPX/IP Gateway, it must be running Novell Client 32 for DOS, Windows 3.1, or Windows 95. The Novell NetWare IPX/IP Gateway protocol is included with the Client 32 software versions. These are part of the NIAS product (on disk 3 of the IntranetWare package), and in all subsequent releases of the clients. The protocol is not included with the Client 32 versions on the NetWare 4.11 disk of the IntranetWare product (disk 1). When you install the NIAS, the client software supporting the gateway is copied to the DOSWIN32 and WIN95 directories found in the SYS:\PUBLIC\CLIENT directory of the server — overwriting any other versions of the clients that are stored there.

INSTALLING THE DOS/WINDOWS 3.1 GATEWAY CLIENT

To install IPX/IP Gateway client support to a Windows 3.1 workstation, you must run the Client 32 SETUP.EXE program from Windows, and select the NetWare IPX/IP Gateway feature in the Additional Options dialog box. You cannot install gateway support from the DOS INSTALL.EXE program. The installation process copies the Novell Winsock.dll module to the workstation, and installs the Gateway Switcher program along with WINPING.EXE (a PING implementation designed to work with the gateway).

The Gateway Switcher enables you to activate and deactivate the client's gateway support at will (see Figure 13-14). When activating the gateway support, you must specify the NDS object name of a preferred gateway server (that is, a NetWare server running the IPXGW.NLM module) using any of the standard NDS object-notation methods. The capability to disable the gateway support, in Client 32, enables you to use a different Winsock module (such as one included in an online service's dial-up software).

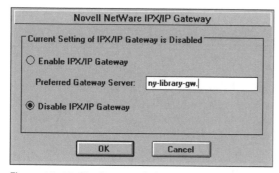

Figure 13-14: The Gateway Switcher application enables you to activate and deactivate the IPX/IP Gateway support in Client 32.

INSTALLING THE WINDOWS 95 GATEWAY CLIENT

In Client 32 for Windows 95, support for the IPX/IP gateway takes the form of a network protocol driver, which you install from the Network Control Panel in the usual manner. As in the Windows 3.1 version of the client, you can specify the name of a preferred gateway server, but in Windows 95, you do so by highlighting the object in the network components list, and clicking the Properties button.

The Windows 95 gateway client includes both 16- and 32-bit Windows Sockets libraries (WINSOCK.DLL and WSOCK32.DLL) to support a full range of applications that can run on the OS. The Gateway Switcher utility in Windows 95 enables you to install the Microsoft TCP/IP client on the system, in addition to Client 32, and switch between the Winsock modules provided by each one. This way, you can connect to Windows network shares using TCP/IP with the Client for Microsoft Networks, or use Dial-Up Networking to connect to a remote system. You may then switch, at will, to the IPX/IP gateway for access to TCP services through the NetWare Multiprotocol Router.

Summary

Novell is migrating its networking products to the TCP/IP protocols, gradually. IntranetWare includes a number of transitional technologies, which enable administrators to add greater TCP/IP functionality to their networks while phasing out the proprietary IPX protocols. The client software included in the IntranetWare product provides TCP/IP solutions for DOS, in addition to all of the Windows computing platforms.

In this chapter, you learned:

◆ How to add TCP/IP functionality to the NetWare DOS Requester with the VLM/IP client

◆ How to use the TCP/IP stack included in Novell's Client 32 for DOS/Windows 3.1

◆ How to implement a NetWare/IP client on any Windows platform

◆ How to use the Novell IPX/IP Gateway to provide IPX clients with access to TCP/IP services

Part V

Tools

Chapter 14

TCP/IP Utilities

IN THIS CHAPTER

Nearly all TCP/IP implementations include some basic utilities that you can use to test the operation of the software, configure its operational parameters, or track the usage of the protocols. Some of the most common utilities are traditionally associated with TCP/IP and included with virtually all implementations of the protocols, while others are designed for use with specific OSs.

There are also a great many TCP/IP network management utilities available as shareware or freeware, or as commercial products. RFC1147, published in 1990, is an informational document published by the Internet Engineering Task Force (IETF) that categorizes the types of utilities available and describes some of the most frequently used titles available for the TCP/IP implementations of the time.

This chapter examines the functions and usage of the TCP/IP utilities in today's OSs, as follows:

◆ PING and TRACEROUTE are the most basic of TCP/IP utilities that have been adapted for use on almost every computing platform.

◆ The Microsoft TCP/IP client includes a standard set of configuration utilities that have been ported to all of the Windows OSs.

◆ Installing TCP/IP support on a NetWare server provides a little-known console utility called TCPCON.NLM that you can use to configure TCP/IP and monitor its performance.

TCP/IP Utility Types

RFC1147 is not an Internet standard. It is an informational document that was designed to inform administrators of tools and utilities that can help them manage their TCP/IP networks. When it was written, Internet access was limited to FTP and Telnet, for the most part. Both of these are useful applications, but not particularly conducive to browsing downloadable files. The document, listing freely available utilities, was intended to prevent other users from having to "reinvent the wheel" by creating their own.

In 1990, TCP/IP was used primarily on UNIX systems. While some of the utilities listed in the RFC have since been ported to the DOS, Windows, and NetWare OSs, many have not. Keywords used in the document to define the functional roles of the TCP/IP utilities are equally applicable to today's applications. These keywords include the following:

- **Alarm** – a tool that triggers a notification event (such as an e-mail or a pager call) as the result of a specified network condition

- **Analyzer** – a program that captures network packets and interprets their contents to examine traffic patterns

- **Benchmark** – a tool that quantifies the performance of a particular network component or process

- **Control** – a program capable of modifying the state or condition of a given network resource

- **Debugger** – a tool that generates and monitors traffic to bring a network, or a component, to a particular state for hardware or software testing

- **Generator** – a program that constructs and transmits packets of a specified configuration to test network components or processes

- **Manager** – a distributed application used to gather operational data from various network components and collate it for output at a central console

- **Map** – a tool that is used to locate specific components, or systems, on a network and report on their configuration, or topology

- **Reference** – a tool used to record system-configuration data for storage at a central location

- **Routing** – a tool used to discover packet-routing information, or configure a system's routing behavior

- **Security** – a program used to analyze systems or networks for security threats, and attempt to prevent them

- **Status** – a tool used to determine the operational condition of network components

- **Traffic** – a program that monitors the transmission of network packets, and compiles traffic statistics

The TCP/IP utilities examined in the following sections are those that ship with the Windows and IntranetWare OSs. There are, however, many other utilities available from third-party vendors (a selection of which can be found on the CD-ROM included with this book).

For more information about the software included on the CD-ROM, see the appendix, "About the CD-ROM."

PING

PING is a generator utility – the most used, and useful, utility associated with the TCP/IP protocols. Virtually every implementation of the protocol stack includes a version of the PING program (whether in a character-based, graphical, or server-console format). There are also many third-party PING implementations that provide additional features or a friendly interface.

By transmitting a request message to a specified system and receiving a reply, PING is a basic test of a system's TCP/IP functionality. If you can PING another system successfully, you know that: the network hardware is functioning on both computers, the link between the two systems is unbroken, and the protocol stack is operational up to the TCP/IP internet layer.

PING usually takes the form of an executable program on the TCP/IP-client system (that is, the system generating the PING request). The server end of the program – the system that replies to the client's request – is almost always internal to the protocol stack. It requires no explicit implementation on the part of the user, or the administrator. The PING client program functions by generating *Internet Control Message Protocol* (ICMP) packets containing a message-type value of 8 (which is defined as an *echo-request message*). On receiving an echo request, a TCP/IP system is required to return an echo-reply message to the sender.

For more information on the Internet Control Message Protocol (ICMP) and its message types, see Chapter 5, "The Internet Layer."

ICMP Echo Messages

ICMP messages are carried within the data field of IP datagrams – without the use of a transport-layer protocol, such as UDP or TCP. The format of the ICMP echo-request and echo-reply messages is shown in Figure 14-1.

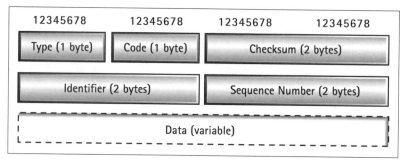

Figure 14-1: ICMP echo-request and echo-reply messages differ only in the value of the message-type field.

The functions of the fields in the echo-request and echo-reply messages are as follows:

- **Type** (1 byte) – The type field identifies the function of the message. The message-type values used by the PING utility are as follows:

  - **8** – echo request

  - **0** – echo reply

- **Code** (1 byte) – The code field is a subclassifier of message types in other ICMP transactions, but echo-request and echo-reply messages always have a code value of 0.

- **Checksum** (2 bytes) – The checksum field contains a value used for error-checking purposes, which is computed on the entire ICMP message.

- **Identifier** (2 bytes) – The identifier field contains a value that can differentiate the messages generated by multiple instances of the PING program on the same system. Windows systems, however, always use a default value of 256 for this field; NetWare servers use a value of 114.

- **Sequence number** (2 bytes) – The sequence number associates specific request messages transmitted to a system, with specific replies received in return. A PING client typically generates a series of echo requests and expects an echo reply in return for each one. Because the IP protocol used to carry ICMP messages does not guarantee delivery, packets may arrive at the destination damaged, or out of order – or not arrive at all. The sequence number ensures that replies are associated with the proper queries. Both Windows and NetWare select a sequence number for the first query transmitted, and increment it by 256 for each subsequent query.

◆ **Data** (variable) — Echo packets contain a data field, composed of random characters, whose default size varies depending on the implementation. The Windows PING program defaults to 32 bytes of data, the NetWare PING.NLM to 40 bytes.

The ICMP protocol operates at the internet layer of the TCP/IP protocol stack — despite the fact that its messages are carried within IP packets, generated at the same layer. When a TCP/IP system receives an echo-request packet, sent by the PING program on another machine, very little processing is involved. The request is passed up only as high as the internet layer of the server system, which changes the type field from a value of 8 (request) to a value of 0 (reply). It reverses the values of the source and destination IP addresses in the IP header, and retransmits the packet back to the sender with the rest of the fields, intact.

PING.EXE

The Microsoft TCP/IP client, for all of the Windows OSs, includes a PING.EXE program that runs from the DOS command prompt. Executing the program with a DNS name (or IP address) on the command line causes four ICMP echo requests to be transmitted to the destination, after the DNS name is resolved. As the echo replies are received back at the sending system, the following information is displayed:

```
Pinging nt4server.mycorp.com [197.10.55.2] with 32 bytes of data:
Reply from 197.10.55.2: bytes=32 time=169ms TTL=249
Reply from 197.10.55.2: bytes=32 time=152ms TTL=249
Reply from 197.10.55.2: bytes=32 time=152ms TTL=249
Reply from 197.10.55.2: bytes=32 time=157ms TTL=249
```

The information included on each result line is as follows:

◆ **bytes** — specifies the number of data bytes included in the request packet and returned in the reply

◆ **time** — specifies the elapsed time between the transmission of the request and the receipt of the reply

◆ **TTL** — specifies the value of the time-to-live field in the IP header of the echo-reply packet

You can modify the properties of the echo-request packets, and control the behavior of the PING program, using any combination of the following command-line parameters:

```
PING [-t] [-a] [-n packets] [-l data] [-f] [-i TTL] [-v TOS]
 [-r hops] [-s hops] [-j hosts] [-k hosts] [-w timeout] destination
```

The function of each parameter is as follows:

◆ –t – causes the PING program to transmit a continuous stream of echo-request packets until interrupted by the user

◆ –a – causes the PING program to resolve an IP address specified in the *destination* parameter into a DNS name, using a reverse look up

◆ –n *packets* – causes the PING program to transmit the number of echo-request messages specified by the *packets* variable; the default value is 4

◆ –l *data* – causes the PING program to include the number of bytes specified by the *data* variable in the data field of each echo-request message; the default value is 32 bytes; the maximum is 8,192

◆ –f – causes the PING program to activate the Don't-Fragment flag in the IP header of each echo-request message

◆ –i *TTL* – causes the PING program to insert the value of the *TTL* variable into the time-to-live field of each echo-request packet's IP header

◆ –v *TOS* – causes the PING program to insert the value of the *TOS* variable into the type-of-service field of each echo-request packet's IP header

◆ –r *hops* – causes the PING program to insert the IP addresses of the intermediate systems the ICMP messages pass through into the Record-route option field of the IP header; the *hops* variable specifies the number of addresses to be recorded and possible values range from 1 to 9

◆ –s *hops* – causes the PING program to insert a timestamp into the timestamp option field of the ICMP packet's IP header (at each intermediate system on the way to the destination); the *hops* variable specifies the number of timestamps to be recorded and possible values range from 1 to 4

◆ –j *hosts* – causes the PING program to route ICMP messages through the intermediate systems specified in the *hosts* variable using loose-source routing (meaning other systems can be accessed in addition to those specified); the maximum number of IP addresses permitted in the *hosts* variable is 9

◆ –k *hosts* – causes the PING program to route ICMP messages through the intermediate systems specified in the *hosts* variable using strict-source routing (meaning no systems can be accessed other than those specified); the maximum number of IP addresses permitted in the *hosts* variable is 9

◆ –w *timeout* – specifies the time interval (in milliseconds) that the PING program should wait to receive a reply from the destination; the default value is 1,000 milliseconds

♦ *destination* – specifies the DNS name, or the IP address, of the system that is to receive the echo-request messages

 In all command-line parameters for the PING.EXE program that use variables, a space should be inserted between the switch and the value for the variable. For example, *–w 10000* would be an acceptable parameter, while *–w10000* would not be acceptable.

PING AND IP OPTIONS

Several of the PING parameters rely on the options made available by the IP protocol – not ICMP. The *–r* parameter, for example, uses IP's record-route option to store addresses of the intermediate systems that the echo-request message encounters on the journey to the destination. When the destination system returns the echo reply, the addresses from the request message are included, and the recording process is duplicated on the return trip. Arriving back at the PING-client system, the recorded addresses are displayed as follows:

```
Reply from 199.10.45.8: bytes=32 time=169ms TTL=248
    Route: 206.119.15.38 ->
           207.60.45.122 ->
           207.60.44.253 ->
           207.60.45.102 ->
           199.10.45.113 ->
           199.10.45.8 ->
           199.1.45.1 ->
           207.60.45.101 ->
           207.60.44.1
```

Notice that the sixth address in the record route field reflects the IP address of the destination system. This means that the five previous addresses identify the routers that the ICMP message passed through on the way to the destination system. The addresses listed after the destination identify the routers that the reply message used on the way back to the client system. Not only does the reply message take a different route from the request, but the listing is cut off because the record-route option can only hold a maximum of nine addresses.

This limitation is not an arbitrary one imposed by the developers of the PING program. Because the internet header-length field of an IP header is only 4 bits long, the maximum length for the IP header is 60 bytes. Twenty bytes are allocated to the standard header fields, leaving 40 bytes for IP options. The record-route option uses 3 bytes for control fields, leaving 37 bytes to store up to nine 4-byte IP addresses (with one byte left over), as shown in Figure 14-2.

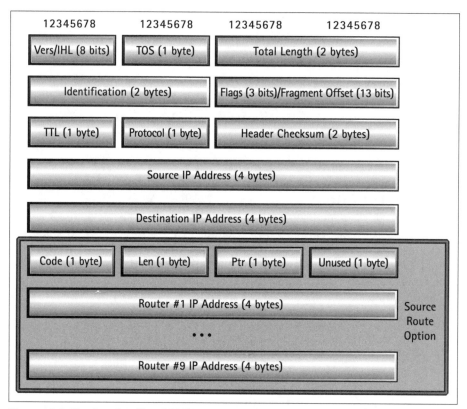

Figure 14-2: The functionality of PING's −r parameter is limited by the size of the options fields in the IP header.

While the −r switch may be useful on a private TCP/IP internetwork, a PING command (specifying an address on the Internet) is likely to exceed nine hops just getting to the destination – without even considering the return trip. This is one reason the traceroute program is more often used to discover the route taken to a specific destination.

PING's −s parameter operates in much the same way as −r, except that it records timestamps from each intermediate system (instead of IP addresses). The IP header's timestamp option functions much like the record-route option. The exception is that the Microsoft PING program causes each hop to record both the router's IP address, and the 4-byte timestamp identifying when the message was processed. This adds up to a total of only four hops, that can be recorded in the option fields of a single message – yielding a display like the following:

```
Reply from 207.50.25.122: bytes=32 time=152ms TTL=253
    Timestamp: 206.119.15.38 : 350778114 ->
               207.50.25.122 : 1140931457 ->
```

```
207.50.33.50 : 1140931457 ->
209.61.45.144: 2968023810
```

The *-j* and *-k* parameters enable you to specify the route that ICMP echo-request messages should take to their destination. These parameters use the IP header's loose-source routing and strict-source routing options to specify the IP addresses of the intermediate systems through which the ICMP messages must pass. These options are also limited to a maximum of nine addresses.

PING ERROR MESSAGES

The error messages PING displays when it cannot complete a transaction are often more significant to the network-troubleshooting process than a successful result. Knowing that communications have failed is not enough; often, PING can tell you why. Some of the most common negative results to PING commands are as follows:

◆ **Bad IP address** – This message is something of a misnomer; PING displays it when the program can't resolve the DNS name specified as the destination into an IP address. This problem can occur when the DNS name is misspelled, when the system's configured DNS servers are not available, or when the name actually doesn't exist in the DNS name space. Because the PING command failed during the name-resolution process, no echo-request messages were transmitted. This result, therefore, provides no indication of the destination system's operational status.

◆ **Request timed out** – This is one of the more ambiguous error messages. It can occur because the echo-request message never reached the destination, or a slow link has prevented the echo-reply message (transmitted by the destination) from arriving before the client's timeout interval has elapsed. This message is displayed when you attempt to PING an address that doesn't exist on the network. It is a good idea to retry the PING command with the *-w* parameter and an extended timeout interval, in case the destination system is very distant, or merely slow in replying.

◆ **Destination unreachable** – The destination-unreachable error results from an ICMP error message returned to the client, by an intermediate system. It is unlike the previous errors, caused by PING's failure to receive a response, and signifies that the destination can't be reached due to a routing problem.

◆ **Packet needs to be fragmented but DF set** – This message is usually generated during the path MTU-discovery process. It indicates that the echo request contains too much data for transmittal (in one packet) over a particular network, and the IP header's Don't Fragment flag has been activated.

PING.NLM

NetWare includes a PING implementation, in the form of an NLM, that runs on the server console. It uses the character-based, C-worthy interface, as shown in Figure 14-3. PING.NLM provides only the most basic functionality in terms of the echo-request packet configuration. In addition to the destination DNS name or IP address, you can specify only the time interval between echo-request transmissions and the size of the packets that are sent.

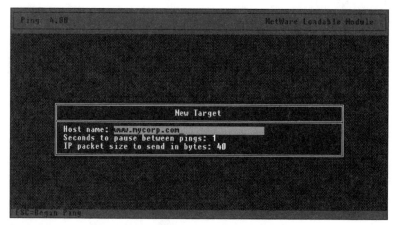

Figure 14-3: NetWare's PING.NLM provides the capability to transmit simple echo requests from the server console.

Once activated, PING.NLM continuously transmits echo requests by default. The process continues until manually interrupted by the user. The results screen displays the following information, in a constantly updated table:

- ◆ Node – specifies the IP address of the destination system

- ◆ Sent – specifies the number of ICMP echo-request packets transmitted to the destination

- ◆ Received – specifies the number of ICMP echo-reply packets received from the destination

- ◆ High – specifies the longest round-trip time of the reply packets received

- ◆ Low – specifies the shortest round-trip time of the reply packets received

- ◆ Last – specifies the round-trip time of the most recently received reply

- ◆ Average – specifies the average round-trip time of the reply packets received

♦ **Trend** – specifies the current trend in round-trip times, or alternatively an informational message, as follows:

  ♦ **No data** – indicates that not enough data is being received to compute results

  ♦ **Down** – indicates that no replies have been received from the destination

  ♦ **Failing** – indicates that two-thirds of the transmitted requests have not received replies

  ♦ **Drop** – indicates that one-third of the transmitted requests have not received replies

One unusual feature of the PING.NLM program enables you to specify additional destinations by pressing the Insert key while the results screen is displayed. This causes the program to transmit echo requests to all specified systems simultaneously, and display the results for all on a single screen, as shown in Figure 14-4.

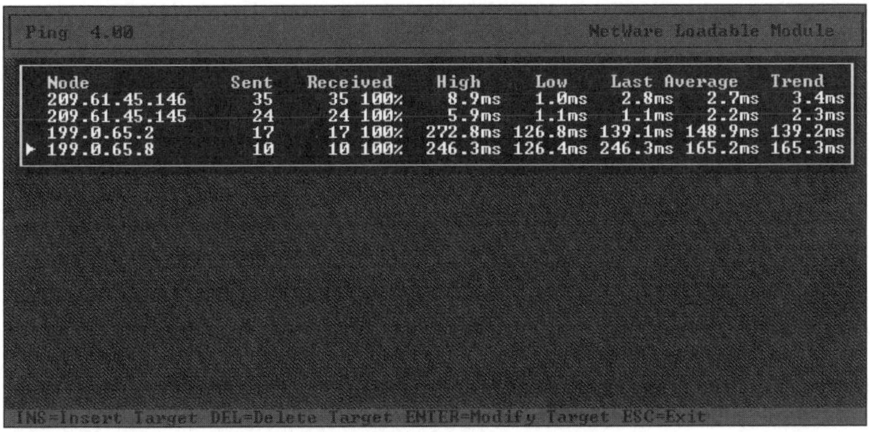

```
Ping  4.00                                          NetWare Loadable Module

   Node             Sent    Received      High       Low   Last Average     Trend
   209.61.45.146      35    35 100%      8.9ms     1.0ms    2.8ms    2.7ms    3.4ms
   209.61.45.145      24    24 100%      5.9ms     1.1ms    1.1ms    2.2ms    2.3ms
   199.0.65.2         17    17 100%    272.8ms   126.8ms  139.1ms  148.9ms  139.2ms
 ▶ 199.0.65.8         10    10 100%    246.3ms   126.4ms  246.3ms  165.2ms  165.3ms




INS=Insert Target DEL=Delete Target ENTER=Modify Target ESC=Exit
```

Figure 14-4: PING.NLM can transmit ICMP echo-request messages to multiple destinations, continuously and simultaneously.

TPING.NLM

NetWare also includes a command-line program for use on the server console, called TPING.NLM. You run TPING on the server using the LOAD command, specifying the destination name or address and (optionally) a packet-size parameter and the number of times the program should attempt to transmit to the destination. By default, TPING sends 64-byte packets and retries up to five times. When a reply is received successfully, TPING specifies only that the destination system is alive, as shown in the following output:

```
Loading module TPING.NLM
  Trivial TCP/IP Ping (IP0200.B02)
  Version 4.00    February 6, 1997
  Copyright (C) 1992-1996 Novell, Inc.  All Rights Reserved
TPING-1.02-8: 199.0.65.2 is alive.
```

WINPING

WINPING.EXE is a variant on the PING program, designed for use with the IPX/IP Gateway client included in Novell's Client 32 for Windows 95 and DOS/Windows 3.1. An IPX/IP Gateway client uses a special Windows Sockets library, and the IPX protocols, to access TCP services through a NetWare server that functions as a gateway to a TCP/IP network. This prevents the client from running a normal PING program, but WINPING.EXE is a Winsock-based program that provides gateway clients with basic PING capabilities, using a graphical interface. WINPING provides no configuration parameters; users may resolve DNS and NDS names, as well as IP addresses, and transmit an echo-request message to the destination.

For more information on the NetWare IPX/IP Gateway, see Chapter 13, "IntranetWare TCP/IP Clients."

Using PING

The basic method of troubleshooting communications problems on a TCP/IP network involves determining exactly where the problem lies. On a complex network (such as the Internet), the inability to communicate with a given system can be due to a problem at the source, the destination, or any of the intermediate networks and systems. The various functions of the PING program can help you isolate the cause of the problem.

In its most basic form, PING is a quick and simple tool that tells you the fundamental elements of the TCP/IP stack on your computer are functioning properly. It also informs you that the destination system is capable of receiving IP communications. Because PING uses ICMP messages, which are generated at the internet layer of the protocol stack, all concerns for the layers above are eliminated from the testing process. If, for example, you are unable to access a particular Web site, but you can successfully PING the site's address, you can be reasonably sure that the problem lies somewhere above the internet layer, on one or both of the systems involved. You can also determine whether or not the problem is in your local system by PINGing the same destination from two different machines.

Unfortunately, in many of today's computing environments, the corollary of this testing procedure is not necessarily true. On an unfiltered connection to the Internet, the inability to PING an address successfully means that you can't connect to that address with an upper-layer application, either. The use of firewalls and proxy servers on business networks complicates this scenario. If your company LAN is connected to the Internet, you may be able to connect to a site with a Web browser, but be unable to PING that same site because ICMP traffic is being filtered out by a firewall, while HTTP traffic is allowed to pass through.

Apart from determining whether a system is operational, you can use PING with additional parameters to create a wide variety of more specific testing scenarios. Many procedures (described in various Internet standards) for discovering certain properties of a TCP/IP network connection are based on PING message variations. The traceroute program, for example, is a utility that generates a series of specially configured ICMP echo-request messages, which are used to identify the intermediate systems accessed during the packets' journey to their destination. See the "Traceroute" section, later in this chapter, for more information.

DETERMINING A PATH MTU

Another standardized use of PING functions is the procedure by which you determine the path MTU of a connection between two TCP/IP systems. The *maximum transmission unit* (MTU) is the largest possible data packet that can be transmitted between two systems. Different types of networks have different MTUs, and the *path MTU* is the size of the largest data packet that can be transmitted from one system to another, across multiple networks, without fragmentation. In other words, both the source and destination of a transmission may be on networks with MTUs of 1,500 bytes, but if one of the intermediate networks has an MTU of 576 bytes, that is the path MTU for the transmission.

Using Microsoft's PING.EXE, you can determine the path MTU for a particular route, manually. To do this, you use the program to transmit echo-request messages to the destination system with the *–f* parameter (to prevent the packets from being fragmented by the IP protocol) and the *–l* parameter (to specify successively larger packets for each request). As you send increasingly larger echo-request messages, you eventually arrive at the point where an ICMP "Packet needs to be fragmented but DF set" error message is returned, signaling that you have exceeded the path MTU. An echo-request message has reached a router that cannot transmit the whole packet at once. Because fragmentation is prevented by the –f parameter, the router has no choice but to discard the packet and generate an error message, as shown in Figure 14-5.

When the path MTU discovery feature is built into a TCP/IP implementation (as in Windows NT), this process is automated and invisible to the user — but the basic technique is unchanged.

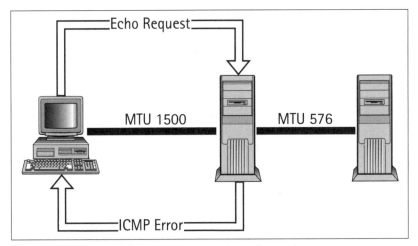

Figure 14-5: The path MTU discovery mechanism relies on the error messages generated by the ICMP protocol.

TESTING ROUTES

With the *–j* and *–k* parameters, you can use PING to test specific routes on your internetwork. When a network is designed with more than one possible route to a destination, it can be difficult to determine whether all routes are operational using standard PING transmissions. PING's capability of using the IP header's source-routing options enables you to specify the addresses of routers that the echo-request messages should use to reach their destination.

The *–j* parameter causes the messages to use the IP loose-source routing option. *Loose-source routing* occurs when you specify the addresses of up to nine intermediate systems. The packets must pass through these systems on the way to the destination, but can also pass through other, unlisted, routers during the trip. If you need to test the functionality of only a single router, you can use this option to ensure that echo requests are routed through it.

With the strict-source routing option provided by the *–k* parameter, on the other hand, you must specify the addresses of all routers used by the echo requests on the way to their destination. This defines the entire route taken by the ICMP packets. If you fail to specify a complete, valid route to the destination, the echo requests are not delivered and an error message is generated.

Denial of Service

Sometimes PING is used on the Internet for less-than-ethical activities. Adding the *-t* parameter to the PING command line causes the program to send a continuous stream of echo-request messages to the destination. When used in combination with the *-l* parameter from multiple client systems, a system can become overwhelmed by processing oversized PING messages. When this occurs, it may be incapable of providing its regular services, or drop its network connection, completely. This is known as "PINGing down" a system or, in more formal terms, a *denial of service* attack.

You can determine whether a system on your network is being attacked by using a traffic utility or a network analyzer to monitor the number of incoming ICMP packets. By examining the contents of the packets, you should be able to discover the attacker's IP address. Then you can take administrative measures to resolve the problem. Deliberately attempting to monopolize, or bring down, a site with incoming traffic is illegal. You can sue the perpetrator, have them prosecuted, or (more realistically) complain to their ISP, which often results in their account being deactivated.

Traceroute

On a relatively small internetwork, the IP header's record-route option is sufficient to identify all intermediate systems between a source and a destination. The Internet, however, is limited to nine IP addresses that can be carried in the IP header. This makes it impossible to record details of a transmission that might pass through 20, or more, routers on the way to a destination system. Not all routers support the IP record-route option.

The traceroute program is a routing utility that was designed for UNIX systems. It provides an alternative means of discovering the route that IP traffic is taking to a particular destination. The program has since been ported to the Windows OSs (as TRACERT.EXE) and to NetWare (as IPTRACE.NLM). Rather than attempting to record the entire route in a single message, traceroute transmits a series of ICMP echo-request messages and displays the results for each, at the client system.

Traceroute relies on the time-to-live (TTL) field of the IP header to accomplish its task. The TTL value specifies the number of hops an IP datagram can make before it is discarded. As a packet is transmitted across an internetwork, each router decrements the TTL value by one (or by the number of seconds it takes to process the packet). The feature is intended to prevent datagrams from endlessly circulating around a network due to accidental routing loops. Normally, a datagram is generated with a TTL value high enough to ensure that the packet reaches its destination.

Traceroute transmits a series of ICMP echo-request packets to the specified destination (the packets are identical except for the TTL value). The first group of three requests contain a TTL value of 1. When a request packet reaches the first router in its journey, the TTL value is decremented to 0. Then, the router must discard the packet, and return an ICMP type 11 error message to the source – informing the traceroute program that the "time-to-live [was] exceeded in transit." This error message is generated by the router and, therefore, supplies traceroute with the IP address of the first router in the path to the destination.

Each subsequent group of three echo requests, transmitted to the destination by traceroute, has a TTL value that is one greater than the previous group (see Figure 14-6). Thus, each successive group of requests travels one hop farther on the path to the destination than its predecessor. The source IP addresses (in the error messages returned by each router) provide traceroute with the identity of each intermediate system. This is done until an echo request is transmitted with a sufficiently high TTL value to reach the destination system. The receipt of a normal echo-reply message, from the destination, signals the traceroute program that the procedure is completed.

Apart from providing fascinating insight into the workings of the Internet, traceroute is valuable for troubleshooting Internet communications difficulties. The inability to PING a system on another network can result from a problem within the remote system, or any of the intervening networks or routers. Traceroute enables you to determine exactly where the problem lies by displaying the traffic's path to the point of failure.

The traceroute program has several important benefits over the record-route method of intermediate system discovery, such as:

◆ Traceroute uses features of the IP and ICMP protocols that must be implemented in all TCP/IP clients. The record-route method, however, uses an IP header option that may not be supported by some routers. Incompatibility with traceroute occurs in the few routers that discard IP datagrams with 0 TTL values, without returning an ICMP error message to the sender. These routers are absent from traceroute's results display, but do not hamper the discovery of subsequent routers.

◆ Because traceroute collates the information from separate ICMP messages transmitted by each router, there is no limit to the number of intermediate systems that can be discovered (theoretically). Most traceroute implementations, however, limit the TTL value to a maximum of 30 hops, by default. This is sufficient to trace the vast majority of possible Internet routes.

◆ Traceroute calculates the round-trip time of each ICMP message exchange, consisting of an echo request and the "time exceeded" error message received in reply. The IP header's timestamp option can hold only four timestamp/IP address combinations.

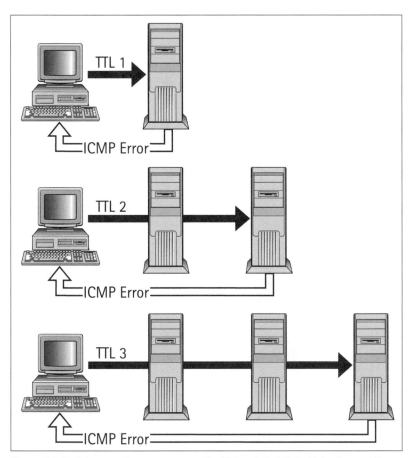

Figure 14-6: A traceroute program uses the IP header's TTL field to discover the address of each intermediate system enroute to a specified destination system.

◆ By default, traceroute performs reverse-name lookups of the intermediate systems' IP addresses and displays them in the program output (in place of the system addresses).

Of course, traceroute does generate more traffic than the record-route method. A route of nine hops, or less, can be recorded in a single message exchange using the record-route option – while traceroute requires a separate exchange for each hop. The increase in the number of packets and the error processing by the intermediate systems also makes traceroute relatively slow. Because the program doesn't run continuously, however, its traffic requirements are transient, and the additional burden on the network is usually negligible.

A potentially more serious problem is traceroute's reliance on the connectionless services of the IP protocol. Because of this, there is no guarantee that successive messages, transmitted to the same destination, will take the same route. Because each hop is identified using a separate exchange of messages, the path displayed by traceroute could be a conglomeration of results from several different routes. Often, this isn't the case, as messages transmitted within seconds of each other usually do take the same route, but there is no mechanism in traceroute to detect or prevent this problem from occurring.

TRACERT.EXE

Microsoft's TRACERT.EXE program runs from the DOS prompt and is supplied with Windows 95, Windows NT, and the TCP/IP-32 protocol stack for Windows for Workgroups. The command-line syntax is as follows:

```
TRACERT [-d] [-h hops] [-j hosts] [-w timeout] destination
```

The functions of the TRACERT command-line parameters are as follows:

◆ **–d** – prevents the program from performing reverse DNS name lookups on the IP addresses received from discovered routers

◆ **–h** *hops* – specifies the maximum possible value for the TTL field of the IP header and, therefore, the maximum number of hops to be traced between the source and the destination; the default value is 30

◆ **–j** *hosts* – specifies the IP addresses of intermediate systems to be inserted into the loose-source routing option field of the IP header, forcing TRACERT's ICMP messages to pass through certain routers on the way to their destination

◆ **–w** *timeout* – specifies the amount of time, in milliseconds, that TRACERT should wait for replies to each of its echo-request messages

◆ *destination* – specifies the DNS name or the IP address of the target system

In all command-line parameters for the TRACERT.EXE program that uses variables, a space should be inserted between the switch and value for the variable. For example, *–w 10000* would be an acceptable parameter, while *–w10000* would not be acceptable.

The TRACERT results display lists the three round-trip times for each hop in the route. These are generated by three separate echo-request messages transmitted for each TTL value. TRACERT also displays the DNS name of each intermediate system, which is discovered using a separate DNS reverse-name lookup for each router. A typical TRACERT results display appears as follows:

```
1      1 ms      1 ms    <10 ms   206.14.76.153
2       *         *         *      Request timed out.
3    135 ms     131 ms    132 ms   core1-ether0.garde.NY.tiac.net [207.
     60.33.50]
4    232 ms     161 ms    132 ms   core3-serial1.newyo.NY.tiac.net [207
     .60.45.121]
5    232 ms     140 ms    247 ms   core1-ether0.newyo.NY.tiac.net [207.
     60.44.1]
6    147 ms     138 ms    148 ms   core1-serial0.bedfo.MA.tiac.net [207
     .60.45.101]
7    146 ms     142 ms    142 ms   core-fddi4-0.bedfo.MA.tiac.net [199.
     0.65.1]
8    146 ms     146 ms    145 ms   903.Hssi3-0.GW1.BOS1.ALTER.NET [137.
     39.135.113]
9    146 ms     146 ms    146 ms   321.atm1-0.cr1.bos1.alter.net [137.
     39.13.234]
10   228 ms     229 ms    226 ms   103.ga000.CR3.LAX2.Alter.Net [137.39
     .74.141]
11   233 ms     234 ms    232 ms   313.atm1-0.gw1.lax2.alter.net [137.
     39.22.45]
12   234 ms     229 ms    224 ms   optuscom-gw.customer.ALTER.NET [157.
     130.224.138]
13   544 ms     543 ms    542 ms   192.65.89.77
14   596 ms     595 ms    601 ms   aarnet-wa-intl1.syd.optus.net.au
     [192.65.88.190]
15   614 ms     598 ms    606 ms   uwa-parnet.parnet.edu.au [203.19.110
     .18]
16   623 ms     647 ms    614 ms   uniwa.uwa.edu.au [130.95.128.1]
Trace complete.
```

This trace lists the routers used by a system in New York when transmitting to a site at the University of Western Australia. Notice how the marked increases in round-trip times enable you to determine when the packets made the transcontinental hop from Boston to Los Angeles (between entries 9 and 10), and the longer intercontinental hop from California to Australia (between entries 12 and 13).

IPTRACE.NLM

Novell added a traceroute implementation to the IntranetWare product in the Support Pack v3.0 release, which is available as a free download from their online services. Called IPTRACE.NLM, the program runs from the NetWare server-console command prompt, using the following syntax:

```
LOAD IPTRACE  destination [HOPS=hopsnumber] [WAIT=time] [PORT=
portnumber]
```

The functions of the IPTRACE command-line parameters are as follows:

◆ *destination* — specifies the DNS name or IP address of the target system

◆ HOPS=*hopsnumber* — specifies the maximum possible value for the TTL field of the IP header and, therefore, the maximum number of hops to be traced between the source and the destination; the default value is 30

◆ WAIT=*time* — specifies the amount of time (in milliseconds) IPTRACE should wait for replies to each of its UDP transmissions; the default value is 5,000 milliseconds

◆ PORT=*portnumber* — specifies the port number on the destination system to which IPTRACE's UDP messages should be addressed; the default value is 40,001

IPTRACE operates in a slightly different manner than does TRACERT.EXE. Instead of sending ICMP echo-request messages to the destination, it sends UDP datagrams addressed to a high port number, unlikely to be used by another process. This does not affect the trace process, because the ICMP error messages returned to the source are the same for any IP packet with an expired TTL. IPTRACE sends a single message (only) with each TTL value, instead of the group of three messages used by TRACERT.EXE.

When you load the IPTRACE program with the name or address of a destination system, the NetWare server console opens a new screen to display the results, as follows:

```
Trace Route (Results logged to file: SYS:\ETC\IPTRACE.LOG)
Max Hops: 30 Max Wait: 5 seconds Dest Port: 40001
From: 206.14.76.177 (219.51.75.127)
To: 194.75.226.17 (FTP.MYCORP.COM)
Hop         RTT        IPAddress
  1       1.002ms      206.14.76.1
  2     115.003ms      207.60.33.59 (DED1.GARDE.NY.TIAC.NET)
  3     115.000ms      207.60.33.50 (CORE1-ETHER0.GARDE.NY.TIAC.NET)
  4     116.007ms      207.60.45.121 (CORE3-SERIAL1.NEWYO.NY.TIAC.
                       NET)
  5     336.009ms      207.60.44.1 (CORE1-ETHER0.NEWYO.NY.TIAC.NET)
  6     126.006ms      207.60.45.101 (CORE1-SERIAL0.BEDFO.MA.TIAC.
                       NET)
  7     126.008ms      199.0.65.1 (CORE-FDDI4-0.BEDFO.MA.TIAC.NET)
  8     128.003ms      137.39.135.113 (903.HSSI3-0.GW1.BOS1.ALTER.
                       NET)
  9     134.006ms      137.39.13.234 (321.ATM1-0.CR1.BOS1.ALTER.NET)
 10     242.008ms      137.39.30.74 (103.HSSI4-0.CR1.SEA1.ALTER.NET)
 11     240.002ms      137.39.13.69 (311.ATM1-0.GW1.SEA1.ALTER.NET)
 12     232.004ms      157.130.176.58 (NWNET-GW.CUSTOMER.ALTER.NET)
 13     236.003ms      198.104.194.49 (SEABR2-GW.NWNET.NET)
 14     221.001ms      204.200.8.5 (SEABR1-GW.NWNET.NET)
```

```
15      238.009ms      198.104.192.9 (MICROSOFT-T3-GW.NWNET.NET)
16      219.002ms      141.167.37.133
```

IPCONFIG

Windows NT and the TCP/IP-32 protocol stack for Windows for Workgroups both include a DOS command-line utility, called IPCONFIG.EXE. This displays the basic TCP/IP-configuration data for the network interfaces on the local system, as shown:

```
Ethernet adapter Elnk31:
    IP Address. . . . . . . . . : 210.51.46.124
    Subnet Mask . . . . . . . : 255.255.255.0
    Default Gateway . . . . . . :

Ethernet adapter NdisWan7:

    IP Address. . . . . . . . . : 212.19.175.88

    Subnet Mask . . . . . . . : 255.255.255.0

    Default Gateway . . . . . . : 212.19.175.88
```

IPCONFIG is particularly useful when using DHCP to obtain TCP/IP-configuration settings for your system. Because the parameter values are not visible in the Network Control Panel, and can change without your knowledge, IPCONFIG is the most convenient method of viewing the current settings. You can also manipulate the current state of the DHCP client by running IPCONFIG with command-line parameters, as follows:

- ◆ /renew *adapter*—This parameter is available only when the DHCP client is active, and causes the IP address lease (for the specified adapter) to be renewed. Replace the *adapter* variable with one of the names specified in the default IPCONFIG display (for example, Elnk31 or NdisWan7). This operation shouldn't be necessary with a normally functioning DHCP client.

- ◆ /release *adapter*—This parameter is available only when the DHCP client is active, and causes the TCP/IP-client configuration (for the specified adapter) to be released. This effectively terminates all current TCP/IP communications on that adapter. Replace the *adapter* variable with one of the names specified in the default IPCONFIG display (for example, Elnk31 or NdisWan7).

◆ /all — This parameter causes IPCONFIG to display a more complete listing of TCP/IP-client configuration parameters, as well as the hardware addresses of the network adapters, as shown:

```
Host Name . . . . . . . . . : cz1.mycorp.com
DNS Servers . . . . . . . . : 179.70.66.2
                              179.70.66.8
Node Type . . . . . . . . . : Broadcast
NetBIOS Scope ID. . . . . . :
IP Routing Enabled. . . . . : Yes
WINS Proxy Enabled. . . . . : No
NetBIOS Resolution Uses DNS : Yes

Ethernet adapter Elnk31:
Description . . . . . . . . : ELNK3 Ethernet Adapter.
Physical Address. . . . . . : 00-20-AF-37-B8-12
DHCP Enabled. . . . . . . . : No
IP Address. . . . . . . . . : 210.51.46.124
Subnet Mask . . . . . . . . : 255.255.255.0
Default Gateway . . . . . . :

Ethernet adapter NdisWan7:

Description . . . . . . . . : NdisWan Adapter

Physical Address. . . . . . : 00-01-B0-E3-5F-80

DHCP Enabled. . . . . . . . : No

IP Address. . . . . . . . . : 212.19.175.88

Subnet Mask . . . . . . . . : 255.255.255.0

Default Gateway . . . . . . : 212.19.175.88
```

WINIPCFG

Windows 95 includes a graphical version of the IP-configuration display utility that provides the same information, and the same capabilities, as IPCONFIG. The WINIPCFG.EXE program is installed to a Windows 95 system's \Windows directory by default, but it is not added to the Start Menu. You must add it yourself, or execute the program from the Run dialog box. When you click the More Info button, you see a window like that displayed in Figure 14-7. You can use the Renew and Release buttons to change the DHCP-client status of a selected adapter, or the Renew All and Release All buttons to change the status of all installed adapters.

CONFIG

NetWare also has an internal server-console command that displays the configuration information for each of the adapters installed in the computer. The command is not IP-specific, but displays the basic IP-address information, as well as hardware information for the network interfaces, as shown:

```
File server name: NY-LIBRARY
IPX internal network number: 0000FFFF
     Node address: 000000000001
     Frame type: VIRTUAL_LAN
     LAN protocol: IPX network 0000FFFF
Server Up Time:  16 Hours 19 Minutes 19 Seconds

SMC Ethernet Adapter Server Driver v7.00 (951207)
     Version 7.00    December 7, 1995
     Hardware setting: I/O ports 240h to 25Fh, Memory C8000h to
 CBFFFh, Interrupt 3h
     Node address: 0000C037675E
     Frame type: ETHERNET_II
     Board name: SMC8000_1_EII
     LAN protocol: ARP
     LAN protocol: IP  address 210.56.85.17  mask FF.FF.FF.0
 interfaces 1
     LAN protocol: IPX network 00000001

Tree Name: NW411TREE
Bindery Context(s):
     CorpNet
```

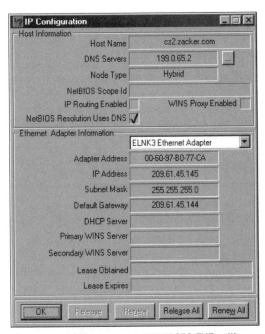

Figure 14-7: Windows 95's WINIPCFG.EXE utility displays the system's TCP/IP-client configuration settings in a graphical format.

NETSTAT

NETSTAT.EXE is a routing and traffic utility that displays protocol statistics and information about a system's current network connections. The program is character-based and runs from the DOS command line in Windows 95, Windows NT, and Windows for Workgroups (with the TCP/IP-32 protocol stack installed).

The syntax for the NETSTAT command is as follows:

```
NETSTAT [interval] [-a] [-p protocol] [-n] [-e] [-r] [-s]
```

With no additional parameters, NETSTAT displays a list of the system's current active connections, as follows:

Proto	Local Address	Foreign Address	State
TCP	cz5:2167	209.61.45.144:nbsession	ESTABLISHED
TCP	cz5:2759	207.87.4.27:80	CLOSE_WAIT
TCP	cz5:2760	207.87.4.27:80	CLOSE_WAIT
TCP	cz5:2776	209.61.45.145:nbsession	ESTABLISHED

The proto column lists the protocol used to establish the connection. The local address and foreign address columns list the host names and port numbers of the sockets used on the two systems to establish the connection, while the state column displays the current state of the connection. The state indicators are taken from the TCP standard, as defined in RFC793.

The TCP standard, and all other RFCs referenced in this book, can be found on the CD-ROM included with this book in HTML format.

The functions of the NETSTAT command-line parameters are as follows:

- *interval* – causes the NETSTAT command to refresh its display every *interval* seconds until the program is aborted by the user

- *–a* – causes the NETSTAT program to display all current connections as well as the listening ports on the local system, as shown:

Proto	Local Address	Foreign Address	State
TCP	cz5:2760	CZ5 :52467	LISTENING
TCP	cz5:2167	219.54.15.154:nbsession	ESTABLISHED
TCP	cz5:137	CZ5 :10469	LISTENING

Proto	Local Address	Foreign Address	State
TCP	cz5:nbsession	CZ5 :58597	LISTENING
TCP	cz5:2759	212.77.54.7:80	CLOSE_WAIT
TCP	cz5:2760	207.77.54.7:80	CLOSE_WAIT
TCP	cz5:2776	CZ5 :35060	LISTENING
TCP	cz5:2776	213.71.145.5:nbsession	ESTABLISHED
UDP	cz5:nbname	*:*	
UDP	cz5:nbdatagram	*:*	

♦ **-p** *protocol* – causes NETSTAT to display only the active connections for a particular protocol

♦ **-n** – causes NETSTAT to identify all systems using IP addresses instead of names; this parameter may be combined with other parameters

♦ **-e** – causes NETSTAT to display traffic statistics for the network interface, as shown:

	Received	Sent
Bytes	249219916	104128840
Unicast packets	354185	352961
Non-unicast packets	28518	638
Discards	0	0
Errors	0	0
Unknown protocols	55229	

♦ **-r** – causes NETSTAT to display the routing table, as well as the current active connections

♦ **-s** – causes NETSTAT to display traffic-statistics summaries for the IP, ICMP, TCP, and UDP protocols, as shown; when used in combination with the *-p protocol* parameter, displays a traffic summary for a particular protocol

```
IP Statistics
   Packets Received                    = 376983
   Received Header Errors              = 0
   Received Address Errors             = 5
   Datagrams Forwarded                 = 0
   Unknown Protocols Received          = 0
   Received Packets Discarded          = 0
   Received Packets Delivered          = 376983
   Output Requests                     = 349317
   Routing Discards                    = 0
   Discarded Output Packets            = 0
   Output Packet No Route              = 8
   Reassembly Required                 = 0
   Reassembly Successful               = 0
   Reassembly Failures                 = 0
   Datagrams Successfully Fragmented   = 0
   Datagrams Failing Fragmentation     = 0
   Fragments Created                   = 0
```

```
ICMP Statistics
                              Received        Sent
    Messages                  603             1052
    Errors                    0               0
    Destination Unreachable   49              360
    Time Exceeded             294             0
    Parameter Problems        0               0
    Source Quenchs            0               0
    Redirects                 0               0
    Echos                     117             572
    Echo Replies              140             117
    Timestamps                0               0
    Timestamp Replies         0               0
    Address Masks             0               0
    Address Mask Replies      0               0

TCP Statistics
    Active Opens                        = 1436
    Passive Opens                       = 6
    Failed Connection Attempts          = 9
    Reset Connections                   = 818
    Current Connections                 = 4
    Segments Received                   = 344418
    Segments Sent                       = 342344
    Segments Retransmitted              = 302

UDP Statistics

    Datagrams Received    = 12666
    No Ports              = 19780
    Receive Errors        = 0
    Datagrams Sent        = 5617
```

NBTSTAT

The NBTSTAT.EXE program is a traffic utility that displays connection information and other statistics concerning a system's use of NetBIOS over the TCP/IP protocols (called NetBT), as defined in RFC1001 and RFC1002. The program is included with all of the Windows network OSs and runs from the DOS command line.

The syntax for the NBTSTAT command is as follows:

```
NBTSTAT [-a name] [-A IPaddress] [-c] [-n] [-r] [-R] [-s] [-S]
  [interval]
```

Unlike most Windows utilities, the switches used in the NBTSTAT parameters are case sensitive.

The functions of the NBTSTAT command-line parameters are as follows:

♦ **–a** *name* – This parameter causes NBTSTAT to display the NetBIOS names registered on a system identified by the *name* variable, as shown:

```
NetBIOS Remote Machine Name Table

      Name              Type        Status
    ------------------------------------------
    CZ1            <00>  UNIQUE    Registered
    CZ1            <20>  UNIQUE    Registered
    WORKGROUP      <00>  GROUP     Registered
    CZ1            <03>  UNIQUE    Registered
    WORKGROUP      <1E>  GROUP     Registered
    ADMINISTRATOR  <03>  UNIQUE    Registered
    WORKGROUP      <1D>  UNIQUE    Registered
    .._MSBROWSE__.<01>  GROUP     Registered
    CZ1++++++++++++<BF>  GROUP     Registered

    MAC Address = 00-20-AF-37-B8-12
```

♦ **–A** *IPaddress* – This causes NBTSTAT to display the NetBIOS names registered on a system identified by the *IPaddress* variable. The resulting display is the same as that of the *–a name* parameter; only the means of identifying the remote system is changed.

♦ **–n** – This parameter causes NBTSTAT to display the NetBIOS names registered on the local machine. The resulting display is the same as that produced by the –a or –A parameter, specifying the name or address of the local system.

♦ **–c** – The –c parameter causes NBTSTAT to display the contents of the local system's NetBIOS name cache.

♦ **–r** – This parameter causes NBTSTAT to display statistics concerning the number of NetBIOS names registered and resolved by the local system. It uses both the broadcast- and name-server methods (as shown), as well as a list of the resolved names:

```
Resolved By Broadcast    = 28
Resolved By Name Server  = 0

Registered By Broadcast   = 5
Registered By Name Server = 0
```

◆ **–R** – This causes NBTSTAT to purge the system's NetBIOS name cache of all entries. It then reloads it by scanning the LMHOSTS file on the local drive for entries containing the #PRE tag.

◆ **–S** – This parameter causes NBTSTAT to display a table of the active NetBIOS sessions, their current status, and the amount of data transferred in each direction. It identifies remote systems using their IP addresses, as shown:

```
Local
Name   State   In/Out     Remote  Host              Input   Output
CZ5    <00>    Connected  Out     209.61.45.144     22MB     13MB
CZ5    <00>    Connected  Out     209.61.45.145      1MB    348KB
CZ5    <03>    Listening
CZ5            Listening
```

◆ **–s** – This causes NBTSTAT to display a table of the active NetBIOS sessions, their current status, and the amount of data transferred in each direction. It identifies remote systems using their host names.

◆ *interval* – The interval parameter causes the NBTSTAT command to refresh its display every *interval* seconds until the program is aborted by the user.

For more information on NetBIOS over TCP/IP, and its use by the Microsoft Windows network, see Chapter 11, "Name Registration and Resolution."

ARP

TCP/IP systems use the *Address Resolution Protocol* (ARP) to discover the hardware addresses of other systems on the network. It does this by broadcasting request messages containing IP addresses and waiting for replies. To prevent redundant ARP transactions, each system on the network stores the hardware addresses of the systems it has already resolved in an ARP cache. Windows network OSs include a control utility, called ARP.EXE, that enables you to view and manage the entries in the cache.

The syntax for the ARP program is as follows:

```
ARP [-a [IPaddress]] [-N interface] [-s IPaddress Hwaddress
[interface]] [-d IPaddress [interface]]
```

The functions of the ARP command-line parameters are as follows:

◆ **–a** [*IPaddress*] – The –a parameter causes ARP to display the contents of
the system's ARP cache, as shown. The *IPaddress* variable is optional, but
if present, causes ARP to display only the cache entry for the specified IP
address:

```
Interface: 209.61.45.146
  Internet Address      Physical Address      Type
  209.61.45.144         00-20-af-37-b8-12     dynamic
  209.61.45.145         00-60-97-b0-77-ca     dynamic
```

◆ **–N** *interface* – This parameter causes ARP to display only the cache
entries, associated with the local network interface specified by the
interface variable.

◆ **–ds** *IPaddress HWaddress [interface]* – This causes ARP to add a new entry
to the cache, associating the IP address specified by the *IPaddress* variable
with the hardware address specified by the *HWaddress* variable. The
hardware address must be specified as six hexadecimal bytes delimited
with hyphens (for example, 00-20-af-37-b8-12). The optional *interface*
variable is used to identify the ARP cache associated with a particular
network interface, to which the entry should be added. Entries added with
the *–s* parameter are static (not dynamic), meaning they are not purged
when the standard ARP-cache timeout period expires.

◆ **–d** *IPaddress [interface]* – This parameter causes ARP to delete the cache
entry associated with the IP address, specified by the IPaddress variable.
The optional interface variable is used to identify the ARP cache
associated with a particular network interface, from which the entry
should be deleted.

If you have network systems, in which IP addresses are permanently associated
with their hardware addresses, you can affect moderate savings in system-
processing time and network bandwidth. This is done by manually adding static
entries to the ARP cache, using the ARP.EXE program. The ARP cache, however, is
stored in system memory, only, and is erased whenever the computer is restarted.
Any manipulations you make to the cache, including the addition of static entries,
must be repeated with each system reboot. You can use a BAT or CMD file to automate the addition of static entries into the ARP cache, but the savings usually aren't
worth the effort.

For more information on the Address Resolution Protocol and the ARP
cache, see Chapter 4, "The Link Layer."

TCPCON

NetWare includes a multipurpose server-console utility, called TCPCON.NLM, that enables you to view TCP/IP protocol statistics, configure advanced protocol parameters, and manage the server's routing table and ARP cache. TCPCON is a menu-driven program that uses NetWare's C-worthy interface. When you load TCPCON.NLM at the server console, you see a screen, like that shown in Figure 14-8. The main screen displays basic server information and a summary of the incoming and outgoing traffic for the IP and TCP protocols.

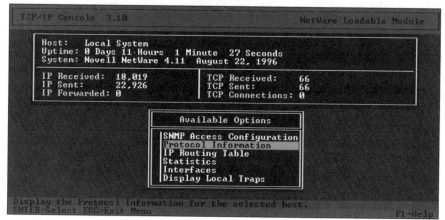

Figure 14-8: TCPCON enables you to perform a wide array of protocol management, configuration, and monitoring tasks from the NetWare server console.

The TCPCON program's routing configuration functions, and the ROUTE.EXE utility included in the Windows network OSs, are covered in Chapter 9, "Routing IP."

Viewing Interface Statistics

TCPCON contains screens that display detailed, continuously updated, statistics on many different aspects of the TCP/IP-communications processes. Comparing the statistics for protocols operating at different layers of the networking stack can help you isolate the source of a communications problem within the server.

When you select Interfaces from TCPCON's Available Options menu, you see a list of the network interfaces installed in the server. When you select an interface, TCPCON displays an Interface Statistics screen like that shown in Figure 14-9. This screen shows basic information about the interface, such as the MTU and the nominal speed of the network to which it is attached. In addition, the display shows the amount of data sent, and received, through that interface measured in bytes, unicast packets, and nonunicast packets.

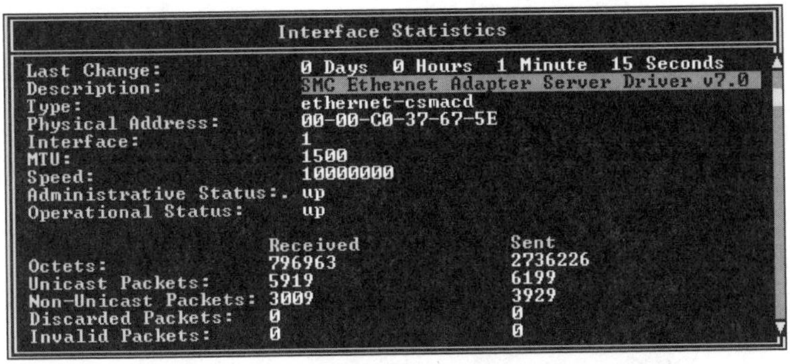

```
                        Interface Statistics
Last Change:         0 Days  0 Hours  1 Minute  15 Seconds
Description:         SMC Ethernet Adapter Server Driver v7.0
Type:                ethernet-csmacd
Physical Address:    00-00-C0-37-67-5E
Interface:           1
MTU:                 1500
Speed:               10000000
Administrative Status:.  up
Operational Status:      up

                     Received              Sent
Octets:              796963                2736226
Unicast Packets:     5919                  6199
Non-Unicast Packets: 3009                  3929
Discarded Packets:   0                     0
Invalid Packets:     0                     0
```

Figure 14-9: TCPCON's Interface Statistics screen displays the total amount of data entering and leaving the system through a particular network interface — regardless of the upper-layer protocol used.

From this screen, you can activate and deactivate the interface by modifying the value of the Administrative Status field. A third setting puts the interface into a Testing mode, a state in which the interface is active, but no operational data is passed through the interface to the network.

Viewing Protocol Statistics

While TCPCON's interface statistics reflect the traffic generated by all protocols installed on the system, the Statistics menu option enables you to choose from among the TCP/IP protocols and view more specific information on network traffic. For example, selecting IP from the TCP/IP Statistics menu displays the screens shown in Figures 14-10 and 14-11. These screens are updated dynamically as displayed, and show the number of incoming and outgoing IP datagrams. More important for protocol analysis and troubleshooting purposes, the screens display the number of datagrams that have been discarded as a result of errors. It also shows the number of packets that have required fragmentation and reassembly at the internet layer.

Selecting other protocols from the TCP/IP Statistics menu displays more specific detail about a subset of the IP traffic, as most of the other protocols are carried within IP datagrams. The ICMP Statistics screen, for example, specifies how many of the incoming and outgoing IP datagrams contain ICMP messages, and itemizes them by message type, as shown in Figure 14-12.

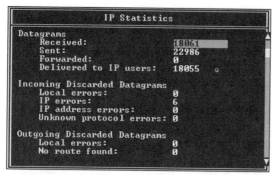

Figure 14-10: The IP statistics screen displays datagram traffic levels, as well as error counts.

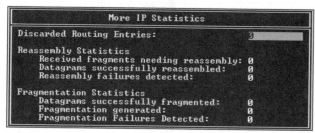

Figure 14-11: The More IP Statistics screen contains information on the IP fragmentation and reassembly process.

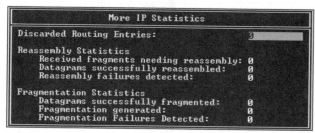

Figure 14-12: The ICMP Statistics screen breaks down the server's ICMP traffic by message types.

The TCP Statistics screen breaks down the traffic by connections in both directions, and the segment transmissions making up those connections (see Figure 14-13). The *Received with Error* and *Retransmitted* values can tell you how efficiently the server is sending and receiving TCP data. In the same way, the UDP Statistics screen enumerates the server's connectionless traffic. The other entries in the TCP/IP Statistics menu are for the *Edge Gateway Protocol* (EGP) and the *Open Shortest Path First* (OSPF) protocol, both of which are activated when these dynamic-routing protocols are enabled on the server.

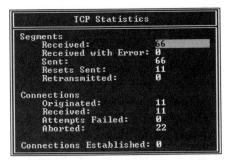

Figure 14-13: The TCP Statistics screen displays the number of currently active connections, and statistics on all previous connections since the system was last restarted.

Configuring TCP/IP Protocols

The TCPCON program's statistics screens are for informational purposes, only. They do not enable you to interactively work with the TCP/IP protocols. To configure the behavior of the protocols, you must select the Protocol Information option from the Available Options menu. Selecting a protocol from list displays an information screen that provides access to various configuration settings, statistics, and tables.

Most of the protocol information screens provide access to the same displays available from the Statistics menu. Some of the configuration parameters are also duplicated in the INETCFG.NLM utility. TCPCON, however, provides the capability to set values for some advanced configuration settings that aren't available anywhere else in the OS.

IP PROTOCOL INFORMATION

The IP Protocol Information screen is shown in Figure 14-14. You can use this screen to modify the default settings for key IP header fields, and to manage the cache of ARP information stored on the server.

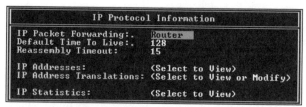

Figure 14-14: The IP Protocol Information screen provides interactive configuration of selected IP settings.

Following are the functions of options on the IP Protocol Information screen:

◆ **IP packet forwarding** – This option is also configurable with the INETCFG utility; it enables you to choose whether the server should function as an IP router or as a multihomed end node. Selecting Router lets IP traffic enter the system through one network interface and exit from another. On an End Node system, all of the installed network interfaces remain active, but their traffic remains segregated within the server.

◆ **Default time to live** – This setting enables you to configure the default value for the IP header's time-to-live (TTL) field in all datagrams generated by the server – except when another protocol (ICMP, TCP, or UDP) specifies a different TTL value. The default value is 128 hops. The TTL value should be at least double the maximum number of hops between the source and its most distant destination. The default value should be more than sufficient, even for Internet use.

◆ **Reassembly timeout** – This setting specifies the amount of time (in seconds) that the server should retain incoming datagram fragments while waiting for the remaining fragments to arrive. The default value is 15 seconds. On lightly trafficked servers, increasing this setting could prevent the need for retransmission of fragmented datagrams being delivered over slow connections. On a busy server, increasing the value causes a greater amount of system resources to be dedicated to the storage of incoming fragments.

◆ **IP addresses** – This option provides informational (that is, uneditable) access to the IP Addresses Table. This table contains entries for the IP addresses bound to each of the network interfaces installed in the server, as shown in Figure 14-15. Each entry contains the following information:

  ◆ **Host name/IP address** – This displays a listing of the server's network interfaces by the host names associated with them, and by their IP addresses.

◆ **Address mask** – This entry displays the subnetwork mask applied to the IP address of the network interface.

◆ **Interface** – This identifies the network interface, to which the IP address is bound, using a unique number that is also shown in TCPCON's Interfaces listing.

◆ **Broadcast** – This specifies the value of the least significant bit of the broadcast IP address used on the network, to which the interface is connected. The standard Internet broadcast address is 255.255.255.255 in decimal form, which is 32 ones in binary notation. Thus, the value of this field is usually 1.

◆ **Maximum size** – The maximum size entry specifies the size (in bytes) of the largest datagram that can be assembled from IP fragments received over this interface.

◆ **IP address translations** – This option provides interactive access to (what NetWare refers to as) the server's IP-address translation table, more commonly known as the ARP cache. You can view, add, modify, and delete entries in the table, just as you can with the Microsoft ARP.EXE program. To add a new entry, press the Insert key and supply values for each of the following fields:

  ◆ **Host name/IP address** – This field is used to specify the host name and/or IP address of the system being added to the table. Press the Insert key to select a system from those listed in the server's HOSTS file.

  ◆ **Physical (MAC) address** – This is used to specify the hardware address of the network adapter associated with the specified host name and/or IP address. Enter the address as 6 hexadecimal bytes, delimited by hyphens.

  ◆ **Interface** – This field identifies the interface on the local system where this table entry is to be used, based on the identifiers shown in TCPCON's Interfaces listing.

  ◆ **Type** – The type field is used to specify whether the table entry is to be static or dynamic. A dynamic entry is purged after a predetermined timeout period expires, while a static entry remains in the table until the server is restarted.

◆ **IP Statistics** – This field displays the same IP Statistics screens available through TCPCON's Statistics menu.

Figure 14-15: The IP Addresses Table identifies the network interfaces in the server to which an IP address has been bound.

TCP PROTOCOL INFORMATION

From the TCP Protocol Information screen, you can monitor the current state of the server's active TCP connections and view advanced TCP-protocol settings (see Figure 14-16).

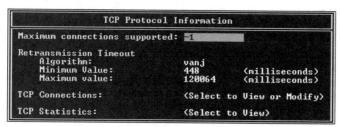

Figure 14-16: The TCP Protocol Information screen enables a NetWare server administrator to view current TCP connections, and disconnect a system, if necessary.

Following are the functions of the TCP Protocol Information screen options:

♦ **Maximum connections supported** – This option displays the number of simultaneous TCP connections the server can support. A value of –1 indicates that the number of connections is determined, dynamically, by the available system resources.

♦ **Retransmission timeout algorithm** – This specifies the algorithm used to compute the timeout period length (that must elapse before the server retransmits unacknowledged TCP segments). A value of *vanj* indicates that the server uses the algorithm developed by Van Jacobson and Robert Braden, defined in RFC1072.

♦ **Retransmission timeout minimum value** – This option specifies the shortest timeout period, which can elapse before the server retransmits unacknowledged TCP segments.

♦ **Retransmission timeout maximum value** – This option specifies the longest timeout period, which can elapse before the server retransmits unacknowledged TCP segments.

◆ **TCP connections** – This displays a table of the server's TCP connections, as shown in Figure 14-17, including those in the Listen state (which indicates they are waiting for incoming traffic to establish a new connection). By pressing the Delete key, you can remove any connection from the list, effectively preventing remote systems from establishing a connection to a listening port, or terminating the access of a currently connected system. The information displayed in each table entry is as follows:

　◆ **Type** – This specifies the network-layer protocol used to carry the connection's TCP data, which is always IP, unless the client is connected using the NetWare IPX/IP Gateway.

　◆ **Local host/IP** – Use the Tab key to toggle between the host name and the IP address used to identify the interface used on the local side of the TCP connection. For a connection in the Listen state, the value 0.0.0.0 indicates that the server will accept a connection through any of its interfaces.

　◆ **Port** – The port entry specifies the service name and/or port number used on the local side of the TCP connection.

　◆ **Remote host/IP** – This entry specifies the host name and/or IP address of the remote system, connected to the server. Connections in the Listen state have a value of 0.0.0.0.

　◆ **Port** – This entry specifies the port number used on the remote system to establish the TCP connection.

　◆ **State** – This specifies the current state of the TCP connection, using the terms defined in RFC793.

◆ **TCP statistics** – This entry displays the same TCP Statistics screens available through TCPCON's Statistics menu.

```
                         TCP Connections Table
   Type Local Host        Port   Remote Host        Port   State
 ▲ IP   0.0.0.0           687    0.0.0.0            None   listen
   IP   0.0.0.0           1024   0.0.0.0            None   listen
   IP   0.0.0.0           6050   0.0.0.0            None   listen
   IP   ny-library        ftp    209.61.45.145      1097   established
   IP   ny-library        80     0.0.0.0            None   listen
   <End of Table>
```

Figure 14-17: The TCP Connections Table lists all remote systems currently connected to the server, as well as the services awaiting connections.

Summary

Many utilities are available for you to use in managing and monitoring the performance of a system's TCP/IP protocol stack. This chapter examined those that are supplied with the operating system providing the TCP/IP support.

In this chapter, you learned:

- ◆ How to classify TCP/IP utilities, according to their function

- ◆ How to use PING and TRACEROUTE to troubleshoot TCP/IP communications problems

- ◆ How to display TCP/IP connection and protocol statistics using NETSTAT and NBTSTAT

- ◆ How to manage the ARP cache on a TCP/IP system

- ◆ How to use the NetWare TCPCON utility to manage a server's TCP/IP protocol stack

Chapter 15

TCP/IP Applications

IN THIS CHAPTER

Hundreds of applications are designed to use the TCP/IP protocols to access network resources, created by OS developers and third parties. Chapter 7, "The Application Layer," examined some of the protocols used to implement application-layer communications between systems. This chapter discusses actual client and server programs that make use of those protocols on TCP/IP systems, particularly those included with the Windows NT and IntranetWare OSs, such as the following:

◆ While there are many third-party implementations with graphical user interfaces, Windows network clients all include a character-based FTP client that employs user commands that are traditional in the TCP/IP world.

◆ IntranetWare's FTP server provides standard TCP file-transfer services using the authentication and access-control facilities provided by Novell Directory Services.

◆ Both Windows NT and IntranetWare include a Web browser, Internet Explorer and Netscape Navigator, respectively. Despite their heated competition, these two programs are fundamentally more alike than different.

◆ Windows NT Server includes the Internet Information Server and Workstation, the Personal Web Server, both of which provide Web, FTP, and gopher services with a unified administrative framework.

FTP

While dedicated FTP clients have been supplanted in popularity by World Wide Web browsers, FTP is still a widely used application protocol. Most links to downloadable files on Web sites actually connect to FTP servers – whether the two services share the same computer or not. Apart from its download speed, FTP is capable of protecting files from access by unauthorized users, by requiring a user name and password. Anonymous access to FTP sites is a long-standing tradition in the Internet community, but authenticated access is used frequently to provide clients with private access to secured files. Another advantage of FTP is that it's designed for bidirectional use. Web sites rarely provide users with the ability to upload files to the server, but FTP clients can upload as easily as download.

While FTP is an efficient means of transferring files between TCP/IP systems, it has always been hampered by its limited capability to locate files. An FTP client could browse the directories of a server, but there was no inherent means of searching, or indexing, the contents of the Internet's many FTP servers – until the World Wide Web came about. Today, FTP clients are used primarily when users know what files they want, and where they are located.

The Windows FTP Client Interface

An FTP client uses a documented series of commands to communicate with an FTP server, and perform activities necessary to access, locate, and transfer files. The user interface of an FTP-client program, however, is isolated from the client/server communications. FTP clients can be graphical or character-based; whatever control the program uses to perform a specific action is translated into the appropriate commands that are transmitted to the server (see Figure 15-1). This makes it possible for developers to create client programs for various computing platforms that use the OS's native idiom (rather than imposing an interface which may be alien to the program's users). It is rare for an FTP client's user interface to use the same command syntax that it employs when communicating with a server.

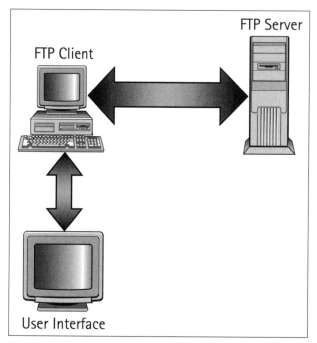

Figure 15-1: The user interface of an FTP client is separated from the client/server communications syntax.

This section examines the command syntax employed by a user with the Microsoft FTP-client program. For information on the communications between the FTP client and server, see Chapter 7, "The Application Layer."

The standards that define the FTP protocol make no attempt to define the command language for a client-user interface. You may find that different clients provide different capabilities. For example, a graphical FTP client may enable you to view the contents of a directory on an FTP server, and select multiple files for download. Once you make your selection, you click a single button to begin the file transfers. While this is a single action to you, the program issues a separate sequence of commands for each file, which initiates a series of individual downloads.

Graphical FTP clients like these are available from many third-party software developers (either as freeware, shareware, or commercial products). Virtually every TCP/IP-capable OS, including Windows 95, Windows NT, and Windows for Workgroups (with the TCP/IP-32 protocol stack installed) includes a character-based FTP client that runs from the command line.

Microsoft's FTP client is based largely on the character-based client used on UNIX OSs. UNIX relies more heavily on FTP for intranetwork file transfers than DOS, Windows, or NetWare, as it doesn't use the drive-mapping metaphor common to PC networking. To accommodate the many different UNIX variants, a collection of FTP client-interface commands evolved into something of a *de facto* standard. Based on standard UNIX command-line conventions, these commands are now used by most character-based FTP clients, including the FTP client included in the Microsoft OSs.

RUNNING FTP.EXE

Most users who are familiar with FTP (even remotely) know that to connect to a server, you enter the FTP command, followed by the DNS name or IP address of the desired destination. There are, however, many useful FTP command-line parameters besides the name of the destination. You run Microsoft's FTP.EXE program from the DOS command prompt using the following syntax:

```
FTP [-d] [-g] [-i] [-n] [-s: filename] [-v] [destination]
```

The functions of the FTP.EXE command-line parameters are as follows:

- ◆ **–d** – The *–d* parameter places the FTP program into debugging mode, which causes the application to display all commands passed between the client and the server, at the user interface. This option is good for exploring the functions of the FTP-protocol process and debugging problems in the client/server communications process.

◆ **–g** – The *–g* parameter causes the FTP client to disable the use of wildcard characters in the specification of file names.

◆ **–i** – The *–i* parameter prevents the FTP client from prompting the user to confirm each operation (when the mget or mput command is used with wildcard characters) to transfer multiple files. This useful, but often-forgotten, command enables you to perform unattended uploads or downloads of multiple files.

◆ **–n** – The *–n* parameter prevents the FTP client from initiating the user logon procedure, automatically, after connecting to a server. To gain access to the server, you must log on manually with the *user* command.

◆ **–s:** *filename* – The *–s* command enables you to specify the name of an ASCII-text file, on the local system, that contains FTP-client commands. The commands are executed in sequence, automatically, when the FTP client is launched.

◆ **–v** – The *–v* parameter causes the FTP client to suppress the display of all command responses sent by the server. This does not include file and directory listings requested with the *ls* or *dir* command, however. These are actually ASCII file transfers – not command responses.

◆ **destination** – The destination parameter is used to specify the DNS name or the IP address of the target FTP server.

The command-line parameters of the Microsoft FTP client affect only the functions of the client's user interface. In no way do they modify the communications between the client and an FTP server. The parameters can, therefore, be used with the client regardless of the FTP server implementation with which it is communicating.

FTP COMMANDS

When you specify a destination on the FTP command line, the client normally begins the authentication procedure as soon as the connection to the specified server is established. Once the logon process is complete, the **ftp>** command prompt appears, and you can issue any of the following user-interface commands:

◆ **!** [*command*] – The *!* command enables you to shell out from the **ftp>** prompt and drop to the DOS prompt on the local machine. When you specify a DOS command with *!*, it is executed from the shell, returning you to the **ftp>** prompt, immediately. Without a *command* variable, you are dropped to the DOS prompt, where you can execute any standard DOS commands before typing EXIT to return control to FTP.

◆ ? [*command*] – The *?* command causes the FTP client to display the function of the user-interface command, specified by the *command* variable. When no *command* variable is supplied, a list of the user-interface commands is displayed. The *help* command performs the same function.

◆ append *source* [*destination*] – The append command transfers the *source* file to the FTP server and concatenates it with the *destination* file. When no *destination* variable is specified, the *source* file is appended to a file of the same name on the server. This command is useful for adding new log information to an existing log file on an FTP server.

◆ ASCII – FTP supports two types of file transfers: ASCII and binary. The *ASCII* command signals the server that the ensuing file transfer(s) will involve text files. ASCII is the default file-transfer mode because FTP transmits file and directory listings as plain text. When a text file is transferred in ASCII mode, nonprinting characters, such as end-of-line markers, are converted to the standard format for the destination OS.

◆ bell – Going back to the days of mechanical keyboards, the *bell* command causes the FTP-client program to generate a beep at the end of each file transfer (when the function is supported by the OS).

◆ binary – FTP supports two types of file transfers: ASCII and binary. The *binary* command signals the server that the ensuing file transfer(s) will involve compiled files that must be transferred byte-by-byte. A binary file is any type of compiled program, image, or data file. While you can transfer an ASCII file in binary mode, the reverse is not the case. Binary files, such as executables or graphics, do not function after being transferred in ASCII mode. Because the FTP-client program defaults to ASCII mode, failing to change to binary mode frequently causes file transfers that appear to complete successfully (but those files actually don't function).

◆ bye – The *bye* command causes the FTP client to terminate the current control connection to the server, and exit the DOS prompt. This can be contrasted with the *close* command, which terminates the control connection and returns the client to the **ftp>** prompt. The *quit* command performs the same function.

◆ cd *directory* – The *cd* command changes the client's working directory, on the FTP server, to the value specified by the *directory* variable. As in DOS, you can specify the full path to a directory from the root, represented by a forward slash ("/"), or the name of a subdirectory of the current directory, with no slash, or use the double period (".") to represent the parent of the current working directory.

◆ **close** – The *close* command causes the FTP client to terminate the control connection and return to the **ftp>** prompt. The *disconnect* command performs the same function.

◆ **debug** – The *debug* command is a toggle that causes the FTP client to display all commands it sends to the connected server, preceded by the characters --->. By default, debugging is disabled.

◆ **delete** *filename* – The *delete* command causes the file on the FTP server, specified by the *filename* variable, to be erased. The account that you used to log on to the FTP server must have sufficient rights in the server file system to delete files.

◆ **dir** [*directory* [*filename*]] – The *dir* command causes the FTP server to transmit an ASCII listing of directory contents, specified by the *directory* variable (including dates, times, owners, and attributes). If no *directory* variable is supplied, a listing of the current working directory's contents is transmitted. By default, the output of the *dir* command is displayed on the client screen, but by specifying a *filename* variable, the directory listing is saved to a file, of that name, on the client system. The *ls* command performs the same function.

◆ **disconnect** – Same as the *close* command.

◆ **get** *serverfile* [*clientfile*] – The *get* command causes the file, specified by the *serverfile* variable, to be copied from the server to the client system. It uses the current file-transfer mode – ASCII or binary – to do this. By default, the file is given the same name on the client system, but you can include a file name in the *clientfile* variable to rename the file during the copy process. The *recv* command performs the same function.

◆ **glob** – The *glob* command toggles the FTP-client program's capability to recognize wildcard characters as part of file names. By default, globbing is enabled.

◆ **hash** – The *hash* command toggles the display of a hash character ("#") at the client, for each 2,048-byte block of data transferred. By default, hashing is disabled.

◆ **help** – Same as the *?* command.

◆ **lcd** [*directory*] – The *lcd* command causes the FTP client to change the local machine's working directory to the value of the *directory* variable. When no *directory* variable is specified, the command displays the name of the current working directory.

♦ literal *command* – The *literal* command sends the string contained in the *command* variable directly to the FTP server, without alteration. The *quote* command performs the same function.

♦ ls [directory [filename]] – Same as the *dir* command, except that *ls* displays a simple listing of file names, only.

♦ mdelete *filenames* – The *mdelete* command enables the FTP client to delete multiple files on the connected server, using wildcard characters in the *filenames* variable. By default, the client prompts for a confirmation before deleting each file. The account used to log on to the FTP server must have sufficient rights in the server file system to delete files.

♦ mdir *filenames localfile* – The *mdir* command causes the FTP server to transmit an ASCII listing of the files that match the contents of the *filenames* variable, including dates, times, owners, and attributes. The *filenames* variable must be included with the command, and may use wildcard characters. To display the contents of the entire working directory on the server, use a hyphen ("-") as the value of the *filenames* variable. The command must also include a value for the *localfile* variable, which specifies the name of the file on the client system, in which the directory listing will be stored. To display the output of the command on the client screen, use a hyphen as the value of the *localfile* variable.

♦ mget *serverfiles* – The *mget* command causes the files specified by the *serverfiles* variable to be copied to the working directory on the client system. It uses the current file-transfer mode – ASCII or binary – to accomplish this. The *serverfiles* variable can use wildcard characters to identify a group of files. By default, the client prompts for a confirmation before transferring each file.

♦ mkdir *directory* – The *mkdir* command creates a new subdirectory in the working directory of the connected FTP server, using the name specified in the *directory* variable. The account used to log on to the FTP server must have sufficient rights in the server file system to create new directories.

♦ mls [*filenames* [*localfile*]] – Same as the *mdir* command, except that *mls* displays a simple listing of file names, only.

♦ mput *localfiles* – The *mput* command causes the files, specified by the *localfiles* variable, to be copied to the working directory on the server. It uses the current file-transfer mode – ASCII or binary – to accomplish this. The *localfiles* variable can use wildcard characters to identify a group of files. By default, the client prompts for a confirmation before transferring each file. The account used to log on to the FTP server must have sufficient rights in the server file system to create new files.

◆ **open** *server [port]* – The *open* command causes the FTP client to establish a connection to the server, specified by the *server* variable. The *server* variable can contain a DNS name or an IP address. The *port* variable can be used to specify a port number other than the default ftp-control port, which is 21.

◆ **prompt** – The *prompt* command toggles the use of confirmation prompts for each file processed by the multiple file commands, such as *mget*, *mput*, and *mdelete*. By default, prompting is enabled.

◆ **put** *clientfile [serverfile]* – The *put* command causes the file specified by the *clientfile* variable to be copied from the client to the server system. It uses the current file-transfer mode – ASCII or binary – to accomplish this. By default, the file is given the same name on the server system, but you can include a file name in the *serverfile* variable to rename the file during the copy process. The account used to log on to the FTP server must have sufficient rights in the server file system to create a new file. The *send* command performs the same function.

◆ **pwd** – The *pwd* command causes the FTP client to display the current working directory on the server to which it is connected.

◆ **quit** – The quit command is the same as the *bye* command.

◆ **quote** – This command is the same as the *literal* command.

◆ **recv** – This is the same as the *get* command.

◆ **remotehelp** *[command]* – The *remotehelp* command causes the FTP client to display the function of the server command, specified by the *command* variable. When no *command* variable is supplied, a list of the server commands is displayed.

◆ **rename** *oldname newname* – The *rename* command gives the file, specified by the *oldname* variable, the name specified by the *newname* variable. The account used to log on to the FTP server must have sufficient rights in the server file system to rename files.

◆ **rmdir** *directory* – The *rmdir* command removes the subdirectory, named in the *directory* variable, from the working directory of the connected FTP server (as long as there are no files or subdirectories contained within it). The account used to log on to the FTP server must have sufficient rights in the server file system to delete directories.

◆ **send** – The send command is the same as the *put* command.

◆ **status** – The *status* command displays the FTP client's connection state, and the state of the transfer mode, bell, debugging, globbing, hashing, prompting, and verbose toggles.

- ◆ trace — The *trace* command is a toggle that causes the FTP client to display all of the procedures involved in processing each command, issued at the user interface. By default, tracing is disabled.

- ◆ type — The *type* command is a toggle that switches the FTP client's file transfer mode between ASCII and binary.

- ◆ user *name* [*password*] — The *user* command causes the FTP client to initiate the authentication process with the connected server. It uses the account specified by the *name* variable and, if necessary, an associated *password*. Ordinarily, this command is not needed because, by default, the user is authenticated, automatically, when connecting to the server. Running FTP.EXE with the –*n* parameter prevents this behavior, forcing the user authentication to be performed manually.

- ◆ verbose — The *verbose* command is a toggle that causes the FTP client to display the responses received from the connected server. By default, verbose mode is enabled.

Most of the FTP user-interface commands can be abbreviated by using the first two or three letters in place of the entire command.

The NetWare FTP Server

Both Windows NT and IntranetWare include an FTP server implementation that enables Internet and intranet users to transfer files (to and from the server), using anonymous or authenticated connections. IntranetWare's FTP server is included as part of the NetWare NFS Services product, a limited version of which is included with the OS. The full NetWare NFS Services product is designed to provide UNIX systems with bidirectional access to NetWare server volumes.

NetWare NFS Services, being a separate product from NetWare itself, is installed only after the OS is fully configured with the TCP/IP protocol stack. You install the product from the server console with the NetWare INSTALL.NLM utility, and manage the various services with the UNICON.NLM program. While the installation process includes all of the modules in the NFS Services product, you can select the services you want to run with UNICON.

The IntranetWare FTP server is implemented as a *NetWare Loadable Module* (NLM), called FTPSERV.NLM. When you activate the service, however, this module remains dormant until a user actually logs in to the FTP server. When a connection is established to the FTP port number, the module autoloads and remains in memory until a two-minute timeout (with no active connections) elapses.

CONFIGURING THE FTP SERVER

After selecting FTP Server from UNICON's Manage Services screen, the Set Parameters option displays the FTP Server Parameters screen shown in Figure 15-2. From this screen, you can configure the basic settings that control the functions of the server. All changes are applied to the running service, immediately; there is no need to restart it.

```
                    FTP Server Parameters
 Maximum Number of Sessions:            9
 Maximum Session Length:                400     minutes
 Idle Time Before FTP Server Unloads:   2       minutes
 Anonymous User Access:                 Yes
 Default User's Home Directory:         VOL1:test
 Anonymous User's Home Directory:       VOL1:test
 Default Name Space:                    NFS
 Intruder Detection:                    Yes
     Number of Unsuccessful Attempts:   2
     Detection Reset Interval:          3000    minutes
 Log Level:                             File
```

Figure 15-2: To administer IntranetWare's FTP service, you use the UNICON utility at the server console.

The configuration parameters for the FTP service are as follows:

◆ **Maximum number of sessions** – specifies how many simultaneous client connections are permitted by the server; the default value is 9

◆ **Maximum session length** – specifies the amount of time (in minutes) that a client can remain connected to the server; the default value is 400 minutes

◆ **Idle time before FTP server unloads** – specifies the amount of time that must elapse without an active client connection before the FTPSERV.NLM module is unloaded from memory; the default value is 2 minutes

◆ **Anonymous user access** – specifies whether or not the FTP server permits clients to log on using the name "anonymous"; the default value is "no"

◆ **Default user's home directory** – specifies the directory that should be used as the root for clients logging in with an NDS name that has no home directory associated with it

◆ **Anonymous user's home directory** – specifies the directory that should be used as the root for anonymous users

◆ **Default name space** – specifies the display format used by the server when generating the directory and file listings that are transmitted to clients; the possible values are DOS and NFS (NFS displays a UNIX-style listing, while the DOS display truncates long file names to the 8.3 format); the default value is DOS

◆ **Intruder detection** – specifies whether a log should be maintained of unauthorized attempts to access the FTP server; the default value is "on," which activates the following two options:

 ◆ **Number of unsuccessful attempts** – specifies the number of failed logins that must occur before a user is considered to be an intruder; the default value is 6

 ◆ **Detection reset interval** – specifies the time interval (in minutes) during which the number of unsuccessful login attempts must occur for a user to be considered an intruder

◆ **Log level** – specifies the amount, and type, of information recorded in the FTP service log; the possible values are as follows:

 ◆ **None** – no information is captured to the log

 ◆ **Login** – only login information is captured to the log

 ◆ **Statistics** – the number of files transferred to, and from, the server is captured to the log, along with the login information

 ◆ **File** – all FTP-command transactions are captured to the log, including the login and statistic information

To display a message screen to FTP clients after they log in to the server, create an ASCII file containing the desired text, name it BANNER.FTP, and place it in the FTP server's SYS:\ETC directory. You can also display a message to users when they change to a particular directory, on the FTP server, by creating a text file called MESSAGE.TXT in that directory.

CONTROLLING FTP ACCESS

On the Internet, anonymous access to FTP sites is the norm, but you can also use FTP to provide protected access to files. The IntranetWare FTP server uses the NDS database to authenticate FTP users. By default, any user with an NDS account can log in to the FTP server with the same user name and password used when logging in to the NetWare network.

NDS users need the same rights to files and directories they access using the FTP server as they have when accessing them with a NetWare client in the normal manner. This is true even for anonymous users. When you enable anonymous access in the FTP Server Parameters screen, a user object called *Anonymous* is created in the NDS tree (with the home directory specified in the Anonymous User's Home

Directory field). Because users are granted full rights to their home directories, automatically, an anonymous user has the rights needed to transfer files to and from the FTP server.

When FTP clients log in to the server using NDS user names, they, too, are placed in their home directories with full rights. Unlike most FTP services, however, these authenticated users have access to directories and files anywhere on the NetWare network. Only when an NDS user does not have an assigned home directory, does a problem arise. In this case, the user is placed into the directory specified in the Default User's Home Directory field. If users don't have the appropriate file-system rights to this directory, they may be able to connect to the FTP server, but they won't have meaningful access to its files and directories.

FTP clients and servers exchange authentication information in clear text — which can be a significant lapse in security when using NDS accounts. Administrators, and other users with high-level network access, can avoid transmitting their passwords by using an alternative NDS account with limited rights for connecting to the FTP server.

By default, all NDS users are granted access to the FTP server. This access is controlled, not by modifying the properties of the NDS objects themselves, but by modifying a text file. This file is called RESTRICT.FTP, and is stored in the SYS:\ETC directory of the FTP server. The file has nothing to do with rights to files and directories on the FTP server that are granted to users; rather, it only determines which user names are permitted to log in to the FTP server. You can edit the RESTRICT.FTP file manually using a text editor, or select Restrict FTP Access from UNICON's FTP Administration screen.

By default, RESTRICT.FTP is installed to the SYS:\ETC directory as a read-only file. You must change its attributes before you can modify it using UNICON or any other program.

The RESTRICT.FTP file is annotated with instructions for its use, and contains only a single active entry – an asterisk that functions as a wildcard, providing access to all users. To modify the file, you can leave the wildcard intact and create entries for users, or workstations, that are to be denied access. Or you can remove the wildcard and list only those that are permitted to log in to the FTP server. You can also limit users to read-only access, or access only, to certain directories.

Internet Information Server

The enormous popularity of the Internet has spawned a great deal of application development activity, but the client and server programs for the basic services, such as FTP and the World Wide Web, remain the core components of Internet technology. Windows NT 4.0 Server includes an integrated package of services called the *Internet Information Server* (IIS), which is administered with a single utility. Windows NT Workstation includes the *Microsoft Peer Web Services* (PWS), a scaled-down version of IIS that provides much of the same functionality.

IIS and PWS both consist of FTP, Web, and gopher servers, as well as the Internet Service Manager – an administrative utility that enables you to manage all IIS and PWS services on your internetwork from a single location. Also included is an HTML version of the manager, which enables you to configure all of the same service parameters using a Web browser on an intranet, or Internet, client system (see Figure 15-3).

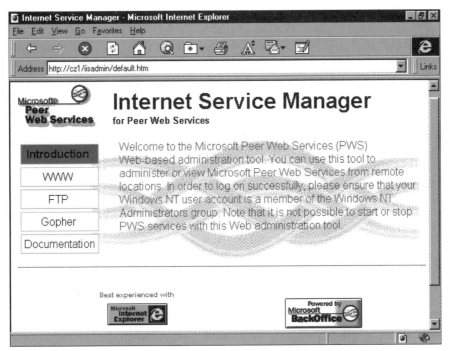

Figure 15-3: The HTML version of the Internet Services Manager provides full administrative access to Windows NT's Internet services.

IIS and PWS are identical when it comes to features and parameters. The only difference is that the Windows NT Workstation product is limited, by its license, to a maximum of 10 concurrent user connections. This is true regardless of whether the users connect with a Windows network client, or a Windows Sockets FTP or Web client. IIS, running on Windows NT Server, supports unlimited connections, and is intended for high-volume use on busy intranets or the Internet.

As is the case with any Internet service, your Windows NT system must have the TCP/IP stack installed and configured to use IIS or PWS. Depending on how you intend to use the services, you may also require one or more DNS or WINS servers to resolve names into IP addresses. On an intranet, users have a choice of using NetBIOS or DNS names to identify a target server. Windows NT Server also includes both DNS and WINS services, which can run on the same system with the Internet services.

Using the Internet Service Manager

When you launch the Internet Service Manager application, you see a listing of the services running on the local system, as shown in Figure 15-4. By selecting Connect to Server from the Properties menu, you can specify the name, or address, of another Windows NT server on your network and add its services to the list. You can also use the Find Servers feature to search the network for other servers running Microsoft Internet services. The Internet Service Manager application can administer both IIS and PWS services from any Windows NT workstation. The Peer Web Server services, however, must be added manually using Connect to Server; the Find Servers feature only locates Internet Information Server services.

Figure 15-4: The Internet Service Manager displays the installed services, and enables you to start and stop them.

From the main screen of the manager, you can start, stop, or pause any of the services displayed in the list. Like any other Windows NT services, they are controllable from the Services icon in Control Panel (where you can also specify whether the services should start up automatically when the system boots).

Each service listed in the manager screen has its own Properties dialog box that you can use to configure the operational parameters of the service. The following sections examine the configuration parameters for the Web and FTP services provided by both IIS and PWS.

Configuring the FTP Service

When you open the FTP Service Properties dialog box, by clicking the Properties button on the main Internet Service Manager screen, you see the Service page shown in Figure 15-5. The parameters on this screen are as follows:

- ◆ **TCP port** — The TCP port field specifies the number of the port used to establish FTP-control connections to the server. By default, the value is 21, the well-known port specified in the "Assigned Numbers" RFC. When you change the value of this field, your users must specify the same port number in their FTP-client software.

- ◆ **Connection timeout** — The connection timeout field specifies the time interval (in seconds) that an FTP client can remain connected to the server, with no activity, before it is disconnected. Possible values range from 0 to 32,767. The default value for IIS is 32,767; for PWS, it is 900.

- ◆ **Maximum connections** — The maximum connections field specifies the number of simultaneous FTP connections supported by the server. Possible values range from 0 to 32,767. The default value for IIS is 32,767; for PWS, it is 900.

- ◆ **Allow anonymous connections** — The allow anonymous connections checkbox specifies whether users should be permitted to log in to the FTP server with the name "anonymous." The *username* and *password* fields identify the Windows NT account used during anonymous logons. This enables you to control the access granted to anonymous users, by modifying the properties of the account. By default, a user called IUSR_<*servername*> is created for anonymous logons during the IIS/PWS installation. If you change the username, you must specify a name with a valid account on the Windows NT system.

- ◆ **Allow only anonymous connections** — The allow only anonymous connections checkbox prevents users from logging on to the FTP server, using any name other than "anonymous."

- ◆ **Comment** — The comment field enables you to specify a descriptive text string that appears in the main service listing of the Internet Service Manager.

By clicking the Current Sessions button on the Service page, you display a screen showing the users that are connected to the server. From here, you can disconnect some users from the server, selectively, or disconnect all users.

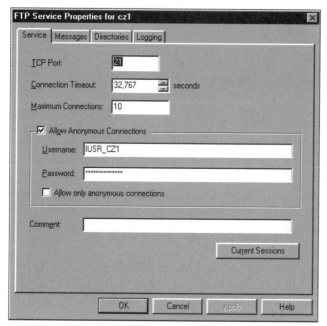

Figure 15-5: The Services page of the FTP Service Properties dialog box controls the basic operational parameters of the FTP service.

DISPLAYING TEXT MESSAGES

On the Messages page of the FTP Service Properties dialog box, you specify the text strings that the server displays to FTP clients when they log on, log off, and exceed the maximum allowable number of connections (see Figure 15-6). You can also configure the server to display text strings, when users change to specific directories, to provide information on the directory's contents – but this is a manual operation.

To display directory information, you must create an ASCII file, called ~ftpsvc~.ckm. This contains the text to be displayed and stored in the selected directory (activating the hidden attribute to make it invisible to users, if desired). For the file to be displayed to clients, however, directory annotation must be enabled on the server, either by the user or administrator.

To permanently activate the directory annotation feature, the service administrator must create a new entry in the Windows NT registry, in the following key:

```
HKEY_LOCAL_MACHINE\SYSTEM
  \CurrentControlSet
    \Services
      \MSFTPSVC
        \Parameters
```

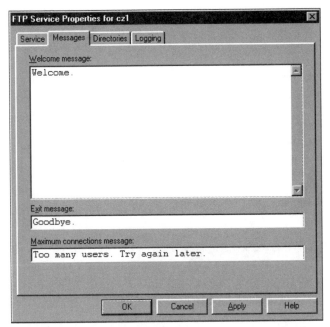

Figure 15-6: The Messages screen enables you to customize the text displayed to FTP service users.

Create a new REG_DWORD entry, called AnnotateDirectories, and give it a value of 1 (true), signifying that directory annotation is enabled. A value of 0 (false), disables the feature.

If directory annotation is not enabled in the registry, users can enable it for their current sessions from the FTP client. After logging in, the client must send the *site ckm* command to the server, but this is a custom command for the Microsoft FTP service – and is not recognized by FTP clients (even Microsoft's). Therefore, to send the command to the server using the Microsoft FTP client, you must use the *literal* or the *quote* command, which sends a string unaltered, as follows:

```
literal site ckm
```

The server responds with a message stating that directory annotation is on, and displays the contents of the ~ftpsvc~.ckm file whenever the user changes to a directory containing one. Directory annotation, however, remains activated only for the duration of the FTP connection.

CREATING CONTENT DIRECTORIES

Every FTP server has a home directory, which can be located anywhere in the server's file system. This, however, appears to FTP clients as the server's root directory. You can create any subdirectory structure you wish under the root directory, and can access any of the files located in those subdirectories. Microsoft's FTP service, however, provides the ability to create virtual directories. These appear, to users, as subdirectories of the root but can actually be located on other drives or Windows network servers.

When you select the Directories tab on the FTP Service Properties dialog box, you see a screen that lists the server's home and virtual directories (see Figure 15-7). By default, the home directories for all Microsoft Internet services are created beneath a directory, called \InetPub. FTP's server's directory is called \ftproot. You can change this directory by highlighting it and clicking the Edit Properties button. You can select any directory to use as the root, but if located on an NTFS drive, the accounts used to access the FTP server (including the anonymous user account specified on the Services page) must have the appropriate rights to that directory.

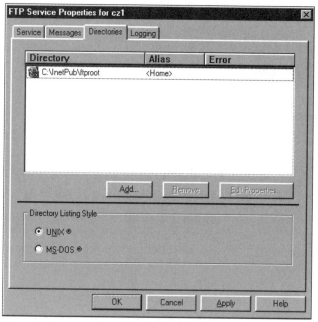

Figure 15-7: The Directories page of the FTP Service Properties dialog box lists both the home and virtual directories configured on the server.

An FTP server can only have a single home directory, but if you want to vary the content provided by the server according to the login name used by the client, you can create subdirectories off of the root. When a subdirectory with the same name as the login name used by a client is created off of the root, that directory is automatically made the working directory for that client upon logon. Thus, a directory called *anonymous* that is created beneath the \ftproot directory becomes the working directory for all anonymous users. This, in itself, is not to be considered a security measure, however. These users have access to the subdirectories below \ftproot\anonymous, but they can also navigate upwards to access /ftproot's other subdirectories. To prevent clients from accessing the directories intended for other users, you must use NTFS permissions.

DISPLAY FORMATS   On the Directories page, you select the display format for the file and directory listings generated by the server. The UNIX format is more familiar to veteran FTP users, because FTP servers traditionally have been UNIX systems. The UNIX display option appears as follows:

```
150 Opening ASCII mode data connection for /bin/ls.
d----   1 owner      group              0 Aug 17 20:54 Anonymous
-----   1 owner      group          13609 Aug 18 21:01 JKYD_12A.JPG
-----   1 owner      group          12620 Aug 18 21:01 JKYD_12B.JPG
-----   1 owner      group          23486 Aug 18 21:03 JKYD_AT6.JPG
-----   1 owner      group          16597 Aug 18 21:03 JKYD_DOG.JPG
-----   1 owner      group          20156 Aug 18 21:01 JKYD_EYE.JPG
-----   1 owner      group        2630328 Jun 10  1:19 MKJ2795.exe
-----   1 owner      group        5818448 Aug  8 22:32 mghjh86.exe
d----   1 owner      group              0 Aug 14 21:30 test
226 Transfer complete.
```

For the many PC users now drawn to the Internet, however, the MS-DOS listing is probably more comfortable. The only problem in using the MS-DOS display option is that there are some GUI FTP clients that rely on the standard UNIX format to create a graphical representation of the file listing. The MS-DOS listing appears as follows:

```
150 Opening ASCII mode data connection for /bin/ls.
08-17-97  08:54PM       <DIR>          Anonymous
08-18-97  09:01PM               13609  JKYD_12A.JPG
08-18-97  09:01PM               12620  JKYD_12B.JPG
08-18-97  09:03PM               23486  JKYD_AT6.JPG
08-18-97  09:03PM               16597  JKYD_DOG.JPG
08-18-97  09:01PM               20156  JKYD_EYE.JPG
06-10-97  01:19AM             2630328  MKJ2795.exe
08-08-97  10:32PM             5818448  mghjh86.exe
08-14-97  09:30PM       <DIR>          test
226 Transfer complete.
```

CREATING VIRTUAL DIRECTORIES   To create a virtual directory, click the Add button on the Directories page of the FTP Service Parameters screen, to display the Directory Properties dialog box (see Figure 15-8). After selecting the Virtual Directory radio button, you specify the directory you want to publish to FTP clients by typing the name in the Directory field, or browsing to the proper directory.

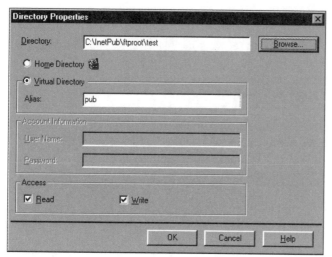

Figure 15-8: To create a virtual directory, you specify a network path name and an alias, by which, the directory should be known to FTP users.

You can select a directory on any Windows network system when creating a virtual directory – but you must supply a UNC path name for directories not found on the local system. This contradicts the functionality of the Browse button, which can incorrectly insert paths containing mapped network drive letters into the Directory field. The service accepts paths to directories on the local system that use drive letters, but no FTP-client access is granted to mapped network drives.

If the directory you select is located on another server, you must supply the user name and password of a valid Windows NT account that has the appropriate access rights to the directory. The FTP service uses this account to gain access to the directory when it publishes the contents to clients.

Once you select a directory, you must supply an alias, by which that directory will be known to FTP clients. This alias name functions, to FTP users, as a subdirectory off of the server's root – regardless of where the directory is actually located. To access a virtual directory, FTP clients use the *cd* command, just as if the directory actually existed as a subdirectory of the root. The only visible difference is that virtual directories do not appear in the file listings furnished to clients by the *dir* and *ls* commands. You must make the users aware of the directories' existence through other means, such as the server's directory annotation feature. As with a home directory, clients automatically inherit access rights to all subdirectories of a virtual directory.

The Directory Properties dialog box for each directory (whether home or virtual) contains an Access box where you specify the rights FTP clients will be granted to the selected directory. The Read and Write rights are granted independently. The Read right permits users to view the contents of the directory with the *dir* and *ls* commands, and download files with *get* and *recv*. The Write right permits users to upload files to the directory, with the *put* and *send* commands, as well as delete files and create new directories. You should assign the Write right to your directories with great care. It is not uncommon for organizations with open Internet FTP servers to discover they've been the unwitting hosts of illicit FTP sites containing pirated software or other unacceptable content.

Granting only the Read right prevents clients from changing the contents of the directory in any way. You may also restrict users rights to only the Write right. This makes it possible for them to switch to the directory using the *cd* command and upload files into it (even though they cannot see the directory or list its contents). Even after a successful file upload, the *dir* and *ls* commands display no files to the client. Companies often use this ability to provide FTP clients with a secure "drop-off box," to which they can upload files without making them accessible to other clients.

The Read and Write rights, which you can assign to FTP server directories, are wholly separate from the rights you can assign in the NTFS file system. If, for example, the account used for anonymous FTP users has no NTFS rights to an FTP server directory, no access to that directory is provided (no matter what the values of the FTP service parameters). If you create a "drop-off box" directory on an NTFS drive that has only the Write right granted by the FTP service, you must ensure that the appropriate users have both the NTFS Read and Write rights to that directory. Without the NTFS Read write, FTP clients cannot switch to that directory using the *cd* command.

Configuring the World Wide Web Service

Many of the configuration parameters for the Microsoft World Wide Web service are nearly identical to those for FTP. Though they use different protocols for client/server communications, the server-side functionality of the two services basically consists of a mechanism for delivering requested files to a client. The graphical nature of Web information is a product of the client technology found in the browser, rather than the server's capabilities.

The Service page of the WWW Service Properties dialog box is shown in Figure 15-9. There, the TCP port, connection timeout, and maximum connections fields have the same functions as for the FTP server. The default port for Web communications is 80.

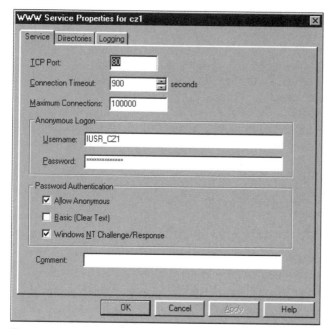

Figure 15-9: On the WWW Service Properties page, you control the authentication procedures clients use to connect to your Web server.

CONTROLLING WEB SITE ACCESS

Although Web clients do not explicitly log in when connecting to a server, they are still authenticated. IIS and PWS use the same IUSR_<*servername*> user account for anonymous access to the Web server as is used for anonymous FTP access. When this user is created in the Windows NT User Manager during the IIS/PWS installation, it is assigned a random password. This is also entered into the Internet Service Manager Password fields. If you change this password in one of these two places, you must change it in the other as well, or anonymous access will not be granted.

The Microsoft Web server supports three types of client authentication: Anonymous access, Basic authentication, and Challenge/Response authentication. You can activate any, or all, of these to control access to the Web server. No matter which authentication method a client uses, the associated account in the Windows NT User Manager must have rights to the files published by the Web server. If the Web site content is stored on an NTFS drive, you must grant these rights to authenticated users, explicitly.

ANONYMOUS ACCESS   When you enable anonymous access by activating the Allow Anonymous checkbox on the Services page, you ensure that all users are granted access to the Web server (as long as the anonymous user name and password are properly configured). If you enable the Windows NT Challenge/Response authentication method as well, clients failing this authentication are logged on anonymously, as a fall-back method.

BASIC AUTHENTICATION   Selecting the Basic authentication option on the Services page enables you to limit Web server access to users that have an account on the server running IIS or PWS. Activating the Basic option causes the Web server to request authentication information from the client. Most browsers respond to this by popping up a login window that requires the user to enter a user name and password before proceeding. This method transmits the user name and password to the server in an unencrypted form – which makes it dangerous to use ordinary network passwords. You can provide a reasonable amount of site security by creating a "guest" account on the Web server. This provides access to the site's home directory, only, and has all clients use that same account.

When you activate the Basic authentication method, together with anonymous access, clients are always logged in anonymously. They are not required to authenticate unless the anonymous user is denied access to a requested document. In this case, the server attempts to authenticate the user.

WINDOWS NT CHALLENGE/RESPONSE AUTHENTICATION   Activating the Challenge/Response authentication method provides the most security with the least effort, as long as both client and server are properly configured. When a Web browser supports this protocol, it authenticates itself to the Web server by transmitting the client's NT user name and password as part of the HTTP header. The password is encrypted and the client is authenticated, automatically, as long as the authentication protocol is enabled on the Web server and a user account exists for the transmitted name.

When you activate multiple authentication methods for your Web server, the Challenge/Response is always used first. This is because browsers supporting the protocol transmit the user name and password in every HTTP request. When Challenge/Response is not supported, the server reverts to anonymous authentication, or to the Basic method (if anonymous access is disabled).

Unfortunately, the only Web client supporting the protocol is Microsoft's Internet Explorer, thus limiting the usefulness of the Challenge/Response authentication method. This option is excellent for use on intranets that require secured access, and that have Microsoft Web servers and browsers deployed throughout the enterprise. It is not practical for use on mixed networks or the Internet.

DEFINING WEB SERVER DEFAULTS   On the Directories page are two options defining the default behavior of the server when responding to client requests. The Enable Default Document option lets you specify the name of the file that is delivered to clients when they request only a DNS name, IP address, or directory name from the client browser. For example, when the client connects to *www.mycorp.com*, the server responds by transmitting the file in the home directory that matches the name in the Default Document field. Although a

long-standing Web tradition calls for index.html to be used as the default document name, Microsoft servers use the file name default.htm.

The Directory Browsing Allowed option controls the server's response to a
request when the target directory doesn't contain a file with the default document
name, or when the default document option is not activated. When directory
browsing is not allowed, the request fails and the server responds with an error
message. When browsing is enabled, the server delivers a listing of the files and
directories in the target server, as shown in Figure 15-10.

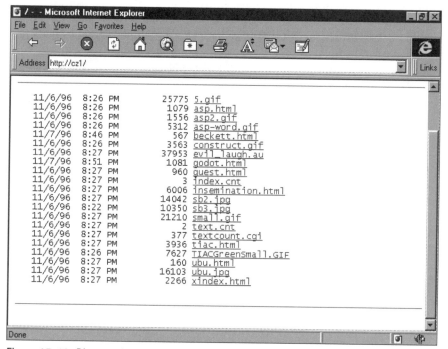

Figure 15-10: Directory browsing causes the Web server to transmit a file listing when no
default file exists in the client's requested directory.

As with the FTP service, virtual directories do not appear in the file listings
generated by the Web server. Users must be notified of the directories'
existence by some other means, such as HTML links.

CREATING WEB DIRECTORIES

The Directories page of the WWW Service Properties dialog box (see Figure 15-11) is very similar to its FTP counterpart, and operates similarly. A Web server has a home directory just like an FTP server; you can create virtual directories using the same procedure described in "Creating Virtual Directories," earlier in this chapter.

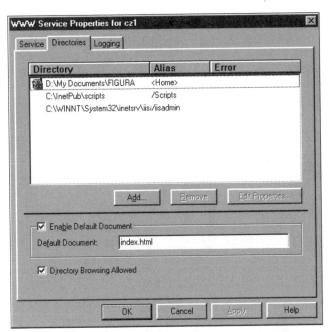

Figure 15-11: On the Directories page, you can create virtual directories and virtual Web servers.

Because you cannot upload files to the Web server, Web directories have Read and Execute rights, instead of the Read and Write rights of FTP servers. The Execute right controls whether users are permitted to run Web applications and scripts found in a specific directory. The Web server is configured with a \Scripts directory by default, which you can use to store your own executable files. Directories with the Execute right should not have the Read right enabled, as this prevents clients from accessing executable files.

CREATING VIRTUAL SERVERS   The Internet Information Server product, because it is designed for use on higher-volume sites, has a capability the Peer Web Services lacks. On an IIS Web server, you can create multiple home directories that function as virtual servers, with their own IP addresses and DNS names. This way, you can run multiple Web sites for different departments or customers that appear to be independent of each other (even though they are all hosted on the same computer).

To create virtual servers, you must assign multiple IP addresses to your Windows NT system, first. You do this from the Network Control Panel by assigning multiple addresses to a single network interface, or use the addresses of the various interfaces on a multihomed system. Once the IP addresses are in place, you must create entries in your DNS server that equate the addresses with the names you want to identify the various Web sites hosted by the system. Even on an intranet, the use of DNS names is preferred for this purpose because you can't assign multiple NetBIOS names to a single Windows NT system.

The process of creating a virtual Web server in the Internet Service Manager is the same as creating a home directory. On the Directory Properties page (see Figure 15-12), you enter a path to a directory anywhere on your network, supply a user name and password if the directory is on another server, and specify the virtual server IP address. When the process is completed, the Directories page lists multiple home directories, each of which has its own root, content, and IP address.

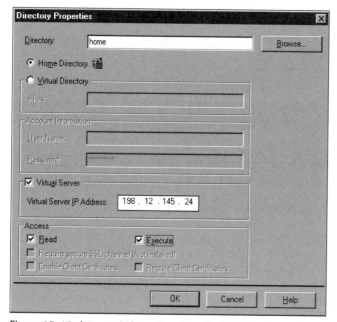

Figure 15-12: Internet Information Server's virtual servers provide the capability to host multiple Web sites using a single computer.

 The default home directory, which is automatically created during the IIS installation, is not associated with any particular IP address. This means that it is accessible from any of the system's IP addresses. If you create virtual servers, you should modify the properties of the existing home directory to ensure that each Web site is configured to use one address, only.

Novell Web Server

IntranetWare includes the Novell Web Server 2.51, which runs on a NetWare server and provides many of the same capabilities as Microsoft's Web server. Since the release of IntranetWare, the Web server product has been upgraded to version 3.1, which is available as a free download from Novell's online services. Like Microsoft's Web server, NWS has the capability to host multiple independent Web sites on a single server, using content located anywhere on the NetWare network. The product also includes a built-in search engine and support for industry-standard development tools, such as the Perl 5 scripting language and the Secure Sockets Layer 3.0 protocol. NWS also works in cooperation with Novell Directory Services to provide secured access to your Web sites.

TIP   Before installing Novell Web Server 3.1, be sure that your NetWare server was upgraded with the IntranetWare Support Pack 3, or Support Pack 2 with the TCPIP.NLM upgrade (found in the TCPN03.EXE patch file). These upgrades are all available from the Novell online services. Novell Web Server 3.1 is found on the Web at `http://www.novell.com/intranetware/-products/novell_web_server`. Support Pack 3 is available from `http://support.novell.com/misc/patlst.htm`.

To install NWS, use NetWare's INSTALL.NLM utility at the server console. The installation process prepares the Web server so it's ready for use on most systems with no additional configuration. You can modify the properties of the software, however, using Web Manager (a graphical utility that is copied to the server's SYS:\PUBLIC directory). NWS also ships with a sample Web site, default scripts, and online documentation in HTML format. By default, NWS creates a directory on the SYS volume, called \inw_web for the content files that are shared by all of the server's Web sites, and a directory called \web for the default virtual server. If you elect to create additional virtual servers, each one has its own home directory, segregating the content for the individual sites.

Installing NWS creates two additional screens on the server console. One tracks the indexing activities of the QuickFinder search engine, and one displays Web server information, as shown in Figure 15-13. Beneath the Information window, the Web server displays real-time status messages, describing errors or events as they occur.

The statistics shown on this screen include the following:

◆ **Uptime** – specifies elapsed time since the Web server was last restarted

◆ **Total requests** – specifies the number of HTTP requests processed by the Web server since it was last restarted

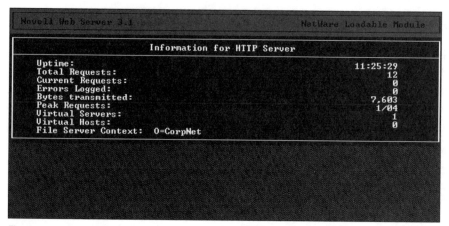

Figure 15-13: The Web Server Console screen displays real-time statistics of your Web sites' activity.

♦ **Current requests** – specifies the number of HTTP requests received by the Web server, and not yet processed

♦ **Errors logged** – specifies the number of HTTP requests received by the Web server that could not be satisfied, for whatever reason

♦ **Bytes transmitted** – specifies the total number of bytes transmitted to Web clients since the server was last restarted

♦ **Peak requests** – specifies the maximum number of HTTP requests simultaneously processed since the Web server was last restarted, followed by the maximum number of requests the server is configured to process simultaneously

♦ **Virtual servers** – specifies the number of virtual servers currently operating

♦ **Virtual hosts** – specifies the number of virtual hosts currently operating in all of the virtual servers

♦ **File server context** – specifies the name of the NDS container object where the Web server is located

Novell Web Server Configuration Files

The configuration parameters for the Novell Web Server are stored in a series of ASCII-text files with CFG extensions. Some of these are modified by the Web Manager utility, and others contain settings that must be edited, manually. As a rule, the commands found under the *#Computer generated* heading are controlled by the Web Manager. While you can edit these parameters manually, your changes may be overwritten the next time you run the manager. Parameters found under a *#Computer preserved directives* heading are designed to be edited, manually. Some configuration files contain one of these headings, while others contain both.

The configuration files are not dynamic; they are read by NWS only when the main server program file, HTTP.NLM, is started. Therefore, whether you use the Web Manager program to change configuration parameters or edit the CFG files manually, you must restart the Web server before the changes take effect. When you use Web Manager to make modifications, you're prompted to save your changes and restart the server. Alternatively, you can select Restart HTTP from the Web Manager's Options menu, or issue the WEBSTOP and WEBSTART commands from the server-console prompt.

Using the Web Manager

NWS consists of one or more virtual servers, each of which functions as an independent Web site (with its own content, root directory, and IP address). Each virtual server can contain one or more virtual hosts, which are subdivisions of a single site. Virtual hosts can also have their own unique URLs or IP addresses, but their content is stored in a subdirectory of the virtual-server directory.

Deciding whether to create separate Web sites using virtual servers, or virtual hosts, should be based on the need for separate configuration settings. If you are creating separate intranet Web sites for the various departments of your company, virtual hosts are preferred because the basic requirements for each site are the same (only the content and the URL differ). If, however, you are hosting multiple Web sites for different customers, with different requirements, virtual servers enable you to maintain completely separate configurations and content directories.

CREATING A VIRTUAL SERVER

The Web Manager utility is a Windows program you can launch by executing the WEBMGR.EXE file, found in the server's SYS:\PUBLIC directory. When you run the program and click the File menu, you see each of the virtual servers that have been created on the system, and some indication of whether that server is currently on or off. The NWS-installation process creates a single virtual server, called *Web*, which is named for its home directory, sys:\web. To create a new virtual server, you select Create Server from the Server menu, to display the Create Virtual Server dialog box, shown in Figure 15-14.

In creating a virtual server, you need only supply the name (by which the server is to be identified), and the location of the server's home directory. All other settings are located in the Server dialog box. You can activate or deactivate a specific virtual server by selecting it from the File menu (so a checkmark appears next to its name) and choosing Enable or Disable from the Server menu.

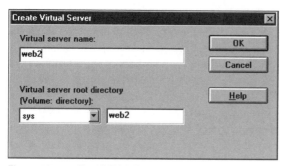

Figure 15-14: Novell Web Server can host multiple
virtual servers, which are separate, independently
configured Web sites.

CONFIGURING A VIRTUAL SERVER

Each virtual server has its own tabbed dialog box, which you open by selecting the
server from the File menu. The Server page of this dialog box (shown in
Figure 15-15) specifies the virtual server name and root directory you specified
during the creation of the server, and the following additional parameters:

◆ **Enable NDS browsing** – This parameter specifies whether Web clients
connecting to this server should be permitted to navigate through the NDS
tree, and access Web pages created for specific objects.

◆ **Enable document indexing and search** – This specifies whether the
contents of the virtual server's directories should be indexed,
automatically, by the NWS QuickSearch engine (so users can perform full-
text searches of their contents).

◆ **Directory containing HTML documents** – This directory specifies the
document root directory for the virtual server. It becomes the functional
root directory for a Web client connecting to this server. By default, the
value of this field is \docs, a subdirectory of the server root directory. You
can, however, specify the full path to another directory, or browse the file
system.

◆ **Directory containing log files** – This specifies the directory in which the
virtual server's access and error log files are stored. The default value is
\logs, a subdirectory of the server root directory. You can, however,
specify the full path to another directory, or browse the file system.

◆ **Enable user documents** – This parameter indicates whether users should
be able to publish their own home pages (by creating documents in a
subdirectory of the home directory, specified in their NDS user objects). It
enables users to control their own Web documents without providing
them access to other Web server files.

◆ **User subdirectory** – This subdirectory specifies the name of the subdirectory that should be created off of each user's home directory, to store their personal Web page contents. The default value is \public.www.

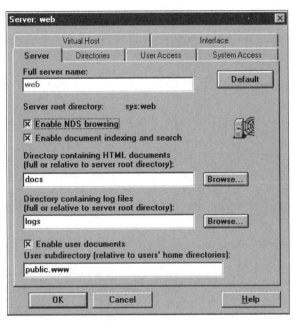

Figure 15-15: The Server page of the Server dialog box contains basic settings, such as the location of the Web site's content files and logs.

THE INTERFACE PAGE   On the Interface page of the Server dialog box (see Figure 15-16), you specify the port number and the IP address (or addresses that will be associated with the virtual server). The well-known port number for HTTP servers is 80. If you change this value, clients must specify the new port number when typing the URL for your site (for example, a port number of 121 would be notated as *http://www.mycorp.com:121*). Using a nonstandard port number is a simple and effective way to prevent casual access to your site – but it is not a strong security measure.

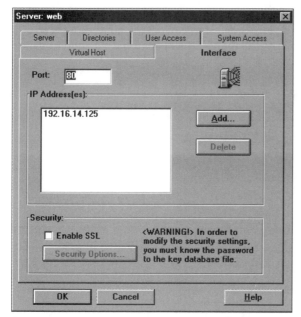

Figure 15-16: On the Interface page, you specify the socket(s) used to connect to the virtual server.

When running only a single virtual server, you can use an asterisk in the IP Address(es) field as a wildcard – providing access to the Web server from any valid server IP address. If you're running more than one virtual server, you must specify different IP addresses for each one. Web Manager displays an error message when you try to save a configuration that contains conflicting sockets. You can use the same IP address for two virtual servers, but you must specify a different port number for each.

You can specify multiple IP addresses for each virtual server, which is recommended when you intend to create virtual hosts that are differentiated by an IP address. All of the IP addresses you enter in the Interface page must be bound to the NetWare server's TCPIP.NLM module. You can bind multiple addresses to a single network adapter using the *add secondary IPaddress* command, from the server console. While the Web Manager program enables you to save configuration changes specifying nonexistent IP addresses, the Web server will generate an error and fail to restart until the IP addresses are changed or properly bound.

You enable the use of the Secure Socket Layer on the virtual server by filling the appropriate checkbox and configuring the Security Options for the server. Using SSL changes the default port number for the server to 443, and requires that you specify the location of a key database file you've created previously. This database contains the public/private key pairs used to encrypt the transmissions between the server and Web clients.

THE DIRECTORIES PAGE   On the simple Web site that is created by the NWS installation program, a single document directory is created for the default virtual server, called sys:\web\docs. When you select the Directories tab on the Server dialog box, you see \docs in the Existing Directories list, as shown in Figure 15-17. The entries in this list define the types of files found in the virtual server's content directories, and the NWS features enabled for each one. You can create any kind of subdirectory structure off of the \docs directory, and each of those subdirectories inherits the settings of its parent. If you want to specify different settings for a particular directory, however, you must add it to the list.

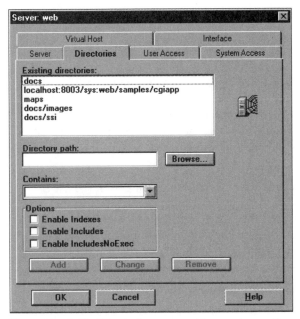

Figure 15-17: The Directories page enables you to specify the type of content found in a particular directory.

To add a directory to the list, browse to the desired directory in the Directory Path field, click the Add button, and configure the parameters for that directory. You can also change the settings of an existing directory by highlighting it, modifying its parameters, and clicking the Change button. Each entry in the Existing Directories list can be configured using the following parameters:

◆ **Contains** – This specifies the type of data files found in the directory. The selector provides the following settings:

  ◆ **Documents** – This parameter specifies that the directory contains the HTML, image, multimedia, and/or other types of content files making up the basic structure of a Web site.

  ◆ **Scripts** – The scripts parameter specifies that the directory contains scripts, which must be processed by an interpreter (such as Perl or NetBasic) at the server before any data is transmitted to a client.

  ◆ **Image Maps** – This specifies that the directory contains graphical images, which are used to create multiple hypertext links, by specifying sector coordinates that define a specific area of the image.

◆ **Enable Indexes** – Enable indexes specifies that the Web server should deliver an index of the directory's contents, as shown in Figure 15-18. These must go to clients requesting that directory in a URL when there is no default document file (such as INDEX.HTM).

◆ **Enable Includes** – This parameter specifies that you permit the use of server-side includes (SSIs) in documents found in the directory. Server-side includes are commands that are executed before an HTML file is transmitted to a client. Typically, they are used to insert customized information into the document, such as the current date and time, or page-counter data.

◆ **Enable IncludesNoExec** – This specifies that you permit the use of server-side includes, only when the files don't contain commands that execute applications. This prevents Web pages from executing SSI commands, such as #EXEC_CGI, which can be used to load an NLM program on the NetWare server.

The default virtual server contains directories intended for image maps, and server-side includes that are entered in the Existing Directories list and properly configured. You need only make changes to the list if you intend to create additional directories using these items.

THE USER ACCESS PAGE   Novell Web Server uses Novell Directory Services for its access-control mechanism. You can select user, or group, objects from anywhere in the NDS tree to provide authenticated access to each directory on your Web site. On the User Access page of the Server dialog box (see Figure 15-19), you can select any of the directories, previously configured on the Directories page, and select the users who will be permitted access.

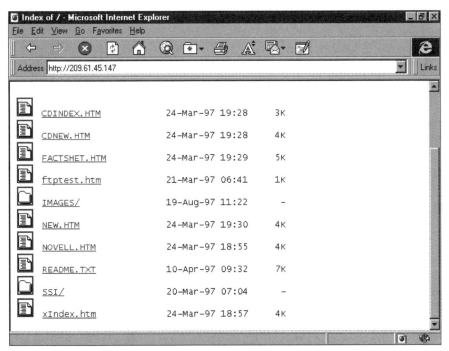

Figure 15-18: You can enable document indexing for specific directories from the Directories page of the Server dialog box.

NWS access control uses NDS on a read-only basis, and is not related to the NetWare file-system rights also using NDS. You can grant users access to a Web site directory, even when they have no NetWare-client rights to that directory.

By default, NWS doesn't list authorized users for each directory. Rather than denying users access to the Web site, however, this provides unauthenticated access to all users. When you add even one authorized user to the list, all clients must be authenticated before access is granted.

To grant user access, you must select a value for the Directory field and specify an NDS context in the Browse Network Users At field. This presents a list of the user and group objects in that context, on which you can highlight the desired objects and click the Add to Authorized Users List button. You can then specify another context to select users in other parts of the NDS tree. Enabling the All Valid Users option disables the individual selection mechanism, and grants all NDS users access to the site. They must authenticate with a valid NDS user account when connecting to the server, however.

When specifying a value for the Default NDS Context field, clients (whose user objects are found in that context) don't have to specify a fully distinguished NDS name when authenticating. Users in containers other than the default context must specify a full path. For example, a client authenticating with the user object

SmithJ.CorpNet must specify only the user name *SmithJ* when the default NDS context is set to *CorpNet*. The user *JonesD.Acctg.CorpNet*, however, must type the entire object name.

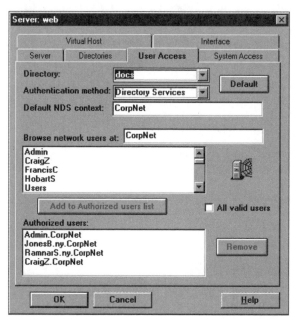

Figure 15-19: On the User Access page, you select to the NDS users, and groups, who will be granted access to each Web server directory.

THE SYSTEM ACCESS PAGE   Access to virtual server directories, based on the IP address or DNS name of the system on which the Web client is running, may also be restricted. On the System Access page of the Server dialog box (see Figure 15-20), you can select a directory and specify the full (or partial) name and address of a system that will be granted access. As with the User Access screen, a blank Authorized Systems list means that all systems are permitted to access the server.

The IP addresses and DNS names that you enter on this page can identify specific systems, entire networks, or domains. An IP address entry of 198.67.9 is interpreted as a network address. It provides access to any system on that class C network. In the same way, an entry with the domain name *mycorp.com* would grant access to any system in that domain.

System-access restrictions are independent of user-access restrictions. The two can be used together to ensure that authorized users are accessing the server from the appropriate systems. Restricting access by IP addresses and DNS names, however, is not a secure system. Once a potential intruder discovers the names or addresses that are permitted access, it is easy to reconfigure a system to use them.

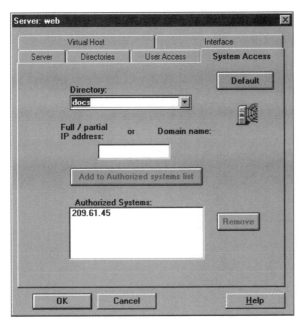

Figure 15-20: You can restrict access to a virtual server based on IP addresses and DNS names, as well as NDS objects.

THE VIRTUAL HOST PAGE   A virtual host is a separate Web site, within a virtual server, that has its own IP address or DNS name, and its own content and log files. A virtual host, however, uses the same configuration files as the virtual server. You can create virtual hosts to publish Web pages for different audiences on a single server, while making the Web sites appear (to users) as if they are completely separate. Virtual hosts are an excellent alternative to creating large, complex Web sites where users must traverse many links, or type long URLs, to access needed documents.

To create a virtual host, you click the Create button on the Virtual Host page, to display the dialog box shown in Figure 15-21. Here, you specify the name that will be used to identify the virtual host, the subdirectories (beneath the virtual server home directory where the site's content and log files are stored), and the DNS name or IP address that clients will use to access the site.

Any IP address you use for a virtual host must be bound to the TCPIP.NLM module, and configured for use by the virtual server. All addresses listed in the Interface page of the Server dialog box are available in the IP-address selector, on the virtual host page. You can also differentiate between virtual hosts by assigning them individual DNS names, instead of IP addresses. To do this, you must add all of the names for your virtual hosts to your primary DNS server, specifying the same IP address for each one. Then, all client requests arrive at the same interface, and the virtual server must forward them to the appropriate hosts.

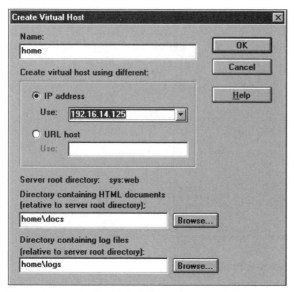

Figure 15-21: On the Virtual Host page, you can create individual Web sites on a single virtual server, with unique IP addresses or DNS names.

Simple TCP/IP Services

Windows NT includes a network service that provides support for several TCP/IP application-layer protocols that are used primarily for system debugging and benchmarking purposes. When you install the Simple TCP/IP Services module from the Network Control Panel, the NT system is able to respond to the following client requests:

◆ **Echo** – The Echo protocol returns the data transmitted in a request back to the source, without alteration. Echo traffic uses the well-known port number 7, with either TCP or UDP as a transport protocol.

◆ **Discard** – The Discard protocol consists of client requests that (when received by a server) are silently discarded. The protocol uses TCP or UDP transmissions, sent to port number 9.

◆ **Character Generator** – The Character Generator protocol consists of client requests that cause a server to return responses containing random ASCII characters. Using port number 19, a TCP request causes the server to return a continuous stream of characters until the client terminates the connection. UDP requests, on the same port, cause the server to generate a single datagram in response. This contains a random number of characters between 0 and 512.

◆ **Daytime** – The Daytime protocol returns the current date and time, as maintained by the server, in response to TCP- or UDP-based client requests, using port number 13.

◆ **Quote of the Day** – The Quote of the Day protocol returns a short text message (less than 512 characters) in response to TCP- or UDP-client requests, using port number 17.

Summary

Both Windows NT and IntranetWare include a collection of TCP/IP applications you can use to access, and host, intranet or Internet services.

In this chapter, you learned:

◆ How to use the Microsoft FTP client to connect to an FTP server

◆ How to host an FTP site on a NetWare server

◆ How to use the Microsoft Internet Information Server and Peer Web Services to host World Wide Web and FTP sites

◆ How to use the Novell Web Server to host Web sites on a NetWare server

Chapter 16

Protocol Analysis

IN THIS CHAPTER

One of the best ways to learn about the TCP/IP protocols, and their communications processes, is to examine the packets transmitted over a network. You can study networking concepts on paper (in the abstract), but when you see a network in action – watching the data pass through the "pipe" – all of the disparate processes come together into a unified whole. You begin to understand how the various protocols fit together into a system that is more than a conglomeration of separate units.

This chapter illustrates some of the TCP/IP-communications processes, described in the book, by looking at live network data. This chapter also examines some of the tools and techniques you can use to analyze the traffic being transmitted over your network, including the following:

♦ Using traffic-monitoring tools to measure the network bandwidth load

♦ Using protocol monitors to capture TCP/IP packets

♦ Examining specific protocol transactions

♦ Improving network performance by modifying protocol behavior

Protocol analysis was once the province of specialized consultants with complex, expensive tools. Now it is possible to analyze your network, yourself, with relative ease. In addition to being a useful learning method, protocol analysis is one of the most powerful troubleshooting tools available to network administrators.

Network Monitoring Tools

A network traffic analysis can be performed on many levels – each of which has its own tools and its own uses. Analyzing traffic involves the use of a software, or hardware, product that scans the data packets as they travel through the network. It then displays information about those packets to the user. Generally, traffic information can be compiled at three levels of detail. The information may be in one of the following forms:

♦ Real-time statistics concerning the total number of packets, using specific protocols, that transmitted during a specific time period

♦ Compiled lists showing the sequence of packets transmitted over the network, in the order in which they occurred

♦ Captured packets that can be opened to display their contents

Traffic Monitors

The simplest form of a traffic-analysis tool is a software module that tracks the total number of packets generated by specific protocols as they are transmitted over the network. Both IntranetWare and Windows NT include utilities that track TCP/IP traffic in this manner. The TCPCON.NLM program runs on a NetWare server and tracks the packet totals for the major TCP/IP protocols, automatically. Windows NT's Performance Monitor application (see Figure 16-1) is a monitoring utility. You can configure this to generate a graph of highly specific statistics concerning many different aspects of system performance, including a wide range of networking protocols.

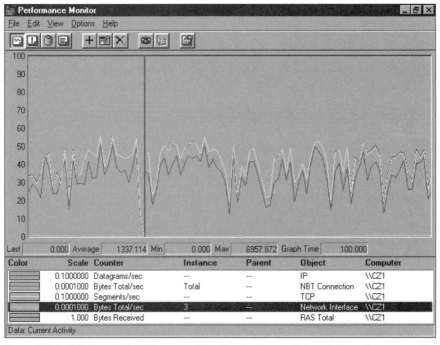

Figure 16-1: Windows NT's Performance Monitor displays real-time information concerning many different network functions.

For more information on viewing protocol statistics using TCPCON.NLM, see Chapter 14, "TCP/IP Utilities."

Both of these tools break down the packet totals for specific protocols to display more specific information (such as the number of errors generated by a protocol). For example, knowing the total number of ICMP messages transmitted over your network is not particularly enlightening, but a program that displays the number of packets containing each ICMP message type is very useful. With this information, you can begin to diagnose routing or flow-control problems that may be affecting your network's performance.

On a network using multiple network-layer protocols, such as a mixed NetWare and Windows NT network, a traffic-monitoring program can also help you track the amount of traffic generated by each OS.

Protocol Analyzers

Traffic analysis is made possible by a more complex tool, called a *protocol analyzer*. A protocol analyzer is a hardware, or software, device that connects to the network and intercepts packets (capturing them to a buffer where they can be examined). In the past, it was necessary to purchase proprietary hardware for this task, or install software that used dedicated drivers for a computer's network adapter. Now, it's possible to capture and analyze network traffic using a standard Windows application.

Both Novell and Microsoft have products that can perform a network-protocol analysis. Novell's LANalyzer is a stand-alone Windows application that performs these functions, while their ManageWise package also includes protocol-analysis features. Microsoft's Systems Management Server (SMS) product includes Network Monitor, a protocol analyzer that ships with the Windows NT Server 4.0 product, in a limited version.

A number of third-party products on the market are, at least, equal to the Novell and Microsoft applications. For example, NetXRay, a product of Network General Corporation, was used to create the screen captures for this chapter.

A trial version of NetXRay is provided on the CD-ROM, included in the back of this book.

PROMISCUOUS MODE

To examine all traffic transmitted on a network, using a standard PC and network interface card, protocol analyzers use a feature, called *promiscuous mode* (which is built into most of today's network adapters). Normally, a LAN adapter scans each packet as it travels through the network, checking the hardware address in the data link-layer protocol header. If this address matches that of the adapter (or is a broadcast address), the packet is passed to the adapter driver, where it begins its trip upwards through the system's network-protocol stack.

If the packet contains an alien address, it is discarded by the network interface hardware and never processed by the system. Putting an adapter into promiscuous mode, however, causes it to accept all of the packets it receives over the network. Once all packets are received, it passes them to the protocol stack – regardless of the hardware address. The packets, themselves, are stored by the analyzer in a buffer on the system's hard disk – a process known as a *capture*. Once the analyzer captures a sampling of the network traffic, it examines the contents of each packet and compiles a chronological display of the network's activity (see Figure 16-2).

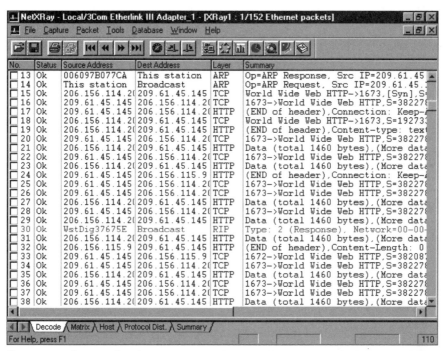

Figure 16-2: A protocol analyzer captures packets traveling over a network and examines their properties.

Depending on the amount of traffic on your network, putting a network adapter into promiscuous mode can have a deleterious effect on a system's network performance. Because the packets normally discarded by the network adapter hardware are now being passed to the system's protocol stack, main system resources are required to process them. On a busy network, your system processor may be dealing with many times its normal number of packets — causing a noticeable drop in performance.

Typically, this display shows the source and destination of each packet, as well as its primary function, in terms of the protocols used to create it. A protocol analyzer not only shows the raw data within network packets, it interprets the data to display the contents in a friendly fashion. The program, therefore, examines all of the protocol headers with a packet and determines which protocol defines the packet's function. For example, a request message generated by a Web browser, and transmitted to a server, appears in the summary display as an HTTP packet (even though it can be called a TCP, IP, or Ethernet packet, and be correct).

With this display, you can trace the exchanges involved in a particular client/server transaction. Such exchanges include the establishment of a TCP connection, the transmission of application-layer requests and replies, and the subsequent closing of the connection. You can view all of the other traffic on your network, as well (including maintenance packets generated by RIP or other routing protocols, ICMP messages, and the traffic generated by other protocol suites, such as IPX). Examining packet exchanges in this manner is one of the best ways to learn about network communications, in general – and about your network's performance, in particular.

PACKET ANALYSIS

From the main packet-capture display, you can select any single packet and display its contents, including all protocol headers and the data carried as the packet's payload (see Figure 16-3). Any program can display the raw data captured from a network, but a good protocol analyzer interprets the data according to standardized message formats for the individual protocols. The result is a visual demonstration of the protocol-encapsulation process, and the method by which a system demultiplexes incoming packets.

The analyzer opens a captured Ethernet II packet, for example, and determines that it's carrying IP data by the value of 0800 in the header's Ethertype field. The program then applies the IP-message format to the Ethernet data field and parses out the various fields of the IP datagram. From the value of the IP header's protocol field, the analyzer determines that the datagram is carrying TCP data. The port number field, of the TCP header, indicates that an HTTP message is the ultimate payload of the packet. Finally, you can see that the HTTP message is a response to a GET request, and can view the contents of the HTML file being transmitted to the client.

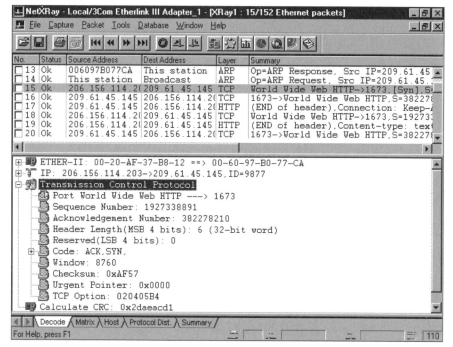

Figure 16-3: Protocol analyzers display a data packet's contents using protocol data-formatting information that is programmed into the application.

A program's capability to interpret the packet contents, in this manner, comes from knowing the message formats used by networking protocols. A good protocol analyzer includes a comprehensive collection of protocol formats, and some means by which you can add formats as new protocols come into use. Most PC-based analysis products support the TCP/IP- and IPX-protocol suites, but if you're using the network to connect to mini- or mainframe computers with other protocols, you should be sure that a product supports those protocols.

You may also encounter products that are slightly out-of-date, and do not support the latest protocols, such as the Point-to-Point Tunneling Protocol (PPTP). This doesn't mean that the program is incapable of processing packets using that protocol. Instead, it displays the data in its raw form, leaving you to interpret the message or obtain an update from the manufacturer.

PACKET FILTERS

Once you get past the novelty of viewing network traffic in its interpreted form, you realize that you are faced with an embarrassment of riches. A protocol analyzer is capable of displaying so much information, you may find it difficult to examine a particular transaction or protocol. For example, you may want to track the progress of a single transaction between a Web client and a server, but the program has captured packets from several different systems on your network – all of which are using browsers to surf the Web at the same time.

What you see in the analyzer's main screen is a large number of TCP-control messages and HTTP requests and replies, all mixed together. This is an excellent illustration of the way communications from multiple computers are multiplexed onto a single, baseband network medium. Of course, this observation does not help you to accomplish your task. To isolate the packets you want to examine, protocol analyzers include filters. You can use these to capture, or display, only the packets you want (such as those containing a specific protocol, or those transmitted by specific IP addresses).

Most analyzers have capture filters, as well as packet filters. *Capture filters* control the type of data copied from the network. This is useful on a busy network, where capturing the entire bandwidth can accumulate many megabytes of data in just a few seconds. Protocol analyzers are not just monitoring the packets as they pass by, they are capturing them – data and all. Typically, analyzers have a buffer with a configurable size. This enables you to prevent the program from filling up your entire hard drive, but you can also isolate the exact data you need by filtering out the unnecessary packets.

Display filters operate in the same way as capture filters, except they control the buffered data shown in the chronological display. This way, you can capture all of the network bandwidth, and then examine specific aspects of the data using one filter at a time.

Packet filters are based on protocols, system addresses, or a combination of the two (usually). You can, for example, filter out all packets, except those containing a specific hardware or IP address as their source or destination, and which carry the IP protocol. Most programs enable you to build complex filters using Boolean operators to specify multiple addresses and/or protocols, and save them for later use.

MOBILE ANALYSIS

When you are administering or troubleshooting an internetwork, the location of the system-capturing network data is critical to the analysis. You may have to capture data on different network segments at different times (a process that is handled by various analyzer programs in different ways). One method is to install the analyzer software on a system connected to each network segment, as needed. This can be inconvenient, because of the multiple installations required, and because the licensing terms of the product may force you to purchase several copies of the software.

A more convenient method is to equip a notebook, or other portable system, with the analyzer software and connect it to the network to be monitored. This method is useful for consultants who may be working at many different sites. Most analyzer programs enable you to capture the data and save it to a file. That way, you can perform the actual analysis at a later time. Only a single software license is required for this method, and your custom packet filters (and other software configuration settings) are available at all times.

A third method is used by Microsoft's Network Monitor product, which employs remote agents that capture data anywhere on the network. Both Windows NT and Windows 95 include a Network Monitor Agent service that functions as a remote capture point for a Network Monitor installation, elsewhere on the network. The system running Network Monitor can connect to any system, with the agent running, and capture the packets being transmitted on that network segment.

PACKET GENERATION

Most protocol analyzers include a packet generator that can create network traffic. Packet generators have two basic purposes: to create large amounts of traffic to stress test a network, and to generate individual packets that are specifically configured for transmission to a particular application, to test its response. Packets generated in this way are consistent and predictable. This makes them better suited for comparisons of hardware or software products than the randomly generated traffic resulting from normal network use.

Using the Windows NT Performance Monitor

Windows NT's Performance Monitor application is a general-purpose tool that displays statistics about a wide range of system functions in a numerical report, or a real-time graph. By selecting criteria (called *counters*) from system-component categories, you create a customized display. This charts the actual activities of the Windows NT computer, as they happen. Installing various NT services and third-party applications adds new categories to the application – ones that are specific to the functions of those services or applications. The Microsoft TCP/IP stack adds the capability to track a system's incoming and outgoing traffic, in great detail.

Creating a Graph

By launching the Performance Monitor application from the Start Menu's Programs/Administrative Tools (Common) group, you see a blank graph. To use the program, you must select one or more counters to add to the display. Selecting Add to Chart from the Edit menu, or clicking the Add Counter button on the toolbar, produces the dialog box shown in Figure 16-4.

Performance Monitor can display information about the local computer, or other Windows NT systems on your network, depending on the system name specified in the Computer field (using a UNC name). You can create a mixed graph of counters from different computers. Doing so enables you to compare the same statistic on different machines, or monitor various attributes of NT systems all over your network.

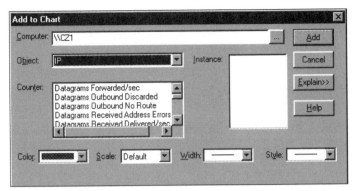

Figure 16-4: From the Add to Chart dialog box, you select the statistics that are displayed by the Performance Monitor program.

 If you prefer to view the system information in numerical form, click the Report button before adding counters. The object categories and the process of selecting counters is the same, except you don't need to consider line colors and styles. The Report display is easier to read than the chart, typically, but it shows only the current value of each counter (rather than the relative values over a period of time). The chart and the report configurations are maintained separately, so you can choose different counters that are better suited to each display medium.

Selecting Object Categories

The Object field in the Add to Chart dialog box contains a list of categories, from which you can choose specific counters. Performance Monitor is by no means limited to the display of networking information; you can track the activities of your system's processor(s), memory performance, memory-caching activities, and other functions. The majority of the object categories, however, are devoted to networking.

Installing network support on the system adds the following object categories:

◆ **Browser** – This provides counters that track the Windows NT Browser service, and network communications, involved in selecting a master browser.

◆ **Network Interface** – This provides counters that track the incoming and outgoing data link-layer packets that pass through the selected network interface adapter (regardless of the upper-layer protocols carried within them), as well as the number of detected errors and discarded packets.

♦ **Server** – The server provides counters that track the system's file-sharing activities on the Windows network, including the numbers of bytes and files sent and received, session logons, and detected errors.

♦ **Redirector** – The redirector provides counters that track the incoming and outgoing packets processed by the Windows NT Redirector (the file system driver that enables Windows network computers to share files and printers).

Installing TCP/IP on the system adds these object categories:

♦ **IP** – IP provides counters that track the incoming and outgoing IP-datagram traffic for the entire system (regardless of the upper-layer protocols carried within them), as well as statistics concerning IP-routing and datagram fragmentation.

♦ **ICMP** – ICMP provides counters that track the total incoming and outgoing ICMP messages for the entire system, and offers a breakdown of the individual message types.

♦ **TCP** – TCP provides counters that track the incoming and outgoing TCP traffic for the entire system, in terms of connections and individual segments.

♦ **UDP** – UDP provides counters that track the incoming and outgoing UDP datagrams for the entire system.

♦ **NBT Connection** – This provides counters that track the number of bytes sent, and received, on each of the systems active NetBIOS over TCP/IP (NBT) connections.

Installing the Internet Information Server or the Peer Web Services adds the following:

♦ **Internet Information Services Global** – This provides counters that track the requests processed by the Internet Information Server services or Peer Web Services, as well as the performance of the IIS/PWS cache.

♦ **FTP Server** – This provides counters that track the usage of the Internet Information Server or Peer Web Services FTP service, in terms of bytes sent and received, numbers of files, connections, and user names.

♦ **HTTP Service** – This provides counters that track the usage of the Internet Information Server or Peer Web Services HTTP (World Wide Web) service, in terms of bytes sent and received, numbers of files, connection types, and user names.

Installing RAS or Dial-Up Networking adds the following categories:

◆ **RAS Port** – This provides counters that track the incoming and outgoing traffic passing through the selected RAS port, in terms of bytes and frames, and the number of errors.

◆ **RAS Total** – **This** provides counters that track the same statistics as the RAS port object for all of the system's RAS ports combined.

Installing the Network Monitor Agent adds the following category:

◆ **Network Segment** – This provides counters that track the total traffic for the local network segment, including the percentage of bandwidth consumed by broadcast and multicast transmissions, and the percentage of the available network bandwidth in use.

Adding Counters

When you select a value for the Object field, a list appears in the Counter field. From this, you can select the statistics to be added to the display. If you select an object, like Network Interface (of which there can be two or more installed in the system), you can choose one object from the Instance listing. This enables you to select counters for each object, separately.

By clicking the Explain button, you can expand the dialog box to display a brief summary of each counter's function. For each counter you select, you must configure the parameters with which it will be graphed. You can select the Color, Width, and Style of the line representing that particular counter, and the Scale by which it should appear on the chart. Because you can add many different counters to the graphical display, being able to distinguish the lines is important.

Depending on your monitor's size, and the capabilities of its video adapter, you may want to modify the program's display defaults. Each counter you add to the chart appears in a legend at the bottom of the main window. This functions as a reference to the various lines on the graph and displays the current values of your selected counters, in numerical form. Once you configure the counters you want to appear on the chart, click the Done button and the graph begins to operate. A vertical red line ticks off the charting interval, which is one second, by default.

Creating an Effective Chart

Using the chart window of the Performance Monitor program, effectively, is a process of trial and error. Naturally, you'll want to select a large number of counters, and display as much information about the system as possible. Too many counters, however, make the chart into a confusing hash of crisscrossed lines. It is best to select a few, related counters to create a coherent display. You can then save the settings in a configuration file (by selecting Save Chart Settings from the File menu) for quick recall later. For the display of a large number of counters, the report window (shown in Figure 16-5) is more practical.

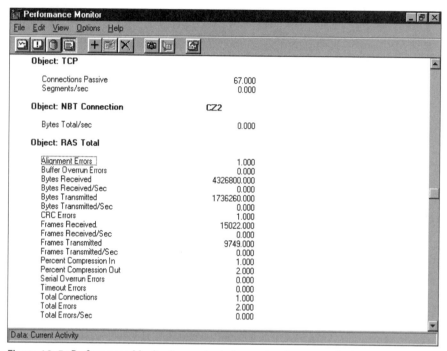

Figure 16-5: Performance Monitor's report window makes it easy to display statistics provided by a large number of counters, on one screen.

The default scale of the graph often makes it difficult to view statistics with any accuracy. By clicking the Options button, or selecting Chart from the Options menu, you display the Chart Options dialog box (see Figure 16-6). From here, you can modify the graph's appearance by selecting the scale for the vertical axis, adding grid lines, altering the data-upgrade interval, or changing the entire display from a line graph to a histogram (a vertical bar graph).

Counters are charted by multiplying the statistical values by a scaling factor you can modify when selecting each counter. This factor is also displayed in the legend beneath the chart. This scaling factor makes it possible to display statistics, using different units of measurement, on a single graph.

A counter that tracks the total number of bytes, transmitted over a network interface, usually yields numbers much larger than a counter tracking the number of active FTP sessions. Adjusting the scale of the graph to display one counter, accurately, would cause the other to be off the scale, or too small to register. The default scaling factor, therefore, is a variable by which the value of each counter is multiplied (to make it comparable with the other counters). If the default scaling factors for certain counters are not appropriate for your system, you can modify them individually from the Add to Chart dialog box.

When using a scaling factor, the graph's vertical-axis values don't necessarily relate to the unit of measure used for each counter. If you want to read the exact value for a particular counter, look at the legend (which displays actual, unscaled statistics), or view the counter in the report window.

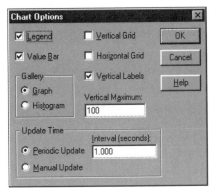

Figure 16-6: The Chart Options dialog box enables you to modify the appearance of the display to suit your hardware, and your taste.

Logging Performance Monitor Information

Apart from displaying statistics in real time, you can use Performance Monitor to create statistical reports and save counter information to log files for later study. To do this, you add counters to the report, or logs, window in the same way as in the chart window. Performance Monitor is also capable of generating alerts, which are triggered when a counter exceeds a predetermined value.

Using NetXRay

NetXRay is a protocol-analyzer and network-monitor program with many features. Its basic packet capture, filtering, monitoring, and decoding functions operate much like those of other, similar utilities. The following sections discuss the procedures for monitoring and analyzing network traffic with NetXRay. You can, however, perform most of the same functions with Microsoft's Network Monitor, Novell's LANalyzer, or other third-party products.

Monitoring Network Traffic

The NetXRay interface is composed of several, different-sized windows that you can display, simultaneously. When you launch the program, you see the Dashboard window, as shown in Figure 16-7. This continuously displays the amount of traffic on your network in packets per second, the percentage of the network bandwidth being used, and errors per second.

Figure 16-7: NetXRay's Dashboard window provides indicators of network-traffic levels at a glance.

For more network-traffic information, click the Host Table button, or select Host Table from the Tools menu. This displays a breakdown of the network's input and output traffic by individual system, using either IP, IPX, or MAC (hardware) addresses (see Figure 16-8).

The Host Table window has other display options, which are accessed from the window's own button bar. These include a Detail window that displays the network traffic for each system, broken down by protocol (see Figure 16-9). You can also display bar and pie charts that list the top 10 systems on the network. These are gauged by the total bytes transferred, total packets transferred, or other criteria you can control from the Host Table Properties dialog box.

NetXRay includes many other traffic-display tools, including the Matrix window, which uses a circular mesh to illustrate which systems are communicating (see Figure 16-10). The Protocol Distribution window breaks down the total traffic for the network segments into the individual protocols. This application also supports other protocol suites, such as IPX, AppleTalk, and SNA, with the same detail as TCP/IP.

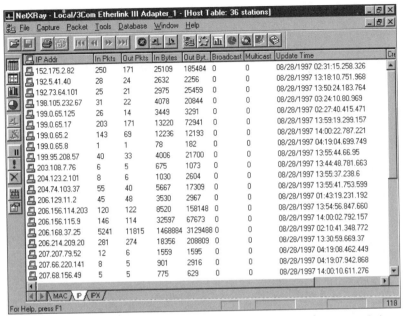

Figure 16-8: The Host Table window displays the network input/output statistics for each system on the network segment— in packets and bytes.

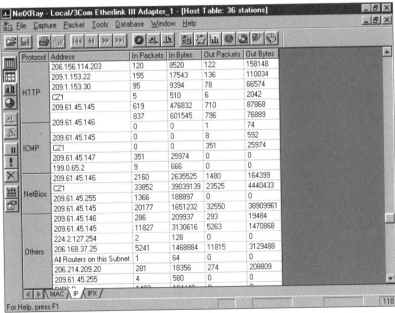

Figure 16-9: The Detail Host Table window displays the amount of input/output traffic experienced by each system for the various TCP/IP protocols.

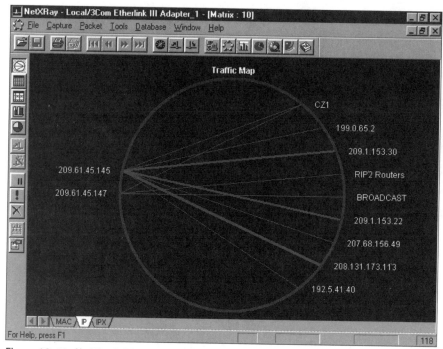

Figure 16-10: NetXRay's Matrix window displays a logical representation of the IP communications between a network's systems.

Capturing Packets

NetXRay's network-monitoring functions operate in real time by continuously compiling traffic statistics. To examine the packets in depth, you must capture a sampling of network traffic to a disk buffer, where it can be decoded and examined offline. The two gauges of the Capture window (see Figure 16-11) appear when you load the NetXRay program. By default, the program captures all of the packets that it detects on the network to a buffer, with a maximum size of 256K. The default buffer fills quickly when you capture all of the traffic carried by an active network. You can modify this behavior by applying capture filters and/or creating a larger buffer from the Filter Settings dialog box, which is accessed from the Capture menu or by clicking the Capture Setting button.

The control buttons on the Capture window operate like a tape recorder, or a VCR. When you click the start button, NetXRay begins copying each packet (entering the selected network interface) to the buffer file on your system's hard drive. The gauges display the number of packets captured and the percentage of filled buffer. By default, the data capture stops automatically when the buffer is filled. You can also configure the buffer to "wrap," (that is, purge) the oldest data to make room for new data when the buffer is full.

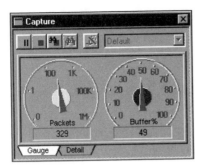

Figure 16-11: From NetXRay's Capture window, you can start, stop, and pause the data-capture process.

Viewing Captured Data

When there is data in the buffer, you can click the Detail tab of the Capture window to display numerical statistics on the current capture. This includes the elapsed time, and number of packets that were excluded from the capture by the application of a filter. When you collect enough data, click the Stop button or the Stop and View button to display the packets in the buffer, as shown in Figure 16-12.

The Packet Viewer window is the heart of NetXRay's protocol-analysis capability. The viewer contains three adjustable-sized panes. The topmost pane displays a one-line summary of each packet in the capture buffer, with the following information:

◆ **Number** – The number field specifies the sequence number of the packet in the capture buffer. When you apply a display filter to remove packets from the summary pane, the sequence numbers remain intact, enabling you to see the gaps where packets were omitted. The checkboxes are used to mark multiple packets for group operations.

◆ **Status** – This field contains the value *[T]* if the packet has triggered the commencement of a data capture by matching an event filter. When you use an NDIS driver (supplied by NetXRay) on an Ethernet network, this field displays the error status of the frame. It uses one of the following values: OK (no error), CRC, Runt, Fragment, Jabber, Oversize, Alignment.

◆ **Source address** – This field specifies the address of the system where the packet originated. Depending on the protocol, the value may be expressed as an IP address, a hardware address, a hardware address with a manufacturer name, or a symbolic name (as found in the program's Address Book).

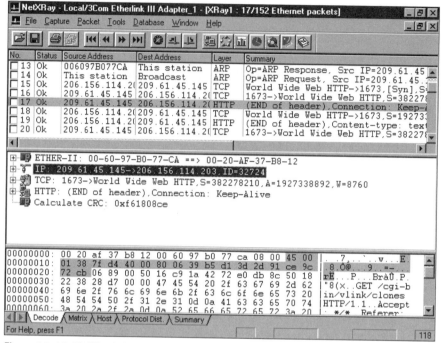

Figure 16-12: NetXRay's Packet Viewer window displays all of the data captured in the buffer, in both summary and detail form.

◆ **Destination address** – This field specifies the address of the packet's ultimate destination, using the same format as the source-address field.

◆ **Layer** – The layer field specifies the highest-layer protocol identified in the packet, and the color of the summary line for this packet.

◆ **Summary** – This field contains a brief summary of the packet's primary function, based on the protocol specified in the layer field. The format varies, depending on the protocol and the type of message contained in the packet.

◆ **Length** – The length field specifies the overall size of the packet, in bytes, minus the 4-byte CRC field applied as part of the data link-layer frame.

◆ **Relative Time** – This field specifies the amount of time elapsed since the beginning of the capture session (in hours, minutes, seconds, and milliseconds).

◆ **Delta Time** – This field specifies the amount of time elapsed between the end of the previous packet's capture and the end of the current packet's capture (in seconds, milliseconds, and nanoseconds).

◆ **Absolute Time** – The absolute time field specifies the date and time the packet was captured, according to the computer's clock.

The middle pane of the Packet Viewer window, called the Detail pane, contains an expandable, decoded version of the protocol headers within the packet. In its collapsed form, the pane shows a list of headers representing all protocols in the packet, in the order in which they are found. Figure 16-12 displays the contents of a Web server reply packet sent to a client, in response to a request. The Detail pane contains headers for the Ethernet II, IP, TCP protocols, followed by the HTTP data, and the CRC trailer that is part of the Ethernet frame.

When a header is collapsed, the Detail pane displays a summary of its contents. You can expand any, or all, of the headers to display the values of the individual fields, as shown in Figure 16-13. Wherever possible, the analyzer decodes the header information. This displays the functions of flag bits, for example, and specifies that the destination port in a TCP header identifies the HTTP service – and not simply the value 80.

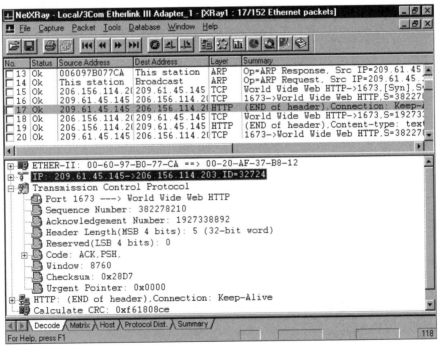

Figure 16-13: The Packet Viewer's Detail pane displays a decoded version of the selected packet's complete header information.

When you view the contents of multiple packets containing the same protocol, NetXRay retains the display characteristics you set in the Detail pane. For example, by expanding the TCP header of a given packet to examine the status of its flag bits, you can select the next packet in the Summary pane to expand its TCP header and highlight the flags. This makes it easy to examine a particular aspect of your captured packets without constantly repeating the same mouse movements for each packet.

The bottom pane of the Packet Viewer is the Hex pane, which displays the selected packet's raw data, in hexadecimal and ASCII form. When you select an element of a header in the Detail pane, the corresponding bits are highlighted in the Hex pane, as shown in Figure 16-14.

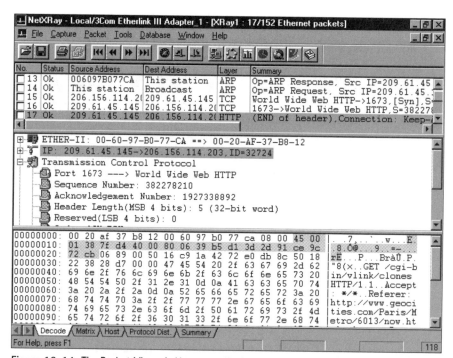

Figure 16-14: The Packet Viewer's Hex pane displays the raw data in a selected packet.

Creating Filters

On a busy network, even a brief data-capture session can add hundreds of packets to the buffer, making it difficult to examine a specific transaction or protocol. Rather than scroll through a Detail pane containing hundreds of entries, you can apply filters that restrict the type of data captured to the buffer or displayed in the Detail pane. The dialog boxes that control NetXRay's capture filters and display filters operate in the same way. They differ only in whether the filter is applied during the data-capture process or afterwards (when the captured data is displayed in the Packet Viewer).

Choosing which type of filter to apply depends on the amount of traffic on your network, and the purpose of your protocol analysis. A consultant visiting a site to perform a general assessment of a network's efficiency might capture an unfiltered traffic sampling. He or she can then take it offsite, where it can be examined later using display filters to isolate specific elements. If you are using NetXRay to learn the various TCP/IP communication processes that occur on a mixed Windows NT and Novell internetwork, applying a capture filter omits the IPX traffic generated by your NetWare systems from the data buffer.

Nearly every protocol analyzer can filter buffered data based on the addresses of network systems, and on the protocols carried in the network packets. Whether you select Capture Filter Setting from NetXRay's Capture menu, or Edit Display Filter from the Packet menu, you see a dialog box like that shown in Figure 16-15.

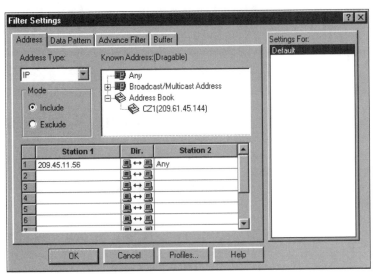

Figure 16-15: In the Filter Settings dialog box, you select the addresses and protocols to view in the Packet Viewer window.

ADDRESS FILTERS

The Address page of the Filter Settings dialog box enables you to select packets based on the source, and destination, addresses specified in the protocol headers. This way, you can opt to display or capture only the traffic involving specific systems and capture incoming or outgoing traffic – or both. By adjusting the setting of the Address Type field, you can select the hardware addresses of systems on the network (as gathered in NetXRay's host table by its network monitoring feature) or by IP addresses. The Mode selector enables you to include or exclude the selected addresses. NetXRay also includes an address book, in which you can record the hardware and IP addresses of network systems, and annotate them with friendly names (such as Windows NT NetBIOS names or NetWare server names) and comments.

To create an address filter, you select a system in the Known Address list and drag it to an open space in the filter listings, at the bottom of the dialog box. You can also select a broadcast address, one of the well-known multicast addresses listed under the Broadcast/Multicast Address heading, or the Any address specifier. By specifying system addresses in both the Station 1 and Station 2 columns, you create a filter that limits the data to only the packets exchanged between those two systems.

By clicking the direction indicator between the two columns, you can select only the data traveling in one direction. Using the Any specifier in one of the columns enables you to create a filter limiting the data to packet exchanges between the selected system and all other systems on the network. You can specify up to 10 address filters in the dialog box, which enables you to create complex configurations displaying only the data you need.

PROTOCOL FILTERS

By selecting the Advance Filter page in the Filter Settings dialog box (shown in Figure 16-16), you can create filters that capture or display particular protocols, only. The default filter settings capture all of the data transmitted on the network. NetXRay supports a wide array of network-layer protocols, from which you select those you want to capture by filling the appropriate checkboxes. When you select a single checkbox in the protocol list, only the packets containing the selected protocols are captured or displayed.

The protocols are listed in an expandable display, according to the layer where they appear within a packet. For example, expanding the IP-protocol entry displays all other protocols that can be carried within IP datagrams. These include the transport-layer protocols TCP and UDP, and other protocols that are carried directly by IP, such as ICMP- and the TCP/IP-routing protocols. Expanding the TCP entry displays, in turn, the application protocols that use TCP for their transport services.

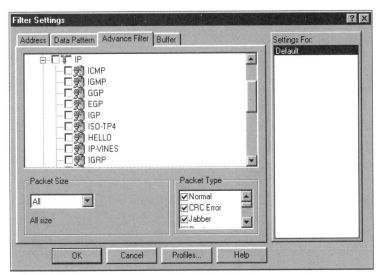

Figure 16-16: On the Advance Filter page, you select the protocols you want to be captured or displayed.

When you select address and protocol filters at the same time, packets must satisfy the restrictions of both filters to be captured or displayed. From this same dialog box, you can also create filters for packets of a particular size (or for the various Ethernet packet types). On the Data Pattern page, NetXRay provides the capability to create filters based on specific data patterns within a packet. You can specify any series of bits and create a filter to capture, or display, only the packets containing those bits. With data-pattern filters, you can capture packets containing protocols that aren't supported by NetXRay. You do this by specifying bits that are unique to that protocol (such as a well-known port number), or even bits in the packet's data field.

SAVING FILTER PROFILES

The many filter options provided by NetXRay enable you to create complex and highly specific configurations – but they can take time to reproduce. The program, therefore, enables you to save filter configurations as named profiles that you can select from the Settings For list in the Filter Settings dialog box. If, for example, you want to monitor the World Wide Web activity of a particular user on a regular basis, you begin by creating a profile. This filters out all network traffic except for the HTTP packets traveling to and from that user's IP address. Once you have created the profile, capturing and examining that user's Web traffic is a quick and simple operation. To create a profile, you click the Profile button in the Filter Settings dialog box and then the New button. In the New Capture Profile dialog box, you specify a name for the new profile (Figure 16-17).

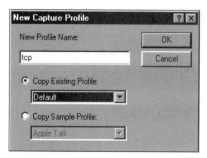

Figure 16-17: You can use capture
profiles to store filter configurations
for easy retrieval.

You can create a new profile from scratch, but often it is easier to modify an
existing profile. By clicking the Copy Existing Profile or Copy Sample Profile radio
button, you can choose from your own profiles, or a preconfigured collection supplied with the software. Once you have created a profile, it appears in the Settings
For list. After selecting it from the list, you can modify the filter settings as needed
and click the OK button to save the changes to the profile.

Analyzing TCP/IP Transactions

Previous chapters examine many of the different communication processes that
use the TCP/IP protocols. In the following sections, you will see the protocols in
action, using live network data. With NetXRay or another protocol analyzer, you
can examine your own network traffic to troubleshoot problems and learn more
about LAN communications.

Examining Implementations of Protocol Standards

Empirical knowledge is the best way to learn how networking products actually
function. Despite the effort that goes into developing protocol standards, such as
TCP/IP, some manufacturers exercise a great deal of freedom in their interpretations
(and implementations) of these standards. It can also be difficult to obtain detailed,
technical documentation regarding the decisions made while developing a networking
product. By exploring the packets that are transmitted over the network, you can see
how closely an implementation resembles the standard on which it is based.

TCP Connections

Because TCP is a connection-oriented protocol that provides reliable service, continual exchanges of control packets are made throughout the life of the connection between two systems. TCP always carries data generated by an application-layer service. The control packets that establish and maintain the connection, however, contain no application data (and are identified as TCP packets in a protocol analyzer).

PACKET ONE

The data capture shown in Figure 16-18 contains a streamlined version of the packets generated by a Web browser (when requesting a URL from a Web server). Before any HTTP data is transmitted, the source system must establish a TCP connection with the Web server. By examining the protocol headers of the first packet, you can see details of the TCP/IP implementation on the client system.

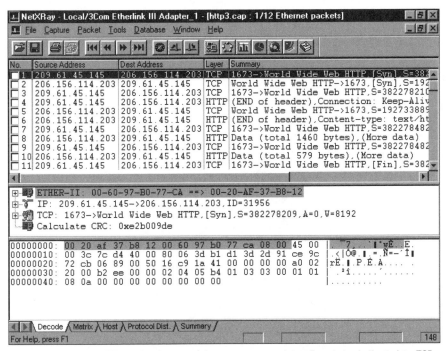

Figure 16-18: An HTTP session between two systems consists of packets dedicated to TCP control functions, as well as the HTTP exchanges.

THE ETHERNET II HEADER

```
Ethernet Version II
        Address: 00-60-97-B0-77-CA -->00-20-AF-37-B8-12
        Ethernet II Protocol Type: IP
```

The client is using the Ethernet II frame on the local network, which has a field specifying the protocol carried within the frame. The other alternative for a TCP/IP system on an Ethernet network is the IEEE 802.3 frame with the additional *Logical Link Control* (LLC) and *Sub-Network Access Protocol* (SNAP) elements. These would show up in the analyzer as two additional headers. The SNAP header contains the code identifying the network-layer protocol, which is required for TCP/IP communications.

Because the Web server being contacted by the client is located on another network (on the Internet), the destination address in the Ethernet II header is not that of the Web server, itself. Rather, it is the address of the router on the local network that provides access to the network where the Web server is located. This Ethernet frame is stripped off by that router, and another data link-layer frame is applied for the trip across the next network. An IP datagram may have many different data-link frames applied and removed during the course of the journey to its destination.

THE IP HEADER

```
Internet Protocol
        Version(MSB 4 bits): 4
        Header length(LSB 4 bits): 5 (32-bit word)
        Service type: 0x00
                000. .... = 0 - Routine
                ...0 .... = Normal delay
                .... 0... = Normal throughput
                .... .0.. = Normal reliability
        Total length: 60 (Octets)
        Fragment ID: 31956
        Flags summary: 0x40
                0... .... = Reserved
                .1.. .... = Do not fragment
                ..0. .... = Last fragment
        Fragment offset(LSB 13 bits): 0 (0x00)
        Time to live: 128 seconds/hops
        IP protocol type: TCP (0x06)
        Checksum: 0x3DB1
        IP address 209.81.65.145 ->207.166.124.203
        No option
```

For more information on the encapsulation of IP datagrams in Ethernet frames, see Chapter 4, "The Link Layer."

The IP header applied by the client system is a typical implementation. The header contains no options, so it is the standard 20 bytes (five 32-bit words) in length. The service types, which are rarely used in normal IP communications, are all set to Normal. Because there is no application-layer data in this packet, the length of the IP datagram is normally 40 bytes: 20 bytes for the IP header and 20 bytes for the TCP header. The total length of this datagram is 60 bytes, however, because of an extra 20 bytes worth of options included in the TCP header.

An IP datagram is assigned a fragment ID, always — even though the Do Not Fragment flag is set, as in this case. Fragmentation should not be necessary when transmitting TCP data from a source system. Because the data stream is segmented at the transport layer, the size of individual datagrams should be appropriate for transmission on the local network. As the datagram travels through routers and across different network types, however, it may need to be fragmented at a later time.

The protocol field contains a hexadecimal value of 06, which the analyzer correctly decodes as the TCP protocol. The IP time-to-live (TTL) value assigned by this implementation is 128 seconds, or hops — which is more than sufficient — but not unusual. Various TCP/IP stacks assign their own values to this field. If you look at one of the packets returned by the Web server to the client, for example, you see that the TTL value it uses is 240 seconds, or hops.

For more facts on the formation of the IP header and its fields, see Chapter 5, "The Internet Layer."

THE TCP HEADER

Transmission Control Protocol

```
Port 1673 --> World Wide Web HTTP
        Sequence Number: 382278209
        Acknowledgment Number: 0
        Header Length(MSB 4 bits): 10 (32-bit word)
        Reserved(LSB 4 bits): 0
        Code: 0x02
```

```
RES: 00.. .... = Reserved
URG: ..0. .... = Urgent Pointer is Invalid
ACK: ...0 .... = Acknowledgment Field is Invalid
PSH: .... 0... = No push Requested
RST: .... .0.. = No reset Connection
SYN: .... ..1. = Synchronize Sequence Number
FIN: .... ...0 = More Data From Sender
Window: 8192
Checksum: 0xB2EE
Urgent Pointer: 0x0000
TCP Option: 020405B4010303000101080A0000000000000000
```

The TCP header identifies the ephemeral port number used by the client system for this particular destination (1673), and decodes the well-known port number (80) for the HTTP World Wide Web service. As this is the first packet in the TCP connection-establishment process, the client system supplies its own sequence number to the server and sets the SYN flag. There is no acknowledgment number because the client is not yet aware of the server's sequence number— or even if the server is reachable.

The length of the TCP header is 40 bytes (ten 32-bit words). This is twice the normal size due to the additional 20 bytes in the option field. The options represent additional features of the client system's TCP/IP implementation that it is proposing to the server. The analyzer has not decoded the options, but by consulting the RFC documents defining the TCP protocol (RFC793), the TCP Extensions (RFC1323), and the Assigned Numbers (RFC1700), you can decode them yourself.

The first 4 bytes of the option field, 020405B4, represent the TCP maximum segment-size option. The first byte (02) specifies the option type, the second byte (04) specifies the length of the option, and the last 2 bytes (05B4) specify the size of the largest segment that the client expects to receive from the server. In decimal form, this is 1,460 bytes.

After the no-operation byte (01) that functions as a delimiter, the second option begins with a 03 byte. This identifies it as the window-scaling option, and another 03 byte specifies that the option is 3 bits long. By including this option, the client is informing the server of its capability to scale the send and receive windows used in the TCP connection. The value of the third byte is 00, indicating that while it cannot scale its receive window, it can scale its send window. Window scaling is not actually performed unless the server includes the option in its acknowledgment of the client's message.

Following the 3-byte window scaling option is a 01 byte that is used to pad the option out to the nearest 4-byte word boundary (followed by another 01, that functions as a delimiter). The third option in the field is identified as type 08, the timestamp option, which is 0A (or 10, in decimal form) bytes long. The two 4-byte fields that should contain the actual timestamps are filled with 0's.

The second field, which is intended to contain an echo reply of the last timestamp received from the connected system, is filled with zeroes. This is understandable, as there have not yet been any packets received from the server. The first field, however, which should contain a timestamp generated by the local system, is inexplicably blank. None of the subsequent packets generated during this connection contain the timestamp option. Discovering such anomalous behavior while analyzing network communications in detail is not unusual. In fact, it can often lead you off on investigative tangents that yield little benefit. Suffice it to say that if a system's behavior does not produce a deleterious effect on the network, the mystery may be better left unsolved.

 For more information on TCP options and their structure within the TCP header, see Chapter 6, "The Transport Layer."

THE ETHERNET II TRAILER   Because there is no application-layer data in this packet, the TCP header is followed immediately by the 4-byte CRC field that is appended to the packet by the Ethernet protocol. As with the Ethernet header, this field is removed by the first router receiving the packet. It may also be replaced with another, in preparation for its transmission across the next network segment.

By examining the headers of this first packet in detail, you learn about the general characteristics of the TCP/IP implementation used on the client system. The elements of the Ethernet and IP headers remain relatively stable throughout the connection, and most of the system's IP transmissions. The focus, in subsequent packets, is on changes in the TCP-header values (during the course of the connection), and the HTTP information carried within the TCP segments once the connection is established.

PACKET TWO

The second packet in the capture is the server's response to the client's connection-establishment request. Aside from reversed source and destination addresses and a different TTL value, the Ethernet II and IP headers are all but identical to those of the first packet. The Ethernet header, of course, represents the data link-layer of the router on the client's local network segment— not that of the Web server, itself.

The TCP header is changed to identify this packet as the second step in the three-way handshake used to establish the TCP connection, as follows:

```
Transmission Control Protocol
Port World Wide Web HTTP --> 1673
       Sequence Number: 1927338891
       Acknowledgment Number: 382278210
       Header Length(MSB 4 bits): 6 (32-bit word)
       Reserved(LSB 4 bits): 0
       Code: 0x12
```

```
            RES: 00.. .... = Reserved
            URG: ..0. .... = Urgent Pointer is Invalid
            ACK: ...1 .... = Acknowledgment Field is Valid
            PSH: .... 0... = No push Requested
            RST: .... .0.. = No reset Connection
            SYN: .... ..1. = Synchronize Sequence Number
            FIN: .... ...0 = More Data From Sender
    Window: 8760
    Checksum: 0xAF57
    Urgent Pointer: 0x0000
    TCP Option: 020405B4
```

With this packet, the server both acknowledges the client's SYN transmission and transmits one of its own. The ACK flag is set, and the server specifies the sequence number it expects in the client's next transmission in the acknowledgment number field. Because the packet last sent by the client had the sequence number 382278209, the server expects the next packet to have the number 382278210. The server simultaneously sets the SYN flag, and specifies its own sequence number to the client. Both systems will keep track of each other's sequence number, as well as their own during the life of the connection.

Notice the server's TCP/IP stack only includes a single option in its TCP header – the maximum segment-size option – with the same value, 05B4 (1460) bytes, as the client. As the windows scaling option was not included by the server, no scaling will be performed between the two systems, nor is there any response to the client's odd timestamp behavior.

PACKET THREE

The third captured packet completes the handshake process, and establishes the TCP connection between the two systems. The client system has acknowledged the server's SYN message by raising its ACK flag, and including the server's sequence number in its acknowledgment field (incremented by one). Notice also that the client's packet contains the sequence number expected by the server in the acknowledgment field of its previous transmission. There are no options included in this message, leaving the TCP header at its minimum length of 40 bytes (five 32-bit words).

Transmission Control Protocol

```
Port 1673 --> World Wide Web HTTP
        Sequence Number: 382278210
        Acknowledgment Number: 1927338892
        Header Length(MSB 4 bits): 5 (32-bit word)
        Reserved(LSB 4 bits): 0
        Code: 0x10
            RES: 00.. .... = Reserved
            URG: ..0. .... = Urgent Pointer is Invalid
            ACK: ...1 .... = Acknowledgment Field is Valid
            PSH: .... 0... = No push Requested
            RST: .... .0.. = No reset Connection
```

```
             SYN: .... ..0. = No synchronize Sequence Number
             FIN: .... ...0 = More Data From Sender
     Window: 8760
     Checksum: 0xC714
     Urgent Pointer: 0x0000
```

PACKET FOUR

With the TCP connection established by the first three packets, application-layer messages can now begin. Depending on the application, the first message can be sent by the client or the server. In the case of the HTTP service, the client begins the process by transmitting a GET request immediately following its acknowledgment of the server's SYN packet.

Transmission Control Protocol

```
Port 1673 --> World Wide Web HTTP
     Sequence Number: 382278210
     Acknowledgment Number: 1927338892
     Header Length(MSB 4 bits): 5 (32-bit word)
     Reserved(LSB 4 bits): 0
     Code: 0x18
             RES: 00.. .... = Reserved
             URG: ..0. .... = Urgent Pointer is Invalid
             ACK: ...1 .... = Acknowledgment Field is Valid
             PSH: .... 1... = Push Requested
             RST: .... .0.. = No reset Connection
             SYN: .... ..0. = No synchronize Sequence Number
             FIN: .... ...0 = More Data From Sender
     Window: 8760
     Checksum: 0x28D7
     Urgent Pointer: 0x0000
```

Notice that the TCP header of the client's message contains the same sequence number as the previous packet. Acknowledgment messages do not occupy sequence number space (although SYN messages do). This makes it possible for a system with a window value of 0 (indicating that it can't accept more data, currently) to continue receiving acknowledgments. The ACK flag is raised again in this header, indicating that the sequence number of the next expected packet is specified in the acknowledgment-number field. The PSH flag is also raised, which requests that the server deliver the incoming data to the HTTP service as quickly as possible.

HyperText Transfer Protocol

```
GET /cgi-bin/vlink/clones HTTP/1.1
     Accept: */*
     Referer: http://www.mycorp.com/Paris/013/index.html
     Accept-Language: en-us
     Accept-Encoding: gzip, deflate
     User-Agent: Mozilla/4.0 (compatible; MSIE 4.0; Windows 95)
```

```
Host: srv2.uln.com
Connection: Keep-Alive
<\r><\n><\r><\n> End of TEST HTTP header
```

The length of the datagram in packet four is specified by the IP header as 312 bytes. This indicates that there are 272 bytes of HTTP data in the packet (after subtracting 40 bytes for the IP and TCP headers). The HTTP message contains the GET request being sent to the Web server by the client, which specifies the URL of the document to be displayed in the Web browser. After the GET command, the client includes a number of optional HTTP headers in the message. These provide additional information about the client, such as the language it is using and the name of the browser running on the system.

When discussing the HTTP protocol, the term "header" does not refer to the protocol-encapsulation process, as in a TCP or IP header. HTTP headers are elements added to a textual command, such as GET, that consist of a label followed by a value.

For more information on the types of headers that can be included in an HTTP message, see Chapter 7, "The Application Layer."

PACKET FIVE

Though packet four is displayed in the Summary Pane of the Packet Viewer as an HTTP packet, the initial response returned by the server is generated by the transport layer. This response takes the form of a TCP-acknowledgment message, with the ACK flag raised and an acknowledgment number of 382278482, indicating that 272 bytes of data have been received.

```
Port World Wide Web HTTP --> 1673
        Sequence Number: 1927338892
        Acknowledgment Number: 382278482
        Header Length(MSB 4 bits): 5 (32-bit word)
        Reserved(LSB 4 bits): 0
        Code: 0x10
                RES: 00.. .... = Reserved
                URG: ..0. .... = Urgent Pointer is Invalid
                ACK: ...1 .... = Acknowledgment Field is Valid
                PSH: .... 0... = No push Requested
```

```
          RST: .... .0.. = No reset Connection
          SYN: .... ..0. = No synchronize Sequence Number
          FIN: .... ...0 = More Data From Sender
Window: 8760
Checksum: 0xC604
Urgent Pointer: 0x0000
```

PACKET SIX

Immediately following the TCP acknowledgment, the server returns an HTTP response message containing a status code of 200. This indicates that the request has been processed successfully. The server then includes headers of its own, identifying itself to the client.

HyperText Transfer Protocol

```
HTTP/1.0 200 OK
          Date: Thu, 28 Aug 1997 17:48:58 GMT
          Server: Apache-SSL-US/1.0.3+1.1
          Content-type: text/html

          <\r><\n><\r><\n> End of TEST HTTP header
```

PACKET SEVEN

The seventh captured packet is a TCP message sent by the client, acknowledging receipt of the HTTP response message from the server. TCP acknowledgments are generated by both systems in response to application-layer messages.

PACKET EIGHT

Finally, in the eighth packet, the server begins sending HTTP data to the client. Because the HTTP protocol operates by sending messages in clear text, you can see the contents of the HTML file being transferred in the ASCII decode, on the right side of the following excerpt:

HyperText Transfer Protocol

```
Data:
  0000: 3c 68 74 6d 6c 3e 3c 68 65 61 64 3e 0a 3c 74 69 | <html>
  <head>.<ti
  0010: 74 6c 65 3e 55 4c 4e 3a 42 75 79 20 4f 6e 6c 69 | tle>RGB:
  Buy Onli
  0020: 6e 65 20 3a 20 4d 65 6d 6f 72 79 2c 52 41 4d 2c | ne :
  Memory,RAM,
  0030: 20 43 6f 6d 70 75 74 65 72 2c 53 49 4d 4d 2c 44 | Computer,
  SIMM,D
  0040: 49 4d 4d 2c 20 50 43 2c 43 44 2d 52 6f 6d 2c 20 | IMM, PC,
  CD-Rom,
```

```
0050: 47 61 6d 65 73 2c 48 61 72 64 20 44 72 69 76 65 | Games,Hard
Drive
0060: 2c 4d 65 6d 6f 72 79 2c 52 41 4d 2c 53 49 4d 4d | ,Memory,
RAM,SIMM
0070: 2c 44 49 4d 4d 20 43 6f 6d 70 75 74 65 72 2c 20 | ,DIMM
Computer,
0080: 50 43 2c 43 44 2d 52 6f 6d 2c 20 47 61 6d 65 73 | PC,CD-Rom,
Games
0090: 2c 48 61 72 64 20 44 72 69 76 65 20 3c 2f 74 69 | ,Hard
Drive </ti
00a0: 74 6c 65 3e 0a 3c 62 6f 64 79 20 62 61 63 6b 67 | tle>.<body
backg
00b0: 72 6f 75 6e 64 3d 22 68 74 74 70 3a 2f 2f 6d 65 | round=
"http://me
00c0: 64 69 61 2e 75 6c 6e 2e 63 6f 6d 2f 69 6d 61 67 | dia.rgb.
com/imag
00d0: 65 73 2f 66 6c 61 67 62 61 63 6b 2e 67 69 66 22 | es/
flagback.gif"
00e0: 20 76 6c 69 6e 6b 3d 22 23 63 30 30 30 63 30 22 | vlink=
"#c000c0"
00f0: 20 6c 69 6e 6b 3d 22 23 30 30 30 30 66 66 22 3e | link=
"#0000ff">
```

This listing displays only a small part of the 1,460 bytes of HTML data carried in this packet. Notice the server is observing the maximum segment size, specified by the client, in the TCP options of packet one.

PACKET NINE

The ninth packet contains the client's TCP acknowledgment of the data received from the server. Following this packet are repeated exchanges between the client and server (which have been omitted from this sampling). HTTP messages containing additional HTML data are sent from the server, and TCP acknowledgment messages are returned by the client.

PACKET TEN

The tenth packet, shown in this capture, contains the end of the HTML file being transmitted from server to client. This is evident by the fact that the HTTP data in this packet totals only 579 bytes (while all previous segments have contained 1,460 bytes – the maximum amount of data receivable by the client, as specified by the maximum segment size option).

Transmission Control Protocol

```
Port World Wide Web HTTP --> 1673
        Sequence Number: 1927362690
        Acknowledgment Number: 382278482
        Header Length(MSB 4 bits): 5 (32-bit word)
        Reserved(LSB 4 bits): 0
        Code: 0x11
```

```
        RES: 00.. .... = Reserved
        URG: ..0. .... = Urgent Pointer is Invalid
        ACK: ...1 .... = Acknowledgment Field is Valid
        PSH: .... 0... = No push Requested
        RST: .... .0.. = No reset Connection
        SYN: .... ..0. = No synchronize Sequence Number
        FIN: .... ...1 = No more Data From Sender
Window: 8760
Checksum: 0x914D
Urgent Pointer: 0x0000
```

Because the server has no more data to transmit to the client, it raises the FIN flag in this last HTTP message. This signals that it is ready to close its side of the connection.

PACKET ELEVEN

Having received the last of the requested data, the client returns a TCP message to the server acknowledging its FIN flag, and sending a FIN flag of its own. TCP connections are full duplex, and both directions must be closed individually to terminate the connection in an orderly manner.

Transmission Control Protocol

```
Port 1673 --> World Wide Web HTTP
        Sequence Number: 382278482
        Acknowledgment Number: 1927363376
        Header Length(MSB 4 bits): 5 (32-bit word)
        Reserved(LSB 4 bits): 0
        Code: 0x11
                RES: 00.. .... = Reserved
                URG: ..0. .... = Urgent Pointer is Invalid
                ACK: ...1 .... = Acknowledgment Field is Valid
                PSH: .... 0... = No push Requested
                RST: .... .0.. = No reset Connection
                SYN: .... ..0. = No synchronize Sequence Number
                FIN: .... ...1 = No more Data From Sender
        Window: 8075
        Checksum: 0x690C
        Urgent Pointer: 0x0000
```

PACKET TWELVE

The server concludes the communications between the two systems by acknowledging the client's FIN flag. In the twelfth packet, the connection between the two systems is now terminated.

Transmission Control Protocol

```
Port 1673 --> World Wide Web HTTP
        Sequence Number: 382278483
```

```
Acknowledgment Number: 1927363376
Header Length(MSB 4 bits): 5 (32-bit word)
Reserved(LSB 4 bits): 0
Code: 0x10
        RES: 00.. .... = Reserved
        URG: ..0. .... = Urgent Pointer is Invalid
        ACK: ...1 .... = Acknowledgment Field is Valid
        PSH: .... 0... = No push Requested
        RST: .... .0.. = No reset Connection
        SYN: .... ..0. = No synchronize Sequence Number
        FIN: .... ...0 = More Data From Sender
Window: 8075
Checksum: 0x690C
Urgent Pointer: 0x0000
```

This capture has demonstrated a simple, abbreviated exchange of HTTP application data between a browser and Web server. In reality, the process is much more complex. In most cases, the HTML code of the URL, requested by the client, contains references to other documents (such as image and multimedia files, and possibly even to information on other Web servers). Depending on the version of the HTTP protocol being used, it may be necessary to establish a new TCP connection for each referenced file — or, at the very least, to negotiate the delivery of additional data over the same connection.

The HTTP 1.0 standard requires that the entire TCP-connection process, documented in the previous sections, be performed for each file requested from a Web server. Version 1.1 of the standard includes a *persistent connections* feature. This feature permits the transmission of multiple files using a single TCP connection, but it is not a requirement for compliance with the standard.

If you perform an unfiltered capture of your network's data as you browse the Web, you will see what appears to be a bewildering stream of packets. The stream is comprised of messages from many different connections, all intertwined by their chronological appearance in the buffer. Multiply this by a dozen or more users on your network, all working simultaneously, and you can see how protocol analysis can be a formidable task.

UDP Transactions

In analyzing TCP communications, you will see a remarkable amount of bandwidth devoted to the control messages used to establish, maintain, and terminate connections. In comparison to TCP, UDP communications are incredibly simple. As a case in point, a DNS transaction used to resolve a name into an IP address consists of only two packets, a request and a reply, as shown in Figure 16-19.

The IP header for UDP messages differs only slightly from that for TCP packets. The value of the protocol field is changed to 11, and the Do Not Fragment flag is turned off. Because UDP doesn't have the capability to segment its transmissions like TCP, this function is provided by IP (should the datagram encounter a network with a maximum transfer unit smaller than that of the packet).

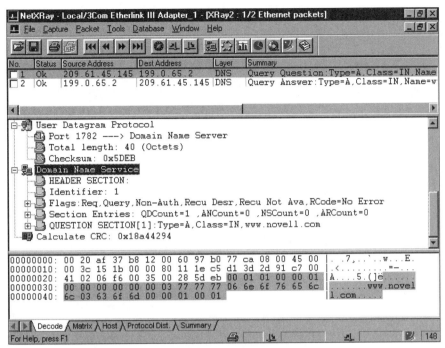

Figure 16-19: UDP transactions do not use the dedicated control traffic required by TCP, and consist only of requests and replies.

Internet Protocol

```
Version(MSB 4 bits): 4
        Header length(LSB 4 bits): 5 (32-bit word)
        Service type: 0x00
                000. .... = 0 - Routine
                ...0 .... = Normal delay
                .... 0... = Normal throughput
                .... .0.. = Normal reliability
        Total length: 60 (Octets)
        Fragment ID: 5403
        Flags summary: 0x00
                0... .... = Reserved
                .0.. .... = May be fragmented
                ..0. .... = Last fragment
                        Fragment offset(LSB 13 bits): 0 (0x00)
        Time to live: 128 seconds/hops
        IP protocol type: UDP (0x11)
        Checksum: 0x1EC5
        IP address 209.81.65.145 ->207.166.124.203
        No option
```

The UDP header is minimal, occupying only 8 bytes. The analyzer displays the ephemeral port number of the system generating the DNS request, and decodes the well-known port number (53) for the DNS service. The length field indicates that the actual DNS message consists of 32 bytes (40 minus 8).

User Datagram Protocol

```
Port 1782 --> Domain Name Server
        Total length: 40 (Octets)
        Checksum: 0x5DEB
```

The DNS message format consists of five sections, as follows:

- **Header** – The header section includes fields that specify whether the message is a request or a reply, indicates the nature of the query, and list the number of entries in the other four sections.

- **Question** – The question section includes fields that specify the DNS name that the server is being asked to resolve, the type of DNS record to seek, and the class of the query.

- **Answer** – The answer field contains a series of resource records that provide answers to the question posed in a request message (that is, IP addresses corresponding to a specified DNS name).

- **Authority** – The authority field contains resource records that identify authoritative sources for DNS information about the domain specified in the question section.

- **Additional** – The additional field contains resource records that contain information pertaining to the DNS name specified in the question section (but these don't necessarily answer the question).

DNS REQUESTS

A DNS request message contains only the header and question sections. The latter of these carries the DNS name that the client system must resolve into an IP address before TCP/IP communications can begin. A captured request message appears as follows:

Domain Name Service

```
HEADER SECTION:
        Identifier: 1
        Flags:
                0... .... = Request packet
                .000 0... = OP Code is 0x00 - Query
                .... .0.. = Non-Authoritative Answer
                .... ..0. = No Truncation Packet
```

```
           .... ...1 = Recursion Desired
           0... .... = Recursion Not Available
           .000 .... = Reserved Bits
           .... 0000 = Response Code is 0 - No Error
    Section Entries:
           Question   Section: 1 Entrie(s)
           Answer     Section: 0 Entrie(s)
           Authority  Section: 0 Entrie(s)
           Additional Section: 0 Entrie(s)
 QUESTION SECTION[1]:
           Domain Name: www.mycorp.com
           Query  Type: 1 = A - a host address
           Query Class: 1 = IN - the ARPA internet
```

The header section contains a transaction identifier, which is used to match up requests and replies, and the flags identifying the message as a request and a standard query (as opposed to a response and an inverse query). Other flags indicate that the message has not been truncated due to excessive length, and that the destination server should use recursive queries, if possible. The section entries field indicates that the message contains only a single question entry, which is typical for a request. The question section, itself, specifies that the resolver is seeking an IP address for an Internet host system with the specified name.

DNS RESPONSES

The DNS response message returned to the resolver consists of the original request message with the answer, authority, and additional sections added to it. The header section of the response appears as follows:

Domain Name Service

```
HEADER SECTION:
        Identifier: 1
        Flags:
               1... .... = Response packet
               .000 0... = OP Code is 0x00 - Query
               .... .0.. = Non-Authoritative Answer
               .... ..0. = No Truncation Packet
               .... ...1 = Recursion Desired
               1... .... = Recursion Available
               .000 .... = Reserved Bits
               .... 0000 = Response Code is 0 - No Error
        Section Entries:
               Question   Section: 1 Entrie(s)
               Answer     Section: 3 Entrie(s)
               Authority  Section: 5 Entrie(s)
               Additional Section: 7 Entrie(s)
```

When a DNS message is designated as a response, the authoritative answer and recursion available flags take on significance, which they lacked in the request. In this sample, the authoritative answer flag indicates that the answer supplied in the message was filled from the DNS server's cache, and not by passing the message to an authoritative server for the requested domain. The recursion available flag indicates that the server is capable of performing recursive queries. The message now contains a total of 15 resource records in the answer, authority, and additional sections, increasing the size of the message to 326 bytes.

If the additional resource records caused the message to exceed its maximum size of 512 bytes, the overage would be omitted and the truncation flag, raised. When the message's receiver detects the truncation flag in a response, it generates a duplicate request using TCP, instead of UDP. Usually, this only happens during DNS zone transfers (that is, server replications).

Each of the resource records in the answer, authoritative, and answer sections of a DNS response appears as follows:

```
ANSWER SECTION[1]:
          Domain Name (w/Pointer): www.mycorp.com
          RR  Type: 1 = A - a host address
          RR Class: 1 = IN - the ARPA internet
          RR Time To Live: 8591 second(s)
          RR Data  Length: 4 Octet(s)
          An ARPA internet address: 137.55.92.36
```

This resource record field represents a DNS server entry for the Internet host system of the type and class requested in the question section. The type and class determine the format and length of the data field, which contains the IP address. The TTL value represents the maximum amount of time the resource record should remain cached.

Subsequent resource records, in the answer section, specify additional IP addresses for the same name. The format of the resource records in the authority and additional sections are the same as answer resource records.

```
AUTHORITY SECTION[1]:
          Domain Name: MYCORP.com
          RR  Type: 2 = NS - an authoritative name server
          RR Class: 1 = IN - the ARPA internet
          RR Time To Live: 20583 second(s)
          RR Data  Length: 5 Octet(s)
          Domain Name (w/Pointer): ns.MYCORP.com is a host has
             the Name Server
ADDITIONAL SECTION[1]:
          Domain Name (w/Pointer): ns.MYCORP.com
          RR  Type: 1 = A - a host address
          RR Class: 1 = IN - the ARPA internet
          RR Time To Live: 20583 second(s)
          RR Data  Length: 4 Octet(s)
          An ARPA internet address: 137.65.1.1
```

The authority entry contains an NS (name server) resource record, containing the name of an authoritative server for information on the mycorp.com domain specified in the question section. The entry's data field provides only the DNS name of the authoritative server, however. This way, a resource record is provided in the additional section that resolves the DNS name into an IP address.

NetWare/IP Communications

The NetWare/IP product presents an unusual problem for a protocol analyzer, in that it uses data structures that (technically) violate some of the basic rules of networking. NetWare/IP uses TCP/IP to transmit NetWare Core Protocol (NCP) file-system traffic, eliminating the IPX traffic from your network. IPX is not actually eliminated, however. Instead, NetWare/IP encapsulates the entire IPX packet within a UDP datagram before transmitting it.

Some protocol analyzers refuse to recognize the IPX protocol when it appears in the data field of a UDP packet — even when they support IPX at the network layer. They refuse to do this because carrying a network-layer protocol within a transport-layer protocol should be impossible. As you can see in Figure 16-20, though, NetXRay processes each protocol independently, and properly displays this unusual configuration.

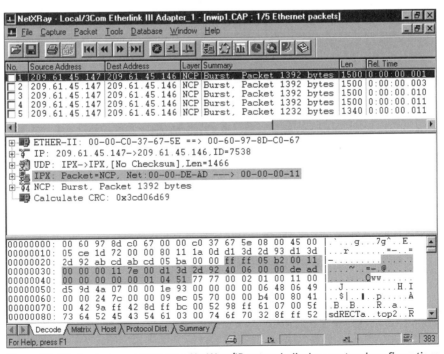

Figure 16-20: Analyzing packets on a NetWare/IP network displays protocol configurations that look like they cannot work.

Summary

There is no better way to learn about TCP/IP networking (and networking, in general) than by examining the packets transmitted by live systems.

In this chapter, you learned some of the basic techniques involved in protocol analysis, including the following:

♦ Using the right tools for the job, such as network monitors and protocol-analyzer software

♦ How to use Windows NT's Performance Monitor application to view network traffic in real time

♦ How to use NetXRay to capture network data for a detailed examination

♦ How to track the progress of a protocol transaction captured by a protocol analyzer

Appendix

About the CD-ROM

Included with this book is a CD-ROM containing extensive documentation for the TCP/IP protocols and other Internet standards. It includes a selection of shareware, freeware, and demonstration versions of TCP/IP-based software products, and links to the World Wide Web sites maintained by the various organizations devoted to the administration and development of the Internet.

The CD-ROM is HTML-based with a main menu file, called **index.htm,** at the root of the disc that contains links to all of the other contents. Although you can read the HTML files with any Web browser by opening the index.htm file, Microsoft's Internet Explorer 4.0 is included on the CD-ROM, in the **\ie4** directory. Internet Explorer enables you to install any of the software products on the disc directly from the HTML file, without locating the appropriate installation program.

For information about how to install the software products from the Index.htm file, see the section "CD-ROM Installation Instructions" in the back of this book.

Requests for Comment

As discussed in Chapter 1, "Building a Network Standard," the standards on which the TCP/IP protocols are based are developed by the Internet Engineering Task Force (IETF). These standards were drawn up using a democratic process and were published as open, public documents called Requests for Comments, or RFCs. The documents cover a wide range of subjects, from the technical to the whimsical, and are available free of charge from hundreds of sites on the Internet. For the sake of convenience, the complete collection of RFCs is included on the CD-ROM. They are indexed and in HTML format, so you can peruse them using your favorite Web browser.

Normally, the RFCs are published only as ASCII files (found on the CD-ROM in the **\rfc\text** directory), but the HTML versions on the CD-ROM are cross-indexed with links to all document references in the text. A few of the RFCs contain graphical material that cannot be reproduced in ASCII format. While there is still a text version, these documents are also published by the IETF in PostScript format. If you have access to a PostScript printer, you can find these documents in the **\rfc\ps** directory on the CD-ROM. For online viewing, however, these documents are provided as Portable Document Format (PDF) files in the **\rfc\pdf** directory – that can be read with the Adobe Acrobat Reader program (found in the CD-ROM's **\adobe** directory).

Software

The software on this disc consists of freeware, shareware, and demonstration versions of selected TCP/IP applications and utilities. The purchase price of this book does not include licenses for these programs. You are encouraged to support the software developers by purchasing the registered versions of any programs that you use beyond a fair evaluation period.

The "install" links for the software products on the disc reference the programs' installation files on the CD-ROM. If you are running Microsoft's Internet Explorer, you can opt to open the linked file, which executes the installation program. Other browsers may not provide this option, prompting you to save the executable file to a local drive, instead. In these cases, to install the program, you should browse to the program's location directory on the CD-ROM using the Windows Explorer, or File Manager, and execute the installation program manually.

Microsoft Internet Explorer 4.0

Internet Explorer 4.0 is the latest version of Microsoft's full-featured Web browser/e-mail client/news reader product. If you do not have a browser installed on your system already, you can use Internet Explorer to read the document files on the CD-ROM.

Adobe Acrobat Reader 3.01

The Adobe Acrobat Reader enables you to display, search, and print documents saved in Adobe's Portable Document Format (PDF). PDF documents retain all of the font, format, layout, and graphic information of the originals – regardless of the platform on which they are displayed.

Network General NetXRay 3.0

NetXRay is a network-monitor and protocol-analyzer application that can capture and analyze the contents of packets from your network, and display a wide range of network-communications statistics. With this demonstration version, you can use your own TCP/IP network to illustrate many of the concepts covered in this book.

Vital Signs Software's Net.Medic 1.2

Net.Medic is a browser companion that works with your Internet browser to monitor, isolate, diagnose, and correct problems that affect Internet communications. You can identify the source of network bottlenecks, whether they exist in your PC, modem, your Internet Service Provider (ISP), the Internet backbone, or in a remote Web site server. Net.Medic identifies problems, offers recommendations for solving them, and in many cases, automatically fixes them.

Globalscape, Inc.'s CuteFTP

CuteFTP is a Windows-based Internet application, supplied in both 16- and 32-bit versions. It enables you to use FTP's capabilities without knowing all the details of the protocol, itself. FTP operations are simplified with the user-friendly, graphical interface – rather than the command-line interface used by the native Windows FTP clients.

FTPx Corp's FTP Explorer

FTP Explorer is a file-transfer-protocol client for Windows 95 and NT 4.0, with a graphical interface that is designed to look and act very much like the Windows Explorer.

Forte Free Agent

Free Agent is the freeware version of Agent (a graphical online/offline newsreader that provides you with access information to thousands of public Internet newsgroups, covering every conceivable topic). FreeAgent is supplied on the CD-ROM in both 16- and 32-bit versions.

TechSmith Corp's NewsMonger

TechSmith Corporation's NewsMonger agent for Microsoft Windows 95 and Windows NT provides complete monitoring of the Internet's largest source of news information – the USENET news service. NewsMonger supports multiple searches, search scheduling, and e-mail notification when new articles, matching your criteria, are discovered.

Khaled Mardam-Bey's mIRC

mIRC is a highly configurable, shareware Internet Relay Chat (IRC) client for Windows. It is available in both 16- and 32-bit versions, and contains all the features other clients on UNIX, Macintosh, and even Windows offer, combined with a clean user interface. mIRC enables you to participate in live, real-time, global chat, and offers full-color text lines, DCC File Send and Get capabilities, programmable aliases, a remote commands and events handler, place-sensitive pop-up menus, a great Switchbar, and World Wide Web and sound support.

Luc Neijens' CyberKit

CyberKit is a 32-bit application for Windows 95 and NT. It provides a graphical interface to standard TCP/IP utilities, such as Ping, TraceRoute, Finger, Whois, Name Server LookUp, and Quote Of The Day.

Net3 Group's IP Calculator

The IP Subnet Calculator is a free, time-saving 32-bit Windows 95/NT utility for computing IP address and subnet-mask values.

Infix Technologies' PingGraph

PingGraph is a multithreaded graphical TCP/IP network monitoring and diagnostic tool for Windows 95 and NT. PingGraph can graph response time within your Local Area Network (LAN) and monitor your Internet Service Provider (ISP) to ensure you are getting the advertised connection quality and stability.

Thinking Man Software's Dimension 4

Dimension 4 is a time-synchronization utility for Windows 95 and Windows NT 4.0. It sets your PC clock using the Simple Network Time Protocol to communicate with a time server (like those at the U.S. Naval Observatory in Washington, DC).

Blue Globe Software's Port Scanner

Port Scanner enables you to scan a group of IP Addresses looking for specific incoming TCP/IP ports. This shows you who (on your network) is running a specific TCP/IP daemon.

Guy Michaud's Subnet Pro

Subnet Pro is a Visual Basic subnetting tool for Windows. It enables you to compute the proper IP address and subnet-mask values for your network environment.

Werner Development's Set MTU Size

Set MTU Size is a utility that modifies the appropriate Windows 95 registry settings to alter the default maximum transfer unit (MTU) size used by the Microsoft TCP/IP client.

Links

Organizations established to govern the Internet, and to develop the standards for the TCP/IP protocols, and other Internet technologies, maintain Web sites offering extensive amounts of information on their activities. The main menu page of the CD-ROM contains links to these Web sites, and to those maintained by other organizations involved in the development of computer networking standards.

Index

S

my2cents.idgbooks.com

Register This Book — And Win!

Visit **http://my2cents.idgbooks.com** to register this book and we'll automatically enter you in our monthly prize giveaway. It's also your opportunity to give us feedback: let us know what you thought of this book and how you would like to see other topics covered.

Discover IDG Books Online!

The IDG Books Online Web site is your online resource for tackling technology — at home and at the office.

Ten Productive and Career-Enhancing Things You Can Do at www.idgbooks.com

1. Nab source code for your own programming projects.

2. Download software.

3. Read Web exclusives: special articles and book excerpts by IDG Books Worldwide authors.

4. Take advantage of resources to help you advance your career as a Novell or Microsoft professional.

5. Buy IDG Books Worldwide titles or find a convenient bookstore that carries them.

6. Register your book and win a prize.

7. Chat live online with authors.

8. Sign up for regular e-mail updates about our latest books.

9. Suggest a book you'd like to read or write.

10. Give us your 2¢ about our books and about our Web site.

Not on the Web yet? It's easy to get started with *Discover the Internet*, at local retailers everywhere.

IDG BOOKS WORLDWIDE, INC.
END-USER LICENSE AGREEMENT

READ THIS. You should carefully read these terms and conditions before opening the software packet(s) included with this book ("Book"). This is a license agreement ("Agreement") between you and IDG Books Worldwide, Inc. ("IDGB"). By opening the accompanying software packet(s), you acknowledge that you have read and accept the following terms and conditions. If you do not agree and do not want to be bound by such terms and conditions, promptly return the Book and the unopened software packet(s) to the place you obtained them for a full refund.

1. **License Grant.** IDGB grants to you (either an individual or entity) a nonexclusive license to use one copy of the enclosed software program(s) (collectively, the "Software") solely for your own personal or business purposes on a single computer (whether a standard computer or a workstation component of a multiuser network). The Software is in use on a computer when it is loaded into temporary memory (RAM) or installed into permanent memory (hard disk, CD-ROM, or other storage device). IDGB reserves all rights not expressly granted herein.

2. **Ownership.** IDGB is the owner of all right, title, and interest, including copyright, in and to the compilation of the Software recorded on the disk(s) or CD-ROM ("Software Media"). Copyright to the individual programs recorded on the Software Media is owned by the author or other authorized copyright owner of each program. Ownership of the Software and all proprietary rights relating thereto remain with IDGB and its licensers.

3. **Restrictions on Use and Transfer.**

    (a) You may only (i) make one copy of the Software for backup or archival purposes, or (ii) transfer the Software to a single hard disk, provided that you keep the original for backup or archival purposes. You may not (i) rent or lease the Software, (ii) copy or reproduce the Software through a LAN or other network system or through any computer subscriber system or bulletin-board system, or (iii) modify, adapt, or create derivative works based on the Software.

    (b) You may not reverse engineer, decompile, or disassemble the Software. You may transfer the Software and user documentation on a permanent basis, provided that the transferee agrees to accept the terms and conditions of this Agreement and you retain no copies. If the Software is an update or has been updated, any transfer must include the most recent update and all prior versions.

4. **Restrictions on Use of Individual Programs.** You must follow the individual requirements and restrictions detailed for each individual program in Appendix, "About the CD-ROM," of this Book. These limitations are also contained in the individual license agreements recorded on the Software Media. These limitations may include a requirement that after using the program for a specified period of time, the user must pay a registration fee or discontinue use. By opening the Software packet(s), you will be agreeing to abide by the licenses and restrictions for these individual programs that are detailed in Appendix, "About the CD-ROM," and on the Software Media. None of the material on this Software Media or listed in this Book may ever be redistributed, in original or modified form, for commercial purposes.

5. **Limited Warranty.**

   (a) IDGB warrants that the Software and Software Media are free from defects in materials and workmanship under normal use for a period of sixty (60) days from the date of purchase of this Book. If IDGB receives notification within the warranty period of defects in materials or workmanship, IDGB will replace the defective Software Media.

   (b) IDGB AND THE AUTHOR OF THE BOOK DISCLAIM ALL OTHER WARRANTIES, EXPRESS OR IMPLIED, INCLUDING WITHOUT LIMITATION IMPLIED WARRANTIES OF MERCHANTABILITY AND FITNESS FOR A PARTICULAR PURPOSE, WITH RESPECT TO THE SOFTWARE, THE PROGRAMS, THE SOURCE CODE CONTAINED THEREIN, AND/OR THE TECHNIQUES DESCRIBED IN THIS BOOK. IDGB DOES NOT WARRANT THAT THE FUNCTIONS CONTAINED IN THE SOFTWARE WILL MEET YOUR REQUIREMENTS OR THAT THE OPERATION OF THE SOFTWARE WILL BE ERROR FREE.

   (c) This limited warranty gives you specific legal rights, and you may have other rights that vary from jurisdiction to jurisdiction.

6. **Remedies.**

   (a) IDGB's entire liability and your exclusive remedy for defects in materials and workmanship shall be limited to replacement of the Software Media, which may be returned to IDGB with a copy of your receipt at the following address: Software Media Fulfillment Department, Attn.: *TCP/IP Administration,* IDG Books Worldwide, Inc., 7260 Shadeland Station, Ste. 100, Indianapolis, IN 46256, or call 1-800-762-2974. Please allow three to four weeks for delivery. This Limited Warranty is void if failure of the Software Media has resulted from accident, abuse, or misapplication. Any replacement Software Media will be warranted for the remainder of the original warranty period or thirty (30) days, whichever is longer.

(b) In no event shall IDGB or the author be liable for any damages whatsoever (including without limitation damages for loss of business profits, business interruption, loss of business information, or any other pecuniary loss) arising from the use of or inability to use the Book or the Software, even if IDGB has been advised of the possibility of such damages.

(c) Because some jurisdictions do not allow the exclusion or limitation of liability for consequential or incidental damages, the above limitation or exclusion may not apply to you.

7. **U.S. Government Restricted Rights.** Use, duplication, or disclosure of the Software by the U.S. Government is subject to restrictions stated in paragraph (c)(1)(ii) of the Rights in Technical Data and Computer Software clause of DFARS 252.227-7013, and in subparagraphs (a) through (d) of the Commercial Computer – Restricted Rights clause at FAR 52.227-19, and in similar clauses in the NASA FAR supplement, when applicable.

8. **General.** This Agreement constitutes the entire understanding of the parties and revokes and supersedes all prior agreements, oral or written, between them and may not be modified or amended except in a writing signed by both parties hereto that specifically refers to this Agreement. This Agreement shall take precedence over any other documents that may be in conflict herewith. If any one or more provisions contained in this Agreement are held by any court or tribunal to be invalid, illegal, or otherwise unenforceable, each and every other provision shall remain in full force and effect.

CD-ROM Installation Instructions

The contents of the CD-ROM included with this book are accessible from an HTML main menu file, called Index.htm, found in the root directory of the disc. To read this file, you must have a World Wide Web browser installed on your computer. If you do not have a browser installed, Microsoft's Internet Explorer 4.0 is also included on the CD-ROM.

Installing Internet Explorer 4.0

To install Internet Explorer 4.0 on your Windows 95 system, follow these steps:

1. Insert the *TCP/IP Administration* CD-ROM into your computer's CD-ROM drive.

2. Double-click the My Computer icon on the Windows 95 desktop. Then, double-click the icon corresponding to your CD-ROM drive, or open the Windows 95 Explorer and expand the CD-ROM drive in the left pane.

3. Open the ie4 folder and double-click the icon for setup.exe file to launch the installation program.

4. Follow the instructions on your screen to complete the Internet Explorer installation.

Installing the Software on the CD-ROM with Internet Explorer

The Index.htm file contains descriptions of the files included on the CD-ROM. It also provides direct links to other HTML documents, TCP/IP resources on the World Wide Web, and the other software products included on the CD-ROM. When you use Internet Explorer as your browser, the "Install" link (for each product in the

Software section) attempts to launch the installation program for that product. This produces the following dialog box:

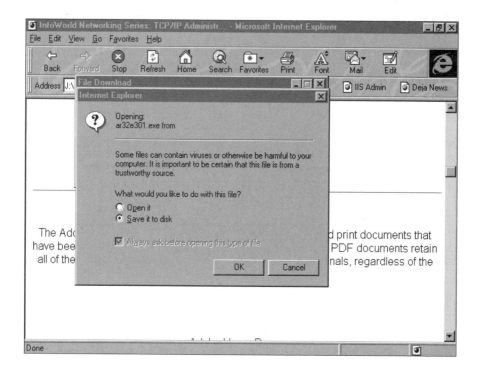

Select the Open it radio button and click OK to execute the program and begin the software-installation process.

Installing the Software on the CD-ROM with other Browsers

Browsers other than Internet Explorer may not be capable of launching an executable file using the links provided. In this case, the name and location of each software product's installation program is provided in the Index.htm file. To install a software product, browse the CD-ROM disc in the My Computer or Windows 95 Explorer window as in the previous procedure. Locate the directory for that product, as shown in Index.htm, and double-click the icon for the specified installation program file. Follow the instructions provided by the program.